The Political Economy of Art

The Political Economy of Art

Making the Nation of Culture

Edited by
Julie F. Codell

Madison • Teaneck
Fairleigh Dickinson University Press

Associated University Presses
2010 Eastpark Boulevard
Cranbury, NJ 08512

The paper used in this publication meets the requirements of the American National Standard for Permanence of Paper for Printed Library Materials Z39.48-1984.

Library of Congress Cataloging-in-Publication Data

The political economy of art : making the nation of culture / edited by Julie F. Codell.
p. cm.
Includes bibliographical references and index.
ISBN 978-0-8386-4168-2 (alk. paper)
1. Art and state—Economic aspects. 2. Federal aid to the arts. 3. Finance, Public. I. Codell, Julie F.
N8600.P635 2008
701.03—dc22 2007043194

PRINTED IN THE UNITED STATES OF AMERICA

Contents

Illustrations

Acknowledgments

ACKNOWLEDGMENT IS GIVEN TO THE FOLLOWING FOR permission to reprint earlier versions of chapters included in this book:

Maria Brown's essay is a version of "Rhetorical Objects and the Stories of the Nation," in Nancy Pedri, ed., *Travelling Concepts III: Memory, Narrative, Image* (Amsterdam: ASCA Press, 2003), 203–15.

Anne Goodyear's essay is a version of "Art, Technology, and the American Space Program," adapted from the original article published in INTERTEXTS 3.2 by permission of Texas Tech University Press.

Daniel Guernsey, "Universal History and Protestant Dissent in Eighteenth-Century England: James Barry's 'The Progress of Human Knowledge and Culture,' 1777–1784," in Daniel R. Guernsey, *The Artist and the State, 1777–1855: The Politics of Universal History in British and French Painting* (Aldershot, UK: Ashgate, 2007).

Andrew Hemingway, "Cultural Democracy by Default: The Communist Contribution to New Deal Art Programs," *Oxford Art Journal*, 30, no. 2 (2007).

Andrew Stephenson, "Palimpsestic Promenades: Memorial Environments and the Urban Consumption of Space in Post-1918 London," *Australia and New Zealand Journal of Art*, 6, no. 1 (2006), 42–61.

I would like to thank Jannelle Warren-Findley, Professor of History and Betsy Fahlman, Professor of Art History, both at Arizona State University, for their helpful suggestions and advice on this project.

The Political Economy of Art

Introduction: Political Economy and the Nation of Culture

Julie F. Codell

The Political Economy of Art

The political economy of art and media has increasingly become a focus of study within the areas of cultural economics and cultural studies.[1] Cultural studies embrace three major areas: political economy, textual analysis, and audience reception.[2] For many scholars the political economy of culture is defined by paths of production and consumption—who makes the art, who are the patrons, how corporate and state interests are invested in funding and promoting culture, and who consumes that culture and in what ways.[3] Economists argue variously about the nature and economic function of the arts, whether they are—macroeconomically—stimulators of jobs and growth, tax bases, tourism, or—microeconomically—public goods, defined as "products that are 'nonexcludable and nonrival,' meaning that their costs cannot practically be recovered through market transactions and that their use by one person does not reduce use by another." This last argument is often used to advocate for state support for the arts.[4]

While Adam Smith argued that the arts were foremost among the means to restore humanity to the workers, putting art "into the category that modern economists call *merit goods*" (goods we may not want personally but believe are socially beneficial anyway), he did not insist that government be responsible for funding or producing the arts, which were not then considered clear public goods, unlike his argument that government should support education, defense, and justice.[5] The first commentary on the political economy of art was by John Ruskin. Drawing on Plato's *Republic* and Xenophon's *Oeconomicus*, Ruskin emphasized the role of the state in culture production and consumption, hoping the state would encourage good art and responsible consumption, but he later felt those responsibilities might best fall on private citizens. Ruskin recognized that production and consumption were interlocked. As Willie Henderson points out, for Ruskin the consumer is an agent capable of (and required to make) moral decisions, "not an economic monad or a mechanistic automation but a member of society enmeshed in moral responsibilities and duties," even when consuming goods, including (especially) art.[6] Economist Alfred Marshall, Ruskin's contemporary, emphasized the economics of consumption as Europe and the U.S. began their long development toward displacing the production of goods with the consumption of goods. Today state and corporate interests actively produce culture often with the intention of shaping consuming spectators to fit into social and national identities and behaviors, not too far from Ruskin's ideal.

Political economy is defined in this volume as collective (state or corporate) support for art and architecture in the public sphere intended to be accessible to the widest possible public. The study of political economy raises questions about the relationship of the state to cultural production and consumption. While government support of the arts began in seventeenth-century absolute monarchies in Europe who centralized art production, it appeared as a discrete subject of inquiry in the eighteenth century in the burgeoning field of political economy in which, when economists even considered art, art was treated as a special economic case. Political economy became tremendously popular in the nineteenth century as it meshed with issues of national identity. In the twentieth century, cultural production has become a regular function of the state often seamlessly blending with a post–World War II corporate economics and blurring distinctions between private and public, corporation and government, and public good and advertising (e.g., the infomercial), as Jürgen Habermas noted over a decade ago.[7]

This collection of essays explores the political economy of art from the perspective of the artist or from analyses of art's production and consumption, emphasizing the art side of the relationship between art and state, unlike many other studies of political economy which take up cultural economics.[8] There are economic issues over the nature of public good, sometimes called "externalities," defined as goods that positively benefit an entire society not just select individuals. As Oliver Bennett notes, the economic notion of public good goes beyond economics:

> Public goods can be defined as "items which, when provided to one person, automatically and unavoidably

> become available to other members of the community as well" (Baumol and Bowen 1966, 380). This causes a "market failure," which can only be overcome if the goods are provided either by public authorities or private organizations on a nonprofit basis. Only a small proportion of cultural amenities—such as historical buildings, monuments, or public art—can be properly described as "public goods." However, the arts, taken as a whole, can be seen to have positive externalities; that is, it can be argued that they benefit not just the individual who "consumes" them but that they enrich society as a whole. Hansen (1995a, 89) suggests that the most important externalities attached to the arts are their educational value and their contribution to a sense of national identity and prestige. In addition, she argues that they may possess "option value" or "bequest value." . . . If the arts have positive externalities, they can therefore be said to be partly public as well as private. William Baumol and William Bowen (1966, 381) describe goods and services with these characteristics as "mixed commodities."[9]

This volume explores art as public good, a central issue in political economy.[10] Artists, art critics, and scholars, like Roger Fry and Kenneth Clark, have commented on economic issues, often raising questions about quality.[11] Victorians with considerable cultural capital like Ruskin, Thomas Carlyle, William Morris, and Matthew Arnold, all early public intellectuals, focused on issues of the dignity of labor and the place of art as labor in political economy. As Bennett points out, Arnold, "puts forward a theory of culture that expounds on what the 'externalities' of the arts actually are."[12] Ruskin's political economy of art has been the subject of many studies, most recently from an economic view by Willie Henderson.[13] For Arnold and Ruskin, art took the place of religion and thus was crowned as the major force for articulating social good and public values. As Gregory C. G. Moore notes, Ruskin "rejected the traditional economic aim of determining the way in which an object's exchange value gravitates toward its long-term cost of production within a world in which consumer preferences are fixed, and set himself the more ambitious aim of determining the way in which an object's exchange value gravitates toward a long-term ethically and aesthetically appropriate value through the adjustments in consumer preferences engineered by a paternalistic authority."[14] That authority was taken up later by politicians as a call for state support for the arts. As Anna Upchurch argues, William Morris, unlike Ruskin, Carlyle or Arnold, "did not believe that capitalism as an economic system held promise for human aesthetic creativity and productivity," and hoped the system would be overthrown for a utopian socialism that could support the arts as creative endeavors without censorship.[15] For many economists, the arts are either a special economic case or a subset of the service industry. But for these Victorians, art was central to social and economic conditions and change.

This book is not a study of public art, focusing on aesthetic issues or on conflicts between a work's aesthetics and public reaction and taste. Also, the essays in this volume do not address private economic exchanges and art historical topics of markets, dealers' galleries, artists' market practices, or particular works' fluctuating market values, all of which are important topics in cultural economics, whose practitioners explore issues such as ticket pricing and finances of arts organizations.[16] Cultural economists argue over the productivity of the arts and problems of their survival, given rising production costs that cannot be met by pricing (the "cost disease"), without government subsidy (similar cases are education and other public services). These topics, especially problematic debates over prices as a function of either exchange or of use value—and the roles that labor, fashion, and desire play in pricing—are fundamental to political economists Adam Smith, Nassau Senior, Alfred Marshall, William Stanley Jevons, John Kenneth Galbraith, among others, including economists active in promoting the arts. John Maynard Keynes and Lionel Robbins (who wrote on the political economy of art[17]) were both deeply influenced by Bloomsbury artists and both advocated for state subsidies to the arts.

Such problems as pricing, however, do not necessarily induce state support. It can be argued that other changes, like the growing political importance of the arts in relation to nation-building and national identities, or mass consumption, have affected decisions about state funding for the arts.[18] Essays in this book examine specific cultural spaces as points of struggle between economics and cultural processes that can seem infinite: art's production includes matters of interpretation and consumption that constitute part of the very nature of art works (as Pierre Bourdieu argues).[19] Our essays focus on three areas of conflict: first, theories of political economy put into practices of state cultural production, exemplified by James Barry's murals and by American art deployed for prescribing/salvaging/promoting national identity in the 1930s New Deal Work Projects Administration (WPA) during the Depression and the 1960s National Aeronautics and Space Administration (NASA), as we tried to catch up with the Soviets. These two American examples occurred during periods when American economic and political and intellectual hegemony seemed to falter. The other two areas of political economy of art examined in this book are sculptural and architectural monuments commissioned by state and corporate entities to shape public identities through public spaces, and conflicts and critiques of state investments in culture by artists and the public.

The state as an essential component of culture derives from one strand of John Ruskin's political economy of art, his initial hope that the state would raise up artists, determine the content and nature of art works in the public sphere, and control consumption both as purchases (costs) and as tangible and intangible benefits, such as tourism, education, or national or local prestige (public good).[20] Essays here explore whether art replicates modern state economics, or contributes to the modern dichotomy of culture as a common good standing against economic greed and power, even openly resisting and undermining the values of its state or corporate patrons. Essays here range historically from the eighteenth to the twentieth century across a variety of political and geographical terrains: eighteenth-century Britain, Napoleonic Milan, Nazi Germany, Japanese corporations, American government projects, and the New Zealand national museum.

We address several forms of state-supported art, such as gifting art to the state or purchases by the state. We should also remember that once a privately produced or privately owned work enters a museum, a transformation occurs as it becomes public property and enters public discourses on that once-private art's moral, social, and political values. Private citizens may create museums out of their own collections or donate works to museums for the public good, often induced by a variety of altruistic and material incentives (tax breaks, avoidance of death duties, etc.). By raising a private gift to public status, the state anoints the private gift as a public good through the authority of the museum as a sanctified site of knowledge and its "experts" whose actions presumably carry out the museum's mission to "reflect and convey a cultural heritage over time," putting the nation's investment into art's accessibility to all and into preservation in perpetuity.[21]

The book's authors consider this issue, while examining works funded by a corporate entity. They also look at artists' uses of state-funded art to comment on political economy, the political and economic issues contained in those art works or their production or consumption in the public space, and public space itself as an artistic and political venue for exhibition and critique of the political economy of art. The authors describe political and ideological—not aesthetic—conflicts sometimes contained within concepts of political economy (Codell, Li, and Norman), art works' very content (Guernsey, Hemingway, and Langa), art production (Norman, Jaskot, Homann, and Snay), or consumption (Brown, Grady, and Goodyear).

State-produced or commissioned art may replicate or express state policies programmatically or conflict with state ideals and policies from within the framework and funding of political economy. Public values expressed as "cultural," as David Throsby points out, can be negative as well as positive.[22] The state may impose monolithic, exclusivist, racist, oppressive, and reductive reifications of culture as a fixed "thing," rather than as collective and multivalent.[23] Those with power and resources often control public cultural consumption, material production, and the symbolic meanings of consumption used to determine communal values. This control, including censorship, was anticipated by Adam Smith who wanted to avoid them by keeping the arts in private hands.[24]

The authors in this volume focus on consequences of conflicting values between state ideologies and art's functions and values through concepts as "public good," "assets," and "symbolic capital." The application of these terms to the arts is not, and has not historically been, self-evident. For example, if a public good as understood by Adam Smith should be both "nonexcludable," that is, free to all, and "nondepletable," available for all time, the arts would not fit this category, as they have been used to mark social distinctions by exclusion and are depletable, if not properly restored. That the arts could be considered public goods, then, means concepts of political economy were subject to historical changes (e.g., eighteenth-century private collections opened to a few to museums as public institutions a century later). Other changes occurred in the role of government as culture producer, in increasing demand for the arts, in the identification of the arts with self-improvement, and in the importance of culture for justifying nationalism and empire.[25] The contents and sites of art works at times convey meanings that threaten the intentions of their commissioning state or corporations to resist state domination despite state patronage.

The modern state has a profound interest in cultural production. The price as value of a work is often dominated by concerns unique to state-funded art and by criteria not enforced on private works—moral content, collective values, representations of racial and/or national identities, aggrandized history, and images of power and authority. The political economy of art assumes that such art produces a public good, as well as public goods, in the expression of civic and national values over individual desires. Economists and critics have attempted to calibrate art's public worth with measures beyond market values. Strict economic measures of production (labor theory) or consumption (marginal utility theory) fail to touch on issues central to the political economy of art: art's contributions to the well-being of the state and its citizens through subjects and styles representative of national or racial hegemony (e.g., the Gothic in England and Germany), artists who embody or idealize national character, states distributing cultural products through its "machinery" (e.g., education, museums, conquest), and art's benefits to national material and symbolic wealth, as promoted by many nineteenth-century philosophers.[26]

Cultural production is often assumed to be outside the market and opposed to it. One form of cultural economic exchange is gifting, a concept introduced by anthropologist Marcel Mauss in 1925. Gifts are a means of ostensible sacrifice or the appearance of individual loss for the greater good that in most cases assures the giver/donor of social prestige in the collective remembrance into the future.[27] Thus gifting can be a form of sublimation for future rewards, one way in which individual economic desire is transformed into the public cultural sphere as a collective public good.[28] Gifting art is often treated as antieconomic, not as a complement to capitalism, which it is. The gifting process becomes idealized as a means to preserve cultural heritage, support social cohesion, maintain historical and geographical continuity, and gain national prestige.[29] State cultural authority is deployed to validate the gift as a public good, a form of government subsidy.[30]

In approaching these topics, political economy becomes not simply a "base" for culture but is a vital part of the circulating system of art discourse. Seeing economics and art as parallel, rather than hierarchic (as both Marxist and capitalist interpretations sometimes see them), allows us to see that state patronage does not necessarily determine art's content, intent, or reception. Often the category of art—presumed to be sanctified and free of worldly motives—can be used to transform and purify state intentions. As Richard Maxwell, among others, argues, "the work of culture has never taken place outside the areas of life determined by particular economic systems and power relations; that is, culture is always *in* political economy."[31]

THE RISE OF POLITICAL ECONOMY OF ART: PRODUCING ARTISTS AND CONSUMERS FOR THE NATION

The eighteenth century is often considered the initial period of expanding public discourse over values, increasingly open to debate and diversity. The opening up or creation of the public sphere, defined variously as a physical urban space and virtual space in the press and in public opinion, was the outcome of economic expansion from local to national to global exchanges. From the early Renaissance or late Middle Ages, economic networks became not only widespread but also independent of existing political control and later instrumental in developing their own political systems.[33]

In the eighteenth century private societies of wealthy patrons and dilettanti began exhibiting art. Public spectating burgeoned in the nineteenth century as it became a matter of national pride and modernity to expose the entire nation to culture for various reasons: to promote unifying values, to socialize (i.e., dominate) the working classes who were becoming voters (the men, at least), and to educate down the social ladder, another means of control in a Europe convulsing in periodic revolutions from 1789 on. Ruskin, the first to articulate a political economy of art, argued that both private and public consumption of art required the same motives of moral and social improvement. For him, aesthetic quality was a "truth" derived from the artist's combined moral character, technical excellence, and poetic vision. The individual artist's vision could then educate the spectator's visual acuity and knowledge of nature, and, in so doing, serve the entire community and the state.

For Ruskin, production and consumption were morally and socially intertwined: production that inflicted cruelty on its workers tainted consumers of that product, and consumption for the sake of mere fashion or frivolity inflicted alienated labor on workers.[33] Similar social and epistemological ideals were upheld by Leo Tolstoy who shared Ruskin's belief that the art market could be corrupting as well as uplifting.[34] These writers sought to saturate the private enjoyment of art with civic, social, and moral ideals. For Ruskin, the artist was in the public domain and genius was a national resource like gold.[35] Marx, who treated art as "an integral part of production in general," considered artistic production to be a good case study of how capitalist fetishization of possession produced an alienated labor.[36] For Marx, art production was part of the material conditions of social life, yet its production was also its consumption, since art created its consumers, supplying not only "'the want with material, but the material with the want.'"[37] In this way, art production includes the production of consumers, as well as of art objects. As Alan Peacock notes, "the purpose of state support for the arts was to inform the public how they could spend their money wisely and well for their own benefit and subsidies could then wither away."[38]

Art also produced the artist. A Victorian critic in the 1856 *Art Journal* defended public scrutiny of successful artists by declaring, "every artist who has reached a high position becomes . . . public property . . . it is not the eye of impertinent curiosity that seeks him out, and that would penetrate even the solitude of his studio and, to a certain extent even the sanctity of his domestic hearth."[39] The distinction between private and public was even blurred regarding the artist's very person.[40] Later, economists planning for state subsidy of the arts would argue, as John Maynard Keynes did, for the artist's work as exemplifying values of "individual and free, undisciplined, unregimented, uncontrolled. The artist walks where the breath of the spirit blows him. He cannot be told his direction; he does not know it himself. But he leads the rest of us into fresh pastures and teaches us to love and to enjoy what we often begin by rejecting, enlarging our sensibility and purifying our instincts."[41] Such a notion of the artist, part and parcel of myths since the Renaissance of the artist as outside ordinary social and economic domains, also implied an opposition between orderly economic behavior and the artist's "nature," a subject mentioned from Giorgio Vasari to Victorian art writings.[42] This "nature," however, was as much constituted by the loss of patronage and the artists' place on competitive open markets, as by working habits that could not easily be regulated (causing, e.g., problems among WPA administrators checking on whether artists were working by visiting their studios).

The political economy of art itself was affected by changing attitudes of nationalism. The blurring of distinctions between private and public was dramatically exposed when private owners tried to sell their Old Master paintings in Britain around 1880. These were largely purchased by American individuals and Continental museums. Aristocratic owners of these paintings were taken to task for their lack of civic-mindedness in selling their pictures, which had become, unbeknownst to them, rather surreptitiously national cultural capital in Britain, at least in the public's opinion by the time of the sale.[43] The feeling that these losses were not private matters but were instead a *national* disgrace prompted the formation in 1903 of Britain's National Art-Collections Fund to raise money to buy Old Masters placed on the market and keep them in Britain as national treasures (even though many of these marketable works were by Continental Old Masters).[44] Whether the purchase was saved for Britain or "lost" to other countries, "although the arguments for retention were—ostensibly—aesthetic and cultural, the outcome was determined by financial and political factors."[45] Other issues such as tariff duties on imported works of art also pulled private consumption into the public domain.[46]

Collectors' private art transactions, whether through auctions or gifting, became matters of national civic duty and entered the sphere of political economy, a sign of the authority the public sphere accrued in the nineteenth century. The spread of education and literacy meant that once-specialized aesthetic discourses, as well as political and economic topics, became discursively available to all citizens for their consideration and commentary, a kind of secular Protestantism (Habermas's bourgeoisie as a "reading public"). Greater numbers of people, the "emerging *public sphere of civil society*" (italics in original), joined debates on topics once reserved for aristocratic consideration.[47] Through an expanding accessibility, the divided and often hostile spheres of commerce and culture, articulated in the Romantic belief that art was "in opposition to commerce," could come together, dialogue, and influence each other.[48]

Throsby distinguishes between the economic sphere, "expressing the individual desires of members of society on their own behalf," even when acting collectively (e.g., providing funds for public services), and the cultural sphere, "gathering together the collective desires of the group or groups within a given society," an expression of a "collective will," even in individual production (e.g., in the studio) or individual consumption (e.g., reading a book alone).[49] Ruskin had hoped to bind these two through his political economy of art, rather than permit their increasing separation. But as the public became a source of opinions and judgments, in the area of art most people believe they are themselves competent aesthetic evaluators.[50] State support for the arts with public funds makes patrons of all the public and further justifies their assessments. Economic and cultural spheres have reversed their nineteenth-century identities: The economic sphere has become collective through the state as art producer, whereas art, once largely collective and public, has become markedly private, even subconscious, expressing individual desires more than collective histories and myths.

Recent studies have highlighted the role of cultural production in the emergence and construction of national identities from the latter half of the nineteenth century in Europe and through the twentieth century throughout the globe. Sergiusz Michalski argues that starting in Republic France in the 1870s, "the erecting of public monuments became an artistic, political and social domain in its own right. Earlier monuments, though often of great political relevance or artistic value . . . had been conceived as individual tokens of respect." After the change, "artistic traditions and ambitions were joined with novel political imperatives, resulting in the creation of a wide and varied system of public statuary" and the "polyvalence of monuments."[51] Artists could be collectively employed to represent a national agenda, often in public mural projects or sculptural programs. The WPA art programs, perhaps exemplary of the problems and conflicts of the political economy of art, often appeared to resolve these problems with subjects from American history, or American ideological values like liberty or progress represented by images of labor or machinery, or racial and cultural diversity (an ideal more virtual than real in the 1930s and 40s), or democracy paraded as the Project's cultural accessibility to all.[52] Our contemporary attention to monuments dedicated to victims of war or the Holocaust, for example, departs sharply from monuments' traditional function of celebrating military or civic leaders by heroizing them.[53] The modern polyvalence of monuments and of their interpretations (e.g., Maya Lin's Vietnam war memorial in Washington, DC) increases the state's imperative to intervene to establish dominant national identities in the public sphere by controlling the spectating and consuming of art, as well as art's production.

The participation of the state in cultural production has historically been a norm, not an exception, first in the interests of local, municipal identities, and later in the interests of national, global, and imperial identities.[54] Public commissions in the Renaissance, for example, were saturated with symbolic civic values—David the giant-slayer representing Florence, for example, or the more mixed private-public representations of church and civic art that included portraits of praying donors or their heraldic signs in sacred paintings in public spaces. From their letters we often find that patrons who commissioned Renaissance art were motivated by a full range of intentions—religious, moral, economic, social, and political. Later public works were often monuments to heroes and thus morphed personal virtues into national virtues embodied and symbolized in the state's most ideal, and idealized, citizens. Art could represent civic ideals symbolically through idealized historical figures, often improving their physical appearance or clothing them in classical dress to elevate such individuals into national symbols. The "higher" order of aesthetics was frequently deployed to bury motives of political power, economic gain, or ethnic inequities.

Nineteenth-century citizens' drive to acculturation coincided with a growing fixation on the nature of national cultural identity, as many argued that the public needs state protection against immoral or seditious cultural artifacts. Art, literature, and music became embodiments of national traits as they were increasingly interpreted in relation to national histories, invented traditions, and differences among nations and their citizen or racial "types." Some scholars argue that national identity was as much the consequence of cultural practices, as of political and social practices and changes. Ernest Gellner argues that appeals to nationalism promote "that similarity of culture" necessary to form crucial social bonds and political identities.[55] Mary Douglas, like Gellner, defines culture as a mutually interdependent set of relationships among its members, "a system of persons holding one another mutually accountable. . . . From this angle, culture is fraught with the political implications of mutual accountability."[56] Benedict Anderson also describes nationalism, or "nation-ness," as a cultural artifact widely diffused and "modular," transplanted "to a great variety of social terrains" through print media and other venues communicating across diverse publics.[57]

As nineteenth-century international exhibitions exposed Europeans to cultures they had colonized or whose markets they had subdued, the production of national identities became a fixation among European countries competing for the same markets. In international exhibitions art and economics were juxtaposed, even joined. As these exhibitions proliferated and began appearing around the globe after the Great Exhibition in London in 1851, the involvement of governments in cultural matters increased in frequency and scale. British schools of design at home and British art schools in India trained Indian artists in European classical art to meet the demands of a burgeoning market for colonial goods under the guise of sharing a superior European aesthetic with Indian artists. European periodicals bulged with essays on and images from cultures around the globe, and the press contributed significantly to both the exposure and constriction involved in defining national cultural identities. The language shaped by media articulated a "norm" for national culture bounded by differences from other nations and a need to appear internally homogeneous and unified, for example, Benedict Anderson's imagined communities, or what Raymond Williams called the illusion of community.[58] Literary scholars have recently addressed the twin births of political economy and the novel as mutually illuminating: the novel in the private sphere and political economy in the public sphere, both marking modern life's gender and class divisions and specialization of knowledge.[59]

Consumer identity could be readily manipulated into cultural, gendered, and national identities by realigning desires as "needs." State-funded culture is often presented as didactically desirable for national identity and not simply as a consequence of consumer insatiability and individuation.[60] Individuals were distinguished in classical economics by their trade and the goods they produced. Marginalist economics leveled everyone as consumers, whose desires were the motives not only for the production of goods, but also for the advertisement of goods and the psychology of desire that became attached to market discourse.[61] Political economy of art complicates economic theories that define consumption as maximizing personal satisfaction because the political economy of art claims to express communal values or needs, an extension perhaps of Adam Smith's "Invisible Hand," invisible altruist forces working within the free market. Studying the concrete processes of the political economy of art may offer "a particular contribution to economic knowledge by showing how people come to 'choose' what they do, by showing how tastes and choices develop and, just as important, are constrained," to further demonstrate, as Regenia Gagnier notes, that "aesthetics means more than the market price of artistic commodities."[62]

As culture and markets merged in international trade and exhibitions, government attention to aesthetic matters was recognized as a means to gain economic prosperity and political domination. Much public art was commissioned to promote a view of culture amenable to a powerful segment of society whose control of public representation and symbolism was essential to its political and economic ambitions.[63] As Throsby recognizes, economics is itself a cultural process with its own various predispositions, such as its faith in the market, and its own representation of the social system.[64] Virtual and material forms of capital can both become subsumed within an ideology of cultural worth to reinforce a national identity as ideal, "natural" and "true."

Whereas monarchs and czars directly commissioned works, or powerful citizens like the Medici indirectly controlled "public" committees, the modern version of state-supported art appears more democratic and consequently more fraught with diverse aesthetic intentions and interpretations that can even subsume more material needs. Douglas argues that consumption is primarily a social act for communication and knowledge, not survival: "Instead of someone who buys for private purposes the consumer would have to be seen as someone engaged in long-term interactions with other social beings and using goods to promote the particular social patterns that he values."[65] Douglas's paradigmatic consumption is buying flowers, not food. In other words, cultural consumption is exemplary of *all* consumption, and a means to share a dominant system of knowledge and to shape social patterns and interactions. Consuming culture is necessary and even primary, not secondary after consumption for survival.[66]

The corporation-funded monument in a public space may appear as a kind of gift, but such public space often remains corporate space in many cases, as in the plazas and atriums of corporate buildings.[67] Not all the public good bestowed by the arts is morally "good," socially cohesive or philosophically ideal. A monument's symbolic meanings may all too readily elide national and corporate values and identities, as when corporate monuments or buildings become symbols of a city's communality (e.g., Rockefeller Center in the city of New York). Tourists are attracted to state-funded monuments that become part of a nation's gross national product, promoted by its description or image in travel guidebooks. One branch of economics studies culture as economic processes, an approach derived from the work of John Kenneth Galbraith. As Throsby notes, in this area of study, "the cultural industries are interpreted using the conventional paraphernalia of economic analysis, albeit with some innovative twists and adaptations to account for the peculiarities of artistic demand and supply."[68] This area of study depends on culture *as* an industry, produced with an eye to profits and consumption. Cultural production generates real money, resources, sales, imports, and exports.

Culture as industry may also be an example of the reciprocity between individuals and social systems in constructing both the individual self and the state.[69] The intersection of cultural values and economic systems can have a virtual life all its own. As Jean Baudrillard has so thoroughly argued, the distinction between an image and its referent often becomes elided, sublimated, or erased, so images can seem more real than the actual object or idea to which they refer.[70] This displacement, a function of consumption in a world of mechanical, and now electronic, reproduction, constructs a knowledge system or epistemology. But within the circulation of these images, spectators' interpretations and significations may be antithetical to the intended meanings that the state thought it purchased when it funded culture. Like objects, meanings circulate, as they are decontextualizd and recontextualized in unpredictable trajectories and provenances to participate in the very production of art.

SUMMARY OF THE BOOK

In the first part of this book, "Political Economy's Interventions in Art Production," essays directly address theoretical issues of government intervention in art production through conflicts between economics and the practices of art production. My essay, "From Culture to Cultural Capital," surveys the development of an active political economy of art, first articulated in full by John Ruskin, and formed as a set of professional, social, and economic practices by Victorian artists themselves. Ruskin's *Political Economy of Art* (1857), later amplified as *A Joy For Ever* (1880), presented an ideal artist—unambitious, innocent, and unworldly. Ruskin hoped to isolate artists from society to protect their susceptibility to market values. To this end, Ruskin struggled with how to adjust market values to the values of creativity he had earlier mapped in *Modern Painters* and *Stones of Venice*. Unfortunately, his political economy of art gutted his earlier ideal of the independent and imaginative medieval artisan, as he articulated a political economy of both the artist and art. Against his recommendations were the actual practices of artists, savvy in economics and in acquiring social status, who redefined art-making as professional, gentlemanly, and lucrative, and became very un-Ruskinian in their effort to participate in the politics and the economics of art production and consumption from the mid-nineteenth century on, exemplified by their creation of professional societies and management of their public images. These activities promoted a new, central role of artists in the creation of national identity.

Focusing on late-twentieth-century artworks, such as Christo and Jean-Claude's environmental artworks and the Brooklyn Museum's Sensation exhibition, Ann Li's "The Political Economy of Art and Culture," surveys some heterodox approaches to fine art(s) as commodity and methodologies that amplify and transform the orthodox analyses of the economics of art. These alternative analyses provide answers to what North American economists Heilbrun and Gray leave as unresolved questions: the role of mass media and arts education in the economics of the arts. Mass media and arts education offer heterodox approaches that render a history of art's political economy more robust and comprehensive. The public sphere in which art exists is also constituted by political communication, which Li sees as influencing cultural criticism's tendency toward being promotional rather than dialectical.

In "Intangible Asset Values," Elizabeth Norman looks at case studies in Japan to assess the terminology used in setting value for contemporary public art. Public art value has conventionally been identified with urban regeneration, property enhancement, and promotion of image and place, benefits that cannot be strictly measured. Norman explores other terminology with which to discuss economic value, a requirement frequently made of public art projects. She considers terms taken from accounting—including goodwill, branding, and intellectual property—known collectively as intangible benefits. Norman argues that by treating public art's values as assets of an enterprise, public art may be made accountable and its values tallied, perhaps permitting a better defense for public art's position as a significant practice of political economy.

The second part, "National Conflicts over Political Economy in the Public Sphere," focuses on the criticism of political economy by artists or the public. Daniel Guernsey ("Protestant Dissent and the Political Economy of Art in Eighteenth-Century England") demonstrates that James Barry's primary purpose in his mural program, *The Progress of Human Knowledge and Culture*, 1777–84, was to historicize the civilizing role of arts, manufactures, and commerce articulated by English and Scottish political economists. Barry constructed a providential vision of intersecting economic and artistic improvements. Barry's narrative contains shifts of emphasis that sometimes subvert the material improvements of British civil society. The primitivist critique of commerce and luxury in James Macpherson's essays on Ossian enabled Barry to uphold William Penn as the quintessential ideal against the abuses of commerce. Through Penn, Barry suggests that cultural institutions themselves can constrain unfettered self-interest and luxury to limit commerce's deleterious effect on the public role of art.

Elizabeth Grady argues in "The Popular Opposition" that the abdication of the Kaiser in 1918 provided an opportunity for the National Gallery's director, Ludwig Justi, to support Expressionism as the leading German modernist style through exhibitions and acquisitions. Grady's study addresses the question of the impact of politicized criticism of the National Gallery's support of modern art on public art opinion, and ultimately on the public acceptance of the National Socialist policy to suppress modern art beginning in 1933. The museum's role in the ideological projection of national identity made it a participant in national politics. Since Expressionism had become linked to political and economic instability during 1918–1923, Justi's rhetoric was intended to make modernism palatable to a nation searching for stability after its World War I defeat, but he met resistance from art critics promoting an heroic and stable image of Germany.

Maria Brown, in her "Art in New Zealand's New National Museum," explores the intersection of cultural and economic agendas in the case of the Museum of New Zealand Te Papa Tongarewa, which used exhibitions to represent and realign the national public sphere and overcome the legacy of colonialism.

The museum deployed divergent systems of display to construct the celebratory narrative of a harmonious society enriched by diverse cultural traditions. Separating Europeanized and native cultures, the museum focused on aesthetic qualities of objects by the indigenous people, while it foregrounded technological achievement for European settlers' material culture. However, the pursuit of this agenda, presumably a public good, was severely constrained by a reduction of public funding that originated in a shift in economic conceptions by a change of government. Forced to operate as a private enterprise, the museum put in place populist strategies that have attracted both large numbers of visitors and strong criticism from art experts and academics.

Part 3, "Public Monuments and the Public Sphere," examines sculpture and architecture and their public roles, emphasizing the difference between government intentions and public interpretations, and how economic value systems can or cannot be applied to art in the public sphere. In "Giovanni Antolini's *Foro Bonaparte*," Joachim Homann investigates the impact of the political economy of art on the creation of public spaces in Napoleonic Milan. Focusing on Giovanni Antolini's *Foro Bonaparte*, an oversized new city center, Homann distinguishes between two levels of the political economy of art, both present in Napoleonic Milan. Through the circulation of money, art and architecture were linked to the general political economy. Architecture was also part of a symbolic exchange of gifts—another level of the political economy of art. By spending unreasonable amounts of money for monuments dedicated to Bonaparte, the Milanese puppet government hoped to define an independent status for their republic.

In "The Panthéon, 1870–1900," Cheryl Snay's study of the decorative program of the Panthéon in the aftermath of the Franco-Prussian War and Commune (1870–71) and undertaken by the state during the Third Republic offers a case study of the government's impact on the political economy of art. The program was conceived by monarchists who dominated the government. Then republicans counterappropriated even more money for a new sculptural program to overwhelm the earlier paintings with sheer scale. Control of the historical message presented in the Panthéon was wrested from the conservatives by the republicans simply by outspending them. Snay's discussion expands our understanding of the power dynamics in a nascent polity and the role of images in articulating political debate.

Andrew Stephenson addresses monuments commemorating the World War I dead caught between shifting modern values and state ideologies of unity and imperial domination in his "Palimpsestic Promenades." The main concern was how prewar commemorative forms and conservative modes of depiction could be rendered appropriate for modern public commemoration, national pilgrimage, and mass participation. Stephenson reveals a post–1919 shift in the processional axes in the City of Westminster. These revised London spatial geographies produced a commemorative route culminating in the Cenotaph as imperial and national shrine, but one that did not simply affirm imperial unity and national integration. These monuments were open to recoding and reinscription, especially by young women, war widows, and gay men, destabilizing state and imperialist symbolism and generating memories that threatened postwar commemoration and its rhetorics of national unity and imperial regeneration.

In "The Political Economy of Hitler's State Architecture," Paul Jaskot focuses on the central ideological and economic value of the building industry to the National Socialist government in Germany. As a means of helping Germany recover from the Depression, the building trades and state projects provided employment and a concentration of resources on a massive scale. Jaskot's subject is the alignment of monumental building aesthetics and technologies with state economic and military policy. In the monumental projects for such sites as Albert Speer's rebuilding of Berlin, the building industry prospered under the ideological projections of various party and state institutions. Monumental projects provided a focus for discussions concerning the integration of building technologies with developing militarization of the German economy.

The last part of this book, "A Case Study: The Political Economy of Art in America," looks at the American governmental commission of art. Essays in this part focus on aesthetic presumptions intended to symbolize democracy's progress and the failure of such presumptions to be imposed. Helen Langa, in her "Constructing Cultural Democracy," examines the New Deal's political economy of art in the 1930s when government funded the production of public art for a mass audience under the banner of "cultural democracy." Advocates sought to legitimate this ideal by drawing on three contradictory sources: progressive ideals of social improvement, leftist valorizations of art as revolutionary, and regionalist affirmation of local values against urban, elitist modernism. Access to diverse cultural experiences did not necessarily translate into popular acceptance of new art forms, but often led to questions about defining and changing values and tastes of a mass audience. Each of the ideological constructs used to support state funding was complicated by underlying complexities and contradictions that left programs vulnerable to oppositional critique, while the pragmatic aspects of their institutional practice also produced intense public debate. Both idealism and dissent assured that the rhetoric of cultural democracy was often belied in the details of its actualization within the larger political economy of cultural development in the United States.

In "Cultural Democracy by Default," Andrew Hemingway examines the apparent confluence between Soviet and American ideologies in the New Deal art programs in the 1930s. To administrators who acted as ideologues for various federal arts projects, these programs were a response to the patent failures of a market-ordered cultural economy to produce truly democratic arts appropriate to America's political traditions, and a first experiment in the use of state power to redress the failings of laissez-faire ideology. The Communist Party's new sympathy for American democratic institutions under the Popular Front was reflected in the party's strong support for the New Deal's cultural programs in which many communists and fellow travelers took part. The unions that the party instigated among introduced an element of democracy beyond anything the administration had ever intended.

Anne Goodyear, in "NASA and the Political Economy of Art, 1962–1974," analyzes how the National Aeronautics and Space Administration (NASA), established to run the U.S. civilian space program, developed an art program in the early 1960s. The agency has long been very focused on the history-in-the-making quality of its work. Support for the art project was argued on historical models of artists accompanying explorers and surveyors to help show Eastern supporters the grandeur of the American West. In addition, the National Gallery was encouraging government agencies to document their work. Goodyear addresses the contradictions between what NASA artists could show and national ideals.

NOTES

1. For a good survey of the literature, see Brigitte H. Bechtold, "Introduction: Art and Political Economy," *Review of Radical Political Economics* 36, no. 4 (Fall, 2004): 461–70. This issue, which focuses on post-WWII art, and the 2005 issue of *History of Political Economy* 37, no. 3, are both devoted to analyses of the political economy of art. For a survey of current issues in cultural economics and public support of the arts, see Crauford D. Goodwin, "Public Support of the Arts in the History of Economics: Introduction," *History of Political Economy* 37, no. 3 (2005): 399–411. Hereafter cited as Goodwin, "Introduction." The most basic studies are Neil De Marchi and Craufurd D. W. Goodwin, eds. *Economic Engagements with Art* (Durham, NC: Duke University Press, 1999); Regenia Gagnier, *The Insatiability of Human Wants: Economics and Aesthetics in Market Society* (Chicago: University of Chicago Press, 2000); James Heilbrun and Charles M. Gray, *The Economics of Art and Culture*, 2nd ed. (Cambridge: Cambridge University Press, 2001); Richard Maxwell, ed., *Culture Works: The Political Economy of Culture* (Minneapolis: University of Minnesota Press, 2001); David Throsby, *Economics and Culture* (Cambridge: Cambridge University Press, 2001); and the pioneering Brian Allen, ed., *Towards a Modern Art World* (London: Yale University Press, 1995).

2. Gail Dines and Jean M. Humez, eds., *Gender, Race, and Class in Media: A Text-Reader*, 2nd ed. (London: Sage, 2003), xiv.

3. Edward S. Herman and Noam Chomsky. *Manufacturing Consent: The Political Economy of the Mass Media* (New York: Pantheon Books, 1988).

4. See Goodwin, "Introduction," 400–1.

5. This quote is from Neil De Marchi and Jonathan A. Greene, "Adam Smith and Private Provision of the Arts," *History of Political Economy* 37, no. 3 (2005): 433; comment on Smith not considering art as a public good, 434. Smith himself was involved in the initiative in 1753 to set up an academy of art in Glasgow, where he taught (445ff).

6. See Willie Henderson, *Economics as Literature* (New York: Routledge, 1995), 9. See also Willie Henderson, *John Ruskin's Political Economy* (New York: Routledge, 2000) and Gregory C. G. Moore, "Evangelical Aesthete: Ruskin and the Public Provision of Art," *History of Political Economy* 37, no. 3 (2005): 483–508, for more on Ruskin's hope for centralized authority in control of art production.

7. Jürgen Habermas, *The Structural Transformation of the Public Sphere*, trans. Thomas Burger (Cambridge, MA: MIT Press, 1991), 141–81.

8. An example of the difference of our approach from that of many studies by economists is in the apology for including Matthew Arnold in the study of cultural economics in Oliver Bennett, "Beyond Machinery: The Cultural Policies of Matthew Arnold," *History of Political Economy* 37, no. 3 (2005): 455. Yet, Arnold and also Ruskin are subjects of essays in this volume, so clearly economists feel the need to look at cultural "sages" in the study of cultural economics and the political economy of art, despite some uncertainty or ambiguity in doing this. Bennett's fine essays trace Arnold's literary career, ideas in *Culture and Anarchy*, and significant contributions to cultural policy into the twentieth century.

9. Bennett, "Beyond Machinery," 456.

10. Some recent books on contemporary art (since the 1980s) employ the term "political economy," but explore a wide range of art production, not all connected to the state as subject or patron; see Jonathan Harris, ed. *Art, Money, Parties: New Institutions in the Political Economy of Contemporary Art* (Liverpool: Liverpool University Press, 2004), an anthology that ranges across museums, galleries, and individual art productions, but does not define political economy and uses an historical sociology as its method (11), and most of its fine essays employ political partisanship and discuss "self-reflective" art that comments on art history, rather than on the political economy of its collective patronage.

11. See, for example, Crauford D. Goodwin, ed. *Art and the Market: Roger Fry on Commerce and Art* (Ann Arbor: University of Michigan Press, 1998).

12. Bennett, "Beyond Machinery," 457.

13. I will examine Henderson's work in my chapter on Ruskin. Earlier studies of Ruskin and economics include J. T. Fain, *Ruskin and the Economists* (Nashville, TN: Vanderbilt University Press,

1956); A. Lee, "Ruskin and Political Economy: Unto This Last," in *New Approaches to Ruskin: Thirteen Essays*, ed. Robert Hewison (London: Routledge and Kegan Paul, 1981), 68–88; Harro Maas, "Pacifying the Workman: Ruskin and Jevons on Labor and Popular Culture," *Economic Engagements with Art*, ed. N. De Marchi and C. D. W. Goodwin (Durham, NC: Duke University Press, 1999), 85–120; J. C. Sherburne, *John Ruskin, or The Ambiguities of Abundance: A Study in Social and Economic Criticism* (Cambridge, MA: Harvard University Press, 1972).

14. Moore, 483.

15. Anna Upchurch, "William Morris and the Case of Public Support of the Arts," *History of Political Economy*, 37 no. 3 (2005): 510. Morris was also an astute businessman himself; see Charles Harvey and Jon Press, *William Morris: Design and Enterprise in Victorian Britain* (Manchester, UK: Manchester University Press, 1991).

16. For a study of the founding of cultural economics, see Gregory Besharov, "The Outbreak of the Cost Disease: Baumol and Bowen's Founding of Cultural Economics," *History of Political Economy*, 37 no. 3 (2005): 413–30.

17. There are many studies of Robbins, the most recent on Robbins's views on state subsidies and his active work in the art world is Susan Howson "Lionel Robbins's 'Art and the State,'" *History of Political Economy* 37 no. 3 (2005): 617–46.

18. What Alan Peacock called "spillover" from culture; cited in Besharov, 421.

19. See especially Bourdieu, *The Field of Cultural Production*, ed. Randal Johnson (Cambridge: Polity Press, 1993) and "The Field of Cultural Production, or: The Economic World Reversed," *Poetics* 12 (1983): 311–56.

20. These are among the arguments made by cultural economists; see Basharov's description and critique of these arguments in the work of William Baumol and William Bowen in Besharov, 423.

21. Heilbrun and Gray, 187.

22. Throsby, *Economics and Culture*, 6.

23. Ibid.

24. De Marchi and Greene, 436. On p. 452, the authors summarized some of Smith's reasons: Government would not encourage independent thought and taste (which the arts should do) and could not provide art that would respond to all individual tastes and desires.

25. For one case of imperialism bolstered by art, see Codell, "Gentlemen Connoisseurs and Capitalists: Modern British Imperial Identity in the 1903 Delhi Durbar's Exhibition of Indian Art," in *Cultural Identities and the Aesthetics of Britishness*, ed. D. Arnold (Manchester, UK: Manchester University Press, 2004), 134–63.

26. Margaret A. Rose *Marx's Lost Aesthetic: Karl Marx and the Visual Arts* (Cambridge: Cambridge University Press, 1984), 12, cites Saint-Simon as an example.

27. Martha Woodmansee and Mark Osteen, eds., *The New Economic Criticism* (London: Routledge, 1999), 29.

28. Among the many interesting studies on gifts are James G. Carrier, *Gifts and Commodities* (London: Routledge, 1994), and David Cheal, *The Gift Economy* (London: Routledge, 1988).

29. Heilbrun and Gray, 227.

30. See ibid., 232. The U.S. suspicion of government subsidies for art is unique among industrial nations (ibid., 250–51).

31. Maxwell, 3.

32. Habermas, 2–17.

33. Mass, 88–89.

34. Goodwin, *Art and the Market*, 161.

35. Ruskin, *A Joy For Ever*, in *Works of John Ruskin*, ed. E. T. Cook and Alexander Wedderburn (London: G. Allen, 1903–12), 16: 29–30.

36. Rose, *Marx's Lost Aesthetic*, 77.

37. Marx cited in ibid., 95.

38. Peacock cited in D. E. Moggridge, "Keynes, the Arts, and the State," *History of Political Economy*, 37, no. 3 (2005): 553.

39. "James Clarke Hook," *Art Journal* 7 (1856): 41.

40. See Julie Codell, *The Victorian Artist* (Cambridge: Cambridge University Press, 2003).

41. Keynes, cited in Moggridge, 552.

42. See Codell, *The Victorian Artist*, chapter 2.

43. Rees, Helen, "Art Exports and the Construction of National Heritage in Late-Victorian and Edwardian Great Britain," 201.

44. On this issue, see Joanna Bailkin, *The Culture of Property* (Chicago: University of Chicago Press, 2004).

45. Rees, in De Marchi and Goodwin, 199.

46. William J. Barber, "International Commerce in the Fine arts and American Political Economy, 1789–1913," in De Marchi and Goodwin, 209.

47. Habermas, 23.

48. Woodmansee and Osteen, eds., 6.

49. Throsby, *Economics and Culture*, 14.

50. Habermas, 2.

51. Sergiusz Michalski, *Public Monuments: Art in Political Bondage, 1870–1997* (London: Reaktion Books, 1998), 8–9.

52. William J. Barber, "'Sweet Are the Uses of Adversity': Federal Patronage of the Arts in the Great Depression," in De Marchi and Goodwin, 240–41.

53. Michalski, 10.

54. Throsby, *Economics and Culture*, 16.

55. Ernest Gellner, *Nationalism* (New York: New York University Press, 1997), 3–4.

56. Mary Douglas, *Risk and Blame: Essays in Cultural Theory* (London: Routledge, 1992), 31.

57. Benedict Anderson, *Imagined Communities: Reflections on the Origin and Spread of Nationalism*, 2nd ed. (London: Verso, 1991), 4–6.

58. Raymond Williams, *The Country and the City* (Oxford: Oxford University Press, 1973), 1–3.

59. Woodmansee and Osteen, 5.

60. Gagnier, 4.

61. Ibid., 2–3.

62. Ibid., 10.

63. Recent studies of gentlemen capitalists under the Raj also stress the collision of cultural and economic interests. See Peter J. Cain and A. G. Hopkins, *British Imperialism, Innovation and Expansion, 1688–1914* (London: Longman, 1993), and Raymond E. Dumett, *Gentlemanly Capitalism and British Imperialism* (London: Longman, 1999).

64. Throsby, *Economics and Culture*, 9.

65. Douglas, *Risk and Blame*, 151.

66. Economists, too, distinguish between absolute needs, which can be satiated, and "positional" needs, which cannot. See Moggridge, 540.

67. Malcolm Miles, *Art, Space and the City: Public art and Urban Futures* (London: Routledge, 1997), 40.

65. Throsby, *Economics and Culture*, 12.

66. Woodmansee and Osteen, 20–22.

67. Jean Baudrillard, *Simulacra and Simulation* (Ann Arbor: University of Michigan Press, 1994), 12–14. See Throsby, 11.

I
Political Economy's Interventions in Art Production

From Culture to Cultural Capital: Victorian Artists, John Ruskin, and the Political Economy of Art

Julie F. Codell

Artists are usually assumed to be born spendthrifts.

—Rudolf and Margot Wittkower, *Born Under Saturn*[1]

The practice of every art is bread-winning as well as aesthetic adventure, and attacks on bread-winning are crimes against citizenship when they cannot be justified by sufficient evidence.

—Walter Shaw Sparrow, *Memories of Life and Art Through Sixty Years*[2]

Artists' Entrepreneurship

In a recent essay, Jonathan Rose ponders the question of whether capitalism was good for Victorian literature. He concludes that it was, generally, and that the scholarly division between high and popular culture, with its concomitant disdain for those who write for money, fails to acknowledge how many "great" authors wrote for money.[3] Capitalism after midcentury was also very good for many Victorian artists, exceptionally good for a handful of them, though only middling for many who emerged in droves to become artists after 1880, inspired by the celebrity and wealth of that handful. Economists B. S. Frey and W. W. Pommerehne point out that successful Victorian painters "received as much for one painting as a university-trained public official earned over a decade, or a minister earned over a year," although such incomes were not typical for a vast majority of artists.[4] For those for whom capitalism was good, it was so because artists actively took advantage of opportunities for self-advertising, press releases, and professional organizations to refine and partition the market so more buyers would pay for more art from more artists. Collusions between artists and dealers could be very lucrative and artists proved themselves fine speculators and investors, as did dealers and collectors. The art press promoted many commercial activities for artists and offered economic information. Like their novelist cohorts, Victorian artists often created their best works under market pressures. Dianne Sachko Macleod has demonstrated that artists were often consummate business negotiators with patrons.[5] As I have shown elsewhere, they actively promoted themselves into celebrity, wealth, and social status.[6]

Attention to money was not new among artists in the nineteenth century. During the Renaissance, Giorgio Vasari's *Lives of the Artists* cited artists' prices and their strategies for increasing profits. In the 1770s James Barry railed against artists corrupted by money and idealized the "real artist" who subordinated personal gain to duty to God and country.[7] Benjamin West and John Singleton Copley were bitterly attacked for their "works of speculation," privately exhibited, intended for reproduction sales, and sometimes with sensationalistic subjects (Batschmann, 29–32). As private patronage was being replaced by impersonal market relations, art buyers hunted for bargains of cheap art "to be bought and sold like any other commodity."[8]

Like writers, artists came to inhabit the split between commerce—what they were doing—and a higher purpose—what they said they were doing. Nineteenth-century literary figures wrote on political economy or incorporated its ideas (De Quincey, Coleridge, Wordsworth) revealing ties between literature and political economy.[9] As Victorian artists became better educated and drew subjects from literature, science, and history, they, too, became interested in political economy. Artists' letters reveal their economic knowledge and activity, even beyond the art market.[10] Edward Poynter in his 1871 lecture "Systems of Education" complained that English art students wanted to sell before they were adequately trained, and French critics condemned English artists as market driven. But Walter Shaw Sparrow's statement at the beginning of this chapter defends breadwinning and, even more, argues that breadwinning inscribed citizenship on artists.

Many Victorians believed artists' sensitivities put them at war with the commercial world, competition, and financial realities. But political economy was not only about money: Adam Smith taught English literature and encouraged his students "to temper their acquisitiveness with the values of sympathy, charity, and taste" (Rose, 490). Victorian artists, too, understood an economics of sublimation for future rewards. As Viviana Zelizer argues, the market is cultural, not just economic.[11] Consumption is a cultural resource, not just a cultural process, and thus generates new meanings, as it did for Victorian artists, art critics, the press, and a public no longer of elites as in the eighteenth-century but a nineteenth-century mass audience.

In this essay I will describe ways Victorian artists controlled their markets and exhibited economic agency. I will then turn to John Ruskin's political economy of art, his attempt to fit art production and consumption into both labor and marginalist economic models. Finally, I will assess these two conflicting views of artists' economic practice to argue that artists transformed culture into cultural capital, by taking on new roles as shapers of national identity and contributors to national well-being, roles commensurate with their own social and economic rise.

Pierre Bourdieu's argument that art world participants disguise or fail to recognize their economic interestedness is only partly true for most Victorian artists who happily paraded financial success as a sign of social respectability and their art's high quality.[12] They seemed to believe, as recent scholars now appear to believe, that aesthetics and commodification were not mutually exclusive (Rose, 493).[13] However, their economic interest was not only material: Many artists abandoned immediate monetary returns on their art "investments" (labor and training), especially in their early years, for long-range, even posthumous reputations—their intangible assets. Victorian artists' market behavior was calculated to serve long-range goals—reputations and social bonds with patrons—as well as immediate economic rewards. Such goals marked them as professionals, not laborers. Victorian artists acted on their own behalf to change their cultural production into cultural capital for themselves and for their consumers. Art market economics became a political economy through artists' efforts and participation in new national roles made possible by their acquisition of money and its perks—grand studio homes and upper-class social circles as friends, not just as patrons.

Present and future successes were collective. Artists had a stake in the value of their colleagues' work. Following artists' deaths, when their works' values were reassessed, fellow artists wrote their posthumous biographies and attended sales and auctions to keep up prices of deceased cohorts. One artist's sales helped all of them.[14] Artists identified each other's forgeries by attending sales to keep up their market and resale values (Mills, 232, 260) and found markets for each other and shared patrons.

Economics could even be a muse. G. D. Leslie insisted that money inspired young artists. He condemned the Royal Academy (RA) for keeping students from selling. The sale of a work for ten guineas, "gave an impetus and energy to my working power." He insisted "in Art, as in other things, the demand commands the supply" and Old Masters "by no means despised the remuneration they obtained for their labours."[15]

Artists were entrepreneurial and their economic activities were broad. They illustrated novels and serialized literature in the press, rejecting the separation between high and commercial art. Making copies or replicas of their popular works, artists insisted these were more valuable than the originals, as the artist had more experience when doing the later replica.[16] Copying was widespread and acceptable until near the end of the century. Artists redefined replicas as new and improved versions to avoid the stigma of potboiling. Richard Redgrave's daughter insisted her father's replicas (the popular *The Poor Teacher* redone four times) were original or semioriginal.[17] Prices provoked by dealers pressured watercolorists to paint in the more lucrative oil and to copy successful works. Ford Madox Brown wrote that "my own work for the last year has, with the exception of two children's head pictures, all been duplicate pieces."[18] Dante Gabriel Rossetti made numerous copies of his works for patrons, and Hunt copied *The Shadow of Death* twice per requests.

Women artists participated as avidly as men in lucrative art ventures across varied venues (e.g., art criticism, portraiture), although with smaller remunerations and fewer opportunities. Lizzie Siddal's "concentration on illustrative subjects suggests a careful assessment of commercial possibilities."[19] Even artists with considerable family wealth, such as Evelyn Pickering, painted to sell. For women, sales were special evidence of their professionalism, a measure that their work was not merely an "accomplishment."

Economic advice abounded in the art press in regular columns and purchases were announced. The art press promoted a political economy of art by condemning the government for failing to raise funds to purchase a work worthy for the nation, whether Old Master or modern British. The language of art in the *Art Journal* and *The Magazine of Art* was professional *because* it was a language of the marketplace. P. L. Simmons in 1872 recognized that "taste is a marketable commodity, which being of so much value is worth getting honestly, and by fair purchase."[20] Simmons demonstrated that, thanks to British art, the balance of trade in 1871 was in the black. Increased demand for art and "artistic" goods abroad and at home supported the national income. Simmons listed the value of imported oil painting, engravings, photos, picture frames, opera glasses, and marble, totaling over £1 million. Exported manufactured art-related goods totaled over £6 million.

Artists and dealers took advantage of the 1860s boom. William Orchardson wrote in 1866 "I have all the 'swell' dealers at me for pictures."[21] Frith made a deal with Louis Victor Flatow to paint *The Railway Station* for £4,500 in 1860 plus exhibition rights of £750.[22] Paying spectators totaled 21,150, and Flatow sold the painting to the print dealer Graves for £16,000. In 1860 Gambart paid Holman Hunt 5,500 guineas for *Finding the Saviour in the Temple*, earned £4,000 in exhibition fees and made £5,000 profit from the engraving before selling the painting for £1,500. Gambart paid Frederick Goodall £6,000 for his sketches done in Egypt in 1869, and the Agnews paid Hunt £11,000 for *The Shadow of Death* (1871–73; see Ferriday, 1576; Reitlinger, 1:147–48). As a marker, the National Gallery bought a Veronese in 1856 for £13,650 (Reitlinger, 1:148). Millais's annual salary was reputed to have been £20,000 to £25,000 between 1868–74, and up to £40,000 in the 1880s, while Landseer, John Linnell, and John Gilbert each left £200,000 after their deaths (Ferriday, 1577; Reitlinger, 1:148).

Success in art was like success in any capitalistic venture; it depended on speculation, risk-taking, and investment. Paintings done on speculation generated new market demands and niches for new subjects like crowds by Frith or military subjects by Elizabeth Butler or archeological religious paintings by Hunt. Hunt and his patron Combe worked as a team to induce purchases of Hunt's works; if his works were purchased by the right people, that would increase the value of Combe's collection of Hunt's paintings. Hunt called their enterprise "the firm"[23] and Combe, its "sleeping partner."[24] William Powell Frith refused to name a price until the work was complete for casual buyers and refused to promise commissions for prearranged prices.

SITES OF EXCHANGE: EXHIBITIONS, DISPLAYS, CRITICS, DEALERS

> In the space of a few months a painting could be seen in an artist's studio, in a London gallery, in a provincial exhibition, in a dealer's showroom, in the house or building of its purchaser; it might be viewed as a print or an illustration in a magazine. Various readings would be made by diverse viewers.
>
> —Deborah Cherry, *Painting Women*[25]

This maze of spectating exchanges described by Deborah Cherry, in which spectating is a form of consumption, was motivated by market conditions requiring multiple sightings. Artists would preexhibit in a Bond Street gallery a painting destined for a patron or for the Royal Academy to display and sell works before the RA exhibition and get press attention, given the likelihood their works would be poorly hung and relatively invisible among thousands of exhibited works. Frederic Smallfield in 1885 praised the gallery as "a picture shop" where artists earned a livelihood. He admonished artists to "sell all your pictures (if you can)," abolish sale-less private views (for elite customers), and charge a shilling entrance fee and sixpence for the catalog to self-select viewers with means.[26] Smallwood wanted to divorce exhibitions from any social purpose and keep their function exclusively economic.

Oskar Batschmann argues that exhibitions require artists to have economic agency, "to define, legitimate and finance their work in public competition with each other . . . adjust to the changing demands of patrons and the requirements of the market . . . calculate or steer public reaction . . . find access to the media and project an interesting image" (9–10). The dominance of the exhibition raised the issue of the nature of the "public" and its role in representing national taste or identity through art consumption. Artists worried about the long-range impact of exhibitions on their reputations and tried to control their works' public display to protect the twins of reputation and market value. Frederic Shields made his purchasers swear not to exhibit his works without his consent (Mills, 119). Artists advised collectors on when to sell their works to get maximum profit and simultaneously raise the artist's works' prices on the market.

Critics often helped artists meet public demands and satisfy their own material needs. Artists, critics, and editors were a close-knit camaraderie. Critics frequented artists' studios to see works in progress—not only to write about them to tantalize the public, but also to suggest which should be sent to the RA and to recommend buyers. The power of reviews is perhaps too well known to require examples: Millais had to accept half the agreed-upon £l,300 price for *The Carpenter's Shop* when his buyer, Henry Farrer, read the scathing reviews of the painting.[27] Critics served multiple economic functions for artists—to introduce them to patrons, find exhibition venues, circulate artists' comments as "press reports," and educate readers about artists' modes of production, their lives, and labor. Artists provided critics with puffs to communicate to the public and often exchanged art works for critical attention, creating a kind of barter or gift economy between artists and critics. Critics sometimes gave financial advice to artists.[28]

These relations had direct economic roles. Gianfranco Mossetto notes that creativity and interpretation are mutually interdependent. Positive critical reviews "have the same effects of a wage increase for artistic labor, even if they are not necessarily accompanied by an increase in the supplied quantity, that is, in the physical productivity of labor":[29]

> artists (who represent their ability to 'create' just as entrepreneurs represent their ability to organize and undertake activities under conditions of risk and/or uncertainty) are a fixed production factor. . . . They can be compared to land. . . . Their earnings are determined through a rent-like mechanism. . . . The rent depends on creativity *and* interpretation. Creativity may produce interpretation, interpretation affects price. . . . The absence of interpretation can lead to an output decrease despite creativity. Artists can be discouraged by people's insensitivity. The returns of creativity are therefore not submitted to any "diminishing law," like the returns on land.[30]

Artists and critics shared self-fashioning identities as focused on aesthetics and sociability; "purely" economic activities, still suspect, were deflected onto dealers who were demonized. C. H. Goodruff in 1890 itemized dealers' corrupt practices, forgeries, lies, and auction house antics: "dealers form a ring and buy the goods at their own prices," being the "shabbiest, sordidest, seediest specimens of the *genus homo* who gather as vultures round a carcase [sic]."[31] Henrietta Ward distinguished between art dealers, "unlovely specimens" and the founder of Christie's, "surrounded by beautiful objects of Art."[32] For Ward and Christie the auction oddly reinforced their transcendental aesthetic values; for dealers it remained just business.

Another demon was the casual buyer. Gallery director Charles Hallé remarked on consumers who cared only about artists' names, propelled by commercialism or status. He considered picture-buying, gambling if done for investment, and prices established by auctions as only economic, compared with exhibitions that established quality. Hallé believed true patrons opened "not only their purses but their hearts," making their purchases forms of social and aesthetic bonding, while picture-buyers' indulged "a highly successful branch of speculation."[33]

The Cultural Capital of Reputation and Sublimation

Clearly, artists' economic activities were inscribed by anxieties and had to be transferred from economic gain to public good through artistic self-sacrifice, social bonds with patrons, serving to educate buyers' tastes, and, ultimately, benefiting the nation. Artists engaged in several forms of capital, which had permeable or overlapping borders, as Mary Douglas notes:

> Cultural capital is based upon educational qualifications but it includes subsequent self-education in various ways. Social capital is the advantage that comes to a child from a home well-endowed with cultural capital. Honorific capital means those forms of civic recognition that accrue to a successful life in the top echelons of industrial society. Symbolic capital is mostly available to writers and artists who can symbolize their virtuous commitment to social criticism without necessarily doing anything to disturb the balance of social forces. It is convenient to think of holdings in these four kinds of capital as spiritual resources; combined with economic resources they form a personal patrimony.[34]

Successful artists accrued cultural and honorific capital and some had social capital from the start. Artists' very names became bearers of multiple capitals for their consumers who gained social capital by their purchases. Artists' economics of reputation and sublimation guaranteed cultural capital—as they gained more economic success, artists were more assertive and authoritative in their dealings with patrons and in their self-fashionings.

The occasional high prices paid to artists were signs of artistic worth for both artists and consumers. Victorian artists' political economy—the national wealth they contributed through reputation or honorific capital—expanded their economic participation in the nation's economic well-being. They often sublimated immediate rewards for "higher" benefits: Frederic Shields and W. B. Richmond abandoned their "clientage to execute a great public work," implying a monetary loss in exchange for public display and reputation.[35] Public murals gave artists a voice in discourses about nationhood; Brown's Manchester murals defined a new industrial urban national history despite not paying well. Holman Hunt complained that for the sake of an anticipated masterpiece he would forego money from salable sketches.[36] Hunt charged Gambart a low price for the copyright to *The Light of the World*, to encourage Gambart to pay for a quality engraving that "will extend to the continent, and will continue for years": [36] "Had you allowed the business interest to be paramount you would have considered only how you could most quickly turn your capital invested in the work. . . . that you have not done this is I really believe a great service to the progress of good taste in England."[38] Hunt's uncanny business acumen put long-term fame above immediate payments. His patron Combe wanted Hunt to paint and sell more quickly. Hunt replied: "My income would be increased as one of the immediate consequences," but his reputation "would never have been what is now—and now a very rapid fall in my income as well as in my reputation would be the result."[39] Hunt's eye was on the economics of reputation, as well as of bread. It took Solomon Hart six months to paint pictures in his early life. He had to make economic decisions "to decline several commissions, . . . with a view of becoming an R.A.," so vital to success was RA membership.[40] As a young artist Hart rented a room for twenty pounds, a large sum, to show a nearly fourteen-foot canvas, on which he spent a year and paid models. He was elected to the RA the following spring.[41]

ARTISTS' ECONOMIC AGENCY: PROFESSIONAL SOCIETIES AND THE POLITICAL ECONOMY OF ART

> Professional life is to some extent public property.
>
> —M. Phipps Jackson, Fine Arts Society catalog[42]

The RA, still functioning under eighteenth-century structures, failed to cope with unwieldy numbers of artists in an increasingly commercial art world. In 1892, Marcus Huish, editor of the *Art Journal*, addressed changing patterns of consumption that aggravated the rivalry between professionals and amateurs.[43] The growing numbers of artists necessitated revised networks, modes of production, and aesthetic rationalizations. As professionals, artists had to understand the economics of art production and consumption. Popular discourse on political economy described the "monopolist" RA against competitive "free market" professional societies. Arguments in the 1850s and 1860s over open exhibitions versus limited memberships expressed conflicts over quality, selling, or trying to match supply and demand modeled on manufacturing.[44] Beginning in the 1860s, Victorian artists felt the effects of an expanding internal art market. A Royal Commission investigated the restricted educational and membership practices of the Academy in 1863 The RA reacted to public criticism by arguing that its members, as professionals, should alone be charged with policing the institution. *Fine Arts Quarterly* critics complained about artists' peculiar professional position that kept them from economic autonomy and left unrecognized their expertise: In the open marketplace any English citizen amateur was free to criticize, judge, or even produce, art. The *Englishwoman's Review* in 1868 took a different tack, encouraging the public to buy relatively cheap works from the Society for Female Artists (SFA) exhibition; clearly women artists had a very different economic position in the Victorian art market.[45]

Economic language in art dovetailed with the new discourse of nationhood. The Aesthete Frederic Leighton, President of the RA, in 1888 argued for a national role for artists in a blend of nationalist and economic language (art's "vital importance to certain branches of national prosperity"). In his view, art contributed to prosperity and artists could improve consumers' taste (not their morality, as John Ruskin had insisted art was to do[46]), to create a discerning "purchaser" who demanded quality.[47] Leighton insisted, too, that good design would address "the waning material prosperity of the country" by improving manufactures. He referred to the public as "purchasers" and artists as "suppliers."[48] For Leighton, the value of a work of art did not lay in its labor, but in a psychological bond between artist and spectator, "producing the emotion and exciting the imagination" for its spectators through form and color, not narrative or didacticism. Leighton's argument fit marginalist theory well and suggested a role for artists in shaping consumption. Critic Marcus Huish in 1890 argued that economic success was evidence of the high quality of British art. State expenditures demonstrated value to "even the most business-like citizen," and public museums "yielded more for the money." Despite an economic slump in the "commercial world," art, he insisted, received "magnificent sums" in the 1880s.[49]

But by the 1880s the boom was over. Artists' professional societies that burgeoned after 1880 demonstrated artists' sophisticated responses to these circumstances as the growing supply of artists had to meet and motivate new demands from consumers of modest means. Professional societies challenged the RA's economic monopoly. Margali Larson points out that as the market increased during the nineteenth century, "a collective effort was needed on the part of the actual or potential sellers of services to capture and control expanded markets. For this, new forms of eliciting and guaranteeing the buyers' preference and trust had to be devised and implemented." Professional organizations sought to "open the ranks of traditional professional elites."[50] The very definition of professional embraced *commodified* knowledge deployed to control market values. Artists increased their market power by acting collectively through new professional societies.[51] James Linton, President of the Institute of Painters in Water Colours set up galleries and cooperatives with commercial venues like the Dudley Gallery (Royal Watercolour Society [RWS] minutes, May 16, 1881), as did other societies. Several galleries offered societies regular places to exhibit in exchange for a percentage of sales and produced prints of popular paintings.

As early as around 1800 Edward Edwardes argued in favor of a free market as the best environment in which artists could thrive and compete. Whereas some considered consumer demand a threat to professional status, an inducement to advertising, and a substitution for training and quality, artists' professional societies attempted to control production and consumption and integrate mass numbers of artists with mass numbers of buyers, while resolving conflicts of artists' professionalism caught between marketing and asserting expertise. Professional societies shaped a market culture professionalism. Organized primarily to sell art, societies were registered with the Board of Trade and served to bring the public and artists into direct communication. Robert Ross in 1911 encouraged artists to "lure rich buyers and rich corporations . . . making a direct appeal to the commercial instinct . . . the public must be won, wooed, not abused."[52]

Societies accommodated mass spectating by decentralizing exhibitions and offering year-round art exhibitions in line with the display rhythms of other consumer venues, like the new department stores. They refined market niches by dividing consumers into small target audiences, unlike undifferentiated crowds at the Royal Academy. They created market niches for small, affordable works by specializing in media (pastellists in 1899, oil painters in 1898, and painter-etchers, 1880) or genres (miniaturists in 1895, medalists in 1891, and portrait painters, 1891). Artists often joined several societies to fit expanding markets at home and abroad. In 1886, the Royal Academy changed its exclusivity rule to allow Academicians to join other societies. Amateur societies also sprang up. In an anonymous essay, "The Business Side of Art," one writer in 1888 recognized the excess of supply over demand and recommended artists divide the market into coteries, what their professional societies were already doing.[53] Andrew Schotter argues that "every evolutionary economic problem requires a social institution to solve it," an idea Schotter derives from the Victorian economist Alfred Marshall.[54] Professional societies were social institutions formed to meet new economic problems of widening spectatorship, competition, and mass consumption.

Like Leighton, many artists argued for a national role in British cultural life. In 1866 Richard and Samuel Redgrave believed art consumption was patriotic and fashioned a cultural national identity that bound consumers to artists through their shared Britishness.[55] Louise Jopling in 1903, describing artists' changed status after 1880, articulated a national role for art "as an important factor in the government of men, in order to bring out all that is best in them."[56]

But despite their intentions to offer alternatives to the Royal Academy, societies often replicated the Academy's organizational structures and practices and used the already existing networks of critics, dealers, and the press, and events like private views, press days, and free advertising in newspapers whose critics wrote catalog introductions for societies' exhibitions.[57] Women governed their professional societies by the same ideals and methods. Harriet Grote, founder of the SFA, wrote on political economy and argued that the progress of art meshed with the progress of commerce for the mass market.[58] Press reviews of the SFA noted its benefits of worthwhile labor and contributions to the circulation of goods and accumulation of capital.[59] A burgeoning market for young, less costly artists reflected the speculation of inexperienced mass buyers. Collectors' clubs formed to bring attention to new promising artists and amateurs. *The Times* in 1909 praised "talented young artists," enabling "art lovers of moderate means" to buy when it was the most helpful to artists and helped the patron "indulge his fancy without sacrificing many of the other luxuries of life."[60]

After 1880, artists' attempts to shape consumer tastes became systematic. Professional societies used their catalogs to articulate a new aesthetic that reshaped consumption as an act of intimacy, desire, and fantasy. Mediating relations between consumer and artist, societies articulated both a labor and a marginalist economy. The theme of labor was prevalent in societies' catalogs by which they increased middle-class empathy with artists by endorsing the work ethic. Clarifications of the exchange value of artists' labor jostled with new aesthetic values of intimacy, sincerity, mystery, and lack of finish (finish, costly in time and materials, was designated as "insincere"). These values, favoring inexpensive and quick media of pencil or watercolor, disguised a capitulation to demand while artists tried to control this demand. Perhaps making a virtue of necessity, critics praised skill as a reflex of temperament, thereby "naturalizing" it to accommodate the uneven training of the armies of amateurs and promoting an art of the ephemeral and mysterious—a writerly text—to borrow Roland Barthes's term, to appeal to consumers' desires to be "co-creators."[61] Promoting the ephemeral appealed to consumers' fantasy *and* ignorance.

As Robert Witkin notes, art turned to "not representing a world but creating one, . . . the participation demanded of the subject in reception is heightened . . . to be something of an 'artist' in respect of everyday experience."[62] Labor's worth, so overt in earlier Victorian paintings with their excessive details, was the residual economics; the aesthetic of the ephemeral was the emerging economics. Art critic Harry Quilter in 1895 noted that critics used to complain, "the picture would have been better had the artist taken *more* pains" but now complain "the picture would have been better had the artist taken *less* pains."[63]

Jean-Joseph Goux points out that generating desire creates an infinite elasticity of demand, whereby the more you get, the more you may want, since the desire is insatiable.[64] This feature was noted by Marshall in 1890 as a pattern among Victorian collectors. Crucial to this new pattern of art consumption was the need "to make the taste for the art dependent on past consumption."[65] Arguing for small-scale works and year-round exhibitions, societies encouraged regular and frequent consumer purchases of art and increased artistic production to meet these demands. As Goux points out, "Demand is all the more elastic when it concerns a 'need,' appetite, or thirst that is not essential to survival—a *substitutable* object . . . the infinity of substitution . . . to the sphere of the symbolic." Thus, "the field of the signifier is the domain of infinitely elastic demand as it operates in the marginalist political economy" (Goux, 201). As Walter Benjamin recognized, the artist's physical labor is intentionally erased by the consumer's dream desire that "makes the transfiguration of things his business . . . obliterating the commodity-like character of things through his ownership of them. But he merely confers connoisseur value on them, instead of intrinsic value. The collector dreams that . . . things are free of the drudgery of being useful."[66] Goux also argues that the marginalist theory erases "the social relations of production by which value and supplementary value are determined—making these relations no more than the subjective effects of an ephemeral relation between a solvent subject of *jouissance* and an object," resulting in an ideological belief "that what ultimately creates surplus value is the manipulation of surplus desire," insolvent desires like sexual desire repressed and resignified by solvent desires (202). Art, like any other valuable object "whose high degree of liquidity has made it a 'quasi money'" (207), can be abstracted to substitute for other and all *jouissance*.

Late-nineteenth century aesthetic theories fed the collector's dream world. Consecrating a modest art that consumers could afford, societies turned market exchanges into exchanges of cultural capital for consumers who could partake of artistic creativity through insatiable consumption of ephemeral works. Societies' intervention also met changes in the oversupply of artists and new, inexperienced consumers. They defined a new aesthetic and then matched "their new products with socially homologous consumers."[67] Artists' societies created socially homologous producers for new consumers and created those consumers by promising to appeal to their fantasies, desires, tastes, and economic means. This marginalist aesthetic replaced labor as a function of time, with labor as a function of knowledge fetishized as creativity: the less time the artist spent painting, the more the painting contained the artist's knowledge-as-intuition, which was taken as a sign of genius. As Whistler noted at the Whistler-Ruskin trial, a painting's value was not measured by hours invested in it—a measure for artisanal work—but by the expertise acquired over a lifetime by the professional artist and ready at the tip of the brush.

Margaret Schabas notes that Stanley Jevons and Marshall recognized, "Introspection and studies of the mechanisms of the mind were thus just the license required by Victorian economists to reorient the discipline around individual agency," unlike classical economy in which individuals were subject to forces of capital accumulation and the rise of commerce.[68] Professional societies promoted a new aesthetic to address consumers' psychological needs to make them regular consumers of art. The two main thrusts of professional organizations, organizing for a market of services and organizing for status and social standing, were intertwined. Larson argues that professions affirm a community in which "professional identity is experienced as shared expertise" and then traded on the market. Since the training of professionals works to exclude the unqualified, "associations of free producers had arisen, in fact, in order to *constitute and control* a new type of market" as they created a new artistic "community" (54–56).

Marginal theory gave artists a new raison d'être. The reevaluation of market value as social, consensual, and psychological inaugurated "a period . . . that took seriously questions of emotion, consciousness, and volition" (Schabas, 80). For late-century Victorians, "All of economic development came from human wants and desires, which were taken to be sui generis, and it was in the act of deliberation that economic phenomena were formed and altered" (82).

TOWARD A POLITICAL ECONOMY OF ART: VILE ARTISTS AND CHASTE ART

For new consumers, buying from living painters was the *modus operandi* influenced by the purchases of the royal family and the growing number of municipal museums that argued for consumption of art as contributing to national wealth and both charitable and patriotic (Ferriday, 1:1458). Huish concluded that "in writing a cheque for a foreign picture we are oftentimes depriving an English artist and his family of a year's support" (1890, 117). Writers attempted to define consumption as a civic responsibility; buying the art of living artists contributed to national culture and wealth and secured the future survival of British culture.

But Victorian anxieties over artists' economic behavior persisted; artists were also bohemians who cared little for money, making them beyond social control, or degenerate, biologically deranged, according to an emerging British psychology. Victorians' anxiety over art production appeared as disjunctions between the mortal artist and sacred precious art object, between art as "uplifting" and its sensuous appeal, and between art as aesthetically aristocratic and appealing to a mass market. The catalog of the 100th Royal Institute of Painters in Water Colours exhibition in 1909 described a chance "to make a bid for the favour of the public—commercially of great value . . . but it also enables him to seek the appreciation of his brother-artists, the intrinsic value of which, only an artist can realise, holding within it, as it does, the incentive to higher aims, . . . for the unattainable."[69] This statement disguises art's commodification with quasi-religious claims ("intrinsic value," "higher aims," "unattainable") and dissembles itself in contradictions between professional cooperation ("brother-artists") and a highly competitive market. Such dissembling exposes residual anxieties about making a bid for the public.

One solution was the Victorians' constructed ideal innocent artist. Alexander Gilchrist's biographies of William Blake (1863, 1880) and William Etty (1855) constructed artists who were naive, innocent, pure, and often solitary. Renaissance artists were believed oblivious to worldly matters of social and economic demands. In 1872 William Davies reconstructed an innocent Botticelli happily working for limited wages in harmony with his patriarchal patron, a Victorian fiction of the Renaissance artist and a foil for what Davies considered market corruption of Victorian artists.[70] For Margaret Oliphant economic success corrupted artists.[71] The conservative critic J. B. Atkinson noted in 1885 that the ideal artist "flees from the tumult of the world, forsakes the vanity of fleeting fashion."[72] These advocacies of artists' economic innocence were diametrically opposed to artists' professional practices of controlling consumers' desires, partitioning the mass market, brandishing their material successes and celebrity.

Perhaps the most adamant defender of a monastic ideal was John Ruskin, notably in his two 1857 lectures delivered in conjunction with the Manchester Art Treasures Exhibition and entitled "The Political Economy of Art." These lectures were subsequently published in 1857 as *The Political Economy of Art* and republished in 1880 with supplementary texts under the title *A Joy For Ever (and its Price in the Market)*. This second version was reprinted in 1887, 1889, and 1895, in a small 1893 edition, and in a 1904 pocket edition, clear signs of its belated popularity.[73] Ruskin's writings on political economy became popular in the last quarter of the century, selling into the tens of thousands.[74] Critics of Ruskin's writings on political economy generally found them utopian, unscientific, ignorant of economics, and filled with unrelated ideas and moral imperatives. Ruskin's thinking on political economy has recently been dissected in the context of political economy, his readership, his wider social criticism, and his own art patronage. My focus is on his views in relation, or opposition, to artists' economic activities described above.

In the 1850s Ruskin experienced doubt whether art could fit the elevated role he prescribed for it and whether purity was possible in capitalist, industrial England. Linda Austin notes that his outbursts against the corruption of money and manufacture in Ruskin's *Academy Notes* form a parallel discourse that threatened the discourse of art. These outbursts "become the new aesthetic terms that both threaten and explain the production, reception, value, and meaning of art in Ruskin's late work."[75] In the context of these changing beliefs Ruskin gave his lectures in Manchester. Defining economy as "the art of managing labour," not simply "spending or saving," Ruskin emphasized the centrality of patrons' and the state's management of future artists (16:18–19). Ruskin's artists were artisanal, cockney, and wool-gatherers who needed direction. Suspicious of artists' corruptibility, he suggested withholding money to punish artists who enjoyed their celebrity with large homes and carriages. High prices led the artist "to dwell on this worldly and wealthy eminence . . . and he gradually loses both his power of mind and his rectitude of purpose" (16:82–83). Artists, whom he called "little boys," were deemed incapable of constructing professional standards and market prices (16:44): Infantilized geniuses must be tended (16:31).

Ruskin essentialized the artist's mode of perception as childlike "infantine sight" (15:28), "of such tenderness and sensitiveness" (11:49), that artists must be kept from society, "a destructive influence" (2:53, 4:394). Ruskin's goal was to keep artists pure, a word with a special meaning for him. As Paul Sawyer notes, purity for Ruskin is a communal force that makes it possible for each part of a system to contribute to the whole.[76] Purity transforms material things into symbolic objects resonant with meanings (Sawyer, 187).[77] Economic and social motives intrude into this organic, ideal (and ideological) mutually beneficial system, breaking it apart by anarchy, individualism, laissez-faire, and competition (172–73). Preciousness, too, had several meanings for Ruskin, including luxuries. Properly disseminated, precious objects were the glue holding a community together; jeweled sacred tabernacles brought communities together to experience sanctity (175, 181).[78] The impure artist, then, could contaminate an entire culture, a fear expressed in theories of degeneracy that spread after 1880 and focused on artists, writers, and composers.

In his political economy of art Ruskin found two precious things: the genius of the young artist that like gold (Ruskin's metaphor) was true wealth to be mined by the state, and the art work itself that needed surveillance in its production and consumption to ensure its goodness (168–169). The artist's character resided in the art work, so the State, Ruskin's "paternal authority," had to shape and restrain the artist's character to ensure a good work of art.[79] Artists did not have the same social and economic needs as others. The artist "differs from us" by "an exquisite complacency in Fasting, and taking infinite satisfaction in Emptiness. You can excite his intense gratitude by the gift of Anything, and if you have Nothing to give him, you will find that Nothing is exactly the thing he most wants, and that he will immediately proceed to make half a picture of it" (Ruskin, 4:388). Ruskin insisted "a real painter will work for you exquisitely," with only "bread and water and salt; and a bad painter will work badly and hastily, though you give him a palace" (16:83–84). Ruskin proposed "a fixed amount of income" for "a certain number of works" (14:488), while also insisting that money was irrelevant to quality: "'The less pay, the better work' . . . for ten pounds you shall have a *Paradise Lost*, and for a plate of figs, a Dürer drawing but for a million of money sterling, neither" (7:449). Taking artists out of the marketplace required government intervention to educate, supply, and commission artists and fix prices for their works. Ruskin's advocacy of public and state restrictions on artists attacked their increasing autonomy, visibility, professionalism, and celebrity. Even the artist's technical skill became so natural that it no longer appeared as a skill, making the artist unable to negotiate on the market for this skill, as other professionals did (Ruskin, 3:22, 6:67). Separating the artist from society and economics was meant to protect artists' vulnerability on the open market: "the best artist is liable to be warped away from what he knows is right by the chance of at once making a vast fortune by catching the public eye, the public eye being only to be caught by bright colours and certain conditions of art not always desirable." Ruskin suggested "an extensive guardianship role for government" but changed this expectation in *Unto This Last* in which he put "more responsibility on the consumer and producers as guardians,"[80] who would be like the kindly housewife who distributed duties or the authoritative father motivated by affection. The state had to protect artists against laissez-faire, "the principle of death."

Art had dangers in its consumption, too. It could be hoarded or devalued through laissez-faire, which encouraged artists to make cheap works for profit and thus keep good art out of public circulation. Consumers were responsible for avoiding hoarding and commodifying art and for protecting artists' innocence by not overpaying or overpraising them (Sawyer, 176–177). Patrons could save money, assure preciousness in art, and improve artists' character by not paying high prices (Ruskin, 16:85). For Ruskin money signified feudal social bonds, making art-buying an act of *noblesse oblige*, and the consumers "arbiters of the will and work of England; . . . whether the work of the State shall suffice for the State or not, depends upon you" (16:102). The state and the art-buying public were conflated here (he later lost faith in government management of art). The government needed to "encourage the private possession of the works of *living* masters . . . to keep down the prices of them as far as you can (Ruskin, 16:81–82). Ruskin insisted that original work is the cheapest and best worth having. Consumers determined the artist's character through "the kind of subjects which you, the public, ask them for, and therefore the kind of thoughts with which you require them to be habitually familiar" (16:35). Ruskin admonished his audience to "conduct yourselves precisely as a manufacturer would, who attended to his looms, but left his warehouse without a roof" (16:76). This helped Ruskin out of the earlier quandary—how art as a luxury item could be a justified purchase (50). Some luxuries were worth the expense, for example, £14,000 for a Veronese was a public good; ball gowns were not.

Goux points out that in Adam Smith and in Hegel, the cost of an object is determined by the pain of the labor invested in its making; for the consumer the cost is measured by the pleasure or *jouissance* the object can give, making an object's value for the producer and for the consumer asymmetrical (210). Ruskin attempted to ameliorate this by insisting that the consumer take on a role with its own "pain"—the moral function of consumption. Ruskin appealed to the consumer's "counterlibido, an *antijouissance*" (211).

Ruskin oscillated between the "necessity" of art, in which case its cost should be low, and its status as a luxury item, in which case its cost should be high. Recognizing that cost was not a function of the artist's labor, but of the patron's desires, Ruskin also argued that it was important "to bring pictures within the reach of the multitude; . . . the subtle balance which your economist has to strike: to accumulate so much art as to be able to give the whole nation a supply of it, according to its need, and yet to regulate its distribution so that there shall be no glut of it" (Ruskin, 16:61).

Artists' own pleasure in their work, their "moral energy" (16:37), was surplus value. Their creative impulses, if left to work, could generate savings because engaged labor was cheaper and done faster (16:42–43). But ultimately Ruskin could not measure artist's labor's worth: "you must, at all events, keep him for six days in bread and water, fire and lodging; that is the lowest price at which he can do it for you, but that is not very dear: and the best bargain which can possibly be made honestly in art—the very ideal of a cheap purchase to the purchaser—is the original work of a great man fed for as many days as are necessary on bread and water. . . . That is the way by which you will always get most for your money" (16:43). Ruskin may have meant this passage as a ludicrous example of applying the labor theory of pricing to artistic labor. He himself admonished artists to do fewer large and many smaller works to make more money and provide works for modest buyers: "paint beautiful water colours from fifty to a hundred guineas each, which could be seen in many places and purchased by people of moderate means."[81] But it was the large work that affected artists' future reputation, got press attention, and attracted powerful collectors, as artists knew.

Determining a picture's price, he mixed classical and utility theories: "For remember always, that the price of a picture by a living artist never represents, never *can* represent, the quantity of labour or value in it. Its price represents, for the most part, the degree of desire which the rich people of the country have to possess it." But Ruskin remained tied to classical economics' "fair price" beyond which he cautioned consumers against paying: "beyond its fair price—that is to say, the price which will pay the painter for his time—you are not only cheating yourself and buying vanity, but you are stimulating the vanity of others" (16:86).

Ruskin's political economy hovers between a labor theory of value linked to belief in an intrinsic worth of things and a need to establish value away from intrinsic worth in the direction of exchange value and marginal utility. The fair price was based on the amount of time the painting took to be done, with a relatively generous ceiling—£500 for an oil, £100 for a watercolor, good prices in 1857, and even in 1880—so the artist should not put in more labor beyond those prices. But many works took years to complete, as many paintings did, and for these a flat fee did not measure labor.

Although utility theory had not yet been articulated in 1857, demand appeared in the classical economics of Adam Smith and David Ricardo. As Willie Henderson and others argue, Ruskin anticipated marginalist theory and Marshall's work.[82] But he dreaded payment for a name that raised prices beyond middle-class means and was wary of consumers' desires as motives. Despite Ruskin's ambivalence toward demand, his political economy recognized that patrons determined valuation and price, but for him consumer demand also affected artists' character and national well-being.

Ruskin's growing awareness of degrading conditions in many areas of life may have impelled his belief that money, neglect, and praise undermined artists and that the state needed to intervene to save artists from capitalism. By the 1880s, when Ruskin's lectures were reprinted, artists had redefined their professional status, economic roles, social circumstances, and public image to invalidate Ruskin's assumptions about them. From the 1860s, Aestheticism offered social and professional identities for artists that opposed Ruskin's childlike artist and economy of preciousness. Names added surplus value to works of art, as they still do. By 1880 art works were becoming the public's and the nation's cultural capital, and the art market was entering a new economic oversupply of art, which necessitated new markets, artist identities, and ways of valuing their labor.

Money is not neutral but carries enormous social and symbolic meanings. Ruskin recognized money as a symbolic language of social relations. Its management and spending shaped social networks, and its ownership reflected class hierarchies. Ruskin grounded his critique of political economy on feudal relations because his concept of political economy was sociological and ethical rather than strictly economic. His inconsistencies in *A Joy For Ever* bespoke the period's changing consumption patterns, the rising social status of artists, the vast numbers of artists and buyers, and culture's alliance with emerging national identities of Englishness. Bourdieu points out that "the art trader cannot serve his 'discovery' unless he applies all his conviction, which rules out 'sordidly commercial' maneuvers, manipulation and the 'hard sell', in favour of the softer, more discreet forms of 'public relations' (which are themselves a highly euphemized form of publicity)—receptions, society gatherings and judiciously placed confidences."[83] Bourdieu's comments apply to both sides of the Victorian political economy of art. Ruskin's hard sell and astringent attitudes toward artists were control mechanisms for maintaining the authority of critics and collectors, like Ruskin, presumably to preserve the moral authority of art. Artists' professional societies offered an aesthetic soft sell to shape buyers' desires and redefine a grander role for artists than servants to collectors like Ruskin. Artists advocated professional identities to transform art making and selling into transactions over art's (and the artist's) symbolic and cultural capital.

VICTORIAN POLITICAL ECONOMY OF ART AND ECONOMICS

It was precisely economic man that Victorian artists aspired to become. Around 1870 attention shifted to consumption as the determinant of surplus value in the economic theories of Jevons and Marshall. Ruskin's ideas were rooted in the labor theory of value but he struggled over the role and nature of consumption. He put an economo-moral onus sometimes on the artist and sometimes on the consumer. A commodity's exchange value was not a measure of its true value, but acknowledged that art's "true" value or vital beauty, a surplus value often indefinable, was distinct from the economic value of its materials and labor.

As Roger Backhouse, Tony Dudley-Evans, and Willie Henderson point out, "in the same way that literary critics have argued over whether meaning is determined by the author, by the reader, or whether it is constructed by a discourse community, so economists have argued over whether value is determined by the buyer, by costs of production or by market processes. . . . Value has no unique meaning. . . . It may be measured, for example by demand-price, supply-price or by a market-price that is equal to neither . . . each appropriate in a different context."[84] For Marshall, "The economy was now depicted in terms of man-made social institutions . . . economic theorists, by discovering the laws that governed the production and distribution of wealth, might also be in a position to change social arrangements" (Schabas, 78). The late-Victorian marginal theory of Marshall and Jevons described value as a psychological function, the money the buyer was *willing* to pay, not simply what the buyer paid. Jevons and his followers merged use and exchange value, a merger especially relevant to luxuries and to art. Economists describing marginal utility theory, like artists in their professional societies, recognized the exchange of money for art was driven by patrons seeking many noneconomic returns—cultural hegemony, social status, intimacy, escape into fantasy, and a share in the power of the creative process, perhaps the most appealing surplus value of art.

NOTES

1. New York: Random House, 1963.
2. London: John Lane, 1924.
3. Jonathan Rose, "Was Capitalism Good for Victorian Literature?," *Victorian Studies* 46, no. 3 (Spring 2004): 489–501. All future references will be cited parenthetically in text.
4. B. S. Frey and W. W. Pommerehne, *Muses and Markets: Explorations in the Economics of the Arts* (Oxford: Blackwell, 1989), 145.
5. Dianne Sachko Macleod, *Art and the Victorian Middle Class: Money and the Making of Cultural Identity* (Cambridge: Cambridge University Press, 1996).
6. See Codell, *The Victorian Artist*.
7. Oskar Batschmann, *The Artist in the Modern World: The Conflict between Market and Self-Expression* (New Haven, CT: Yale University Press, 1997), 26. All further references will be cited parenthetically in text.
8. Ann Pullan, "Public Goods or Private Interests? The British Institution in the Early Nineteenth Century," in *Art in Bourgeois Society, 1790–1850*, ed. A. Hemingway and W. Vaughan (Cambridge: Cambridge University Press, 1998), 36–37. Frey and Pommerehne argue that sharing risks allows dealers to support unknown artists, not all of whom will become famous, while benefiting living artists who have a prospect of becoming known (17). But even for successful Victorian painters, "the real monetary rate of return on paintings lies below that of financial assets, whereas the risk is higher" (113).
9. Willie Henderson, *John Ruskin's Political Economy*, 26.
10. William Holman Hunt's letters in the Bodleian Library, University of Oxford, are filled with stock market suggestions to his friends. Further citations to letters will be abbreviated in these notes.
11. Viviana Zelizer, "Beyond the Polemics on the Market: Establishing a Theoretical and Empirical Agenda," *Sociological Forum* 3 (Fall 1988): 628.
12. In *Field of Cultural Production*.
13. Rose claims Paul Delaney's *Literature, Money and the Market from Trollope to Amis*, 2002, endorses this liaison between literature and commodification.
14. Rossetti painted on James Smetham's unfinished pictures to sell them and raise money for the ill Smetham and his family; see Ernestine Mills, *The Life and Letters of Frederic Shields, 1833–1911* (London: Longman, Green, 1912), 227, 243–44. All further references will be cited parenthetically in text.
15. G. D. Leslie, "The Artist in Relation to his Work," *Art Journal* (1882): 71–72.
16. Hunt assured Combe that Rossetti's "replica" contained "certain improvements in design . . . since completing the first [painting]" (Bod. ms. Eng. lett. c. 296, Hunt to Combe, December 30, 1852).
17. F. M. Redgrave, *Richard Redgrave, C. B. R. A.* (London: Cassell, 1891), 35. Frank Holl's daughter defended his replicas as "finer than the original pictures," Ada M. Reynolds, *The Life and Work of Frank Holl* (London: Methuen, 1912), 129–30.
18. Letter to critic F. G. Stephens, Bod. ms. don. e. 61, March 20, 1877. Cited with permission from the Bodleian Library, University of Oxford.

19. Jan Marsh and Pamela Gerrish Nunn, *Women Artists and the Pre-Raphaelite Movement* (London: Virago, 1989), 68; see also 49, 62, 108.

20. Simmons, P. L., "Art-Aids to Commerce," *Art Journal*, n.s. 11 (1872): 295.

21. Peter Ferriday, "The Victorian Art Market: The Profits of Painting," *Country Life* 2 (June 16, 1966), 1577. All further references will be cited parenthetically in text.

22. Gerald Reitlinger, *The Economics of Taste, Vol. 1: The Rise and Fall of Picture Prices, 1760–1960*, 3 vols. (London: Barrie and Rockliff, 1961), 150. All further references will be cited parenthetically in text.

23. Bod. ms. don. c. 296, March 13, 1854, Bodleian Library.

24. Bod. ms. don. c. 296, February 26, 1859, Bodleian Library.

25. London: Routledge, 1993, 13.

26. Frederic Smallfield, "A Private View of Private Views," *Temple Bar* 74 (June 1885): 255.

27. Mary Lutyens, "Selling the Missionary," *Apollo* 86 (November 1967): 380.

28. Codell, "'The Artist's Cause at Heart': Marion Harry Spielmann and the Late Victorian Art World," *Bulletin of the John Rylands University Library of Manchester* 71 (1989): 139–63.

29. Gianfranco Mossetto, *Aesthetics and Economics* (Dordrecht: Kluwer, 1993), 127.

30. Mossetto, 131–32.

31. C. H. Goodruff, "The Collector on the Prowl," *Blackwood's Magazine* 147 (1890): 680, 679.

32. Henrietta Ward, *Memories of Ninety Years*, ed. Isabel G. McAllister (London: Hutchinson, 1924), 31.

33. Charles Hallé, *Notes from a Painter's Life* (London: J. Murray, 1909), 178–79, 184.

34. Douglas, *In the Active Voice* (London: Routledge and Kegan Paul, 1982), 129.

35. Bod. 86: #173–74, 5/6/05 from Bodleian Library.

36. Bod Eng. letters d. 40, #32–33 [ND].

37. Bod. ms. don. c. 296, July 10, 1854.

38. Bod. ms. don. c. 83: #18–19, September 11, 1867.

39. Bod. ms. don. c. 296, December 24, 1867.

40. Solomon Hart, *The Reminiscences of Solomon Alex Hart, R. A.*, ed. Alexander Brodie (London: Wyman and Sons, 1882), 17.

41. Hart, 109–110.

42. London: Fine Art's Society, 1893, 8.

43. Huish, "Whence This Great Multitude of Painters?" *Nineteenth Century* 32 (1892): 720.

44. Christopher Newall, *Victorian Watercolors* (Oxford: Phaidon, 1987), 27.

45. *Englishwoman's Review*, April 7, 1868, 467.

46. Emilie Barrington, *The Life, Letters and Works of Frederic Leighton*. 2 vols. (London: George Allen, 1906), 2:343–44.

47. Ibid., 2:350–51.

48. Ibid., 2:358–61.

49. "Ten Years of British Art," *Nineteenth Century* 27 (1890), 102–3, 105, 111. All further references will be cited parenthetically in text.

50. Magali S. Larson, *The Rise of Professionalism: A Sociological Analysis* (Berkeley and Los Angeles: University of California Press, 1977), 10. All further references will be cited parenthetically in text.

51. A few societies appeared early in the century: The Royal British Artists established in 1819 "as a protest" against the Royal Academy, two watercolor societies in 1804 and 1832, a Society of Engravers in 1802, and the British Institution in 1805. See Wendell V. Harris, "A Handlist of Nineteenth-Century London Art Societies and Their Predecessors," *Nineteenth-Century Studies* 18 (2004): 139–62; and Codell, "Artists' Professional Societies: Production, Consumption and Aesthetics," *Towards a Modern Art World*, ed. B. Allen (London: Yale University Press, 1995), 169–87.

52. Robert Ross, *Present and Future Prospects of English Art*, lecture delivered before the Sandon Studios Society, Liverpool, October 10, 1910 (London: Sandon Studios Society, 1911), 31.

53. *Art Journal*, 1888, 249.

54. Andrew Schotter, *The Economic Theory of Social Institutions* (Cambridge: Cambridge University Press, 1981), 3.

55. Richard and Samuel Redgrave, *A Century of Painters of the English School* (London: Smith, Elder, 1866); see Codell, "Righting the Victorian Artist: The Redgraves' *A Century of Painters of the English School* and the Serialization of Art History," *Oxford Art Journal* 23, no. 2 (2000): 93–118.

56. Louise Jopling, "On the Education of the Artistic Faculty," in *Education and Professions*, vol. 1, The Women's Library (London: Chapman and Hall, 1903), 113.

57. William Laidlay, *The Origin and First Two Years of the New English Art Club* (London: Bodley Head, 1907), 6, 10, 53, 164, 193.

58. Harriet Grote, *Collected Papers* (London: John Murray, 1862), 196–200.

59. *English Women's Journal*, 1858, 205. See the following for more on this, including where women exhibited and their purchasers: Marsh and Nunn, *Women Artists*, 28, 29, 43, 60, 62, 82, 102, 108, 119–20, 123, 142, 147. Jan Marsh and Pamela Gerrish Nunn, *Pre-Raphaelite Women Artists* (Manchester: Manchester City Art Galleries, 1997), 47.

60. June 21, 1909, 1.

61. Roland Barthes, *S/Z* (New York: Hill and Wang, 1974), 5.

62. Robert Witkin, *Art and Social Structure* (Cambridge: Polity Press, 1995), 81.

63. Harry Quilter, "The Relation of Criticism to Production in Art," *National Review* 2, no. 25 (June 1895): 468.

64. Jean-Joseph Goux, *Symbolic Economies: After Marx and Freud*, trans. Jennifer Curtiss Gage (Ithaca, NY: Cornell University Press, 1990). All further references will be cited parenthetically in text.

65. David Throsby, "The Production and Consumption of the Arts: A View of Cultural Economics," *Journal of Economic Literature* 1 (1994), 3.

66. Benjamin, *Reflections: Essays, Aphorisms, Autobiographical Writing*, trans. Edmund Jephcott (New York: Schocken Books, 1986), 55.

67. Pierre Bourdieu, "Field of Cultural Production, or: the Economic World Reversed," *Poetics* 12 (1983), 336.

68. Margaret Schabas, "Victorian Economics and the Science of the Mind," in *Victorian Science in Context*, ed. B. Lightman (Chicago: University of Chicago Press, 1997), 85. All further references will be cited parenthetically in text.

69. *Catalogue of the 100th Royal Institute of Painters in Water Colours* (London: Mall Galleries, 1909), xvii.

70. William Davies, "The State of English Painting," *Quarterly Review* 17 (June 1872): 329–33. See my book *The Victorian Artist* for more on these issues.

71. Margaret Oliphant, "An Artist's Autobiography," *Blackwood's Magazine* 136 (November 1884): 614, 631.

72. J. B. Atkinson, "Decline of Art," *Blackwood's Magazine* 138 (July 1885): 25.

73. I will be using John Ruskin, *Works of John Ruskin*. All further references will be to volume and page numbers and cited parenthetically in text.

74. In the 1880s *Unto This Last* sold over 2,000 copies a year. *A Joy For Ever* and *The Two Paths* each had sales of about 75,000, and *Munera Pulveris* sold between 35,000 and 50,000 copies.

75. Linda. M. Austin, *The Practical Ruskin: Economics and Audience in the Late Work* (Baltimore: Johns Hopkins University Press, 1991), 47–49.

76. Paul Sawyer, *Ruskin's Poetic Argument: The Design of the Major Works* (Ithaca, NY: Cornell University Press, 1985), 171. All further references will be cited parenthetically in text.

77. The rich dress on Veronese's figures described in *The Political Economy of Art* is not simply material wealth but also nobility by which others could be educated.

78. The flow of art circulating as described in *The Political Economy of Art* was restricted only scarcity of precious things transformed their owners through preciousness.

79. See Henderson, Chapter 1.

80. Henderson, 34.

81. Ruskin letter to Hunt, Bod ms. Eng. lett. c. 46, June 22, 1883.

82. Henderson, 167, 169.

83. Bourdieu, *The Field of Cultural Production* (New York: Columbia University Press, 1993), 77.

84. R. Backhouse, T. Dudley-Evans, and W. Henderson, "Exploring the Language and Rhetoric of Economics," *Economics and Language*, ed. Henderson, Dudley-Evans, and Backhouse (London: Routledge, 1993), 11.

The Political Economy of Art and Culture: Virtual Capital in the Postmodern Period

Ann Z. Li

> "Our perception of art is basically Victorian. The object, the commodity as a work of art is a completely recent perception."
>
> —Christo, 1979, quoted in *Twentieth-Century Artists on Art*[1]

In the modern period, the conventional disciplinary framework for analysis of the political economy of art is twofold: the private sector's corporate form of collection and presentation, including retail gallery venues, and its public sector partner, the civic arts venue and museum. The field of arts and cultural management services both sectors and the economics of art and culture determines their organization. The common threads in both sectors are the roles of producers, distributors, and consumers, given that cultural production exists within a larger market for commodities and capital that often cannot be differentiated from other commodity forms.

However, scholars have largely emphasized orthodox approaches to economics. One recent example is the magisterial text by James Heilbrun and Charles Gray largely informed by the dominant paradigm of neoclassical economics, which emphasizes the efficiency of demand and supply.[2] Heilbrun and Gray suggest that "individuals and firms that consume or produce art behave like producers and consumers; in some significant ways, they behave differently."[3] While they claim significance on behavioral terms for the choices of individual agents in a neoclassical paradigm, it is the ideological differences that suggest the need for a political economy perspective that critiques this dominant paradigm.

The dominant art world institutional structure is supported by wealth based in profit and nonprofit entities, all of which fit this paradigm. "Art world," in this context, is defined as that entity outlined by institutionalist theories of art by George Dickie and Howard Becker.[4] Alternative or heterodox approaches to a political economy of art have always existed from Marx's commentaries on the role of art in society to Veblen's studies on the leisure class.[5] These theories resemble the institutionalist theories within the history of economic thought because the artistic avant-garde has shared the goals of heterodox political economy analyses of art.[6] But alternative analyses of political economy address what Heilbrun and Gray leave as an unresolved question: the role of mass media and arts education in the economics of the arts. As neoclassical economists, their argument about what constitutes "American" art and culture relies on excluding the causal and problematic elements that produce anomalies in their analysis, including those artworks that challenge or resist the commodifiable nature of art production.[7] Heilbrun and Gray suggest that certain not-for-profit activities are more appropriate or "coherent" for economic analysis than other forms of art and culture, and that key media industries such as motion picture production are "inherently complex" and therefore excludable. Although important in terms of controlling and limiting the data under scrutiny, their selective analysis delimits the mediated effects reproducing all art and culture in an age of mass media.[8]

In this chapter I will examine the heterodox approaches to art(s) as commodity and provide an overview of methodologies that critique, amplify, and transform orthodox analyses of the economics of art. The public spheres of modern art worlds are fields of political communication that affect cultural criticism and historiography as criticism becomes more promotional than dialectic.[9] I will emphasize contemporary art sometimes designated as late modern, or postmodernism, or antimodernism. Late-modern, antimodern, or postmodern art works are those that address typologies or taxonomies of forms to signify a problematic public nature of art production and its reception. Fredric Jameson and David Harvey connect postmodernity to "late capitalism" or "flexible accumulation," including art that resists the celebration of modernity and industrialization.

Movements involving performance or critiques of art as commodity also critique the "material object" paradigm and the associated conventions of art presentation. These "resistant" artworks, often called avant-garde, are produced synchronously with works produced for conventional markets. Even avant-garde or postmodern works perform spectacular and promotional roles that support the same markets Heilbrun and Gray examine more closely, even though such artworks, whatever their form and content, position themselves politically in opposition to art's conventional role in the production of mass culture.[10] The concepts of avant-garde and arrière-garde, as espoused by Rosalind Krauss, constitute a set of conflicts between creative individuals and their cultural ecology. These conflicts pit social institutions supported and constituted by a capitalized, cultural logic against individuals situated in contemporary, cultural, self-defined resistance to global economic power. Heilbrun and Gray's argument misses variables of mass media and arts education that are key to the concept of virtual capital and evident in many modern artworks' problematic relationships with cultural institutions and the public sphere. Their discussion of specifically nonprofit forms ignores the necessary relation between nonprofit and for-profit cultural institutions.

Within the historical convergence between the art world and political movements addressing social justice issues, the originality of individual artworks as a form of scarcity is critiqued not simply as unique but also as representing privilege. Krauss describes the avant-garde as "not those who have new ideas but by those who challenge their time's hegemonic conceptualization of art."[11] In conceptualizing the avant-garde as a vanguard social institution, political economy has been complicit, whether as in pre-Stalinist constructivism or in the democratic socialism of the Bauhaus. In constructivism, the Soviet promotion of official, revolutionary culture in social engineering of cultural production promoted mediated style and arts institutions that were both modernist in style and in proposed method, whether as imitative of or integrated into modernist mass production processes. The Dessau Bauhaus as a political economic institution was identified with the ideological and financial support of local government and the associated sheltering of the same Bolshevik styles promoted by Soviet constructivism.

VIRTUAL CAPITAL AND ART

The problem for a political economy of art in the modern period is a problem of virtual capital, the conflict between fictitious capital forms and functional capital forms. Fictitious capital here refers to the kinds of value wagered on production that does not yet exist. The institutions embodying such discursive conflicts range from the artist's loft on "open space" day to the museum and the university class, and all engage in cultural reproduction of virtual capital. Cultural reproduction includes not only educational institutions but is also the basis for how such structures of activity create value and hence capital.[12]

Art is one form of virtual capital in the modern period. "Virtual capital" characterizes a materialist body of thought ranging from concepts of fictitious capital, seen as a form of finance capital, to knowledge flows as capital, and, finally, to information and telecommunication technology as capital factors.[13] Marx examined the problem of creating fictitious capital—money put into circulation without material reference in production or commodities.[14] This "credit money" signifies a deeper problem of the relations between money as an abstract expression of value and commodities as the concrete embodiment of value.[15] Modern artwork functions like money as an indexical measure of values, especially in the auction context, and can function as a medium of exchange, albeit not clearly or absolutely fungible. In that context, artwork produces differential value in the form of rents over the life of its circulation as property whether displayed and amplified in the context of exchange (e.g., auctions, exhibitions). As Marx indicates for fictitious capital, the circulation of exchanged representations or proxies for capital is more important. The irony of such transactions can be seen in Andy Warhol's synthetic polymer and silkscreen print of Chairman Mao from 1972 with its November 2006 Christie's auction sale of $17.37 million to a Hong Kong executive.[16] The economics of art literature tracks such prices as conventional research on appreciating commodities or luxury goods. Art is a medium of exchange in this circulation of the representations of exchange.

The classical political economy of the eighteenth and nineteenth centuries distinguished between use value and exchange value. Marx in *Das Capital* describes this in general and in *Grundrisse* comments more passionately about the irony of the historical value of artwork, despite the reduction of alienated labor to the material status of a commodity. Marx retained a relatively autonomous view of artists as creators resistant to material appropriation of artwork. This becomes problematic in the consideration of fetishistic relations among humans and commodities that invest complex meanings in all things, making ironic the art object's and its creator's relative autonomy. Art objects, then, do not have the same forms of commodity exchange values as other commodities because of this underlying fetishism.[17] Walter Benjamin attempted to address this with the concept of the aura and hoped to recover the utopian and revolutionary potential of artwork as capital resources that were socially redemptive for the masses mired in false consciousness.[18] Later Marxists of the Frankfurt School also drew upon this notion of cultural capital as an industrial form capable of creating mass illusion.[19] Similarly, Pierre Bourdieu defined symbolic capital as mirroring wealth, status, and class. The circulation of symbolic capital is reproduced as capital in educational institutions and media industry. Virtual capital, much as nineteenth-century paper bills of exchange, have become the electronic exchange markets that include international art auction houses and blockbuster museum exhibitions.

While artwork and the arts as objects and performances are a small part of the entirety of capital, their relations to capital are important, particularly in the entertainment industries which subsume other arts and culture industries.[20] The arts signify the circulation of commodity capital but do not constitute it when we consider the massive divisions of labor and capital investment required to train and produce, for example, computer graphics–based movies along with their promotion and merchandising.

Art and Its Systems

Artistic training remains a combination of careerism and romantic ideologies.[21] The dependencies of both modern and postmodern art and culture on mass media and arts education, my main topics, persist in Dadaism, conceptualism, minimalism, earth art, feminist art, and performance art. The art world as an institution has been a disciplinary focus for philosophy and sociology, as in the theory of art worlds proposed by George Dickie's institutional analysis of artwork. Marcel Duchamp's ready-mades are often cited as examples of conferred art status that may be compared to the institutionalist economic theory of Thorstein Veblen in their family resemblance to functional objects of less than fully intended aesthetic purpose. Such movements have emphasized the importance of exemplars like Duchamp who disavowed his connection to Dada's social, political, and psychological aims. Duchamp's works have figured centrally in philosophical concepts like the art world. His choices of object from mass culture signify Benjamin's suggested resistance to the ritual object. Some of Duchamp's works explicitly addressed the art object as commodity form, but, despite their sense of play and critique of formalism, these works ultimately became what they critiqued, precious and scarce museum acquisitions. The manipulation of the social network of arts institutions, patrons, and personnel is replicated in lives and careers of individual artists, no matter what claims of marginalization as resistant "new genres" these artists may make.[22]

Contemporary art production exists at multiple levels of autonomous and mass production with relative time lags in their distribution and effect. Artists retain the image of working isolated in their studios, yet require the collaborative division of labor and capital necessary to the production of any industrial product. The massive nature of urban building projects with subsequent and related cultural programs has helped to proliferate a mass consciousness of art, yet reproducing these uneven developments is best represented by extremes of artisanal craft activity and subcontracted design production for manufacturing.

The modern and postmodern art object or activity and its audiences have transformed the value, or perceptions of their value, as public goods toward a "heterodox" economics, that is, the theories claiming to explain phenomena described as economic but having more diverse and comprehensive definitions of value. Heterodox approaches include media distribution, economic and political perspectives in artists' statements, cultural criticism, and academic analyses practiced within or outside academic institutions. They represent a variety of implicit and explicit conceptual frameworks and include, but are not limited to, institutionalist, Marxian, and neo-Ricardian economics, among others. The unevenness of cultural production allows the legitimation and marginalization of ideological positions within dominant institutions such as having a token Marxist within an academic department's faculty, which, in some cases, is a pastiche of academic freedom. Resistant ideological positions are tolerated because their critique still depends on shared terms from the dominant discourse, despite resistance to that discourse.[23]

In Thorstein Veblen's theories the social and moral context is important when interpreting artworks' status. Veblen's concern is the effect of economic activity on the quality of human life. His book on the leisure class reified the notion of "conspicuous consumption," the purchasing for status display rather than for personal use.[24] For George Dickie, the aesthetic aspect is constrained by its contingent social and cultural contexts and the possibility that mediation by language displaces direct aesthetic experience. Dickie notes that to claim something as a work of art trumps other aesthetic considerations, especially when confronted by an object such as a Duchampian ready-made in a museum. But an institutionalist theory suggests that the problem of aesthetics is not circular; visual art formalism, like literary formalism, refers to an internal logic of the artwork itself and cannot be understood simply by an appeal to the formal, essentialist characteristics of an art object, but by appeals also to alternative discourses.

Art's Socioeconomics and Virtual Capital

Art's histories and controversies are aligned with the political economy of art, which embraces public relations and persuasion in the allocation of public funds.[25] In this context, promotion ranges from press quotes of President Roosevelt on Duchamp's work at the 1913 Armory Show to 1999 public policy controversies in New York City at the Brooklyn Museum's Sensation show, in which the Mayor attempted to withhold funding as a punitive measure.[26] In such controversies, the effect of statements on the artist's reputation and the price and value of artwork reveal the important role of political economy in the *historical* analysis of the arts.

The study of art's social role has been increasingly the focus of cultural studies scholars. Howard Becker, Paul DiMaggio, and Janet Wolff advocate a more comprehensive approach to value in an age of technological reproduction. Most art historians now incorporate cultural, political, and social elements into their historicist analyses. This discourse has been further expanded by discussions ranging from the social production of art as a sociology of art to considering social production as aesthetics, within the more traditional philosophical discipline of value theory.[27] Other cross-disciplinary influences include economic geography, which considers the location of objects, or sites as objects. For David Harvey the art world is an "image production industry." In his institutional framework, Harvey poses concepts of transforming "images into material simulacra" and "collapsing time horizons," representing the "acceleration of turnover time" through the production and marketing of images. The loft as artist's garret is more than a living space; it can be seen as the site for subcontracted flexible production that functions as gallery, salesroom, studio, and a new form of incubator industrial site.[28]

Other evidence of the centrality of political economy in the arts is new royalty laws that reinforce institutional promises of intergenerational, sustainable, cultural value. Regulation, taxation, and matters of standing for corporations make the corporate venue attractive to both artists and patrons. Public incentives for entrepreneurial support in the form of the production of symbolic goods encourage public interest in expanding cultural industries that Bourdieu has identified as a "structural homology" between dominant classes and the institutions producing and marketing cultural goods.[29]

I consider works by Christo (Hristo Yavashev) and Richard Serra as representative of the volume of complex works and meanings presented in modern and postmodern art movements, which address central issues of political economy in the twentieth- and twenty-first centuries. These two artists signify the complex, layered expectations for modern artwork such as Serra's *Tilted Arc*, which become postmodern in their political and cultural conflicts with institutional apparatuses such as the legal system. There are but scant treatments of political economy when artistic style is situated within legal discourse. The argument for a modern political economy of art easily extends to artwork beyond the scope here.[30]

Christo and Jean-Claude (Jeanne-Claude Denat de Guillebon), the duo whose oeuvre emphasizes complex environmental artworks, are prime examples of the corporate, institutional form of art-making and of the importance of virtual capital in the artists' means of financing artwork. All of Christo's temporary large-scale urban and rural environmental works contain elements of painting, sculpture, architecture, and urban planning. They are financed by the artists through the sale by CVJ Corporation (Jeanne-Claude, President) of preparatory pastel and charcoal drawings, collages, lithographs, and early works.[31] The artists have had accompanying documentary films recording their production process. The distribution of such secondary and multiple manifestations of the artwork as cinema, public relations, or other mass media forms make institutional roles paramount.[32] While they clearly state that they "do not participate in the films' marketing and do not share in any financial gain from the selling of these films," this disclaimer refers to a trivial difference created by their disavowal, since these works serve to promote their celebrity reputation that in turn creates virtual capital. Virtual capital in this context takes many forms: from the cinema distribution system; the television distribution as public television and private television news coverage; the print media coverage as local regional, national, and international newspapers and magazines; and the mass merchandising of the work as souvenir through all media conduits. In addition, the canonizing of the work in art reviews, criticism, and art history distributed among academic outlets completes the mass distribution of virtual capital. The collectible nature of all of the former artifacts can only improve the material value of the art object or event. This represents the idea that other media reproductions of artwork become valorized; intangible assets increase their value in other media marketplaces by association. Some of these markets have their own production, circulation, and consumption circuits as in the market for rare art books or associated products including exhibition-related merchandise.

Christo's 1973 *Valley Curtain* in Rifle Gap, Colorado, is an example of the corporate style as revealed in the documentary film by Albert and David Maysles. It was filmed in the context of local business, and, in one scene, we see the juxtaposition of the artwork to a golf course. The didactic elements of such works—like *Surrounded Islands* of 1984 that featured ancillary marketing of package tours to Florida as an ecotourist destination, or as spectacle—are more institutionalized versions of the programmatic or propositional artwork of the period. Art groups such as Art & Language emphasized a conceptual art viable in its proposition as language not only as hypothetical but also as material in its distribution as published print to be consumed in the act of reading. This combination of production, distribution, and consumption functions is possible not only in the commodity form of preparatory drawings, as in the case of Christo, but in the publication of project programming by a wide variety of conceptualists. Financially successful artwork is clearly connected to developing wealth. Whether cultural benefits are equitably distributed is, of course, another question considered by numerous studies of gallery and museum malfeasance of artists' estates, as in the case of Mark Rothko's estate, or through the acquisition and authentication scandals suffered by major museums.[33] These events became legal battles over the undervalued and hidden works of Rothko by Marlborough Gallery and the legal control over collection dispersal by the Barnes Foundation.

Christo's works are site-specific and time-specific, yet are symptomatic of the productivity lag common to the mounting of large-scale cultural arts projects, including operas or motion pictures. Each work requires tremendous capital resources in the planning and logistical preparation, despite its relatively short duration as an event, and positions itself with extreme self-referentiality in relation to its place in the history of art. Christo controls corporate institutional costs, whether transactional costs in terms of its bureaucracy, as in the environmental permit process, or its social costs in terms of the environmental impact. In each instance, a regulatory state apparatus and a mass media culture help constrain the process.

Christo's project management challenges come in a variety of strategies and tactics at levels ranging from international to local politics. In each project, whether wrapping the Reichstag or proposing artwork placed on public lands like Central Park in New York City, the institutional role of the artist is to incorporate a *relative* autonomy of the art world within other social forces. In this context, the projects as promotional events sustain the unit prices of the artifacts used to finance the work. A more crass analogy lies in those artworks created and promoted by creative individuals skilled in one discipline (such as theatre) who choose to market creative products in other disciplines, using their celebrity as an added value to the purchase of such artworks. Such ancillary commodity forms are indeed reliquary but are more than souvenirs in the case of Christo, although pieces of the 1978 *Running Fence* in Marin County, California, were made available to those recruited from local art colleges to assist in the artwork's installation.

The connection between celebrity and celebration comes closest when the oeuvre of Christo is seen as public works. Unlike urban design, the accountability and fixed or sunk costs are minimized, making his works on paper not dissimilar to an initial public offering of finance capital, although they reside like financial bearer bonds in collections as a kind of provenance. This documentation of ownership has its own speculative value in terms of connoisseurship and the ability to revalue artworks, according to the volume of information and knowledge of its activity as transferred capital from patron to patron, often as hereditary wealth ultimately validated by auction pricing.

Richard Serra's 1981 *Tilted Arc* was a work contesting both figurative and literal terrain. A federally subsidized artwork, this site-specific sculpture in the plaza of a New York City government office building was removed by administrative fiat. As site-specific and clearly legitimated by the selection institution, the National Endowment for the Arts, the work came under attack as having questionable merit on a variety of premises, motivated by the legal power of public officials and the prevailing political climate. Serra comments that the "relocation would in fact transform Tilted Arc into an exchange commodity in that it would annihilate the site-specific aspect of the work. Tilted Arc would become exactly what it was intended not to be: a mobile marketable product."[34] In Serra's case the "destruction" of his artwork was the removal of a legitimately chosen and contracted sculpture installation in an act abusing legal authority.

In what is called neo-institutionalist economics, the questions here revolve around transaction costs. The contractual, legal superstructural forms and conditions for creative industries serve as virtual capital's regulatory infrastructure.[35] Since principal in the form of rights of expression rather than patronage payment for property rights was in dispute, the matter depended on a variety of ancillary institutions and activities, including the role of art critics of major newspapers in framing discourses. Ultimately *Tilted Arc*, like Christo's works, has become a mobile, marketable product; it exists historically less as a monument mediating environmental perceptions than as a mediated document. As a cautionary tale of public policy, the artwork as virtual capital enters art history as an exchange commodity, but one that reinforces certain other institutional myths regarding the subjugation of individual artistic creativity in a democratic country. Historically, the public artwork has always been collaborative and never the sole product of the artist's autonomy. Protection of the marketplace of ideas clearly has ironic constraints, even as the marketplace for commodities serves a legitimate and legitimating role in the production of public art.

Since their inception in the 1960s, most earth artworks have similar corporate institutional elements. They range from the pastiche of ecological art as university research with the works of Helen Mayer Harrison and Newton Harrison to the hermetic, monumental works of Michael Heizer, Robert Smithson, Nancy Holt, James Turrell, and Walter De Maria. Published and distributed print and film media become the primary discursive field for their analyses.[36] De Maria's 1977 *Lightning Field* achieved a minor celebrity by having its photo in *Rolling Stone* magazine and is known in a variety of mass media contexts, including works by most of the previous artists featured in the travel section of the *New York Times*.

De Maria's 1977 *New York Earth Room* and 1979 *Broken Kilometer* suggest the complex political economy of urban real estate in its support by the Dia Foundation.[37] In this instance, the Dia Art Foundation was established as a financial entity to support the collection and development of artworks that often were exhibited or situated in locations *only* accessible by media images. In each case the artwork was used to affect the tax liability of the property as an asset of a nonprofit entity, especially in a transitional rental market. Not unlike the creation of central business district parking lot empires as surplus capital and land rent intermediaries in reserve for large-scale, high-rise building projects, the role of artwork to provide nonprofit cost savings to foundations as spatial tax "write-offs" signals a type of virtual capital at work. In the case of Art & Language, the concept of transfer of development rights often referred as "air" rights is used in a variety of conceptualist projects proposing the creation or manipulation of features or attributes of a hypothetical artwork.[38] Here, it is possible to define an artwork by invoking its dimensions in a specific location, which, in a real estate context, renders it also a legal form of virtual capital.[39] The political economy of urban space as defined not by rent as in the orthodox case, but by more heterodox institutional elements, such as the use of regulation or law, is evident in a number of such works.

Robert Smithson's *Installation Art*, while contemporary with De Maria's, used the dialectic of gallery and environment to suggest the problematic relationship of site-specific work as virtual capital. He used photography or film to produce absent or fictive values mediated by representational forms like video, cinema, or photography as a method of increasing value. Photographic reproduction, whether static or dynamic, plays a significant role in that process.[40] Some objects meant as revisionist history also serve as promotional and celebrity status as in the works of Judy Chicago. It is ironic that her celebration of what is presented as antiessentialist art activism devolves into essentialist self-promotion in a political economic analysis. Her 1972 *Dinner Party* was as much an event planner's spectacle as it was a political photo opportunity.[41] Journalistic photo opportunities constitute the discourse on the proper role of photography in the canon of art.[42] Analog and digital photography function as artifacts of virtual capital in the case of Cindy Sherman. The concept of documentation, whether documented performance or cinema, stills affirms the sign system appropriate to mass media.[43] Such a sign system is suggested by Hjelmslev as the language system through which all other signs may be translated because of its breadth.

The 1999 public policy controversies in New York City at the Brooklyn Museum's Sensation show in which the Mayor attempted to withhold funding as a punitive measure support a theory of virtual capital. Such controversies address the public policy problems that the economics of art present in an age of advanced technology such as intellectual property, censorship, and the role of the state. In this case, the fiduciary responsibilities of public institutions and of their elected and appointed officials come into conflict with public interest as ensuring public morals. Then, disputes become engaged as a regulatory discourse.

The law and economics discourse, though largely regulatory, is also a transaction and contract conflict, a property discourse that restates the conflicts of ownership. Because the law functions linguistically, it embodies virtual capital as language product and as such provides the cultural context for fictitious capital that contractually represents those imaginary values exchanged in virtual markets and then is saved, invested, and sold. Artwork's consigned values as produced and then placed often have a credit and debt relation, as evident in the changing nature of art gallery ownership or names. In this instance, galleries go bankrupt due to the shifting fortunes of cash flow only to transfer or restructure their assets in a new, merged partnership or acquired ownership. This activity often reveals the complex financial character of lent artwork by individual or corporate collectors and applies in greater scale with the institutional context of the traveling museum exhibition as a massive capital import/export operation. Artwork as an asset with lagged productivity culturally defines the difference between productive and unproductive forms of fictitious capital.

The many alternative discourses including semiotics and structuralism bring a new dimension when art and the art world can be seen as a political economy of signs.[44] In *Sensation*, the collusion of museums and collectors representing global advertising empires are not simply coincidental but are correlational. The large scale, "blockbuster" art exhibition is a key element in the analysis of the institutional role of the museum, not only as spectacle, but also as a financial necessity for the museum as a corporate institution. Baudrillard's view of museums is as sites of consecration and legitimation in which cooperation and co-optation coexist.[45] What Harvey calls "anti-auratic," postmodernist art functions as promoter and appropriator of such forms. The concept of simulacrum, defined as replication in which the difference between original and copy becomes indeterminate, is dominant. Duchamp's ready-mades qualify as heuristic examples confounding original and copy, but it is the large-scale commodification of virtual representations of museum artwork and their associated cultural events which creates new markets for simulacra. The production of such information goods is stimulated by a succession of events performed and staged like exhibitions.

Political economies of art match the changing landscape of capitalist industrialization of collective memory in the mediation of forms as fictitious capital. As a museum show travels, its path produces meaning in a locality. The show is distributed as mass media and becomes consumed by a status-conscious public. The museum spectacle emits documentation in print and electronic form and as a collective memory, like other mass culture forms, is often concurrently presented with ancillary media such as music, performance, or cinema. Civic pride as economic development is part of the urban transformation facilitated by public art and blockbuster exhibitions. A blockbuster show as temporary, yet monumental in the public memory, has been part of the historical analysis of public art with examples like the Armory show or the Sensation exhibition. Other more culturally explicit or less art-identified media help to consecrate public art at rock festivals and political demonstrations.[46] In each example, the effect of such events produces virtual value in spatial and temporal forms for entrepreneurs, local and global economies, and the capital market itself. The built environment frames this formation of fictitious capital and is emphasized as monumentalizing that activity; public spaces are cultural transgressions that historically invent traditions.[47] Those traditions are transient forms of virtual capital that are commodified and reproduced for consumption.

Neoclassical principles and techniques can provide supplemental means for analysis. The function of the art world as a capitalist institution is clearly covered by Heilbrun and Gray in their deliberately restricted field of analysis. Holding other related media as external to the analysis is more problematic because of the highly integrated nature of modern art world production, which relies on mediated forms to distribute and produce spectacle. In the same way that conceptual art considered Duchamp paradigmatic and itself "post-Duchampian," the dominant paradigm of economics as scientific has assumed that heterodox, oppositional political economy has a marginalized role. Heterodox economics comes in a variety of non-Marxist subdisciplines that while generally materialist in outlook consider more diverse perspectives on the discourse of material exchange than the orthodox and homogenous dominant discourse of economics. Post-Keynesian economists are only a part of those contributing to such heterodox discourse. In the case of Duchamp and any putative paradigm shift, some speculative methodologies from other disciplines remain useful. Writers such as Annamma Joy and John F. Sherry suggest that "while the market operates on a narrative that valorizes the latest trend in image making, aided by the creation of new technologies, it is neither the only nor the most important arbitrator of value for the viewer."[48]

Art world analysis incorporates a political economy and sociological perspective as modern art histories have shown. Since the art world is a category of a larger entertainment industry, it can be used to examine the role of audience in legitimating the art world in a political economy of art. Cultural audiences, consuming bodies, and ratings points become the measure of success of a cultural project, and in some media those audiences become the commodity bargained between network and advertiser. In this context, the individual artist as an agent in a social system is also a celebrity with business managers and agents, just like other media personnel.

The inclusion of cinema, video, and photography among other multimedia artifact forms in the modern museum's collection has made orthodox economic analysis impractical. Heilbrun and Gray consider the museum or gallery as a venue containing valuable objects visited by demographic data. However, the concepts of elasticities, price-discrimination, and externalities are among the useful tools available for heterodox issues, such as considering the impurity of art as a public good and its exclusionary character, like ticket rationing or control among entertainment industry venues.[49] The complexity of the art world's relation to culture and society confounds orthodox economics based on conventional explanations of a restricted concept of cultural capital. As Heilbrun and Gray indicate by exclusion, any inclusion of the role of mass media in the analysis of the economics of art and culture is contradicted by the role of electronic media in shaping public taste, and the same media's potential for financing and presenting the arts. Conceptual art in the latter half of the twentieth century represents one metatheoretical discourse in a redefined political economy of art and the problematic institutional and economic relationships among artists, patrons, and audiences in a deeper and wider cultural field for the "arts."

NOTES

1. See http://www.artcyclopedia.com/artists/amberger_christoph.html/ for complete quote: "Our perception of art is basically Victorian. The object, the commodity as a work of art is a completely recent perception. . . . What is important with the Running Fence or the Reichstag or the Valley Curtain is that they are outside of that art system, and they are thrown directly into the everyday life of the country, of the community, of politicians, of the army, of circulation on streets and highways" (Christo, 1979, qtd. in *Twentieth-Century Artists on Art)*.

2. Heilbrun and Gray, *Economics of Art and Culture*; Arjo Klamer, ed., *The Value of Culture On the Relationship between Economics and Arts* (Amsterdam: Amsterdam University Press, 1996); Christine Rider, "Art, Ethics and Economics," *Review of Social Economy* 57 (1999): 263–32; Tyler Cowen and Alexander Tabarrok, "An Economic Theory of Avant-Garde and Popular Art, or High and Low Culture," *Southern Economic Journal* 67, no. 2 (October 2000): 232–53; Wilfred Dolfsma, "A Status Quo in the Economics of Art and Culture? —A View of Some Recent Developments," *De Economist* 145, no.2 (July 1997): 243–54; *Review of Radical Political Economics* 36, no. 4 (2004), special art and political economy issue.

3. Heilbrun and Gray, 3.

4. See Peter Gyorgy, "Between and after Essentialism and Institutionalism," *The Journal of Aesthetics and Art Criticism* 57, no. 4 (Autumn 1999): 421–37; Howard S. Becker, *Artworlds* (Berkeley and Los Angeles: University of California Press, 1984); George Dickie, *Art and the Aesthetic: An Institutional Analysis* (Ithaca, NY: Cornell University Press, 1974); and Howard S. Becker, "Art As Collective Action," *American Sociological Review* 39, no.6 (December 1974): 767–76. See also Charles T. Griffin and Brenda S. Griffin, "Art Worlds and Social Types," *American Behavioral Scientist* 19, no.6 (1984): 703–19.

5. G. M. Hodgson, W. J. Samuels, and M. R. Tool, eds., *The Elgar Companion to Institutional and Evolutionary Economics* (Aldershot, UK: Edward Elgar 1994); G. M. Hodgson, *Economics and Institutions: A Manifesto for a Modern Institutional Economics* (Cambridge: Polity Press, 1988).

6. In Thorstein Veblen *The Theory of the Leisure Class: An Economic Study in the Evolution of Institutions* (New York: Macmillan, 1899), viii. Subtitle changed in 1912 by Veblen to: *An Economic Study of Institutions* (at http://de.geocities.com/veblenite/txt/tlc.txt). The theory of conspicuous consumption can be linked institutionally to John Commons, "Institutional Economics," *American Economic Review* 21 (1931): 648–57. See http://xroads.virginia.edu/~HYPER/VEBLEN/veblenhp.html/ and http://socserv2.socsci.mcmaster.ca/~econ/ugcm/3ll3/commons/institutional.txt: "If we endeavor to find a universal circumstance, common to all behavior known as institutional, we may define an institution as collective action in control, liberation and expansion of individual action. . . . From this universal principle of collective action in control, liberation and expansion of individual action arises not only the ethical concepts of rights and duties and the economic concepts of security, conformity, liberty and exposure, but also of assets and liabilities. In fact, it is from the field of corporation finance, with its changeable assets and liabilities, rather than from the field of wants and labor, or pains and pleasures, or wealth and happiness, or utility and disutility, that institutional economics derives a large part of its data and methodology. Institutional economics is the assets and liabilities of concerns, contrasted with Adam Smith's *Wealth of Nations*."

7. The critique of neoclassicism, the orthodox dominant ideology of economics, is addressed by a variety of heterodox ideologies. Peter M. Lichtenstein, *An Introduction to Post-Keynesian and Marxian Theories of Value and Price* (Armonk, NY: M. E. Sharpe, 1983); Antonio Callari and David F. Ruccio, *Postmodern Materialisms and the Future of Marxist Theory* (Middletown, CT: Wesleyan University Press, 1996). In the case of late capitalism, artwork deconstructs the ideological homogeneity of economic relations. As imaginary concepts represented as referents, art resists and transforms social homogeneity (also referred to as capitalist hegemony). Orthodox Marxism is no different than orthodox neoclassical economics in its essentialist and teleological strategies and totalistic discourse. Heterodox approaches as critical and dialectic resist those tendencies; see http://www.hetecon.com/

8. Heilbrun and Gray, 11.

9. Donald Kuspit has written on promotional forms of criticism while seeking new more authentic methods of providing critical discourse. See also John A. Walker, *Art and Outrage: Provocation, Controversy and the Visual Arts* (London: Pluto, 1999).

10. Fredric Jameson, *Postmodernism, or, the Cultural Logic of Late Capitalism* (Durham, NC: Duke University Press, 1991), 15, 61; David Harvey, *The Condition of Postmodernity: An Enquiry into the Origins of Cultural Change* (London: Blackwell, 1989). As Jameson states, "the new political art (if it is possible at all) will have to hold to the truth of postmodernism, that is to say, to its fundamental object—the world space of multinational capital—at the same time at which it achieves a breakthrough to some as yet unimaginable new mode of representing this last, in which we may again begin to grasp our positioning as individual and collective subjects and regain a capacity to act and struggle which is at present neutralized by our spatial as well as our social confusion."

11. Rosalind Krauss, *The Originality of the Avant-Garde and Other Myths* (Cambridge, MA: MIT Press, 1985).

12. Michael W. Apple and Lois Weis, *Ideology and Practice in Schooling* (Philadelphia: Temple University Press, 1983); M. W. Apple, *Education and Power* (Boston: Routledge and Kegan Paul, 1982); Liz Gordon and Paul Willis, "Education, Cultural Production and Social Reproduction," *British Journal of Sociology of Education* 5, no. 2 (1984): 105–15.

13. Guglielmo Carchetti, *Problems in Class Analysis* (London: Routledge, 1983) and *Frontiers in Political Economy* (London: Verso, 1991); P. Sraffa, *The Production of Commodities by Means of Commodities* (Cambridge: Cambridge University Press, 1960); David Harvey, *Limits to Capital* (London: Verso, 1999).

14. Marx considers that certain instruments of capital have no "eventual transformation into actual money": "These do not rest upon the circulation of money, be it metallic or government-issued paper money, but rather upon the circulation of bills of exchange."

15. Harvey, *The Condition of Postmodernity*, 241.

16. *People's Daily*, November 16, 2006, http://english.peopledaily.com.cn/200611/16/eng20061116_322025.html/.

17. Susan Buck-Morss, Julian Stallabrass, and Leonidas Donskis, "Money, Disembodied Art, and the Turing Test for Aesthetics," in *Ground Control: Technology and Utopia* (London: Black Dog, 1997), p. 13.

18. Walter Benjamin, *Illuminations*, ed. Hannah Arendt, trans. H. Zohn (New York: Schocken, 1969).

19. Theodor Adorno and Max Horkheimer *Dialectic of Enlightenment* (London: Verso, 1979), 120–67.

20. Reflexivity means a process of examining, questioning and monitoring the behavior of the self and others promoted by the social conditions and experiences of late modernity. See Tony Bilton et al., *Introductory Sociology*, 3rd ed. (London: Macmillan, 1996), 668. Also see http://www.soci.canterbury.ac.nz/resources/glossary/reflexiy.shtml.

21. Frederic Jameson, *Postmodernism or, the Cultural Logic of Late Capitalism* (Durham, NC: Duke University Press, 1991).

22. Michael C. Fitzgerald, *Making Modernism: Picasso and the Creation of the Market for Twentieth Century Art* (Berkeley and Los Angeles: University of California Press, 1995).

23. Institutional economics is a field represented by a variety of economic theories and viewpoints, including Thorstein Veblen and John Commons, among others, and views the evolution of economic institutions as part of the broader process of cultural development. See http://www.msu.edu/user/schmid/commons.htm/; The Frankfurt School position on art and aesthetics is best represented in English by the works of Martin Jay (see http://artsci.wustl.edu/~anderson/criticaltheory/3rdGeneration.htm/).

24. Dickie, *Art and the Aesthetic*, Dickie, *The Art Circle: A Theory of Art* (New York: Haven, 1984); Robert Yanal, ed. *Institutions of Art: Reconsiderations of George Dickie's philosophy* (Philadelphia: Pennsylvania State University Press, 1994).

25. John Frohnmayer, *Leaving Town Alive: Confessions of an Arts Warrior* (New York: Houghton Mifflin, 1993); Richard Burt, "'Degenerate Art': Public Aesthetics and the Simulation of Censorship in Post-Liberal Los Angeles and Berlin," in *The Administration of Aesthetics: Censorship, Political Criticism and the Public Sphere*, ed. R. Burt (Minneapolis: University of Minnesota Press, 1994), 216–49.

26. Lawrence Rothfield, *Unsettling "Sensation": Arts-Policy Lessons from the Brooklyn Museum of Art Controversy* (New Brunswick, NJ: Rutgers University Press, 2001). The *Sensation* exhibition in Brooklyn has a considerable body of analysis available representing a broad spectrum of political opinion. See http://www.artsjournal.com/issues/Brooklyn.htm/. As David M. Merszenhorn of the *New York Times* noted, "Although a few major museums have restrictions that would have kept the exhibit, 'sensation,' out of their galleries and prevented an auction-house sponsorship, the Brooklyn Museum and other institutions are free to show any private collection without fear of violating an industrywide ethics code" ("Brooklyn Museum Accused of Trying to Spur Art Value," September 30, 1999, sec. A, col. 2, 1).

27. Becker, *Artworlds*; Sharon Zukin, *Loft Living: Culture and Capital in Urban Change* (New Brunswick, NJ: Rutgers University Press 1989); Sharon Zukin and Paul DiMaggio, eds., *Structures of Capital: The Social Organization of the Economy* (Cambridge: Cambridge University Press, 1990); Paul DiMaggio, *Nonprofit Enterprise in the Arts: Studies in Mission and Constraint* (Oxford: Oxford University Press, 1987); Walter W. Powell and Paul J. Dimaggio, eds., *The New Institutionalism in Organizational Analysis* (Chicago: University of Chicago Press, 1991); Janet Wolff, *The Social Production of Art*, (New York: New York University Press, 1993) and *Aesthetics and the Sociology of Art*, 2nd ed. (Ann Arbor: University of Michigan Press, 1993).

28. Harvey, *The Condition of Postmodernity*, 290–92. Harvey's chapter 17, "Time-Space Compression and the postmodern condition," is especially important in discussing this. See also Macleod, *Art and the Victorian Middle Class* for analyses of how the successful Victorian artist's studio became a site of business negotiations, however genteelly disguised.

29. Bourdieu, *Field of Cultural Production*.

30. Problems of cultural context and cultural literacy are at the center of any economics of art and culture in relation to the social system. One only has to look at the history of the Bauhaus, its sources in the arts and crafts and secession movements, and of Soviet art to consider other political economy perspectives.

31. Ann Monroe, "CVJ Corperation," *Wall Street Journal*, July 12, 1984, sec. 1, col. 1, 1. This is a firm established by Christo to finance his expensive art projects and his portrait. See David W. Dunlap, "'The Gates' Promote Nothing, Except Maybe the Artists," *New York Times*, February 17, 2005, sec. B; col. 1, 3:

> "I would have had a much more difficult time going to community boards, the Municipal Art Society and other civic groups making a case for it if there had been corporate logos on it," said Adrian Benepe, the parks commissioner. "The artists are paying the estimated $21 million cost of the 16-day installation. They refuse sponsors, they say, because they want to work 'in total freedom.' Of course, in one sense, their work promotes themselves. Whether on the gray smocks worn by monitors along the walkways or in the piles of merchandise at the gift shops, there is no mistaking who gets top billing: Christo and Jeanne-Claude. But the couple are not trying to sell real estate or financial services, airline or museum tickets. To the extent that they may be trying to move 'Gates' merchandise—or at least to satisfy the demand for it—they are not receiving income from the sales, which largely benefit city parks," said Megan Sheekey, a spokeswoman for the project. And the 16-foot-high orange gates are free of advertising. . . . "In other projects, we have received offers of sponsorship and have always said a flat no," Jeanne-Claude said in a telephone interview on Tuesday. "But for 'The Gates,' we have not received any offers of sponsorship because we think—Christo and I— that by now, they know we don't say yes, ever. So nobody even bothered." Asked about the proliferation of commercial imagery elsewhere in the city, Jeanne-Claude conferred briefly with her husband before she returned to the phone. "Christo answered, and I repeat word for word, 'I never think of advertising.'"

32. Jacob, Baal-Teshuva, *Christo and Jeanne-Claude* (Cologne: Tashen, 2001). Other links to Christo are http://www.christojeanneclaude.net/, http://prelectur.stanford.edu/lecturers/christo/links.html#beakman/, and http://users.deltanet.com/~plockton/christo_bibliography.html/.

33. John Conklin, *Art Crime* (New York: Praeger, 1994); Mark Jones, ed. *Fake? The Art of Deception* (Berkeley and Los Angeles: University of California Press, 1990); Thomas Hoving, *False Impressions: The Hunt for Big-Time Art Fakes* (New York: Simon and Schuster, 1996); James Breslin, *Mark Rothko: A Biography* (Chicago: University of Chicago Press, 1993); Dore Ashton, *About Rothko* (New York: Da Capo Press, 1996). *Mark Rothko*, exhibition catalog (Washington, DC: National Gallery of Art, 1998); http://www.francis-bacon.cx/articles/03a_00.html/ and http://www.artvault.com/1055/1057/10464/11200.asp/.

34. Clara Weyergraf-Serra and Martha Buskirk, eds. *The Destruction of Tilted Arc: Documents* (Cambridge, MA: MIT Press, 1991), 5.

35. Richard E. Caves, *Creative Industries: Contracts Between Art and Commerce* (Cambridge, MA: Harvard University Press, 2000).

36. Jeffrey Kastner and Brian Wallis, eds. *Land and Environmental Art (Themes and Movements)* (London: Phaidon 1998); Blake Stimson and Alexander Alberro, eds. *Conceptual Art: A Critical Anthology* (Cambridge, MA: MIT Press, 1999); Tony Godfrey, *Conceptual Art* (London: Phaidon, 1998); Alexander Alberro and Sabeth Buchmann, eds. *Art After Conceptual Art* (Cambridge, MA: MIT Press, 2006). See also http://www.rodencrater.org/intro2.htm/.

37. http://www.diacenter.org/dia/history.html/.

38. Art & Language, "Voices Off: Reflections on Conceptual Art," *Critical Inquiry* 33 (2006): 113–35. Online version of *Art & Language* work referred to as "Blurting in A & L" is located at http://container.zkm.de/blurting/annotations.html/.

39. Lucy Lippard, *Six Years: The Dematerialization of the Art Object from 1966 to 1972: A Cross-Reference Book of Information on Some Esthetic Boundaries* (Berkeley and Los Angeles: University of California Press, 1977).

40. Erika Suderburg, ed. *Space, Site, Intervention: Situating Installation Art* (Minneapolis: University of Minnesota Press, 2000).

41. Judy Chicago at http://www.fsus.fsu.edu/chicago99/hisofart.html/.

42. John Tagg, *Grounds of Dispute: Art History, Cultural Politics, and the Discursive Field* (Minneapolis: University of Minnesota Press, 1992).

43. Cindy Sherman at http://csw.art.pl/new/98/shermeg.html/.

44. Winfred Noth, *Handbook of Semiotics* (Bloomington: Indiana University Press, 1995), 443–44. Signs in this context are the interpretable commodity forms identified by the discipline of semiotics. From a political economy perspective, in the field of semiotics, the use value and exchange value were observed by a number of classical political economists including Marx who spoke of relational "meaning" and the "language of commodities." A sign in this case has a signifier that is an object susceptible of exchange within a consumption system of commercial signs, each sign composed of signifier and signifieds. See Jean Baudrillard, *For a Critique of the Political Economy of the Sign*, trans. Charles Levin (St. Louis, MO: Telos, 1981).

45. Baudrillard, *Critique*, 120–22.

46. Maxwell, ed., *Culture Works*; http://www.chelt.ac.uk/cwis/pubs/landiss/vol12/page2.htm/.

47. Peter Stallybrass and Allon White, *The Politics and Poetics of Transgression* (Ithaca, NY: Cornell University Press, 1986); Terence Ranger and Eric J. Hobsbawm, eds., *The Invention of Tradition* (Cambridge: Cambridge University Press, 1992).

48. Annamma Joy and John F. Sherry, "Disentangling the Paradoxical Alliances between Art Market and Art World," *Consumption, Markets and Culture* 6, no. 3 (September 2003): 155–81.

49. Harold L. Vogel, *Entertainment Industry Economics*, 4th ed. (Cambridge: Cambridge University Press, 1998). Here it is possible to use the financial analysis of industries including publishing, amusement theme parks, and movie theaters to assess art world industries.

Intangible Asset Values: Three Public Art Projects in Tokyo

Elizabeth Norman

THE STARTING POINT OF THIS ESSAY IS THE IMPLICATION found in Neil De Marchi's and Craufurd D. W. Goodwin's *Economic Engagements with Art* (1999), and more particularly their concluding remarks in the introduction:

> We have seen in a variety of ways and contexts that writers on economics have consistently found themselves conflicted over art. On the one hand, art is acknowledged to possess and convey civilizing value. On the other, no place for it has been found in economic analysis. Economists are left with a choice. They can develop terminology such that the social, historical, aesthetic, symbolic, or other sorts of value added by art can be discussed and decisions affecting resources can be made in terms comparable to measured, market value. Or they must accept to exclude this whole realm, in the same way as an exclusive focus on known costs automatically limits any serious discussion of novelty.[1]

I take De Marchi's and Goodwin's remarks as a challenge. I explore how the particular value of a particular art practice, such as public art, may be discussed by using terminology acceptable to the economist. Public art is chosen because it is an art made public, that is, made for the public good and sited in a public space, and accountable to how so-called public (state or corporate) money is spent. In other words, evidence of value for money is a principal issue for public art. How can subjective claims such as promoting a sense of identity, place, and well-being be given value using economic terminology? I am, of course, referring to contemporary public art, now more commonly identified with urban and rural regeneration schemes than with pieces standing in parks as monuments and commemorative statuary.

Mark Blaug, reviewing De Marchi's and Goodwin's book, points out that cultural economists are already interested in and working on ways of analyzing economic value.[2] Indeed, David Throsby introduces a discussion of value by identifying a fourth form of capital within contemporary economic analysis, which he calls cultural capital. As capital, it can be considered an asset, tangible or intangible. Buildings, sites, artworks, and related services are tangible assets. Intangible assets are understandably less concrete—ideas, beliefs, values held by a community or group—and artworks "which occur as public goods."[3] It is worth noting how descriptions of intangible assets in other basic economic accounts begin: they "may seem invisible,"[4] "cannot be seen or touched,"[5] or are "stealth assets."[6] However, determining public art as public goods, having what Throsby calls "public-good benefits," places a discussion of value or benefit for the practice within a political economic discourse.[7] Indeed, in her introduction to this volume, Codell speaks of art as public good being one of the central issues in political economy. The focus of this essay is public art and how its public value may be "measured," or at least discussed. But I look first at the terms of value public art has been conventionally given in the West before focusing on three public art projects in Tokyo conceived during the "bubble economy" period and thus begun under optimum economic conditions: Faret Tachikawa (1994) in Tachikawa; Shinjuku i-LAND (1995) in Shinjuku; and Obayashi Corporation's Head Office (1999) in Shinagawa.

Public Art in the West

A search for terminology that might be used to discuss the economic value of art began well before Sara Selwood's iconic but ironically titled *The Benefits of Public Art* (1995) was published. In 1976, Blaug predicted that economics of the arts might become "one of the most rewarding branches of applied economics."[8] In 1988, a documented measure of the economic benefits of the arts was attempted by examining the arts in the marketplace. John Myerscough's report, *The Economic Importance of the Arts in Great Britain*, was pioneering, but the methods used and the findings were soon questioned. In an early critical investigation, Gordon Hughes proposes terms by which a nonmarket value of the arts might be discussed. Of the three terms identified, two assist in an understanding of the values or benefits of public art. These are "spillover benefits,"[9] defined as "the indirect effect on another person(s) of a gain or loss to the original person," and "merit goods—goods or services whose consumption is thought to be desirable for the community as a whole." Sara Selwood acknowledged the usefulness of Hughes' work for her later study of the benefits of public art. Myerscough, however, did not completely disregard the arts' softer economic values. In his report he mentioned another economic study which he called "the 'economics of the quality of life,' the kind of effects which generate so-called 'external benefits.'"[10]

The purpose of *The Benefits of Public Art* was to evaluate the contemporary practice to date. Selwood studied public art projects throughout England with the stated objective: "to consider the perceived social, cultural and political benefits of public art."[11] It was not an oversight that the economic value was omitted. Selwood knew Myerscough's findings that the arts helped to regenerate cities, to create greater employment, and to stimulate tourism were already being used as arguments for public art's economic value.[12] Belief that public art could help with urban regeneration was a contributing factor in public art's early adoption as a political policy by many cities. Selwood, however, begins her report on a critical note by stating that "expansive claims are made for public art," principally as "a cultural investment, vital to the economic recovery of many cities."[13] The claims she lists are indeed ranging: public art provides landmarks and a sense of cultural identity and place, which attracts business and tourists; it enhances and safeguards property value; and it humanizes the environment for the greater enjoyment and respect of all its users.[14] The list indicates how varied public art's roles are believed to be and how social, cultural, and political benefits cannot be separated from the economic ones.

Selwood's case studies are selected to detail and interrogate the benefits. For example, in a study of Centenary Square in Birmingham, the issue of social benefit is raised. Selwood asks: Who benefits? Centenary Square opened in 1991 as an artist-designed public space filled with artwork and was much admired as a pioneering urban regeneration project. It was acclaimed as having raised the profile of the city, attracted new investment, and increased the number of visitors—all accepted political, cultural, and economic benefits. Yet Selwood points out that research conducted the year after it opened found that the project, like similar civic squares created elsewhere, actually created an uneven distribution of benefits and costs.[15] The environment is impressive and very public, but oddly cold. One of the most contested pieces, a Soviet-style peoples' monument by Raymond Mason titled *Forward*, was set on fire in 2003 and totally destroyed. Another revealing case study concerns the property enhancement scheme at Broadgate in the city of London in the late 1980s. Best known as the site of Richard Serra's *Fulcrum* (1987), Broadgate was designed for status and distinctiveness as a new city development and public space. Selwood raises several questions about this case: Did the project enhance the environment? Did it create good economic returns and social outcomes? Did it improve the image of the area?[16] The political and economic benefits are evident. Serra's *Fulcrum* is a successful landmark for Broadgate, identifiable and not as confrontational as his *Tilted Arc* because the work complements the architecture and the scale of the buildings. Serra's well-known name and those of other major artists represented on-site, added quality and prestige to the development, immediately attracting wealthy occupants and achieving almost full occupancy, Selwood claims, at the time of her publication.[17] While artwork by Serra, Barry Flanagan, George Segal, and others may represent a significant cultural endowment, the social benefit is less clear. The imported artwork seems to speak for corporate ambitions more than community interests.

One of the best examples of the expansive claims made for public art, however, postdates Selwood's study. In 1998, *The Angel of the North* by Antony Gormley was installed at Gateshead and is now considered a landmark for the whole Northeast region of England. The once depressed region has since acquired cultural status as the home of some outstanding new venues for the arts. It also has assumed political ambition by bidding for the European City of Culture 2008 Award, and has developed a sense of local pride and identity. Claims made for *The Angel of the North* were eerily previewed in an early and theoretical study of public art to appear in England. In *Art for Public Places* (1989), Malcolm Miles proposes several arguments for public art. These are:

> It gives a sense of place;
> it engages the people who use the place;
> it gives a model of imaginative work
> it assists in urban regeneration.[18]

Selwood's benefits are closely related to Miles's arguments. Each list serves to reinforce and validate the other. Benefits or arguments now have a well-established role in public art theory, but, in practice, are without proof. Miles, like Selwood, represents them as claimed rather than assured values.

An attempt was made in 1993 to quantifiably measure the effect of one claimed benefit for public art—property enhancement. The School of Urban Development and Planning at the University of Westminster undertook to verify the claim using real estate data, but too many subjective judgments were found to be involved and no conclusive results were achieved.[19] A reexamination of the benefits of public art was undertaken in 2000 and conducted by the British organization, Public Art Forum, when it hosted a symposium directed to "conceiving and evaluating benefit in a complex environment."[20] Questions proposed for discussion were quite exploratory, for example, "What is the link between benefit and quality in public art?" and "Why are environmental issues increasingly thought to be as important as social and economic values?" The benefits the symposium identified ranged from "developing a sense of self-worth" and "promoting ecology" to "nurturing grass roots culture."[21] These benefits describe agendas more closely identified with what is known as new genre public art. "New genre" is intended to signal a different order of public art. When it was announced in the mid 1990s, public art was well established as having an important role in urban regeneration schemes and being of economic value. The new form, however, was more socially committed; it concerned engaging and empowering communities through programs and projects and addressing social and political issues.[22]

PUBLIC ART IN JAPAN

Public art in Japan has only recently begun to explore the agendas identified as new genre agendas. Contemporary public art was first largely inspired by much-publicized Western models of the 1980s engaged for urban regeneration schemes to promote place and purpose. These roles fit nicely with a practice already in place in Japan, the familiar city beautification programs initiated in the 1960s to combat ugly urban development caused by the rapid rebuilding of Japan.

The first of these programs, more formally called "City Planning with Sculptures" programs,[23] is said to have been pioneered at Ube in 1961 with Kobe and other cities following.[24] Beautification meant ornamenting parks and streets with sculpture, improving a city's appearance and appeal to citizens and visitors alike. These programs were at once popular and political. There was an inevitable element of competition in the undertakings because the programs varied in terms of quality and management. For example, Hachioji's program lacked a strategy and consequently the sculpture was placed quite haphazardly about the city.[25] The city of Sendai, however, had a well-conceived program that ran successfully until 2000 and one feature, an avenue of trees and sculpture, is said to have been "praised both in Japan and abroad, as the 'Sendai Way.'"[26]

The term "public art" was first used in Japan in 1987, according to Sokichi Sugimura, now president of the Tokyo-based Public Art Research Institute, but was then a manufacturer of street furniture who had just returned from touring several American cities. Eager to promote public art, he founded the Public Art Research Library, which he later developed as the Public Art Research Institute. For the Institute's first bulletin in 1994, Sugimura highlighted public art as though it were a new word: 'Public Art' is a work of art that utilizes the value it has and its power to fascinate people to create a society. In fact, in a number of cities in the world, real 'Public Art' in that sense started to appear. We sincerely hope that there will be many people who will continue to show interest and participate in 'Public Art' and that they will utilise the power of art with enthusiasm and perseverance in the making of the city and scenery."[27] Sugimura seems to describe a practice that closely resembles the city beautification programs when he refers to art in relation to "city and scenery." But "real" public art he makes clear is about people and participation.

By 1994, when Sugimura wrote this statement, contemporary public art was a recognized practice in Japan, but largely seen as Western, patterned after the urban development and regeneration schemes. A few years earlier, a scheme to promote public art in Japan by providing an opportunity for discussion and display of international examples was initiated by the organizers of the International Contemporary Art Fair, Japan. Between 1992 and 1994, the fair, which was held in Yokohama, provided a venue for an annual display and discussion of public art and funding for a series of publications with related data. The inaugural *Public Art Proposals I*, with its focus on the environment and art, set public art in a context of city and town politics and policies. It gave recognition to public art's contribution to town planning and saw it operating under a percent for art policy. Thus, the opening words of *Public Art Proposals I* give public art an important position in modern Japan:

> In recent years, as Japan has achieved economic success, the creation of urban environments which are not merely functional and efficient but afford spiritual rewards as well, has assumed greater importance as a goal of public policy-making. The movement towards allocating 1% of publicly-funded architectural budgets for sculpture and design of public spaces, and towards closer collaboration with renewal activities by local city, town and village governments, can be seen as an attempt to meet this goal, reflecting a new awareness of the role of aesthetic values in town-planning.[28]

The proposal goes something like this: Public art can play a strategic role in improving the appearance of the built environment, not just parks and roadsides, which were targeted under the city beautification schemes. Public art, assisted by a percent for art policy, can contribute to the "aesthetic value" and by implication the overall value of the adoptive city or town.

One of the first major schemes to attempt to use public art in the manner advocated by *Public Art Proposals I* was the hugely political undertaking, the New Tokyo City Hall Complex (1991). When Tokyo moved its seat of government from the Marunouchi district in the heart of the city to Shinjuku, it relocated to a site of new, impressive high-rise development. The architect, Kenzo Tange, was commissioned to design a complex of impact, proclaimed "the symbol of Tokyo's administrative autonomy and culture."[29] The complex contained the highest tower in Tokyo at the time; the urban space was claimed to be the largest in the world. Generously scaled terraces and walkways, along with Citizen's Plaza, were opened to public access and display of sculpture. These were quite traditional spaces for sculpture and the sculpture project itself seemed quite tentative in purpose. A plan for the selection of artwork was not apparent and placement for the most part seemed random. Only Bukichi Inoue's contribution, *My Sky Hole 91 Tokyo* (1991), identified as one of his Sky Hole works, appears to be site-specific (Figure 1). Two arcs are positioned at either side of the enormous Citizen's Plaza to reach out across the vast space. Their suspension dramatizes not only the huge space of the plaza but also the political might of Tokyo's new government site and autonomy. Very soon after the New Tokyo City Hall Complex opened, however, the sculpture project was criticized for being ineffectual. Blame was laid on the much-used, committee-led style of public art management, steered by men of influence with individual priorities, which guaranteed confusion of purpose. Consequently and as if on purpose, the next prestigious urban development projects in the Tokyo metropolitan area were managed quite differently.

The effectiveness of the art director system of management secured the place of contemporary public art in Japan. The art director system is one which put aesthetic decisional control into one person's hands, not a committee pulled in many directions. This system grants single authority over the concept of the project, choice of artists, location of the work, and negotiations between client and steering committee. As a professional in the art world with curatorial experience and knowledge of the contemporary art market, the art director ensures value for money. Indeed, for one project, the Tokyo International Forum Art Project, the art director was able to keep to a tighter budget than anticipated because he was able to act without a middleman.[30]

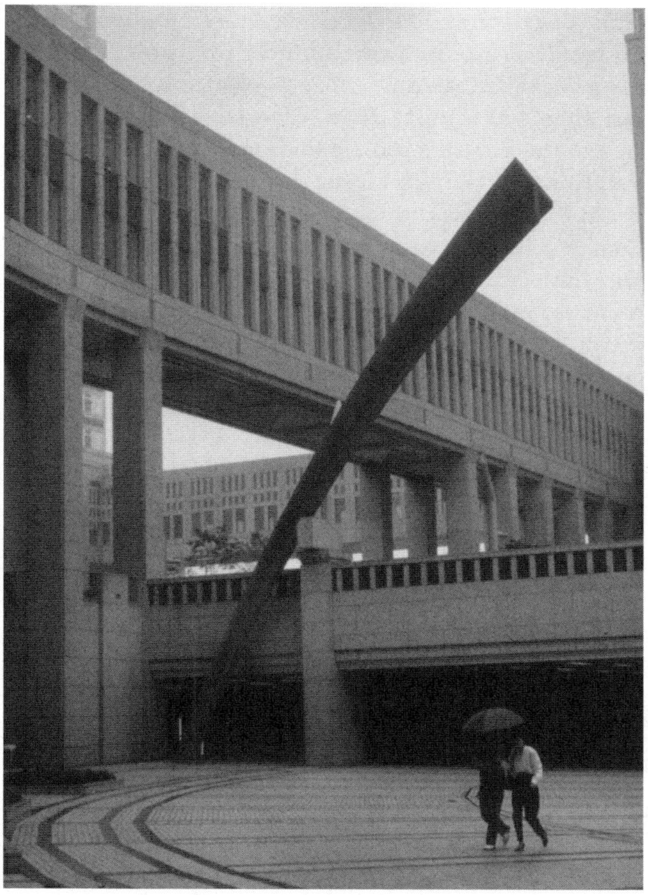

1. Bukichi Inoue, *My Sky Hole 91 Tokyo*, 1991 (one of two identical parts), painted corten steel, 17 × 17 m, Citizen's Plaza, New Tokyo City Hall Complex, Shinjuku, Tokyo. Photo courtesy of the author.

From the start in the early 1990s, contemporary public art was promoted as something new and fashionable. What was new was not public art itself, but the perception of it. Public art was seen to bring glamour and attention to the big urban development projects. These projects attracted newspaper and journal coverage at home and some publicity abroad, engaged internationally famous artists to submit work, and became popular sightseeing destinations. One of the factors for taking up public art at this time was that proportional funding could be more or less ensured under a somewhat informally recognized Percent for Art policy for local government projects. Substantial sums of money during and even after the collapse of the so-called bubble economy—an aptly named phenomenon of economic buoyancy extending from the mid-1980s to the start of the 1990s, were given to architecture and construction projects. It is no accident that public art was taken up when Japan seemed to have money in excess of need. The budget for the artwork alone at the New Tokyo City Hall

Complex is said to have been over ¥1.6 billion.[31] That budget was unique; the budgets for subsequent art projects did not come close to matching that level, but they were more than adequate. In the case of two of the projects to be examined, Faret Tachikawa and Shinjuku i-LAND, the developer was the Tokyo branch of the national government's Housing and Urban Development Corporation (HUDC), as it was then called.[32] Both projects were urban developments of importance for enacting government policy. Faret Tachikawa was created to draw business and commerce to a new site away from overly congested central Tokyo. Shinjuku i-LAND was planned as a prestigious housing and commercial development suitable for the capital's interest in expansion by high-rise development. Faret Tachikawa was allocated a budget that one reviewer called a mere ¥900 million[33] while Shinjuku i-LAND received a similar amount.[34] At the time, the sum was given in dollars as 9 million. The budget for the third case study to be examined was not disclosed. As a privately funded project for a custom-designed new head office for Obayashi Corporation in Shinagawa, the company would only reveal that funds for artwork were found within the overall construction budget. It admitted that the creation of what the company publicized as an art-filled environment was an experiment for the company.[35] The undertaking was explained and funds were allocated as a corporate investment in public and company relations.

My analysis and further description of the three projects' political economic importance are based on the claims already made for public art and cited by Selwood. These are: Public art creates a sense of place and identity for urban developments and regenerated sites in general as landmarks or representations of civic values; it attracts new business and tourists as a strategic investment in culture; and it raises the quality of life, operating on the most straightforward level as a public amenity and on the most complex level as a source of public enjoyment, social pride, and imagination. The claims are numerous, as Selwood noted, but before proceeding with the case studies they are repeated here to point out and to recall some of the various ways public art may serve the political economy.

FARET TACHIKAWA ART PROJECT

There was a definite economic incentive for the project Faret Tachikawa (1994). The project was part of a political strategy involving the economic remapping of the Tokyo metropolitan area. Tachikawa was one of five cities earmarked for urban redevelopment under a national plan to attract new business and commercial and cultural development to areas less congested than Tokyo.[36] Tachikawa is a suburb less than an hour by train west of Tokyo. One of the reasons Tachikawa was chosen as the site of new development was because there was land available for it. 480 hectares (one hectare equals 2.47 acres) had been returned to the city after the closure of a United States Army base in 1977. Nearly six hectares were appropriated to construct a mini-city containing hotel, department stores, cinema, and offices. After the plans were drawn, the Housing and Urban Development Corporation decided the buildings had insufficient character to establish a specific identity for the new site. Fram Kitagawa, director of an important contemporary art gallery in Tokyo, Art Front, was selected to devise a plan for the inclusion of artwork. It was the first major public art project Kitagawa

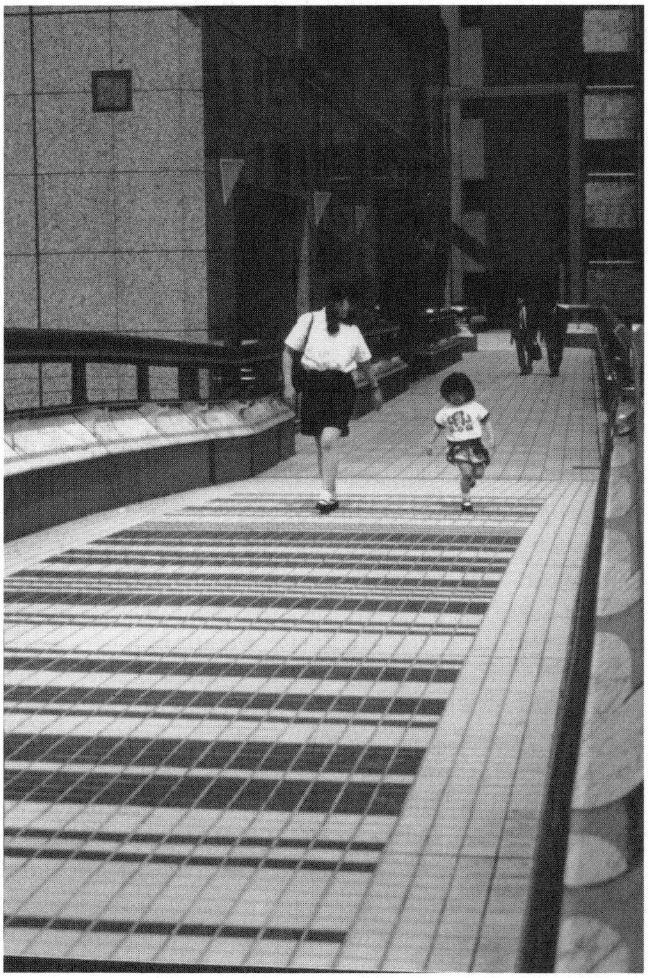

2. Hirotoshi Sakaguchi, *Barcode Bridge*, 1994, ceramic tile. 3400 × 2000 cm, Faret Tachikawa, Tachikawa. Photo courtesy of the author.

directed although he has since become one of the leading figures in the field. The project had "the purposes of 1) changing the image of Tachikawa from a 'military base town' to a cultural town, and 2) creating a cultural center for the Tama area."[37] Kitagawa's solution was to cover the site with over 100 pieces, creating what he described as a "forest" of artwork for the relatively small site.[38] The work had to be entirely exterior because the building designs had already been approved. Many new ways in which art could function in a city were devised: as signage, lighting, utility covers, benches and bollards, all radical ideas for Japan at the time. Some landmark pieces were also installed such as Claus Oldenberg's *Lipstick with Stroke Attached (to M. M.) 1967–71*. Forgoing any homogeneity, Faret Tachikawa provided an idiosyncratic mix of purpose, material, and cultures (artists from thirty-six countries were represented). All elements at Faret Tachikawa adhered to Kitagawa's unusual "fact and fantasy" requirements, a blend of the practical and the imaginative.[39] For example, Robert Rauschenberg's flashing neon bicycle, *Bicycloid VI*, is positioned as a signpost at the entrance to an underground bicycle parking lot; Hirotoshi Sakaguchi's design for the tiled paving of a pedestrian bridge is simply an enlarged barcode, a work called *Barcode Bridge* (Figure 2); and Vito Acconci's so-called bench is a reduced scale-concrete car situated, or "parked," on a sidewalk and halved to offer its open side as a bench. Kitagawa treated the selection and placement of the huge number of works systematically, devising a system of categories that would create some organization for the large number and variety of objects and spaces involved. For example, it was a calculated decision to place the work of a young Nigerian sculptor, Sunday Jack Akpan, never before shown in Japan, in a prime but also busy and distracting location. Kitagawa saw Akpan's life-size seated "chiefs," referred to as *Objects (Strangers)* (Figure 3) in the project catalog as a piece of necessary impact. It is also a good example of the kind of witty disregard for normative public art displayed at Faret Tachikawa.

Faret Tachikawa's most obvious values—economic and political—were immediately acclaimed. "All in

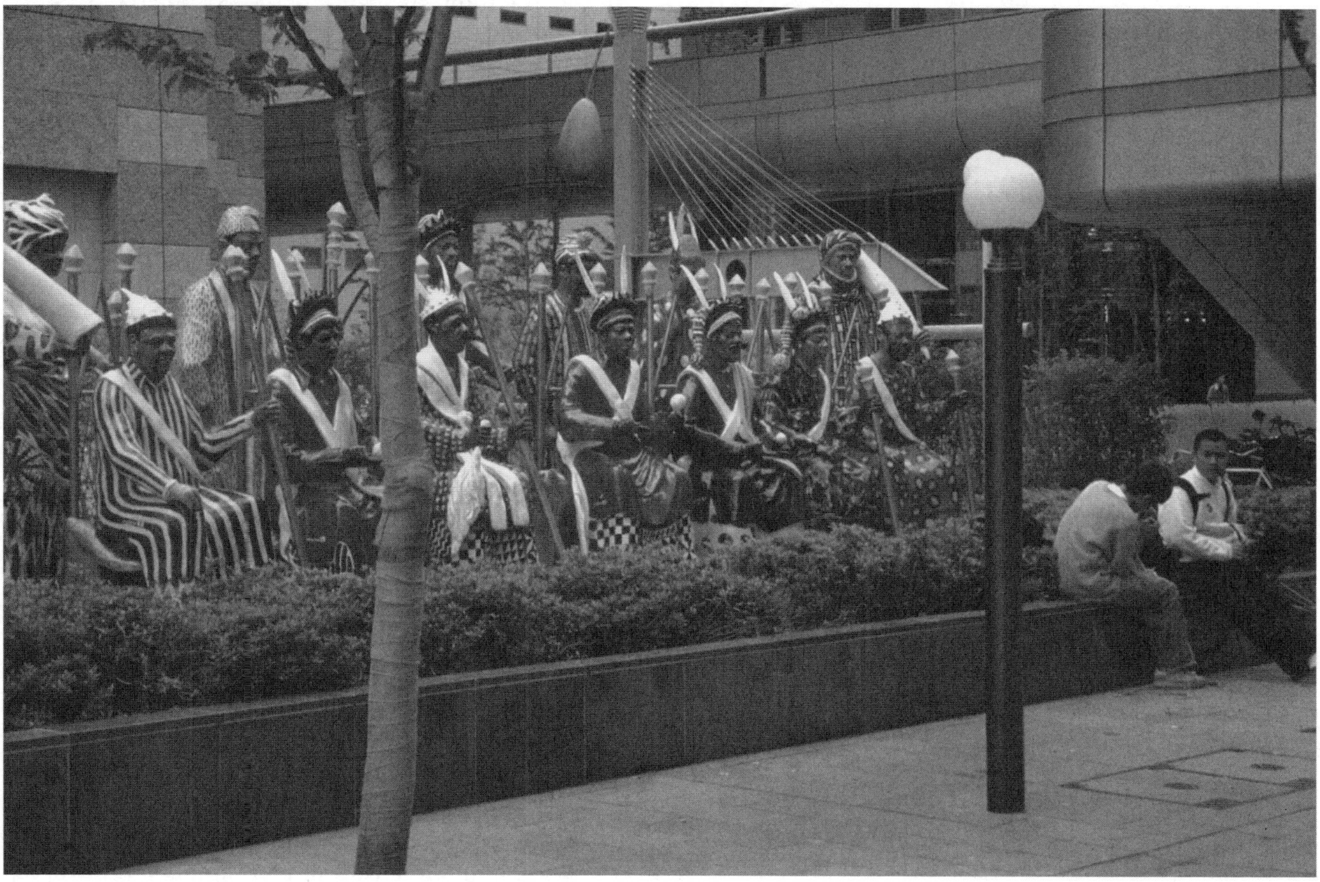

3. Sunday Jack Akpan, *Objects (Strangers)*, 1994 (seven pieces), painted concrete, 2000 × 1000 × 800 cm overall, Faret Tachikawa, Tachikawa. Photo courtesy of the author.

all, the project is a hopeful, new role model for the future of public art in Japan" announced a reviewer of the newly opened Faret Tachikawa.[40] A similar verdict was reached even prior to its completion: "HUDC and Art Front will have achieved something that few modern projects have done. They will have put forth a noble model on which future generations of designers and planners can build . . . the size and scope of the redevelopment and installation has provided the opportunity to re-invent the modern city."[41] Despite the hype of this statement, almost everything said about the project was true. Prior to Faret Tachikawa, major public art projects showed little conceptual unity, a lack of purpose in the selection of artists, and slight regard for their place siting. Kitagawa's instincts were to use untested, even unknown artists as well as proven ones; to commission rather than buy work; and to work directly with officials/politicians, architects, and artists.

None of this could have been achieved without the art director system, which placed the responsibility for the selection of artists in Kitagawa's hands who responded to his vision of street furniture and city utilities as potential artwork. The process occupied him for two years, assisted by others advising, researching, and advertising for artists while also publicizing the project. The final selection represented a set of priorities, which included first looking for various genres and as wide a selection of media as possible to reflect contemporary practice, then seeking types of work and finally suitable locations.[42] In the end, Kitagawa could safely say, "Faret Tachikawa was planned to be a model redevelopment project."[43] On another occasion, Kitagawa spoke for public art in general: "Public art is essential to urban development and will be important in urban planning from now on."[44]

Years after it was completed, Faret Tachikawa remains a distinctive place. Weekly tours of the site, initially conducted by Kitagawa himself, built up a following, and media coverage was intense in the first year. The site is now known and visited for itself; a site art map printed only months after the opening has gone through at least two editions. While there is little way to measure the economic impact of the project precisely, the near lack of vandalism close to ten years later suggests some recognition of the value added. Public art created a personality and a sense of community for a town which in itself was a creation.

SHINJUKU i-LAND ART PROJECT

Shinjuku i-LAND (1995) was another urban development project, which was located in Shinjuku and set among fellow high-rise buildings, corporate offices, and commercial properties. The development was an architect-designed complex consisting of two skyscraper towers, several outlying buildings, and a large sunken plaza. The compact site, roughly the shape of a triangle, occupied approximately 21,500 square meters of high-value land.[45] It had once supported housing for hundreds of people; the numbers, houses, and the years of negotiations by the HUDC is recounted in several sources.[46] In keeping with its location in one of the most expensive real estate areas in Tokyo, the artwork chosen for Shinjuku i-LAND was intentionally select, elegant in appearance, and of quality material. It was intended to be a lasting endowment, not merely a temporarily fashionable dressing for the site.[47] Criteria for selection were very specific. Foreign artists were to be well known and experienced; Japanese artists were to have had two international exhibitions.[48]

Only ten artists were engaged. Fumio Nanjo, the art advisor and founder of Nanjo and Associates, now Deputy Director, Mori Art Museum, worked with the architect, Masaharu Rokushika, of Nihon Sekkei, Inc. Together they selected and sited the work as the buildings were being designed, a first for Japan and a relative rarity in any country.[49] Thus, many of the pieces are part of the structure's fabric. In the main building, a wall drawing by Sol LeWitt's *Wall Drawing #722* was realized permanently in granite and extends the full two-story height of the lobby. A design by Giulio Paolini, *Meridiana*, was set into the floor. The signature stripes of Daniel Buren were used to trace a path from the sidewalk into and throughout an events hall, its title describing the way it works: *From One Place to Another, From One Material to Another, Passages In and Out* (Figure 4). Other pieces were installed in the open spaces that surround the i-LAND buildings to mark the property's boundaries, principally Robert Indiana's iconic *LOVE* (Figure 5), or to act as what Nanjo called site guardians. These were Gilberto Zorio's *Le Stelle di Tokyo* positioned at the three corners of the site. As the site map explains: "The lines of the stars are connected together to keep the energy over the whole site."[50] Nanjo felt there was a need to make the space at Shinjuku i-LAND more humane, so Roy Lichtenstein's vibrant *Tokyo Brushstrokes' I and II* were installed in a dreary side street approach.[51] To ensure Shinjuku i-LAND remained an environment that would continue to allure occupiers and visitors, thought was given to i-LAND's long-term maintenance. A manual detailing material, manufacture, forms, and levels of repair for every piece was produced.[52] Apart from a bit of repainting and a crack in the glass of one of the pieces,

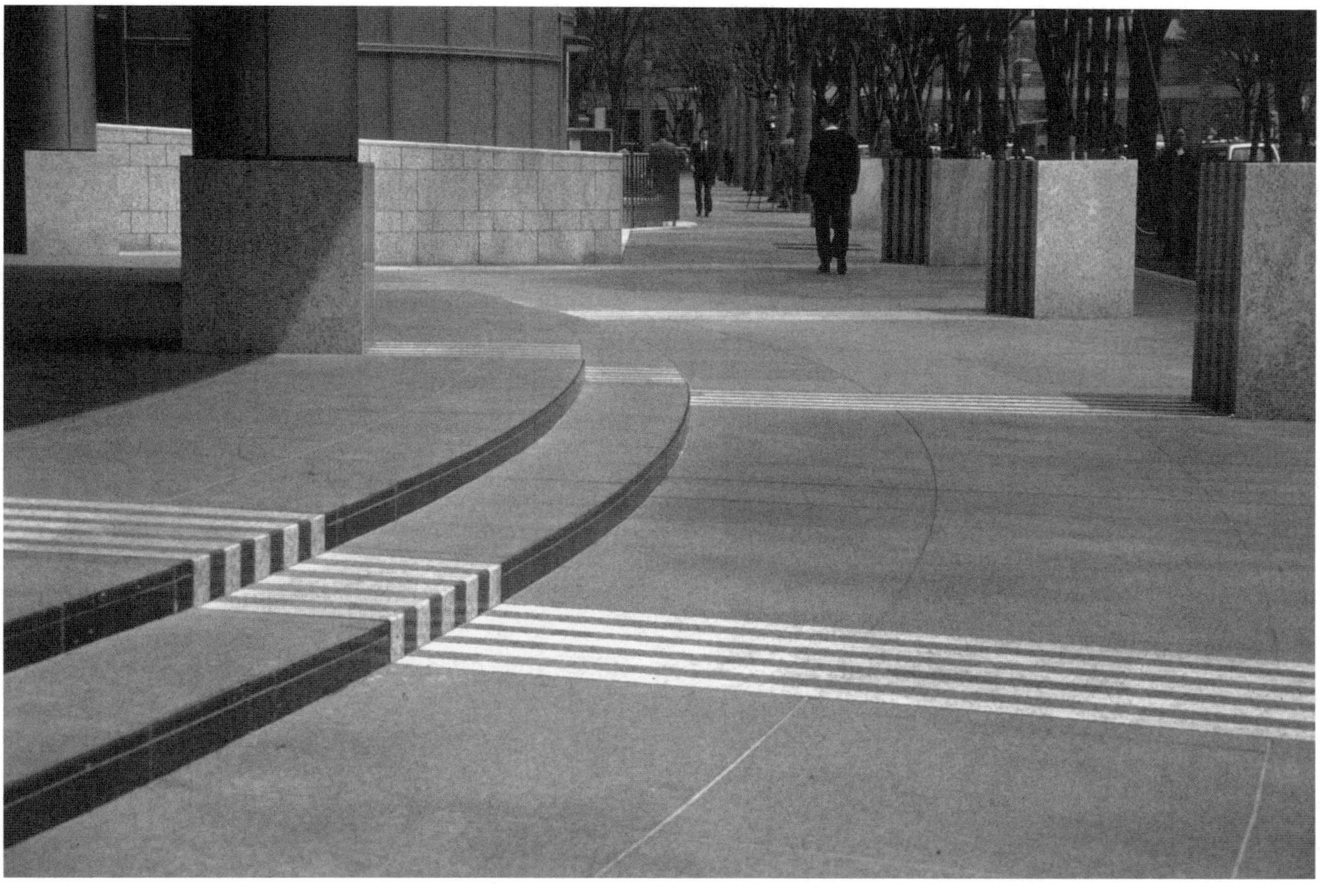

4. Daniel Buren, *From One Place to Another, From One Material to Another, Passages In and Out*, Work in situ, Shinjuku, Tokyo, 1993–94, granite, aluminum panel, glass, marble, plastic tape. Photo courtesy of the author.

observed in 2004, no need for major repairs seems to have arisen. Maintenance was only one of many safeguards provided for the investment in art at Shinjuku i-LAND. The architect lists several in his statement for the project's promotional CD: to select artists of renown; to create a good relation between art and architecture; to ensure a unified concept; and to produce a pleasant environment for visitors.[53] Much care was taken to determine spaces for artwork and to choose the artists. Drawing upon his experience and knowledge, Nanjo proposed certain artists and then, with Rokushika, discussed, interviewed, and visited them. The process was a carefully conducted and prolonged undertaking, confirming a procedure very different from that taken earlier at the New Tokyo City Hall Complex. Nanjo's choices were artists representing various, major contemporary art movements. In his own statement for the project's promotional CD he explained, "It is a specialist's task" to ensure that public art offers works which are "worth future esteem."[54] Certain belief in i-LAND as a landmark project prompted Nanjo's statements about quality and permanency found in the promotional material, and surely led Nanjo to conduct a site tour the year Shinjuku i-LAND opened for a limited, fee-paying audience. Nanjo believed the project marked a departure from the conventional view of public art as decoration. In a statement echoing Kitagawa's concerning Faret Tachikawa, Nanjo concluded for the CD: "I will be contented if the project marks a step towards future development of public art in Japan."[55]

Both Shinjuku i-LAND and Faret Tachikawa were included as "Recent Public Art Projects" in a report undertaken in 1994 by NLI (Nippon Life Insurance Co.) Research Institute entitled *Incorporating the Arts into Urban Development*. The report was directed to look at the impact of the arts upon urban development in both Japan and the U.S., in particular economic impact. "Public art originally referred simply to artworks placed in public spaces. Recently, however, in recognition of its large impact upon the image of the city, it is being used more actively and purposefully in urban spaces. For example, a collection of artworks expressing a particular theme may be placed throughout a given area or artworks may

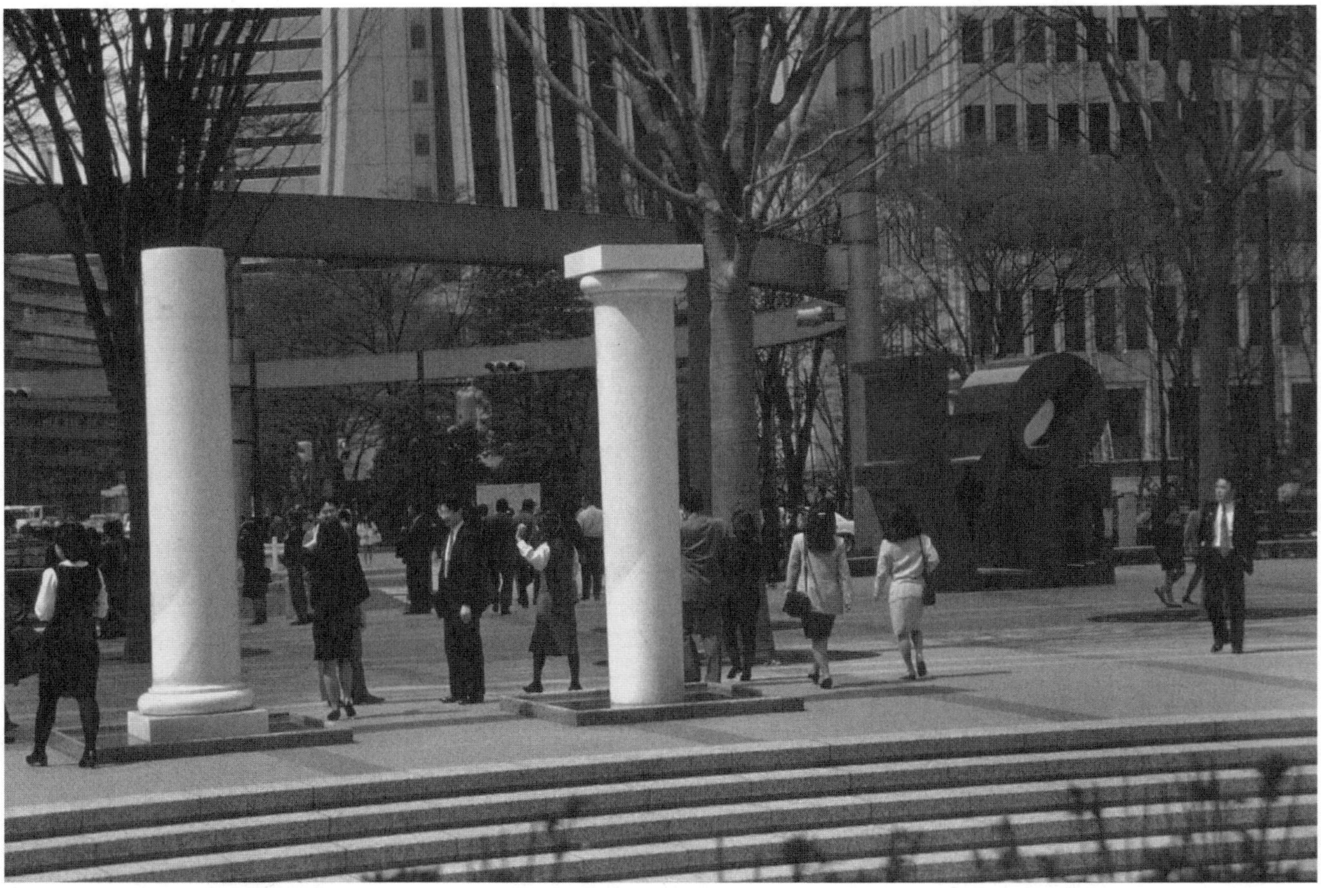

5. Robert Indiana, *LOVE*, 1993 (1968), painted aluminum, 360 × 360 × 180 cm, Shinjuku i-LAND, Shinjuku. Giulio Paolini, *Caleidoscopio*, 1993 (two columns), marble, stainless steel, 355 × 85 × 85 cm each, Shinjuku i-LAND, Shinjuku. Photo courtesy of the author.

be commissioned specifically for a particular location. In any event, public art is giving artworks an increasingly important role in urban development."[56] Singled out for mention was public art's "impact on the image of the city." This citation helps to explain the reason Nanjo and Kitagawa saw their projects representing the future of public art in Japan. It also helps to explain why Shinjuku i-LAND's and Faret Tachikawa's impact may be considered both political and economic. The projects brought purpose and identity to new property developments. They provided businesses with the assurance of good investment marked by quality and innovation. And together they raised the status of public art in Japan and demonstrated Japan's singular prosperity even after the collapse of the bubble economy. Obayashi's Tokyo Head Office project may also be seen to have political economic significance, for the company anyway. The new location was designed for impact upon the company output and image as a quality think tank environment, and hence enhance Obayashi's creative reputation worldwide.

OBAYASHI CORPORATION ART PROJECT

Obayashi Corporation is one of the leading construction companies in Japan. It chose to relocate its head office in 1999 to one of the towers of a new multipurpose complex called Shinagawa Intercity, an area undergoing extensive redevelopment close to Shinagawa's excellent transport network. The property was in itself a good investment; the company saw Shinagawa as "designated to become Tokyo's new urban core in the 21st century."[57] However Obayashi further invested in the design of the space in the tower it now occupies (3F, 14–28F). The company used its own interior designers, and its architects worked in consultation with another construction company, Nihon Sekkei, Inc. Nanjo was invited to be art advisor though not the single decision maker.[58] As it had only partial ownership, Obayashi felt the need to make a professional imprint on its portion of the building. It was an entirely interior environment. There was no space for a large corporate display piece; there were no company grounds. The main lobby on the third

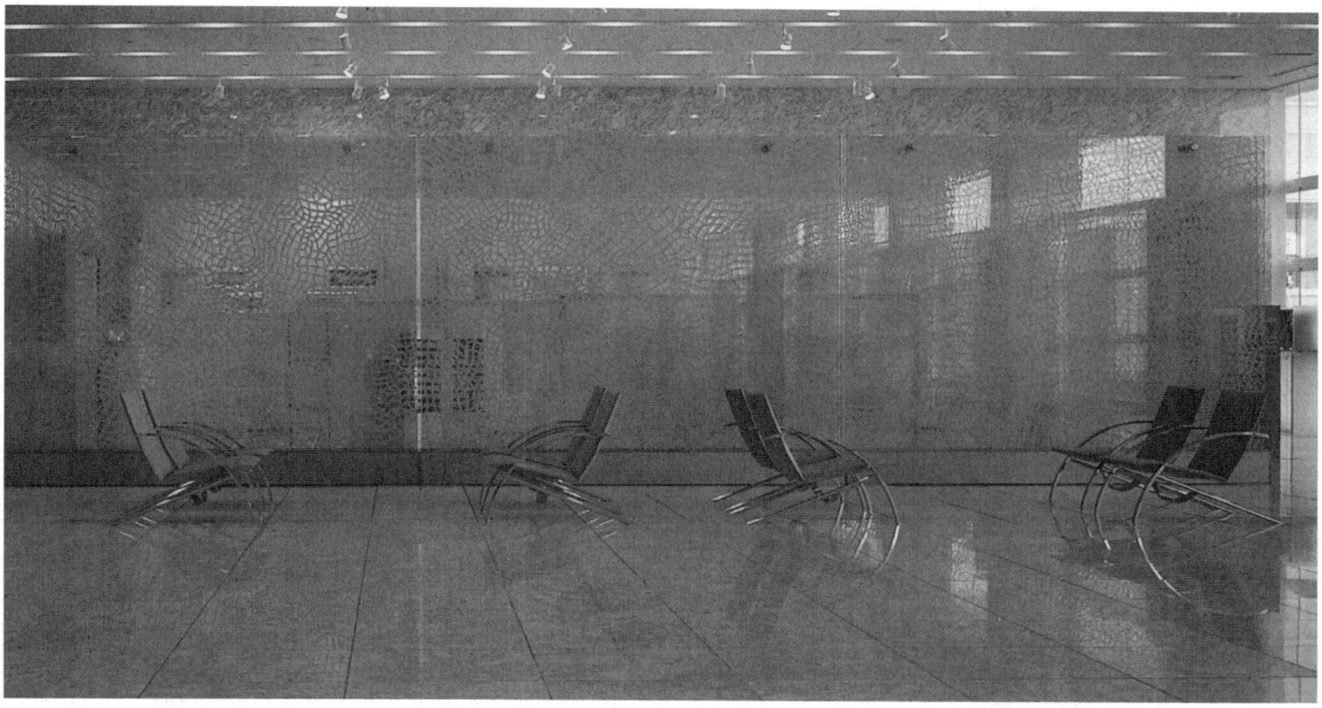

6. Yayoi Kusama, *Infinity Net*, 1998 (three panels), etching on glass, 248 × 300 × 41 cm each, Obayashi Corporation, Shinagawa. Yayoi Kusama, *Infinity Net* 1998 (detail). Photo courtesy of the author.

floor served to project the corporate image where the publicly accessible art work was installed, notably an etched glass screen of layered netting entitled *Infinity Net* by Yayoi Kusama (Figure 6), one of the few Japanese contemporary artists who are as well known in the West as in Japan. Her work served to provide a meeting point secluded from the main thoroughfare. In that space was installed another Western work, Rem Koolhaas's wall drawing, a text entitled *Bigness*, and on a balcony by the escalator to the ground floor entrance a series of pale-colored abstract forms by Ettore Spalletti, *Collezione, Passagio* can be viewed from both levels.

There was also a space for a changing display of work. Other artwork not readily accessible to the public was custom-designed, commissioned, or permanently installed and spread throughout the upper floors: in reception, conference, or presentation rooms; in the two cafes; along corridors; and in a multistory atrium. The atrium was designed to serve as a light well and act as a space where communication could take place between employees. The artwork by François Morellet, colored vinyl threads set in glass producing huge arcing lines across and through the floors opening onto the atrium, seemed a spatial visualization of communicating between different levels. Its title, *35 Jumping Arcs of the Rising Circle*, describes interaction. Indeed, all the open spaces in the building—whether café, corridor, or atrium—were designed to act as places of creative exchange of ideas, an even more radical idea for the company. One of the most trafficked spaces in the building, a corridor leading from one café to another, was filled with a large, eye-catching cibachrome print entitled *Last Departure* by the pop artist Mariko Mori. In a lounge, the wood and steel furniture and vinyl floor were designed by Langlands and Bell, wonderfully entitled *Moving World*.

Some eighteen works were commissioned for the executive floors, marked by the core atrium, which runs from the eighteenth to the twenty-eighth floors, the last two floors set aside for a presidential suite. In addition, fifty purchased works of contemporary art are displayed. The company's philosophy was made clear: A collaboration between architecture and contemporary art produces a creative and communicative environment.[59] By design, Obayashi affirmed innovative thinking and exchange may be generated. Not only art itself but spaces may stimulate creative communication between employees.

Obayashi's art-filled spaces were not to be considered capital investment in artwork, an undertaking associated with a number of large institutions. Obayashi said its substantial investment was designed to embody company philosophy and to perform as "a place where people meet, work and interact, exchanging ideas that will serve as a foundation for innovation and the creation of a new value."[60] The phrase "new value" often appeared in the company literature but not in reference to the artwork. It was not speaking of the value of art itself but the experience of having it part of the working environment.[61] Obayashi said it was designing for improved quality of life and work for its employees, ensuring social and economic benefits for both employees and company. Yet Obayashi's high-minded claim for investment in art was clearly related to the fact that designing environments is the company business.

VALUES AND MEASURE

Returning to the stated issue of measure and value in public art, it should be clear that this chapter is not concerned with price value, but intangible value. As De Marchi and Goodwin point out: "There is a gap between what the theory of price can *explain* and the sense that value is created by art."[62] The gap between actual and perceived value is considered in an Arts Council discussion paper of 1991. It points out the weaknesses of Myerscough's study: only short-term benefits were considered ("job creation and income generation"), there was a generous reading of secondary effects or multipliers ("ratio of income generated to the initial investment made"), and it attempted to be an all-inclusive arts study.[63] Cameron recommends using a cost-benefit analysis (a weighing up of benefits set against costs) because, for example, an impact study will only reveal that the arts can enhance property values, but not that the enhancement may be at the expense of other kinds of effects.[64] A cost-benefit analysis may include some social effects in an economic measure, while others may be possible to analyze but not exactly measure. For example, it is impossible to present some of the social benefits of urban regeneration in exact economic terms. Selwood prefers to speak of public art's economic values as perceived values and identifies these as social, cultural, and political. The purpose of the research is "to contribute to the evaluation and formulation of public policy in respect of public art."[65] By implication, the purpose is not to strictly measure public art's value. To speak of public policy is to speak in part in political economic terms.

The field studies in *The Benefits of Public Art* reveal some of the variables effecting an evaluation of public art. For instance, public art's long-term value is rarely considered. Public art is often created, sited, and then forgotten. Then too its symbolic value may alter in response to changing situations—whether social, cultural, economic, or political—and this factor is often overlooked.[66] More recently, Selwood has remarked on the difficulty the arts are currently experiencing in the cultural sector, faced with "measuring the unmeasurable"—its social value—and being involved in time-wasting, pointless searches for evidence.[67] What Selwood describes is a classic example of conflict between what the state expects of art and what art can deliver as evidence of its value.

An aggressive defense of public art's "unmeasurable" value is made by Jack Becker, Executive Director of *Public Art Review*, in an address to The Fifth National Public Art Forum organized by the Public Art Research Institute in Tokyo. "Public art at the end of the millennium is as much the dialogue that occurs amongst those engaged in a project as much as it is about any finished product."[68] In other words, public art has a problematic and elusive value. Becker concludes by speaking of what he calls public art's public value. He uses words no more explicit than those used to describe intangible assets when he writes that it is a value "which for so long has remained elusive or unrecognized. Given that public art will eventually infiltrate almost every facet of our culture in one form or another (education, community development, public policy, the environment and so on), and given that support continues to increase, public art is poised to win a cultural revolution . . . in its myriad ways, public art can help all the arts to regain a position of value and priority in our society."[69]

While nothing so radical can be identified as being the agenda of the three Tokyo projects, the projects do seem to show a strong commitment to public value or public good. The commitment is apparently devoid of political and funding pressures and this might well be explained by the economically prosperous period in which these projects were initiated. Indeed, the statement Nanjo made for the Shinjuku i-LAND CD reveals an optimum situation for public art. He speaks of art as added value or a kind of amenity, and then provides an illustration. "If efficiency and economy alone were pursued in designing a many-storied building, the best result would have the lowest ceilings with no superfluous space. But this is unbearable to human beings. Even if useless, a higher ceiling provides us with comfort. Superfluity generates ease . . . this argument must be judged according to values which are more human and sensible than sheer economy and rationality."[70] Nanjo is of course describing Shinjuku i-LAND and its "extras." He sees i-LAND as an environment carefully constructed to project generosity of spirit and purse. For example, the project theme is love. "i" sounds like the Japanese word for love and Indiana's famous *LOVE* icon spells it out in English.

i-LAND is conceived to differentiate the development from its competitors in the area and to demonstrate it is interested in people more than profit.

Kitagawa argues likewise for Faret Tachikawa. There is something of the fairy tale in his description of Faret Tachikawa for the site's Art Map: "Faret Tachikawa is a new functional urban space. The aspiration to create a space whispering to the five senses of the people who work in and visit that town was the starting point of the Faret Tachikawa art plan. A town where early in the morning old people take a walk, during the daytime children play, at dusk young people have a talk . . . couldn't art be involved in making such a town?"[71] He personalizes the art plan so that a promising future may be easier to imagine at Faret Tachikawa. Kitagawa describes the new urban space as an ideal space, pursuing his fact-and-fantasy philosophy. The art project is once again represented as value added. The Obayashi project is similarly argued. The company Web site proclaims that in an art-filled environment, no doubt one of its own creations, a "new value" is produced. The corporate mission is to add new value to space. "This stance reflects our belief that the new value that arises in an everyday environment surrounded by contemporary art provides the wellspring from which the future is built."[72] The statement translates the company's business into a concern that transcends any notion of profit.

CONCLUSION

There are two points to make here with regard to public art and the political economy. First, the projects in Tokyo are represented deliberately and openly as public good. They can be read as unusually altruistic endeavours, Obayashi's above all because company profits were involved. In addition, the art projects exemplify that an economic argument based on hard evidence is unreasonable to expect. The University of Westminster investigations closed without finding proof of economic benefit for real estate companies investing in public art. Obayashi's goodwill investment might well have been inspired by Nanjo's essay, *What Can Art Do For Corporations?*, written for the *Public Art Proposals II* series in the early days of seeking support from all sectors, and influenced by the part Nanjo had in steering the art project.[73] "By appropriating part of its profits for the support of culture or art, a company is in effect giving up part of those wholly independent operations and casting its gaze outside the profit treadmill. It is a symbolic indication that the company's managers are not cogs of a monstrous profit-making machine, but are aiming at the creation of a better quality of life, for themselves as well as the company's employees and the public. It also signifies that the company subscribes to various values and criteria separate from the economic yardstick."[74]

Obayashi's mission statement supports this idealism. Put briefly, the mission at corporate level is "to improve global standards of living while contributing to the advancement of society and development of the world"; at management level, "to make a contribution to society"; and for the employee to "improve yourself."[75] Obayashi presents its art-filled head office as an example of the kind of creative and caring environment it sees itself providing worldwide. The mission is to bring the Obayashi philosophy of good design to all people. Management represents the missionaries, while the employees are the grateful and responsive natives.

It is interesting that Nanjo does not also ask: What can art do for the state? This may be explained by remembering Nanjo was writing when Japan was still under the spell of the "bubble economy." There is now a different economic and political climate in Japan. It seems more difficult than ever to secure funding for public art. One pessimistic suggestion has been that cultural tourism may be one way for public art to survive as there is an ever-increasing number of over-sixty-year-olds, people who have time and money to travel and are interested in culture.[76] The recently completed art project at Murou, conveniently close to Nara, which, according to a Western guidebook, "deserves a pilgrimage by anyone really wanting to know Japan," promises to become a cultural attraction in its own right and a good investment.[77] The project introduces Dani Karavan's sculptural landscaping to an already much visited and revered temple site. However, the success of an earlier project may have first prompted an idea of public art as a political and economic asset for the state. The Echigo-Tsumari project, a much-needed regional regeneration scheme in northern Japan, is chiefly identified by an art fair it holds every three years. The stature of the triennial has increased over the years; it is now a recognized event in the art world, attracting big-name artists, and becoming more widely known to the Japanese public. While it cannot be said that the fairs make much money, they have changed the image of the region and have given Japan a new cultural platform.

Second, the Japanese projects demonstrate Codell's point that state and corporate commissioned art can be used to shape public identities through public space. David Harvey considers "place-bound identities" important for a sense of location and belonging in an increasingly complex world. How such places are created and what kinds they are, Harvey believes, has particular significance because places communicate the various identities and values of community, city, or state.[78] The relevance of his ideas for public art is obvious. Public art's acknowledged role in establishing a sense of place and identity comes to mind. Harvey understands place to be a social construct assisted by many means, one being to introduce "new works of art which celebrate or (as with artefacts in the built environment) become symbolic of place."[79] At a time when public art is becoming ever more involved in the design of the built environment and ever more identified with community dialogue and engagement, according to Becker, Harvey's words seem to describe public art's changing forms and places in the political economy.

Criticism for "a new breed of public art" appears in a recent document published by an independent policy think tank. The essay title, "Who owns public art?" is as much an accusation as it is a question. The author describes what she sees as a lack of commitment by the state to public value. The real question seems to be: Who benefits?

> This new breed of public is different to public art of the past, and indeed from other forms of contemporary art. Today's public art has new funders: state and quasi-state bodies, such as local authorities, the Arts Council, the National Lottery, development corporations and arts-consultancies. Together, this group could be described as "the regeneration industry": it funds public art on the basis that it will help regenerate communities, by forging new connections and public identities, and improving local conditions. . . . However, today's public art is not really the expression of community values or desires: it's driven by officialdom, and its spirit springs from the policy specifications of bureaucrats. Such art is about officialdom's *image* of the public, not real communities of living, working men and women.[80]

A mean-spirited public art is here described. It has no vision or message for the public; it is all about state interests and value for money.

The issue of who benefits should be an issue that concerns long-term benefits, a point Selwood makes in her study of public art benefits. The wonder of Harvey's position is that long-term benefit is precisely what he is talking about. He sees public art's value as helping us to imagine how we want to live: "How we imagine communities and places of the future becomes part of the jigsaw of what our futures can be."[81] This is the intangible value of public art. Harvey is confident enough to acknowledge it as such for he is describing the very best practice of art in the political economy.

NOTES

1. De Marchi and Goodwin, eds., 28.
2. Mark Blaug, Book review of De Marchi and Goodwin, *Journal of Cultural Economics* (May 25, 2001), 154–55.
3. Throsby, *Economics and Culture*, 46.
4. Karl Erick Sveiby, *The New Organizational Wealth* (San Francisco: Berrett-Koehler, 1997), 12.
5. John Black, *Dictionary of Economics* (Oxford: Oxford University Press, 1997), 241.
6. Charles Leadbeater, *Living on Thin Air: The New Economy* (London: Penguin Books, 2000), 46.
7. Throsby, *Economics and Culture*, 23.
8. Mark Blaug, ed., *The Economics of the Arts* (London: Martin Robertson, 1976), 21–22.
9. Gordon Hughes, "Measuring the Economic Value of the Arts," *Policy Studies* 9 (Spring, 1989): 39.
10. John Myerscough, *The Economic Importance of the Arts in Britain* (London: Policy Studies Institute, 1988), 5.
11. Sara Selwood, *The Benefits of Public Art* (London: Policy Studies Institute, 1995), xv.
12. Ibid., 26.
13. Ibid., 1.
14. Ibid., 2.
15. Ibid., 156.
16. Ibid., 118.
17. Ibid., 117.
18. Malcolm Miles, ed., *Art for Public Places* (Winchester, UK: Winchester School of Art Press, 1989), 8.
19. Marion Roberts, Chris Marsh, and Miffa Salter, *Public Art in Private Places: Commercial Benefits and Public Policy* (London: University of Westminster Press, 1993).
20. The subtitle of the symposium held in London, March 29, 2000, was "The Benefits of Public Art."
21. Davina Thackara, ed., *The Benefits of Public Art,* Public Art Forum Symposium transcript, 27, 35.
22. Suzanne Lacy, ed., *Mapping the Terrain: New Genre Public Art* (Seattle, WA: Bay Press, 1995).
23. Sokichi Sugimura, "Art at City Corners," *The Aurora*, Kansai Forum 21(1997): 4.
24. Naoki Takeda, *Public Art in Japan* (Tokyo: Seibundo Shinkousha, 1995).
25. M. Arima and A. Hirano, letter to author from Lifestyle and Culture Division, City of Hachioji, May 16, 1995.
26. Toru Ishii, "Greeting," in *Sculpture and Foliage* (Tokyo: Spatial Design Consultants, 1991).
27. Sugimura, "The Art: From appreciation to City Making and Revelation," *Public Art* 2 (1994): n.p.
28. Masami Shirashi, foreword to Ritsuko Segawa, Sachiko Kodama, and Yasuko Maekawa, eds., *Public Art Proposals 1* (Tokyo: International Contemporary Art Fair, 1992), 9.
29. Anon. *The New Symbol of World Metropolis Tokyo* (Tokyo: Tokyo Metropolitan Government, 1994). Government brochure.
30. Tatsumi Shinoda, interview with the author, Tokyo, May 22, 1995.
31. Catherine Osborne, "The Public Eye," *Asahi Evening News*, September 8, 1994, weekend edition.
32. "HUDC, established and financed by the Japanese government, has undertaken many of the country's housing and (re) development projects, with the aim of bringing a comfortable and

delightful atmosphere to communities and creating beautiful and integrated landscapes," in "Outline of the Art Project," (English summary), in Mitsuhiro Kimura and Fram Kitagawa, supervisors, *A "New Century" for City and Public Art: Faret Tachikawa Art Project* (Tokyo: Gendaikikakushitsu Publishers, 1995), 244.

33. Kay Itoi, "A Forest of Public Art," *Sculpture* 15 (April 1996): 29.

34. Steven Brull, "Bringing Public Art to Japan," *International Herald Tribune*, March 25–26, 1995.

35. Ko Uehara, Design Department, Obayashi, interview with the author, Shinagawa, April 20, 2001.

36. "Outline of the Art Project," in Kimura and Kitagawa, 243.

37. Kitagawa, "Art in a City: Development of Urban Public Art after Faret Tachikawa," in Kimura and Kitagawa, 52.

38. Kitagawa, *Faret Tachikawa Art Map* (Tokyo: Housing and Urban Development Corp., 1994).

39. "Outline of the Art Project," in Kimura and Kitagawa, 244–45.

40. Julia Cassim, "Open-air, Public-art Project in Full Bloom," *Japan Times*, December 17, 1994, 15.

41. "Art into Function," Japan Supplement, *Asian Art News* 4, no. 4 (July/August 1994): 13.

42. "Outline of the Art Project," in Kimura and Kitagawa, 245–46.

43. Kitagawa, "Urban Public Art in Japan," transcript of paper delivered at Building Legible Cities Conference, Bristol, March 15, 2001.

44. Kitagawa, tour talk on-site, Tachikawa, June 7, 1995.

45. *Shinjuku i-LAND Public Art Project* (Tokyo: Housing and Urban Development Corp. 1995), 4.

46. *Shinjuku i-LAND Public Art Project* and Masaharu Rokushika, "Architects and Art Planning," in *Shinjuku i-LAND Public Art Project CD* (Tokyo: Housing and Development Corp., 1996), 3.

47. Fumio Nanjo, interview with the author, Tokyo, April 5, 1995.

48. Fumio Nanjo, "i-LAND," in *Public Art Scene*, ed. Achi-ken Bunka Jōhō Sentā (Nagoya: Aichi Prefecture Culture Information Center, 1995), 5–12

49. Nanjo, interview with the author, Tokyo, April 5, 1995.

50. *Shinjuku i-LAND Art Guide Map* (Tokyo: Housing and Development Corp., 1995).

51. Nanjo, interview with the author, Tokyo, April 5, 1995.

52. Nanjo, interview with the author, Tokyo, 5 April 5, 1995.

53. Rokushika, "Architects and Art Planning," in *Shinjuku i-LAND Public Art Project CD*, 10.

54. Nanjo, "Concept of 'Public' and Its Practice in Art," in *Shinjuku i-LAND Public Art Project CD*, 3.

55. Ibid., 11.

56. Mitsuhiro Yoshimoto and Mami Kataoka, "Incorporating the Arts into Urban Development," *NLI Research* 5, no. 73 (December 1994): 9.

57. *Obayashi in Shinagawa Intercity* (Tokyo: Obayashi Corp.), 3.

58. Uehara, interview with the author, Shinagawa, April 20, 2001.

59. *A Collaboration between Architecture and Contemporary Art* (Tokyo: Obayashi Corp. Public Relations Dept., 1999).

60. *Obayashi in Shinagawa Intercity*, 10.

61. Uehara, interview with the author, April 20, 2001.

62. De Marchi and Goodwin, 11.

63. Samuel Cameron, "Review of Literature and Research on the Socio-Economic Effects of the Arts," in *National Arts and Media Strategy Unit*, ed. Alan Peacock and Samuel Cameron (London: Arts Council of England, 1991), 18–20.

64. See "Uneven Development: Public Art in New York City," in Rosalyn Deutsch, *Evictions: Art and Spatial Politics* (Cambridge, MA: MIT Press, 1996).

65. Selwood, 6.

66. Ibid., 250–251.

67. Sara Selwood, "Unreliable evidence: The Rhetorics of Data Collection in the Cultural Sector," in Munira Mirza, ed. *Cultural Vultures: Is UK Arts Policy Damaging the Arts?* (London: Policy Exchange, 2006), 48–50.

68. Jack Becker, "Public Art as a Cultural Revolution," in *Public Art Forum* (Tokyo: Public Art Research Institute, 1998), 20.

69. Ibid., 21.

70. Nanjo, "Concept of 'Public,'" 4.

71. Kimura and Kitagawa, *Faret Tachikawa Art Project* (Tokyo: Gendaikikakushitsu Publishers), 1995.

72. "Introduction," in *A Collaboration between Architecture and Contemporary Art*, .

73. Uehara, interview with the author, April 20, 2001.

74. Nanjo, "What Can Art Do For Corporations?" in Segawa et al., *Public Art Proposals II*, 19–20.

75. http://www.obayashi.co.jp

76. Hiroko Shimizu, interview with the author, Tokyo, August 21, 2006.

77. Jack Altman, *Japan* (Lausanne, France: Editions Berlitz, 1988/1989), 123.

78. David Harvey, "From Space to Place and Back Again: Reflections on the Condition of Postmodernity," in John Bird et al., eds., *Mapping the Future* (London: Routledge, 1993), 27.

79. Harvey, "From Space to Place," 24.

80. Josie Appleton, *Who Owns Public Art?* in Mirza, ed., *Cultural Vultures*, 54.

81. Harvey, "From Space to Place," 28.

II
National Conflicts over Political Economy in the Public Sphere

Protestant Dissent and the Political Economy of Art in Eighteenth-Century England: James Barry's *The Progress of Human Knowledge and Culture*

Daniel R. Guernsey

JAMES BARRY'S MURAL PROGRAM, *THE PROGRESS OF Human Knowledge and Culture*, in the Adelphi complex of The Society for the Encouragement of Arts, Manufactures, and Commerce in London (hereafter, the Society of Arts[1]) was the most ambitious depiction of Western civilization in the eighteenth century.[2] From 1777 to1784 Barry worked on six large murals, painted on canvas, for the four walls of the Society's large meeting room. Barry's written account of the program makes clear his intent: to chart the evolution of Western civilization from ancient Greece to eighteenth-century England and America.[3] Barry devoted the first three murals of the program to the progress of civilization in ancient Greece. The first depicts the mythic origins of civilization, *Orpheus Instructing the Savage Greeks in the Arts of Theology and Social Life.* The second mural, *A Grecian-Harvest Home,* is devoted to Greek agriculture and fertility ritual. The third mural depicts the full maturation of the Greek polis in the fifth-century BC, *Crowning the Victors at Olympia.* In the fourth and fifth murals, Barry shifts the evolutionary focus to eighteenth-century England with the allegory *Commerce, or the Triumph of the Thames* and a group portrait entitled, *The Distribution of Premiums at the Society of Arts*, both of which appear on the wall opposite *Orpheus* and *A Grecian-Harvest Home.* The evolutionary narrative concludes with the sixth mural, *Elysium and Tartarus, or the State of Final Retribution*, a quasi–last judgment scene of redemption and damnation. *Elysium and Tartarus* appears on the wall opposite *Crowning the Victors at Olympia.*

Such a comprehensive sequence, encompassing past, present, and future, evokes what Immanuel Kant called "universal history," or the speculative search for an underlying pattern to historical development as it moves inexorably toward the fulfillment of some transcendental end.[4] On one level, Barry's speculative scheme appears to promote the civilizing aims of the institution that sponsored the program: namely, the promotion of the mechanical arts, indeed, for the arts of manufactured goods in general. On another level, however, Barry's universal history did not, as one might expect, merely legitimize the civilizing role of commerce and manufactures. A close exegesis of the narrative reveals shifts of emphasis that at times challenge, rather than blindly sustain, the material improvements of civil society. Indeed, Barry viewed the rise of the mechanical arts as one of considerable portent, for his universal scheme was bound up with what he believed was the diminished support for history painting and its public role in the growing market for the mechanical arts.

For him, ceasing to paint in the grand manner was at stake, since the demise of history painting was symptomatic of what Barry saw as the unfavorable side effects in civil society caused by commerce and industry—social inequality, demoralization of wealth, dehumanization that arises in refined cultures, the erosion of communal citizenship, and artistic alienation.[5] Recent scholarship on Barry's art theory has shown that he was well versed in civic humanist and economic ideas to address this crisis.[6] However, what has not been fully appreciated is how Barry organized his universal history around the converging discourses of religion, politics, and political economy that shaped the civilizing process in the *Progress of Human Knowledge and Culture*. To appreciate Barry's achievement necessitates understanding how he responded to the religious, economic, and political turmoil of the 1770s and 1780s. Before discussing the convergence of these discourses in the mural program, it is first necessary to say a few words about Barry's sponsoring institution, the Society of Arts.

THE SOCIETY OF ARTS AND THE *DOUX-COMMERCE* THESIS: UNIVERSAL BENEVOLENCE IN THE COMMERCE OF NATIONS

In 1754, William Shipley, a Northampton philanthropist and drawing teacher, established the Society of Arts in London. He subsidized technological inventions and the applied arts with prizes to encourage new discoveries as well as to enhance the public's knowledge of the relationship between free trade and humanitarianism.[7] Although he sought state support for his objectives, Shipley established the institution through subscriptions as a voluntary organization in civil society.[8] In his *Proposals*, Shipley envisioned the Society of Arts as a philanthropic association of private individuals who would organize themselves into what he called "a body of generous and public spirited persons [in order to provide civil society the] effectual means to embolden enterprise, to enlarge science, to refine Art, to improve our manufactures, and extend our Commerce."[9] Shipley argued that these material improvements would generate "the esteemed . . . ornaments of nations"[10] and function as "the necessary sweetener of life" in civil society at large.[11] These aims reflected Shipley's ambitious attempt "to render Great Britain as the school of instruction as it is already the center of traffic to the greatest part of the known world."[12] What Shipley's *Proposals* suggest is that the uniqueness of the Society of Arts lies in the attempt of its members to link their cosmopolitan and philanthropic outlook to developments in free trade that was inextricably connected to the emerging discipline of political economy.

Shipley's views toward free trade in the *Proposals* are consistent with many statements produced by key eighteenth-century thinkers who viewed the civilizing role of commerce, or what Albert O. Hirschman calls the "*doux-commerce* thesis," as the driving force behind the social construction of human values.[13] In eighteenth-century thinking, these values produced by economic trade became associated with enlightened civility—particularly, the refinement of the arts, sciences, manners, and morals. These thinkers' views on the constructive role of economic trade reflected much discussion in eighteenth-century England and France about the douceur of commerce. In English, the French word "douceur" had multiple meanings, denoting sweetness, mildness, softness, gentleness, and peacefulness. The word "commerce" went beyond economic trade to encompass the cultivation of polite conversation, good manners, sociability, philanthropy, and aesthetic refinement.[14] As Hirschman and J. G. A. Pocock have demonstrated, when linked together, *doux-commerce* denoted two main principles in eighteenth-century thought. First, that economic trade would sweeten material life, rendering it more luxurious, and second, that through social interaction produced by economic trade people would become more humane and polite, even as their taste and refinement were sensitized. In this, Pocock identifies how the polishing and softening of manners evidenced a redefinition of virtue in eighteenth-century thought. Apologists for commerce, Pocock argues, developed an ideology of "commercial humanism"[15] that attempted to differentiate these *civil virtue*s associated with economic trade from the civic humanist's cult of *civic virtue*, or fraternal participation in politics modeled on the ancient republics of Sparta and Rome.[16] In this redefinition of virtue, *doux-commerce* thinkers insisted that economic trade would enlarge people's sense of their moral purposes so that the cosmopolitan value of universal benevolence becomes a defining characteristic of their behavior.

What is significant about Shipley's *Proposals* is how he availed himself of *doux-commerce* thinkers in his attempt to institutionalize the idea that free trade was the most effective means to promote global friendship. Malachy Postlethwait, political economist and supporter of the Society of Arts, reinforced Shipley's humanitarian vision. In his influential *Universal Dictionary of Trade and Commerce* (1730–55), Postlethwait identified not only the pivotal role that commerce played in the formation of the Society of Arts, but also how it figured prominently in the historical transformation of Europe from feudalism to commercialism, from war to peace. Indeed, as a *doux-commerce* theorist, Postlethwait maintained that societies that were organized to facilitate trade were inclined more to peace than war, a conviction that many Enlightenment thinkers thought distinguished modern commercial societies from martial societies of the ancient and feudal worlds. While the latter tried to secure wealth by way of conquest and plunder, the former tried to secure wealth by peaceful commercial means. The combination of peace and prosperity became a distinguishing mark of the foundation of what Enlightenment thinkers called "civilization,"[17] and what Benjamin Constant later called "modern liberty."[18] For Postlethwait, "it appears that in those countries, where there is no commerce, the human species seems to be little superior to brute creation; but, wherever trade and navigation flourish . . . there we find mankind civilized and capable of all the social virtues. So that commerce should seem to be the original parent of the arts and sciences . . . which alone is capable of knitting mankind together in a mutual intercourse of good offices, distributing gifts of nature, finding work for the poor, and wealth for the rich, and magnificence to the great."[19]

Several things are noteworthy in Postlethwait's statement about the civilizing role of commerce. The notion that commerce appears to be "the original parent of the arts and sciences" meant that social and cultural life is organized around economic trade. It also suggests an interplay between free trade and culture that links commerce to prosperity, prosperity to leisure, and leisure to increased possibilities for human self-realization in the arts and sciences. This process alludes to a *doux-commerce* sequence—a semantic chain—that Pocock has examined as running "commerce, leisure, cultivation" of arts and manners.[20] In *doux-commerce* thinking, wealth and virtue were deemed compatible because commerce engendered a more polished human type—one who was aesthetically refined frugal, industrious, tolerant, polite, helpful, and sociable.

In this, Postlethwait suggests that as commerce pushes the civilizing process forward in history, the citizens of commercial societies become progressively more civilized in a moral sense, with the result that leisure comes to be viewed less as a chance for consumer (i.e., bourgeois) indulgence than as an opportunity to develop what Hirschman has identified as "the nonmaterial and nonconsumptionist" dimension of the human personality.[21] This dimension served, in Hirschman's words, to "facilitate the smooth functioning of the market"[22] by providing it with what Fred Hirsh has termed "a supporting social morality."[23] That Postlethwait identified as a moral by-product of economic trade a new host of "social virtues" suggested that governments who regulate too much hindered free trade's ability to "knit mankind together in a mutual intercourse of good offices." What both Shipley and Postlethwait postulated, then, was a socioeconomic means of reforming society whereby commerce would "refine the manners of men, by . . . cultivating the politer arts, which embellish and adorn human life; and which are its external ornaments and perfection."[24]

In the heady aftermath of the Jacobite Rebellion of 1745, a period that "witnessed the peak of eighteenth-century anti-Catholic feeling,"[25] it appears that Shipley drafted the *Proposals* to advance a cosmopolitan agenda that linked *doux-commerce* thought and humanitarian religious values, particularly the economic and religious universalism associated with English dissenters.[26] During the American Revolution, many reform-minded Dissenters shared Shipley's view that free trade is a main agent of humanitarian reform, particularly in how it knits nations together in a single community of cosmopolitan fellowship. In his text, *An Essay on the First Principles of Government, and on the Nature of Political, Civil, and Religious Liberty* (1771), the famous English Dissenter, Joseph Priestley, summed up the cosmopolitan spirit of friendship among Protestant nations. According to Priestley, Catholic "France was greatly hurt by the revocation of the edict of Nantz whereas England was a great gainer on both occasions, by granting an asylum for those persecuted industrious people [i.e., the French Huguenots]; who repaid us for our kindness, by the introduction of many useful arts and manufactures, which were the foundation of our present commerce, riches, and power."[27] In viewing French religious and mercantilist policies toward the French Huguenots as illiberal—that is, selfish, particularistic, competitive, and oppressive—Priestley presented English free trade as benevolent, universalistic, cooperative, and tolerant. Priestley's call for religious toleration, universal benevolence, and free trade evidenced a cosmopolitan view of global friendship contrary to France's reason of state policies.

Moreover, when Priestley stated that the French Huguenots "introduced [into England] many useful arts and manufactures" that were "the foundation of our present commerce, riches, and power," he tacitly referred to how their doctrine of laissez-faire revitalized British economic life. Priestley was not alone in this view in that his linkage of free trade and Christian benevolence in the 1770s operated in a discursive tradition going back to the 1750s. It was in the mid-1750s that leading members of the Society of Arts and prominent Dissenters encouraged French laissez-faire as a policy recommendation for economic and humanitarian reform.

Not insignificantly, the Society of Arts did much to disseminate laissez-faire policies articulated by one of its most influential members, Benjamin Franklin. Having joined the Society of Arts in 1756,[28] Franklin took advantage of his unique situation as a diplomat in France and England to assimilate and spread French thinking about laissez-faire to his circle of English friends.[29] William Shipley's elder brother, Jonathan Shipley, was a close friend of Franklin, and popularized Franklin's laissez-faire views in the early 1770s in circumstances that were to promote American independence. Jonathan Shipley, who was also close to the reform-minded finance minister Lord Shelburne, held liberal religious and economic views that appealed to Shelburne as well as to many Dissenters who were part of Franklin's network of English friends.[30] He recommended a plan that mixed humanitarian religious and utilitarian economic concerns in improving Anglo-American relations. Using the language of laissez-faire, he argued that the key to better relations between the two peoples lies in the "true art of . . . not governing too much."[31] In this, Jonathan Shipley criticized English trade policymakers for pursuing selfish ends through force rather than ones that would promote the "laws of justice and equity" through mutual trade, a pursuit that was consistent with "benevolent Christian morals."[32] The linkage of free trade and Christian benevolence, he maintained, was indicative of the "great liberal commanding spirit" of the present age.[33]

For humanitarians and cosmopolitans associated with the Shipley brothers, the Pennsylvania Quakers, especially, exemplified the intersection of liberal religious and liberal economic thinking. Priestley and his fellow Dissenter Richard Price advocated laissez-faire trade and religious toleration as a policy recommendation for how the English could keep the Americans in common fellowship with them without England having to resort to force to secure American loyalty. In the early 1770s, Priestley and Price were closely associated with Shelburne, who applied their political, religious, and economic philosophy of universal benevolence to government policy.[34] When he was under Shelburne's patronage, Priestley claimed that the Pennsylvania Quakers and their English brethren were at the forefront of promoting Anglo-American concord. In his view, "Pennsylvania flourished much more than . . . any other of the English settlements in North America, evidently in consequence of giving more liberty in matters of religion. . . . England has also been much more flourishing and happy, since the *establishment* . . . of the dissenting method of worship, by what is commonly called the *act of toleration*."[35] In keeping with this, Priestley contended that religious mutualism between England and North America encouraged the possibility that a market friendship between the two parts of the Empire would evolve into a friendship of true benevolence.

In this context, evidence suggests that Barry was attuned to these discussions about Anglo-American relations. In a letter he sent to the Dissenter and Whig leader Charles James Fox, Barry states that in 1771–72 he frequented a favored venue of English reformers, St. Paul's Coffee House. In his words, "it was my good fortune to be acquainted with some of your principle Dissenters in London, who made me a member of their Clubb at S. Paul's Coffee house, where Dr. Price occasionally came & where I had frequently the opportunity of hearing interesting Constitutional Questions honestly & ably discussed. About this time your political conduct [on the] American questions was much distinguished."[36]

In addition to Fox and Price, Priestley, Franklin, Shelburne, and Thomas Amory (among others) frequented St. Paul's Coffee House, providing Barry the opportunity to absorb their pro-American views.[37] Although he was an Irish Catholic, Barry appears to have associated his own sense of religious persecution in the 1770s and 1780s with that of Dissenters. It was in the haven of Dissenters where Barry learned advanced thinking about religious toleration and free trade, all of which, for him, comprised the ensemble of values associated with civil liberty and how the Enlightenment presented itself as a humanitarian and cosmopolitan age. These acquaintances further indicate that his ties to Dissenters appear to have been strongest during the concurrent moments of the American Revolution and work on the mural program for the Society of Arts.

In decorating the walls of an institution whose members encouraged free trade, American independence, and humanitarian religious values, Barry attempted to legitimize the civilizing aims of Protestant Dissenters. Barry and many Dissenters viewed the American Revolution as a momentous religious event in world history, a millenarian moment indicative of God's providential plan to realize Anglo-American cooperation in the future. From this religious perspective, Barry located the civilizing aims of the Society of Arts within a providential scheme to reveal how God had sanctioned the institution to assume a leadership role in fulfilling humanity's long quest for universal benevolence in human history. Suffice it to say, a providential format in the mural program enabled him to celebrate "the generous, liberal views of the Society . . . [with] a work, which should be *one* and *entire*, comprehending a *beginning*, a *middle*, and an *end*, illustrative . . . [of its] pursuit of truth and justice . . . [Truth and justice were] necessarily required as the foundation of civil society, in lieu of that brutal violence, fraud, and consequent miseries of the savage state."[38] That the entire program comprised a "*beginning*, a *middle*, and an *end*" was another way of saying how the narrative unfolds according to a three-age scheme of historical evolution: past, present, and future, respectively.

As we shall see, Barry employed the three-age scheme to delineate the providential development of art, manufactures, and commerce in Western history from ancient Greece (the past), to eighteenth-century England (the present), to America (the future). For him, the shift in human understanding—which registers itself in each age in art, economics, and philosophy—constitutes the concrete manifestations of humanity's awareness of its telos in and through history. The providential and teleological structure allowed Barry to read an evolutionary process into recent English history to make the laws of historical change more accessible, and, hence, make future developments more predictable. It is with Barry's three-age sequencing of historical understanding that we proceed to interpret the convergence of religion, economics, and politics in the *Progress of Human Knowledge and Culture*.

THE ECONOMIC ORIGINS OF ART IN ANCIENT GREECE: "KNOWING THE PAST"

In the first three murals dedicated to ancient Greece, Barry depicted how humanity gradually evolved from the state of nature to civilized association. His first mural of the program, *Orpheus Instructing the Savage*

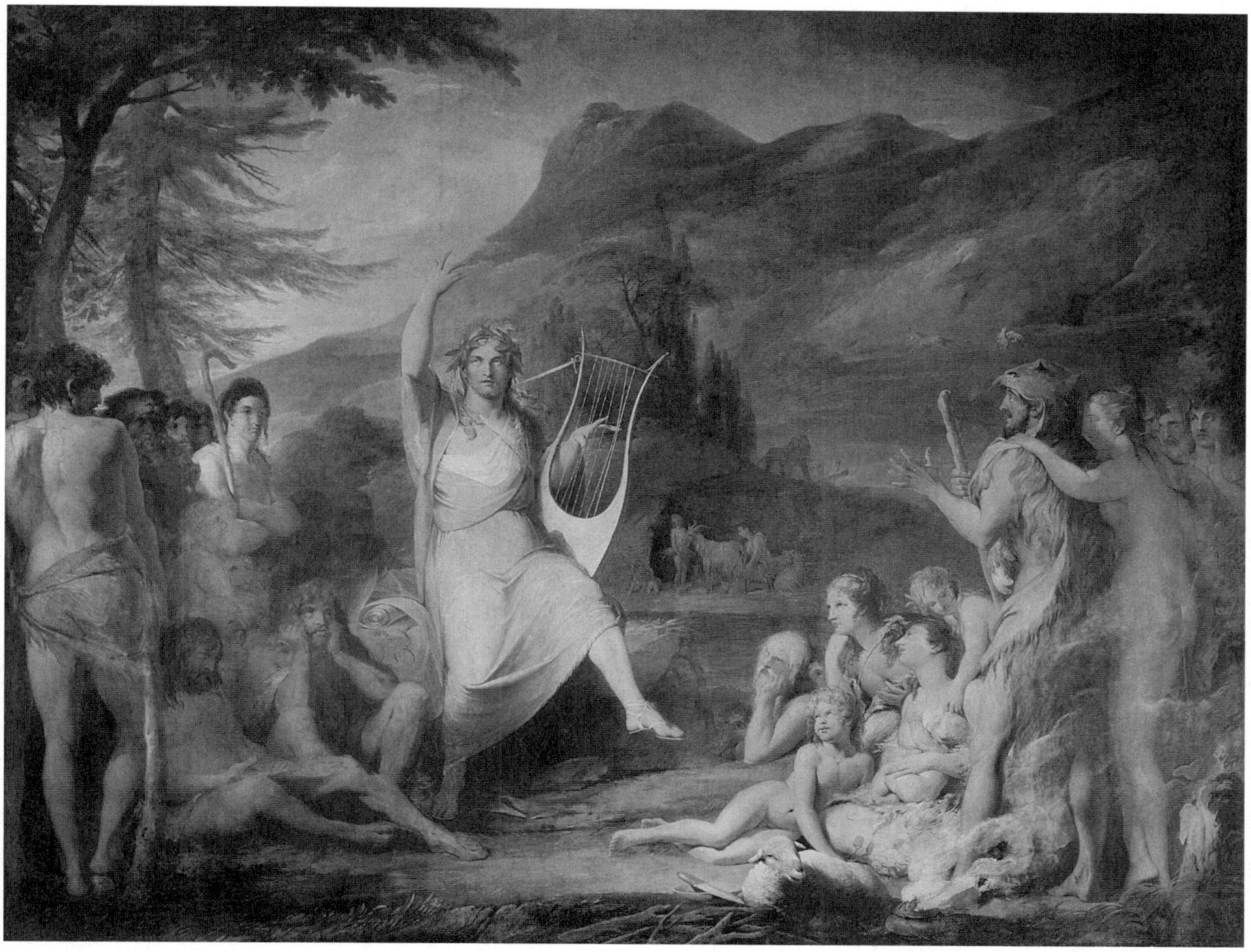

7. James Barry, *Orpheus Instructing the Savage Greeks in the Arts of Theology and Social Life*, 1777–84, oil on canvas, 360.68 × 462.28 cm (11 ft 10 in × 15 ft 2 in), Royal Society of Arts, London, UK/Bridgeman Art Library.

Greeks in the Arts of Theology and Social Life (Figure 7), depicts the transition of humanity from a state of savage primitivism to a civilized community. Set in the state of nature, the poet-lawgiver instructs the savage Greeks in the civilizing influence of culture. The dark shadows on the left-hand side of the picture represent "the state of nature . . . far short of the golden age," while the supernatural light of Orpheus—the brilliant source of revelation in the center of the painting—symbolizes his civilizing influence bestowed to the astonished humans partially illuminated on the right side of the mural.[39] In Barry's words, Orpheus "is impressing on the savage Thracians those lessons of *theology* and *morality*, which substitute the ardor for *truth* and *justice* in place of selfish *fraud* and *violence*, and of social institutions."[40]

As humanity moves from the barbaric state of self-love and violence to morality and peaceful association, Barry sought to link the civilizing role of Orpheus to that of the Society of Arts in the civilizing process. He states: "Appointed for the administration of justice [by Providence], Orpheus had persuaded his savages to associate into a civil polity; and what can afford a surer prospect of success and honorable reward, either in the world at larger, or in the Society for the encouragement of arts, than a solid foundation of early domestic culture, and industrious useful applications."[41] For Barry, the figure of Orpheus functioned as an artist-seer who unifies humanity because he himself "unite[s] in the same character, the legislator, the divine, the philosopher, and the poet, as well as the musician."[42] In other words, Orpheus represented the original unity of labors—ideal and mechanical—given to barbaric humanity.[43] Indeed, the transition from barbarism to civilization in *Orpheus* denotes a fertile informative stage in history wherein humanity's quest for social unity on a higher plane had begun.

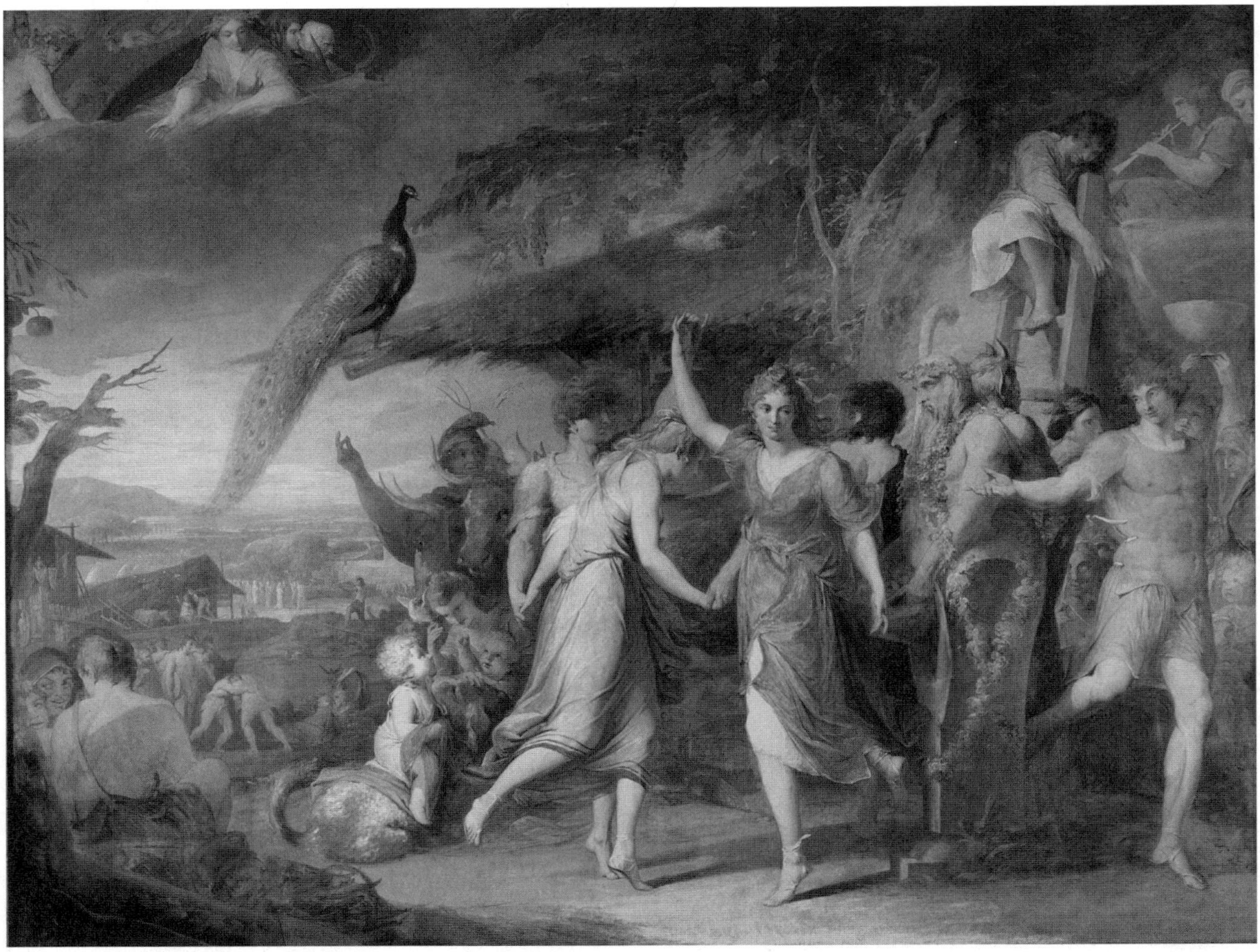

8. James Barry, *A Grecian-Harvest Home*, 1777–84, oil on canvas, 360.68 × 462.28 cm (11 ft 10 in. × 42 ft 11 in), Royal Society of Arts, London, UK/Bridgeman Art Library.

Humanity's quest for social unity continues with the advancements in agriculture and fertility ritual in the second mural of the program, *A Grecian-Harvest Home* (Figure 8), and comes to an even higher fulfillment in the third, *Crowning the Victors at Olympia* (Figure 9). As noted, *Crowning the Victors* depicts the high point of ancient civilization, the Golden Age of the Greek polis in the fifth-century BC. The scene is the Olympic Games, where Barry combines the finest competitors, thinkers, and artists spanning several generations in one ideal game of fraternal brotherhood. Reminiscent of the heroic procession in the Parthenon frieze, the athletes in the painting parade from left to right in communal action, or praxis, on their way to be crowned by the judges seated aloft on the far right side of the mural. The central focus is on an elderly man, a former champion, and his two sons, both of whom have just won competitions and have hoisted their father on their shoulders. Two colossal painted statues set off this heroic procession on either ends of the mural. At the far left is Hercules treading down Envy and at the far right is Minerva, the goddess of wisdom, war, and patron deity of the arts and sciences. Placed adjacent to the judges' seat, Minerva functions as the exemplar by which they choose the heroic victors. In the center, just to the right of the rearing horseman, Barry depicted prominent Athenian orators, philosophers, and playwrights, all of whom partake in the festive procession of athletes and musicians.

The expansion of light from the partial brightness in *Orpheus* to the nearly full illumination in *Crowning the Victors* suggests a Christian subtext of special note. It represents, in the words of Price, "the system of nature and the plans of Providence"[44] [whereby] "light and knowledge have been gaining ground."[45] "Such are the nature of things," Price continues, "that this progress must continue. . . . , [for, in] an enlightened age . . . , the light, after being smothered for a time,

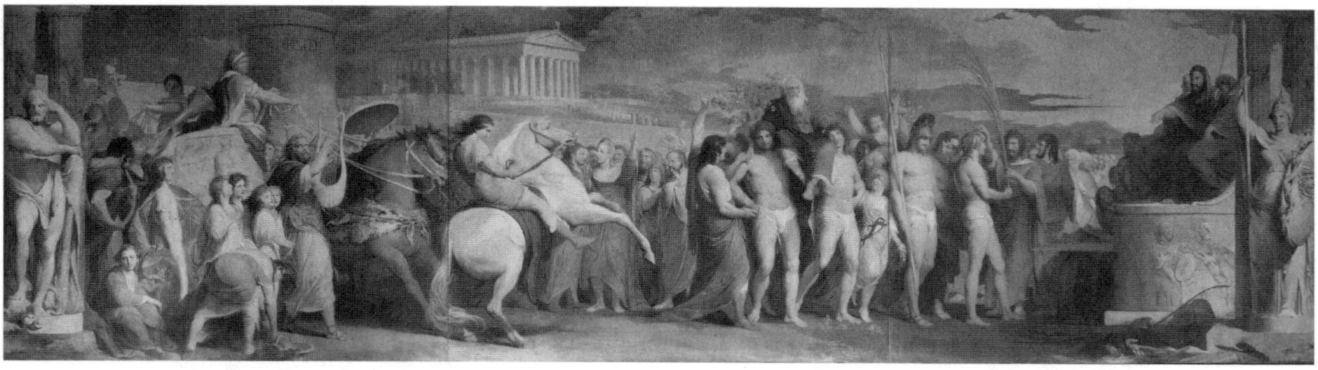

9. James Barry, *Crowning the Victors at Olympia*, 1777–84, oil on canvas, 360.68 × 1308.1 cm (11 ft 10 in × 42 ft 11 in), Royal Society of Arts, London, UK/Bridgeman Art Library.

will break out again with a brighter luster."[46] The even distribution of light in *Crowning the Victors* alludes to humanity's mature state, evidencing what the famous Anglican Bishop Joseph Butler called "the moral administration of nature, . . . [for] everyone shall be dealt [with] equitably. [Otherwise,] all shadow of injustice, and indeed all harsh appearances, in this various *economy of Providence*, would be lost"[47] (my emphasis).

The prominent feature of this linkage of economics and religion—the "economy of providence"—was the emphasis it placed on the slow, measured pace of divine dispensations. Many English Dissenters in the eighteenth century referenced the economy of providence to the Creator's long-term investment in humanity's capacity to achieve ethical perfection in and through history. As exemplified with Price's statement, Protestants often used the visual analogue to the economy of providence—the economy of light—to signify how God accommodated the human race in history, in which the Creator reveals more light in the world incrementally as humanity gradually matured from the state of nature to civilization. The light metaphor was also presented to eighteenth-century readers to signify a series of educational experiences that manifests humanity's growing awareness of what Price called the invisible "government of the Deity," for the light of God "proceeds gradually and slowly. As he does not bring the individuals of the human race on the stage of human life, before they have been duly prepared for it, by passing through the instruction and discipline of infancy and childhood, so neither does he bring the species to that finished state of dignity and happiness for which it is intended without a similar introduction and education."[48]

Given his ties to English Dissenters, it is not surprising to find Barry using the economy of providence as a governing motif in the mural program. In his writings, Barry linked religion and economics in terms of the moral education of the human race, for, in his view, it is only when humanity is properly prepared will the Creator shower the "fruits and blessings of industry . . . down upon us [as a] . . . distinct view of that *infinite economy*, which . . . will be everywhere manifest through *all the works of God*"[49] (my emphasis). Otherwise, according to Barry, if "brutal violence, injustice, and partialities [prevail], . . . these blessings will never be given to us . . . whenever we have rendered ourselves unworthy of the Divine favour."[50] Such unworthiness, in his view, would "obstruct human nature in its progress to destined perfection."[51] "Destined perfection," for Barry, was God's dispensation for the human race to participate in its own salvation—that is, the achievement of ethical perfection—in the here and now through its own economic improvements. For this reason, it is safe to conclude that the pictorial equivalent to the economy of providence, or the economy of light, denotes how God reveals more light in the world incrementally as humanity gradually matured from the state of nature in *Orpheus* to the Greek polis in *Crowning the Victors*.

In this context, Minerva played a significant role in Barry's thinking about the origins and improvement of the mechanical and fine arts in ancient Greece. He was especially interested in the economic origins of high-minded painting, particularly how painting as a fine art evolved from the mechanical art of textiles. According to Barry, Minerva was not only the goddess of war and patron deity of the arts and sciences, but also a benefactor of many household crafts, especially spinning and weaving. Around the base of the Minerva statue and prominently positioned in the right foreground of the *Crowning the Victors* are accoutrements of war and the peaceful arts (Figure 10). A helmet, a shield, and protruding arm of a bow represent the arts of war. In front of these martial images, a shepherd's staff with vessel, a porkpie hat, and a rumpled pile of textiles reference the cultivation of the peaceful arts. One of the textiles appears to be a solid

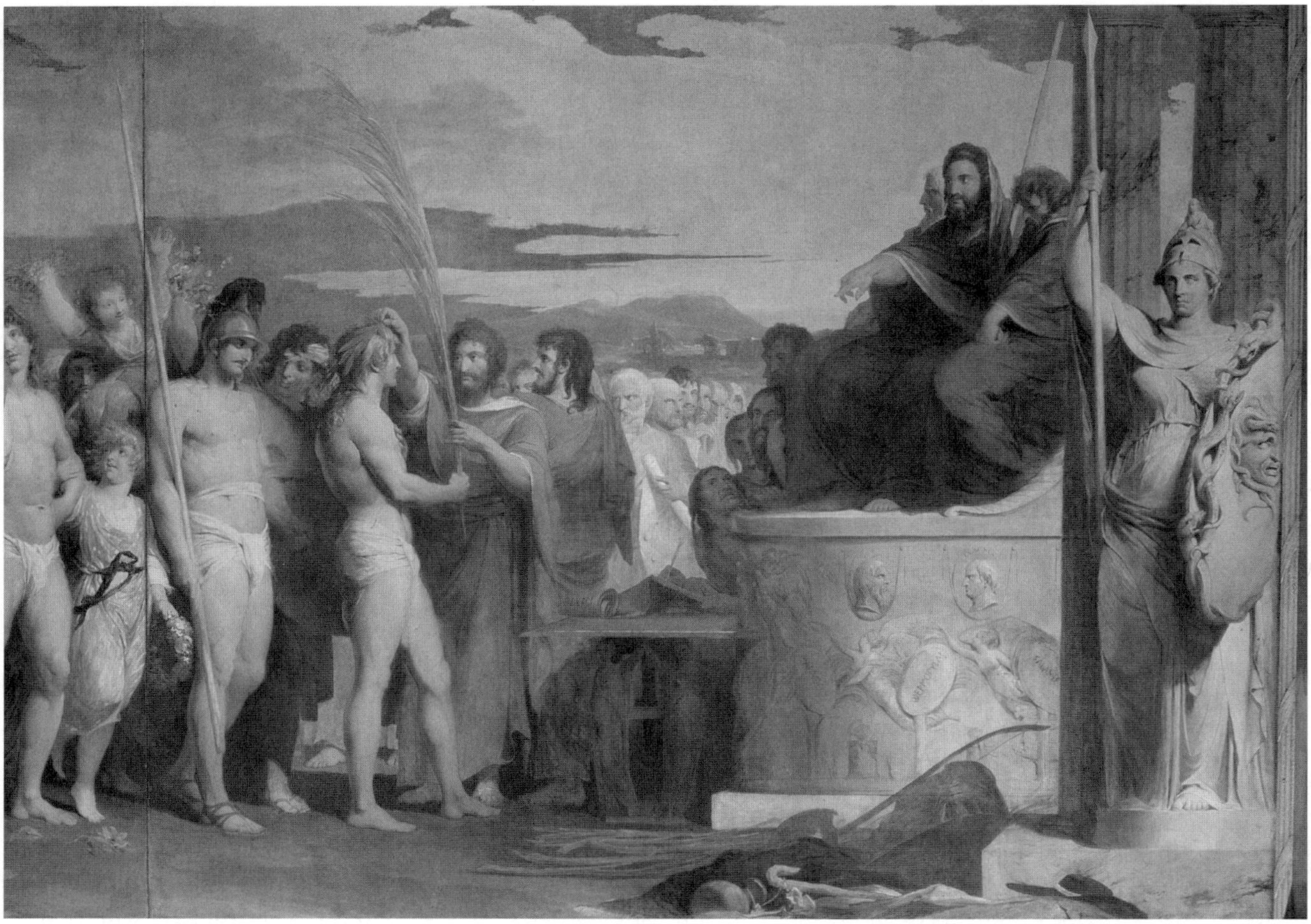

10. James Barry, *Crowning the Victors at Olympia*, detail of right side, Royal Society of Arts, London, UK/Bridgeman Art Library.

blue, gold-trimmed carpet, which is juxtaposed to another rug with sinuous patterns that extends to the male athletes. In this high moment of the economy of providence, or what the ancient Greek philosopher, Xenophon, termed the "Intelligence in Nature,"[52] Minerva served as a tacit reference to the economic origins of painting, emanating from what Barry called the goddess's "skill in the labours of the loom."[53] For him, Minerva embodied the linkage of economics and morality by means of textiles, for she was "skillful in the art of painting in tapestry, and employ[ed] that universal language of forms . . . [for] all the grand, ethical purposes of . . . persuasion and instruction."[54]

An anthropological approach to Greek myth and history seems to have allowed Barry to interpret Minerva's union of the ideal and the mechanical in textiles as evidence of the Greek's living attempt to coordinate the moral and economic spheres of public life in the polis. Barry's linkage of this union in textiles evidences his core view that "art is of a two-fold nature, consisting of the *ideal* and the *mechanical*," and that their coordination is, historically, what generated art's civilizing role in society.[55] Going beyond the private household, or the *oikos*, the textiles in *Crowning the Victors* are incorporated into the public festivity along with their brethren of the ideal in the fine arts and letters: sculpture, architecture, music, theater, and philosophy. Minerva functioned as Barry's ideal embodiment of that artistic unity in active civic life in the fifth-century BC, a unity that signified a high golden moment in Western civilization.

Moreover, in viewing the goddess as responsible for creating "the art of painting in tapestry" as a "universal language" for the "ethical purpose of persuasion and instruction," Barry also understood Minerva as possessing a teleological aspect. In this, Minerva represented not only the ancient origins of painting rooted in textiles, but also the telos of high-minded history painting that unfolded in human history from ancient Greece to the eighteenth century. According to Barry, like ancient textiles, the aim of history painting was to uphold this "universal language" (i.e., the ideal) for the "ethical purpose of persuasion and instruction" in human history.

Barry's teleology may account for why he portrayed himself (anachronistically) in *Crowning the Victors* as a civic hero of history painting. He sits to the left at the base of Hercules' statue in the character of the classical Greek artist Timanthes, holding the ancient painter's celebrated picture of the *Sleeping Cyclops*. Although Barry presents himself in the mural on a slightly smaller scale, his choice of Timanthes as a persona shows the herculean estimation of his artistic and intellectual stature. Barry associated himself with this ancient masterpiece, which offered a heroic statement on the importance of artistic genius and the sublime.[56] Indeed, Barry sought to emulate the lofty genius of his mentor to generate his own colossal figures of civic virtue in *Crowning the Victors*. In so doing, he believed the mural surpassed, in sheer scale, the cyclopean masterpiece of old. In addition, Barry revealed his genius at this stage of the narrative as a variation of the civilizing role of Orpheus. Just as the mythic artist taught social unity through the power of music and poetry, Barry, in turn, presented a grand exemplum of civic virtue on canvas to the members of the Society of Arts, educating those proponents of free trade about civilization's communal origins and the artist's pivotal role in shaping human association. Indeed, *Crowning the Victors* served to remind Barry's viewers that it was during the Golden Age of Athens when the "philosopher, the poet, the sculpture, and the painter, went hand in hand, mutually enlightening and perfecting each other; and the collision of all these emulations could not fail of producing with the public at large the most highly cultivated and expansive mode of thinking. . . . To this end, all the abilities and faculties of men were, with the most indefatigable industry, employed in all the various pursuits of knowledge."[57] The Greek's "indefatigable industry" allowed Barry to view the heroic paintings of Timanthes (as well as his own) as lofty by-products emanating from Minerva's honest industry in textile production.

Given her civic role in *Crowning the Victors* as patron deity of the arts, Minerva represented not only the unity of the mechanical and fine arts, but also served as a moral guide in what Barry called "good stewardship." Barry maintained that artistic unity could only function if a wise manager of the economy, or a "good steward, . . . disposes the great overplus of wealth which has been entrusted to [him]" to enrich not only civil society, but also the state, or the commonwealth, with sufficient revenue for public services.[58] Barry's notion of stewardship was commensurate with his notion of the "infinite economy" of Providence in that he viewed the wise management of the nation's wealth as a divine calling to ensure frugality and moderation in society at large.

He may have found an antecedent for stewardship in the writings of Xenophon. Perhaps in response to Bernard Mandeville's scandalous apology for conspicuous consumption, Richard Bradley—a distinguished professor of botany and writer on husbandry, trade, arts and sciences—advocated Xenophon as a model to promote good stewardship in English society to check the tendency toward decadence and decline that accompanies periods of opulence.[59] In his influential translation, *The Science of Good Husbandry: Or, the Oeconomics of Xenophon* (1727), Bradley argued that although "by oeconomy we mean . . . the wise management of [one's] possessions, or of [one's] household, . . . it is not enough, says Xenophon, to know how to get money. [Rather, it is important to know] how to apply it to the best advantage . . . for establishing rule and good order in every degree of life."[60]

Although he referred to "stewardship [as primarily] the good management . . . of everything belonging to a house," Xenophon maintained that it also promoted public benefits since it "breeds good men, and occasions generosity of spirit and good will towards one's friends and country."[61] It is true that Xenophon castigated "handicrafts" for their potential to erode "government and moderation" since they multiplied those luxurious "invaders of our liberties," including "gluttony," "vanity," and "want of public spirit."[62] Yet, despite Xenophon's criticism of the mechanical arts, Barry and his Protestant associates found the *Oeconomics* relevant to contemporary attempts to instill good stewardship in advanced commercial societies.

One of Barry's apparent acquaintances at St. Paul's Coffee House, Thomas Amory, a leading Dissenter in radical politics and in the wool industry, translated Xenophon's *A Conversation of Socrates, Wherein he proves A God and a Providence* (1746) to educate British merchants that Providence sanctioned the coordination of private and public wealth.[63] In so doing, Amory was careful to distinguish stewardship from the unnatural pursuit of narrow pleasure and entertainment as ends in themselves—that is, those activities associated with consumer pleasures and with the ideology of what C. B. Macpherson has called "possessive individualism."[64] In Xenophon's dialogue, Socrates asked the effete Alcibiades that if "private favors demand acknowledgement from private persons, ought not public benefits, those the commonwealth jointly receives from the favor of heaven, to be jointly acknowledged? As everyone shares in the happiness of a good government, a prosperous administration of affairs . . . , is it not fit everyone should join in the acknowledgment . . . in common [of] the Deity?[65]

For Amory, the economy of providence denoted a unifying ethos, preparing stewards to administer the commonwealth properly, and, hence, protect the public welfare from the unnatural tendency toward decadence and decline in times of great prosperity.

Given this broad understanding of stewardship in eighteenth-century thinking, it is not surprising that Adam Smith made tacit reference to it in the very title of his famous text, *The Wealth of Nations* (1776). As Laurence Dickey has shown, Smith viewed the commonwealth of nations as more than just the aggregate wealth of laissez-faire individuals, for, in Smith's words, "every prodigal appears to be a public enemy, and every frugal man a public benefactor."[66] Moreover, the notion of an impersonal "invisible hand" in economic development must take into account moral character and choice that, in the long run, can serve the public good as long as the habit of frugality becomes a sociocultural measure of good conduct, one that can be "depleted" only at great risk to society. It is, therefore, the human choice and conduct of frugal people who advance commercial societies in an ethically responsible manner. Such behavior was the sure means in advancing the economy of providence as a "system of natural liberty" in economic development.[67] Priestley, likewise, reminded readers in his *Institutes of Natural and Revealed Religion* (1772–73) that "it is very common to forget the use of money as a means" to improve the public welfare rather than as a narrow "*end* [in itself] without any regard to the proper use of it."[68] Xenophon's notion of stewardship in the *Oeconomics* was relevant to these modern attempts to apply ancient wisdom to market societies because, in Bradley's words, it was "one of the most useful tracts that ever appeared . . . for establishing rule and good order in every degree of life."[69]

With this ideological context in mind, it is not surprising that Barry believed good stewardship provides opportunities for artists to serve the public good in the widest sense. As for the public role of the fine arts, Barry perhaps heeded Xenophon's prescription that "[the] wise and benevolent artist . . . ascribes to design, that which is most useful [to humanity, including the] . . . *Epick Poetry* [of] Homer, . . . the *Tragedy* [of] Sophocles, . . . the *Statuary* [of] Polycletus, and the *Painting* [of] Zeuxes.[70]

This statement may account for Barry's claim that the Athenian "philosopher, the poet, the sculpture, and the painter, went hand in hand, mutually enlightening and perfecting each other." As noted, for Barry, this unity emanated from Minerva's integration of the ideal and the mechanical, of the universal and the particular, of morality and materialism. Because she integrated both, Minerva represented the quintessence of art's communal role in the Greek polis. The music of Orpheus's lyre, which tamed the savages, initiated civilized society. In turn, the honest industry of Minerva continued the civilizing process—one that evolved from her "painting in tapestry"—to the heroic integration of the ideal and the practical in the Grecian fine arts. As we shall see, Barry extended this union of the various arts to contemporary England in his linkage of history painting and the luxurious, manufactured carpets prized by the founder of the Society of Arts, William Shipley.

CONTEMPORARY ENGLAND AND THE LEGITIMACY OF THE SOCIETY OF ARTS: "KNOWING THE PRESENT"

As noted, Barry dedicated the fourth and fifth murals in the program to the progress of arts, commerce, and manufactures in eighteenth-century England. In the first of these murals, *Commerce, or the Triumph of the Thames* (Figure 11), Barry identified economic trade as the dominant mode of economic life that distinguished modern commercial societies from ancient agrarian ones. Seated slightly left of center, the allegorical figure of "Father Thames, steering himself with one hand, [and guided by a] mariner's compass," is propelled by such illustrious seamen as Sir Walter Raleigh, Sir Francis Drake, Sebastian Cabot, and Captain James Cook. To the rear "Nereids carry several articles of our manufactures and commerce of Manchester, Birmingham, etc." to the four trading continents personified on the far left side of the painting: Europe, Asia, America, and Africa.[71] In turn, "brought together" by "modern navigation," the Continents "pour their several productions into the lap of the Thames."[72] In the upper left corner is "Mercury, or commerce, summoning the nations together" as he flies swiftly above with a caduceus and trumpet, echoing the assured movement of Father Thames and his agents of economic trade.[73]

Although religion is not overtly portrayed in Barry's juxtaposition of classical allegory, portraiture, and productive wares, the mutual exchange of goods and the festive movement of these figures toward "mutual intercourse" suggest Providence at work. In his *Institutes of Natural and Revealed Religion*, Priestley identified a hidden providential structure that is commensurate with Barry's economy of providence in *Commerce*. Priestley asserted that,

> [although] incomprehensible by our finite understanding, . . . the great design of the divine being, in all the *works of his hands*, was to produce happiness. That the world is in a state of improvement is very evident in the human species. . . . Knowledge [has] . . . been increasing from the time of our earliest acquaintance with

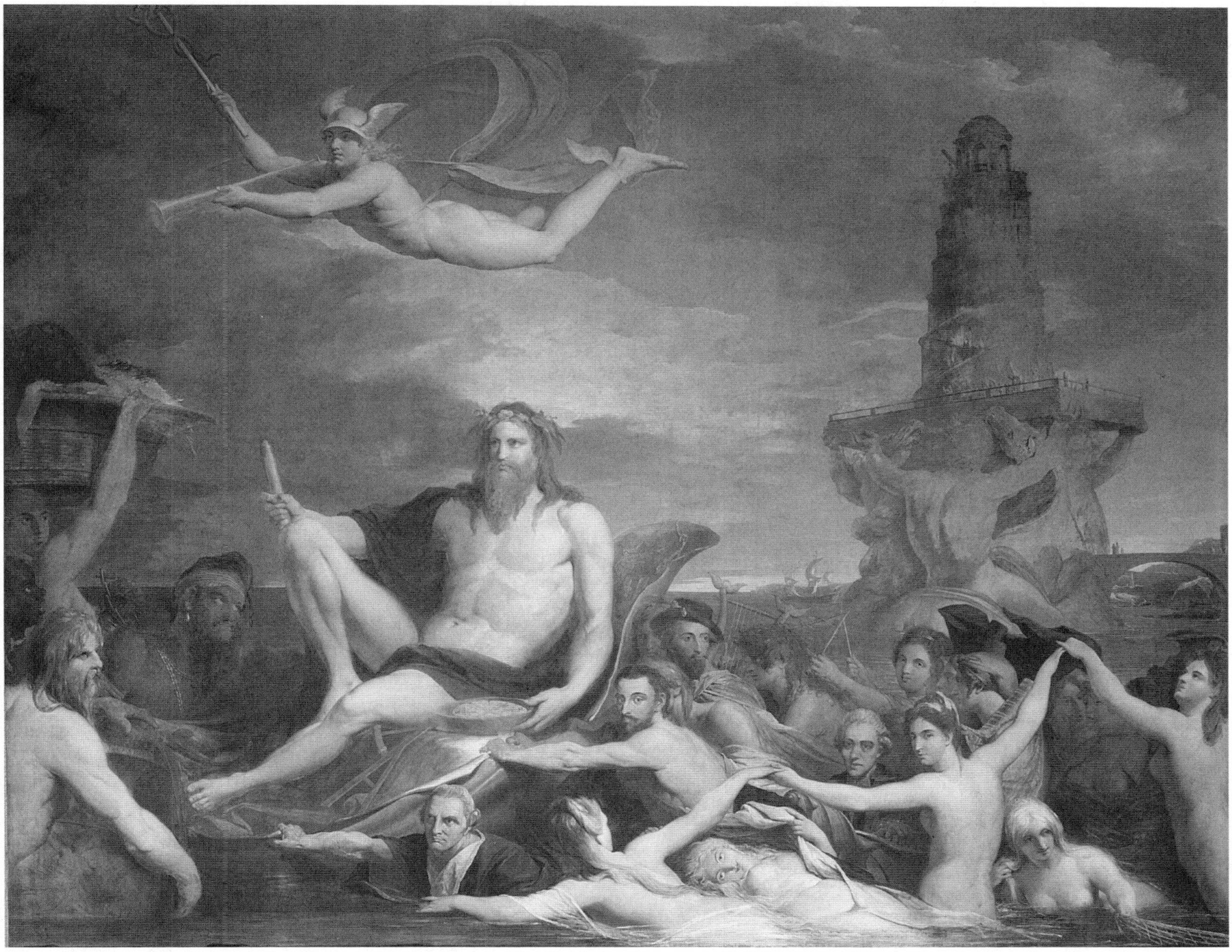

11. James Barry, *Commerce, or the Triumph of the Thames*, 1777–84, oil on canvas, 360.68 × 462.28 cm (11 ft 10 in × 15 ft 2 in), Royal Society of Arts, London, UK/Bridgeman Art Library.

> history to the present; and in the last century this progress has been amazingly rapid. By means of increased commerce the valuable productions of the earth become more equally distributed . . . to the great advantage of the whole family of mankind. It is partly in consequence of this improvement of the human species . . . that the earth itself is in a state of improvement, the cultivated parts continually gaining ground on the uncultivated ones.[74] (my emphasis)

Not surprisingly, Barry's *Commerce* supported the encouragement of economic trade articulated by the Society's founding father, William Shipley, whose objective was "to render Great Britain as the school of instruction as it is already the center of traffic to the greatest part of the known world."[75]

It is difficult to view *Commerce* as entirely benevolent, however, if we consider Barry's critical views toward the slave trade. In his description of the work, he tacitly referenced the abuses of English colonial policies, stating that "the supplicating action of the poor Negro slave [in the left-hand side of *Commerce*], or more properly of enslaved Africa, the cord around his neck and attached heavy chain on his wrists . . . denote the agonies of his soul, before the abolition of slavery became the subject of public investigation [in our own day]."[76] If mutual intercourse is the overarching theme of the mural, it is devoid of mutual equality, visually, in terms of scale and hierarchy. The triumphant figure of Father Thames dominates the four continents as they take on a subservient role to Britain in the margins of the picture, invoking Shipley's view that Britain "is already the center of traffic to the greatest part of the known world."

Yet, it would be misleading to conclude that Shipley endorsed England's reason of state policies toward the colonies. As noted, in the ideological context of debates about Anglo-American relations within the British Empire, many of England's leading Dissenters in the Society of Arts clearly associated laissez-faire not only with anti-imperial ideas, but also with humane policy recommendations that were in the service of cosmopolitan rather than national values. To that end, the Shipley brothers, Franklin, Lord Shelburne, Price, and Priestley criticized England for governing the colonies with force rather than kindness. Moreover, it was within the convergence of liberal economic thinking and religious humanitarianism that many Dissenters criticized colonial abuses of the slave trade.

Indeed, when Barry stated that "the abolition of slavery became the subject of public investigation" in his own day, he probably referred to the humanitarian research done by the Society of Friends, the Quakers. These Dissenters not only supported free-trade policies against British imperialism, but also played an active role in the abolitionist movements in England and America. England declared slavery illegal in 1772, but in the colonies, where it was regarded as vital for the production of economic goods such as cotton and tobacco, there were many obstacles to overcome. During the 1770s, the Society of Friends purged its own membership first of those involved in the slave trade and then slave owners. By 1783, a London-based group, The Meeting for Sufferings, responded to a request from their Philadelphia counterpart and established the first abolitionist organization in England called the Committee on the Slave Trade.

Given his close ties to English Dissenters and his pro-American sentiments, it appears that Barry did not intended to associate the slave trade in *Commerce* to the free trade recommendations of the Society of Arts. Rather, it seems likely he linked the slave trade to England's illiberal policies toward the colonies prior to the emerging liberal economic principles encouraged by the Society of Arts during the 1760s and 1770s. It is no coincidence that Barry's statement about public investigations into the slave trade appeared at the very moment when the converging discourses of free trade and benevolent Christian morals were at their peak during the American rebellion. It appears that Barry had appreciated how emphasis on the ideological connection between free trade and universal benevolence on the one hand and between free trade and laissez-faire on the other could turn economic liberalism into a potent anti-imperial and antislavery ideology. In this way, Barry's *Commerce* suggests how free trade and universal benevolence, a major theme of the policy recommendations of the Society of Arts, comprised the ensemble of humanitarian values associated with civil liberty and the eighteenth century as a cosmopolitan age.

The second and final mural in the sequence dedicated to contemporary England is a group portrait entitled, *The Distribution of Premiums at the Society of Arts* (Figure 12). Located adjacent and to the right of *Commerce*, it forms a logical place in the civilizing narrative of the mural program. The structural sequence evokes Postlethwait's idea "that commerce . . . seem[s] to be the original parent of the arts and sciences" as one moves left to right from economic trade in *Commerce* to human cultivation in *The Distribution of Premiums*. Indeed, Barry foregrounds the Society's distinguished members rewarding projects meant to stimulate free inquiry in arts, agriculture, commerce, and manufactures.

The group portrait is indebted to seventeenth-century Dutch examples, which blends many individuals into a unified composition without having any one person dominant. To achieve this end, Barry avoided a central focus and instead arranged the figures across the entire length of the canvas.[77] Barry's portrayal of social unity is a fitting tribute to the philanthropic objectives established by Shipley, whose Society of Arts, in the words of political economist Robert Dossie, attempted to serve "the public interest . . . in many employed hands, not in the accumulated wealth of the few."[78] Appropriately, Barry includes the magnanimous Shipley in the bottom left-hand corner of the painting, seated below the ordinary farmer, holding his *Proposals for the Society of Arts* while gazing inquisitively at the adjacent mural dedicated to commerce. Near Shipley's feet is a sumptuous English carpet, an object worthy of the Society's premiums in promoting the decorative arts. The carpet also forms a meaningful connection to Minerva's textiles on the right-hand side of *Crowning the Victors*, underscoring the affinity between the material improvements in ancient Greece and those in eighteenth-century England. To extend his beneficent support, Shipley encouraged the production of other luxury items to sweeten domestic life—Rococo clock designs, arabesque mirror frames, embroidery, upholstery, cameos, and florid wallpaper. Such luxuries, Shipley insisted, would "be the esteemed . . . ornaments of nations"[79] and function as "the necessary sweetener of life,"[80] thus functioning as exemplary products that extend the *doux-commerce* thesis in civil society. Similarly, in his written account of the picture, Barry asserted that such goods were "the amiable charms of domestic life, and the graces of social friendly conversation."[81]

The Distribution of Premiums further suggests Barry's view that a moral by-product of commerce would be the support for high-minded history painting. Dominating the center of the painting, therefore, are two large works of art Barry deemed worthy contenders for awards, both based on the artist's own oeuvre: *The Fall of Satan* of 1777 and *The Birth of Venus* of 1772.[82]

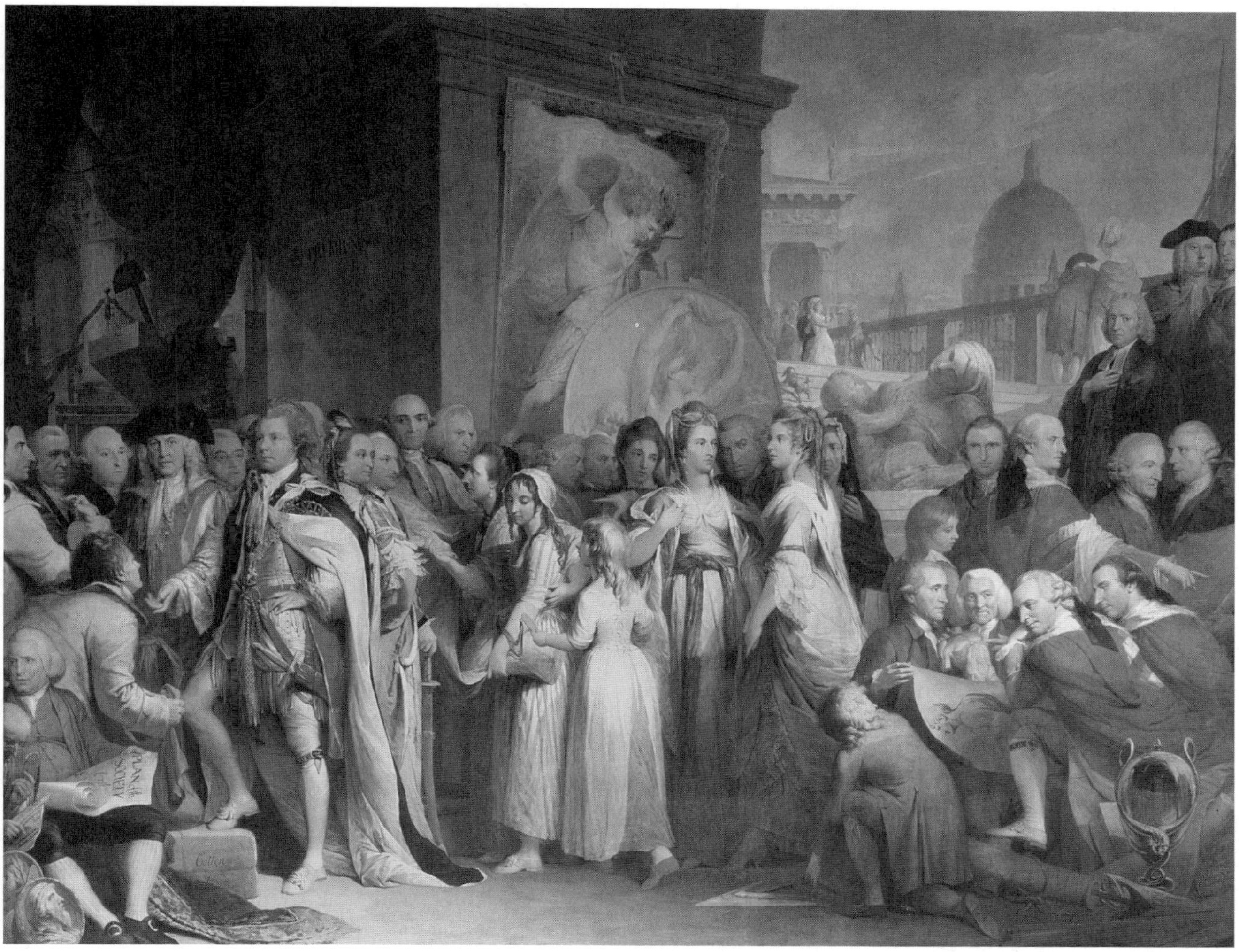

12. James Barry, *The Distribution of Premiums at the Society of Arts*, 1777–84, oil on canvas, 360.68 × 462.28 cm (11 ft 10 in × 15 ft 2 in), Royal Society of Arts, London, UK/Bridgeman Art Library.

The heroic scale of *The Fall of Satan* on the central pier in the group portrait alludes to his continued interest in Edmund Burke's notion of the sublime in art whereas the ovular shaped relief of *Venus* just below *Satan* denotes the Burkean ideal of the beautiful.[83] Towering above the mortal humans below, *The Fall of Satan* offered the Society of Arts a compelling image of divine justice and retribution in the figure of St. Michael, the archangel, who bursts forth from the flat plane of the canvas to vanquish, presumably, Satan.

Moreover, Barry believed that even the grand manner could accommodate the art of industrial design, thereby investing history painting with significance for contemporary commercial society. In the right foreground of the *Distribution of Premiums*, four men admire a contestant's drawing of a heroic nude figure as the youthful prizewinner kneels before them, his left arm extended to a portfolio of drawings. This group affirms the importance of continuing the grand tradition so valued by the Shipley, but within the larger context of art's commercial application. The vignette of the apprentice artist suggests one who will eventually design objects like the grand hydraulic pump that dominates the left background, or, more humbly, the functional and elegant globed teapot depicted in the painting's bottom right corner.[84]

These examples of art's industrial and commercial application provided a model of art's utility as it contributed not only to the material ease in the private sector, but also promoted public benefits. In the Preface to his *Memoirs of Agriculture, and other Oeconomical Arts*, Dossie provided one of the most comprehensive views of the role of drawing in the Society of Arts. In one instance, he wrote, "Awards were offered [to youths] for human figures, birds, beasts, fruit; all connected with designs or ornaments for trades, and equally leading to the higher departments, of which drawing is the basis."[85] Similarly, in his writings, Barry linked the grand tradition to the applied arts to underscore his notion of artistic unity. He stated that the "small and trifling particulars are no longer such when . . . dignified by . . . exalted associations," for, "art is of a two-fold nature, consisting of the *ideal* and the *mechanical*" to reiterate Barry's notion of artistic unity.[86]

Barry redirected these traditional precepts of art theory, aligning them to the commercial role of art and manufactures as defined in Postlethwait's *Universal Dictionary of Trade and Commerce*. The *Universal Dictionary* stated, "*Art*—signifies a profession, or trade. Two forms: 1) liberal arts of painting, architecture, etc. and 2) mechanical arts, such as trades of turners, carpentries, etc."[87] By integrating history painting, portraiture, and the mechanical arts in the *Distribution of Premiums*, Barry democratized the hierarchy of genres into what he called a "confederation and union of [diversified] talents."[88] This confederation was to produce an intimate knowledge of the various arts and sciences, practical and theoretical, as the basis of social difference and as the basis for building social cooperation.[89] Thus, by coordinating the ideal, the grand tradition of painting to textile production with its origins in Minerva's "painting in tapestry," Barry established in his program a seamless continuity between ancient Greece and eighteenth-century England. In this way, he legitimized Shipley and the Society of Arts and promoted the institution as the destined vanguard of an emerging, liberal social order.

OSSIAN AND THE POLITICAL ECONOMY OF ARTISTIC DECLINE

In discussing the continuities between the past and the present in the murals, we have seen how the evolutionary narrative of the *Progress of Human Knowledge and Culture* affirmed the civilizing role of commerce and manufactures in human understanding. Yet, as discussed in *Commerce*, Barry was attuned to the underside of English commercial policy, which, as noted, not only knows "how to get money," individually, but also "how to apply it to the best advantage [of the] commonwealth," publicly. For him, the crucial problem of commercial society is when "the vast influx of wealth. . . . , or overplus, . . . exceeds what is necessary for the conservation of [human] existence."[90] As we shall see in the concluding section of this essay, Barry concentrated this criticism most explicitly in his vision of the future, *Elysium and Tartarus, or the State of Final Retribution* (Figure 13), though the theme of cosmic war between good and evil in the *Fall of Satan* in the *Distribution of Premiums* already suggests an underlying anxiety. The unease involved not only Barry's concerns about religious turmoil, but also his view that the public role of history painting was on the wane in British society. The portentous St. Michael could perhaps be seen as a sublimated form of the artist's retribution against English society for its excessive support for the mechanical arts. An implied discontent with the mechanical arts in the *Distribution of Premiums* is indeed explicit in his writings. Barry contended that the "good providence of God, having already enabled me in one great work deposited with the society, [allowed me] to do something of a deeper and more serious reference to the interests of national education in the proper exercise of the human faculties, than the general run of mere amusement productions, to which our art has hitherto been too much confined."[91]

According to Barry, such "amusements" and monetary "overplus" "produce such a corruption of public principles, as must finally end in a worse than savage ferocity, and the consequent utter subversion of all civil establishments."[92] For him, such degradation of wealth signified a regression of humanity to an animal condition, or to a "worse [condition] than savage ferocity" in the state of nature. In his seminal study on ancient Greek and Roman primitivism, Arthur O. Lovejoy employed the idea of "cultural primitivism" to explain such negative views towards "overplus" occurring within high-civilized moments: "the discontent of the civilized with civilization."[93] It is the belief that a life far simpler and less sophisticated in most respects is a more desirable one than a highly evolved cultural condition in the present. Yet, Barry did not merely retreat into an escapist nostalgia. He was, to apply Lovejoy's term, a "primitivistic reformer" who attempted to teach moral culture to preserve civilization against the degradation of commercial society.[94] For Barry, the free market seemed to produce, in Bradley's words, the lack of "good oeconomists . . . of my own country . . . [and of] the multitude who live without rule."[95] The apparent anarchy of the laissez-faire market stemmed from merchants' failure "to read Xenophon's *Oeconomics*," or from their inability to "have [the] courage enough to practice it" to avoid divisive self-love.[96]

Although he believed economic trade refines and improves culture, Barry maintained that, if left uncoordinated, commerce ultimately depoliticizes citizens and art's civic capacity. For him, depoliticization had reached the point where civil society sadly lacked the sense of a common public purpose, one that united art and industry rather than divided it. Barry identified the problem as distinctively modern, indicative of the broad transformation of art's role in Western civilization from the *civic* to the *civil*, from the political to the social, from the ancient polis to modern market societies. Indeed, Barry insisted that artistic "talents

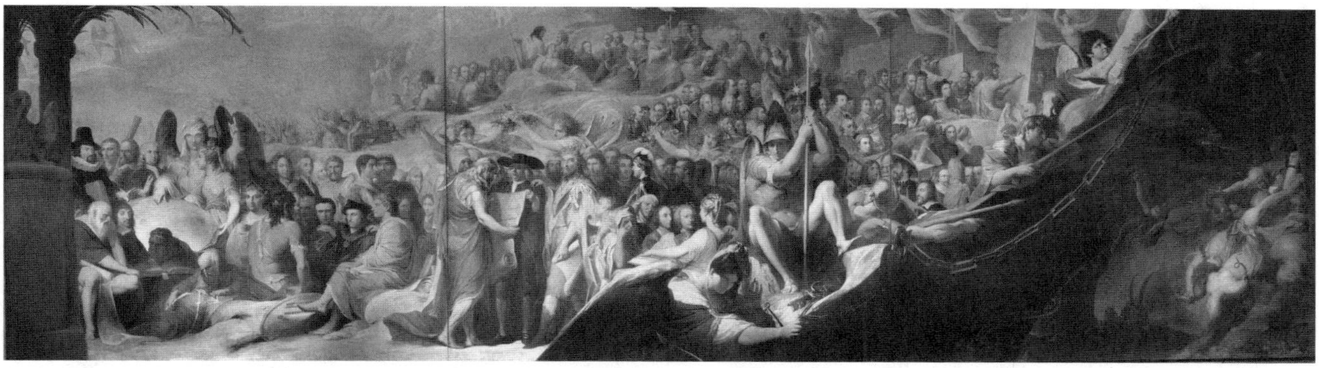

13. James Barry, *Elysium and Tartarus, or the State of Final Retribution*, 1777–84, oil on canvas, 360.68 × 1308.1 cm (11 ft 10 in × 42 ft 11 in), Royal Society of Arts, London, UK/Bridgeman Art Library.

. . . belong to the country at large and . . . cannot, in justice, be monopolized, or converted into private property."[97] Accordingly, he blamed self-seeking merchants for reducing artistic practice to "mere . . . mechanical principles, as their entire stock of trade, and thus bring[ing] about a separation between the body and soul of art, with very little prospect of their being happily reunited afterwards."[98]

Barry's pessimistic account of the split "between the body and soul of art" generated by private property was consistent with the writings of the Scottish poet, James Macpherson. In his dissertation to *The Works of Ossian, The Son of Fingal* (1765), Macpherson criticized the underside of the *doux commerce*, anticipating what Fred Hirsch has called "The Depleting Moral Legacy" of capitalism.[99] It is the idea that the very strength of commerce as an economic system depletes, or "erodes," the moral foundation needed for its functioning. Reminiscent of Rousseau's social theory of hypocrisy in the *Discourse on Sciences and Arts* (1750), Macpherson asserted that "those manly pursuits from which barbarity takes its name, are highly favorable to a strength of mind unknown in polished times. In advanced society the characters of men are more uniform and disguised. The human passions lie in some degree concealed behind forms, and artificial manners; and the powers of the soul, without an opportunity to exert them, lose their vigor. The times of regular government, and polished manners, are therefore to be wished for by the feeble and weak in mind."[100]

Macpherson historicized ancient Scotland to present an alternative account of how commercial society evolved and declined. The Scottish process fit into Macpherson's general theory of universal history wherein all collectivities move through the same stages of socioeconomic development, each with its own superstructure of language, laws, and customs. Macpherson maintained that there "are three stages in human society" whereby civil states, like natural products, have periods of growth, decay, and renewal. "As the first is formed on nature," Macpherson argued, "so, of course, it is the most disinterested and noble."[101] Whereas the moral purity of the first age (i.e., the past) resulted from the "natural affection of the members of a family to one another," the second age (i.e., the present), according to Macpherson, "begins when property is established and men [fall into] injustice, [a sign of] . . . complete barbarism and ignorance."[102] As a champion of the Scottish Highlanders, Macpherson "fix[ed] the beginning of the decay of heroism . . . in the days of Ossian," a decline caused by "the invasions and injustice of neighbors" that occurred during the transition from the first age to the second.[103] From this comparative perspective, Macpherson interpreted the decay of Ossianic virtue in the remote past through the lens of his own century, during which it seemed that the introduction of commerce and manufactures in Scotland had dislocated the rustic unity and ancient customs of the Scottish Highlanders. He hoped that the regenerative third age (i.e., the future) would allow the Highlanders to have the "leisure to cultivate the mind, and to restore it, with reflection, to a primeval dignity and sentiment."[104]

In a Rousseauian gesture, the leisure to cultivate high-minded reflection, or true culture against corrupt civilization, eclipses the weariness caused by property's degenerative import: excessive douceur of modern urban life. It appears that Rousseau's *Discourse on the Origin and Foundations of Inequality Among Men* (1755) allowed Macpherson to provide an economic rationale (i.e., the introduction of private property) in explaining social atomism and the decline of wholesome creativity during the second age of human history.[105] In his comparative anthropology, then, Macpherson linked the gloomy world of Ossianic myth to the cultural degradation in eighteenth-century Scotland, a period in which it seemed wealthy proprietors had eroded the Highlander's social and artistic traditions.

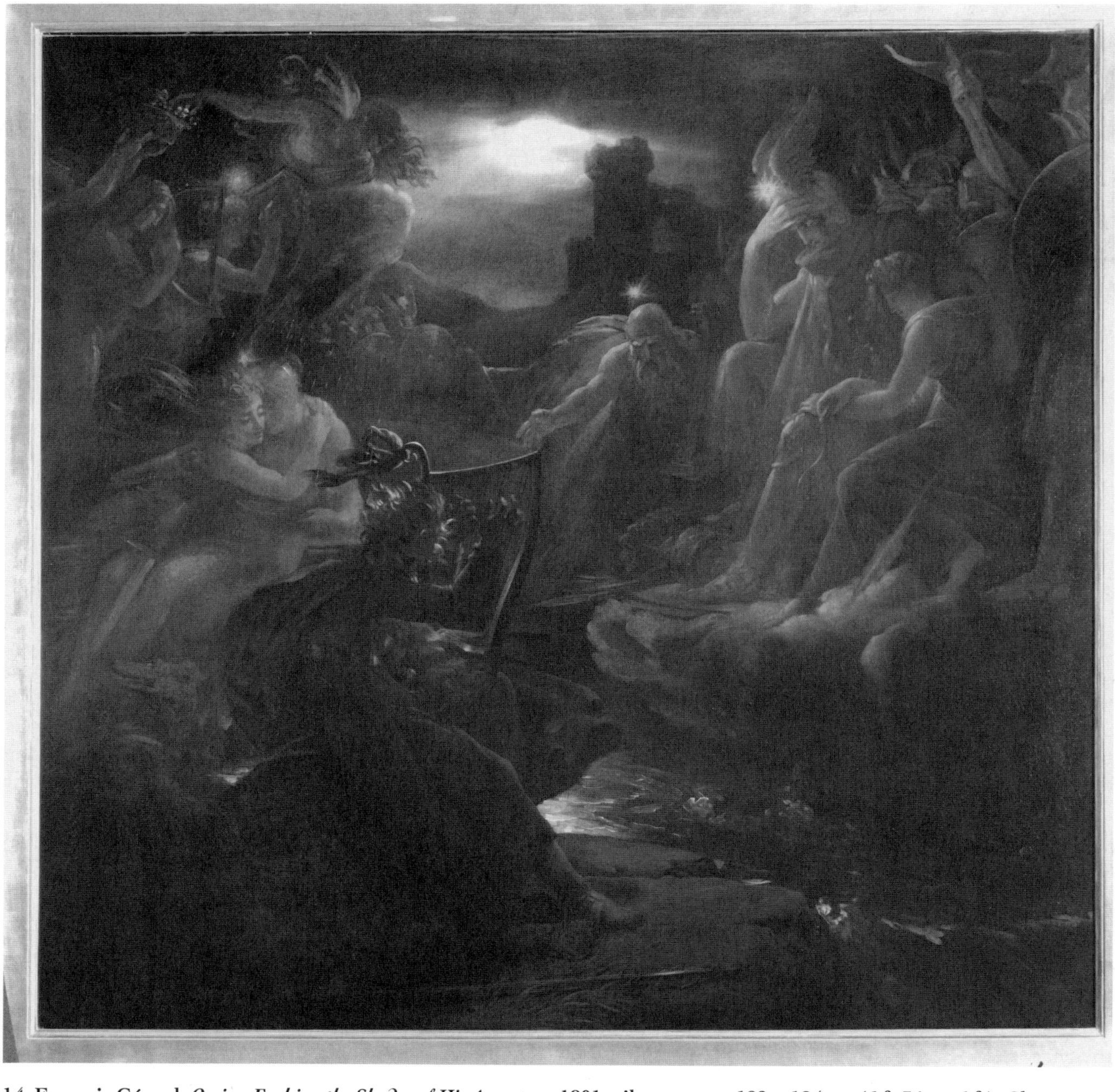

14. François Gérard, *Ossian Evoking the Shades of His Ancestors*, 1801, oil on canvas, 192 × 184 cm (6 ft 3 in × 6 ft), Chateaux de Malmaison et Bois-Preau, Rueil-Malmaison, France. Photo: © Erich Lessing/Art Resource, New York.

The Ossian poems and later Romantic depictions of them, such as François Gérard's painting, *Ossian Evoking the Shades of His Ancestors* (1801; Figure 14), expressed this sense of dislocation and spiritual decay. In Gérard's work, dark introspection pervades the estranged mood of the lonely bard, Ossian, who conjures up the ghosts of his ancestors through the musical prowess of his lyre. In contrast to Barry's *Orpheus*, Gérard's *Ossian* is not a radiant lawgiver connected to humanity, but rather a shadowy loner longing for a remote past, a lost Golden Age when the artist was fully integrated into society—heroic, ennobled, virtuous.

Although he disparaged "those miserable rhapsodies published by Macpherson under the name of Ossian" and Hugh Blair's "national prejudice of the Scotch," Barry, nonetheless, agreed with the latter's linkage of property and artistic decline.[106] As Macpherson delegitimized *doux-commerce* in terms of Scottish myth, Barry presented a similar contrast between primitive unity in the past and social atomism in the present. Unlike Macpherson's nostalgia for a

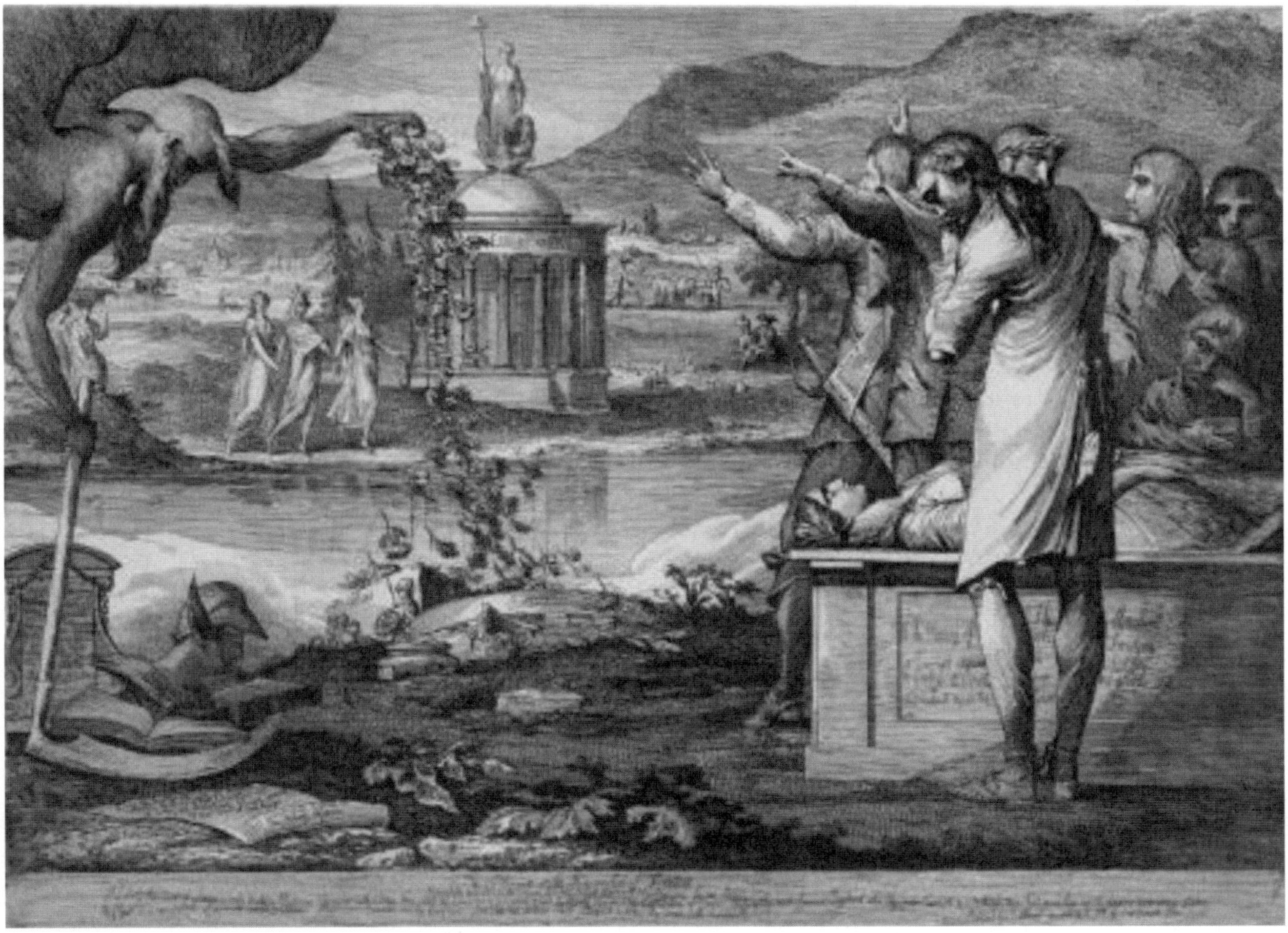

15. James Barry, *The Phoenix, or the Resurrection of Freedom*, 1776, etching and aquatint, 43.2 × 61.3 cm (17 × 24 in). Photo: © the Trustees of The British Museum, London.

lost Golden Age, however, Barry maintained that the Golden Age lay in the future. The artist, in his view, has to confront degradation in the present to reeducate humanity to live according to "the natural order of things," or to the economy of providence, as the proper course to fulfill human redemption in history. Accordingly, Barry hoped to regenerate a new artistic ideal, one that would reintegrate humanity in the future. For him, if ideal art was to be revived, "perhaps the glory of obtaining this palm is reserved for some other new people, where the shoot[s] of vigor and virtue may have ample room to expand themselves."[107]

Barry's aquatint, *The Phoenix, or the Resurrection of Freedom* (1776; Figure 15), implies just this: the new "shoot[s] of vigor and virtue" have been transplanted from England to America.[108] In the upper left, Father Time honors the memory of classical Athens, republican Rome, and Renaissance Florence, where political liberty and art's communal role had once flourished. On the right, English mourners of the seventeenth century, mostly Dissenters, assemble around the bier of Britannia while in the background the Three Graces dance before the Temple of Liberty now on America's shores. Among the English mourners are Algernon Sydney, John Milton, Andrew Marvell, a brooding John Locke, and Barry himself on the far right. This work was an impassioned endorsement of republican virtues, which encouraged public art, and a lament that the attacks on luxury preached by these persecuted heroes had failed to reform England but would take root in America. Barry employed dramatic contrast between dark and light to reference pessimistic gloom in England and sunlight optimism in America, respectively. Barry's regenerative image presents America as a future paradise from which public art thrives once again.

REPUBLICAN MILLENNIALISM AND AMERICAN INDEPENDENCE: "KNOWING THE FUTURE"

This vision of America as the land of the future informs Barry's concluding mural to the program, *Elysium and*

Tartarus, or the State of Final Retribution. Although he made overt reference to classical subject matter in the mural, Barry employed an apocalyptic subtext to make tacit judgment on contemporary events, particularly England's refusal to grant American independence. His written account described *Elysium* as a grand "apotheosis" dedicated to "the generous labors of those personages [of all ages and nations in human history], who had worn themselves out in the service of mankind."[109] Here, civic heroes and divine revelation meet in a heavenly union. Supernatural light unifies humanity, signifying how God revealed divine dispensations to the human race as humanity matured through the centuries. The radiant light also suggests the ultimate fulfillment of what Barry called the "infinite economy" of Providence in human history. Related to the light-dark contrast in the *Phoenix, or the Resurrection of Freedom*, the energized world of heaven in *Elysium* contrasts sharply with the hellish darkness of *Tartarus* on the far right side of the mural. According to Barry's description, some of the figures in hell include a "miser," a "spendthrift," and those who "represent the abuses of power"—most notably an "absolute king" and a "pope"—as they fall into a "fiery cataract."[110] Barry reinforced the redemptive message of *Elysium* with the colossal guardian angel, who sits on the rocky threshold in the right-central foreground with spear and helmet as he calmly waits for the moment of retribution. Just below this figure and partly cut off at the bottom edge of the mural is another gigantic archangel holding the scales of divine justice. In the words of William Pressly, it "is beneath this awesome figure, poised to weigh men's souls in the balance that every visitor to the Great Room must pass."[111] Barry presented in *Elysium* an ideal world of humanity reunited, a virtuous community of legislators, artists, scientists, and philosophers, who, "full of active good," advanced human culture toward a common ethical end.[112]

This ideal community centers on the two lawgivers depicted in the right-central foreground in *Elysium* (Figure 16). Dressed in black attire, the American Dissenter and Quaker William Penn, whom Barry described as "the greatest and best of lawgivers," shows the constitution of Pennsylvania to his classical counterpart, the Spartan legislator Lycurgus.[113] Barry foregrounded Penn in the center of the composition to reference his duel role as founding lawgiver of America and prophetic harbinger of the American Revolution. According to Barry, it was "William Penn, who in an age of illiberality and intolerance [of the late seventeenth century], . . . establish[ed] a code of laws, and a government in Pennsylvania, which . . . may be of service to future ages."[114] By "service to future ages," Barry appears to suggest how Penn's virtuous laws of the late seventeenth century set in motion historical

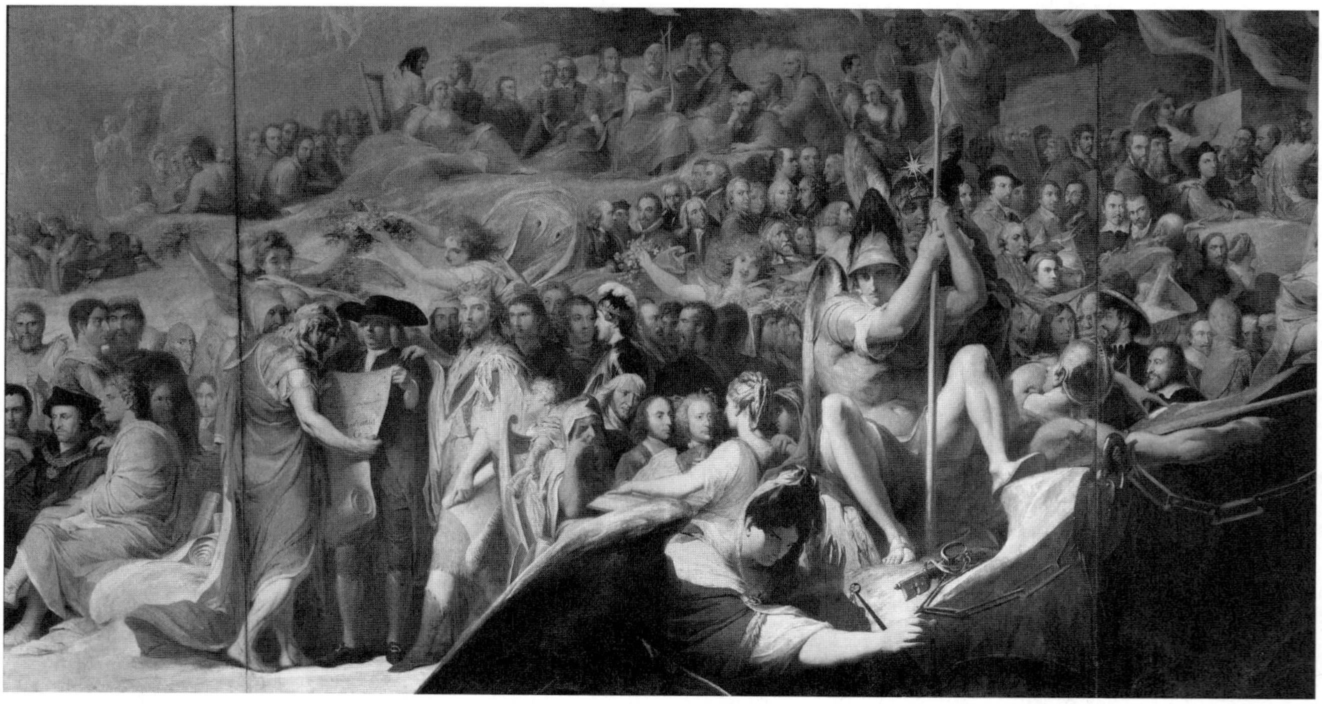

16. James Barry, *Elysium and Tartarus, or the State of Final Retribution*, detail of center, Royal Society of Arts, London, UK/ Bridgeman Art Library.

process that contributed to the American struggle for independence in the 1770s. In this, he may have heeded Penn's call upon the virtuous in the Quaker's *England's Present Interest Considered* (1675) to advance "Moderation and Virtue [as humanity's] Course . . . for the future, [for they] shall steer [a] Free People . . . in the Haven of Eternal Blessedness."[115]

There was also a millenarian aspect in Barry's apology of Penn that lent legitimacy to Dissenters' demand for American independence. In 1784, Price attached millenarian expectations to the American rebellion, which he viewed as a revolt "ordained by Providence to introduce these time [the millennium]."[116] Price also prophesized that America—the worldly agent that fulfills humanity's quest for religious and economic universalism—was to become "a confederation of States prosperous and happy, without Lords—without Bishops—and without Kings."[117] Price's views provide tacit support for why Barry gave Penn (a symbol of American independence) such a prominent position among the elect in *Elysium*, and why the artist discarded "illiberal" kings, popes, misers, and spendthrifts of Europe into the dark abyss of *Tartarus*. Barry's encomium to Penn also served the Shipleys' cosmopolitan agenda at the Society of Arts, for, as noted, they sought to unite Christian benevolence and economic universalism in bringing about the "great liberal commanding spirit" of the age.

For Barry, then, Penn signified humanitarian virtues that were antithetical to English colonial and commercial abuses. In viewing English religious and economic policies toward America as illiberal—that is, selfish, particularistic, and competitive—Barry presented Penn as "the greatest and best of lawgivers" to underline the Quaker's humanity as benevolent, universalistic, and cooperative. Penn's call for religious toleration, Christian fellowship, free trade, and the abolition of the slave trade evidenced a cosmopolitan disposition of global friendship contrary to English Machiavellian policies. Related to his image of the African slave in *Commerce*, Barry juxtaposed Penn and Lycurgus in *Elysium* to make implicit reference to the English slave trade, reminding contemporary viewers that Penn's benevolent laws contributed to the recent emancipation of slaves by the Pennsylvania Quakers in 1776.[118] Quoting Montesquieu, Barry had linked Penn, the "honest legislator, who formed a people to whom probity seems as natural as bravery to the Spartans,"[119] to the "enthusiastic eulogism"[120] of the Quaker written by the renowned abolitionist in France, the Abbé Raynal. Barry also quoted Raynal's celebration of Penn, for the Quaker represented "in America an example of justice and moderation that the Europeans have not even imagined until now.— The humanity of Penn . . . extends . . . to the splendor of states and to the felicity of citizens, property, and liberty."[121] Such humanitarianism evidenced the call for universal benevolence among nations, a disposition that would emerge only if economic universalism freely formed the world into what Montesquieu called "a single [cosmopolitan] state of which all nations are members."[122]

In this, Barry's *Elysium and Tartarus* also confronted the ambiguity found in the implementation of a bourgeois ideology within English civil society—that is, the spread of those apparent civil values he associated with narrow "amusement" and what David Hume called "vicious luxury."[123] For Barry, because of the difficulty in uniting wealth and virtue, the ancient conception of virtue continued to be relevant to modern commercial society as it provided a link to tangible historical visions: the virtuous citizens of Sparta and their modern progeny, the Pennsylvania Quakers. Barry included Lycurgus at this juncture of the narrative to reinforce his prophetic warning against excessive luxury. In this, he may have availed himself of Penn's *England's Present Interest Considered*, in which the Quaker maintained that "a Promotion of General Religion [i.e., communal religion in the present], which, being itself practical; brings back ancient *Virtue* [of the scriptures] . . . , [for they embody those of] *Lacedaemon* [before] Luxury [and] a Pompous Living had eaten out their Severity and . . . Excellent Laws."[124] Penn indeed intended to instill a precommercial ethic into the modern market as a prescription for responsible economic development—the "moralization of money."[125] Penn's moralization of wealth exemplifies what Margo Todd argues was the "Christian humanists intent on applying ancient wisdom to contemporary [economic] problems" to check the tendency toward corruption that accompanies periods of monetary surplus.[126] Accordingly, Penn and Lycurgus in *Elysium*, along with their angelic hosts and the dark abyss of *Tartarus*, served as ominous warnings to those self-seeking merchants who transgressed the collective good of humanity. Set within an apocalyptic context, these lawgivers functioned as an exhortation to the new barbarians who lurk within advanced civilization.

In all, Barry's coupling of Penn and Lycurgus suggests a dialectical union of ancient and modern virtue, a union that completes the historical process that the first two ages had begun. The union emboldens the mural's message of "Moderation and Virtue [as humanity's] Course . . . for the future, [for they] shall steer [a] Free People . . . in the Haven of Eternal Blessedness."[127] Indeed, it was the hero-painter, Barry, who grasped the providential unfolding of universal history as a three-age process, evolving from unity in ancient Greece (the past), to division in contemporary England (the present), to the reachievement of unity on a higher level in America (the future). With his encomium to Penn, Barry provided the Society of Arts with an ideal model for its civilizing role in the promotion of cooperative social ends, an ideal that in turn would re-revitalize liberalism's public role in shaping didactic art.

NOTES

1. The institution was granted the prefix "Royal" in 1908. This essay uses its eighteenth-century title.

2. Portions of this essay appear in Daniel R. Guernsey, *The Artist and the State, 1777–1855: The Politics of Universal History in British and French Painting* (London: Ashgate, 2007). I thank Ashgate for granting me permission to use portions of my book for this article.

3. On Barry's murals, see William L. Pressly, *The Life and Art of James Barry* (New Haven, CT: Yale University Press, 1981), 86–122 and *James Barry: The Artist as Hero* (London: The Tate Gallery, 1983); William L. Pressly, "Barry's Murals at the Society of Arts," in *James Barry, 1741–1806: "The Great Historical Painter,"* exh. cat., ed. Tom Dunne (Cork, Ireland: The Crawford Art Gallery, 2005), 47–55.

4. Immanuel Kant, "Universal History from a Cosmopolitan Point of View," in *On History*, ed. Lewis White Beck (New York: Macmillan, 1963), 23–26.

5. For the "de-moralization of luxury" in eighteenth-century political economy, see Christopher J. Berry, *The Idea of Luxury: A Conceptual and Historical Investigation* (Cambridge: Cambridge University Press, 1994), 101–95.

6. On Barry's political theory of art, see John Barrell, *The Political Theory of Painting from Reynolds to Hazlitt: 'The Body of the Public"* (New Haven, CT: Yale University Press, 1986), 163–221. For the socioeconomic role of art in eighteenth-century England, see David H. Solkin, *Painting for Money: The Visual Arts and the Public Sphere in Eighteenth-Century England* (New Haven, CT: Yale University Press, 1992).

7. For a comprehensive discussion of the early history of the Society of Arts, see D. G. C. Allan and John L. Abbott, eds., *The Virtuoso Tribe of Arts and Sciences: Studies in the Eighteenth-Century Membership of the London Society of Arts* (Athens: University of Georgia Press, 1992).

8. On the relationship between the Society of Arts and governing agencies, see David Guy Charles Allan, "The Society of Arts and Government, 1754–1800: Public Encouragement of Arts, Manufactures, and Commerce in Eighteenth-Century England," *Eighteenth-Century Studies* 7, no. 4 (Summer 1974): 434–52.

9. William Shipley qtd. in D. G. C. Allan, *William Shipley: Founder of the Royal Society of Arts* (London: Scolar Press, 1968), 43.

10. Ibid., 42.

11. Sir Henry Cheere, "A Plan for an Academy for Sculpture and Painting laid before the Society of Arts," in Dr. Templeman, *Transactions*, vol. 1 (London, 1754–58), 32.

12. Shipley qtd. in Allan, *William Shipley*, 7.

13. I base my discussion of *doux-commerce* on the following studies: Albert O. Hirschman, *The Passions and the Interests: Political Arguments for Capitalism before Its Triumph* (Princeton, NJ: Princeton University Press, 1977) and "Rival Views of Market Society," in *Rival Views of Market Society and Other Essays* (Cambridge, MA: Harvard University Press, 1992), 105–41; J. G. A. Pocock, *Virtue, Commerce, and History* (Cambridge: Cambridge University Press, 1985); Laurence W. Dickey, "*Doux-Commerce* and Humanitarian Values: Free Trade, Sociability, and Universal Benevolence in Eighteenth-Century Thinking" in *Grotius and the Stoa*, ed. Hans W. Blom and Laurens C. Winkel, vols. 22/23 (2001/02), 271–318; Laurence W. Dickey, "Pride, Hypocrisy and Civility in Mandeville's Social and Historical Theory," *Critical Review* (Summer 1990): 387–431; Laurence W. Dickey, "*Doux-Commerce* and the 'Mediocrity of Money' in the Context of the Wealth and Virtue Problem," in Adam Smith, *An Inquiry into the Nature and Causes of the Wealth of Nations*, ed. Laurence W. Dickey (Indianapolis, IN: Hackett, 1993), 243–59. For a discussion of *doux-commerce* and sociability in pre-Revolutionary France, see Daniel Gordon, *Citizens without Sovereignty: Equality and Sociability in French Thought, 1670–1789* (Princeton, NJ: Princeton University Press, 1994).

14. It is no accident that the discipline of aesthetics appeared in the eighteenth century as an autonomous field of human inquiry, a discipline that Enlightenment thinkers viewed as closely associated with the refinement of commerce.

15. Pocock, *Virtue, Commerce, and History*, 50.

16. For the crucial distinction between *civic* and *civil virtue* in eighteenth-century thought, see J. G. A. Pocock, "Cambridge Paradigms and Scotch Philosophers: A Study of the Relations between the Civic Humanist and the Civil Jurisprudential Interpretation of Eighteenth-Century Social Thought," in *Wealth & Virtue: The Shaping of Political Economy in the Scottish Enlightenment* ed. Istvan Hont and Michael Ignatieff (Cambridge: Cambridge University Press, 1981), 235–52.

17. The word "civilization" was first coined in the middle of the eighteenth century. For a discussion of its various meanings in eighteenth-century thought, see Jean Starobinski, "The Word Civilization," in *Blessings in Disguise; or the Morality of Evil*, trans. Arthur Goldhammer (Cambridge, MA: Harvard University Press, 1993), 1–35. See also Gordon 4, 19, 89–92, 155–59.

18. Benjamin Constant, *Political Writings*, ed. B. Fontana (New York: Cambridge University Press, 1989), 309–28.

19. Malachy Postlethwait, *Universal Dictionary of Trade and Commerce*, vol. 1 (London, 1730–55), 1.

20. Pocock, *Virtue, Commerce, and History*, 49.

21. Hirschman, *Passions and the Interests*, 108.

22. Hirschman, "Rival Views of Market Society," 109.

23. Fred Hirsh, *The Social Limits to Growth* (Cambridge, MA: Harvard University Press, 1976), 12, 120.

24. "A Letter to the Members of The Society for the Encouragement of Arts, Manufactures, and Commerce" (London, 1761), 53–54.

25. J. C. D. Clark, *The Language of Liberty, 1660–1832: Political Discourse and Social Dynamics in the Anglo-American World* (Cambridge: Cambridge University Press, 1994), 254 and *English Society, 1660–1832*, 2nd ed. (Cambridge: Cambridge University Press, 2000), 91–92, 107.

26. It appears that Shipley's *Proposals* were indebted in part to the pedagogic ideas of the celebrated dissenting minister from Northampton, Philip Doddridge. Although he was not directly under his tutelage, Shipley absorbed Doddridge's educational ideas while a member of the Northampton Philosophical Society. Not only was Doddridge the most prominent Dissenter of the 1740s, but his dissenting academy at Northhampton was also the most influential center of learning for clergymen and laymen in England during the mid-eighteenth century. Northampton was arguably the most active center of Calvinist rebellion in England during the sixteenth and seventeenth centuries, a reputation in-

dicative of what Alan Clifford calls Northampton's "long republican tradition." See Alan C. Clifford, *Good Doctor: Philip Doddridge of Northampton* (Norwich, UK: Charenton Reformed Publisher, 2002), 81, 110. During the Jacobite Rebellion of 1745, Doddridge published his widely popular text, *The Rise and Progress of Religion in the Soul* (1745), a work that wedded progressive theology, scientific inquiry, and practical knowledge. In emphasizing useful knowledge, Doddridge used the text as a weapon against a university curriculum that stressed formalized Aristotelian reasoning transmitted through an uncritical method of instruction. Moreover, Doddridge established the first charity school outside London that was paid for by voluntary subscriptions, a model that Shipley used to fund the Society of Arts. For more on Doddridge and dissenting academies in eighteenth-century England, see David L. Wykes, "The Contribution of the Dissenting Academy to the Emergence of Rational Dissent," in *Enlightenment and Religion: Rational Dissent in Eighteenth-Century Britain*, ed. Knud Haakonssen (Cambridge: Cambridge University Press, 1996), 99–139; Thomas P. Miller, *The Formation of College English: Rhetoric and Belles Lettres in the British Cultural Provinces* (Pittsburgh, PA: University of Pittsburgh Press, 1997), 62–116; Irene Parker, *Dissenting Academies in England: Their Rise and Progress and Their Place among the Educational Systems of the Country* (Cambridge: Cambridge University Press, 1914; reprint, New York: Octagon Books, 1969).

27. Joseph Priestley, *An Essay on the First Principles of Government, and on the Nature of Political, Civil, and Religious Liberty*, 2nd ed. (London, 1771), in Joseph Priestley, *Political Writings*, ed. Peter Miller (Cambridge: Cambridge University Press, 1993), 54.

28. On September 15, 1755, William Shipley wrote to Franklin, offering him membership in the Society of Arts. His letter praised Franklin's efforts to establish economic mutualism between England and North America. Shipley stated: "I make no doubt but if your plan was in Execution in America and a Correspondence Carried on with ours and many other Societies in Great Britain that it would occasion such a circulation of most useful and Beneficial Knowledge as might exceed our warmest Expectations." Shipley's letter to Franklin is reproduced in Allan, *William Shipley*, 195–98.

29. On Franklin's dissemination of French laissez-faire ideas in England, see Dickey "*Doux-Commerce* and Humanitarian Values," 293–97.

30. Dickey, "*Doux-Commerce* and Humanitarian Values," 294–95. Jonathan Shipley suggested that the center of civilization might possibly shift from Europe to America. In his view, as a result of the "gracious dispensation of Providence," the people of America had made "considerable advances in the arts of civil government and the conduct of life." Jonathan Shipley qtd. in David Spadafora, *The Idea of Progress in Eighteenth-Century Britain* (New Haven, CT: Yale University Press, 1990), 225.

31. Jonathan Shipley quoted in Dickey, "*Doux-Commerce* and Humanitarian Values," 296.

32. Ibid.

33. Ibid.

34. Dickey, "*Doux-Commerce* and Humanitarian Values," 295.

35. Priestley, *First Principles of Government*, 54.

36. Barry qtd. in Pressly, *Life and Art of James Barry*, 81.

37. For a discussion of political radicalism in London coffeehouses, see Verner W. Crane, "The Club of Honest Whigs: Friends of Science and Liberty," *William and Mary Quarterly*, 23, no. 2 (April 1966), 210–33.

38. James Barry, *The Works of James Barry*, vol. 2 (London, 1809), 574.

39. Ibid., 325.

40. Ibid., 422.

41. Ibid., 436.

42. Ibid., 324.

43. Barrell, 212.

44. Richard Price, *The Evidence for a Future Period of Improvement in the State of Mankind, with the means and Duty of Improving It, in a Discourse Delivered on Wednesday, the 25th of April, 1787 at the Meeting-House in the Old Jewry, London, to the Supporters of a New Academical Institution Among Protestant Dissenters* (London, 1787) in Richard Price, *Political Writings*, ed. D. O. Thomas (Cambridge: Cambridge University Press, 1991), 159.

45. Richard Price, *Observations on the Importance of the American Revolution and The Means of making it a*

Benefit to the World, London, 1785, in Richard Price, *Political Writings*, ed. D. O. Thomas (Cambridge: Cambridge University Press, 1991), 118.

46. Price, *Political Writings*, 118.

47. Joseph Butler, *The Analogy of Religion, Natural and Revealed to the Constitution and Course of Nature* (London, 1788), 303. Butler's "economy of providence" evidences a Christian inflection given to Xenophon's treatise on the wise management of the household, or *oikos*, the *Oeconomicus*. In *The Analogy*, Butler stated that "Parts . . . of this economy [of Providence] are the miraculous mission . . . of the invisible government, which Christ at present exercises over his church: that which he himself refers to in these words, 'In my father's house are many mansions—I go to prepare a place for you . . . [to] re-establish the Kingdom of God'" on earth (259). Although the first edition of Butler's text appeared in 1736, this chapter refers to the 1788 edition, which was roughly contemporary to Barry's murals. Pressly suggests that Butler was the main source for Barry's thinking on light metaphysics in the mural program; see his "A Chapel of Natural and Revealed Religion: James Barry's Series for the Society's Great Room Reinterpreted," *Journal of the Royal Society for the Encouragement of Arts, Manufactures, and Commerce* 132 (August 1984), 636–37.

48. Price, *Evidence*, 159–60.

49. Barry, 2:572, 364.

50. Ibid., 2:572.

51. James Barry, *The Works of James Barry*, vol. 1 (London, 1809), 363.

52. Xenophon, *A Dialogue on Devotion after the Manner of Xenophon; in which The Reasonableness, Pleasure and Advantages of it are considered. To which is prefixed, A Conversation of Socrates, Wherein he proves A God and a Providence*, trans. Thomas Amory (London, 1746), 16.

53. Barry, 2:585.

54. Ibid., 2:585

55. Barry, 1:480.

56. Pressly, *Life and Work of James Barry*, 98.

57. Barry, 1:364.

58. Barry, 2:344.

59. Richard Bradley (c. 1688–1732) wrote widely on husbandry and trade, including his text, *The Weekly Miscellany for the Improvement of Husbandry, Trade, Arts and Sciences* (London, 1727).

60. R. Bradley, preface to Xenophon, *The Science of Good Husbandry: Or, the Oeconomics of Xenophon*, trans. R. Bradley (London, 1727), 1, 2. As far as I have been able to determine, Bradley's 1727 translation of Xenophon's *Oeconomics* was the standard English version available in eighteenth-century Britain. The first English translation appeared in the sixteenth century.

61. Xenophon, *Science of Good Husbandry*, 3, 39.

62. Ibid., 37, 9, 8.

63. Barry mentions Amory in passing in *Works*, 1:277. For Amory's religious and political activities during the American Revolution, see James Bradley, *Religion, Revolution, and English*

Radicalism: Non-Conformity in Eighteenth-Century Politics and Society (Cambridge: Cambridge University Press, 1990), 351. See also Knud Haakonssen, ed., *Enlightenment and Religion: Rational Dissent in Eighteenth-Century Britain* (Cambridge: Cambridge University Press, 1996), 71, n. 36.

64. C. B. Macpherson, *The Political Theory of Possessive Individualism* (Oxford: Oxford University Press, 1962).

65. Xenophon, *A Dialogue on Devotion*, 83.

66. Adam Smith qtd. in Laurence W. Dickey, "Economics and Ethics in Smith's Theory of Capital Accumulation," in *Adam Smith, An Inquiry into the Nature and Causes of the Wealth of Nations*, ed. Laurence W. Dickey (Indianapolis, IN: Hackett, 1993), 217.

67. Dickey, "Economics and Ethics," 218.

68. Joseph Priestley, *Institutes of Natural and Revealed Religion*, vol. 1 (London, 1772), 105, 82.

69. Bradley, "Preface," Xenophon, *Science of Good Husbandry*, 2.

70. Xenophon, *A Dialogue on Devotion*, 15, 13, 12.

71. Barry, *Works*, 2:332, 333.

72. Ibid., 2:332.

73. Ibid., 2:332–333.

74. Priestley, *Institutes*, 1:19–21.

75. Shipley qtd. in Allan, *William Shipley*, 7.

76. James Barry, Portfolio of Prints, c. 1808, Royal Society of Arts.

77. Pressly, *Life and Art of James Barry*, 105–6.

78. Robert Dossie, *Memoirs of Agriculture, and Other Oeconomical Arts*, vol. 3 (London, 1782), vii.

79. Shipley qtd. in Allan, *William Shipley*, 42.

80. Cheere, 32.

81. Barry, 2:344.

82. Pressly, *The Art and Life of James Barry*, 107.

83. Ibid., 32–33, 107.

84. Barry added the tea urn in the mural in 1801. He introduced it "as an improvement on those in general use . . . , [for it] is of the simplest and least complicated kind." Barry, 2:660. See also Pressly, *Life and Art of James Barry*, 291.

85. Dossie, xx.

86. Barry, 1:477, 480.

87. Postlethwait, 115.

88. Barry, 2:145.

89. Barrell, 211–12.

90. Barry, 2:515, 514.

91. Ibid., 1:279.

92. Ibid., 2:515.

93. Arthur O. Lovejoy and George Boas, *Primitivism and Related Ideas in Antiquity* (Baltimore: Johns Hopkins University Press, 1935), 7.

94. Lovejoy, 16–19. For this reason, I contend that Barry's thinking was not merely an example of what Lovejoy termed "chronological primitivism," which "is essentially a backward-looking habit of mind" (7).

95. Bradley, "Preface," Xenophon, *Science of Good Husbandry*, 2.

96. Ibid.

97. Barry, 2:343.

98. Ibid., 1:480–81.

99. Hirsch, 117–58. For more on the Hirsch thesis, see Hirschman, "Rival Views of Market Society," 109–17. On the demoralization of wealth in the eighteenth-century, see Berry, 101–95.

100. James Macpherson, "A Dissertation Concerning the Poems of Ossian" (1763), qtd. in James Macpherson, *The Poems of Ossian and Related Works*, ed. Howard Gaskill, intro. Fiona Stafford (Edinburgh: Edinburgh University Press, 1996), 205. See also Fiona Stafford, *The Sublime Savage: A Study of James Macpherson and the Poems of Ossian* (Edinburgh: Edinburgh University Press, 1988).

101. Macpherson, 211.

102. Ibid.

103. Ibid.

104. Ibid.

105. In *Sublime Savage* (158–59), Stafford argues that Macpherson's views on property and decline were influenced by Ferguson's *Essay on the History of Civil Society* (1767). Although Ferguson published the *Essay* after the 1765 edition of *Ossian*, the two men conversed prior to the publication of their respective works. Macpherson may have had Rousseau in mind for the degenerative role of property. In his *Discourse on the Origin and Foundations of Inequality Among Men* (1755), Rousseau identified the introduction of private property as an essential factor in the decline of civil society. For the relationship between Rousseau and the Scottish Enlightenment, see Peter France, "Primitivism and Enlightenment: Rousseau and the Scots," *Yearbook of English Studies* 15 (1985), 64–79.

106. Barry, 1:266.

107. Ibid., 1:453.

108. For a discussion of Barry's *Phoenix, or the Resurrection of Freedom*, see Pressly, *Life and Art of James Barry*, 77–78.

109. Barry, 2:361.

110. Ibid., 2:393, 402.

111. Pressly, *Life and Art of James Barry*, 113–14.

112. Barry, 2:363.

113. Ibid., 2:369.

114. Ibid.

115. William Penn, "England's Present Interest Considered," in William Penn, *The Political Writings of William Penn* (Indianapolis: Liberty Fund, 2002), 74.

116. Price qtd. in Jack Fruchtman, Jr., "The Apocalyptic Politics of Richard Price and Joseph Priestley: A Study in Late Eighteenth-Century English Republican Millennialism," in *Transactions of the American Philosophical Society* vol. 73, no. 4 (Philadelphia: The American Philosophical Society, 1983), 83.

117. Fruchtman, Jr., 83.

118. On the relationship between Providence and the emancipation of slaves by the Pennsylvania Quakers, see Jacob Viner, *The Role of Providence in the Social Order: An Essay in Intellectual History* (Princeton, NJ: Princeton University Press, 1972), 83.

119. Montesquieu qtd. in Barry, 2:440.

120. Barry, 2:440.

121. Abbé Raynal qtd. in Barry, 2:440.

122. Montesquieu qtd. in Dickey, "*Doux-Commerce* and Humanitarian Values," 286.

123. David Hume, "Of Refinement in the Arts," in *Essays: Moral, Political, and Literary* (Indianapolis, IN: Liberty Classics, 1987), 269, 280.

124. Penn, 72–73.

125. Dickey, "*Doux-Commerce* and the 'Mediocrity of Money,'" 250.

126. Margo Todd, *Christian Humanism and the Puritan Social Order* (Cambridge: Cambridge University Press, 1987), 174. Todd writes: "The attitudes of both Protestants and humanists . . . were a partial sanctification of the market-place—encouraging discipline, productivity and thrift, but suspicious of profit-making and accumulation. Poverty was no longer praiseworthy, but neither was financial success" (174). For the influence of stoicism on Dissenters, see Margo Todd, "Seneca and the Protestant Mind: The Influence of Stoicism on Puritan Ethics," *Archive für Reformationsgeschichte* 74 (1983): 182–99.

127. Penn, 74.

The Popular Opposition: Politicizing Modern Art in the National Gallery in Berlin, 1918–1933

Elizabeth M. Grady

PARADIGMS AND THEORIES ABOUT THE FUNCTIONING of political economies as they relate to art are useful only insofar as they may be brought to bear on particular cultural situations in specific historical moments. An especially clear example of the interaction between government funding for art, its manifestation, and its reception may be found in the National Gallery in Berlin during the Weimar Republic. Here, the tradition of government funding of an ideologically stable and rigid program of exhibition and acquisition in the museum was turned on its end in the service of the democratic values of the new government that was instituted after the abdication of the Kaiser. With the introduction of modern art into the National Gallery came a strong, nationalist public criticism of its new direction, suggesting the power that had been exerted by government-funded culture in the past in determining the definition of national identity. This public criticism indicates the importance that was accorded the power of government-funded culture in continuing to influence and shape that identity. The battle over the form that the programming of the National Gallery took contributed significantly to debates over the political direction of the nation, and was used self-consciously by the National Socialists as a tool in gaining electoral support.

With the end of World War I came enormous political and economic changes in Germany. The revolution that began in November 1918 brought about the downfall of the monarchy, and the establishment of a democratic government. And several factors conspired to ensure that the results of the end of the war and the revolution went far beyond the political realm. The terms of the Treaty of Versailles were punitive, imposing massive reparations payments and trade restrictions on an already weak economy. To make matters worse, the government was also struggling to make welfare payments, however limited, to the masses of war widows and veterans returning home, crippling any efforts it might otherwise have made to turn the nation's economic woes around. The initial result was chaos: widespread unemployment accompanied by runaway inflation. The first years of the Republic were characterized by political upheaval, violence, and financial desperation among its citizens.

It was under these circumstances that the National Gallery in Berlin made profound changes in its policies of exhibition and acquisition. Acquisition policies were the first to change, as the museum's director, Ludwig Justi, was unbound from the restrictive policies of Kaiser Wilhelm II, who had all but forbidden any art not traditional and German from entering the collection of the museum. Justi began to purchase, and then to exhibit, the work of living modern artists. This art differed radically from that previously seen in publicly funded museums, and the changes were widely reported in the daily newspapers and art press. The extensive debates that ensued were frequently marked by criticism, raising public awareness of the museum's activities, but often having a negative impact on public opinion. This chapter will examine the ways that the political and economic instability of the period, coupled with the ideological function of the National Gallery's collections as a representation of German culture, worked to popularize and politicize negative opinions of the introduction of modern art into the National Gallery in Berlin.

The National Gallery's figurehead status is key to understanding the heated tone of the debates that accompanied policy decisions made by its director. Any government institution with the power to control the ideological projection of the nation's self-image was a participant, willing or not, in national politics. The museum's special status was due in part to its location in the nation's capital near the government district and imperial residences, making clear its connection to those with power and influence. It served as both a symbol of the generosity of the former ruling family and as the arbiter of an inherently German national culture.[1]

The history of the museum's use for ideological purposes before the war provides the basis for how it was viewed as the single most important site of the projection of national cultural identity, even after the founding of the Weimar Republic. Among the first sights to greet any visitor to the museum from the moment of its opening were two full-length portraits of the Emperor Wilhelm I and Empress Augusta painted in 1873 by Bernhard Plockhorst.[2] Most of the art shown could be seen as inherently German, and much of it approached blatant propaganda. Even when the building was still in the planning stages, the State Art Committee had commissioned artists to produce grand battle scenes associated with key Prussian victories that were instrumental in consolidating power, like Christian Sell's *At Königgrätz*, 1872, and Emile-Joseph Hünten's *Battle at Wörth 6 August 1870*, 1877. In addition, it purchased academic or traditional genre scenes and landscapes, which were exclusively by German artists.[3] Thus the art found in the National Gallery since the opening of its main building was of a specifically German, nationalist, and academic or traditional sort. This early rejection of foreign work, while seemingly not codified as official policy, may be seen as a tacit acknowledgment of the museum's task to express and promote German cultural identity.

Regardless of their opinions of the National Gallery's new policies, many accorded it a great deal of importance in contributing to the formation of German society.[4] The art chosen and the way it was presented was held to be of paramount importance by the government and nationalists in presenting an ideal view of German culture, as evidenced by their interest in and enthusiasm for the institution. The ideological force of this presentation was made clear by the contentious debates that raged over it.

By presenting academic art, those who had advocated or sympathized with its choice for the National Gallery before the war believed that a coherent, historicized view of society could be presented—a view with which many longed to identify, especially in the face of the loss of the war and the subsequent revolution. Many paintings on view in the National Gallery were intended to project not only a glorious image of the nation but also of the role of the Prussian monarchy as its leader.[5] For conservatives, Justi's choice to exhibit modern art was highly problematic because they saw such art as expressing violence and social chaos.[6] They attributed these values to the formal features of the works, which included coarse brushwork and crowded, unbalanced compositions, and to their subjects, which included scenes of urban decadence and revolution. This sharp contrast from the nationalist paintings that had been favored by the Kaiser was viewed as an ideological shift from promoting stability and national coherence to accepting chaos as the new social order.

The relationship of the National Gallery to the government is the most obvious factor that ensured that any action of the museum had a political impact. Funded by the State of Prussia, the National Gallery had an historical relationship with the government. Justi himself acknowledged the political component of this financial relationship, citing the influence of the Foreign Office and the *Landtag* (provincial assembly) on the National Gallery in an article of 1922.[7] That the staff of the National Gallery was charged with selecting the work to be shown in two exhibitions organized in cooperation with the Foreign Office confirms this influence.[8]

The National Gallery also served as the most visible outward representation of the government's nebulous cultural policy, which was essentially to allow cultural institutions relative freedom in a spirit of democratic inclusiveness. The promotion of modern art by Justi was thus supported by the various cultural ministers under whom he worked during the Weimar Republic. Generally politically left of center (most were members of the SPD, the Social Democratic Party), if culturally conservative, they believed strongly in artistic freedom.[9] They were also likely to have supported the alteration of the pro-imperial ideology on display until the abdication of the Kaiser in 1918, an ideology all but antithetical to the new government. Since the public knew that the National Gallery was administered by the state, the freedom it was allowed implied to the public that it had active state support for its programs.

With the revolution of 1918 had come a radical change in governance, from monarchy to democracy. This accompanied a structural change in the way that the government made its decisions and fulfilled its obligations, and fundamental changes in most ministries followed. The National Gallery was a notable exception to these changes. Its administrative stability ensured that its traditional ideological function also remained relatively unaltered, in spite of the changes initiated by Justi. The ideology it represented was the cultural continuity of the German people, from the time when the nation was a fragmented group of principalities through the unification of 1871 to the Weimar Republic. It drew a lineage of leading styles in German art, beginning with the often fiercely nationalistic Romantic painting made in the face of the Napoleonic occupation in the early nineteenth century.[10] The interest in its actions was so acute, and its critics so impassioned, because of its central role in constructing and propagating the myth of an historical German identity.

In the wake of the national traumas of war and revolution, many of those who had been resistant to modern art before—such as museum director Wilhelm von Bode and critic Karl Scheffler (who will both be discussed in greater detail below), in addition to broad sectors of the middle class—became adamantly opposed. They feared the dissolution of the national government as a result of the revolution.

They feared losing their social position as they saw the value of their cash assets dwindle due to the inflation that had begun during the war. And they were fiercely defensive of their national pride, which had been tarnished by their collective defeat. Those who felt this way saw modern art as a signal of precisely the kind of change they wanted to avoid—that is, a change in the moral standards and class structures of their society.

Continuity in the National Gallery reassured them of the nation's stable past by presenting an unbroken lineage of accomplished artistic production in an unchanged cultural fixture whose history stretched back well into the nineteenth century. Particularly because the National Gallery was one of very few institutions to survive the revolution intact, any policy changes made in it were likely to be seen in a negative light in the general context of political upheaval that prevailed in 1918–19, thus mirroring political and social turmoil.

Partly in response to the demands of some modernist artists who had organized into revolutionary councils on the Soviet model, such as the Working Council for Art and the November Group, to push for the introduction of modern art into public museums, and partly due to his own taste and to budget restrictions, Justi made profound policy changes in the museum at the end of World War I. The most controversial change was the decision to acquire modernist contemporary art. He initiated this new policy almost immediately, exploring the purchase of modernist paintings for the first major round of acquisitions to come before the commission in June, 1919. These included four paintings by Karl Schmidt-Rottluff, and works by Max Beckmann, Erich Heckel, Ernst Ludwig Kirchner, Franz Marc, Emil Nolde, and Max Pechstein.[11] It is notable that the artists that particularly interested Justi were Expressionists, and this tendency (with the exception of Beckmann) to favor the artists of the *Brücke* and *Bläue Reiter* groups continued throughout the Weimar Republic. Old Master works had become prohibitively expensive, and foreign art was out of the question due to the deflated state of the currency. By purchasing the work of younger, less well-known artists, the National Gallery would be buying the cheapest work available at the same time they were helping those who were struggling.[12]

He changed the museum's exhibition policies similarly, showing not only the newly acquired work of living modern artists, but also borrowing work to supplement these acquisitions. This decision was facilitated by the government's decision to put sections of the former palace of the crown prince—the Kronprinzenpalais—at the disposal of the National Gallery. Conscious of the potential for negative reactions and criticism if he were to introduce the most extreme modernist art into the hallowed halls of the main National Gallery building, Justi actively sought another venue. Located within easy walking distance of the main museum building, the Kronprinzenpalais was ideal.

In response to the new imperatives that had resulted from a change to a democratic government, and in an effort to promote acceptance and understanding of contemporary art, Justi instituted a number of measures to increase accessibility to the museum. Free tours, lectures, and inexpensive guides provided new or expanded opportunities to the museum's audiences. Free days were offered, and evening and weekend hours were expanded to accommodate workers' incomes and schedules. And especially in times of economic distress, such as the periods from 1918–23, and 1930–33, the museum's audiences took advantage of these opportunities.[13] Thus, just as changes were being made in the museum, Justi saw to it that the largest possible number of people would be made aware of them.

The active interest of the press in cultural enterprises, as well as the director's energetic publicity, guaranteed public awareness of the changes. The result was extensive publicity that reached its most contentious form in press debates over the introduction of Expressionism into the National Gallery. Unsurprisingly, artists could be counted both among those supportive of the museum, and among those critical of it. The state had historically supported artists with tax breaks and by purchasing their work, often for the National Gallery. After the war, in the face of desperate hardship, art was no longer a top priority, so the budget of the National Gallery was cut. To make matters worse, in Berlin during the Weimar Republic there were an extraordinary number of artists, far more than could ever be supported by the art market. The market was fairly strong during the years of hyperinflation, as those with money sought to shelter it by converting it into tangible assets. But the financial circumstances of even the most favored artists were precarious as a result of the very inflation that fueled the market. Thus, both the glut of art available and the instability of the market ensured that very few artists made a decent living at their chosen profession. In this weak market, artists nonetheless expected a measure of government help, yet due to the weak economy and tight budget, none was forthcoming. This naturally led to resentment against both the government and the museum, especially on the part of those artists whose work was no longer in favor.

Some had fought long and hard for the introduction of modern art into the museum, only to find, in the case of the artists of the Berlin Secession, that they were no longer modern enough and had been passed over. Others, especially traditional and academic artists who had been favored under the monarchy, felt that the rug had been pulled out from under them. Although the National Gallery did support some prominent Secessionists, notably Slevogt and Corinth, the newly extensive press coverage of Expressionism overshadowed these acquisitions.

Initially, many modern artists, such as Erich Heckel, who served on Justi's first postwar acquisition commission, remained supportive of Justi's new policies. However, on the occasion of the 1929 exhibition, "New German Art from Berlin Private Collections," some modern artists had cause to protest. In this exhibition Justi pursued his interest in Expressionism as the most authentically German art on the contemporary scene. Like critics, artists protested against his exclusion of abstract art. On behalf of its members, who represented a wide variety of styles, the *Reichsverband bildende Künstler Deutschlands* (Reich Organization of Visual Artists of Germany), published a protest letter in the press. Calling on the National Gallery as a government-sponsored institution, the group claimed the museum had a responsibility to include *all* contemporary German art.[14]

This situation led to a number of developments. Some artists appealed directly to the director of the National Gallery, Ludwig Justi, to invite him to exhibitions and offer work for sale.[15] But most significantly, the resentment of artists was recognized by right-wing extremists who saw an opportunity in it. Seeing the masses of struggling artists and acknowledging that a resentment against modernism was widespread among traditional artists and their audiences alike, the National Socialists began preaching an ideology intended to appeal to these groups, of the reestablishment of an inherently German national culture.[16] So, in this way, the negative impact of economics and market changes on art led to the politicization of the issue of the financial support of artists by the state.

By far the harshest, most vocal, and most damaging of Justi's critics were those on the political right. Oftentimes they preyed on the fears of wide sectors of the population, in the hope of making their cultural criticism as relevant as possible, as found in their criticism of acquisitions. Although in reality Justi was extremely careful in his use of the National Gallery's funds, the public image of his financial management skills was not always very favorable. Artists, especially academic artists motivated by hardship, protested when large sums were spent that did not benefit them. On the rare occasions when Justi made imprudent decisions, they were widely publicized by indignant critics, making him seem incompetent. This was the case in the controversy over the purchase of Van Gogh's *Garden of Daubigny*, for a rather large sum from a Parisian dealer. Critics, along with the President of the Prussian Academy of Arts, Max Liebermann, lambasted Justi's decision to acquire the work.[17] This purchase provoked additional criticism since it was made outside Germany, in the very nation most responsible for hobbling Germany with unmanageable reparations payments. He was criticized for wasting public money, when in fact he had used money from private donations. Therefore, a combination of opposition to Justi's policies and confusion about the details of his expenditures fueled conservative critics and artists in their complaints of his misuse of government funds, and in their nationalist defense of the old guard.

One of the most damaging forces at work against the National Gallery was the press's widely disseminated nationalist criticism of the museum, through which the museum's opponents reached the public. The critique of the museum on this basis employed public resistance to modern art to win sympathy for conservative political concerns. And the reverse was also true; nationalist sympathies were deployed to win support for the critique of modern art.

Modern art had certainly been criticized long before Justi's policy changes, as prominent critics like Karl Scheffler interpreted Expressionism as a rejection of bourgeois values.[18] However, the criticism took on a nationalist tone only *after* Justi implemented his new policies in the National Gallery. Thus this politicized response to modern art was more a function of its having been embraced by the director of a national institution, which had historically promoted the ideology of German nationhood, than as a political reaction against the art. Critics believed that there was an identifiable path that German art had followed since the Middle Ages, and that by embracing Expressionism Justi was interrupting the development of the nation's cultural heritage.[19] The common belief that Expressionism was morally, and after the revolution even politically, subversive led to a series of nationalist diatribes against the art, and the institutions and museum officials who supported it in cities across Germany. Because of Berlin's significance as the capital of both the nation and the German art world, its National Gallery and the actions taken by its director provoked particular ire among some of Germany's most prominent critics.

One such critic was Wilhelm von Bode, who, as a former director of the City Museums of Berlin, had an impeccable reputation as an art administrator.

However, by the early 1920s he was also a staunch conservative in artistic and political matters. His harsh and well-publicized words against both modern art and the public institutions that supported it were assured of making an impact, coming as they did from such a well-respected and influential man.

> Artists and art historians now work together with novelists, poets, musicians, decadent art enthusiasts, . . . in order to "fulfill" themselves under the common flag of Expressionism or Dadaism. That in so doing they arrive, almost without exception, at political radicalism may not be taken badly, but the scholarly efforts of this mixed propaganda society truly cannot be promoted. And no one will venture to claim that their industry is stimulated by this, their morals strengthened by it. People will doubtless object, "morality is a private affair"; however for the state, therefore also for the government, it certainly isn't that. . . . Does anyone believe that Germany's renewal can come from this quagmire? Is the power to recover, in spite of the annihilating peace and in spite of all of the shackles that have been placed on us through this "peace," supposed to gather here?[20]

Radicalism and lack of morality expanded what might have begun as a mere critique of the introduction of modern art into public museums into a harsh and politicized diatribe against progressive cultural forces in Germany in general.

Bode's view of immoral forces as not only negative in themselves, but as thoroughly incapable of aiding in a German renewal that was to follow the "annihilating peace agreement" of World War I, is ideologically significant. By 1920 hostility toward modern art had become explicitly politicized, making art opinion a matter of national interest and concern.

Karl Scheffler, the critic and editor of one of the leading art magazines, *Kunst und Künstler*, was also important as a promoter of the nationalist opposition to Justi's new policies in the National Gallery. Scheffler had been critical of Justi even before he made policy changes, but his opposition became significantly sharper thereafter. He criticized nearly every move Justi made, from choices about which artists to show and collect to the hanging of the National Gallery's collection.[21] Scheffler's frequent articles appeared in his own magazine, but came to an early head in a pamphlet he published in 1921, *Berliner Museumskrieg*. Here, he condensed his arguments against Justi and his actions into one long diatribe, in which he engaged in a point-by-point critique of Justi's tenure, culminating in a dramatic call for the removal of Justi as director of the National Gallery.

Scheffler's criticism also took on a clearly nationalist tone. He linked revolutionary art and revolutionary museum policies, saying that such policies as Justi's would be detrimental to the well being of the German nation.

Scheffler's criticism of Justi and modern art in general continued unabated throughout the Weimar Republic. By 1930 he was referring to the National Gallery's exhibition of the work of Nolde as *landverderbend* (ruinous of the country). This article was also widely publicized, having appeared in Scheffler's own magazine, and having received (somewhat critical) commentary in both *Der Tag* and *Weltbühne*. Publicity enhanced Scheffler's nationalist arguments even as they became more extremist, making them more convincing.[22]

The final, and by far the most virulent, attackers were the right-wing, middle-class, cultural organizations, which tended to be small but numerous.[23] The most important of these were the *Deutsche Kunstgesellschaft* (German Art Society) and the *Kampfbund für deutsche Kultur* (Fighting League for German Culture). These groups disseminated their ideas through lectures and cultural evenings, which included concerts and theatrical performances. But one of the most effective means of spreading their message was through the *Deutsche Kunstkorrespondenz* (German Art Correspondence). Run by Bettina Feistel-Rohmeder of the *Deutsche Kunstgesellschaft*, this organ published a short newspaper distributed to the press and to other *völkisch* (folkish) groups, with preapproval for free reprinting of articles. Major and minor right-wing extremist publications alike—including the National Socialist *Völkischer Beobachter*—made use of its reports.[24]

Typical of the traits favored in its strongly worded and intensely critical diatribes was the inherent "Germanness" that art was meant to evidence, while avoiding any Bolshevist political influence. An anonymous article published in the Völkischer Beobachter in 1925 is typical: "All of the famous master paintings that have been removed from public painting collections and city galleries are to be re-hung in their previous places. All kitsch has to disappear. Establish your own art committee and give the Jew-serving sham-Germans your conditions! Art must remain free of politics, therefore all people who carry party politics into the art committees are to resign from their previous posts."[25] This demonstrates the preference for older, more traditional art, while modernist art is by implication kitschy and "sham-German." By the reference to "party politics," the author means leftist politics of the sort espoused by many modernist artists in the days following the November 1918 revolution, in their spontaneous support for the Working Council for Art and the November Group. These leftist groups pushed for the introduction of modern art into public museums.

Hitler himself influenced right-wing cultural groups, making connections between art and politics in *Mein Kampf*. He railed against the "Bolshevized" art of "Bolshevized" states, suggesting that government, national identity, and art were thoroughly interconnected, and that government was responsible for a nation's culture.

> Art Bolshevism is the only possible cultural form and spiritual expression of Bolshevism as a whole.
>
> Anyone to whom this seems strange need only subject the art of the happily Bolshevised states to an examination, and, to his horror, he will be confronted by the morbid excrescences of insane and degenerate men, with which, since the turn of the century, we have become familiar under the collective concepts of cubism and dadaism, as the official and recognized art of those states.
>
> No more than a political collapse of the present magnitude would have been conceivable sixty years ago was a cultural collapse such as began to manifest itself in futurist and cubist works since 1900 thinkable. . . . This plague could not appear at that time, because neither would public opinion have tolerated it nor the state calmly looked on. For it is the business of the state, in other words, of its leaders, to prevent a people from being driven into the arms of spiritual madness.[26]

Thus the opposition to modern art became a moral imperative against destructive political and economic forces.

Many believed that the leading styles in art expressed the political conditions and the economic situation in Germany and the state of society in general. By altering the kinds of art shown in the National Gallery, Justi was implying that dramatic social and political changes were under way. That people at opposite ends of the political spectrum viewed art and its representative function in this way suggests the significance that was accorded decisions about art—especially in the nation's flagship museum.

Those on both sides of the debate over modernism believed that one of the primary functions of art was to express social values. Justi believed that museums should lead their audiences by the example of the art exhibited, educating them and providing inspiration for their creative impulses. Conservatives, on the other hand, believed that it was the responsibility of anyone who wanted to contribute positively to the political situation to care also for the intellectual and cultural needs of the people. That is, they believed that culture, economics, and politics were inextricably linked.[27]

As many Expressionists had claimed, Justi believed that formal innovations in art had indicated the dramatic social and political changes that were to occur during and after World War I, presaging a dramatic change to come. "The rise of this new art preceded the powerful shocks and restructurings of the state and social world, which we have now experienced, and in that one feels a deeper connection. The leading artists of the new sentiment . . . stood personally close . . . to the new efforts and hopes in the totality of the spiritual and social life, they felt their creations to be a sudden flash of the future that was to come, that would bring existence to another path, externally and above all internally."[28] For the many who feared further change, the art presented in the National Gallery must have seemed threatening, suggesting the imminence of further upheavals.

As a reflection of the state of society, Expressionism was both embraced and rejected in the first years of the Republic. Its idealistic visions of social change could represent the hope of a spiritual revitalization of culture and society, or it could be seen as the expression of the tumultuous times in which it was produced. As it happened, it became associated with the immediate postwar years when it was introduced into the National Gallery. Expressionism—not least due to its own rhetoric—had also been linked to left-wing politics and revolution. The image of instability and revolution associated with Expressionism came to be seen as a threat by a populace weary of conflict and longing for the images of national stability ideologically projected at times by traditional and academic art.

The Expressionists who were engaged with the revolution were extremely vocal about their intentions and allegiances, and their political involvement became quickly apparent to the public. The awareness of their activities was both reflected in the press and extended by it. Sometimes reports were merely informative, but most were critical of the connection between art and left-wing politics.[29] Many came to believe that to be an Expressionist was tantamount to being a Spartacist [a member of the Communist *Spartakus-Bund*] or a Bolshevist.[30] Even though Expressionism was already nearly twenty years old, it seemed as if it was emerging for the first time with the opening of the *Kronprinzenpalais* in the summer of 1919, that it was a brand new movement which had emerged along with political instability.

In a 1931 review of Justi's *Vom Corinth bis Klee*, one critic wrote: "The artists of today certainly appear to be children of their time. Yes, that they are, perhaps all too much, and they haven't wanted for critics that had to brand several of them as dangerous revolutionaries, as form-smashers, that have participated in the "disintegration of the spiritual world." These critics of modern art are not so terribly wrong."[31] This perception was certainly encouraged by works that depicted street fights, violence, death, and war. But it was extended to modernist work of all stripes.[32] Expressionists' own claims to a visionary modernism were used against them, as were the claims of the desire to rebuild the connection between art and life. To make art expressive of the political and social instability of Germany was, for some, to pervert the function of art.

The middle class experienced a great deal of anxiety in the wake of World War I. Salaries and savings accounts of civil servants and others were rapidly losing value as a result of inflation. There was therefore a great deal of perceived erosion in the financial well-being of this group, and Expressionism became a symbol of their difficulties. From its negative political and economic associations with the postwar period to its leftist tendencies, Expressionism seemed threatening.

In contrast, there appears to have been sympathy with traditional and academic art. This preference was reflected in the press and in private correspondence by those on both sides of the debate over the introduction of modern art into public museums. Citing the first exhibition organized in the National Gallery by Justi's assistant Ludwig Thormaehlen, his correspondent, the artist Erich Buchholz, recounted an experience he had had in the Kronprinzenpalais, where the majority of viewers had expressed disfavor of the art on display. He had rebelled against them. "I might remind you of your first exhibition directorship in the Kronprinzenpalais. You certainly know how the public accepted the thing then. I was there myself and had to observe how the better part of the public let loose against the things, until the affair became too colorful for me, and I rebelled against it; among other things also stressed that the public really ought to be happy that someone gave them the possibility to see things that were certainly controversial, but absolutely new in their form, and at least make the effort to engage with the things instead of simply to make fun of them without judgment."[33] This belies the apparent popularity of such modernist work that high attendance numbers might otherwise suggest. Although the Kronprinzenpalais undoubtedly drew large numbers of visitors, this account—by someone sympathetic to the National Gallery administration's goals—suggests that they were not necessarily there out of love for the work.

On the right, Bettina Feistel-Rohmeder, founder of the German Art Society, describes the results of a survey handed out at the *Große Berliner* (a major annual juried exhibition) in 1928, which came out (if we are to believe her) strongly in favor of traditional work and against modernist art: "The questionnaire, which was to be filled out by the visitors, which each was handed at the entrance, resulted in the unambiguous decision for the art of the old school and the rejection of 'modern madness', sometimes expressed in the harshest words."[34] If this report stood in isolation, it might be dismissed as an exaggeration, or even a fabrication. However, those supporting modern art cited similar stories.

It seems, then, that the preference for traditional art over modernism was a prevalent one, exhibited by those who feared the dramatic social changes that were underway, or who lacked either the education or the desire to make sense of the work in question. This preference, coupled with a new level of exposure to modernism, and the fact that most people were still forming their opinions about it, laid the groundwork for the impact of negative and politicized criticism of modern art on public art opinion.

Without the deeply felt economic hardship that impacted the middle class and artists alike, the criticism of modern art in the Weimar Republic would have been far less severe and politicized. The middle class, who made up much of the traditional market for art, suffered from social instability due to the massive inflation of the immediate postwar years, and the Great Depression of the last years of the period. Artists, too, felt the pinch as their ever-swelling ranks found fewer and fewer serious collectors to buy their work. In response to this pressure, conservative artists protested the introduction of modernism into the National Gallery. The middle class walked in step with them, rejecting modern art in their longing for images of a retrospectively idealized past in the years of the monarchy that were to be found in the art they preferred. The impact of the economic situation on the formation of public opinion on art was therefore exponentially increased.

As with most sectors of the economy, the market for art was profoundly impacted by the economic crises of the first and last years of the republic. Many of those who had traditionally bought art were no longer in a position to do so. Those who, on the other hand, had made money by profiting from the war economy and by engaging in speculative ventures made possible by inflation—largely industrialists—did not have the same allegiance to traditional art. Rather, they were interested in modern art.[35]

The negative and politicized opinion of modern art that became evident in the daily press in the last years of the Weimar Republic, reinforced by the opinions of respected art experts, was created by a combination of widespread public critique, economic desperation and allegiance to the past. The changes in acquisition and exhibition policies to include modern art in the National Gallery, especially in its affiliate in the Kronprinzenpalais, received a great deal of press attention, not least because of Ludwig Justi's own efforts to try to make people aware of the new changes and programs. This resulted in a sudden and rapid exposure to modernism for the public.

With the shock and awareness of the new policies came criticism, and the nationalist critics were the most aggressive in politicizing public opinion toward modern art. Because of the museum's role in the ideological projection of national identity, it was of particular importance to nationalists. This also made it vulnerable to attack, as its taste for modernism was seen as inappropriate in representing the nation.

The questionable (for the nationalists) implications of Justi's placement of Expressionism at the end of a long line of national styles were exacerbated by the leftist political connotations that the style had for many people. This ensured that Expressionism would be irrevocably associated with economic and political chaos. Accustomed to seeing traditional and academic art in the National Gallery, and being instead faced with work associated with leftist politics and political, social, and economic chaos, a great many people reacted negatively to the new work. That the work was being presented as the contemporary manifestation of German national culture, the end of a long and proud artistic lineage, made the shock all the more objectionable.

Finally, the negative opinion that large sectors of the public had of modern art was exacerbated by the economic conditions under which these events took place. For the middle class, the art shown in the National Gallery as a new part of their artistic heritage was a bitter reminder of the instability they had experienced in the wake of the revolution. They were predisposed, in part due to the slippage in the stability of their financial situations, to disapprove of major changes—especially in one of the few government institutions to remain intact from the Wilhelmine era. This negative opinion was mirrored by artists who were also experiencing hardship in the face of government budget cuts.

It was, then, the combined effect of all of these factors that led to the formation of a negative and politicized opinion both of modern art and of the new acquisition and exhibition policies of the National Gallery's director, Ludwig Justi. And it was precisely the negative public opinion of modern art that was to make tenable the reactionary measures taken against it by the National Socialists beginning in 1933.

NOTES

1. See Françoise Forster-Hahn and Kurt W. Forster, "Art and the Course of Empire in Nineteenth-Century Berlin," in *Art in Berlin 1815–1989* (Seattle: University of Washington Press, 1989), 41–60.

2. Françoise Forster-Hahn, "The Politics of Display or the Display of Politics?," *Art Bulletin* 77, no. 2 (June 1995): 176; Forster-Hahn "Shrine of Art or Signature of a New Nation? The National Gallery(ies) in Berlin 1848–1968," *Studies in the History of Art* 47(1994): 84.

3. Forster-Hahn, 1994, 90–92.

4. von Bode, Wilhelm. "Eine neue deutsche Kunst in Sicht?", *Der Sammler (Unterhaltungs—und Literaturbeilage der München—Augsburger Abendzeitung)*, April 4, 1923, qtd. in Adolph Donath, ed., *Der Kunstwanderer* (n.p., n.d.).

5. Forster-Hahn, "The Politics of Display," 174–79. See esp. 176–77.

6. N.a., *B.Z. am Mittag*, "Bode gegen den 'Modernismus' öffentlicher Kunstpflege," April 21, 1920.

7. "Indeed from within the country and without, urgent requests for loans from the National Gallery come continually, one almost every week. Other museums fundamentally refrain from it [loaning work], and for the most part, fewer claims are made on them. The National Gallery is the only collection of recent art which is supported by the Prussian state, and which is therefore exposed to political influences through the Foreign Office, the State Parliament, etc." ["Allerdings kommen fortgesetzt vom Inland und vom Ausland dringende Ersuchen um Darleihungen aus der National-Galerie, fast jede Woche eins. Andere Museen sehen grundsätzlich ab, und zumeist werden sie weniger in Anspruch genommen. Die National-Galerie ist die einzige Sammlung neuerer Kunst, die vom preussischen Staat unterhalten wird, und die daher politischen Einflüssen ausgesetzt ist durch das Auswärtige Amt, den Landtag, usw"] Justi, "Kunst und Politik," *Kunstchronik und Kunstmarkt* 57, n.s. 23, no. 35 (May 26, 1922): 569–74, 570.

8. The exhibitions were the "Four-Nation Exhibition," and an exhibition of contemporary German art to be shown in Oslo, Norway.

9. The SPD cultural ministers Haenisch and Becker supported Justi in his efforts to expand the kinds of art shown in the National Gallery.

10. See Albert Boime, "Caspar David Freidrich: Monk by the Sea," *Arts Magazine*, November 1986, 54–63.

11. Justi visited the atelier of Ernst Ludwig Kirchner in Berlin in December 1918. See correspondence in SMBPK/ZA, Gen. 10, Bd. 11, 1918–20 on the initial activity. On the acquisitions of June 1919, see Beratungsliste zur Ankaufs-Sitzung am 17. Juni 1919 im Kronprinzen-Palais, SMBPK/ZA, Gen. 10, Bd. 11, 1918–20.

12. For an example of the effect of inflation on art prices, see letters from the Karl Haberstock Kunsthandlung in Berlin to Justi: "I would be very thankful to you if you would kindly inform me when the decision about the sale of the Zorn will be made. The constantly changing currency values make it impossible for me to maintain my offer for an indefinite period. I would therefore be very obliged to you for expediting the matter." ["Ich wäre Ihnen sehr dankbar, wenn Sie mir freundlichst mitteilen würden, wann die Entscheidung über den Verkauf des Zorn fallen wird. Die ständig wechselnden Valutaverhältnisse machen es mir unmöglich, mein Gebot auf unbestimmte Zeit hinzuhalten. Ich wäre Ihnen daher für eine Beschleunigung der Angelegenheit sehr verbunden."] And November 22, 1920, "The ongoing changes in currency valuation and the resulting call for the improvement of our

Mark make it unfortunately impossible for me to keep to my offer on the Zorn. Unfortunately, at today's rates I cannot spend more than 175,000 Marks." ["Die fortlaufenden Valutaschwankungen und die dadurch hervorgerufene Verbesserung unseres Markkurses machen es mir leider unmöglich, mein Gebot auf den Zorn zu halten. Bei dem heutigen Kursstand kann ich leider nicht mehr als 175,000 Mark geben."] Both in SMBPK/ZA, Gen. 10, Bd. 11, November 16, 1920, And Justi himself discussed the issue, "it's still the worst with foreign art, of which our collection has such valuable holdings from earlier decades. The official 20-year restriction ended in the year 1918, but then the devaluation of the currency followed, until 1923. Then came money shortages. During these years the gallery occasionally got no acquisition funds at all. At the same time the prices sought on the world market for artworks that were desirable to us rose from month to month. Sums that were required for masterworks of foreign art, such as Norwegian Kroner for Munch, were, in view of the possibilities offered to us, thoroughly fantastic: such acquisitions belonged in the realm of utopia." ["Am schlimmsten ist is noch um die ausländische Kunst bestellt, von der unsere Sammlung aus früheren Jahrzehnten so kostbare Bestände enthält. Jene zwanzigjährige amtliche Hemmung hörte zwar mit dem Jahre 1918 auf, aber nun folgte die Geldentwertung, bis 1923. Dann kam die Geldverknappung. Während dieser Jahre erhielt die Galerie zeitweise überhaupt keine Ankaufsmittel. Gleichzeitig stiegen die Preise der Kunstwerke, die auf dem Weltmarkt gesucht und für uns erwünscht waren, von Monat zu Monat. Summen, welche für Meisterwerke ausländischer Kunst erforderlich gewesen wären, etwa norwegische Kronen für Munch, . . . waren angesichts der uns gegebenen Möglichkeiten durchaus märchenhaft: solche Ankäufe gehörten ins Reich der Utopie."] Justi, "Die Ankäufe des Vereins 'Freunde der Nationalgalerie' zu einer Ausstellung im Kronprinzenpalais" (n.p., n.d., sometime after the group was founded in 1929), 20.

13. "Regarding number 6. The difficulty of the time forces the population to use free days for visiting the museum more than before, therefore the income is going down steadily. In the first quarter of the current fiscal year 1932 the entrance fees amounted to 1,121 RM less than in the same period of the previous year."

["Zu Nr. 6. Die Not der Zeit zwingt die Bevölkerung die eintrittsfreien Tage stärker als früher zum Besuch der Museen zu benutzen, daher gehen die Einnahmen ständig zurück. Im ersten Vierteljahr des laufenden Rechnungsjahres 1932 betrugen die Eintrittsgelder 1 121 RM weniger als in der gleichen Zeit des Vorjahres.] GstA PK I. HA Rep. 151, Finanzministerium. Kassen- und Rechnungswesen, 1932–44, Zu U IV 12442/32. Nationalgalerie und Rauch-Schinkel-Museum in Berlin. Kap. 34 Tit. 9, Nr. 6.

14. "We expected that the much advertised exhibition of post-Impressionist art would bring an actual overview. Two exhibitions actually came about—noted nearby as loans from private collections—but if these exhibitions were supposed to signify an overview, then peculiar viewpoints were standard: the entire movement, which was the continuation of the already shown beginnings (in part Constructivism, called pure abstraction) was silenced. . . . We feel that we are obliged to the state as the upholder of cultural work, however that you remember your duty as an official of the state, as the steward of artistic holdings." ["Wir erwarteten, daß die groß angekündigte Ausstellung nachimpressionistischer Kunst einen tatsächlichen Überblick bringen würde. Es kamen wohl zwei Ausstellungen zustande— nebenbei bemerkt Leihgaben aus Privatbesitz—aber wenn diese Ausstellungen einen Überblick bedeuten sollten, dann waren sonderbare Gesichtspunkte maßgebend: die ganze Bewegung, die die Fortführung der schon gezeigten Anfänge war (teilweise Konstruktivismus, reine Abstraktion genannt) ist totgeschwiegen. . . . Wir fühlen uns dem Staat als Träger kultureller Arbeit verpflichtet verlangen aber, daß Sie als Beamter des Staates, als Verwalter künstlerischer Güter sich ihrer Plicht erinnern."] Hermann Pling, as representative of the Reichsverband bildender Künstler Deutschlands, letter of May 17, 1930, n.p. (clearly a newspaper clipping), SMBPK/ZA, Allgemeiner Schriftwechsel, Spec 20, Bd. 9, January 1930–December 1931.

15. "My present desperation compels me to try everything to sell something. I know that this is the song of artists today—still I don't want to leave it untried, to appeal to you." ["Meine augenblickliche Notlage zwingt mich, alles zu versuchen, um etwas zu verkaufen. Ich weiss, dass es d a s Lied der Künstlerschaft heute ist—dennoch möchte ich es nicht unversucht lassen, an Sie zu appellieren."] Oskar Schlemmer, letter of July 21, 1931 to Justi, SMBPK/ZA, Gen. 10, Bd. 15, 1930–32, Ankäufe.

16. "Hitler's agitation in the years of the Weimar Republic was, that the art trade, art criticism, and the press were under Jewish control, from which the terrible economic situation of nationally minded German artists and those participating in the art business followed." ["Agitation Hitlers in den Jahren der Weimarer Republik war, daß Kunsthandel, Kunstkritik und Presse unter jüdischer Kontrolle seien, woraus die schlechte ökonomische Lage national gesinnter deutscher Künstler und am Kunstbetrieb Beteiligter folge."] Thomas Mathieu, *Kunstauffassungen und Kulturpolitik im Nationalsozialismus, Studien zu Adolf Hitler, Joseph Goebbels, Alfred Rosenberg, Baldur von Schirach, Heinrich Himmler, Albert Speer, Wilhelm Frick* (Saarbrücken: Pfau Verlag, 1997), 37.

17. "For a (certainly great) work of the dead van Gogh one pays over 200,000 Marks. But for living artists nothing is there! May they starve!" ["Für ein (gewiß großartiges) Werk des toten van Gogh zahlt man über zweimalhunderttausend Mark. Für lebende Künstler aber ist nichts da! Mögen sie hungern!"] N.a., *Berlin am Morgen*, "Kunst unterm Knüppel. Preußens Verdienste um die bildenden Künste," April 22, 1932; "The price of 240,000 Marks for Van Gogh's, 'Garten of Daubigny,' is certainly an enormous price when one considers that three years ago the highest sums which had been spent on the first and best Van Goghs fluctuated between 70,000 and 80,000 Marks. But in the last three years the sources of help of the German galleries [read: publicly funded museums] have run so dry that under today's economic conditions it would no longer occur to any gallery director to use hundreds of thousands for a single painting, even if the miracle could happen that a private friend of art would advance the means." ["Der Preis von 240 000 Mark für Van Goghs 'Garten von Daubigny' ist allerdings ein Riesenpreis, wenn man bedenkt, daß vor drei Jahren die höchsten Summen, die man für erste und beste van Goghs angelegt hat, zwischen 70 000 und 80 000 Mark schwankten. Aber in den letzten drei Jahren sind die Hilfsquellen der deutschen Galerien so gründlich versiegt, daß es heute wohl keinem Galerieleiter mehr einfallen dürfte, unter den heutigen wirtschftlichen Verhältnissen Hunderttausende für ein einziges Bild aufzuwenden, selbst wenn das Wunder geschehen könnte, daß ein privater Kunstfreund die Mittel vorstrecken würde."] N.a., *Berliner Tageblatt*, "Die Künstler an den Reichskanzler. Van Gogh und der Ruf nach einer Notverordnung," April 28, 1932.

18. Klein places this early moment of resistance on the part of Scheffler on the occasion of the Erste Deutsche Herbstsalon of 1913. She wrote: "Besides the irritation of the viewing habits of the viewers, the criticism of tradition, of the bourgeois perception of the world inclined toward 'order and security' that was brought to expression through the works was decisive for the negative valuation of this art. . . . Even before the collapse of the bourgeois order had become a matter of historical fact through

the first world war, it had already been realized in the prescient spirit of the artists. In the magazine *Kunst und Künstler* the journalists who shared the expansionist and pro-war conception of the bourgeoisie therefore fought against 'Expressiveness.'" ["Ausschlaggebend für die negativ Bewertung dieser Kunst war neben der Irritation der Sehgewohnheiten des Betrachters auch die durch die Werke zum Ausdruck gebrachte Kritik am herkömmlichen, auf 'Ordnung und Sicherheit' gerichteten, bürgerlichen Weltempfinden. . . . Ehe noch der Zusammenbruch der bürgerlichen Ordnung durch den Ersten Weltkrieg zu einer geschichtskundigen Tatsache geworden war, hatte er sich in dem ahnenden Geist der Künstler bereits vollzogen. In der Zeitschrift *Kunst und Künslter* kämpften daher die Journalisten, die die Auffassung des expansionsfreudigen und kriegsbegeisterten Bürgertums teilten, gegen 'Expressives' an."] Iris Klein, *Vom kosmogonischen zum völkischen Eros: Eine sozialgeschichtliche Analyse bürgerlich-liberaler Kunstkritik in der Zeit von 1917 bis 1936* (Munich: Tuduv, 1991), 23.

19. See Julius Elias, "Berliner Kunstglossen," *Der Tag*, June 11, 1921.

20. "Künstler und Kunthistoriker arbeiten jetzt zusammen mit Literaten, Dichtern, Musikern, dekadenten Kunstenthusiasten, . . . um unter der gemeinsamen Flagge des Expressionismus oder Dadaismus sich 'auszuleben.' Dass sie dabei fast ausnahmslos ins politisch Radikale gelangen, mag nicht schwer genommen werden, aber die wissenschaftlichen Bestrebungen können in dieser gemischten Propagandagesellschaft wahrlich nicht gefördert werden. Und dass ihr Fleiss dadurch angeregt, ihre Moral dadurch gestärkt würde, wird auch niemand zu behaupten wagen. Man wird zweifellos einwenden, die 'Moralität sei Privatsache'; für den Staat, also auch für die Regierung ist sie das aber gewiss nicht. . . . Glaubt man, dass aus diesem Sumpf Deutschlands Erneuerung kommen kann? Soll es hier die Kraft sammeln, um trotz dem Vernichtungsfrieden und trotz aller Fesseln, die uns durch diesen 'Frieden' angelegt sind, sich allmählich wieder zu erholen?" Reprinted in Germania, Abendausgabe, April 22, 1920 as "Ein Notruf Bodes."

21. On these protests against modern art and against Justi's publicity efforts, see Karl Scheffler, *Berliner Museumskrieg*, (Berlin: Bruno Cassirer, 1921), 94, 95.

22. Dr. D., "Blick in die Kunstzeitschriften," *Der Tag*, May 20, 1930; Adolf Behne, "Karl Scheffler und das Kronprinzenpalais," *Die Weltbühne*, June 10, 1930.

23. "The KfdK was but one of many groups advocating völkisch culture. One estimate places twenty such groups in Saxony, Bavaria and Baden alone in 1930." Jonathan Petropoulos, *Art as Politics in the Third Reich* (Chapel Hill: University of North Carolina Press, 1996), 28.

24. See, e.g., Merker's remarks: "(the) *Deutsche Kunstkorrespondenz* lived almost exclusively from the negative attractive power of "degenerate" art and the activity of Mrs. Feistel. The paper was sent for free to around 100 "folkish" organs, who were given the right to reprint [from it] for free (of which the Völkischer Beobachter of the NSDAP made use, among others.)" ["(der)*Deutsche Kunstkorrespondenz* lebte fast ausschliesslich von der negativen Anziehungskraft 'entarteter' Kunst und der Aktivität Frau Feistels. Das Blatt Wurde kostenlos an rund 100 'völkische' Organe erschickt, die zum freien Nachdruck berechtigt waren (wovon u.a. der *Völkische Beobachter* der NSDAP Gebrauch machte.)"] Reinhard Merker, *Die bildenden Künste im Nationalsozialismus: Kulturideologie, Kulturpolitik, Kulturproduktion* (Cologne: DuMont Buchverlag, 1983), 78.

25. "Alle aus öffentlichen Gemäldesammlungen, städtischen Galerien entfernten berühmten Meisterbilder sind an ihren früheren Plätzen wieder aufzuhängen. Aller Kitsch hat zu verschwinden. Gründet eigene Kunstausschüsse und stellt den judendienerischen Scheindeutschen euere Bedingungen! Kunst muss sich von Politik freihalten, deshalb haben alle Personen, die Parteipolitik in die Kunstausschüsse hineintragen, von ihren bisherigen Posten abzutreten." N.a., *Völkischer Beobachter*, "Kampf gegen den Kunstbolschewismus," vol. 64, June 14–15, 1925, repr. in Gerhard Koehler, *Kunstanschauung und Kunstkritik in der nationalsozialistischen Presse: Die Kritik im Feuilleton des "Voelkischen Beobachters" 1920–1932* (Munich: Zentralverlag der NSDAP, Franz Eher Nachf, 1937), 35; see also: "A real artist, who creates timeless artworks, will always be free of (negative) tendencies, that means that for him it is quite unimportant, which political strains are right there. But he will have his roots as a German in Germany . . . the great artist, the great personality stands above everything momentary, as well as above appearances, as above the political situation of every period." ["Ein wirklicher Künstler, der zeitlose Kunstwerke schafft, wird immer tendenzlos sein, d.h. es ist für ihn ganz unwichtig, welche politischen Strömungen gerade da sind. Er wird zwar seine Wurzeln als Deutscher in Deutschland . . . haben . . . der grosse Künstler, die grosse Persönlichkeit steht über allem Augenblicklichen, sowohl über der Erscheinung wie über der politischen Situation jeder Zeit."] Fritz Behne, "Kunst und Tendenz," Völkischer Beobachter 94, (April 24, 1929), repr. in Koehler, 38; "Justi himself has put together an exhibition of newer, supposedly 'German' art from private collections as a payment on account for the coming establishment of this building as a museum. . . . In spite of the fact publicity heralds of these artists continually lied to the public that their art is no longer controversial at all, even more that it is already perceived as a 'classical expression,' it is once more ascertained, that that part of the German people with art expertise rejects this sort of 'art,' that it protests against its designation as 'German art,' and perceives giving up historically meaningful German sites for the showing of such anti-art as robbing them of their dignity." ["Justi hat daselbst im Obergeschoss als Abschlagszahlung auf die kommende Einrichtung dieses Hauses als Museum eine Ausstellung neuerer, angeblich 'Deutscher' Kunst aus Privatbesitz zusammengebracht. . . . Trotzdem der Öffentlichkeit von Reklameherolde dieser Künstler ständig vorgelogen wird, dass ihre Kunst gar nicht mehr umstritten, vielmehr bereits als 'klassischer Ausdruck' empfunden werde, sei wieder einmal festgestellt, dass der kunstverständige Teil des Deutschen Volkes diese Art 'Kunst' ablehnt, sich gegen ihre Bezeichnung als 'Deutsche Kunst' verwahrt und die Hergabe geschichtlich bedeutungsvoller deutscher Stätten zur Vorzeigung solcher Unkunst als eine Entwürdigung empfindet."] Bettina Feistel-Rohmeder, "'Deutsche Kunst' im Berliner Kronprinzenpalais," *Deutsche Kunstkorrespondenz*, 8/9, December 1927–January 1928, repr. in Bettina Feistel-Rohmeder, Im *Terror des Kunstbolschewismus: Urkundensammlung des "Deutschen Kunstberichtes" aus den Jahren 1927–33* (Karlsruhe: C. F. Müller, 1938), 30.

26. Hitler, Adolf, *Mein Kampf*, intro. D. C. Watt, trans. Ralph Manheim (London: Hutchinson, 1969), 234, originally published as *Hitler, Mein Kampf: Eine Abrechnung* (Munich: Zentralverlag der NSDAP, F. Eher Nachf, 1925–27).

27. "The *Deutsche Allgemeine Zeitung* maintains, therefore, (that) the economic crisis is at the same time the expression of an intellectual crisis. Therefore an answer must be found here to more general ethical-political problems. In this sense the demand is always resurfacing, that party propaganda must not only address and reach the people in the social sector. . . . Now an answer must be sought here out of the idealism of the right, and the Germans [must be] made newly familiar with the national train of thought. It appears, however, that this work cannot be performed by the political parties. Therefore our newspapers,

particularly the expressly non-partisan organs, the *Deutsche Allgemeine Zeitung, Deutsche Tageszeitung*, and the *Kreuzzeitung*, hope for not only an improvement in the economic situation, but the fulfillment of these intellectual-spiritual requirements of a national movement." ["Die Deutsche Allgemeine Zeitung stellt daher fest, die Wirtschaftskrise sei zugleich Ausdruck einer Geisteskrise. Hier müsste daher eine Antwort gefunden werden auf allgemeinere ethisch-politische Probleme. In diesem Sinne taucht immer wieder die Forderung auf, die Parteipropaganda müsse das Volk nicht nur auf dem sozialen Sektor ansprechen und erreichen. . . . Hier sollte nun aus dem Idealismus der Rechten eine Antwort gesucht und die Deutschen neu mit nationalen Gedankengängen vertraut gemacht werden. Diese Aufgabe scheint jedoch von den politischen Parteien nicht geleistet werden zu können. Daher erhoffen unsere Zeitungen, zumal die betont parteilosen Organe, Deutsche Allgemeine Zeitung, Deutsche Tageszeitung und Kreuzzeitung, nicht nur eine Besserung der wirtschaftichen Lage, sondern eine Erfüllung dieser geistig-seelischen Bedürfnisse von einer nationalen Bewegung."] Eva Pfeifer, *Das Hitlerbild im Spiegel einiger konservatier Zeitungen in den Jahren 1929–1933* (Heidelberg: Ruprecht-Karl Universität, 1966), 183.

28. "Das Aufkommen dieser neuen Kunst geht den gewaltigen Erschütterungen und Umbildungen der staatlichen und sozialen Welt, die wir nun erlebt haben, kurz voraus, und man empfindet darin eine tiefere Verbindung. Die führenden Künstler der neuen Gesinnung, nicht allein in der Malerei, und die Freunde solcher Kunst, standen vielfach persönlich den neuen Strebungen und Hoffnungen in der Gesamtheit des geistigen und gesellschaftlichen Lebens nahe, sie fühlten ihr Schaffen als Wetterleuchten der Zukunft, die da kommen sollte, die äußerlich und vor allem innerlich das Dasein auf andere Bahnen bringen sollte." Justi, *Neue Kunst: Ein Führer zu den Gemälden der sogenannten Expressionisten in der National-Galerie* (Berlin: Amtliche Veröffentlichungen der National-Galerie im Verlag von Julius Bard, 1921), 5.

29. For example, Theodor Heuss, "Kunst, Revolution, Staatsform: Randbemerkungen," *Deutsche Allgemeine Zeitung,* April 2, 1919.

30. See Christian Gries, "Johannes Molzahn (1892–1965) und der 'Kampf um die Kunst' im Deutschland der Weimarer Republik," PhD diss., University of Augsburg, 1996, 84.

31. "Die Künstler von heute scheinen also doch rechte Kinder ihrer Zeit zu sein. Ja, sie sind es vielleicht allzu sehr und es hat nicht an Kulturkritikern gefehlt, die einige von ihnen als gefährliche Revolutionäre brandmarken mußten, als Formzertrümmerer, die den 'Zerfall der geistigen Welt' mit vorbereitet hätten. So ganz unrecht haben diese Kritiker der modernen Kunst nicht." Hugo Kubsch, "Vom Corinth bis Klee," *Deutschen Tageszeitung,* August 8, 1931.

32. "In opposition to the very 'conservative' exhibition of the Academy, they offer a true reflection of today's anarchy in art, which is further a mirror of the anarchy of life." ["Dafür bietet sie im Gegensatz zu der ganz 'konservativen' Ausstellung der Akademie ein treues Spiegelbild der heutigen Anarchie der Kunst, die wieder ein Spiegel der Anarchie des Lebens ist."] Paul Friedrich, "Die Juryfreie Kunstschau 1923," *Berliner Börsen-Zeitung,* October 1, 1923.

33. "Ich bin Ihnen nicht ganz unbekannt ich möchte Sie nur an Ihre erste Ausstellungsleitung im Kronprinzenpalais erinnern. Sie wissen ja wie das Publikum die Dinge damals aufnahm. Ich war selbst dort und musste beobachten wie der grösste Teil des Publikums gegen die Dinge loszog bis mir die Sache zu bunt wurde und ich mich dagegen auflehnte; unter anderm auch betonte dass das Publikum sich doch eigentlich freuen sollte dass man ihm die Möglichkeit gab Dinge zu sehen die zwar umstritten aber doch absolut neu in ihrer Formung wären und wenigstens doch den Versuch machten sich mit den Dingen auseinander zu setzen anstatt einfach wahllos zu schimpfen." Erich Buchholz, letter of June 14, 1928 to Ludwig Thormaehlen, SMBPK/ZA, ad Spec 20, Bd. 62/1, Ausstellung Nachimpresionistische Kunst aus Berliner Privatbesitz.

34. "Die von den Besuchern auszufüllenden Fragebogen, die jedem beim Eintritt überreicht wurden, ergaben die zweifelsfreie Entscheidung für die Malerei der älteren Schulen und die zum Teil in schroffsten Worten ausgedrückte Ablehnung des 'modernen Wahnsinns.'" Bettina Feistel-Rohmeder, n.t., *Deutsche Kunstkorrespondenz,* 11/12, August–September, 1928, repr. in Feistel-Rohmeder, 38.

35. See Junge on collectors who made money as industrialists, esp. Ida Bienert in Henrike Junge, ed., *Avantgarde und Publikum: Zur Rezeption avantgardistischer Kunst in Deutschland 1905–1933* (Cologne: Böhlau Verlag, 1992); "[Art historians] mostly become trailblazers of the most modern directions of our German art and intermediaries of the same with the buying public. However, since the war this has basically changed; the old, independent collectors remain almost entirely aloof, while the masses of the new rich, in their severe ignorance, namely the feminine part of this society, to whom the new business people and profiteers gladly assault art as mockery and a means of publicity, let themselves be talked into the art of the many 'isms' out of the quest for the new and fashion foolishness. In this way they become the strongest promoters of our unhealthy newest strains in art, especially in visual art." ["(Kunsthistoriker) werden Schrittmacher meist der modernsten Richtungen unserer deutschen Kunst und Vermittler derselben an das kaufende Publikum. Dieses ist aber seit dem Kriege gründlich verändert; die alten, selbständigen Sammler halten sich fast ganz fern, während die Masse der Neureichen in ihrer starken Ahnungslosigkeit, namentlich der weibliche Teil dieser Gesellschaft, dem die neuen Geschäftsleute und Schieber die Kunst als Spott und Reklamemittel gern überfallen, aus Neuerungssucht und Modenarrheit sich die Kunst der vielen 'Ismen' einreden lassen. Sie werden so zu den stärksten Förderern unserer ungesunden neuesten Kunstströmungen, auch in der bildenden Kunst."] Bode.

Art in New Zealand's New National Museum: An Inquiry into the Identity of a Nation

Maria E. Brown

THE MUSEUM OF NEW ZEALAND TE PAPA TONgarewa (MNZ-TPT) opened in Wellington in 1998. It is a multidisciplinary institution that aims to represent New Zealand's environment and cultures.[1] Since its opening, it has faced mixed evaluations. While it has been praised for the number of visitors it has attracted, its critics point to the low informational and scholarly content of its exhibits. The strongest and most frequent criticism has centered on the Museum's approach to the visual arts.

In this chapter I will examine the permanent art exhibitions of the MNZ-TPT, in particular, the complex interactions between cultural, political, and economic factors that determined the multiple and sometimes contradictory roles assigned to art in these exhibitions. I will outline how art was used to serve national interests when the exhibitions functioned as grounds to resolve symbolically the ethnic tensions that prevailed during the period when the Museum was designed. This entails special consideration of the intersection between discourses on national identity and the display strategies of postcolonial art exhibitions. All these determinants played a part in the rationale for committing public funds to the MNZ-TPT project, as well as changes in economic policies toward cultural consumption. I suggest that it is fundamental to take into account the interdependence of these economic and cultural agendas to understand how the Museum prioritized its multiple goals.

THE REPRESENTATION OF NATIONAL IDENTITY

The representation of a national identity accepted by all the groups that inhabit a given territory is always problematic. The problem is compounded in ex-colonial countries where ethnic groups with diverse cultural traditions have been obliged to coexist under the rule of colonial powers, which founded these countries upon the dispossession of the indigenous inhabitants, leaving deep social divisions.[2] Such divisions threaten the functioning and stability of modern nation states that rely for their viability not on explicit coercive powers, but on inducing the effective cooperation of their citizens. In this context, it is in the state's interest to support the idea of a unified nation endowed with a distinct identity that reflects the aspirations of all social groups.

The recent wave of new national museums in excolonies such as Canada, New Zealand, and Australia confirms that visual representations are powerful means for the assertion of national identity, or in Benedict Anderson's terms, for the creation of "imagined communities."[3] In New Zealand a new museum constituted an opportunity to construct the image of a bicultural nation, one in which Maori, the indigenous people of New Zealand, and the descendants of the British colonizers live in harmony. The symbolism of art was deemed one of the most significant devices for the articulation of this ideal.

The planning of the Museum began in the 1980s, a time of political changes implemented to manage the social tensions created by ethnic conflicts arising from the country's colonization process.[4] New Zealand became a British colony in 1840 when a number of Maori chiefs and a representative of the British monarch signed the Treaty of Waitangi; in return, Maori were granted British citizenship and the protection of all their possessions. Despite these terms, Maori had lost most of their land by the end of the nineteenth century, a significant proportion through illegal confiscations.[5] Since then, with their economic base nearly destroyed, many Maori have occupied a secondary place in New Zealand society, reflected in low incomes, low levels of education, and, until recently, the devaluation of their culture. Commonly held views among the European settlers characterized the culture of the indigenous people either as an obstacle for the development of the nation, or as a curious relic from the past.[6] The Maori language was in danger of disappearing by the late 1970s, under the pressure of an assimilation policy pursued by the New Zealand government for more than one hundred years.[7]

The decade of the 1970s, however, also marked a turning point; it saw the emergence of a generation of very vocal Maori leaders who denounced the long history of domination of their people by the population of British descent. They demanded respect for their property rights and culture.[8] The most radical were prepared to call for full Maori sovereignty.[9] While massive demonstrations in support of these claims intensified throughout the 1980s, the reactions among New Zealanders of European background were far from uniform, ranging from total rejection of Maori demands to committed support for them.[10] Such divisions added to the climate of social unrest. One response of the state to these pressures was the passing of legislation establishing the Treaty of Waitangi as the founding document of New Zealand. Thus Maori were recognized as equal partners of the British settlers in the creation of the nation state. Additionally, a bicultural policy was adopted with the intention of ensuring that Maori culture and interests would be considered in the running of official agencies.[11]

The project to build the MNZ-TPT was closely related to these measures. It took form between 1985 and 1989 just after the Treaty legislation was completed and the policy on biculturalism formulated. The concept adopted for the Museum reads: "The Museum of New Zealand Te Papa Tongarewa will be a national museum that powerfully expresses the total culture of New Zealand. It will express the bicultural nature of the country, recognising the mana and significance of each of the two mainstreams of tradition and cultural heritage and providing the means for each to contribute effectively to a statement of the nation's identity."[12] This concept structures the space of the MNZ-TPT, forming the base of the iconographic program that articulates its fundamental message.[13] The visitors who reach the Museum's main floor face a bifurcated arrangement that images the bicultural nation. When they emerge from the elevators, or from the central staircase, they see a huge facsimile of the Treaty of Waitangi in front of them. To their left, an impressive waharoa (gate) signals the entrance to the displays of Maori art and culture. To their right, is the area dedicated to the art and culture of the descendants of British settlers.[14]

Art historian Carol Duncan argues that art museums are places for the enactment of rituals that transmit social values.[15] The MNZ-TPT, with its iconographic program, is an excellent example of a public space for the dispensation of civic lessons. Chief among those lessons is the definition of a national identity as constituted by two equally important cultures, Maori and European. Despite its apparent harmony, this union is not easily accepted by a society with a history of colonial domination and racial discrimination. However, once colonialism becomes indefensible, either the state recognizes the sovereignty of the ethnic groups it formerly dominated, or it obtains their support by accommodating their demands for equal participation in the civic life of the nation. In New Zealand the latter path has been followed; it has been labeled "biculturalism," which is one of the corporate principles of the MNZ-TPT.[16]

Museums are one of the organs of modern civil society, and as such are ideally placed to disseminate information that fashions identity and contributes to "produce social commitments."[17] It is not surprising, then, that this museum project was undertaken during a time of serious social conflicts in the 1980s. According to William Tramposch, former Director of Museum Resources at the MNZ-TPT, "the New Zealand government has supported the museum and accepted that museums and culture can help alleviate the pernicious conditions caused by racism and prejudice."[18]

MANA WHENUA: MAORI ART

Art has been chosen as the principal means by which Maori culture is represented and reevaluated at the MNZ-TPT. Mana Whenua, the Maori exhibit hall, is the most spectacular part of the museum. The predominant mode of display in this section is typical of many art galleries. Objects are singled out by dramatic lighting, and there is enough space around them to allow for concentrated contemplation of their formal features, presenting these objects as valuable works of art, as "masterpieces." Although some glass cases resemble the traditional displays found in ethnographic museums, they are few, and do not dominate this area.

The practice of staging art exhibitions to improve the standing of a country, or people, is related to the belief that art is one of the indicators of the degree of a nation's level of "civilization."[19] The practice was well established by the late nineteenth century, when art exhibitions were important elements of the international expositions characteristic of the epoch. Those events had as one of their multiple goals the demonstration of the state of development of the participating nations.[20] A connection was assumed between artistic excellence—as defined by the European elites—and intellectual sophistication. Somehow this assumption seems to continue today in the phenomenon that Brian Wallis calls "cultural diplomacy."[21] Wallis refers to art exhibitions from a particular country that circulate internationally with the intention of transforming negative stereotypes into positive national images.[22] In the case of the MNZ-TPT, the packaging of Maori culture is done primarily for domestic consumption, although the attraction of foreign visitors was also contemplated in the planning of the institution.

By the time the museum project was approved, the concentration on the aesthetic aspect of Maori objects had already proven to be an effective mechanism to present Maori culture in a positive light, disciplined by museum display and art historical recognition. This concentration on formal qualities—identified with modernity, cultural sophistication, and market values—was a feature of the exhibition Te Maori, organized by New Zealand museums and Maori groups in cooperation with the Metropolitan Museum of Art.[23] It opened in New York in 1984 and went on to St. Louis, San Francisco, and Chicago. According to Douglas Newton, curator at the Metropolitan, the show received great public acclaim on its tour of the United States.[24] Its focus on Maori objects as art is underlined by the comments of Ian White, director of the de Young Museum in San Francisco, who reportedly described the works in the exhibit as "world class" sculptures.[25] Similarly, critic Charles Miedzinski found many of the works outstanding, but referred to one in particular—*Uenuku*—as a "highly abstract and mysterious form" that for him was "a living remainder of what great art aspires to become."[26]

In New Zealand, Te Maori was hailed as a success for the nation. "It was a time for all New Zealanders to stand tall, to feel a not-often-allowed national pride in seeing our art alongside that of some of the world's greatest civilisations," asserted one of the local organizers of the show.[27] Undoubtedly, it did much to change the perception of Maori material culture among New Zealanders. On this point, Bernie Kernot, an expert on Maori art, wrote, "The publicity [around *Te Maori*] seemed to shatter our complacency because as a nation we had always regarded the carvings more as curios than art," and he added, "the New Zealand public suddenly woke up to the reality that those old familiar carvings were being acclaimed by the big out-there world as high art."[28] Back from the United States, Te Maori traveled to the country's four major cities, where record attendances demonstrated that it was a source of pride for Maori and non-Maori alike.[29] Amid the social tensions, mentioned earlier, the show created a sense of unity. Several of the Museum's planning documents refer to Te Maori as an example of the outcomes sought by the project.[30]

The art exhibitions in the MNZ-TPT function also as statements of a new nationalist discourse that tries to distance itself from the ideology of colonialism. From the 1950s, the art galleries of the country began to focus on representing a unique New Zealand identity, but they almost exclusively exhibited art made in the European tradition. Maori material culture, like the material culture of many indigenous peoples around the world, was seen in museums devoted mostly to natural history. Anthropologist Michael Ames claims that assigning the label "art" is a political act and that to exclude the arts of native peoples from art galleries is "to collaborate in the suppression of their identity and their continued exclusion from the full life of a country."[31] The political statement of the MNZ-TPT is particularly poignant, considering that it replaces the former National Gallery and National Museum, which many associated with colonial domination.[32] The two institutions shared one building, the Museum occupying the ground floor and exhibiting Maori objects as part of its ethnographic collections. An imposing staircase led to the National Art Gallery and its collections of objects labeled "fine art." For most of the sixty years of its existence, the National Art Gallery collected and displayed mainly British art and art made by New Zealanders of European origin. The new museum presents Maori and European art on the same level.

One could even argue that the new museum reverses the earlier situation by displaying Maori artifacts as fine art, and the artifacts produced by non-Maori as ethnographic documents. Indeed, one of the recurrent themes in the controversies surrounding the MNZ-TPT has been precisely that it privileges Maori art, both in the area assigned to it and in its mode of display. The very central place accorded to Maori art in the new museum can be seen as part of New Zealand's efforts to solve a "postcolonial" crisis precipitated by the collapse of colonialism. Left without ideological support, the descendants of the colonizers faced feelings of guilt and questions about their right to occupy appropriated lands.[33] To an extent, the narratives in the MNZ-TPT respond to their search for ways of reaffirming the legitimacy of their presence in the country.[34] The museological narratives fulfill their aspirations when they tell the story of a unified nation that was born with the first Maori settlements, nearly eight hundred years before the colonial period. In this extended history the arrival of the British settlers is celebrated as part of a smooth progression that seems to lead, naturally, to the nation that we know today.[35]

Thus Maori art appears to be of the first phase of the history of all New Zealanders. Maori artistic achievements are now the achievements of the nation, even those that took place centuries before the British settlers brought with them the concept of "nation." This has not gone unnoticed among some Maori. For instance, Maori scholar Paul Tapsell has criticized the way the MNZ-TPT uses Maori symbols and concepts to pursue the state's political agenda.[36] For him, this is a misappropriation that "demonstrates that the Museum's biculturalism is in reality no more than a monoculturally governed vehicle for the 'Maorinization' of post-colonial New Zealand."[37]

The Maori exhibit hall, however, should not be seen as expressing solely the social ideals of the descendants of the European settlers. Rather, it is the outcome of a negotiation process in which many Maori took a leading role. Unsurprisingly, Mana Whenua does not represent the views of all Maori, for Maori are a complex and evolving ethnic formation, and all its members do not share a single vision of their identity. Nevertheless, the exhibition reflects one line of Maori views, since its development was left almost completely in the hands of Maori staff who consulted Maori groups from all over New Zealand. Undoubtedly, the agenda(s) of those groups influenced the resulting exhibition. It is probably their influence to deploy current art gallery conventions (dramatic lighting, objects spaced far apart, and aesthetic narrative) to convey the image of a people with a long and refined artistic tradition. This representation endorsed by a national institution both reflects and adds to the weight of Maori political demands.

Commendable as the intentions of the Maori exhibit hall may be, the results are, nonetheless, problematic. Arguably, the display of Maori works is so successful in foregrounding their aesthetic qualities that it obscures their cultural significance. The Maori gallery achieves its goal of imbuing Maori material culture with the prestige of fine art, paradoxically, at the expense of adequate information that would otherwise promote much needed cross-cultural understanding. A more disturbing effect of this focus on art is that it helps the Museum's narratives gloss over important events in the history it purports to tell. The rupture and violence caused by the colonial occupation do not have a place in this celebratory narrative, for example, even though they marked the "historical" beginning of the present nation state. Sociologist Ben Dibley points out that the MNZ-TPT project articulates "a discursive reorganisation of the national past to meet political and cultural aspirations of the present."[38] A reorganization of this nature avoids confronting current Maori grievances originating in colonialism and its legacy by excluding the evidence of old conflicts, still affecting the present. Thus, it allows the construction of a past in line with today's bicultural agenda, which seeks to assert the unity of a nation that embraces the cultures of the country's two main ethnic groups.

PARADE: THE ART OF THE SETTLERS

I would like to consider now the other side of the bicultural equation, as proposed by New Zealand's national museum during its first three years of operation. Facing the Maori exhibit hall during that period, the visitor found Parade, the area dedicated to the art and culture of European Zealanders. Fully independent teams planned each of the two permanent art exhibitions, with strikingly different results. Whereas Mana Whenua has received much praise, Parade provoked such criticism that it was closed in May 2001.[39] The main cause of the discontent, I would suggest, can be traced back to its rather conflicting goals.

Parade was basically an exhibition designed to tell a story of cultural change in New Zealand from the arrival of the British settlers to the present day. The exhibition's planning documents made clear that the fundamental function of works of art displayed in this area was to illustrate events in that story.[40] But art was not the only protagonist. Objects from the former national art collections and social history collections were combined as manifestations of the human creativity that drives cultural change. One found there, for example, oil paintings, domestic appliances, prints, furniture, pottery, sculptures, textiles, a yacht, and plastic figurines.

One of Parade's objectives was to convince its visitors that all these cultural manifestations were equally valuable.[41] This notion is central to discourses on national identity that present New Zealand as an egalitarian society, where the fine arts, and other intellectual pursuits, are not above more practical endeavors. The presence of a yacht in the exhibition underscored one of the tenets of this view, namely, that industrial design is an aesthetic activity as creative as the production of fine art. For many years, supporters of these views deplored the practices of the National Art Gallery, the predecessor of the present Museum. The former institution focused primarily on the fine arts. It followed practices common among art museums that tend to enhance the perceived prestige of the objects on display, such as sparse hanging, which favors concentrated contemplation of each object. The designers of Parade broke decidedly with those practices. They juxtaposed crafts, fine art, and objects of everyday use; nothing was set apart for special aestheticized contemplation.

Parade's crowded exhibits not only offered a supposedly egalitarian representation of a range of objects, they also addressed the criticism of art museums emphasizing formal qualities to the detriment of context. The emphasis on formal qualities, according to some critics, promotes the distorting view that art is better appreciated on its own terms, disconnected from the sociopolitical events that shape the world outside art galleries.[42] Certainly, the presentation of art in a cultural context can be an enriching experience. Yet, this approach can result in very complex exhibits, which require comprehensive interpretative strategies to convey the wealth of information that visitors need to understand objects in a wide cultural context.[43]

In Parade's case, the search for popular appeal worked against the provision of such levels of information. Most museums strive to achieve a balance between popular appeal and their scholarly, educational functions. For the MNZ-TPT popular appeal has an overriding priority; visitor attendance is the criterion most frequently invoked to assess its performance. Of course, a large participation rate in the consumption of museum services is an important outcome for a project funded with public resources. But for this new museum a large number of visitors was not only important, they also became absolutely essential for its survival.

In this set of conflicting demands, the museum's complex role in a national political economy of culture emerges. By the time the project entered its final design phase, New Zealand had a new conservative government that espoused the "free market" ideology. Its economic policy treated art, higher education, and cultural activities in general more as private goods than as public good.[44] In other words, such services were considered of benefit mainly to their individual users. A report commissioned by the MNZ-TPT on admission charges explains this succinctly: "The market view states that museum visitors enjoy the educational and exhibition outputs of a museum exclusively, and, as the direct beneficiary [*sic*] should be expected to pay for this service. These outputs are realised as private goods that can be assigned a commodity value, and the marketing of which offers scope for generating revenue."[45] Under this conception there is no justification for the use of public funds to subsidize private consumption. In the case of the MNZ-TPT, however, it was difficult to support the argument that its activities created benefits exclusively for its individual users, rather than for the community as a whole, since one of the Museum's fundamental goals was the fostering of a sense of national identity and pride, presumably, a public good.[46]

The government that inherited the project agreed to provide most of the funds necessary for its completion, but it required the Museum to recover a substantial proportion of its operating costs from visitors and other private sources.[47] This decision came in 1994, after more than nine years of planning.[48] Understandably, it had a major impact on an already complex design process. The Museum had to transform itself into a business-like organization with corporate principles that include being "commercially positive."[49] Nevertheless, most of the funding for the Museum building still came from government sources and certain conditions were imposed on the institution. The Museum's Board of Governance was charged with the mission of attracting wider audiences than the normally highly educated public that frequents most museums.[50] So if the Museum was to be an investment for the communication of important social messages, it had to be an effective mechanism, one capable of transmitting those messages to all levels of society. The Board, then, confronted the problem of ensuring access to the Museum for as large a proportion of the population as possible, while generating revenue from its visitors. A marketing study, commissioned by the Board to assess the implications of admission charges, concluded that an admission fee could reduce the number of potential visitors to such an extent that it was likely to affect adversely not only the total revenue opportunities of the Museum, but also its ability to fulfill its mission to serve a wide audience.[51]

In light of these findings, the Museum planners decided not to charge admission fees. To reach the imposed financial goals, they opted instead for a combination of sponsorship deals and commercial enterprises. This means that visitors pay once they are inside the Museum. They are offered a range of options in which to spend their money. Examples of such options include special exhibitions, guided tours, audio guides, floor maps, thrill rides, restaurants, and stores. Evidently, the success of these revenue-generating operations depends crucially on visitor numbers. Similarly, visitor numbers are critical in the competitive market for corporate sponsorship, given that the incentives for the sponsors of the Museum increase with the size of the audience to which their brands are exposed.

The concern with popular appeal was evident throughout Parade, as part of the rationale for displaying a seemingly incomprehensible mixture of objects. The exhibition aimed at making all visitors feel comfortable, interested, and included by presenting objects to which many could relate, even the uninitiated.[52] One of the MNZ-TPT's press releases described Parade as a place where "High culture meets the stuff of everyday—the good, the bad, and the undecided—in a wonderful walk through New Zealand's rich and quirky visual history."[53] The exhibition's title was an invitation to "join the parade and make art happen."[54] Moreover, the Museum actively tried to dispel the notion that the appreciation of art requires specialized knowledge: Everybody has an opinion on art and all opinions are equally valid, the visitor was told. Statements such as "Different people like different things" and "What you value depends on who you are" were scattered throughout Parade, with no further explanation.[55] These populist strategies met with widespread disapproval, sparking intense debates that did not stop until the exhibition was eventually closed. For example, art historian Jenny Harper wrote of the MNZ-TPT: "The museum too often becomes puerile in its efforts to be populist."[56] Whereas art philosopher Denis Dutton charged this museum with "trying never to exceed its own dumbed-down conception of public taste,"[57] critic Theodore Dalrymple characterized it as an "institutional exemplar of the lowest common denominator turned into official cultural policy."[58]

At any rate, Parade's populist slant preempted the accusations of elitism often leveled at art museums. Many empirical studies have demonstrated that art museums are visited, mainly, by a highly educated public.[59] As a consequence, low-income groups are normally underrepresented among museum visitors. Some critics, notably sociologist Pierre Bourdieu, have even charged art museums with reinforcing arbitrary social distinctions.[60] An institution with a public mission, such as the MNZ-TPT, can hardly afford to be associated with elitism. So it put in place display strategies that sought to overcome those accusations and to draw a representative cross-section of the population. But unfortunately, in Parade's case this was done in a rather simplistic manner, trying to avoid a didactic tone, which its designers believed could make the exhibition less appealing, less popular. Information was kept to a minimum despite the number of complex messages they intended to transmit. One of those messages, for instance, was the view that taste and social class are interrelated in such a way that the most affluent classes maintain control of the criteria sanctioning artistic quality and taste. Another message was the conception of art as a phenomenon that exceeds formal concerns, and is linked to developments in other aspects of social life such as moral values, patterns of consumption, and technology, to name just a few. The conjunction of this level of complexity and minimum information produced a confusing exhibition that visitors confronted without any significant guidance, generating such a controversy about Parade's lack of informative depth that the government commissioned an independent review of the Museum's presentation of the national art collections and the exhibition was eventually closed.[61]

The roles of art at the MNZ-TPT have been varied and sometimes contradictory. This museum celebrates the nation and intends to foster a sense of national unity, but the nation's colonial past contains important episodes that both contradict such unity and can hardly be celebrated. Focusing on Maori art helped the Museum to construct a continuous and unproblematic history of the nation. In its attempts to overcome the divisions left by colonialism, the institution foregrounds the formal aspect of art as an indicator of Maori cultural sophistication. However, on its European side, the MNZ-TPT represented a "national" culture that rejected as elitist the association of art with sophistication. Furthermore, on that part of the museum the formal qualities of works of art were downplayed; outside an aesthetic narrative, they took the role of symbols of national characteristics. Works of art, displayed without information that may have prompted reflection, also functioned as complements to the range of amusement options on offer in a museum that acts as a commercial enterprise, maximizing revenue by catering to the entertainment needs of its customers.

The variety of these roles reflects complexities faced by public institutions that aim to define national identity in a master narrative in which art plays a crucial part of the public sphere, in this case, a site of social unrest brought in the wake of the collapse of colonialism and the concomitant rise of Maori activism. A national agenda determined that art serves national interest by modifying the discourse on nationhood that had become untenable under the new political circumstances. In the nation defined by the MNZ-TPT, Maori and the descendants of the European settlers are equal partners, while until recently relations between them were marked by the inequalities resulting from colonial domination. The Museum, then, operates as a compensatory space. Its permanent art exhibitions are the most important means of balancing—if only symbolically—power relations between these groups.

On the Maori side, the prestige of fine art is invoked to reevaluate the culture that has occupied a subordinate position. Meanwhile, in the initial exhibition dedicated to the culture of the New Zealanders of European ancestry, which is now closed, art gallery conventions were carefully avoided. In a sense, this strategy rejected one of the fundamental pillars of the colonial enterprise, namely that the European settlers were heirs to the most refined civilization. Instead, the ethnographical mode of display, which debunked the notion of fine art, reinforced the popular myth that they had created a classless society.[62] The rhetoric of the art exhibitions of the MNZ-TPT was instrumental also in demonstrating to the institution's audience the potential benefits of the bicultural message. The unified nation, as proposed by these exhibitions, was enriched by the contributions of two distinct, but supposedly complementary members.

The Museum enforced this complementarity by placing side by side the cultural representations of the country's two main ethnic groups, which emphasized certain qualities attributed to each group. Aesthetic refinement and spirituality are salient features of the Maori exhibit hall, whereas the exhibition of the art and culture of the European settlers emphasized technological change and ingenuity. Within this narrative, Maori provided the nation's spirituality and the European settlers its drive for material development. This image, however, undermined the Museum's intended message of equality, since it may have been seen as a justification for the blatant economic disparities between the two groups. The continuous history of the nation's artistic achievements, as represented at the MNZ-TPT, may also help the descendants of the European settlers face the uncertainties of a postcolonial crisis. In a way, this narrative legitimizes their presence in the country by inserting their history into an unproblematic progression that culminates in the nation that they have fashioned. At the same time, the narrative allows the settlers to claim a distinct cultural identity that originates in their new country in the Pacific, rather than in a distant motherland.

These complex messages were disrupted, and their reception complicated, however, by display strategies lacking in informative depth. Changes in economic policies toward cultural activities affected the planning of the Museum, in particular, the level and scholarly quality of the information that it provides. The museum concept was developed by a government that saw art and other cultural activities as public goods. That is, as services that deliver benefits for society as a whole. By contrast, the administration that inherited the project treated cultural activities as private goods. From that perspective, there is no justification to subsidize individual enjoyment with public money. Consequently, funding was reduced and the institution was forced to operate as a commercial enterprise. To compete in the entertainment market, the MNZ-TPT developed strategies that focus on visitor numbers. For the most part these strategies have been successful; the Museum has become, primarily, a popular attraction that in its first two years of operation received more than four million visitors.[63] However, this has been achieved at the price of deemphasizing the scholarly and informative side of its art exhibitions. Moreover, the construction of a popular and celebratory narrative of nationhood required the erasure of crucial parts of New Zealand's colonial history. Those selective omissions preclude not only a sustained critique of colonialism in the past, but also, and perhaps more importantly, of its consequences in the present.

NOTES

1. *Museum of New Zealand Te Papa Tongarewa Annual Report 1999–2000* (Wellington, NZ: Museum of New Zealand Te Papa Tongarewa, 2000), 1.

2. Colonialism can hardly be considered a phenomenon with uniform characteristics in all the countries where it occurred. Nicholas Thomas argues that it acquired distinct characteristics in places where European settlers eventually outnumbered the indigenous population. He calls these territories "settler countries," in contrast to countries such as India or South Africa where this was not the case. In settler countries colonization cannot end with the restitution of sovereignty to the original inhabitants; this is at the base of many of New Zealand's ethnic conflicts. For a discussion of the culture of settler countries in the South Pacific, see Nicholas Thomas, *Possessions: Indigenous Art/Colonial Culture* (London: Thames and Hudson, 1999) and *Colonialism's Culture: Anthropology, Travel and Government* (Cambridge: Polity Press, 1994).

3. For Anderson, "imagined communities" is not the opposite of "real communities." He contends, rightly I believe, that except for very small communities, all communities are created by ties that their members apprehend intellectually, i.e., in their imagination. See Benedict Anderson, *Imagined Communities*, 6–7.

4. For a discussion of New Zealand's ethnic conflicts since the colonial period, see David Pearson, *A Dream Deferred: The Origins of Ethnic Conflict in New Zealand* (Wellington, NZ: Allen and Unwin, 1990).

5. Maori owned 66,400,000 acres of land in 1840 when the Treaty of Waitangi was signed. By 1891 they owned approximately 11,000,000 acres and only 3,000,000 acres in 1975. Ruth Naumann, Lyn Harrison, and Te Kaponga Winiata, *Te Mana o Te Tiriti: The Living Treaty* (1990; Auckland, NZ: New House Publishers, 1997), 47 and 55.

6. Pearson, 38–72. See also Leonard Bell, *Colonial Constructs: European Images of Maori 1840–1914* (Auckland, NZ: Auckland University Press, 1992), 205–7.

7. Ranginui Walker, *Ka Whawhai Tonu Matou: Struggle Without End* (Auckland, NZ: Penguin Books, 1990), 146–48.

8. Pearson, 190–97, and Walker, *Ka Whawhai Tonu Matou*, 209–19.

9. Donna Awatere, *Maori Sovereignty* (Auckland, NZ: Broadsheet, 1984), 10.

10. The Maori word *Pakeha* is sometimes used to refer to New Zealanders of European origin, in particular to those of British origin. However, not all the members of these groups accept the term's political connotations. Those who refer to themselves as *Pakeha* tend to be part of the fraction that supports Maori demands. The problematic application of this term reflects both the divisions within the majority of the population regarding Maori claims and the difficulties of attributing a single identity to such a heterogeneous group as New Zealand's white population. To avoid confusion, I am not using the term here. See Paul Spoonley, "Constructing Ourselves: The Post-Colonial Politics of Pakeha," in *Justice and Identity: Antipodean Practices*, ed. Margaret Wilson and AnnaYeatman (Wellington, NZ: Bridget Williams Books, 1995), 96–115.

11. Wilson and Yeatman, introduction, *Justice and Identity*, xv.

12. Museum of New Zealand. Project Development Board, *A Concept for the Museum of New Zealand Te Papa Tongarewa* (Wellington, NZ: Museum of New Zealand, 1989), 1. Mana is a Maori word with connotations of prestige and power. It is not italicized in the original to emphasize that Maori is an official language of New Zealand.

13. I draw upon Carol Duncan and Alan Wallach's seminal discussion of the museum experience as a ritual guided by an iconographic program. See Carol Duncan and Alan Wallach, "The Museum of Modern Art as Late Capitalist Ritual: An Iconographic Analysis," *Marxist Perspectives* 1, no. 4 (1978), 28–51.

14. There were a few works by European artists of nationalities other than British in this exhibition, but for the most part they referred to New Zealand as a British colony, and not to the artists' country of origin. This part of the Museum was in the process of refurbishment at the time of writing. Originally, four artworks from the 1980s and 1990s marked its entrance.

15. Carol Duncan, *Civilizing Rituals: Inside Public Art Museums* (London: Routledge, 1995), 5–6.

16. The origin of the terms "biculturalism" and "bicultural" is traceable to the ethnic conflicts of the 1980s between Maori and European New Zealanders. The country, however, is multicultural rather than bicultural. In the 1996 census, about 10 percent of the population identified themselves with Asian or Pacific Island ethnic groups. Statistics New Zealand, *New Zealand Official Yearbook 1997* (Wellington, NZ: Government Printer, 1997), 124.

17. Ivan Karp, introduction, *Museums and Communities: The Politics of Public Culture*, ed. Ivan Karp, Christine Mullen Kreamer, and Steven D. Lavine (Washington, DC: Smithsonian Institution Press, 1992), 5.

18. William Tramposch, "Exact Imagining: The Museum as a Journey," *Museum News* 77, no. 2 (1998), 49.

19. See Maria Brown, "Representing the Body of a Nation: The Art Exhibitions of New Zealand's National Museum," *Third Text* 16, no. 3 (2002), 285–294, and Brown "Rhetorical Concepts and the Stories of the Nation," *Travelling Concepts III: Memory, Narrative, Image*, ed. Nancy Pedri (Amsterdam: ASCA Press, 2003), 203–15.

20. Tony Bennett, *The Birth of the Museum: History, Theory, Politics* (London: Routledge, 1995), 67.

21. Brian Wallis, "Selling Nations: International Exhibitions and Cultural Diplomacy," in *Museum Culture: Histories, Discourses, Spectacles*, ed. Daniel J. Sherman and Irit Rogoff (London: Routledge, 1994), 265–67.

22. An example of this type of exhibition was the show Mexico: Splendors of Thirty Centuries that toured the United States in the early 1990s, when Mexico was being evaluated as a potential partner in the NAFTA (Wallis, 272–74).

23. Sidney Moko Mead, ed., *Te Maori: Maori Art from New Zealand Collections* (Auckland, NZ: Heinemann; New York: American Federation of Arts, 1984).

24. Douglas Newton, "Old Wines in New Bottles, and the Reverse," in *Museums and the Making of "Ourselves": The Roles of Objects in National Identity*, ed. F. E. S. Kaplan (London: Leicester University Press, 1994), 285.

25. Jerry Carroll, "Maori Magic at the de Young," *San Francisco Chronicle*, July 10, 1985, qtd. in Hirini (Sidney) Moko Mead, *Magnificent Te Maori: Te Maori Whakahirahira* (Auckland, NZ: Heinemann, 1986), 79.

26. Charles Miedzinski, "The Art of the Maori: An Undiminished Power," *Artweek*, August 24, 1985, qtd. in Mead, *Magnificent Te Maori*, 81.

27. Mattie Wall, "Te Hokinga Mai," *Art Galleries and Museums Association of New Zealand Journal* 17, no. 3 (1986), 18.

28. Bernie Kernot, "Te Maori Te Hokinga Mai: Some Reflections," *Art Galleries and Museums Association of New Zealand Journal* 18, no. 2 (1987), 3.

29. Newton, 285.

30. Examples of these documents are Project Development Team for the National Museum of New Zealand/Te Marae Taonga o Aotearoa, *Nga Taonga o te Motu: Te Marae Taonga o Aotearoa. Treasures of the Nation: National Museum of New Zealand: A Plan for Development* (Wellington: Department of Internal Affairs, 1985), 7; and Joanne C. Horgan, *Museum of New Zealand: Report of the Interviews* (Boston: E. Verner John, 1988), 23–25.

31. Michael M. Ames, "Biculturalism in Exhibitions," *Museum Anthropology* 15, no. 2 (1991), 8.

32. Project Development Team, 13.

33. If colonialism took different forms in each country where it occurred, the subsequent postcolonial experiences are also diverse. For a discussion of the postcolonial crisis in New Zealand, see Simon During, "Postmodernism or Postcolonialism?" *Landfall* 39 (1985), 366–80.

34. Ben Dibley, "Museum, Native, Nation: Museological Narratives and Postcolonial National Identity Formation," Master's thesis, University of Auckland, 1996, 6–7.

35. For a discussion of narratives of nationhood in museums, see Bennett, *Birth of the Museum*, 148–53.

36. Paul Tapsell, "Taonga: A Tribal Response to Museums," PhD diss., University of Oxford, 1998, 211–15.

37. Ibid., 215.

38. Dibley, 5.

39. At the time of writing, a new exhibition of visual culture created by the European settlers is planned for the place formerly occupied by Parade. It had a separate art section and is entitled Made in New Zealand. For an in-depth analysis of Parade, see Paul Williams, "Parade: Reformulating Art and Identity at Te Papa Museum of New Zealand," *Open Museum Journal* 3 (May 2001): 1–28.

40. Museum of New Zealand Te Papa Tongarewa, *The Exchange Concept Design*, Archives of the MNZ-TPT, 1995, 5–8. The Exchange was the working title of the exhibition that eventually opened as Parade.

41. Museum of New Zealand Te Papa Tongarewa, *Parade—90% Developed Design Part One A*, Archives of the MNZ-TPT, 1996, 7.

42. See, e.g., Douglas Crimp, *On the Museum's Ruins* (Cambridge, MA: MIT Press, 1993), 236–81; and Brian O'Doherty, *Inside the White Cube: The Ideology of the Gallery Space* (Santa Monica, CA: Lapis, 1986), 14–17.

43. Philip Wright, "The Quality of Visitors' Experience in Art Museums," in *The New Museology*, ed. Peter Vergo (London: Reaktion Books, 1989), 124–32.

44. For a discussion of the economic terms "private goods" versus "public good" and how they apply to museum services, see Don Fullerton, "Tax Policy Towards Art Museums," in *The Economics of Art Museums*, ed. Martin Feldstein (Chicago: University of Chicago Press, 1991), 199–201; and Christopher T. Duffy, "The Rationale for Public Funding of a National Museum," in *Cultural Economics*, ed. Ruth Towse and Abdul Khakee (Berlin: Springer, 1992), 37–48.

45. Museum of New Zealand Te Papa Tongarewa, *Admission Charges: The Issues: Audience New Zealand, Identity New Zealand*, comp. Mark Lindsay (Wellington, NZ: Museum of New Zealand, 1994), 18.

46. Horgan, 9–10.

47. *Museum of New Zealand Te Papa Tongarewa Annual Report 1996–1997* (Wellington, NZ: Museum of New Zealand, 1997), 6; and Tramposch, "Exact Imagining," 47.

48. William Tramposch, "Te Papa: Reinventing the Museum," *Museum Management and Curatorship* 17 (1998), 342–43.

49. *Museum of New Zealand Te Papa Tongarewa Annual Report 1998* (Wellington, NZ: Museum of New Zealand, 1998), 2.

50. *Museum of New Zealand Te Papa Tongarewa Annual Report 1998–1999* (Wellington, NZ: Museum of New Zealand, 1999), 2.

51. MNZ-TPT, *Admission Charges*, 36–37.

52. MNZ-TPT, *The Exchange-Concept Design*, 9.

53. Museum of New Zealand Te Papa Tongarewa, "Press Kit: Parade," *Te Papa Our Place*, July 3, 2001, http:// tepapa.govt.nz/ communications/press-releases/pr-parade.html/

54. MNZ-TPT, "Parade," 21.

55. "Debate poles" provided a number of conflicting judgments on some artworks. The authors of the statements ranged from high school students to recognized art critics. The Museum did not give any opinion on such views, nor did it attempt to help its visitors to make sense of them.

56. Jenny Harper, "For the Sake of Your Art," *Dominion (Wellington, NZ)*, June 2, 1999, 10.

57. Denis Dutton, "New National Museum Resembles a Junk Shop," *New Zealand Herald (Auckland, NZ)*, May 21, 1998, A15.

58. Theodore Dalrymple, "An Amusement Arcade Masquerading as a Museum," *New Statesman*, February 12, 1999, 33.

59. For a review of a number of empirical studies conducted in art museums in the United States and Europe, see J. Mark Davidson Schuster, "The Public Interest in the Art Museum's Public," in *Art in Museums*, ed. Susan Pearce (London: Athlone, 1995), 109–42. The situation in New Zealand is assessed in McDermott Miller Ltd, *Non-users of Museums in New Zealand: A Survey and Guide for Museums* (Wellington, NZ: Museum Directors Federation of Aotearoa New Zealand, 1996).

60. Pierre Bourdieu and Alain Darbel, *The Love of Art: European Art Museums and Their Public*, trans. Caroline Beattie and Nick Merriman (Cambridge: Polity Press, 1991), 109–12.

61. The review team concluded that Parade's interpretative strategies needed improvement. New Zealand Ministry for Culture and Heritage, *Report of Specific Issues Relating to the Museum of New Zealand Te Papa Tongarewa*, by Des Griffin, Chris Saines, and T. L. R. Wilson, June 16, 2000. It is fair to mention that the lack of informative depth was more a problem of presentation and ease of access than a problem of total absence of information. The Museum has a library and electronic databases that visitors can use, however, these are in areas completely separate from the exhibition areas.

62. For an overview of social myths in New Zealand, see Claudia Bell, *Inventing New Zealand: Everyday Myths of Pakeha Identity* (Auckland: Penguin Books, 1996).

63. *MNZ-TPT Annual Report 1999–2000*, 3.

III
Public Monuments and the Public Sphere

Giovanni Antolini's *Foro Bonaparte*: Constitution of Public Space in Napoleonic Milan

Joachim Homann

THIS CHAPTER EXAMINES THE MOST AMBITIOUS MILANESE plan for public architecture from the Napoleonic period: if realized, the proposed public buildings, monuments, and squares would have radically redefined public space in Milan. The public space of the new, postrevolutionary society constituted itself not only as an architectonically shaped place where citizens interacted, but also as a new system of political and economic relations between people and their social institutions. Consequently, public monuments were considered as tools for the political education of the citizens and for the economic improvement of the working class. Since public life in Milan then depended on the goodwill of the French, the organization of public space was always motivated by the goal of visually defining its relation to France. Dedications of built and planned public monuments played an important part within the diplomatic relation to Napoleon and the French administration.

An analysis of the complex functions of public architecture in Napoleonic Milan includes elements of a specific political economy developed at that time. Public architecture can be characterized with the following model, in which the political economy of art consists of two different levels. First, prizes for material and salaries for artists linked art production, like any other production, to economic circulation, itself based on the exchange of money. Second, art was, as symbolic capital, involved in symbolic exchanges between people, institutions, and even nations. These exchanges, in turn, created values and identities for the donors and recipients. Within this exchange of gifts, the value of public art and monuments was not defined through the stimulation of the circulation of money; it was, rather, rooted in the accumulation—and destruction of—capital. Symbolic values were only to be gained if capital would be withdrawn from the circulation. In this essay, I show how the conflict between both levels, the economic and the symbolic, became productive for the definition of public space in Napoleonic Milan.

This model is indebted to philosopher Boris Groys's analysis of two aspects of cultural economy which coexist in a productive tension. He distinguishes a commercially motivated, profane level of production and consumption from a "neo-sacred" second level based on sacrifices, aggressions, and occupations. Using Marcel Mauss' *Essai sur le don* (1925) and Georges Bataille's interpretation of the potlatch, Groys argues that calculated sacrifices play a critical role in the formation of cultural value systems, so cultural economy cannot be fully understood if described only in terms of the marketplace, since it encompasses older and more comprehensive economic relations.[1] In her introduction Julie Codell similarly interprets gifting not as "anti-economic" but as complementary to the market, and I want to further understand this interdependence within the political economy of art by focusing on urban planning in Napoleonic Milan.

Located in the fertile plain of the river Po in northern Italy, the city of Milan served during the eighteenth century as a political, economical, and military center for the Habsburgian domination of Lombardy. In 1796–97 the French army invaded northern Italy to expel the Austrians and force them to accept a peace treaty which would shift the balance of power in Europe. In this campaign the French army was far more successful under its general, Napoleon Bonaparte, than the Parisian Directory had expected.[2] The government was unable to give orders to the military because there was not yet a prepared strategy for what to do with the occupied territories. Bonaparte seized the opportunity and created new, Italian sister republics of the French Republic by himself, among them the *Cisalpina* (Cisalpine Republic), with the capital in Milan. To win the support of the Italian people he promised to bring freedom, civil rights, and political independence.[3] In the proceeding "revolution from above," implemented by government officials and the French military, privileges of the church and the aristocracy were abandoned, men of all classes and religions were granted equal rights, and private property was guaranteed. Through these politics, Bonaparte earned the sympathy of many Italian democrats, or as they called themselves, patriots. Leftist intellectuals came from all over Italy to join the local Jacobins and the French army in their attempt to form a new society. Support also came from liberal members of the local elite, among them aristocrats and members of the developing middle class, who saw advantages in the liberalization of the market.[4] Both parties, radical Jacobins and more moderate liberals, supported Bonaparte for different reasons, but for the moment the French general could overlook the conflicts between these interest groups. What counted for him was that he could report to Paris that the Italian people accepted the French as liberators.[5] Bonaparte strengthened his influence in Paris enormously through his Italian success.

Since the Austro-Russian Coalition was able to reconquer northern Italy in 1799, when the attention of the French army was bound in Egypt, the French had to start a second campaign in 1800. Napoleon presented himself again as a military genius. His troops conquered the northern peninsula for a second time and he reestablished the Cisalpine Republic. Although he declared the Republic would be democratic, Bonaparte did not give any power to its bodies. Instead, he chose all of its representatives and thereby ensured that he was elected president. The officially independent state was in reality only a satellite of the French Republic. The provisional government, built by three men who had made political careers in the first Jacobin years of the *Cisalpina*, found itself confronted with a chaotic political and economic situation (Hearder, 24–27). Giovanni Sommariva, Francesco Visconti, and Francesco Ruga managed to improve the financial situation of the *Cisalpina*, despite hefty contributions, through the organization of the successful *Banca di Napoleone*. The economy was strong for some years, partly because of Milan's geographical location close to France. The capital's population grew.[6] The members of the provisional government were eager to define the status of Milan as a democratic capital of an independent republic. This political goal was as important as the economical strategy, since the *Cisalpina* could only survive with the support of its people against inner and outer enemies. It was crucial to remind Bonaparte to fulfill his promises of the *Cisalpina's* independence.[7]

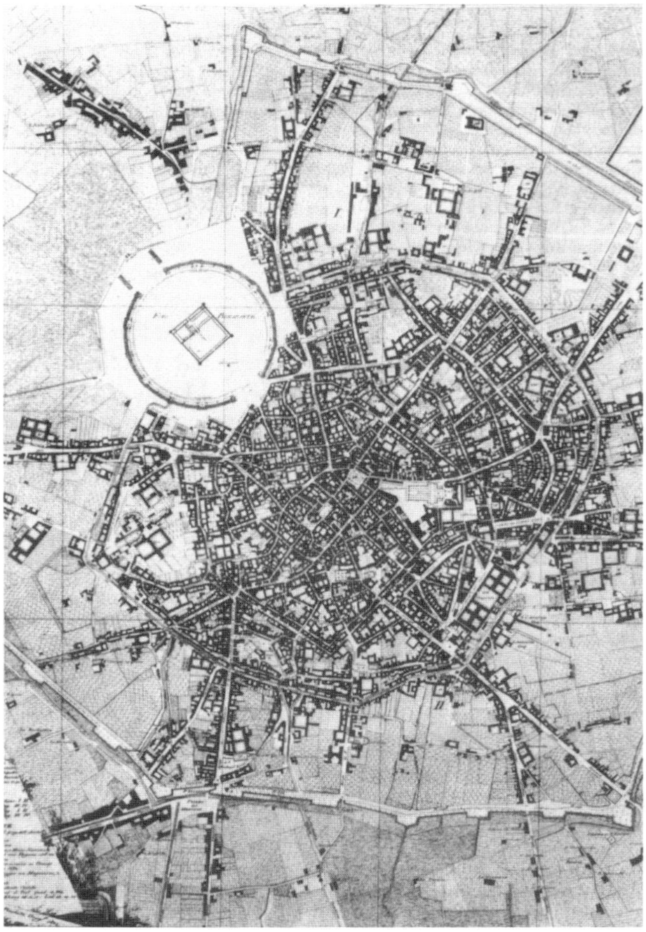

17. Giacomo Pinchetti (drawing) and Giuseppe Caniani (etching), *Milan City Map*, Milan 1801, original scale 1:6200, 79 × 56.5 cm, etching, Civica Raccolta delle Stampe Achille Bertarelli, Milan. Photograph from Saporetti, Milan, published with permission from Milano, Civica Raccolta delle Stampe Achille Bertarelli. Pinchetti's map shows Antolini's circular *Foro Bonaparte* (never built) in the city's northwestern area, on the site of the then partly demolished *Castello Sforzesco*. The *Lazaretto*, a former quarantine used in the Napoleonic period for political festivals, is visible in the Northeast as an expansive structure in form of a square.

The most ambitious architectural projects of the *Cisalpina* were developed for the site of the *Castello Sforzesco*, which dominated the northern part of the city with its huge star-shaped bastions, until Bonaparte for strategic reasons ordered the breakdown of its ramparts in June of 1800 (*Milan City Map*, Figure 17). Suddenly there was a vast empty space close to the city center, which immediately provoked several proposals for its development. This huge expanse functioned as a projection screen for the politicians' dreams of Milan's political and economic future. Pragmatic proposals by the national architect Luigi Canonica and the local building contractor Giuseppe Antonio Cassina were rejected by the government.[8] Although Canonica suggested dedicating the new suburb to Napoleon as *Città Bonaparte*, and although he planned a square decorated with a triumphal arch commemorating the victories of the French army in Italy, his proposal was not appreciated, since in the eyes of the members of the local government it was not inspired enough by the new postrevolutionary conditions.

Canonica saw the area's economic potential and wanted to encourage economic development by private business, public administration, and the military.[9] In his plan, the unification of two canals would be of outstanding importance for the Milanese economy and would create conditions for the formation of a new commercial center. Canonica developed the outlines for a public initiative to stimulate private investment. Reduced prices for plots in attractive locations and reduced taxes could be used to win the investors' interest for the development schemes of the administration. Public expenses would return through the disposal of the land and building materials, which would be obtained during the demolition of the fortification. The strong economic aspects, which dominated Canonica's development plan, influenced later suggestions.

Even more pragmatic was the proposal of the building contractor Cassina. Together with his offer to prepare the ground and to organize the building activities, the experienced businessman handed in a calculation of all costs and a time schedule, which promised the completion by the end of 1802. Although he included in his plans a round piazza for public celebrations, located between the barracks and the inner city, his proposal was turned down because the politicians worried it would serve the contractor's financial interests, not the city's beauty.[10]

Giovanni Battista Sommariva encouraged the architect Giovanni Antolini (1753–1841), who had come to Milan one year before as a member of the hydraulics commission, to draw more imaginative plans.[11] Born and trained in the province of Bologna, Antolini had spent twenty formative years in Rome, where he published archeological treatises, carried out hydraulic work, and produced several architectural designs for members of the European nobility. For a short time he went to Faenza to build mansions for the Jacobin patron Count Achille Laderchi and a triumphal arch for the city. In Faenza he also made a proposal for the development of a whole new suburb, which was thought to reflect the conditions of a democratic society.[12] Later, in Milan, he was a two-time winner of competitions initiated by the governing committee with designs for memorial pyramids and columns to honor the French army and its general Napoleon Bonaparte. As Antolini wrote to a friend, he was highly motivated to come up with a more demanding plan, which would win him not only a prize, but a pension.[13]

In December, 1800, Giovanni Antonio Antolini presented his proposal to the governing committee of the Cisalpine Republic, drawing praise as well as criticism by an officially appointed board of experts as well as independent competitors (*View of the Bonaparte Forum*, Figure 18).[14] Antolini partly dealt with the same questions Canonica had to face, such as financing construction work and attracting businesses to a new economic center, but he framed them quite differently. He understood the socioeconomic dimensions of construction works in a positive way and wanted to work with them to form a new society. The buildings should be constructed with an effort that would unify the nation, and when they were finished, they should provide the city and the republic with an economic and political center suitable for a democratic and capitalistic society. He also wanted his architecture to be more than useful. It should prove that the Italian nation still could produce monuments of antique grandeur. Both aspects, the functional and the representative, found their unification in the building type of the forum, which was described in Diderot's and d'Alembert's *Encyclopédie* and in contemporary architecture theory as the ideal public space of the Greek and Roman cities. For these reasons, he presented his plans for the site of the castle as an *Economic and Political Plan for the Foro Bonaparte*.[15]

In his proposal he reminded the government of its duty to strengthen the economy especially in times of war, when, as he said, civil commerce was interrupted and the price of goods was high: "The best way to ensure the circulation of money is through commerce," he wrote, "or through the erection of new buildings." The architect explained how construction could stimulate economic growth. The money spent for construction work would enable the "needy classes" to take part in consumption and, as a result, the money would start to circulate in town. "When the bricklayer works, all the arts work: when the artisans and shopkeepers earn, calamity is unknown, money is spent, commerce has its part, and everyone is content." In a later, published version of his plans, Antolini enriched his argument by directly addressing the artists. He thought of them when he designed the *Foro Bonaparte*, Antolini wrote, because he wanted to provide them with a possibility to work and to earn money in times of common unemployment: "When money is circulated among the most useful class of people [the artists], it can strike fire in many minds and give vigor to many arms that, at present, for lack of employment, languish in inertia and demoralization."[16]

His plans for the Foro Bonaparte showed a model of perfect circulation, as if Antolini wanted to illustrate his political economic ideas (*General Plan of the Foro Bonaparte to Be Constructed in Milan*, Figure 19). Obviously he was interested not only in the functional organization of space, but also in the demonstration of its functions to the visitors. With the following description of the Foro Bonaparte, which emulates the same order as Antolini's own paper, I explain how Antolini tried to serve the economic and political needs of the rising republic. Antolini's strategy can be discussed as the transformation of public space into a display of the primary forces that constituted the *Cisalpina*: the people, the economy, and its political and cultural institutions.

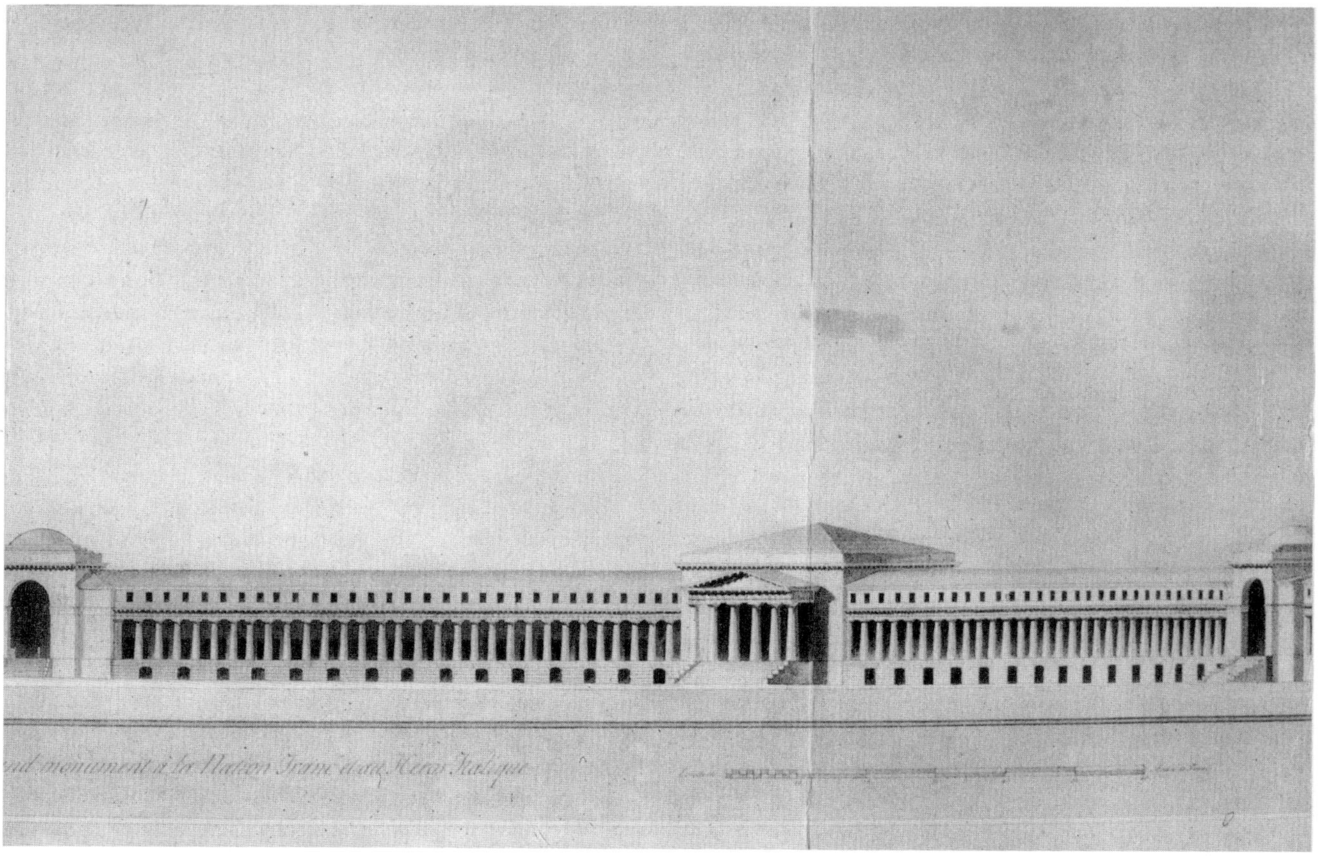

18. Giovanni Antonio Antolini, *View of the Bonaparte Forum, Presupposing the Total Demolition of the Castle and the Construction on the Same Site of a Large Monument of the French Nation and to Bonaparte*, detail, 1801, ink and watercolor on paper, 39.2 × 168.7 cm, Paris, Archives Nationales, Cartes et Plans. Photograph published with permission from Archivio FMR, Bologna.

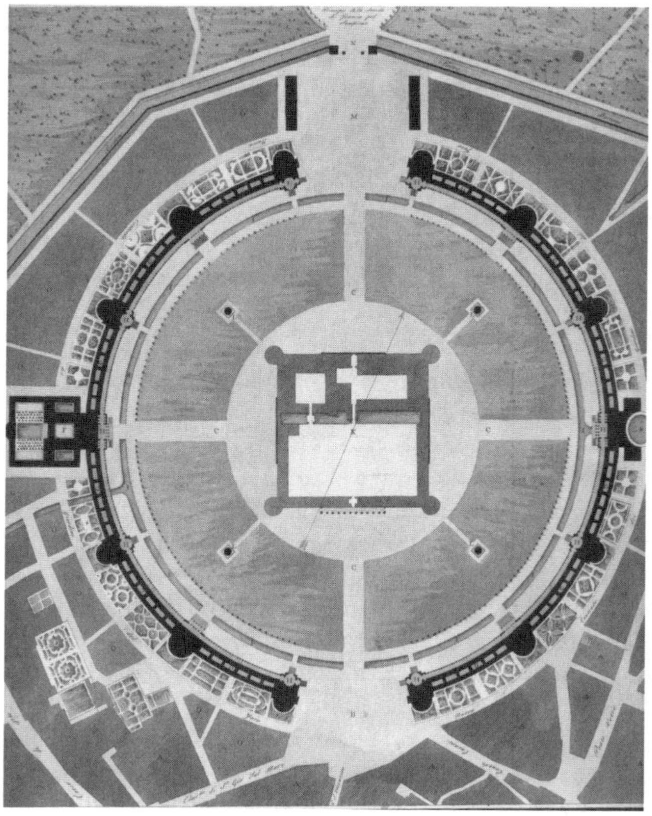

19. Giovanni Antonio Antolini, *General Plan of the Bonaparte Forum to be Constructed in Milan*, ink and watercolor, c. 1801–05, c. 75 × 45 cm, Paris, Bibliothèque Nationale de France, Cabinet des Estampes. Photograph published with permission from Archivio FMR, Bologna.

The economic exchange between the city and its territory and the city and the countries north of the Alps would have been presented as a spectacle. Antolini proposed to build a whole new city center at the site of the Castello Sforzesco. He envisioned a huge circle, which would consist of public, commercial, and private buildings, connected through a continuous colonnade. Only two spacious gaps would open the vast square to the city and to the country. The traffic from the northeast, including all the travelers from France who arrived via the new Simplon road, would have to enter the square, as if it were an arena. To guarantee a dynamic economy, Antolini wanted to enforce a circular canal, placed within the larger circle of the buildings. The canals would be linked, as Canonica already had suggested, to the most important waterways in the area. It would not only make the Foro Bonaparte a center for commerce, but would also, at first, simplify the transportation of construction materials. The necessary excavation work and the construction of banks, bridges, and outlets should be carried out, as Antolini wrote, by both militia and prisoners condemned to forced labor. This was probably the cheapest way to do it, and it had a pedagogical effect as well. Right at the beginning of the construction work it was shown to the Milanese people that the society could use everyone and that behavior against the common good was not tolerated. The canal was the first element to be realized under the guidance of the government, but the government was not in charge of the whole development project.

Antolini proposed strategies to finance the building activities that suited their different functions. Eight assembly halls were to be used and constructed by the city's eight districts. Their supervisors had to manage the financing by selling the old meeting places and by collecting taxes. These officials had to organize the construction of the assembly halls following the plans of the government. The building process was decentralized probably not for practical, but for political reasons.

Antolini wanted to institutionalize what was practiced as a festival. During the first Cisalpine Republic, public festivals often took place as parades of the districts' representatives—for example, children, young couples, and old people—who had to meet in their neighborhoods and were picked up by members of the national guard. They were guided to a meeting point where they were brought together with people from all the other areas of the city. From there they marched to the city center, usually to the square in front of the cathedral, to attend public ceremonies. The Jacobin government of the *triennio rivoluzionario* (Revolutionary Three-Year Period) visualized, through these mass spectacles, the belief in a democratic system based in public consensus, not in political representation.[17] With the assembly halls for the districts centered around one public square, the society was shown as a sum of its parts, where every citizen had a place and could either make his or her voice heard or be reached through public education. Governmental residences or offices for the administration were not integrated in the *Foro Bonaparte*. As institutions of a representative society they did not belong to Antolini's ideal of the democratic society to come. The government was indispensable in the building process, however. The two buildings facing each other on the most prominent axis in the middle of the two colonnades, the thermal baths and the customs office, were both to be erected by the government.

The public baths were located in the most complex and expensive building of the *Foro*, and Antolini hoped that the profits from sold tickets would reimburse the construction expenses. He was so confident that he thought it would be worthwhile offering this project to private investors. As an incentive, Antolini recommended that any such party would receive the site for free and would be rewarded with tax reductions on the construction materials. There was only one stipulation: The investor had to follow the original construction plans. Although there were no actual architectural precedents for this building type in modern times, baths were described in contemporary medical studies as necessary for the public welfare. Since it was a nation's genuine interest to have healthy citizens, it had to provide sports facilities to strengthen peoples' bodies. Architects could answer the doctors' admonitions with references to the Greek gymnasiums and Roman baths. The Greek sports grounds were well known through Vitruvius's descriptions, and the Roman *thermae* (baths) had been studied for centuries as examples for the organization of architectural space in general.[18] Academic students of architecture in Rome were familiar with them and learned to design *thermae* for academic competitions. As Antolini wrote in a later explanation of his plans for the *Foro Bonaparte*, he did not copy the luxurious Roman models from the imperial period for he believed that they pampered the people, instead of educating them. Instead, his goal was to invent a new type of bath through the combination of Greek and Roman schemes and the addition of new elements like individual bathtubs, which would be adequate for contemporary hygienic needs. In his *Economic and Political Plan*, Antolini expressed his belief that physical and moral life is inseparable and he ensured that his *Foro Bonaparte* would have "both these objects in view."[19]

The second of the two "major constructions of public interest" was the customs house. According to Antolini, it was to be constructed by the government on commission from the Department of Finance. The city was still a special tax zone, protected by a wall against smugglers, and all imported or exported goods had to be checked by the customs officers. Customs was the most important source of wealth for the public treasury, Antolini reported, and as such, deserved to be placed prominently, facing the thermae. The canal would run directly through the custom house. On exiting the house, it would form a circle around the forum, and would feed into the thermae swimming pools. The circulation of water could be seen as a metaphor for the economy, which was founded in the circulation of goods and money. The water flowing from the customs house to the thermae would therefore symbolize the unity of economic circulation and the physical well-being of the people. Again Antolini found a solution for a practical need, and used it in a didactic way. The underlying hydraulic concept of the forum was understandable as an explanation of the society's new functioning.

Other public buildings had specific purposes. The stock exchange building was to be assigned to the traders (until then such a commercial center did not exist in Milan and, as Antolini mentioned in his later explanation, there was not even an Italian word for it). The traders, in turn, would build and use it. Referring to ancient models, Antolini introduced three new building types on behalf of the nation, to suit functions related to a new civic religion. The theater was thought of as a democratic institution to raise the citizens' morals. People were to attend moral plays, which were secular services. The Pantheon was dedicated to the remembrance of important men after their death. Honored men would be immortalized through portrait busts and sculptures, and not with monuments in churches, as it had been common practice until now. The museum presented precious products of art and nature. Instead of looking at altarpieces presenting religious wonders, visitors would marvel at artworks and precious products of the natural world, showing the creative potential of nature and the skills of mankind. With the theater, Pantheon, and museum, Antolini would have filled the gaps left through the exclusion of churches from the *Foro* and from future society in general. The different functions of religious spaces were to be transferred into public institutions.

These various public buildings were connected through twelve colonnades, named after the twelve departments of the *Cisalpina*, which visualized the unity of the *inseparable* republic, as it was called in official documents. Antolini wrote that the colonnades, with their spaces for shops, storehouses, and private homes, should be constructed by merchants and all other citizens. The investors would again receive the construction site for free and would be exempt from taxes on construction materials. This would potentially allow every member of society to participate in the building process, which was thought to be an act of unification and homogenization of the citizens. All shops and houses would have been designed alike both in decoration and size. Neither the differences between spatial needs of various businesses nor the distinctions between more or less financially strong investors were reflected in this vision, which was nourished by the conviction that the market would create a strong, homogeneous middle class.

Colonnades were the favorite features of public architecture at that time. They were useful as a protection against the sun and bad weather, and they were appreciated as embellishments of singular beauty for city squares and public buildings. Antolini's interest in this building type was even more multilayered. He was fond of colonnades, for they allowed the *Foro* to function as a theatrical space: The colonnades would provide masses of people with a good viewpoint from which to watch public ceremonies or the spectacle of everyday life in the huge square.

Here I focus on three different aspects of Antolini's concept of public space. First, I argue that Antolini could have referred to a famous city-renewal program in nearby Padua as a model. Second, by analyzing Antolini's formal choices, I emphasize that the normative character of the construction process was to be reflected in rigid architecture, thought to educate the people through strong sensual impressions. Third, I suggest that public space itself was defined as a space of simultaneous control through perfect visibility. These three observations will hopefully lead to an understanding of Antolini's architecture as an educational arrangement that improves the identification of the people with their role in their society's political economy.

Antolini was most likely inspired by a famous project of regeneration of public space for the benefit of the local economy: Antonio Memmo's Paduan *Prato della Valle* (Figure 20).[20] Here, a former damp meadow close to the city center was drained through a circular canal and developed as a new economic center. The *Prato della Valle* was used as a splendid setting for trade fairs and as an elegant park for the pleasure and education of the inhabitants and their guests. Although he was familiar with the most advanced theories of architecture in his time, Memmo was not a trained architect; he was the governor of

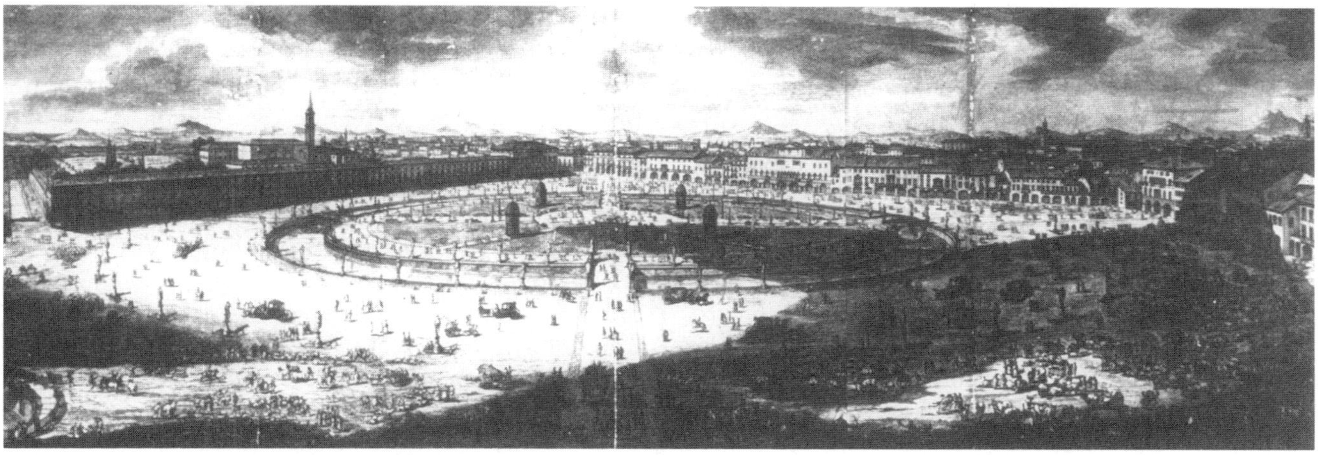

20. Francesco Piranesi, after Subleyras, *Prato della Valle*, c. 1786, etching, London, British Museum. Photograph from Joseph Rykwert, *The First Moderns: The Architects of the Eighteenth Century*, 4th ed., Cambridge, MA: MIT University Press, pp. 320–21. Published with permission from MIT University Press and © Copyright the Trustees of The British Museum.

Padua on behalf of the Venetian republic.[21] As such, he was an expert on economic stimulation through the reorganization of public space. His project was remarkable, because Memmo found a way to attract private capital to fund his public project. The erection of eighty-eight statues of city benefactors, for instance, which gave the square the appearance of an open air museum, was funded mainly by donations. When Memmo published his ideas in a monograph (officially written by his secretary), he illustrated it with a huge panorama view of the *Prato della Valle* from the workshop of Piranesi, at that time owned by Giovanni Piranesi's son.[22] This panorama was an idealized version of the project, depicting the *Prato* from such a perspective that it was impossible to discern if the park was a circle or an oval (it was in reality an oval). Aldo Rossi paid tribute to the *Prato della Valle* as the only authentic experience of successful coordination in eighteenth-century Italian urbanism.[23] Although Antolini did not refer to Memmo's plans in his texts, his fantasy obviously was stimulated by them, and he tried to answer Memmo's problems by a radicalization of the *Prato's* concept.

Carroll W. Westfall's iconographic investigation of the meaning of the *Ordine Dorica* in Antolini's *Foro* revealed that the Doric, or heroic, order was appropriate for a forum dedicated to the hero Napoleon Bonaparte.[24] In addition, the use of the Doric order was not only guided by interests in decorum and style, but, above all, in strategies of rationalization of space. The Doric order was considered a rational one, which helped to systematize space and show the principles of its construction. Antolini's contemporary, Quatremère de Quincy, wrote that since it relied on the simplest principles for construction and exposed them visually, the Doric order could be seen as the perfection of construction in Greek architecture.[25] For Antolini, too, the Doric order was rooted in natural principles of creation. In the plan for a suburb in Faenza, discussed earlier, he had shown how a row of Doric columns could turn into an alley of trees. In Milan he demonstrated the rationality of the Doric order with the use of basic geometric forms. The functional organization of space dominated his interest. In his point of view, architecture was defined through necessity. Beauty resulted from functionality.[26]

The circle-shaped city square, although it was not yet commonly used in Italy, was the favorite form in French-inspired city planning in Europe. To combine the circle—the simplest and most universal of all geometric forms—with the purified Doric order must have given Antolini the feeling of having finally reached the *point zero* of public architecture. The Italian architect did not fill this pure form with emotional content, as Boullée and Ledoux did, when they attributed expressions to their plans and tried to stimulate specific sentiments in their viewers.[27] The step from Blondel's doctrine of the building's *charactère* to the poetics of the so-called revolutionary architects was not taken by Antolini. In his design, the façade of the *thermae* was the same as that of the customs house. They were not distinguished by architectural elements, but by the sculpture.

What was more important to Antolini than the association of building types with specific emotions was that the visitor could grasp the whole complex at first glance. The visitor should be overwhelmed by the beauty and vastness of the construction, without being distracted by the details. In a book published as early as 1785, Antolini had explained the dependency of the sensation of beauty on the geometrical simplification of architectural structures. Only the perception of simple forms would stimulate the human nerves intensely. The perfect object would be simple, would unify all its parts, and would be accessible for the viewer through one sensation. Disparately combined entities produced, as Antolini wrote, a monstrous idea.[28] These remarks were made concerning architecture in general, but described the concept for the *Foro Bonaparte* in so far as Antolini used geometric forms in a simple and intelligible arrangement. They even help clarify why Antolini was so interested in the circle: There were no hidden corners or overlapping volumes in a complex organized in a circle. Every part of the architecture was ideally exposed to the eye. One glance could include the entire circumference, stimulating a strong and pure sensation, which was thought to function as an impulse for the moral elevation of the viewer.

Antolini's ideal, which motivated the plans for the forum, lay at the vanishing point of nature and of reason and was therefore untouched by history, place, individuality, or any other distinction. Its ambition was absolute. The quoted declaration of principles was given at the end of his essay on the topic of the *Ordine Dorico*. The appeal for purification and simplification of architecture was still based on the idea that Doric architecture could be the model of this process. Antolini's architecture was not free enough to become poetic in the sense of the designs of Ledoux and Boullée; it remained imitative. Antolini's choices were not rhetorically justified; terms of decorum did not play a decisive role, but they were thought to be compelling with sensual and rational immediacy. The strong normative attitude of the *Foro*, which was expressed in its functional display, was also the driving force of the development of its architectural form.

The understanding of architecture's power, mediated through its visual perception, allowed him to develop a concept for the education of the viewer through architecture. As Julie Codell points out in the introduction to this volume, "state-produced or commissioned art may replicate or express state policies programmatically, or conflict with state ideals and policies from within the framework and funding of political economy" (15). In the case of the Foro Bonaparte, state ideals were propagated, but ultimately the project collided with the funding policies of the political economy in continuous change. To illustrate the normative aspect of Antolini's architecture, I would like to explain the "male" character of Antolini's planned buildings as the attempt to form ideal citizens. There was no question for Antolini that the vocabulary of his architecture, gained in a process of formal reduction following the principles of reason and nature, would bear a distinctive, masculine character. For Vitruvius the Doric column represents the male body, since for him the relation of the foot to the male body was reproduced in the relation between the column's diameter and its height (1 to 6). The Ionic column was considered "female" because of its slender proportions. In addition, Vitruvius described the unadorned Doric column as nude and the fluted Ionic one as dressed with women's garments.[29] The public, Doric space Antolini created was a male space, which matched perfectly the rhetoric of the time. The return to ancient virtues, as it was conjured in Bonaparte's and in his politicians' speeches, was avowedly tantamount to a restitution of virility.

To understand that public spaces had to be masculine by definition, Antolini only had to read the guidelines of Francesco Milizia for the renewal of the *magnificenza civile*. Milizia defined the ancient ideal of splendid public squares and buildings as a combination of the "male" and the "great" to reach the "sublime." His remarks described Antolini's *Foro* very well. As criteria for male architecture he named: a simple composition, decent forms without an overload of decoration, right angles, and clearly lined parts that caused great shadows. Magnificent architecture should consist of only a few monumental parts—the sublime in architecture was constructed through the masculine and the magnificent. To illustrate his thesis he compared the emotional effect of architecture to the impression of magnificence aroused by the uniformity of a parading regiment. The crowd of the visitors, taken individually, may have been dressed in a much fancier manner than the soldiers, but without the regiment's order and scale. Magnificence, he concluded, was nothing other than order on a large scale, existing without affluence and extravagance. Comparing the effect of successful public architecture with that of parading soldiers, Milizia led his readers to understand that military values, like uniformity and discipline, also counted in public architecture.[30] Architectural and military magnificence served equally to make an impression on the people and to guide them to masculinity and grandeur. This motivation obviously stood behind Antolini's severe concept. With the ideal of magnificent public place he inherited and sustained the legacy of the unquestioned exclusion of the feminine.

In his designs Antolini defined public space literally as the space needed by the people to come together and constitute the nation. The public festivals of the French army in Italy provided a model for this emphasis of mass gatherings. When Bonaparte founded the Cisalpine Republic in 1797 he organized

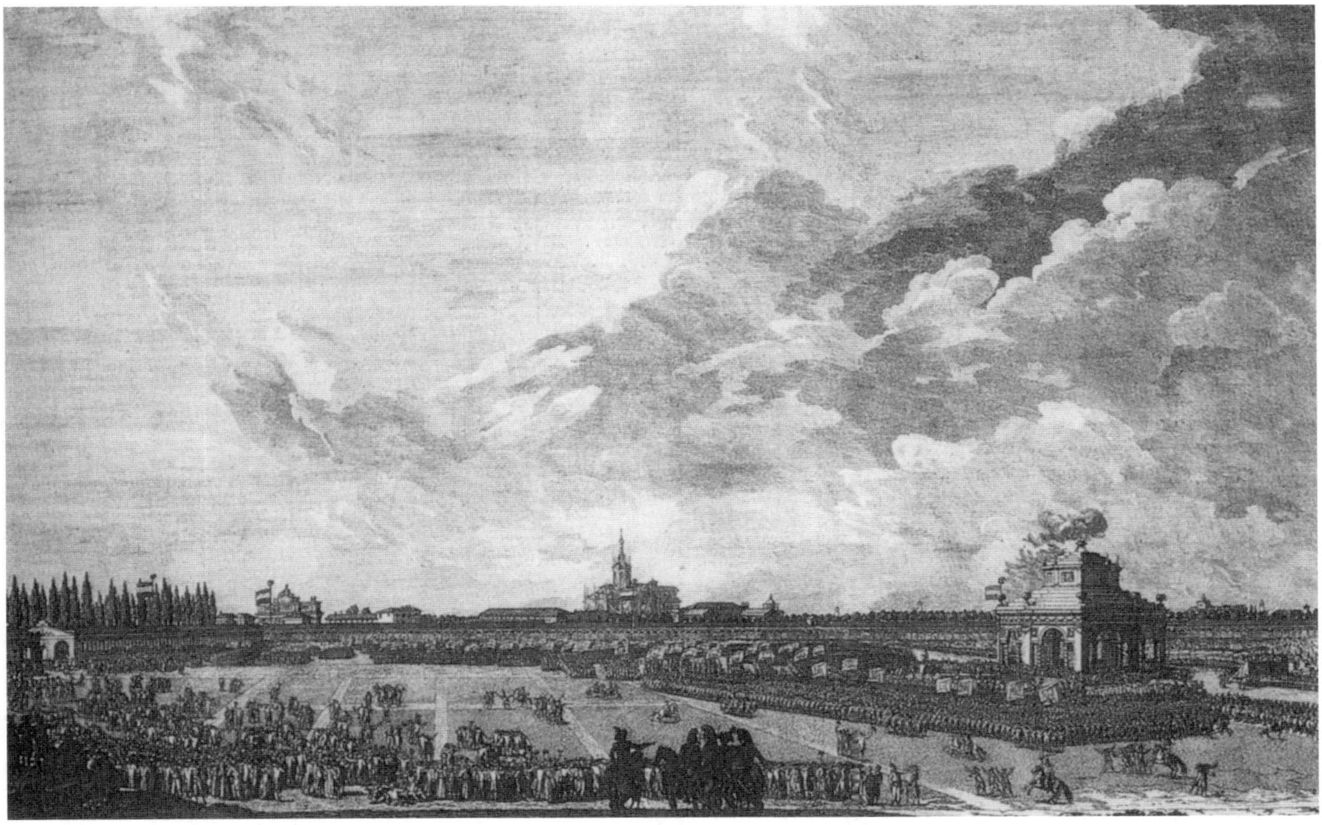

21. Domenico Aspari, *The Festival of the Federation of the Cisalpine Republic*, c. 1797, etching, Milan, Museo del Risorgimento (photograph: Raccolte Bertarelli). Published with permission from Biblioteca delle Civiche Raccolte Storiche, Milan.

a *Festa della Federazione*, similar to the festivities of the 1790s in France, in which politicians took oaths to the constitution to be witnessed by the multitudes of citizens. While in Paris and other French cities the *Champs de Mars* were used to gather together the city's populations,[31] in Milan *il Lazaretto*, the former quarantine in front of the *Porta Orientale*, was decorated as *Campo della Federazione* (*The Festival of the Federation of the Cisalpine Republic*, Figure 21). The vast rectangular square, surrounded by colonnades, offered everything the festival organizers needed.[32] There was enough space for thousands of visitors and a parading military. The uninterrupted space provided good visibility for everyone. It was easily accessible and easy to control at the same time. Although the *Lazaretto* had a remarkable history, its homogenous construction did not offer any distractions from the Napoleonic spectacle, as the city space would have done. It was a neutral stage for festivals. Antolini wanted to create a space close to the city center, which would copy and optimize the *Lazaretto*'s advantages. His goal was to transform daily city life in the heightened order of the festival, where everybody could see himself acting in a play of "democracy." From the revolutionary festivities he learned to define public space as theatrical space. His architecture provided an artificial horizon for a vast area of total visibility.[33]

The idea behind the ambitious festivals like the French *Fête de la Fédération* had its origin in Rousseau's description of a revolutionary celebration. Rousseau had proclaimed that for a perfect revolutionary spectacle there was nothing needed but a simple decoration to indicate a location where the crowd could meet. The most interesting spectacle for the people would be the people themselves.[34] It has to be mentioned that in reality the military played an important part in all revolutionary festivities. In Paris, and even more so in Milan, the people actually were assembled to see not only themselves as citizens, but also to cheer the ideal of the self-sacrificing patriot in the person of the soldier. However, Rousseau's enthusiasm for the people becoming aware of themselves in a situation of seeing (I see all the others) and being seen (I feel myself seen as part of a crowd) was reflected in Milizia's remarks on the moral qualities of the theater in its function as public space. One of the most important advantages of public theaters was, for Milizia, that they forced people to stay in a public space for an extended period of time. He explained that everyone would behave differently, and hopefully better,

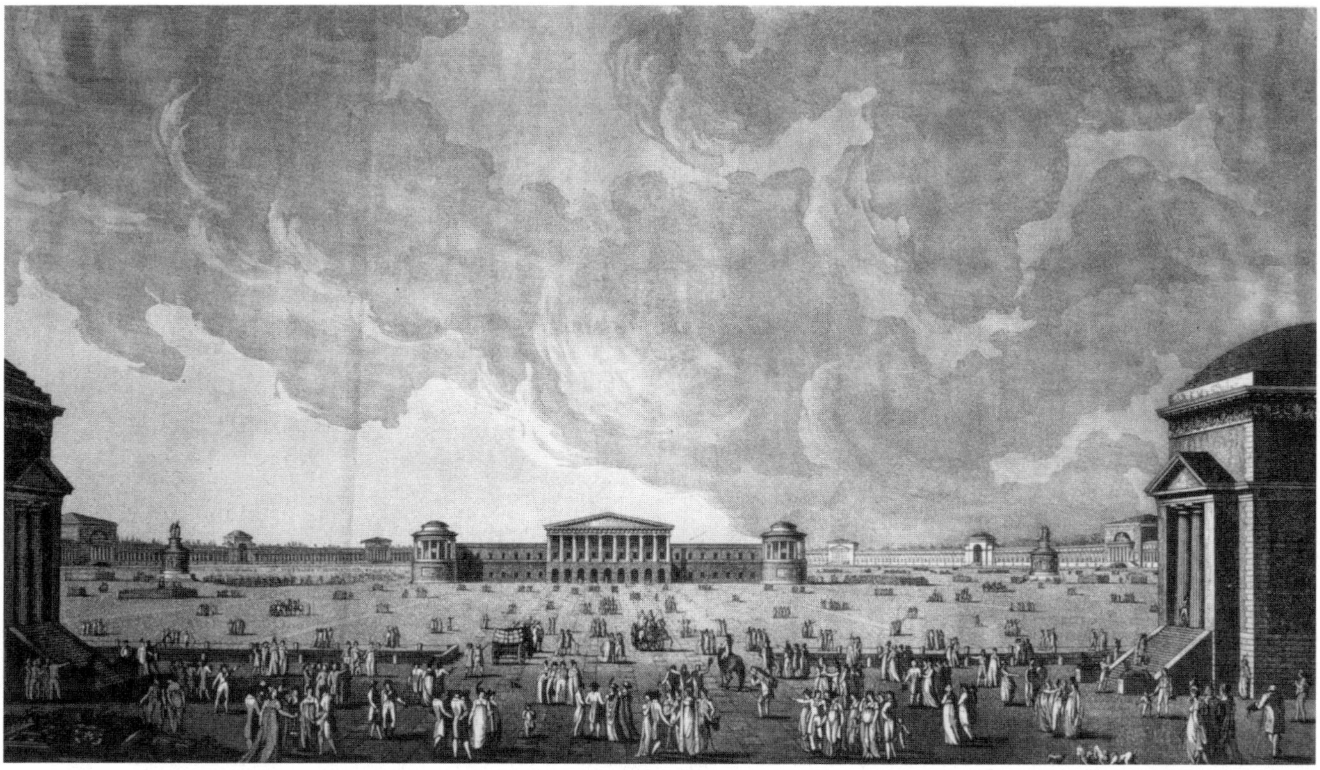

22. Giovanni Antonio Antolini, *The Bonaparte Forum in Milan*, 1801–05, ink and watercolor, c. 45 × 75 cm, Paris, Bibliothèque Nationale de France, Cabinet des Estampes. Photograph published with permission from Archivio FMR, Bologna.

in a public space than at home. At home, when they felt comfortable, people would not try to discipline themselves, he argued; they would not care how they looked and if their behavior was appreciated. Public space, on the other hand, would function per se as a space of control. If people suspected that they could be controlled without their knowledge, simply because they were exposed and not hidden, they would behave differently. To be in a public space would mobilize mechanisms of self-control, even if no actual external control was present. Milizia generalized: the more the citizens were exposed to public space, the better for the individual and for society. Public space had the power to improve morals permanently.[35]

In this understanding of public space Antolini's *Foro* was legitimized as an arrangement for viewing (*The Foro Bonaparte in Milan*, Figure 22). It would have allowed the visitors to see Milanese society with all its political and economic functions as a unity, not structured by a prestabilized hierarchy, but accessible for everyone in all of its parts, coherent through an ongoing circulation of people, goods, water, and ideas. And it would have exposed the visitor to others as part of that ideal society at work. In feeling exposed, the visitor would have tried to behave according to the severe principles that the architecture imposed on everyone. This challenging new world would have strengthened individuals physically and morally by stimulating them to identify themselves with their participation in society's circulation.

This envisioned unity of the people in fulfillment of the principles of the new order was a monument in itself for the newly risen grandeur of the liberated Italian people, comparable only to the magnificence of ancient Rome. In the second, later published version of his *Piano economico-politico*, Antolini tried to justify the huge expenses for the proposed *Foro Bonaparte* with reference to antique practice. Addressing the artists, he wrote: "You will defend my plans from the attacks of those ice-hearted souls who are so little lovers of the Fatherland, and of the honor of the name Italian, that they consider as squandered whatever sum might be invested in grandiose public works, without reflecting that it is precisely and solely because of such works that Italy has risen to such heights of fame."[36] With this phrase Antolini changed his perspective. As his goal he mentioned the representation of the Italian nation—not yet politically unified—in a monument, which would impress foreign visitors, among them the French occupying forces.

This patriotic argument introduces the second level of political economy of art in the model I outlined earlier. On the first level, expenses for art seemed to be reasonable, because the spent money would allow artists to participate in consumption. The money would soon be part of the economic circulation again. Architecture was here used as an integrative process for the formation (and normalizing) of a new society. On the second level, Antolini suggests that it would be inadequate to expect a yield from an investment in art as from investments in other economic fields. Art and monumental architecture—Antolini made no difference between them—produced fame and honor instead. They were part of a symbolic economy. Antolini's underlying interpretation of this symbolic economy was that it was based on squander, that is, on expenses that were no longer justifiable through functional reasons. In this economy the destruction of accumulated money generated symbolic capital.

The plans for the *Foro Bonaparte* were indeed deeply rooted in a symbolic economy, which evolved from an exchange of gifts between Paris and Milan. Antolini started his plans as a participant in a competition for a memorial column.[37] The government of the Cisalpine Republic opened this competition in June of 1800, a few days after the decisive French victory of Marengo over Habsburg, to show its gratitude to the French army and its chief, Napoleon Bonaparte, who had just freed Lombardy a second time. Antolini's design of a memorial was approved. At the same time, Bonaparte ordered the destruction of most of the fortresses in Lombardy for strategic reasons, among them the star-shaped *Castello Sforzesco*, which had dominated northern Milan for centuries. The government, which found itself confronted with a challenge in the city's urban situation, asked Antolini to develop plans for a square around the monument, which could redefine the vast empty space so close to the city's center. The former site would be dedicated to the French army and its general and would show the city's gratitude.

When Antolini visited Napoleon in Paris to show him the plans for examination, Napoleon was more than skeptical. The First Consul estimated that the costs were far too high for the Cisalpine Republic, and he explained it would be more reasonable to spend the money for dikes on the Po and urgently needed fortification against Habsburg. Antolini replied that there should be no exclusivity between the different projects. If there were peace, all of the projects could be realized. For the *Cisalpina* no effort was too great to express its gratitude to Bonaparte.[38] It is remarkable that Antolini did not mention that there could be an economic sense behind the realization of the *Foro*. In his summary of his conversation with Bonaparte in a letter to the governing committee in Milan, Antolini described Napoleon as being moved by the glory of the design (for it was truly meant as a gift of thanks), but also as being too modest to accept such a grandiose gesture of thanks. It was the latter feeling that dominated his feelings, wrote Antolini.

I see this scene as a failed attempt to establish an economy of gifts between the *Cisalpina* and Bonaparte. The dedication of the project to Bonaparte would have allowed the new republic to prove not only its gratitude, but also to force Bonaparte to accept the *Cisalpina*'s status as an independent state. An investment in new dikes for the Po would not have had any effect on the symbolic status of the Italian republic in relation to France. The *Cisalpina* could hope to gain symbolic value only through the waste of money for a project not to be justified in economic terms. But as long as Bonaparte controlled the financial policy of the *Cisalpina*, the puppet government could only announce its intentions, but could not realize them.

Without waiting for Bonaparte's approval, the Cisalpine government celebrated the foundation of the *Foro Bonaparte* on April 30, 1801. Paolo Bargigli, an architect who was experienced in the field of ephemeral monuments for political festivities, decorated the space between city and castle with a symbolic landscape.[39] During the celebration, the city's authorities moved from one monument to another, interrupted by speeches, songs, and the sound of cannons. The victories of the French army were glorified in spiral-reliefs on a column that decorated the site of the altar of the nation. It was similar to Trajan's column in Rome. A small temple was dedicated to Bonaparte's victories as the fundament for eternal freedom. A nearby pyramid commemorated the French war victims. The cornerstone of the *Foro* was carried to the site by young men in Roman clothes. The general of the French troops in Milan spoke before three members of the *Comitato di Governo* symbolically laid the stone. In the evening the people were entertained with fireworks and events in the main theaters. The official report in French and Italian, authorized by Minister Pancaldi, summarized the day: "The *vaghezza* of all of its elements and the deeply felt joy of the people made this festivity, which can be named twice: a celebration of humanity and of thankfulness, so delightful and brilliant."[40] Not surprisingly, not all visitors were as enthusiastic as Pancaldi assumed. Stendhal mentioned the day only very briefly in his diary. He noted: "On a posé la première pierre du foro Bonaparte. Le soir, feu d'artifice mesquin. Scène lyrique assez ennuyeuse au grand théatre [La Scala] et bal où les femmes honnêtes ont dansé."[41] He was obviously bored by this ceremony, which was one of the most ambitious propagandistic efforts of the Cisalpine republic in the short time of its existence.

Pancaldi, Minister of Foreign Affairs, was proud of this special day which gave the government of the *Cisalpina* the opportunity to show itself side by side with the officials of the French army. He reported to the Cisalpine ambassador in Paris, Ferdinando Marescalchi, that the people were even more overwhelmed by the spectacle than the official article could express. Pancaldi instructed the ambassador to let Bonaparte and his politicians know how honestly thankful the Milanese people were for their liberation. He attached to his letter many prints of the several ephemeral monuments and asked Marescalchi to hand them out to Bonaparte and to the influential politicians around him (descriptions would follow). Together with the prints, Pancaldi sent a large sum of money to his ambassador to enable him to show the gratitude of the Milanese government through generous gifts to many senators, other politicians, and people who would make decisions about the future of the Italian republics.[42]

After the cornerstone was laid in a grandiose ceremony and the propagandistic effect of the project was widely used, the plans were, so to say, buried. The architect had—not willingly—wasted his energy and imagination on a building project which was condemned to remain on paper. Antolini was at least rewarded with the post of professor of architecture at the University of Bologna. The *Foro* was remembered as an unfulfilled dream and compared to the dream of Italian independence itself. As such, it was seen as the fruit of Jacobin idealism, which was destroyed with the foundation of the Italian republic in 1802, when Jacobin patriots were expelled from public functions. Soon it was forgotten that from the beginning, Antolini's project oscillated between the attempt to modernize public space in Milan and the temptation to centralize the city's capacities in one great but ruinous gesture toward the French. It was the same political, economic condition that stimulated the creation of the plans and their failure. The generative and the destructive forces were both linked to the two functions of art as part of two economies, the circulation of money and the exchange of gifts.

NOTES

1. Boris Groys, *Über das Neue: Versuch einer Kulturökonomie* (Munich: Hanser, 1992), 14–16, 127–38.

2. Harry Hearder, *Italy in the Age of the Risorgimento: 1790–1870*, Longman History of Italy, vol. 6 (London: Longman 1980), 16–24; Carlo Zaghi, *Il Direttorio Francese e la Repubblica Cisalpina*, 2 vols. (Roma: Istituto storico italiana per l'età moderna e contemporanea, 1992), 2:1189.

3. Ettore Rota, "L'età napoleonica: 1796–1814." in *Storia di Milano*, 18 vols. (Torino: Fond. Treccani degli Alfieri per la Storia di Milano, 1953–96), 13:29–30.

4. Franco Della Peruta, ed., *Storia illustrata di Milano*, 5 vols. (Milan: E. Sellino, 1993), 5:1541–60.

5. Napoléon I, *Correspondance de Napoléon Ier publié par ordre de l'Empereur Napoléon III*, ed. A. Du Casse, 32 vols. (Paris: Impremerie Imperial, 1858–69), 2:264.

6. Giovanni Montroni, "L'età napoleonica," in *L'Italia giacobina e napoleonica*, ed. Bruno Anatra et al. (Milan: Teti, 1985), 262.

7. Fernando Mazzocca, "G.B. Sommariva o il Borghese Mecenate," *Itinerari* 2 (1981): 145–277.

8. Anna Maria Brizio and Marco Rosci, eds. "Interventi urbanistici e architettonici a Milano durante il periodo napoleonico," in *Napoleone e l'Italia*, Convegno Accademia dei Lincei Roma, 1969 (Rome: L'Accademia Nazionale dei Lincei, 1973), 412; Gianluca Kannès, "Il Foro Bonaparte tra l'Antolini e il Canonica: Un progetto di concorso ma non di esecuzione," in *Milano Parco Sempione: Spazio, pubblico, progetto, architettura 1796/1980* (Milan: n.p., 1980), 106–13; Gianni Mezzanotte, *L'architettura neoclassica in Lombardia* (Naples: Edizione scientifiche italiane, 1966), 244–45, 287–88; Luciano Patetta, ed., *Idea della magnificenza civile: Architettura a Milano 1770–1848*. Rotonda di Via Bersana Milano, October–November, 1978 (Milan: Electa, 1978); Giorgio Simoncini, "Aspetti della politica napoleonica dei lavori pubblici in Italia," in *Villes et Territoire pendant la période napolèonienne: France et Italie*, Actes du colloque organisée par l'Ecole française de Rome avec la participation de la Maison des Sciences de l'Homme, Rome, May 3–5, 1984 (Rome: L'Ecole, 1987), 1–21.

9. Jean Soldini, "Il Foro Bonaparte di Luigi Canonica" *Storia della Città* 7, no. 22 (1982): 89.

10. Aurora Scotti, *Il Foro Bonaparte. Un' utopia giacobina a Milano*, trans. R. E. Wolf (Milan: F. M. Ricci, 1989), 94.

11. Francis Haskell, "An Italian Patron of French Neo-Classic Art," in *Past and Present in Art and Taste: Selected Essays* (New Haven: Yale University Press, 1987), 47–64, and "More about Sommariva," *Burlington Magazine*, October, 1972, 691–95; Rota, 486.

12. Franco Bertoni, "L'Architettura a Faenza dalla Repubblica Cispadana alla Restaurazione: Giovanni Antonio Antolini e Pietro Tomba," in *Giuseppe Pistocchi (1744 –1814) architetto giacobino*, ed. Ezzo Godoli (Florence: Rotografia Fiorentina, 1974), 63–76.

13. Gianluca Kannes, "Un acquarello per il Foro Bonaparte in Milano ed altri inediti di G.A. Antolini," *Storia della Città* 7, no. 22 (April–June 1982): 85.

14. Giuseppe Pistocchi, "Riflessioni architettoniche sopra il premiato disegno della trionfale colonna de erigersi in Milano," Milan, 1800, in *Giuseppe Pistocchi (1744–1814) architetto giacobino*, ed. Ezzo Godoli (Faenza: Palazzo delle Esposizioni, 1974; Florence: Rotografia Fiorentina, 1977), 89–92.

15. Scotti, 144–46; Patrizia Giudicelli Falguières, "Espace privée et espace public à Milan: 1796–1814," in *Villes et Territoire pendant la période napolèonienne: France et Italie*, Actes du colloque organisée par l'Ecole française de Rome avec la participation de la Maison des Sciences de l'Homme, Rome, May 3–5, 1984 (Rome: L'Ecole, 1987), 261–84; Orietta Rossi-Pinelli, "Il Foro Bonaparte: Progetto e fallimento di una città degli uguali," *Ricerche di storia dell'arte* 3 (1976): 43–65.

16. Giovanni Antonio Antolini, *Descrizione del Foro Bonaparte*, (Parma: Tipi Bodoniani, 1806), as reprinted in Scotti, *Foro*, 102.

17. Maria Domenica Genovese, "Milano 1796–1815: Feste pubbliche e concorsi nel primo periodo napoleonico," in *La cultura a Milano tra riformismo illuminato e rivoluzione*, ed. Raffaele De Grada et al. (Milan: Vangelista, 1989), 99–105; Luciano Guerci, "'Democrazia rappresentativa': Definizioni e discussioni nell'Italia del triennio repubblicano 1796–1799," in *L'Europa tra illuminismo e restaurazione: Scritti in onore di Furio Diaz*, ed. Paolo Alatri (Rome: Bulzoni, 1993), 227–75.

18. Vitruvius, *Ten Books on Architecture*, trans. Ingrid D. Rowland, commentary and illustrations Thomas Noble Howe (New York: Cambridge University Press, 1999), 5:10.

19. Antolini, *Piano economico-politico del Foro Bonaparte presentato coi disegni al Comitato di Governo della Repubblica Cisalpina* (Milan: n.p., 1801).

20. Lionello Puppi, ed., *Prato della Valle: Due millenni di storia di un'avventura urbana* (Padua: Signum, 1986).

21. Andrea Memmo, *Elementi di Architettura Lodoliana o sia l'arte del fabbricare con solidità scientifica e con eleganza non cappriciosa* (Rome: Pagliarini, 1786).

22. Vincenzo Radicchio, *Descrizione della general idea . . . dall'eccellentissimo signore Andrea Memmo . . . sul materiale del Prato, che denominavasi della Valle* (Roma: Antonio Fulgoni, 1786).

23. Rossi, *Scritti scelti sull'architettura e a città: 1956–1972*, ed. Rosaldo Bonicalzi (Milan: Cooperativa libreraria universitaria del politecnico, 1975).

24. Carroll W. Westfall, "Antolini's Foro Bonaparte in Milan," *Journal of the Warburg and Courtauld Institutes* 32 (1969): 366–85.

25. Antoine Chrysostome Quatremère de Quincy, "Architecture," in *Encyclopédie Méthodique*, vol. 1 (Paris, 1801); Joselita Raspi Serra, ed., *Paestum and the Doric Revival 1750–1813: Essential Outline of an Approach*, 2 vols. (Rome: Centro Di, 1986).

26. "l'architettura ha per base il necessario, chiaramente ne siegue, che tutto il bello prenda il carattere della necessità, che gli ornati derivino dalla stessa natura dell'edifizio: che niente sia fuori d'uffizio: che quanto vuolsi rappresentare tanto dev'essere in azione. Non far mai cosa senza poterne rendere sode ragioni, ma ragioni evidenti." Giovanni Antolini, *L'ordine dorico ossia il Tempio d'Ercole nella città di Cori* (Rome: Stamperia Pagliarini, 1785), 19.

27. Michel Gallet, *Claude-Nicolas Ledoux: 1736–1806* (Paris: Picard, 1980); Rossi, 352–53.

28. Antolini, *L'ordine dorico ossia*, 18–19.

29. Vitruvius, 170.

30. Francesco Milizia, *Principi di architettura civile*. 3 vols. Finale: Stamperia di Jacopo de' Rossi, 1781, repr. "Collana anastatica 3," 5 vols. (Milan: Sapere, 2000), 2:44–45.

31. James A. Leith, *Space and Revolution: Projects for Monuments, Squares, and Public Buildings in France 1789–1799* (Montreal: McGill-Queen's University Press, 1991), 35–57.

32. Vicenzo Cavenago, *Il Lazaretto: Storia di un quartiere di Milano*, 2nd ed. (Milan: NED, 1989).

33. Mona Ozouf, "La fête révolutionnaire et l'espace urbain," in *Stadt und Fest: Zu Geschichte und Gegenwart europäischer Festkultur*, ed. Paul Hugger (Unterägeri, Switzerland: W and H; Stuttgart: J. B. Metzler, 1987), 89–108.

34. Jean-Jacques Rousseau, *Lettre à d'Alembert sur les spectacles* (Paris: Garnier freres, 1926), 232–33.

35. Milizia, *Del Teatro* (Rome, 1771; Venice: Giambattista Pasquali, 1773), 83–85; Michael Gollwitzer, "Francesco Milizia: Del Teatro. Ein Beitrag zur Ästhetik und Kulturgeschichte Italiens zwischen 1750 und 1970," PhD diss., Cologne, 1969.

36. Antolini, *Piano economico-politico*. Translated by R.E. Wolf in Scotti, *Foro*, 102.

37. Scotti, 120–23; Kannès, "Il Foro Bonaparte," 110–11.

38. Scott, 149–50.

39. Rosella Grassi, "Paolo Bargigli architetto: 1760c.–1815c.," *Parma nell'arte* 1 (1982): 47–67.

40. Articolo estratto dalla descrizione generale della festa per la celebrazione della Pace, e per la collocazione della prima Pietra del Foro Bonaparte. Biblioteca Ambrosiana, Milano, S.C.V.VIII.1:17°

41. Stendhal [Henri Beyle], *Œuvres intimes* (Paris: Gallimard, 1955), 436: "Today the first stone of the Bonaparte Forum was laid. In the evening, shabby fireworks. Very annoying lyrical scenes at the grand theatre [La Scala] and a ball where honourable women danced."

42. Scotti, 149.

The Panthéon, 1870–1900: Public Monument as Political Machine

Cheryl K. Snay

Conceived in the aftermath of the Franco-Prussian War and Commune (1870–71), the decorative program of the Panthéon (Interior of the Panthéon, Figure 23) represented a significant political and financial investment on the part of the government of the Third Republic. The state had only just finished paying five billion francs in war reparations to Prussia when it allocated more than one quarter of its annual budget for the fine arts for four years to the Panthéon project alone; this amount was in addition to the cost of structural repairs made necessary when the building was bombed during the war and subsequent civil unrest.[1] This chapter resituates the new decorative program planned after 1870 within the context of the legislative debates on its appropriations and artistic content. Julie Codell points out in her introduction that state-sponsored art, such as that in the Panthéon, was meant to socialize and nationalize citizens. The present essay goes beyond a conventional art historical reading of the monument focusing on style and narrative subject and looks instead at how the process of production and consumption unfolding in France's nascent and tenuous democracy provides a case study in the political economy of art.

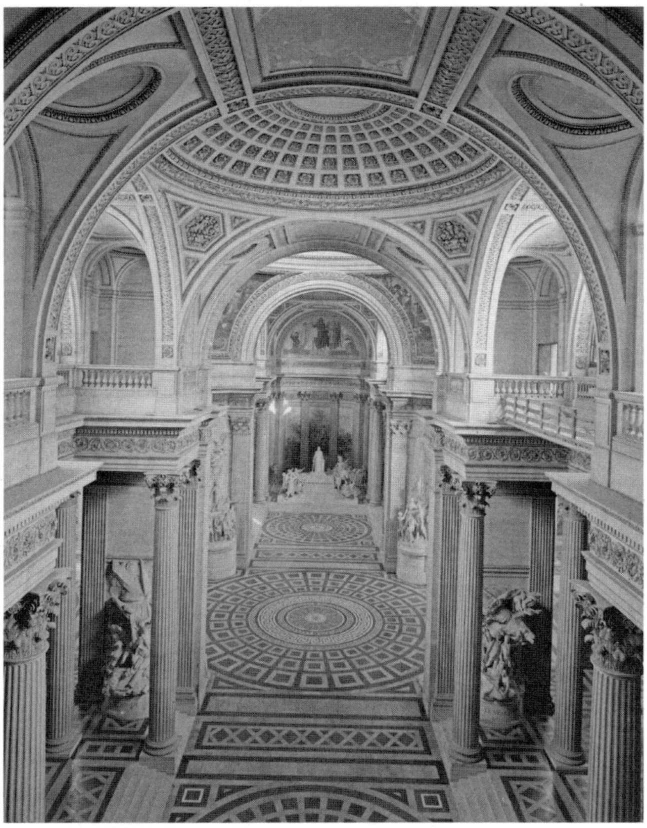

23. Interior of the Panthéon, Paris. Photo: © Caroline Rose, Centre des monuments nationaux, Paris.

The newly formed government of the Third Republic reorganized the administration of the fine arts, placing it under the auspices of the Ministry of Public Education, Cults and Fine Arts.[2] Policy decisions were made by the director of fine arts or his undersecretaries (if he had them), but the finances were determined by the legislature, which authorized credits and passed budgets. Approving the annual budgets or supplemental chapters occasioned parliamentary debate. Rarely did legislators' opinions affect the execution of the director's policies—except in the case of the Panthéon. There, the expression of political ideology through public expenditures is easily discernible.

The Franco-Prussian War left in its wake a political and social chaos in France that took decades to set straight. In 1873 Marshal Patrice MacMahon, the Duke of Magenta, was elected president, and his policy of reestablishing moral order was carried out with missionary zeal. The idea of moral order was based on the assumption that the organization of society is naturally hierarchical.[3] Its objectives were to curb radicalism as it had manifested itself in elections, to restore the monarchy to France, and to return temporal power to the pope.[4] The administration of the fine arts was equally affected by this conservative shift in government. Charles Blanc, liberal in his politics and the brother of the radical Louis Blanc, resigned as Director of the Fine Arts in December 1873 and was replaced by a legitimist, the Marquis Philippe de Chennevières.

Chennevières had held various posts within the arts administration of Napoleon III and wrote prolifically about artistic matters, but rarely proclaimed outright his position on political issues. The one exception to this was a series of letters, *Lettres rurales*, written in 1871 and 1872 and published in a provincial newspaper.[5] In these, he showed himself to be vehemently opposed to republicanism, an advocate for the active role of the church in society, and an adherent to traditional social structures, including the aristocracy. In other words, he was the perfect candidate for Director of Fine Arts when MacMahon's government took power and Blanc resigned. In the Marquis' view, public order was more important than the liberals' concept of equality, "a gilded synonym for envy."[6]

In March 1874, a scant four months after his appointment, Chennevières proposed a grand decorative scheme for the Panthéon that bore all the hallmarks of MacMahon's ambitions to restore moral order. It became the latest in a succession of attempts by previous regimes to leave their impression on one of the city's most prominent structures.[7] Begun in 1755 by Soufflot under the patronage of Louis XV, the building was originally designed as a church. In 1793, however, the revolutionary government dechristianized the monument and rededicated it to "Great Men." With each change of government thereafter, the building's function switched from church to civic monument and its decoration was modified accordingly. When the Third Republic came to power, the walls of the Panthéon were bare (occasionally tapestries were hung for special events) and only the dome and pendentives were painted with the *Apotheosis of Ste. Geneviève* by Baron Antoine Gros and allegorical figures by Baron François Gérard.

Chennevières gave de Fortou, Minister of Public Instruction, Cults and Fine Arts, three reasons for undertaking the project to decorate the Panthéon.[8] First, he believed it his duty as director to promote the careers of French artists by combining their talent to one of France's greatest— and, in terms of decoration, most neglected— monuments. Second, the impact of such an ambitious program would reach beyond the country's boundaries, and France could impress Europe with her resilience after defeat at the hands of the Prussians. Finally, Chennevières argued that the project would restore France's credibility as an artistic force, and by extension a political force, among its European neighbors. France could not maintain its position as a cultural leader if it continued to expend its artistic resources on frivolous projects, such as the recently inaugurated Opéra. The reference to the Opéra is significant. Charles Garnier's masterpiece was regarded by conservatives as a "monument to decadence" and an "outrage to public decency."[9] Chennevières offered the Panthéon as a corrective to the architectural offense to social order represented by the new opera building.

> As when, M. le Ministre, you had inaugurated the stately monument of the Opéra, where our country wanted to show, without skimping, and in bringing together a group of its most brilliant artists, what its genius is capable of when applied to the architecture of theatrical festivals, it will be interesting to note that works which demand more particularly gravity and solid vigor are still suitable to our artists, and that after providing proof in the eyes of Europe, of inestimable gifts of spirit, grace and elegance, they are capable of climbing back up to the most rigorous and most noble summits of religious and political art.[10]

Chennevières's juxtaposition of the Opéra and the Panthéon opens the door for us to compare the budgets of these two projects, but such doors must remain closed. The Opéra is fundamentally a Second Empire building even though it was not finished and inaugurated until after the Third Republic was declared. The Opéra was also an entirely new building, built from scratch, whereas the Panthéon had a long, complicated architectural and political history and was already partially decorated when Chennevières adopted it as his cause. The function of each building is significantly different and therefore calls for different approaches to their decoration. Moreover, the method of selecting the artists who would provide the decoration was different. Garnier was allowed to select the painters, sculptors, and mosaicists with whom he wanted to work, and he carefully coordinated their production. By doing so, he was able to create a sumptuous and harmonious foil for the display of capital accumulated by the middle class under Napoleon III's laissez-faire policies. In contrast, Chennevières resigned long before the Panthéon program was finished, and the directorship of the fine arts changed hands no fewer than nine times after his resignation. Instability within the fine arts administration and the ideological shift that resulted had a definite impact on the monument's decoration. Finally, the Panthéon and the images contained in it were addressed to the broadest section of the French public, and appealed especially to the conservative constituents of MacMahon's government.

The walls of the nave and transept where the eight main cycles of the program are installed are divided by engaged columns creating four separate panels. After consulting with the architect of the Panthéon, Chennevières agreed that three of the panels could be treated as a continuous scene while the fourth, isolated from the main axis, could be treated with a different scene relating to the same subject. A frieze depicting a procession of French saints, similar to that by Hippolyte Flandrin at St. Vincent de Paul, was deemed the most suitable treatment for the continuous band above the level of the impost blocks. Painted frames around the friezes further establish their visual integrity. And by enlivening their processions with portraits of their (often controversial) contemporaries, the artists added an overt political dimension to their work. None of the paintings are done in traditional fresco technique, but rather are painted on canvases that were later pasted to the wall (*marouflage*).

With the help of Abbott Bonnefoy, the dean of Ste. Geneviève, Chennevières devised a program "where the legend of the patron saint of Paris is combined with the religious history of France" (Figure 24).[11] Two scenes from the life of St. Denis, who introduced Christianity into Gaul, on either side of the narthex, provide a visual preface to the epic that would unfold beyond the entrance. On the south wall of the nave, Chennevières proposed the education and pastoral life of Ste. Geneviève, and on the north wall, the march of Attila toward Paris with Ste. Geneviève calming the masses. Beyond the transept and continuing on the north wall, visitors would find the saint at the siege of Paris by the Franks. The sequence culminates on the south wall of the choir in the death and funeral scene of the saint attended by Queen Clotilde. Chennevières introduced the second theme of the program, the religious history of France, primarily in the guise of the monarchy, in the transept of the church. In the south wing Clovis is shown at the Battle of Tolbiac, and, in the separate panel, being baptized. On the opposite wall, Charlemagne is crowned emperor by the pope in Rome. In the north wing of the transept *St. Louis Rendering Justice and Founding the Institutions That Established His Glory* would be juxtaposed with panels showing Joan of Arc before Orléans or in prison at Reims. Finally, altars dedicated to Ste. Geneviève in the south transept, the Virgin in the north transept, and in the apse Christ showing a vision of the destiny of its people to the angel of France provided the climaxes for the narrative design.

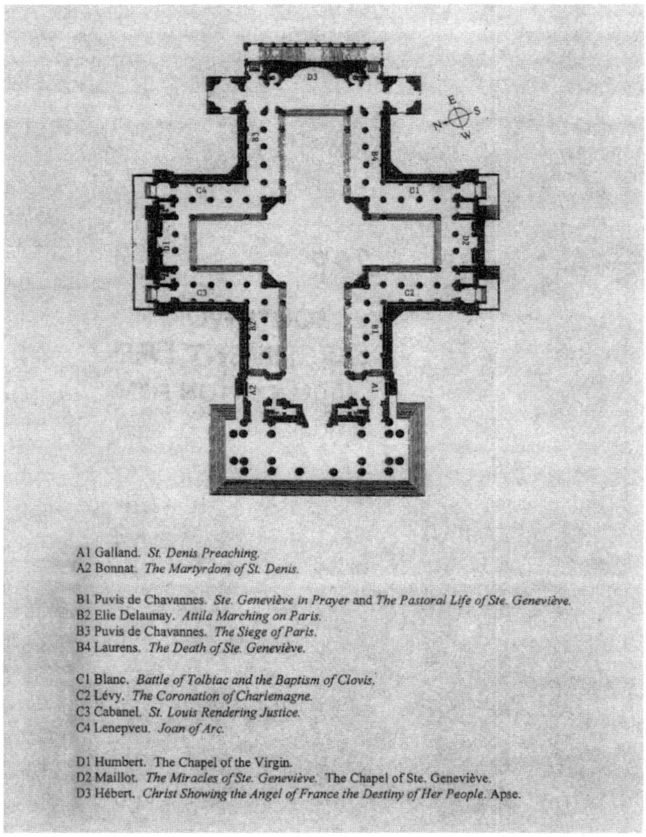

24. Diagram of the Panthéon reflecting Chennevières's narrative decorative program.

To date, the duality of this narrative and its spatial organization have not been adequately addressed in the critical literature. The program is dismissed for its lack of cohesion and originality, both in content and in style; but these assessments are based on an unintentional marginalization of the beholder relative to the narrative.[12] Visitors to the monument today must skirt the periphery of the interior and are forced to shift between scenes from the life of Ste. Geneviève and scenes of the history of religion in France. These are essentially two different, albeit related, themes organized along axes that intersect yet retain their integrity. Visually, the difference between the two themes is made clear by the direction of the procession of saints in the friezes above the main panels in the transept, which progress towards side altars, not towards the apse as do the processions in the friezes of the nave. Even the organization of Chennevières's description of the program in his letter to the minister assumes a central location for the spectator, who actively participates in the narrative and is not marginalized by it.[13]

Eschewing the republican method of selecting artists for public commissions by open competition, Chennevières simply invited those artists whom he believed bestowed the greatest glory on France to paint the murals.[14] Several of the artists he asked declined immediately and were replaced. Paul Chenavard, having designed an entire program for the building in 1848, was not content to be given only a "morsel," even if it was the apse and was visually and conceptually the most important part of the program.[15] Ernest Hébert, former director of the French Academy in Rome, was chosen to replace the older artist. Offered the commission for the altar of the Virgin, Gustave Moreau claimed a lack of experience in painting large murals and was succeeded by Ferdinand Humbert who had shown his work well at the Musée du Luxembourg. Henri Lehmann declined his invitation to paint the cycle of Charlemagne due to ill health, so Chennevières turned to Henri Lévy whose religious paintings had been well received at St. Denis. Jean-Léon Gérôme enjoyed great success with his easel paintings and private commissions and saw no advantage in taking on government work. Chennevières then awarded the cycle showing the death and burial of Ste. Geneviève to Jean-Paul Laurens because the artist "possessed an instinct for the Merovingian era."[16] Chennevières's choice of Laurens is an interesting one. If the artist had a talent for making motifs "of sinister majesty," as the director observed, he was also decidedly anticlerical—a strange choice, then, for a commission to paint a religious subject destined for a church.[17] Millet accepted his commission to paint the chapel of Ste. Geneviève but died in 1875 leaving only a few sketches. Théodore Maillot, who had just painted one of the chapels at Notre Dame de Paris, succeeded Millet. Similarly, Lenepveu assumed the commission for the scenes of Joan of Arc after Paul Baudry died in 1883. Pierre Puvis de Chavannes, Alexandre Cabanel, Joseph Blanc, Paul Galland, Léon Bonnat, and Elie Delaunay accepted their commissions. Puvis de Chavannes completed not only his own work, but finished that of Meissonier, who died before providing the sketches for *Ste. Geneviève and the Siege of Paris*.

In a separate letter Chennevières outlined the budget for the project: 820,000 francs for the paintings and sculptures and almost 300,000 francs for ornamentation, scaffolding, and pedestals for a total of 1,100,000 francs.[18] With an estimated annual budget for the fine arts of at least 915,000 francs, 275,000 could be set aside for each of the next four years (1875–78) for the Panthéon program and still leave 640,000 francs for other expenses and projects, such as commissions to decorate other public buildings both in the capital and the provinces, purchases of existing works from exhibitions, and organizing the salons and other exhibitions that provided artists with much needed commercial opportunities. His projection that the decorative scheme could be finished by 1878 proved overly optimistic and the budget overruns mounted.

To put these figures into some context, we might look to an interim report Charles Blanc put before his minister in 1871.[19] Out of 930,000 francs allocated for works of art and the decoration of public buildings, 232,250 francs were either already expended or were committed to commissions that were not yet finished. The remaining 623,374 francs would be distributed as follows: 200,000 for commissions and acquisitions of original sculpture; 150,000 for commissions and acquisitions of original paintings (sculptors were believed to be in more dire need than painters of governmental assistance); 80,000 for engravings after masters; 30,000 for engraving and striking medals; 60,000 for copies of masterpieces in the Louvre; and 100,000 for copies of ancient and modern masterpieces for the Musée Universel. The Musée Universel was Blanc's answer to the brain drain that he witnessed after the recent war and civil strife. To stem the tide of French artists emigrating to England, Russia, Austria, and even to America (which he found particularly insulting to French superiority) to seek work, Blanc resurrected the idea he had proposed twenty years earlier for a museum of copies. Under his plan, French artists would be employed to make copies of about a dozen of the works deemed most beautiful throughout the world. In this way, the poor and rich alike could be instructed in the history of art, and artists would be paid a modest sum (8,000 to 10,000 francs inclusive of travel expenses!) to use the skills they had developed in the Ecole des Beaux-Arts and at the French Academy in Rome.[20] It is difficult, if not impossible, to draw many conclusions from such a comparison given that the variables are so numerous and the figures unreliable. What is interesting to note is how each director approached the task of creating what amounts to a financial aid package for artists. In an era when originality was the watchword, Blanc occupied his artists with making copies. The return on this investment was the educational benefit it provided to the general public. It was Chennevières, the royalist, who allowed his artists the most latitude in interpreting the program he had written, accepting their changes and digressions and going so far as to commission an artist, Jean-Paul Lauren, whose ideology was diametrically opposed to his own. Chennevières was also more interested in teaching the history of France than he was the history of art—and his version of French history was particularly controversial.

Chennevières devised the decorative program for Ste. Geneviève at a time when a restored monarchy was still a possibility, but the manner in which it would be effected was very much in question. Two opportunities to achieve this goal had already slipped away in 1871 and again in 1873 when the Comte de Chambord, the pretender to the throne, refused to return to Paris under the tricolor flag, a symbol of acquiescence to the Chamber of Deputies. The director proclaimed his aversion to politics and repeatedly asserted that his main concern was the promotion of French artists; nevertheless, his program can be read as a declaration of allegiance to the legitimists. For him, it was obvious that only a divinely ordained monarch could save French society from the recent disasters of the Franco-Prussian War and the Commune. He reminded his audience that in similar occasions in the past (as with

Attila, the Franks, the Romans), salvation came from an appeal to God through his representatives (saints and kings) on earth. Chennevières rehearsed these historic battles and disasters not only as evidence that the French had always survived such onslaughts, but more importantly as a demonstration of the means by which those triumphs had materialized.

The program in Ste. Geneviève presents the legitimists' case at precisely the moment when a resolution to these issues was being negotiated. During the first year of his presidency (1874), MacMahon found himself trying to repel advances by the Left with no legitimate basis for power or authority. He resorted to promoting a conservative constitution, which was finally adopted in February 1875.[21] The constitution provided for a strong president and a senate comprised in part by members appointed for life, thereby ensuring the conservative nature of the body. Equally important was the provision that the president, with the consent of the Senate, could dissolve the Chamber of Deputies. With these elements in place, MacMahon believed he would be able to thwart the liberal tendencies of the Chamber and eventually secure the restoration of the monarchy. The very principle of a constitution alienated the extreme right; it passed by only one vote.

In light of the political maneuvering taking place in the Chamber of Deputies as well as in Frohsdorf, Austria, where the Comte de Chambord lived, could Chennevières's and Abbott Bonnefoy's choice of subject matter for Ste. Geneviève be regarded as a compromise as it is sometimes characterized?[22] In scripting the program, the two men go beyond a mere celebration of the monarchical history of France,[23] or the reality of the alliance between the church and royalty, and locate the origin of a state's power in God.[24] Clovis invoked God's name and defeated the Romans. Subsequently, he was baptized, and the dove of the Holy Spirit descended on him. Charlemagne was crowned by the pope and ushered in an era of cultural glory. St. Louis devoted himself to God, and his benevolent reign was marked by social harmony. Clearly, in Chennevières's view, there was no need for a constitution. It was a moot issue. A monarch's authority to rule derived from God, not from a National Assembly.

The first fruits of Chennevières's decorative scheme were presented at the Salon of 1876. Puvis de Chavannes exhibited the finished panel of *Sainte-Geneviève in Prayer* and cartoons of the other panels.[25] He was heralded as one of the "moderns," and his painting was called "a composition of incomparable purity."[26] Zola regarded him as the only one among French artists who could really make "grande peinture."[27]

The drawings submitted by Blanc and Maillot at the same time received far less critical attention than those of their illustrious colleague.[28] Blanc, a student of Cabanel and a Grand Prix winner in 1867, exhibited drawings that were complex in their narrative and organization.[29] The three main panels of *The Battle at Tolbiac* are filled with images of death and destruction (Figure 25). The isolated panel of the *Baptism of Clovis* is appropriately serene.[30] But it, too, is replete with minutiae: winged helmets, brocade cope, jeweled book cover, mosaics in the pendentives, composite capitals. For all this effort, one critic said only that the high degree of finish would make Blanc's work a superb pendant to that of Puvis de Chavannes.[31]

Maillot's panels for the altar of Ste. Geneviève in the south side of the transept received much the same cursory treatment as Blanc's. He was charged with depicting scenes of the power of the patron's relics in times of disaster. Of the two miracles depicted, the earlier miracle to the right of the altar shows a procession in 1130 led by St. Stephen, the bishop of Paris, to the church where the saint was asked to deliver the people from a plague that ravaged the city. The second panel of this scene shows a priest at an altar surrounded by his acolytes. To the left of the altar, Maillot showed the occasion when the saint's powers were invoked to stop a flood that was devastating the city. In the first panel located on the wall perpendicular to the altar, a procession winds its way through the streets of a medieval town and continues in the second panel.

There is a remarkable resemblance between Maillot's compositions and a depiction of the closing of a novena dedicated to Ste. Geneviève at the Panthéon shown in a print dated 1874. Similarities include the bird's eye perspective, the general movement of the procession from upper left to lower right, the isolation of the celebrant created by his costume and gesture of holding an open book, a male spectator seen from the back and a soldier leading the procession in the lower right foreground. There are differences as well, most notably the setting (exterior vs. interior). This comparison is not meant to show that Maillot was influenced by or was copying the printmaker's image, or even to argue the relationship between high and low culture. Rather, the point is that Maillot's picture of a religious ceremony in the very place where such religious ceremonies still occurred proved a very real connection between past and present and reinforced the moral order. Believers and skeptics alike looking at Maillot's picture would have recognized in it echoes of recent events. After the war, Catholics advocated the undertaking of a "National Vow." Only with acts of penance could the faithful obtain the deliverance of the sovereign pontiff and secure the well-being of France.[32] The most obvious manifestation of the National Vow is the construction of Sacré Coeur on

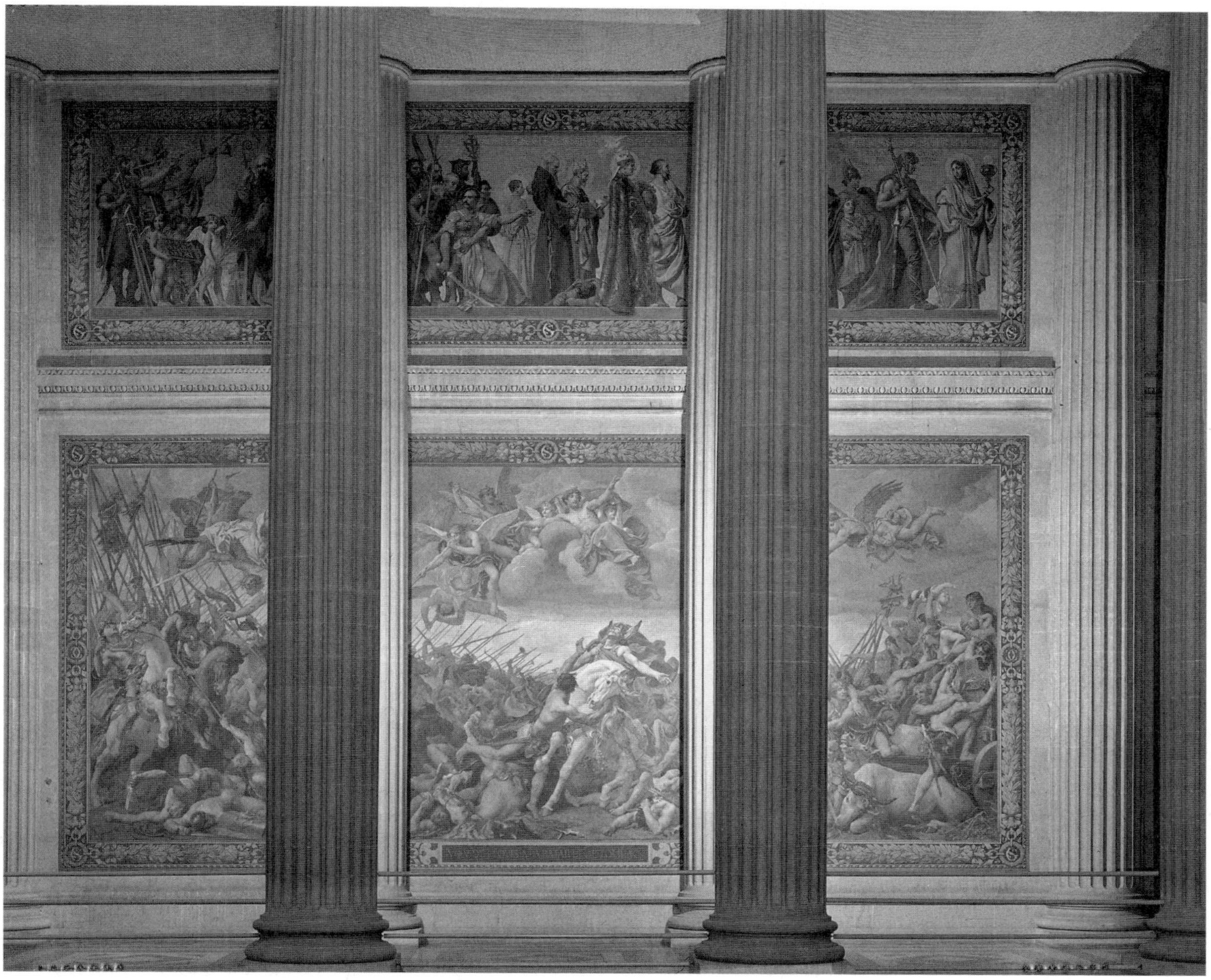

25. Joseph Blanc, *The Battle of Tolbiac,* 1881. Panthéon, Paris. Photo: © Caroline Rose, Centre des monuments nationaux, Paris.

Montmartre; but it also expressed itself in ritualistic behavior, such as the celebration of the novena. Maillot's fastidious drawing, obsession with details, use of vertical perspective, diminutive, dolllike figures, and jewellike colors earned him the label of *primitif*. The sharp contrast with the monumental simplicity exercised by Puvis led one critic to conclude that Maillot's and Blanc's works were "modest" by comparison.[33]

In his review of the Salon, Jules Castagnary, who became Director of Fine Arts himself in 1887, called on Chennevières to suspend work at the Panthéon, not for aesthetic reasons, but for political ones. He argued that the return of the monument to a civic function was inevitable and therefore the funding of religious paintings at taxpayer expense was irresponsible.

> The Panthéon is by no means a religious monument. The Revolution in dedicating it to the memory of great men has marked it as its own. . . . But, at the Panthéon, the State pays. And the republican deputies will be voting for funds to let the paintings of Mr. Maillot scream out next to those of Mr. Joseph Blanc, and those of Mr. Joseph Blanc next to those of Mr. Puvis de Chavannes! They will vote for funds to cover with a feudal legend the walls of a monument that the revolution claims. The transformation of the temple of philosophy into a Christian basilica will be accomplished with the money of the taxpayers. No, no If it is established that, each time that the reaction[aries] triumph in France, the church seizes the Panthéon, it is no less certain that each time the revolution prevails, the Church gives it back. . . . After all, what good is it that the Genevieves keep their flock conversant with St. Germain? The director of fine arts must, with wisdom and prudence, declare the works suspended, to render an account, and tell the artists that they no longer have to linger over useless compositions. This is not the first time, he knows it well, that political events have nipped the decoration of the Panthéon in the bud.[34]

Deputies in the Chamber joined the battle cry. On August 10 and 11, several republican members addressed some of the issues raised by Castagnary. Emile Bouchet proposed an amendment to an appropriations bill that the 400,000 francs allocated to the decoration of public buildings in 1877 should not be used to pay for the paintings and sculptures in Ste. Geneviève, objecting on the grounds that the program was exclusively Christian.[35] Citing the "universality" of Chenavard's aborted program of 1848 as a model, he argued that the amount was too high a price for a decorative project that represented such a narrow political perspective. It was not the religious nature of the content that offended Bouchet—Chenavard's cycles included images of Christ—so much as its conservative tone. His proposal was tabled until the following day's session, when Antonin Proust (who became Minister of Fine Arts from November 14, 1881, until January 30, 1882) and Madier de Montjau elaborated on Bouchet's arguments.[36] Going even farther than Castagnary, who called the Panthéon expenses irresponsible, Proust began by casting the proposed appropriations as illegal: "Everyone is in agreement on this point that these funds are badly appropriated, that it is absolutely illegal."[37] In addition to budgetary concerns, he added aesthetic ones. He was one of the first to point out that the styles of the artists proposed to carry out the commissions were too disparate to provide a unified program. He described Chennevières's project as "an eccentricity."[38]

Madier de Montjau joined Proust in opposition. He was not convinced by the administration's assertions that its intentions were benign or that its concerns were anything other than aesthetic. He rightly perceived in Chennevières's program an attempt to rekindle the memory of a long and glorious monarchical tradition in France and the many benefits that the monarchy, in tandem with the Church, could bestow. Madier de Montjau mocked the selective—or revised—history as well as the religious content of the program. He reasoned that the legislature was under no obligation to continue paying for a project that had been proposed by a previous minister (de Fourtou had since been replaced; the minister in office while this debate unfolded was Wallon). Indeed, the legislators had an obligation, he continued, to correct an abuse of power once it was discovered.

> You are opposed, he said to us, to the teaching of history through painting. But, then, let's see what history will be taught to us in the decoration of Ste. Geneviève? The martyrdom of St. Denis, says the list before my eyes: 20,000 francs. This is so little for a martyr. The Sermon of St. Denis, 20,000 francs. St. Denis is decidedly the cheapest, as you are going to see. . . . Here is Ste. Genevieve at the siege of Paris—the former siege—I wish she had been more present and active at the last one,—50,000 francs for services rendered . . . against Attila! The last moments of Ste. Geneviève, 50,000 francs. Always 50,000; a sum round and fixed, like the price of bread at the baker's. . . . History—Clovis. Ah! The grandeur of Clovis—of that barbarian chief of savage hordes! Clovis offers an example to our children and to our descendants as classical and poetic language relates. Let's see Clovis, "having killed many other kings, his close relatives, fearing that they might strip him of his empire, he extended his power throughout all Gaul. The story is told that one day he gathered his subjects, and spoke thus of his kin whom he had killed: Unhappy would I be in protecting myself if adversity were to come! But it was not that he was distressed by their death; he spoke thus only as a trick to discover if he had still more relatives to kill." What examples! What models? . . . This is the history that you want to teach us! . . . This is the decorative painting that our children are taught to regard as great and glorious! [39]

Recognizing that Madier de Montjau is being supremely sarcastic, his diatribe nevertheless illustrates precisely the problem of determining remuneration for such commissions. He seems inclined to allocate funds based on the validity of the subject and mocks Chennevières's more objective criteria by scale: "a sum round and fixed, like the price of bread at the baker's." The amendment prohibiting the use of the 400,000 francs allocated for the decoration of public buildings from being used for the Panthéon was defeated 163 to 252. Chennevières's project was funded for another year.

Work at Ste. Geneviève continued at a snail's pace. Puvis de Chavannes finished his cycle and installed it in May and the frieze in December of 1877, eliciting a fresh wave of favorable reviews each time.[40] Commentators still predicted that all the murals would be finished in time for the Universal Exposition in 1878 as Chennevières had proposed four years earlier. Cabanel was the only one to keep to this schedule, submitting *St. Louis Rendering Justice* (Figure 26) to the exhibition.[41] Instead of treating the three main panels as one continuous scene with the fourth as a separate but related subject as Chennevières had suggested and as Puvis had done, Cabanel confined the continuous scene to the two central panels and treated the two flanking panels as if they were both isolated. This modification to the composition allowed the introduction of a new subject: *The Education of St. Louis*. Despite the discontinuity of the three separate images, the frame extends around all four panels. The result is somewhat confusing and causes an awkward break in the cartouche below the central panels depicting the main theme. The author of this deviation in subject

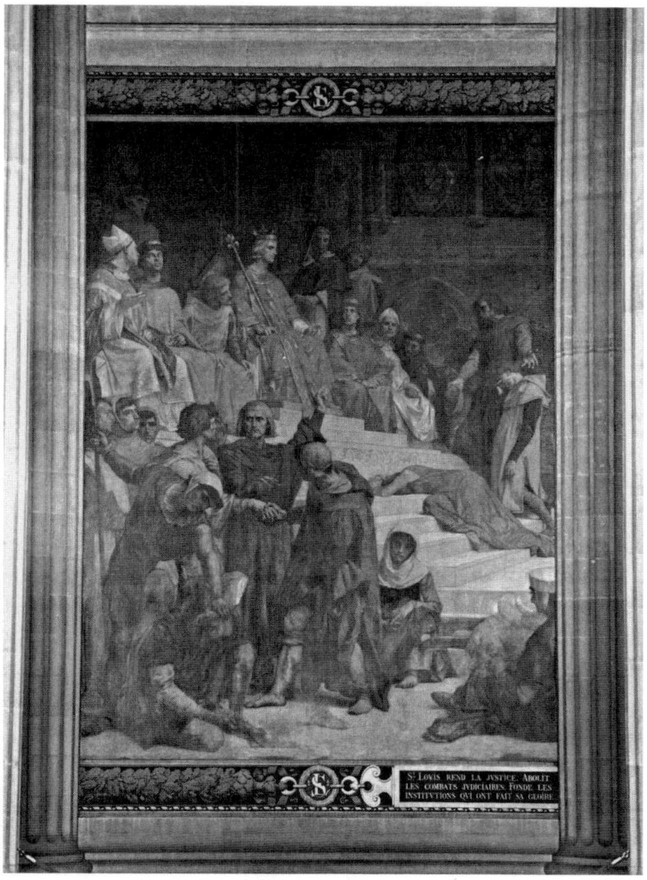

26. Alexandre Cabanel, *St. Louis Rendering Justice*, 1879. Panthéon, Paris. Photo: © Patrick Cadet, Centre des monuments nationaux, Paris.

and composition is unclear. In the original plan submitted to de Fourtou in May 1874 and again in a letter to Puvis de Chavannes detailing his commission, Chennevières specifically identified the first panel on the right side of the nave before the dome as *The Education of Ste. Geneviève*.[42] Puvis ignored that dictate, choosing instead to show *Ste. Geneviève in Prayer*.[43] No such comparable subject of education is mentioned in Cabanel's commission. Nevertheless, *The Education of St. Louis* appears as the first panel of his cycle. Whether Cabanel was asked or whether he took it upon himself to rectify Puvis's lapse is unknown.

In the panel Louis sits in profile to the right of his mother Queen Blanche of Castille surrounded by the prelates and by the Dominicans Jourdain de Saxe and Vincent de Beauvais. That the education of the sovereign is administered by members of the clergy surely raised the ire of republicans, who had made lay education and the expulsion of the clergy from the teaching profession a hallmark of their platform. It was a battle begun during the Commune and bitterly waged by the republicans throughout the 1870s. Moreover, it was not only a matter of who should teach, but also who should be taught. Liberals believed that positive social change and development depended on all members of society, regardless of class or gender, being educated (to what extent is another matter altogether). Conservatives, on the other hand, believed that anyone aspiring to rise above the station into which he—or she—was born was evil. Such aspirations violated the moral order and were as dangerous as armed insurrection.[44]

Cabanel's image of a young boy fidgeting with the ties of his cape, intent on the lessons provided by priests and monks, participated in a political debate, which advocates of moral order ultimately lost. The political fortunes of the republicans improved after MacMahon exercised his right to dissolve the Chamber in 1877 (known as the *coup d'état seize mai*) and subsequent elections swept them into power.[45] Jules Ferry, a moderate republican, became Minister of Education and initiated legislation that transformed the state educational system. From 1879 to 1882, the control of the clergy over everything from primary schools to universities was eroded. Primary education became compulsory, free, and lay. Secondary education for girls was established. In the course of the 1880s approximately 300 Catholic schools were closed.

In 1879 in the Chamber of Deputies, Benjamin Raspail launched a campaign for the return of the church of Ste. Geneviève to a civic status. On May 21, 1880, the twentieth Commission led by Raspail and composed of fifty-four other members, including Madier de Montjau and Louis Blanc, proposed a law that would "suppress the metropolitan chapter of the Chaplains of Sainte-Geneviève and return the Panthéon to the purpose intended by the National Assembly in 1791."[46] While the effort failed, the repeated attacks began to take their toll on Chennevières who finally resigned as director the same year. He continued to rally support for the project by writing a series of articles, the first of which appeared in the *Gazette des Beaux-Arts* in October, 1880, explaining the history of the monument and justifying the present program; but, in a letter written to Lévy in 1881, Chennevières conceded that the tide had turned against his decoration of the Panthéon.[47]

No doubt, Chennevières felt that his efforts were undermined by the very artists whom he had entrusted with performing the work. At the Salon of 1881, Blanc exhibited the first two panels of the frieze for his Clovis cycle in the Panthéon. Entitled *The Triumph of Clovis*, the king leads a procession, which includes Theodoric, Clotilde, and his sons, Clodomir, Childebert, and Clotaire. In the next panel are Aurelianus, St. Rémi, St. Avitus, St. Wast Galactorius, Verus, and Volusianus. St. Martin of Tours, St. Hilaire of Poitiers, and three allegories of victorious battles, followed by soldiers bring up the rear of the procession.

Blanc antagonized both the faithful and the leftists by casting republicans and anticlerics as the saints and royalty in the frieze. It was not uncommon for artists to insert portraits of their friends, family, students, or patrons in their work, sometimes to demonstrate deference or gratitude. The gesture was always meant to confer honor on the model. For example, in the frieze above the *Childhood of Ste. Geneviève*, Puvis de Chavannes had astutely cast Chennevières as St. Paul of Narbonne and included his own self-portrait as St. Trophime, the two deep in conversation. Although conceptually, these two figures are at the tail end of the procession that heads down the nave and toward the apse, they are the first two saints in the frieze to be seen by visitors to the church.[48]

But Blanc approached caricature with his high concentration of recognizable portraits of people overtly hostile to the church. Ste. Clotilde was identified as Mme. Edmond Adam, an editor of *La nouvelle revue* and a prominent figure in literary circles. Her salon was renowned for its gathering of republicans, chief among them Léon Michel Gambetta, who appears in the frieze as a catechumen. Georges Clemenceau is shown in the guise of the wounded soldier falling back into the arms of people tentatively identified as Paul Bert and Edouard Lockroy. Bert was a close colleague of Jules Ferry and worked with him on educational reform to exclude the clergy from the system. In 1881, Bert was named minister of public instruction and cults. Lockroy formed the core of the radicals at the extreme Left with Clemenceau and, along with twenty-four other deputies in the Chamber, issued an anticlerical manifesto in 1876. Lockroy and Clemenceau were also members of the commission headed by Raspail that had just proposed the law to return the monument to its civil function. Coquelin aîné strikes a pose as Aurelianus, Clovis's advisor—an apt role for the well-known actor who tutored Spuller and Waldeck-Rousseau in elocution and rhetoric. Antonin Proust (who, it will be remembered, questioned the legality of the expenditures for the decoration of the Panthéon in 1876 after Blanc, Maillot, and Puvis de Chavannes had exhibited in the Salon), Geoffroy Saint-Hilaire, and Louis Pasteur all make an appearance in the procession. Blanc's satire—if that is what it was, for even the critics seem a bit confused about the artist's motive—went beyond good taste and backfired:

> it exceeded acceptable limits in identifying a quasi religious scene—since the prelates of Clovis's court are found in there—a scene which is supposed to adorn a church, with characters who never passed as zealous defenders of religion. We even find in doubtful taste to have shown, dressed in the linen tunic of the Levites, an actor, certainly without rival in the theater, but whose place is not here. It is not good to have Crespin [Pierre-Noel-Adolphe Crespin was a deputy from Loiret who sat to the center left of the Chamber] or Mascarille walking side by side with the confessors of the faith.[49]

The artist's mocking tone could not have been meant to be malicious as he included portraits of his wife, father, and himself, as well. In the absence of any documentation that might provide some insights, we can only speculate on Blanc's intentions. Was he sympathetic to the republican cause—a closet anticleric—and was this an attempt to redeem the republicans by associating them with national heroes? The critic Buisson suggested as much in his discussion of Blanc's frieze: "Maybe this was the only way that the painter could introduce his friends into the church without damaging their [chances for] reelection."[50] Or was the irony intended as a critique of the republicans who preached a new social order while appropriating the methods and means of the tyrants against whom they bellowed in the Chamber? Was it the artist's revenge for the insults he had endured at the hands of Castagnary, Proust, and Madier de Montjau when he exhibited the main panels of the cycle in 1876, or perhaps for the recent attempt to return the Panthéon to a civil function spearheaded by Raspail? We know only the reaction to his "monumental prank."[51] Chennevières seemed not to have been offended by having enemies of both the church and the monarchy infiltrate the sanctity of the national basilica. Rather, he was disappointed because the gesture compromised the gravity of the program and opened it up to unnecessary criticism. Nevertheless, he defended Blanc's work against the caprice of the critics.

> Mr. Blanc must have understood the ruckus raised by the intrusion—a little too marked perhaps—into a religious painting of figures who were not exactly friends of the Church. If his frieze had gone directly from his studio to the Panthéon, without going through the inevitable epilogues of the critics of the salon, I do not doubt that the superb qualities of art would have dominated all this noise and would even have been extinguished by the gravity of his vast composition's ensemble. But this salon is a terrible seduction, and sometimes pretty dangerous for monumental paintings which do not know to escape from it.[52]

Henri Lévy completed his cycle, *The Coronation of Charlemagne*, and exhibited it in the triennial exhibition of 1883.[53] In the center of the composition the pope stands in profile holding the crown in his outstretched hands silhouetted against a backdrop obscured by incense and heavenly clouds. Charlemagne stands to the right on a step lower than that of the pope, followed by his sons Charles and Pepin and his daughters who bring gifts to the pope. In the right panel, members of Charlemagne's court and soldiers raise their swords in salute. A red banner emblazoned with an imperial eagle hovers over the crowd. The pope's entourage comprised of priests and bishops occupies the left panel. With the temporal and religious powers divided, the two men meet in the center where St. Peter carried by angels descends on them, "symbolizing the alliance of Carolingian France and the papacy."[54]

Lévy's cycle soon became an anachronism. With the death of the Comte de Chambord in 1883, the Comte de Paris became the pretender to the throne. Ongoing debates about the constitution culminated on August 14, 1884, with a series of constitutional amendments. Article 2 of the law reads: "The Republican form of Government cannot be made the subject of a proposed revision. Members of the families that have reigned in France are ineligible for the presidency of the Republic."[55] "It [the monarchy] was definitively killed and buried on 13 August at Versailles, in the very palace of Louis XIV and henceforth it remains only as a bad and distant memory."[56] Worse still from a Catholic's point of view was the about-face of Pope Leo XIII's church policy toward the French Republic. Although the encyclical formally announcing the *ralliement* did not arrive in Paris until 1892, the pope made it clear shortly after his election in 1878 that French Catholics should drop their resistance to the republican government in the hope that this would reduce the antagonism between Rome and Paris.

The fate of the Panthéon was finally decided when Victor Hugo, France's most esteemed poet and politician, died on May 22, 1885.[57] The day after his death the Chamber of Deputies met to discuss arrangements for his funeral. The government of Jules Grévy proposed that a national funeral be held and that the Chamber allocate 20,000 francs for its expenses. Several members from the Right protested the use of funds for a ceremony that was clearly political and overtly antireligious. Claiming to speak for the thirty-five million Catholics in the country, one deputy expressed condolences for the death, but concluded, "As a royalist, I cannot knowingly associate with a republican demonstration; as a Catholic, I cannot participate in a funeral from which religion and God are banished."[58] Their objections were dismissed, and the budget for the funeral was passed 408 to 3. In the Senate, too, the measure received overwhelming support: 210 voted for it; only one member voted against it.[59]

Republicans in the Chamber used Hugo's atheism as a pretext for returning the Panthéon to purely civic use. Following the vote for the budget of the funeral, a law was proposed by Anatole de la Forge to return the monument to its "first and legal" function so that the poet's body could be buried there and still comply with the deceased man's last wishes for a civil funeral. Royalists protested the obvious ambush. "[This proposal] is no longer about national funerals, it is about whether the Panthéon will be stripped of its Catholic cult; and it comes at a time of mourning apparently, without discussion, without preparation, in a moment of legitimate passion, if you want to put it succinctly!"[60] They succeeded in postponing a vote. When the deputies returned to the issue several days later, the Right knew that they were on the losing side of the battle, and they attempted to block the movement with procedural objections and disputes over legality and precedence.[61] The debate reached fever pitch, with the specter of the *drapeau rouge* raised and several conservative members threatened with sanctions for their disruptive behavior. The tactics failed. The vote to reject the government's decree stripping the Panthéon of its function as a Catholic church was 81 in favor and 369 against. The second vote taken to affirm the government's decree was 330 in favor and 88 against; 32 members abstained.

Chennevières let fly his fury with a new series of articles on the Panthéon, this time published in *L'Artiste*. He vehemently denied all accusations that he used the decorative program at the Panthéon to advance a particular philosophic or political ideology, insisting that the religious content was in keeping with the purpose of the edifice and that such content had "satisfied the daily needs as well as the most noble impulses of the human soul for 18 centuries."[62] He argued that the civic function proposed for the monument was incompatible with its original function as a church. The distinctive character of a church derived from its consecration to a particular saint while a pantheon is constantly changing with the addition of each new altar or tomb. "The transformation of the church Sainte-Geneviève into a Panthéon makes then a puerile and ridiculous esthetic."[63] Finally, Chennevières damned the republicans for their failure in logic: "What is a great man? Are there any great men? . . . In the thought of the Revolution and from the perspective of the Republic, the idea of great men is nonsense."[64]

In his criticism of Bonnat's painting of the *Martyrdom of St. Denis* exhibited in the Salon of 1885, André Mitchell raised the critical question, "What is going to happen to the decoration of the Panthéon now that the edifice has again become secular?"[65] No commission was more affected by the political reshuffling that occurred between 1879 and 1885 than that of Ferdinand Humbert.[66] Assigned to decorate the altar of the Virgin in the north arm of the transept, Humbert's first orders from Chennevières were to provide various manifestations of the Virgin in France: Notre Dame de la Garde, Notre Dame du Puy, Notre Dame de Fourrières and Notre Dame de Lourdes. But in 1877 while Chennevières was still director, the program was changed because the subjects were neither historical nor national.[67] Instead, the administration selected great Christian women of France including St. Blandine (the martyr of Lyon), St. Radegonde in her monastery at Poitiers, Jeanne de Hachette at the siege of Beauvais and Mme. Legras, the founder of the Daughters of Charity. The corresponding frieze for each panel would have shown allegories of faith, science, civilization, and charity. In 1881, with Proust succeeding Chennevières as Director of the Fine Arts and Lockroy as the reporter of the budget, both of whom had shown considerable hostility toward the Church, the subjects of the commission were revisited and deemed unsuitable. Humbert, despairing that he would never be able to finish his project, suggested a program that would surely please the republican administrators then dominating the committee: Work, Devotion, Patriotism, and Family for the main panels and Prosperity, Humanity, Liberty, and Peace in the frieze (Figure 27). Stripped of all religious connotations, Humbert's suggestion was ratified, and the artist set to work on his cycle, completing *Pro Patria* in time for the Salon of 1886.[68]

With the complete overhaul of Humbert's commission, republicans within the arts administration began to articulate their position in the public debate Chennevières had begun more than a decade earlier. These efforts, however, did not go far enough. The cycles of paintings that made up the decorative program at the Panthéon were too far advanced to abandon completely or even to influence significantly. Instead, Gustave Larroumet, the Director of Fine Arts, submitted a plan in February, 1889 to Edouard Lockroy, the anticleric who was then the Minister of Public Education and Fine Arts, proposing a sculptural program that would temper the conservative narrative of the murals and reflect the monument's new, secular function.[69] Moreover, in recognition of the centenary of the French Revolution, the Chamber passed a law approving the transfer of the remains of "revolutionary heroes" to the Panthéon. A sculptural program honoring them was in order.

Larroumet rehearsed the familiar justification that the return of Ste. Geneviève to a civic function was legitimate because it was deemed so by the Constituent Assembly of 1793.[70] He characterized the

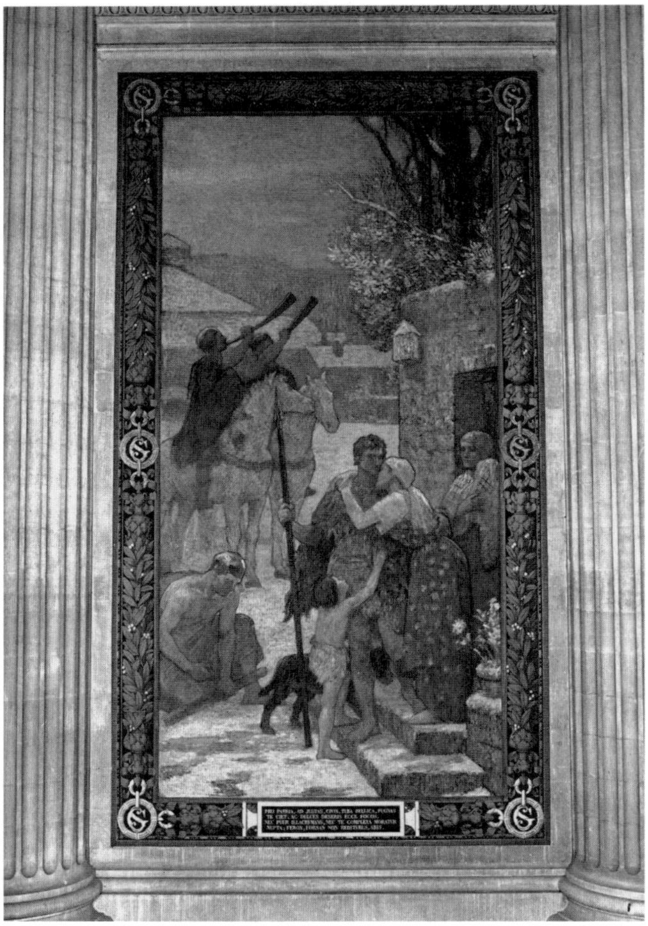

27. Ferdinand Humbert, *Pro Patria*, 1886, Panthéon, Paris. Photo: © Patrick Cadet, Centre des monuments nationaux, Paris.

sculptural portion of Chennevières's complete decorative program, consisting of only twelve statues, as "restrained" and therefore subject to elaboration.[71] Furthermore, the new sculptural project could address the issue of French history from "an entirely new point of view."[72] Larroumet, fully aware that the content of what he was about to propose might seem "shockingly antithetical," cast the proposed program as a "continuation" of the wall paintings, a "logical conclusion" of the ensemble, rather than as a repudiation of them. A plan of the monument appended to his report shows where the new sculpture would be placed, but gave no evidence that the existing sculpture completed under Chennevières's tenure was incorporated into the proposal.[73]

Larroumet proposed four high reliefs of allegories depicting the Middle Ages, Renaissance, Seventeenth Century, and Eighteenth Century to cover the piers of the central bay, each of which would consist of three or four figures and would be executed in a style befitting its subject, that is, the Middle Ages would have a gothic character, and so on.[74] In addition to the reliefs, five freestanding cenotaphs (for Descartes, Voltaire, Rousseau, Mirabeau, and Hugo[75]), two funeral monuments applied to the walls (one dedicated to Lazare Carnot;[76] the other to be shared by Foy, de Manuel, and d'Armand Carrel), and about eighty sculptures would pay homage to the great men of France. The climax of the proposed program was to be a monument in the hemicycle dedicated to the French Revolution and comprised of allegories of France, Liberty, Equality, and Fraternity mounted on a base covered with reliefs showing the proclamation of a new social law, the defense of territory, and the expansion of new ideas.[77] The program seemed particularly timely in a year in which the French celebrated the centennial of the Revolution.

Following the model Chennevières had established with his budget in 1874, Larroumet explained that they would not have to request special funding from parliament to carry out the proposed sculptural project.[78] Of one million francs allocated for works of art in the annual budget, 600,000 francs were earmarked for the decoration of public buildings and divided equally between paintings and sculpture. Half of the amount designated for sculpture could be spent on the Panthéon project; the remaining half on other projects in Paris and the provinces. This sum, 150,000 francs, would be appropriated for about fifteen years for a total expenditure of 2,250,000 francs on sculpture alone. Larroumet's sculptural program celebrating republican heroes and virtues and conceived to eclipse Chennevières's royalist themes promoting moral order cost more than twice that of the original plan, which included both paintings and sculpture. In Chennevières's four-year plan, a total of 240,000 francs was allocated for twelve sculptures of saints. The republican's plan proved too ambitious, however. Few of the works were ever commissioned and even fewer were executed and placed in the Panthéon.[79]

The decorative program of the Panthéon underwent a profound iconographical evolution over the course of a quarter century. It was initially conceived as a visual treatise on moral order, locating the legitimate source of political authority in a monarch who derived his power directly from God and constructing a rigid social hierarchy into which all French men and women fit. Artists selected from the ranks of the Academy provided murals addressed to specific contemporary issues, namely educational policies, the justice system, the Franco-Prussian War, and the Catholic Church. At the outset republicans challenged the underlying assumptions that motivated the monarchist authors of the program by introducing legislation that would have cut the project's budget. Failing that, they appropriated even more money for a new sculptural program with the intention of overwhelming the earlier paintings by its sheer scale and number; the murals would have faded into the background. The issue was never about whether to fund a program or about the validity of the academic system or style to represent contemporary France. There was never a doubt that the government's support of artists had anything but a salutary effect on society. Control of the historical narrative presented in the Panthéon was wrested from the conservatives by the republicans simply by outspending them. The nexus of art and politics in late nineteenth-century France and its implications for modernism have long been of interest to historians of visual culture. The study of the decorative program at the Panthéon expands our understanding of the dynamics of power in a nascent polity and the role of images in articulating political debates.

NOTES

1. In a report to the Minister of Public Works dated October 30, 1872, the Director of Civil Buildings asked for an appropriation of 100,000 francs to repair the Panthéon, which had been used as an ammunition depot during the war and Commune and had sustained heavy damage. In 1873, another 30,000 was appropriated and in 1874, another 30,000. After the repairs were made, the amount allocated to maintain the building dropped significantly: 1875, 15,600; 1876, 16,800; 1877, 12,000; 1878, 13,000; 1879, 20,000; 1880, 11,000. Archives nationales [hereafter AN] F^{21} 845.

2. For a discussion and analysis of the administration of the fine arts under the Third Republic, especially the impact of the parliament on policy, see Pierre Vaisse, *La troisième république et les peintres* (Paris: Flammarion, 1995), 34.

3. Robert R. Locke, *French Legitimists and the Politics of Moral Order in the Early Third Republic* (Princeton, NJ: Princeton University Press, 1986), 46.

4. John Lough, *An Introduction to Nineteenth-Century France* (London: Longman Group, 1978), 142.

5. For a summary of these, see Jane Mayo Roos, "Aristocracy in the Arts: Philippe de Chennevières and the Salons of the Mid 1870s," *Art Journal* 48, no. 1 (Spring 1989), 55-56.

6. As qtd. in Roos, "Aristocracy," 56.

7. The evolution of the construction, decoration, and historical significance of the monument are thoroughly addressed in the exhibition catalog by the Centre Canadien d'architecture and Caisse nationale des monuments historiques et des sites, *Le Panthéon: Symbole des revolutions* (Paris: Picard, 1989).

8. Letter from Philippe de Chennevières to de Fourtou, Minister of Public Instruction, Cults and Fine Arts, dated February 28, 1874, AN F^{21} 4403.

9. As qtd.in Locke, 151, n. 20.

10. Letter from Chennevières to de Fourtou dated February 28, 1874, AN F^{21} 4403.

11. Letter from Chennevières to de Fourtou dated May 7, 1874, AN F^{21} 4403.

12. The most scathing attack was launched by Boinet, who regarded the artists, with the exception of Puvis de Chavannes, "a

pitiable sample of talents of which many were completely inept at decorative painting." A. Boinet, *Les églises parisiennes* (Paris: Éditions de minuit, 1963), 3:313. Vaisse did not criticize the subjects chosen for the Panthéon but remarked that "all of these subjects, even the last two [Attila marching on Paris and the Siege of Paris], were nothing new." See Vaisse "Le peinture monumentale au Panthéon sous le IIIe république," *Panthéon: Symbole*, 255.

13. Letter from Chennevières to de Fourtou dated May 7, 1874, describing the proposed decorative program for the Panthéon, AN F[21] 4403. Chennevières reproduced the letter in *Les décorations du Panthéon* (Paris: Aux Bureaux de *l'Artiste*, 1885), 70–78.

14. Vaisse seems to indicate that Chennevières made an attempt to hold a *concours*, but none of the letters I saw refer to an open competition. *Panthéon: Symbole*, 252–53.

15. For a monograph on the artist, see Joseph C. Sloane, "Paul-Marc-Joseph Chenavard, artiste de 1848" (PhD diss., University of North Carolina, 1962). For discussions of this commission, see Marie-Antoinette Grunewald, *Paul Chenavard et la décoration du Panthéon de Paris en 1848* (Lyon: Musée des Beaux-Arts, 1977), and Jean Richer, "Une collaboration inconnue: La description du Panthéon de Paul Chenavard par Gautier et Nerval," *Archives des lettres modernes* 3, no. 48 (1963): entire issue. The cartoons are in the collection of the Musée des Beaux-Arts in Lyon. Additional sketches are in the collections of the Musée Fabre in Montpellier and in the Ecole nationale supérieure des Beaux-Arts in Paris.

16. Chennevières, *Décorations*, 81.

17. Ibid.

18. Letter from Chennevières to de Fourtou dated May 7, 1874, AN F[21] 4403.

19. Vaisse, *Troisième république*, 445.

20. Ibid, 443.

21. Charles Currier, trans., "Contitutional and Organic Laws of France," *Annals of the American Academy of Political and Social Sciences* 3 (March 1893): 160–69.

22. See, e.g., Brian Petrie, *Puvis de Chavannes* (Brookfield, VT: Ashgate, 1997), 94.

23. Kimberly Jones, "Resurrecting History: Jean-Paul Laurens and the Politics of History Painting During the French Third Republic, 1871–1914." (PhD diss., University of Maryland, 1996), 261.

24. François Vergnette, "Anticléricalisme et naturalisme au Panthéon: Le décor de Jean-Paul Laurens," *Histoire de l'art* 28 (December 1994), 52.

25. Listed as entry numbers 1694 and 2868 respectively in *L'Exposition des oeuvres des artistes vivants: Salon de 1876: Compte rendu du Journal des Art* (Paris, 1876), 85–86. See also *Explication des ouvrages de peinture, sculpture, architecture, gravure et lithographie des artistes vivants exposées au Palais des Champs-Elysées le 1er mai 1876* (Paris: Imprimerie nationale, 1876), 210, 359. For a brief summary of the commission and a full discussion of preliminary sketches, studies, and reduced versions relating to the cycle, see Aimée Brown Price, *Pierre Puvis de Chavannes* (New York: Rizzoli, 1994), 146–57.

26. Jean Prouvaire, "Peintures sacrées" in *La République des lettres: Le Salon de 1876* (Paris, 1876), 180–81. For another positive review, see Th. Veron, *Mémorial de l'art et des artistes de mon temps: Le Salon de 1876* (Paris, 1876), 33–34.

27. Emile Zola, *Salons* (Geneva: Librarie E. Droz, 1959), 178.

28. None of the previously cited critics mentioned Blanc or Maillot in their reviews of the Salon.

29. Exhibited as number 192 in *Explication des ouvrages*, 24–25.

30. Studies for this panel are in the Musée du Louvre, Dessins.

31. Victor de Swarte, *Lettres sur le Salon de 1876* (Saint-Omer, France, n.p., n.d.), 74.

32. H. Rohault de Fleury, *Historique de la Basilique du Sacré Coeur: Pièces et documents* (Paris: F. Levé, 1903), 1:29. The idea to initiate a National Vow originated with Guibert, Archbishop of Paris, before the Franco-Prussian War, but it became a mission after he returned from exile in 1871. In addition to undertaking the construction of a basilica, the committee formed to study the project published a monthly tabloid called *Le Bulletin de l'oeuvre du Voeu nationale*.

33. "Il nous a paru intéressant de rapprocher de la grande oeuvre de Puvis de Chavannes les plus modestes projets de Mm. Maillot et Blanc destinés à la même décoration" "Le Salon de 1876," *Zigzags*, May 7, 1876, 4.

34. J. Castagnary, "Salon de 1876," *Salons* (Paris, 1892), 2:223–25.

35. *Journal officiel* (August 11, 1876), 6236–37.

36. *Journal officiel* (August 12, 1876), 6294–96.

37. "Tout le monde est d'accord sur ce point que la dépense a été mal engagée, qu'elle est absolutement illegale."

38. *Journal officiel* (August 12, 1876), 6294. Vaisse makes the point that the "spatial autonomy" of each of the arms reduces the validity of this criticism because no spectator can see all of the cycles simultaneously. As a result, one isn't entirely aware of the disparity of styles; see Vaisse, in *Panthéon Symbole*, 257.

39. *Journal officiel* (August 12, 1876), 6296.

40. Arthur Baignères, "Les Peintures de l'Eglise Sainte-Geneviève par M. Puvis de Chavannes, *Journal officiel* (May 25, 1877), 3999; Maurice Vachon, "Les peintures de M. Puvis de Chavannes au Panthéon," *La France*, May 28, 1877, 2. Vachon, "L'oeuvre de M. Puvis de Chavannes au Panthéon," *La France*, December 11, 1877, 3. Jules Comte, "Les peintures murales du Panthéon," *L'Illustration* 1832 (April 6, 1878): 216–19.

41. *Saint-Louis, Roi de France* is listed as entry number 160 in *Exposition universelle de 1878 à Paris: Catalogue officiel publié par le commissariat général. Volume I: Groupe I: Oeuvres d'art* (Paris: Imprimerie nationale, 1878), 17. A reduction of the cycle is listed and the artist's description of the scenes is reproduced in Henry Fouquier, *Catalogue de tableaux, aquarelles et dessins provenant de l'atelier Alexandre Cabanel* (Paris, 1889), 22–23. On preliminary studies for this cycle, see Musée Fabre, *Dessins d'Alexandre Cabanel 1823–1889* (Montpellier, France: Musée Fabre, 1990), 39–42.

42. Letter from Chennevières to Puvis de Chavannes dated May 15, 1874. Documentation Musée d'Orsay.

43. Puvis informed Chennevières of the change in subject matter, but offered no explanation for it. For a translation of the letter and brief discussion of Puvis' Panthéon commission, see Petrie, 93–96.

44. Locke, 47–48.

45. A study for the figure of the Louis as a child was reproduced in the Georges Lafenestre, "Alexandre Cabanel," *Gazette des Beaux-Arts* 1 (April 1889): 274ff.

46. Rapport Sommaire, no. 2761, AN F[21] 845.

47. Chenevières, *Décorations*, 102.

48. In addition to Puvis de Chavannes, Cabanel included portraits of his students in the frieze he provided; Laurens inserted portraits of Chennevières and Rodin in his. According to Chennevières, the face of Christ in the apse mosaic by Hébert was modeled after Joseph Péladan, a writer for *l'Artiste*; Uckermann identified the model for Christ as Mounet-Sully, an actor at the Comédie-Française. René Patris d'Uckermann, *Ernest Hébert* (Paris: Réunion des musées nationaux, 1982), 160.

49. *L'Exposition des Beaux-Arts: Salon de 1881* (Paris, 1881), 122.

50. "Peut être le peintre a-t-il jugé malicieusement que c'était là le seul moyen de fair entrer ses amis à l'Eglise, sans nuire à leur reelection." J. Buisson, "Le Salon de 1881," *Gazette des Beaux-Arts* 23, no. 6 (June 1881): 504.

51. Ibid.

52. Chennevières, *Décorations*, 101.

53. The paintings are in a state of serious deterioration. The canvases suffer from water damage as well as vandalism. The cracks in the central panel are so pronounced as virtually to obscure the figures of the acolytes. Test patches indicate that much-needed restoration is being considered.

54. Chennevières, *Inventaire général des richesses d'art: Volume II Monuments civils* (Paris, 1889), 347.

55. Currier, 168.

56. "Elle a été définitivement tuée et enterrée le 13 août à Versailles, dans le palais même de Louis XIV et désormais elle ne reste plus qu'un mauvais et lointain souvenir." Ph. de Grandlieu, "N'en parlons plus!," *Le Figaro*, August 19, 1884, 1.

57. Hugo went into self-imposed exile in Belgium after Louis-Napoleon's coup d'état. He wrote invectives against the regime and became increasingly liberal. In 1871, he opened his home to the Communards fleeing Paris and was asked by the government of Belgium to leave for doing so. When he returned to Paris, he was elected to the Senate. David Bell, ed., *A Biographical Dictionary of French Political Leaders since 1870* (New York: Simon and Schuster, 1990), 207.

58. "Royaliste, je ne saurais m'associer à une manifestation républicaine; catholique, je ne peux participer aux enterrements dont la religion et Dieu sont bannis." Baudry d'Asson, *Chambre des Députés: Débats Parlementaires* (May 24, 1885), 899–905.

59. *Journal officiel*, Sénat, Débats Parlementaires (May 24, 1885), 608.

60. Ibid. In Jolibois's words: "Il ne s'agit plus maintenant d'obsèques nationales, il s'agit de savoir si le Panthéon sera enleve au culte catholique; et c'est à l'instant même, en signe de deuil apparemment, sans discussion, sans preparation, dans un moment d'entrainement légitime, si vous le voulez, qu'on va trancher une pareille question!"

61. *Journal officiel,* Chambre des Députés: Débats Parlementaires (May 28, 1885), 924–31.

62. Chennevières, *Décorations*, 140.

63. "ne fut donc d'une esthétique puérile, ridicule . . ." Ibid., 142.

64. Ibid.

65. Ibid., 11.

66. In his well-documented study of this particular commission, Pierre Vaisse validated the "official" art produced by the government of the Third Republic by demonstrating Humbert's successful "synthesis" of vibrant color associated with the impressionists and stark composition characteristic of Puvis de Chavannes. Pierre Vaisse, "Styles et sujets dans la peinture officielle de la IIIe République: Ferdinand Humbert au Panthéon," *Bulletin de la Société de l'Histoire de l'art français* (1977), 306.

67. Vaisse, *Panthéon: symbole*, 255.

68. Vaisse, "Styles et sujets," 302.

69. For a detailed discussion of this proposal, see Jane Mayo Roos, "Rodin, Hugo and the Panthéon: Art and Politics in the Third Republic" PhD diss., Columbia University, 1981, chapter 2.

70. Rapport au Ministre sur la continuation des travaux de décoration intérieure du Panthéon (Paris: Imprimerie nationale, 1889), 4, AN F[21] 6160.

71. Chennevières included twelve statues of saints in his program, eight of which had been installed by the time Larroumet made this report.

72. Rapport au Ministre, 4, AN F[21] 6160.

73. For an illustration of this plan, as well as that of Chennevières, showing the distribution of sculpture in the monument, see Anne Pingeot, "Le décor sculpte du Panthéon sous le Second Empire et le IIIe Republique," *Panthéon: Symbole*, 269.

74. Rapport au ministre sur les séances de la sous-commission des travaux d'art chargée d'examiner le projet de décorations sculpturale du Panthéon (Paris: Imprimerie nationale, 1889), 5, AN F[21] 2381.

75. The controversy surrounding this commission involving Rodin and Dalou is examined in detail in Roos "Rodin's Monument to Victor Hugo: Art and Politics in the Third Republic," *Art Bulletin* 68, no. 4 (December 1986): 632–56.

76. Lazare Carnot's grandson, Sadi Carnot, was president of the Republic when Larroumet made this proposal.

77. Rapport au ministre sur les séances, 4, AN F[21] 2381.

78. Rapport au ministre sur la continuation des travaux de décoration intérieure du Panthéon (Paris: Imprimerie nationale, 1889), 7, AN F[21] 6160.

79. The first two works commissioned in 1889 were the monuments to Mirabeau and Victor Hugo to be carried out by Injalbert and Rodin respectively. Each artist was to have been paid 75,000 francs. Rapport, 10, AN F[21] 2381.

Palimpsestic Promenades: Memorial Environments and the Urban Consumption of Space in Post–1918 London

Andrew P. Stephenson

While the end of the Great War and the Armistice in November 1918 marked out a traumatic moment in British and Western European histories, simultaneously many writers and critics claimed it as a turning point that would launch a "new renaissance" for the visual arts in Great Britain under state and government patronage.[1] The two most enduring emblems of this artistic renewal were commemorative sculptures and collections of state-commissioned war art, such as those now housed in the Imperial War Museums in London and Salford.[2] In the post-Armistice years, almost every parish of the 16,436 in Great Britain commissioned some form of commemorative sculpture to be located in a central public space and incorporated within a respectful memorial environment. In this chapter, I will examine the intricate ways in which political economy narratives of memorial environments, urban space, and subjectivity intersected in these locations and the role that sculpture might occupy in these transactions. Dedicated to upholding the collective memory of those local citizens who had fought and given their lives in the conflict, these memorials were often positioned on consecrated land in churchyards or outside churches. Alternatively, they were found in prominent positions, most usually in town squares or on village greens. Extolling the virtues of national resilience during wartime and dedicated to venerating social ideals to which future generations could aspire, these civic monuments were financed by public subscription, as well as by private donation.[3]

Given the ubiquity of memorial forms, I will also explore the diversity of political meanings engendered by memorial sculpture and how its potential contradictions challenged the postwar desire to align a divided nation with acceptance of a celebratory cause that reaffirmed a "just" military victory for the British and their allies. Although there was no explicit legislation passed by the British government directing the selection criteria for the artist or materials they should employ or features and scripts they should display, the formats that these memorial sites might take was overseen by local government and military representatives and monitored by diocese wardens as well as major private donors. Proposals were carefully vetted by professional bodies, such as the Royal Academy's War Memorials Committee and the council of the Royal Society of British Sculptors.[4] Furthermore, any decisions about scale and landscaping were subject to local planning regulations and council bylaws. The outcome was also substantially informed by popular taste with the opinions of local people—notably ex-servicemen and widows—ratifying the whole selection and construction process and being extensively reported in the local and national press.

Erected in huge numbers, memorials not surprisingly exhibited a diversity of styles and formats; some recorded details and rank of those who died, while others provided no specific mention of the deceased whatsoever. Equally remarkable was that although they frequently depicted military personnel or personifications of peace, valor, or sacrifice, the memorials did not contain the bodies of soldiers killed abroad. Exhumations and the repatriation of the deceased had been banned during the war and this restriction continued after its cessation. Instead, the British and colonial dead were buried in huge cemeteries near the battlefields in northern France and Flanders that from 1917 came under the control of the Imperial War Graves Commission.[5] As a consequence, there was an urgent need to build permanent memorials to the fallen in Great Britain to register their valor as well as to provide a focus for mourning. On or around Armistice Day (November 11), these memorial sites became the special centerpieces of elaborate military and civilian parades that confirmed commemoration in peacetime as a meaningful acknowledgment of self-sacrifice and also reshaped it as an act of responsible citizenship on the part of combatant nations in the postwar era.

As Alex King argued in his essay, "Remembering and Forgetting in Public Memorial of the Great War," "the function of commemoration is to give authority to one interpretation of social reality against competitors. . . . Officials as holders of municipal or state power, remain the dominant power in these negotiations."[6] Given the previously unimaginable scale of bereavement and human loss that the Great War produced, the main issue for government officials and artists alike was to determine the most decorous and respectful representations of sacrifice. In response to the growing desire of the British public to commemorate through ritual processions, such as the laying of flowers or wreaths by local veterans, war widows, and community groups, practical considerations also had to be accommodated. Official publications, such as A. Clutton-Brock's *On War Memorials* (1917) and the Royal Academy's *Suggestions for the Treatment of War Memorials* (1919), alongside exhibitions such as the Victoria and Albert Museum's two-part War Memorial show (Summer 1919) offered guidance on the most appropriate sculptural forms and Christian symbolism that a nation in mourning should adopt while safeguarding the sensitivities of female mourners, war widows, and bereaved families.[7] Linked to this design issue were issues of precedence: how previous Victorian funerary devices—prewar idealized forms for depicting martyrdom and earlier conventions linked to male sacrifice—could be modernized and made relevant to the scale of the Great War.

What emerged in response to government and professional guidance and popular reaction was that two simple rules were to be rigidly adhered to. First, by demonstrating the "birthrights of our own flesh and blood, [Memorials] of the British School . . . [should be] . . . executed by a sculptor of purely British descent."[8] Second, in the planning of memorial environments and in selecting monumental forms and styles, esoteric symbolism and foreign precedents should be disregarded. Not unsurprisingly, it was insisted that "we shall naturally avoid the limitations of the German" and any signs of "Germanness" in manufacture or embellishment.[9] In addition, subjects such as homicidal acts or depictions involving extreme violence, which were unbecoming to the military dead and might give a dishonorable impression, should also be avoided.

In Spring 1919, it became clear that the public wanted a national memorial to the British Empire dead of the Great War to be erected in the capital in preparation for the international peace celebrations that were to be held in London on July 19. Cabinet records underline government anxieties about the need to retain control over the artist's selection and over the location and sculptural format employed to avoid a processional "Siegesallee" in central London.[10] Initially it was decided that a temporary catafalque be designed to stand in Whitehall. The prime minister, Lloyd George, approached the British architect Edwin Lutyens in early June since Lutyens had had experience designing Boer War memorials in South Africa. Lutyens rapidly produced a design for a structure some thirty-three feet high made of wood and plaster with a sarcophagus on top. Submitted for approval to Chief Architect to the Government Office of Works, Sir Frank Baines, this design was only slightly amended by Lord Curzon before being given government approval. It was this monumental structure lined with flags that was unveiled on July 19 and delineated saluting point for both Allied troops and their leaders during the Allied peace procession.[11]

Nevertheless, the main focus for the 1919 peace celebrations was the Mall—the route from Trafalgar Square to the Queen Victoria Memorial in front of Buckingham Palace—where a series of commemorative pylons had been erected with the names of key naval and land battles and British victories. Culminating in a review by the king outside the palace itself, the peace procession was a highly militaristic event comprised of contingents of Allied troops displaying the latest in tanks, guns, mortar launchers, and military hardware. However, what was noteworthy was that for weeks after the procession, mourners and pilgrims continued to bow their heads and stand in silence or lay wreaths at Lutyens's temporary monument. Contemporary press reports noted that contrary to expectations, it was the temporary Cenotaph in Whitehall, rather than the Queen Victoria memorial in the Mall or Nelson's Column in Trafalgar Square, which emerged as the site where people felt closer to the bereaved. Events and mass media coverage confirmed that the Mall was now seen as "an avenue of triumph" whereas the Cenotaph had been elevated as the "national shrine." "From a memorial," declared the *Leeds Mercury*, "it [the Cenotaph] has become a shrine."[12]

Following a petition to the Cabinet from twenty-three members of the House of Commons to retain the Cenotaph as an enduring national shrine and as the centerpiece of an annual ritual of remembrance, it was agreed on July 30, 1919 that a permanent replica be erected on its present site in Whitehall.[13] Lutyens's permanent version, *The Cenotaph* (Figure 28), consisted of a severely geometrical, monumental empty tomb made of Portland stone decorated by laurel wreaths and by Union and military flags. Engraved upon its sides were the date and (upon Lloyd George's suggestion) the words, "The Glorious Dead." While its detractors christened the Cenotaph a dreary "tombstone," its supporters praised its unassuming and "distinctively British" styling. As the *Times* applauded on November 11, it perfectly fulfilled two of the criteria set out as appropriate for war memorials. It had been completed by a British subject (Lutyens) and the memorial was "simple, massive, unadorned," and spoke "of the qualities of the race."[14] Lutyens's success was further reinforced when he received the Royal Institute of British Architects' gold medal in

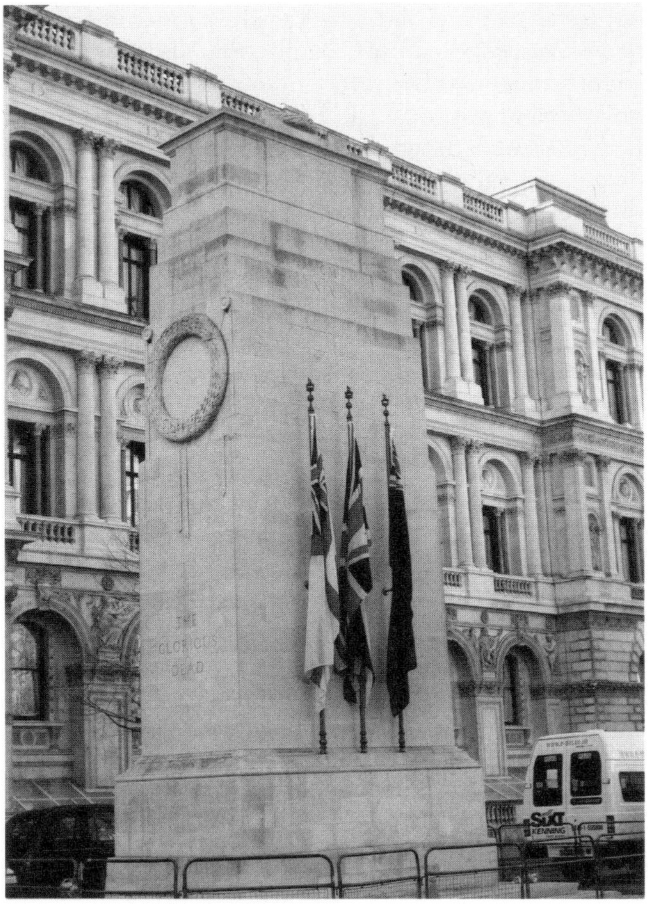

28. Edwin Lutyens, *The Cenotaph*, 1920. Whitehall, London.

1921. In his speech, President J. W. Simpson applauded Lutyens's vision and extolled the Cenotaph's appropriate scale, simplicity, and proportion because "precisely suited to its site and its surroundings, austere yet gracious, technically perfect, it is the very expression of repressed emotion."[15]

With the unveiling of this permanent Cenotaph in Whitehall at the same time as the dedication of the Tomb of the Unknown Warrior in Westminster Abbey on November 11, 1920, there was an emphatic shift in the prewar memorial axes in the city of Westminster that revised the dominant westward spatial geographies of Edwardian London.[16] What was produced was a memorial path that bypassed the "great processional way" from Buckingham Palace, past the Queen Victoria memorial down the Mall through the newly built triumphal Admiralty Arch into Trafalgar Square and to Charing Cross. Instead, this new commemorative route upheld the Cenotaph as the imperial and national shrine for British mourners and then moved southward down Whitehall to Westminster Abbey and to the Tomb of the Unknown Warrior. The politically significant and culturally meaningful nature of this "continuous memorial avenue," as contemporary commentators dubbed it, was confirmed by the annual Armistice Day parade and in its accompanying ritual of two minutes' silence in front of the Cenotaph instituted on the first anniversary of the cease-fire at 11:00 a.m. on November 11, 1919.[17]

Cabinet records reveal that as late as October, 1919 the British government failed to fully realize the significance to ordinary people of the Armistice anniversary and the enormous emotional response it would engender.[18] It became a key date to review the cost of the war to Great Britain, its colonies, and its allies. What were required were modern forms of memorialization that offset any sense of government culpability and military incompetence and, instead, emphasized social harmony, national continuity, and popular unity. In the face of a costly and disruptive war after which—as many war veterans, war widows, and mourners asserted—nothing could ever be the same again, the disparity between government intention and popular reaction could not be easily ignored.

Even though officials hoped that the political economy of these imposing commemorative environments would reaffirm continuity, the modern rituals they generated had to be carefully orchestrated to shape and support an integrationist, postwar public discourse. As Daniel Sherman recently emphasized, "the construction of memory as a form of representation is a political and social process" and it is one that is always rich and complex in its political associations.[19] Sherman also proposed, in relation to postwar French culture, "for commemoration to have the larger political and social resonance with which historians credit it, it must subsume individual memories and other cultural materials into a larger narrative about the commemorated event, in this case the Great War. To the extent that commemoration grew out of and sought to reshape both individual and collective knowledge of the war, moreover knowledges with a direct bearing on the future cast of [French] society, the oppositions it entailed were central to its larger stakes, power."[20] Following the Armistice, any return to late Victorian and Edwardian funereal traditions and mourning practices seemed to many postwar commentators in Britain outmoded and irrelevant given the scale of events and popular emotion. While the demand for memorials was enormous, the formats employed by the "war-memorial industry" frequently appeared overstylized and inappropriate to the experience of modern warfare. During the war, the impulsive appearance of temporary street shrines and wayside crucifixes, often incorporating photographs and personal mementos, had signaled the emergence of less staid vernacular forms of mourning, primarily because of the lack of access to human remains around which traditional burial rituals revolved.[21] In addition, given the previously unimaginable scale of loss that the Great War had produced, there were concerns about overcommercialization and the quality of manufacture of mass-produced memorials. What was needed were updated memorial forms that registered the huge sacrifice of and enormous respect for the dead, but which retained and allowed for some degree of individualized response.

To act together at a moment of national crisis did not automatically assure an agreed language of commemoration, especially given the postwar divide between ex-servicemen who had enlisted and fought, and those civilians who had not. Private memories and personal dissent based on individual experience gained as a result of battle experience (for male war veterans or women volunteers) or not (for those who remained at home), deflected intended patriotic meanings and the dominant expectation that commemoration would be simply a reassertion of the status quo.

The reproduction of the dominant memorial discourse was more fragile and more problematic in the cases of many young single women, homosexual men, pacifists, and conscientious objectors who had not been conscripted during the war and whose attitudes frequently questioned the uncritical nationalism and patriotism that the war had engendered. Many individuals from these social groups were located outside conventional bourgeois family formations and they were disenfranchised either because of their sex, their sexual preferences, or their political or religious beliefs. Their diverse wartime experiences frequently involved encountering discrimination head on: overt sexism in the workplace, political scapegoating in public, and a pervasive and entrenched homophobia. As a consequence, these groups harbored wartime memories that approached postwar modes of secularized commemoration in a more critical way. Their marginal social positioning, minority political convictions, and nonnormative sexual preferences contributed toward an outlook that questioned postwar reaffirmations of a domesticated and conservative vision of British identity with its ideals of national unity and imperial regeneration.[22]

For certain passersby, their prewar political attachments and wartime experiences became vividly reexperienced within such memorial environments. Set apart from those groups who were the main addressees of memorial sculpture—war widows, bereaved families, and ex-servicemen—theirs could not have been an easy acceptance of the dominant commemorative narratives authorized by the state. For war widows and veterans, any visit to the Cenotaph or the Tomb in Westminster Abbey was inevitably marked by two or more minutes of silence that was remarkably profound: it was "the silence of memory" (to use a phrase coined by Adrian Gregory),[23] shaped by and through the bereavement of a lost member or members of family, community, or fellow comrade in arms. For those who had not fought or who opposed warfare, what this silence reinforced was their absence of loss and their position outside these bereaved "communities." What was also highlighted was the gap between others' firsthand experience of war, and their own very different experiences on the home front. Instead of memory comforting them through exposure to familiar rhetorics of idealization and Christian martyrdom, such commemorative forms reiterated their ambivalent positions in relation to the status quo and their distance from the ideal of self-sacrifice celebrated within postwar British commemorative culture.

Cultural historians have also distinguished the end of the Great War in November 1918 as a major turning point in the history of death and in attitudes towards memorialization and commemoration. As David Cannadine concluded, one of the key features in the aftermath of the hostilities was that "inter-war Britain was probably more obsessed with death than at any other period in modern history."[24] Given the scale of the casualties incurred by the nations involved—some 722,785 dead and 1,676,037 injured and wounded among the British troops alone—this phenomenon was shared between nations even if it was inflected differently by distinct national and localized traditions, and various shifting national and imperial identities in the postwar decades.

In central London, the City of Westminster was the area in which the major state memorials of the Cenotaph in Whitehall and the Tomb of the Unknown Warrior in Westminster Abbey were situated. National commemorations have been held since 1919 on the anniversaries of the Armistice. The location of these memorials in Whitehall and near the Houses of Parliament meant that, as I have already noted, there was a displacement of earlier processional axes in the metropolis. Overriding Edwardian London's "great processional way" from Buckingham Palace to Trafalgar Square and Charing Cross, as David Lloyd has shown, "in the 1920s and 1930s, the Cenotaph and the Grave of the Unknown Soldier replaced Trafalgar Square as the central place in London" not only for the British, but for citizens from throughout the British Empire.[25] It quickly attained the status, claimed the *Glasgow Herald* in November 1920 of being "one of the Empire's hallowed places."[26]

While the annual Armistice Day service defined British national and imperial identity by staking out a conspicuous memorial route through the heart of

London, some contemporary commentators recognized that it was, at the same time, symbolic of the many other processional routes to war memorials, churches, and chapels that had grown up throughout the country. Although few permanent memorials had been erected within the first year of the Peace, the speed of construction was remarkable. By 1928, according to C. S. Cooper's *The Outdoor Monuments of London: Statues, Memorial Buildings, Tablets and War Memorials*, there were at least sixty within a five-mile radius of Charing Cross.[27] By 1931, so plentiful were such sculptural landmarks and memorial markers that one commentator described how "every English highway is now one continuous memorial avenue. The cumulative effect upon the traveler's mind is almost inconsiderable."[28]

Although used as a state memorial route only temporarily around key dates such as November 11 and on the anniversaries of great battles (such as the Somme or Verdun), the symbolic importance of such processional avenues as theaters for national remembrance was quickly established. It is revealing that when in October 1920, disabled and unemployed ex-servicemen demonstrated against the government's treatment of war veterans, the location chosen for this public display of their feelings of betrayal and bitterness was Whitehall, close to the recently built Cenotaph. In the following year, another large crowd of over twenty-five thousand unemployed and disaffected ex-servicemen demonstrated on Armistice Day by again marching to the Cenotaph through Whitehall waving their medals.[29]

The centrality of the Cenotaph as the hub of national remembrance was reconfirmed when the suggestion of a two-minute silence in front of the Cenotaph by Sir Percy Fitzpatrick, a former high commissioner to South Africa, was supported by the king and taken up by the government.[30] As a relatively modern "invented tradition" surrounded by rhetorics of religion, empire, king, and country, the patriotic sentiments and populism associated with the Armistice Day parade generated strong opinions. Evelyn Waugh recorded in his diary on Tuesday, November 11, 1919: At 11 am today we had the King's amazing proposition of two minute's silence to commemorate last year. It was really a disgusting idea of artificial nonsense and sentimentality. If people have lost sons and fathers they should think of them whenever the grass is green or Shaftesbury Avenue brightly lighted, not for two minutes on the anniversary of a disgraceful day of national hysteria."[31]

The Silence, as it became known, was a highly political gesture. It occupied a distinctive position in the service as an overtly public moment of personal contemplation on the topic of bereavement, sacrifice, and mass death.[32] This new cultural form in attempting to make commemoration "visible," government-orchestrated, and politically "meaningful," simultaneously left these minutes open to reinscription by personal memories and desire. At such moments of capture and intensity as the Armistice Day's silence provided, London's crowded streets and their spatial environments became haunted by other stories. As the *Daily Herald* on November 11, 1922 asked of its readers, "What will you be thinking of while silence falls upon the country for two minutes at eleven o'clock today? Perhaps a son or a husband, or a brother or a close friend who died in the belief that the war was to make a better world."[33] With the radio broadcasting of the memorial service from the Cenotaph in 1928, the two minutes' silence achieved even greater symbolic significance as the nation was able (through radio) to coordinate and synchronize its ceremonies and to hear the silence reverberate across the nation following the last strokes of Big Ben at eleven o'clock in London.[34]

Nevertheless, although the state carefully orchestrated the Armistice parade and ritual protocols, the dominant narrative could incorporate less prescribed imaginings. As one contemporary journalist recalled after the Armistice parade, the projection of more personal meanings onto the "empty" shell seemed to be encouraged by the blank and austere severity of Lutyens's memorial. In particular, with the piling up of over one hundred thousand wreaths and floral tributes, the formal geometry of the monument was recast (Figure 29), "[During the two minutes silence, the Cenotaph] was no longer a cenotaph, an empty tomb. You could vow that the deep flowers took the shapes of the dead they covered, and the sweet heavy scents spread from a flowered battlefield."[35]

As a newsreel film of the 1919 Armistice Day procession illustrates, given the size and social diversity of the crowd and the heightened emotionalism of the event, issues of appropriate decorum and how to behave during the two minutes' silence were significant.[36] For royalty and politicians, public experience and social background dictated a somber and stoic public decorum and respectful bodily posture. Likewise for the military personnel present, drilling and regimentation secured a uniformed and dignified gravitas maintained in orderly ranks and evidenced by disciplined behavior. Among the civilians in attendance, the war widows' and demobilized war veterans' behavior was less restrained and less predictable. From the evidence of the film, sobbing, sighing, and talking plus the sounds of police horses repositioning punctuated the two minutes' silence.

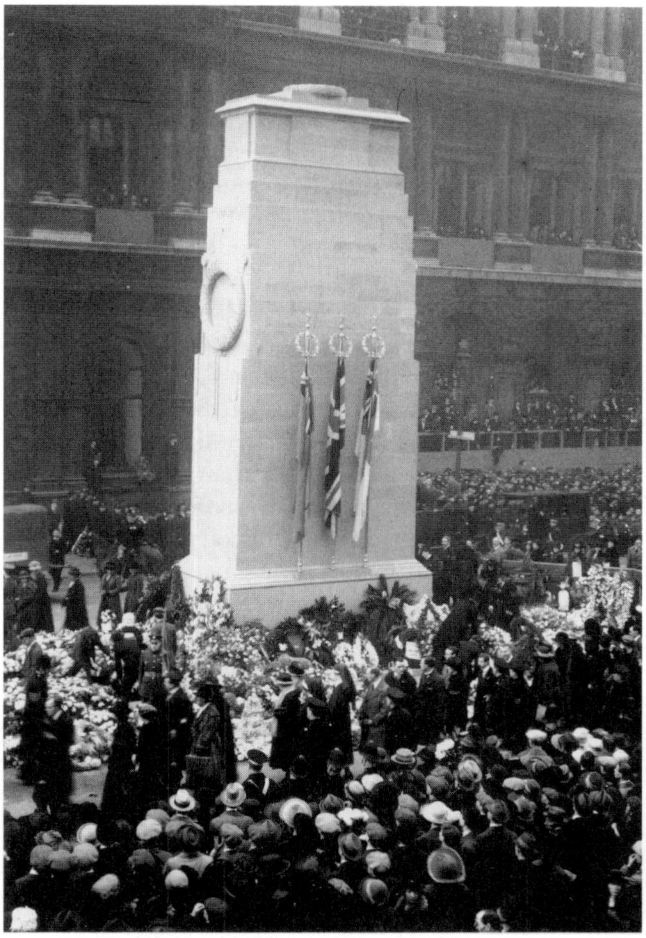

29. Scenes at the Cenotaph just after the unveiling ceremony. Photo courtesy of the Photograph Archive, Imperial War Museum, London. IWMQ31494.

Newspaper reports also recorded that two women shrieked hysterically throughout the ceremony, contravening codes of appropriate behavior for such an event. Furthermore, legal records documented that one man committed suicide overcome by the scene at the Cenotaph.[37]

This new and emotional postwar reaction to death contrasted markedly with the brevity and seemly reserve that funeral crowds had adopted during the war. To some reviewers, such emotionalism seemed excessive and un-British, and far beneath the standards for public behavior that were to be expected. For others, the immense scale of war death and the extreme trauma of bereavement mitigated against such harsh judgments on public behavior. The collective outpouring that the Armistice parade and the entombment of the Unknown Warrior allowed for seemed cathartic, demonstrating solidarity among those who had been bereaved as well as those who had not. The scale of the 1920 event again took organizers completely by surprise with thousands of mourners and pilgrims eager to file past the Cenotaph or to pay tribute to the Tomb of the Unknown Warrior in Westminster Abbey. It is estimated that over 1,250,000 people visited the Abbey in the period on or after Armistice Day, 1920, and many more would have paid their respects at the Cenotaph if it had not demanded such long hours of queuing to gain access.[38]

While the Cenotaph harbored no corpse, the Tomb of the Unknown Warrior contained human remains disinterred and repatriated from the battlefields of northern France and Flanders (Figure 30). In a carefully orchestrated procession captured in newsreels and extensively described in the contemporary press, the body of the Unknown Warrior placed in a coffin of English oak was returned via Boulogne Quay on the destroyer *Verdun* to Dover on November 10, 1919. Amid large crowds and highly emotional scenes, and following precedents established for the state burials of royalty or national heroes, there was a formal funeral

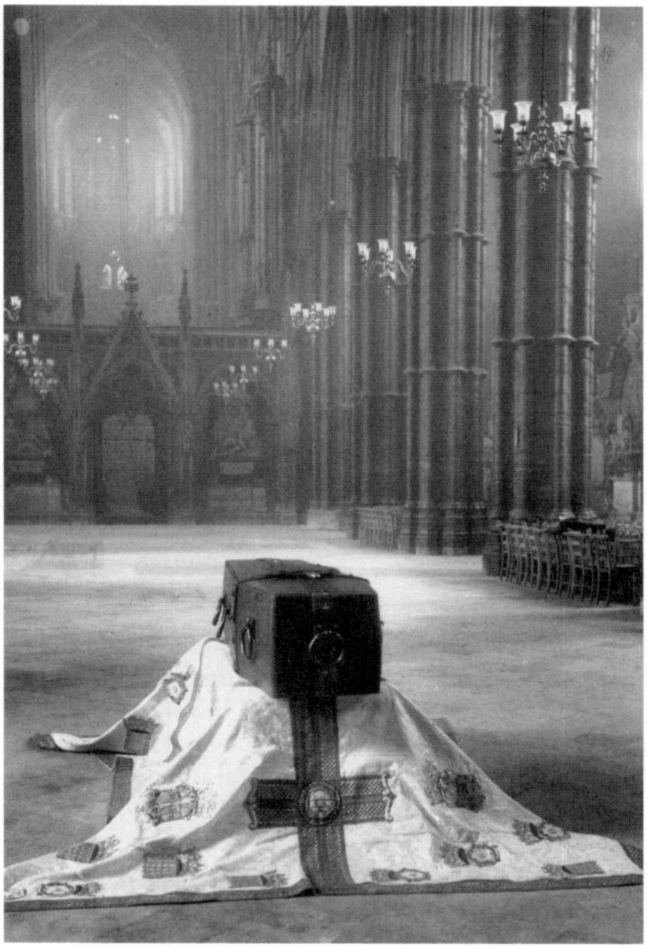

30. The Tomb of the Unknown Warrior in Westminster Abbey, London. Photo courtesy of the Photograph Archive, Imperial War Museum, London. IWMQ31514.

procession through the streets of London before interment. The accompanying entourage arrived from the coast by train to Victoria where the coffin was placed on a gun limber pulled by six black horses for the procession to the Abbey. The coffin was covered by the Union Jack flag with a simple trench helmet, belt, and bayonet placed on top, and over a thousand members of the armed forces including the Guards Bands and the Pipers of the Scots Guards followed the body in procession through the London streets. Behind these ranks were over four hundred representatives of war veterans and ex-servicemen groups as well as leading military commanders deployed as pallbearers.[39]

In the absence of corpses to bury, the Tomb provided a surrogate body for those who had been bereaved, especially war widows. At its dedication on Armistice Day, 1920, as the Minutes of the Memorial Committee (November 1, 1920) underscore, priority at the service in Westminster Abbey was given to women: "a) to women who had lost a husband *and* a son, b) to women who had lost only sons and c) to other widows."[40] As Adrian Gregory argued, the order of these priorities is revealing. Bereaved members of Parliament were the only fathers present alongside a small number of male members from the armed forces. This hierarchy reiterated Lord Curzon's reasoning in cabinet discussions that since the dedication was a funeral service of sorts, "the bereaved were more deserving of consideration" than war veterans, ex-servicemen, or military personnel.[41] As the rhetoric of memorialization evolved and was established in the years immediately after the Armistice, it became clear that in such memorial environments the bereaved, usually women, were the main subjects of address. It also became obvious that the language of consolation used in such commemorative services adapted imagery of Christian idealism and imperial destiny to the cause of national service and personal sacrifice, again aimed primarily, though not exclusively, at women who were themselves largely excluded from such service and sacrifice.

Given what some commentators perceived as the increasing militarization and bureaucratization of the Armistice Day services at the Cenotaph throughout the early 1920s, this prioritizing of the bereaved, especially bereaved women, at the Tomb acted as a counterbalance to demilitarize remembrance. Different emphases were at play in Westminster Abbey from those dominant at the Cenotaph in Whitehall. Such a distinction seems to have been recognized by war veterans who focused their attention upon the latter rather than the former. Although never declared, newspaper reports speculated endlessly about the identity of the body contained within the Tomb. They carried stories of women who firmly believed that their husbands or sons were indeed buried in the tomb. And it was noted by journalists that in the cards attached to flowers and wreaths placed in the Abbey rarely were they addressed to the Unknown Warrior but more frequently to named deceased family members or to those lost or missing and believed dead.[42] Throughout the interwar decades, these two locations in central London—the Cenotaph and the Tomb of the Unknown Warrior—became established as the most significant sites of national pilgrimage. Positioned at the heart of the empire, close to the seat of British Parliament and within the sacred chapel where the kings and queens of Britain were crowned and buried, these arenas infused the residues of imperial and state histories into modern rituals of remembrance that were performed and consumed annually.

As Alex Potts argued in his essay, "Male Phantasy and Modern Sculpture," modern sculpture achieves an alluring immediacy both through its literal presence within the viewer's world and through its close spatial proximity to the viewer's body. At the same time, sculpture generates a complex and contradictory tension in that its materiality offers a resistance to this intimacy and to the aesthetic promise of "unmediated communion between object and viewer, of an unframed experience of the thing in itself."[43] As Potts maintains, this anxiety is particularly acute when the sculptural form represents a human figure since its apparently three-dimensional "realness" makes the sculpted body amenable to projective fantasies and imaginings that break down the distance between viewing subject and viewed object.

While neither the Cenotaph nor the Unknown Warrior's tomb employed figurative sculptures, the ordinary soldier was one of the most numerous and familiar features on British war memorials. The *Royal Artillery Memorial* (Figure 31), located at Hyde Park Corner not far from Whitehall, was a conspicuous example of his incorporation into a commemorative site. Unveiled by Prince Arthur, the Duke of Connaught, on October 18, 1925 in the presence of huge crowds, this memorial had been commissioned by the Royal Artillery War Commemoration Fund (RAWCF) to remember the 49,076 men of the artillery ranks who had died in the Great War. Forty-three feet long, twenty-one feet wide, and thirty feet high, the imposing main structure was designed by Lionel Pearson with four life-size artillerymen, and elaborate side panels and pedestal friezes completed by the sculptor, Charles Sargeant Jagger. Surmounted by a larger-than-life howitzer made of Portland stone, this monument subsequently became known as the "special 'Cenotaph' of the gunners" (Figure 32).[44]

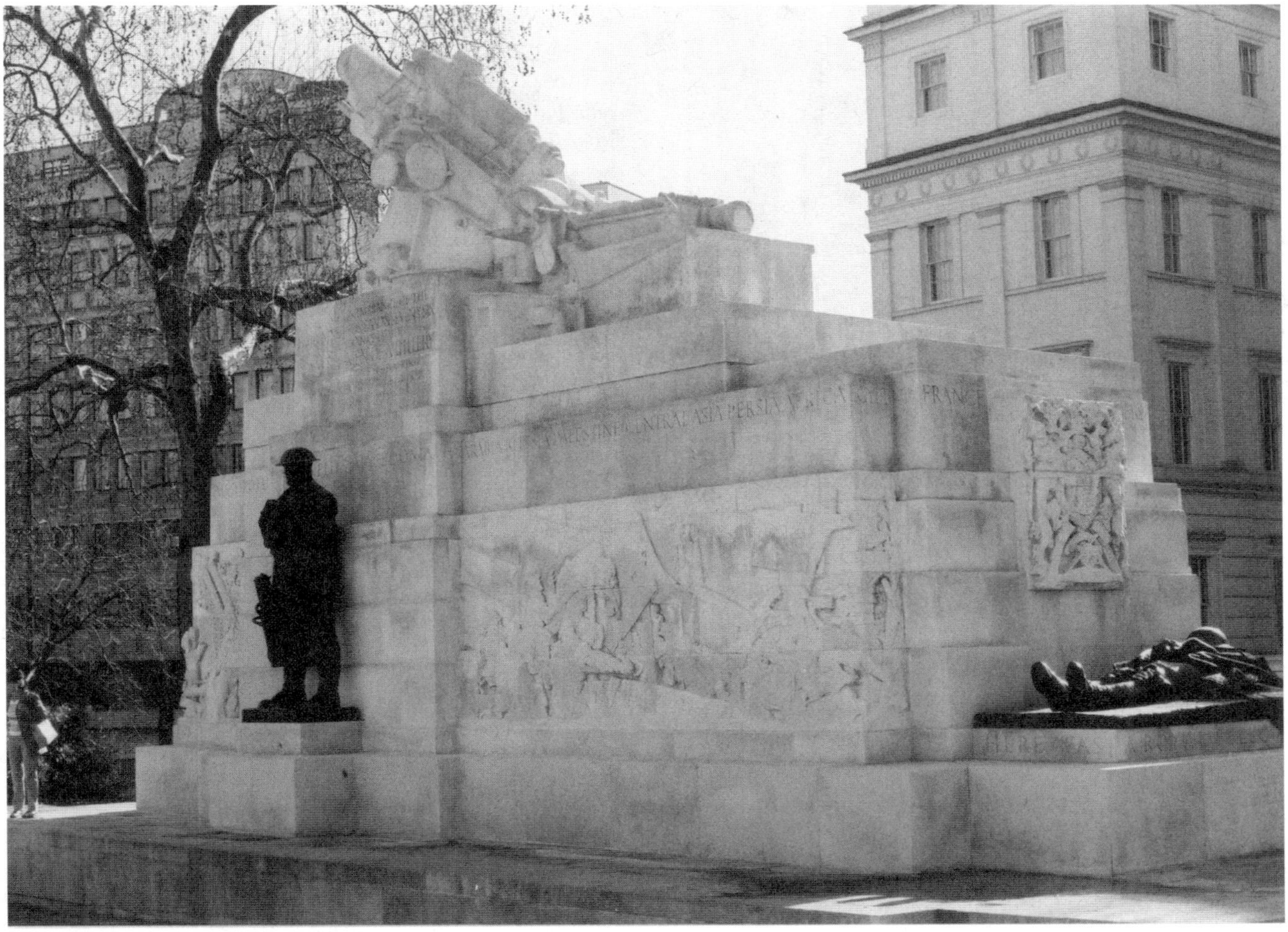

31. Charles Sargeant Jagger, *Royal Artillery Memorial*, 1925, Hyde Park Corner, London.

What attracted particular discussion in Jagger's work were the four bronze pedestal artillerymen, one placed on each side of the memorial's base: a driver on the western side, a shell carrier on the eastern side, an artillery captain on the southern side, and—most provocatively, wrapped in a trench coat—the recumbent figure of a dead gunner at the northern end (Figure 33). As Jonathan Black writes, Jagger's vivid depiction of "war without the gloss" was highly controversial.[45] In his critics' eyes, the figurative sculptures came too close to being seen as "real" men and the Portland stone howitzer was too convincing as a replica of one of the most effective killing machines of the Great War.

What had convinced the RAWCF's committee of professional soldiers to accept the sculpture was the evidence of Jagger's own army record and that he had been decorated with the Military Cross for exceptional bravery in action. When countering press criticism that Jagger's characterization was "coarse" and "callous" in its realism and his men "stocky, sordid, bluntly formidable figures" and too close in conviction to "real tommies," it was argued that the sculpture was the privileged testimony of an infantryman who had experienced the war directly.[46] Jagger's approach was that of an artist who had not just observed war, as some war artists had, but of one who had actively participated in and knew its sacrifices firsthand. This claim for Jagger's memorial as incorporating frontline observation and as embodying the voice of authenticity was evidenced in the "strong and realistic" modeling, in the inclusion of the convincing mock howitzer, and in the accuracy of the relief detail. In an article in the *London Illustrated News* on October 3, 1925, accompanied by photographs showing Jagger working on the monument, the artist's integrity was robustly defended since "the sculptor's main idea has been to combine art with history so that the memorial may form a record of uniform and equipment, as well as ordnance and weapons used in the war. . . . The side panels employ much detail including field guns, trench mortars, Lewis-guns, rifles, signalers, and warning posts."[47]

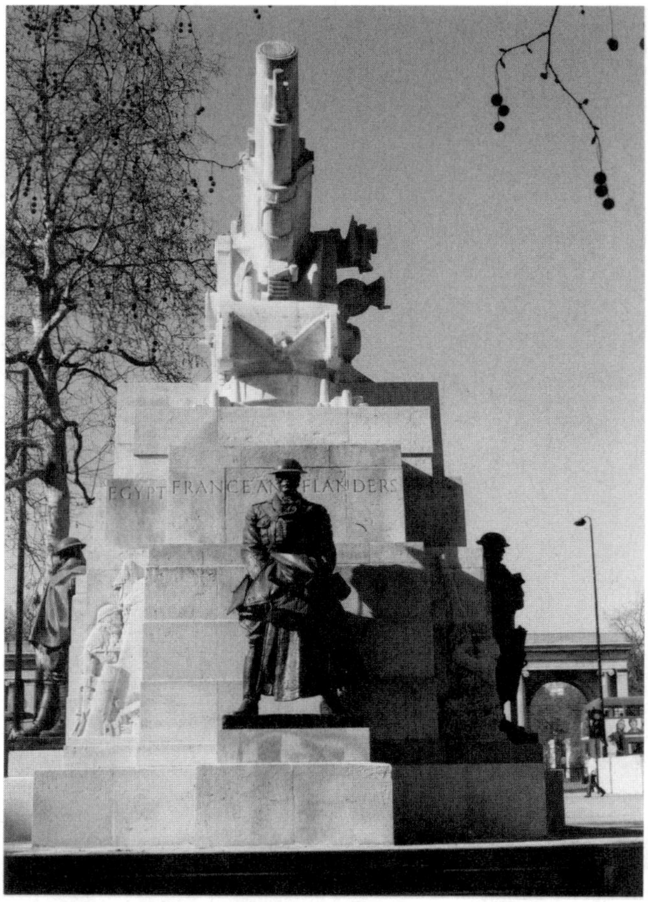

32. Detail of the *Royal Artillery Memorial* showing mock howitzer and artillery officer.

In Potts' terms, this response signals an overidentification that highlights the narrowing of any objective distance between viewer and sculpted body. Such a collapse between art and life could testify to dissolution of sculpture's proper aesthetic boundaries, ultimately producing dissatisfaction and disappointment. Too lifelike by far, the figures appeared to be no more than "dolls" in uniform on a pedestal and the carved howitzer, an ornate military replica. Moreover, if one crucial role of the sculptural aesthetic was to counter an overmasculinization of the body and to defer the threat of unhealthy sexual desire, then Jagger's "rough" privates were troublesome indeed, not least for their failure to respect the sensitivities of the female mourner.[48]

Nevertheless, key members of the Armed forces supported Jagger's work because it avoided the overly glamorous, excessively theatrical and saccharine "fashion-plate" characterization of military masculinity that many active servicemen found sentimental and offensive in a number of war memorials. As General Sir Ian Hamilton argued in a letter to the *Morning Post*, many memorials had to their detriment incorporated "the best looking lads with delicate Greek features and smooth chests. The result has been all over England a sort of bastard Greek sculpture. Now these Royal Artillerymen . . . on the memorial . . . are the real thing and not only the real thing, but the real thing in the rough."[49]

Produced in the same year though unveiled in 1926 and occupying the same space between the Wellington Memorial and St. George's Hospital just opposite Jagger's work was the *Machine Gun Corps Memorial* (Figure 34). By Francis Derwent Wood, Professor of Sculpture at the Royal College of Art and Jagger's tutor, the memorial depicted a full size nude figure of David with his right hand on his hip and his left hand holding an impressive ceremonial war sword. On either flank of the bronze, contrapposto-stanced youth there were decorative wreaths that discretely covered the artifacts of military service: machine guns, helmets, ammunition, and military packs. In contrast to Jagger's stark realism, Wood's restrained classical nude clearly emulated the sculptural precedents of Michelangelo, Donatello, and late nineteenth-century aestheticism. It elevated ancient Greek and Renaissance exemplars rather than contemporary uniformed tommies as providing the correct models for depicting the beautiful and the manly in modern British sculpture.[50]

Unlike the Tomb of the Unknown Warrior that was aimed chiefly at women mourners, the two military memorials at Hyde Park Corner were primarily, though not exclusively, addressed to men although, as I have underlined, there was no consensus about how British heroism should be configured. Applauded by military commanders such as Hamilton and the RAWCF's committee, the *Royal Artillery Memorial* through its gritty realism and its minute detail appealed to a viewer who had, like Jagger, experienced fighting firsthand and who would recognize the accuracy of trench warfare transcribed into convincing sculptural form. To its detractors, however, the monument was too close to life and Jagger's vulgar realism marked out a "callous" approach that dishonored the dead and would upset female mourners. By representing "the real thing in the rough," even a soldier's corpse, Jagger's sculpture had not only ignored appropriate artistic and aesthetic precedents, but, according to some observers, it had failed to adhere to agreed codes of decency and propriety applauded in public memorials.

By contrast, Wood's *David* transcended the brutish by adopting the ideal proportions of the contemplative adolescent under the guise of a historical hero. For Hamilton, it was neither the nudity that was controversial nor the allusion to David's victory over Goliath, but the vapid characterization and shallow

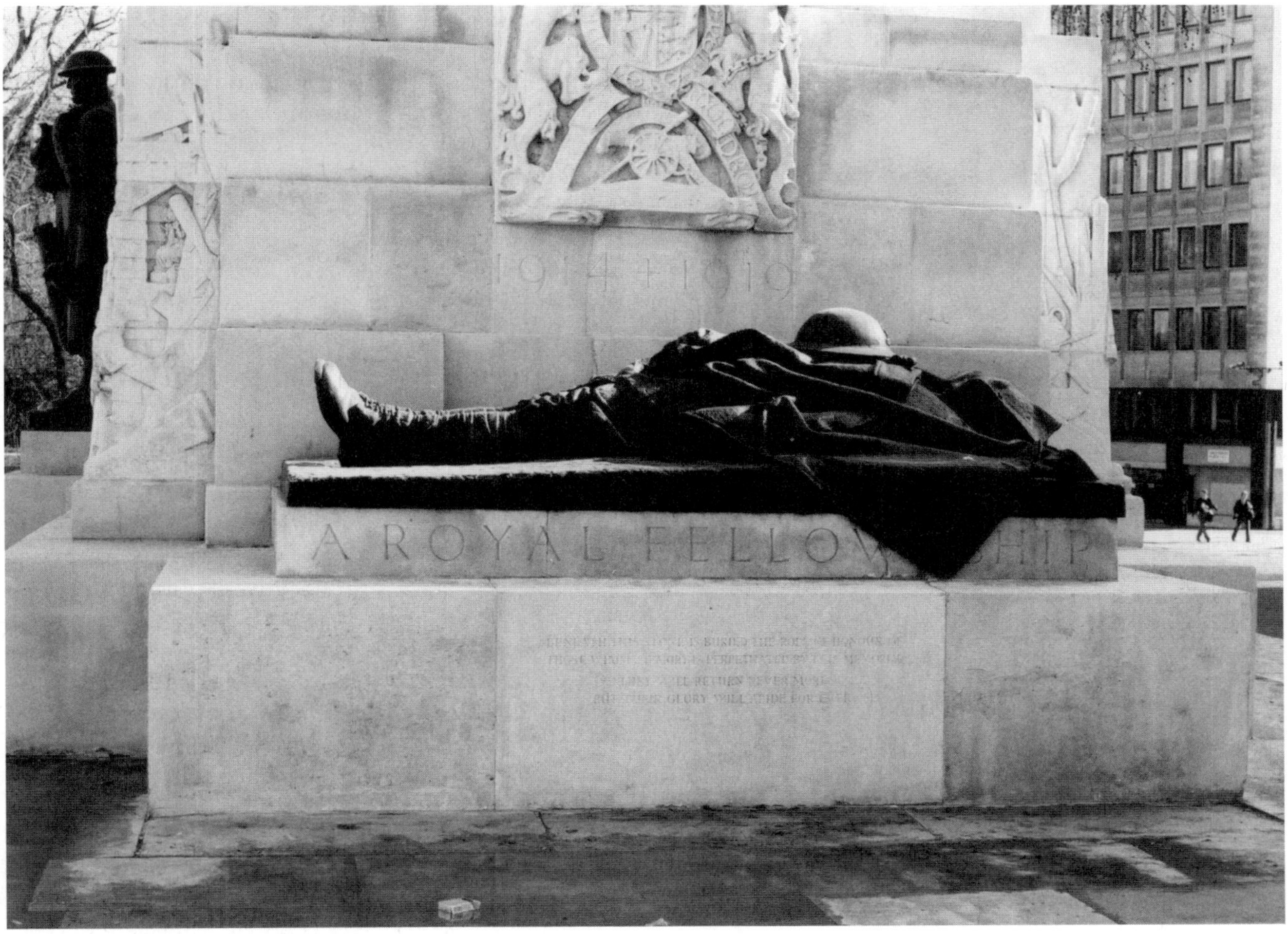

33. Detail of the *Royal Artillery Memorial* showing fallen soldier in battle dress.

veneer of Antiquity that it espoused. As he had stated in the press, works like Wood's *David* with "delicate Greek features and smooth chests" produced "a sort of bastard Greek sculpture" that seemed ill-suited to the job of characterizing British fighting men and commemorating Great War bravery.

As younger generation sculptors such as Jagger developed contemporary languages in opposition to these earlier sculptural conventions and aesthetic legacies, the issue of how to appropriately portray decent British manliness on large-scale memorials was a complex one. As the sculpted male body became the vehicle for, and the focus of, remembrance, male physique, manly proportion, racial features, and masculine styling assumed particular significance. Moreover, Wood's mixture of naturalism and classicism demonstrated indebtedness to late Victorian aestheticism that was increasingly unserviceable as the means of fashioning military authority. Tarnished by associations with effeminacy and intellectualism, government statistics further discredited it by revealing that "artistic types highly strung people and imaginative city types" had been more likely to break down under trench warfare than ordinary working-class men.[51]

Within the multivocality of British commemoration, one urban community with a particular fascination in the sculptural male body and in military masculinity that so far has not been mentioned is homosexual men. While sexual geographies remain difficult to map in interwar London because of the illegality of homosexuality and the illicit nature of sexual tourism, the memorials at Hyde Park Corner, like those in Whitehall, were positioned close to the well-known cruising areas of Trafalgar Square, St. James's Park, Speaker's Corner, and Hyde Park Corner. The fountains in Trafalgar Square were an established location for picking up "renters" or "ruffs." Other "trolling" grounds were Birdcage Walk running from Parliament Square south of St. James's Park up to Buckingham Palace, the public baths in Great Smith Street near Westminster Abbey, and the toilets and bushes on Hyde Park's eastern fringes

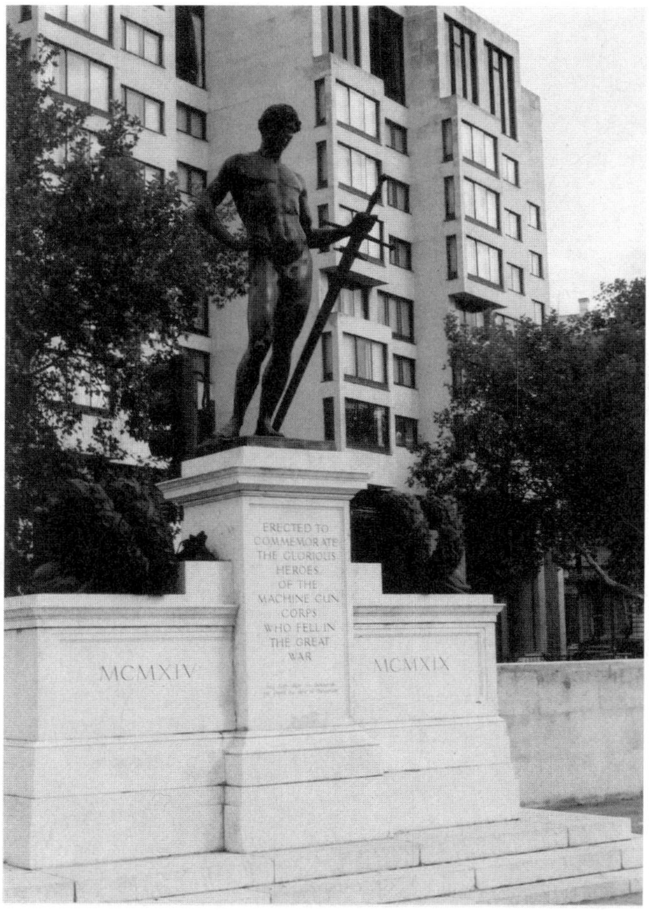

34. Derwent Wood, *Machine Gun Corps Memorial*, 1926, Hyde Park Corner, London.

paralleling Park Lane.[52] For those homosexual men whose interests focused on soldiers—especially the potent homoerotic appeal of the Household Cavalry and Guards Regiments—the public houses near the Wellington Barracks across from Buckingham Palace and the Grenadier pub on Wilton Place close to the Knightsbridge Barracks were favorite haunts for encountering off-duty guardsmen.[53]

Given the evidence of a contemporary homosexual man, Montague Glover, a veteran of the Artists Rifle Regiment who was awarded the Military Cross for bravery during the Great War and who, after graduating in architecture from London University, worked as an assistant in the War Graves Commission from 1923–26, these vicinities in the heart of the City of Westminster spawned and supported vibrant homosocial and homosexual communities.[54] Operating alongside and overlapping with an avowedly public urban culture, these metropolitan spaces mapped out a sexual economy encountered only fleetingly through a cautious, if recognizable, system of glances, gestures, and slang. What is apparent from Glover's letters, biography, and photographs is that this clandestine London incorporated many of the major commemorative thoroughfares and memorial sites into its geographies. Its communities appreciated the erotic and aesthetic components of military memorials and their commemorative rituals.

The reception of Jagger's and Wood's work, like that of the Cenotaph and the Tomb of the Unknown Warrior, reveals numerous postwar tensions: tensions between generations of sculptors whose artistic languages, figurative or not, exploited different traditions and aesthetic frameworks: tensions in the altered approaches to memorials of those who had seen active service and those who had not, and tensions between the genders and between groups of different sexual preferences regarding the most appropriate artistic means needed to memorialize the Great War dead. "They were a wall unto us," extolled the *Illustrated London News* captions over photographs of Jagger's *Royal Artillery Memorial*: the dilemma was how military masculinity might be represented within the evolving visual idioms of the war memorial to convey this sacrifice and how sculptural forms could be conveniently joined with postwar social and political ideals in the eyes of its diverse spectators.[55]

In *The Practice of Everyday Life* Michel de Certeau draws attention to the complex ways in which pedestrians experience and negotiate the spaces of the modern city.[56] He describes how in contrast to the systematic layouts of the city favored by town planners and urban cartographers (evidenced in clear street maps and neat grid patterns), pedestrians transform the metropolis as they move through it by erratic changes in direction and unpredictable maneuvers. As their bodies respond in unruly motion and unpremeditated gestures to the objects, people, and circumstances they encounter, any imagined coherence and urban logic is disturbed. In the chapter "Walking in the City," de Certeau emphasizes how walking approached through such a framework can be figured as an "absence." "To walk is to lack a place. It is the indefinite process of being absent and in search of a proper. The moving about that the city multiplies and concentrates makes the city itself an immense social experience of lacking a place."[57] Employing the term "trajectory" to suggest both a movement through and simultaneously a transcription of these changes, de Certeau asserts that though mirroring the structures of language such "trajectories form unforeseeable sentences, partly unreadable paths across a space . . . the trajectories trace out the ruses of other interests and desires that are neither determined nor captured by the systems in which they develop."[58]

To grasp these subjective ways of urban walking in greater depth, de Certeau introduces a crucial distinction between two forms of urban circumlocution: between what he terms a "trajectory" and a "tactic."[59] The first, the trajectory, is a kind of tracing of volition across "proper" sites and "named" locations. It records acts of decision making, however casual or arbitrary, within the urban environment and conceives of them as plotted in a quasi-behavioral way. The second mode, the tactic, is a more provisional operation. It is a strategy for city locomotion that is constantly frustrated by watching out for casual opportunities and promiscuously engaging in unpredictable revisions. In its reorientations, the subject frequently eschews a knowledge based on systematic geography and official routes in favor of one open to the vicissitudes of chance and desire, to licit and illicit exchanges. As a consequence, it is possible to reconceive of Whitehall, Parliament Square, and Hyde Park Corner not only as centers of government, established religion, and monarchy, but as spaces that are continually rendered foreign and displaced. As the tactic is able to "insinuate itself into the other's place, fragmentarily, without taking over its entirety, without being able to keep it at a distance," the social and sexual significance of metropolitan space and place is reformed.[60]

Elaborating these proposals further, de Certeau argues that crucial to any interrogation of urban spatial orders and their signifying practices, three factors demand consideration: the *believable* (understood through knowledge and legend), the *memorable* (recorded within memory), and the *primitive* (reemerging in dreams).[61] In a phrase that has direct links to the study of commemorative environments, de Certeau declares, "the memorable is that which can be dreamed about a place. In this place that is a palimpsest, subjectivity is already linked to the absence that structures it as existence and makes it be 'there.'"[62]

Retaining these different ways of recording and interpreting metropolitan mobility, of appropriating otherness, and of shaping sexuality and subjectivity within urban spaces it is possible to conceive of the Armistice Day parade, the laying of wreaths and floral tributes at the Cenotaph, the two-minute silence followed by trumpet solo and gun salute, the procession to the Tomb of the Unknown Warrior in November 1920, and the unveiling of the Royal Artillery and Machine Gun Corps memorials as less secure forms of performance than might be envisaged, rituals in which the reproduction of particular commemorative identities was not guaranteed. Following de Certeau, as trajectories through the metropolis, such rituals of remembrance were also constantly open to unforeseeable change precipitated by an unexpected view of a once familiar sculpture; by a casual, unrehearsed social interaction; or by the reconfiguring of the city landscape as a sexualized space. Although scheduled to take place at a historically significant time and date through a highly symbolic, predetermined route, and, at the same time, designed to produce respectful mourning in an impressive memorial avenue marked by imposing sculptures of historical and contemporary figures, participation remained open to alternative inscriptions.

As Steve Pile emphasizes in *The Body and the City: Psychoanalysis, Space and Subjectivity* (1996), it is clear that the state-sanctioned rituals at the Cenotaph, the Tomb, and the military memorials made the political economy of urban space more conspicuous: "Monuments in trying to make urban space incontestable both by closing off alternative readings and by drawing participants into the presumption that the values they represent are shared . . . make visible power relations, but they do so in ways which also tend to make and/or legitimate and/or naturalize those relationships."[63]

That such visibility opened up the rituals of remembrance to alternative possibilities seems equally plausible at this enormously complex and contested historical moment. It exposed a *memorable* that was not always about an uncritical endorsement of state-sanctioned histories or shared social values. Rather, individual responses emerged palimpsesticly through the potency of location and sculptural forms to give shape and meaning to intense memories of imagined bodies lost in war. Intended to install idealized social bonds and to reaffirm heroic national histories, urban trajectories also opened up the city spaces to new pleasures and desires: to the possibility that the Tomb might contain *his* body; to the fantasy that the wreaths and flowers at the Cenotaph might evoke the dead on a Flanders battlefield; to the longings that a troubled intimacy with strangers in front of Jagger's "rough" privates or Derwent Wood's restrained classical *David* might stimulate, or to the homosocial bonds that at least two minutes of heightened emotionalism in front of Lutyens's stark monument might allow.

In her 1930 book on street rambling entitled *Street Haunting: A London Adventure*, Virginia Woolf declares that wandering through the streets of London constitutes one of the greatest of all modern pleasures.[64] Ostensibly about going out to buy a new pencil, Woolf records the fluctuating desires and fantasies generated by urban loitering experienced in the form of window shopping, browsing in second-hand book stalls, or searching through antique markets. What is perhaps remarkable in her promenade from Bloomsbury to the Strand is that there is neither mention of nor attention paid to the war memorials that so prominently marked London thoroughfares and which she could not have ignored had she undertaken such a walk in real life. In Woolf's imaginative psychogeography of London, memorials attract no attention or play any significant part. In her address to the modern young woman reader, they are, therefore, conspicuous by their absence.

In 1925, the British Legion believed that commemoration was declining in popularity and that there was a need to reassert the debt that postwar British society owed to war veterans for their national loyalty and self-sacrifice during their military service.[65] The visibility of ex-servicemen as beggars on London streets and as the disabled demonstrating in front of the Cenotaph signaled in public the failure of the government to respect and reward responsible citizenship.[66] Against the "rough" naturalism of Jagger's powerful, stoic and able-bodied artillerymen and contrasting with the idealism of Derwent Wood's ephebic *David*, the spectacle of maimed and disfigured war veterans was a startling visual reminder. It was a reminder of how in spite of the different masculine aesthetics offered by memorial figuration, the Great War had physically remolded the male body in less aesthetically pleasing ways as evidenced in the scarred faces, the mangled anatomies, and the mutilated human limbs of the war disabled.[67]

By the end of the decade, following the publication of a spate of books based on firsthand experience of the Great War by fellow combatants in 1927–28, the earlier claims made by and for British soldiers as exemplars of self-sacrifice, moral excellence, and unquestioned patriotism became open to question. Generating considerable controversy, these published testaments stressed the human cost, undisciplined behavior, and morally feeble nature of the men fighting at the front. It left their military leaders and politicians under suspicions of incompetence and unprofessionalism. By 1929–30, not only did the power of earlier forms of historical memorialization—its well-rehearsed rituals and its patriotic platitudes—appear less convincing, but the history of remembrance took a new turn in the light of contemporary social and political events.[68] With the onset of the Depression and with the increasing realization that the Treaties of Versailles and Locarno held few certainties in relation to European politics, idealistic commemoration, rather than unifying national identity and reinforcing collective memory, rubbed against the glaring evidence of the betrayals of the past, haunting the uncertainties of the present, and fears about the future. Faced with the complex legacies of the Great War in the shifting politics of the late 1920s and 1930s, the annual Armistice Parade to the Cenotaph and its Silence became not only a moment of considered reflection, but an instance of recognition concerning the inability to speak meaningfully about the traumas of modern war; the repetition of which seemed increasingly imminent from 1933. In a similar vein, John Berger later in the 1970s reflected that "the sculptured war memorials are like no other public monuments ever constructed. They are numb . . . monuments to an inexpressible calamity."[69]

Maybe this response in the face of such stark and obdurate forms offers a way into understanding their absence in Woolf's essay. On the one hand, it reflected her feminist ideals and her avowed antimilitarism and, on the other, it signaled Woolf's own changing concerns with London as an arena for forging a conspicuously contemporary postwar feminine identity in a public culture freed from the grief and mourning of war and from its sexually inhibiting Victorian legacies. If the decade after the Great War marked out major shifts in attitudes toward remembrance and the British approach to death, it also "constituted a pivotal transition moment in the history of European gender relations during which Victorian gender arrangements met their final demise and a reformed gender order gradually was established."[70] Just as the Great War had destabilized masculine norms and transformed attitudes toward manliness, it had also emphasized the gulf between the male and female experience of modern warfare (even when some men had not participated in it and some women volunteers had).

In the postwar years, this difference had manifested itself again in contested approaches to idealized images of male heroism and self-sacrifice, and in the different degrees of access young women, war widows, homosexual and pacifist men, and war veterans had had to the public cultures of commemoration. Conservative calls supported by war veterans and many postwar governments to return to prewar conditions within the family and women's subordination in the workplace merely exacerbated these divides. They openly demonstrated the strong resentment felt by many returning soldiers about the gains made by women during the war and to their newly found social and sexual freedoms.[71] In Woolf's account, the liberation of the modern single woman (like that of the metropolitan heterosexual man) is allied to financial independence, to social mobility and the potential pleasures of consumerism, and to the sexual freedoms of "sudden capricious encounters" with strangers who quickly vanish.[72] It is not as a consequence of participating in a war to defend and uphold a discriminatory status quo or to reinstate traditional family values that such gains were achieved. Nor did this stance readily subscribe to the idealism of Armistice Day or to its postwar rhetoric of slaughter as sacrifice being the harbinger of a new, more democratic social order.

In such dynamic and unpredictable memorial environments, bodies moving through urban spaces sanctioned sidelong glances that mobilized fears, pleasures, and desires beyond those fully rehearsed and prescripted by military and government agencies. These rituals of remembrance held the potential for a brief, if casual and sometimes dangerous, intimacy with strangers in public places in ways that could not always be anticipated. Moreover, the evolving idioms of commemoration gave a license to look at bodies, sculptural or fleshy, real or imagined, mutilated or disfigured, in a new light. These updated ways of looking were informed by shifts in attitudes toward both male and female sexuality, and they were inflected through experiential differences and modernized sexual manners. Such revisions could not always be restrained by the aesthetic conventions of monumental sculpture or readily be harnessed in a compulsory way through the polite protocols of commemoration to the political exigencies of the postwar state.

NOTES

1. For discussions of the Great War and national identity, see Paul Fussell, *The Great War and Modern Memory* (Oxford: Oxford University Press, 1977); Bob Bushaway, "Name Upon Name: The Great War and Remembrance" in *Myths of the English* ed. Roy Porter (Cambridge: Polity, 1992), 137–67; Thomas Laqueur, "Memory and Naming in the Great War" in *Commemorations: The Politics of National Identity* ed. John R. Gillis (Princeton, NJ: Princeton University Press, 1994), 150–67; and Jay Winter, *Sites of Memory, Sites of Mourning: The Great War in European Cultural History* (Cambridge: Cambridge University Press, 1996). The notion of a postwar renaissance in the arts is examined in Sue Malvern's *Witnessing, Testimony and Remembrance. Modern Art, Britain and the Great War* (London: Yale University Press, 2004).

2. These artistic legacies are examined in Meirion and Susie Harries, *The War Artists: British Official War Art of the Twentieth Century* (London: Michael Joseph and Imperial War Museum, 1983); Richard Cork, *A Bitter Truth: Avant-Garde Art and the Great War* (New Haven, CT: Yale University Press, 1994); and Sue Malvern, "War, Memory and Museums: Art and Artefacts in the Imperial War Museum," *History Workshop Journal* 49 (2000): 177–203.

3. The most extensive analysis of war memorials are Derek Boorman, *At the Going Down of the Sun: British First World War Memorials* (York, UK: Ebor Press, 1988); and Alexander King, *Memorials of the Great War in Britain: The Symbolism and Politics of Remembrance* (Oxford: Berg, 1998).

4. Christine Moriarty, "Christian Iconography and First World War Memorials," *Imperial War Museum Review* 6 (1991): 63–75.

5. For the history of the War Graves Commission, see Philip Longworth, *The Unending Vigil: A History of the Commonwealth War Graves Commission 1917–67* (London: Constable, 1967).

6 .Alexander King, "Remembering and Forgetting in Public Memorial of the Great War," in *The Art of Forgetting*, ed. Adrian Forty and Susanne Kuchler (Oxford: Berg, 1999), 149.

7. Moriarty, 68–70.

8. Quote from Minutes of the Council of the Royal Society of British Sculptors, June 28, 1917.

9. *The Church Times*, March 3, 1916, qtd. in Alexander M. King's PhD thesis "The Politics of Meaning in the Commemoration of the First World War in Britain, 1914–39" (University College, University of London, 1993), 191.

10. Ibid., 193–94. In the plans for the postwar redevelopment of the city of Westminster, concerns were expressed that it might look like Berlin's "Siegesallee" in *The Builder*, June 6, 1919, 563.

11. For Lutyens's Boer War Memorials, see Alan Borg, *War Memorials from Antiquity to the Present* (London: Leo Cooper, 1991), 70; and for Lutyens's negotiations with the Cabinet about the Cenotaph, see Arts Council of Great Britain, *Lutyens: The Work of the English Architect Sir Edwin Lutyens 1869–1944* (London: Hayward Gallery, 1981–82), 148–55.

12. *Leeds Mercury*, July 23, 1919.

13. This petition and its consequences is discussed in David W. Lloyd, *Battlefield Tourism: Pilgrimage and the Commemoration of the Great War in Britain, Australia and Canada 1919–39* (Oxford: Berg, 1998), 54–55.

14. *The Times*, November 11, 1920.

15. King, "The Politics of Meaning," 198.

16. For a detailed analysis of the architectural redesign of Victorian and Edwardian Westminster as part of an Imperial metropolis, see M. H. Port, *Imperial London: Civil Government Building in London 1851–1915* (New Haven, CT: Yale University Press, 1995), 23–25, 192–93.

17. E. Homberger, "The Story of the Cenotaph," *Times Literary Supplement*, November 12, 1976, 1429–30; and Winter, 102–5.

18. Gregory, *Silence of Memory: Armistice Day, 1919–1945* (Oxford: Berg Publishers, 1994), 8.

19. Daniel J. Sherman, *The Construction of Memory in Interwar France* (Chicago: University of Chicago Press, 1999), 2.

20. Ibid., 6.

21. Wayside crosses and street shrines had appeared from early 1916 and the Society for Raising Wayside Crosses was established in mid-1916. See Moriarty, 67.

22. For the shifting roles of single women, see Deidre Beddoe, *Back to Home and Duty: Women between the Wars 1918–39* (London: Pandora, 1989), 12–14. For the pacifist movement, see Martin Ceadel, *Pacifism in Britain 1914–45: The Defining of a Faith* (Oxford: Clarendon Press, 1980), 38–39. For postwar discourses of national and imperial continuity, see Raphael Samuel, "Exciting to be English," in Samuel, *Patriotisms: Britain 1900–1939: The Making and Unmaking of British National Identity. Volume 1: History and Politics* (London: Routledge, 1989), xviii–xxviii; and Lloyd, 9–10.

23. Gregory, 6–7.

24. David Cannadine, "War and Death, Grief and Mourning in Modern Britain," in *Mirrors of Mortality: Studies in the Social History of Death*, ed. Joachim Whaley (London: Europa, 1981), 189, 231. See also Lloyd, 4.

25. Lloyd, 50.

26. *Glasgow Herald*, November 13, 1920.

27. C. S. Cooper, *The Outdoor Monuments of London: Statues: Memorial Buildings, Tablets and War Memorials* (London: The Homeland Association, 1928).

28. I. Hay, *Their Name Liveth: The Book of the Scottish National War Memorial* (London: John Lane, 1931), 4.

29. Gregory, 54–59.

30. Ibid., 9.

31. Evelyn Waugh, *The Diaries of Evelyn Waugh*, ed. Michael Davie (Harmondsworth, UK: Penguin Books, 1982), 37.

32. Gregory, 8–13.

33. *Daily Herald*, November 11, 1922, qtd. in Gregory, 60.

34. Gregory, 133–34.
35. *Daily Mail*, November 12, 1919.
36. The newsreel film capturing the unveiling of the Cenotaph is in the collection of the Imperial War Museum, London.
37. Reported in the *Leeds Mercury*, November 12, 1920 and in the *Daily Express*, November 16, 1920.
38. Lloyd, 73.
39. Ibid., 63–75.
40. Minutes of the Memorial Services Committee, November 5, 1920, Public Records Office, Cabinet Papers CAB 27/29, 22.
41. Minutes of Memorial Services Committee, November 1 and 3, 1920, Public Records Office, Cabinet Papers CAB 27/99, 45, 48.
42. Gregory, 27–28.
43. Alex Potts, "Male Phantasy and Modern Sculpture," *Oxford Art Journal* 15, no. 2 (1992): 46.
44. Richard Francis, "War Memorials," in *British Sculpture in the Twentieth Century*, ed. Sandy Nairne and Nicholas Serota (London: Whitechapel Art Gallery, 1981), 63–65. For a detailed examination of the memorial, see Ann Compton, ed., *Charles Sargeant Jagger: War and Peace Sculpture* (London: Imperial War Museum, 1985), and esp. James Steven Curl's "The Royal Artillery Memorial at Hyde Park Corner," 81–100.
45. Jonathan Black, "'War without gloss?' Masculinity, the Feminine Ideal and the Image of the Vulnerable British Soldier in First World War Memorial Sculpture c. 1919–1925," *Objects* 2 (1999/2000): 40–45.
46. Black, 40.
47. *London Illustrated News*, October 3, 1925, 626–27.
48. Potts, 46.
49. Letter from General Sir Iain Hamilton to the *Morning Post*, October 20, 1925 qtd. in Black, 42.
50. Sandy Nairne and Nicholas Serota, eds., *British Sculpture in the Twentieth Century* (London: Whitechapel Art Gallery, 1981), 44.
51. Report of the War Office Committee of Enquiry into Shellshock under Lord Southborough, 1922, qtd. by Daniel Pick, *The Rationalisation of Slaughter in the Modern Age* (New Haven, CT: Yale University Press, 1993), 251.
52. This notion of overlapping sexual geographies is explored in the special issue, "Sexual Geographies," of *New Formations: A Journal of Culture/Theory/Politics* 37 (1999) in the introduction by Frank Mort and Lynda Nead. With respect to homosexual cultures of a later period, see also Frank Mort's "Mapping Sexual London: The Wolfenden Committee on Homosexual Offences and Prostitution 1954–57," *New Formations* 37 (1999): 92–113. The parameters of this territory in interwar London draws upon James Gardiner, *A Class Apart: The Private Pictures of Montague Glover* (London: Serpent's Tail, 1995).
53. Gardiner, 50-58.
54. Ibid., 9–10.
55. *Illustrated London News*, November 14, 1925, 957.
56. Michel de Certeau, "Walking in the City," in de Certeau, *The Practice of Everyday Life*, trans. Steven Rendall (Berkeley and Los Angeles: University of California Press, 1988), 91–110. My approach has also been informed by Dolores Hayden, *The Power of Place in Urban Landscape as Public History* (Cambridge, MA: MIT Press, 1995).
57. Certeau, 103.
58. Ibid., xviii-xix.
59. Ibid., 98–99.
60. Ibid., xix.
61. Ibid., 105.
62 Ibid., 109
63. Steve Pile, *The Body and the City: Psychoanalysis, Space and Subjectivity* (London: Routledge, 1996), 213.
64. Virginia Woolf, *Street Haunting: A London Adventure* (San Francisco: Westgate Press, 1930). For a searching analysis of Woolf's position, see Rachel Bowlby, "Walking, Women and Writing: Virginia Woolf as *flaneuse*," in *New Feminist Discourses: Critical Essays on Theories and Texts*, ed. Isobel Armstrong (London: Routledge, 1992), 26–47.
65. Lloyd, 217. For the growth of the pacifist movement, see Ceadel, 62ff.
66. Winter, 80, 95.
67. Trudi Tate, *Modernism, History and the First World War* (Manchester, UK: Manchester University Press, 1998), 96. On shifting attitudes toward the male body and categories of disability, see Joanna Bourke, *Dismembering the Male: Men's Bodies, Britain and the Great War* (London: Reaktion Books, 1996), 31–39, 250–52.
68. These books included R. C. Sherriff's *Journey's End* and Robert Graves's *Goodbye to all That*. For an analysis of the ways in which these books revised earlier and received histories of the Great War, see Samuel Hynes, *A War Imagined: The First World War and English Culture* (London: Bodley Head, 1991), 424, and Gregory, 119.
69. John Berger, "The Untellable," *New Society*, May 11, 1978, 317.
70. Brigitte Soland, *Becoming Modern: Young Women and the Reconstruction of Womanhood in the 1920s* (Princeton, NJ: Princeton University Press, 2000), 6.
71. See Beddoe, 12–13. For a fascinating study of George Frampton's *Edith Cavell Monument* in the light of these changing gender issues, see Sue Malvern's essay "For King and Country": Frampton's *Edith Cavell* 1915–20 and the Writing of Gender in Memorials to the Great War," in *Sculpture and the Pursuit of the Modern Ideal in Britain, c. 1880–1930*, edited by David J. Getsy (Aldershot, UK: Ashgate, 2004).
72. Woolf, 23.

The Political Economy of Hitler's State Architecture

Paul B. Jaskot

The study of political economy has seemingly been implicit in much of the art history of the last decades. State and party policies and institutions have interested art historians as much as markets, patronage, and other economic factors. And yet, the real essence of political economy in its emphasis on the permeation of economic conditions with political and social actions has rarely been taken up in its totality in art historical scholarship. Focusing rather on the explication of movements, artists, and objects, art history remains interested primarily in the significance of culture rather than in the functional relationship between cultural work and political economic forces. Such a functionalist art history still deals with questions of particular artists, objects, and aesthetic choices. But these are merely the starting points of the analysis. An art historical political economy must use cultural work as a means of explaining the legitimization and conflict of broader conditions of society thus breaking free of the very limitations analytically imposed on a focused study of culture per se. This, too, is a crucial art historical project.

Let us take, for example, the monumental building projects of the National Socialist Party and state. The building industry was of central ideological and economic value to the National Socialist government upon coming to power. As a means of helping Germany recover from the Depression, the building trades and state or party projects provided employment and a concentration of production and resources on a massive scale. And in the monumental projects for such prestige sites as the Party Rally Grounds at Nuremberg and the rebuilding of Berlin, the building industry prospered under the ideological projections of various party institutions and leaders wishing to connect themselves to Hitler's favorite peacetime program. While not the largest industry in the Third Reich, building production was nevertheless one of the most high-profile state and party tasks and thus became a key point for consensus among leading institutions or for the power-politics that occurred between these institutions.

Building technologies—or, more precisely, the question of what kind of construction techniques to use—became a central point of departure for the consensus and conflict that marked the building industry. Engineers and architects, bureaucrats and labor leaders all made decisions for particular sites and made arguments against each other based on the developing building policies of the state and the contingent economic plans occurring because of rearmament. These discussions and debates intensified with the very public promotion of monumental building projects that increased dramatically in the late 1930s and into the war. Monumental projects favored by Hitler provided a high-profile symbolic focus to contemporary discussions concerning the integration of building technologies with the developing strength and militarization of the German economy. As one of Hitler's major peacetime initiatives, the reconstruction of specific cities on a massive scale and with particular aesthetic materials (above all, stone) helped revive segments of the building economy, a revival that was thoroughly aligned with the broader policies of the state.

It is this alignment of monumental building aesthetics and technologies with state economic and military policy which is the subject here. Analyzing the integration of monumental building with political economy must work from such valuable early studies as that of the New Reich Chancellery by Angela Schönberger, Alex Scobie's investigation of the meaning of neoclassicism in the buildings of Hitler's Germany, as well as the work of Joachim Thies in which the integration of architectural policy with state and party concerns was first thematized.[1] Yet, while each of these authors and those who have followed them have noted the conjunction of building and broader political goals, nevertheless, scholars have most often been interested in either: (1) how such a synchronism helps to explain the ideological significance of built forms, or (2) providing additional evidence of the general integration of economic and political goals in the development of Nazi Germany. In either case, the specific political economy of state architecture or the legitimation of expanding architectural production in political economic terms remains peripheral to the main argument.

Certainly, in the case of monumental architecture, political economy must be part of our analysis as such architecture involves the mobilization of vast resources and labor that so often was influenced, shaped, or directed by other political goals. The question revolves around how unstable economic variables like available resources are subjected to compelling or conflicting policies, institutions, and agents and what function culture has within this historical dynamic. Or, as Charles Maier has stated, political economy can most effectively be used "not to account for politics according to criteria of alleged economic rationality, but to analyze economic choices in terms of political forces. Those who advocate this approach . . . ask what power relations underlie economic outcomes."[2] This historical political economy also poses a challenge for art history as it means extending our investigations beyond an explanation of the significance of particular forms or the biographies of specific artists or artistic institutions. Historical political economy as an analytic tool thus allows us to explore not only how buildings get built or artworks get made but also what effects the production of works of art and architecture have on other, seemingly nonartistic, state and economic policies, and how these policies are culturally legitimized. That is to say, I would argue that historical political economy necessitates breaking away from an elite and isolating focus on objects or artists toward a more synthetic—and hence historical—understanding of the function of culture. Nowhere is this question more necessary than in analyzing the link between culture and state policy in the development of National Socialist Germany. A failure to examine the political economic significance of culture in this period is a failure to analyze more completely the power relations that are inextricable from architectural production.

The importance of such specificity becomes clear if we consider the crucial years of 1937–39. Following Hermann Göring's pronouncement in late 1936 of the Four-Year Plan (which introduced regulations that affected the building industry), debates concerning building materials went through a decided shift toward a promotion of masonry construction. In conjunction with this, it was precisely in these years that Hitler and his main architect, Albert Speer, dramatically increased the number of monumental building projects to be undertaken in peacetime Germany and to be built mostly with limestone and granite. Hence, this moment in which the building industry was further centralized under state regulation and in which key highprofile privileged projects were promoted almost daily in Party speeches and the press is a moment in which architects and engineers reconsidered construction techniques and redefined the importance particularly of stone construction for state and Party goals. At no other point in Nazi Germany were design decisions, technological considerations, and economic factors so thoroughly and broadly integrated with one another. Analyzing the debate concerning the ideological significance and economic possibilities of masonry construction in these years clarifies this moment of concomitant interests. Further, it also indicates the ways in which the choices for monumental state and Party architecture not only legitimated but at times also became central to many of the policy decisions and goals of the building industry as well as Hitler's dreams for a peacetime Nazi state.

Of course, the specific decisions made in 1937–39 did not rise out of thin air but rather developed from the particular limitations and conditions of the broader German building economy. In this regard, we can identify roughly three distinct phases in the building industry which correspond to the German economic recovery, militarization, and the conditions of war: (1) the early years of Nazi rule up to full employment in 1936, characterized by a concern with getting laborers into jobs and promoting autarkic state policy; (2) the conjunction of the military economy and the monumental building economy before the outbreak of war in September 1939 based on specific goals of worker allocation as well as the division of key material resources; and (3) the prioritization of architectural goals to complement the Blitzkrieg strategy during the early war years and up to the turn in the war on the eastern front beginning in 1942. In this last phase, labor allocation and the use of war-important materials like steel were the major concerns. Notably, in each phase, the two key factors were available workers and choices of materials for construction.[3]

Keeping these factors in mind, a brief overview of the German building economy up to 1937 helps to clarify the kinds of changes in building technologies that were promoted in those years.[4] The German economy in general started out sluggish but significantly began to pull out of its 1929 crash in the fall of 1932, months before Hitler came to power. In the initial recovery, however, unemployment remained high, and National Socialist candidates made the issue central to their campaign promises and criticism of the Weimar Republic. Employment had significant political import because by 1932–33 only two out of every five people with a job in 1929 were still working. This ratio was even higher in some geographic areas of Germany with strong building industries. In Bavaria, for example, well-known factors such as the rural crises and a disenchantment with the parliamentary democratic system proved influential in turning citizens to vote for the National Socialist German Workers' Party in the 1932 elections (with support at just over 37 percent in July 1932). But in addition to these concerns, economic distress and unemployment obviously became important as well for voters rejecting the republican political parties. As the largest sector of the Bavarian industrial economy, the building trades suffered from the Depression at even greater rates than many other comparable industries; according to the 1933 census, 39 percent of building trade workers were unemployed.[5] A crucial campaign issue, the unemployment situation provided fodder for the Nazi Party leaders in general and with sectors of the building economy in specific.

As a major concern of the new National Socialist regime, the unemployment situation and stimulation of production formed the core of economic policy as they had in the previous republican governments. From 1933–36, work-creation schemes and the stimulation of trade were astonishingly successful in the recovery of the German economy. Furthermore, Hitler promoted the construction industry as a central component of this directed government spending effort. In this regard, while no one sector of the economy was sufficient on its own for causing the recovery, construction nevertheless grew at a much greater rate than the economy as a whole. The bulk of this construction was in new housing and road construction (particularly the Autobahn), but industrial and commercial construction as well as a few high-profile public buildings formed a significant contribution to the overall economic effect. Government expenditure in the construction industry not only had the desired economic impact of stimulating businesses related to and reliant on building activity but also helped achieve the political goal of marking the National Socialists as the party that had brought Germany back from the economic brink.[6]

Through such means as work creation and directed state investment, the employment situation was eventually stabilized by 1936. At that time, the reverse problem arose of an increasing demand on the available labor pool. Public works projects (particularly the Autobahn and building construction) and the growing importance of armaments production as a percentage of total economic output strained the labor market even further.[7] The competition for labor in these years had considerable influence on decisions concerning state and party construction projects and the infighting over labor allocation between government administrations pursuing individual and institutional interests.

Monumental party and state construction prospered from the initial impetus to direct government spending toward building; yet, by late 1936, such construction was also restricted by the crisis in labor markets and limitations on materials. Hence, aesthetic choices combined with political economic policies. This situation can be elucidated by looking at the stone industry, stone being the key aesthetic material promoted by Hitler and his architects. Paul Ludwig Troost's House of German Art in Munich (*Haus der deutschen Kunst*, Figure 35), Hitler's first major commission after he came to power in 1933, relied on vast quantities of German limestone for its façade, a material Hitler had chosen himself. In these cases as in others, Hitler's belief in the permanence of stone and its connection (unlike modernist structures) to a craft tradition, which he associated with powerful political regimes and a "German" style, obviously influenced aesthetic choices made by state and party architects. Though many different materials were used throughout the National Socialist period, the high-profile projects of the party and state remained exclusively stone buildings with modified neoclassical forms, and they influenced a broad range of building types including major residential and public structures.[8]

And yet, before the end of 1936, the ideological justifications for using stone were generally distinct from arguments for an autarkic economic policy and work-creation measures. Put another way, cultural decisions at this time were largely separated from what were seen as more pressing political economic priorities. As an example, in May of 1936 a provincial building official (*Landesbaurat*), one G. Steinlein, wrote a revealing article in the pages of *Der Deutsche Baumeister*, the main professional journal for architects and structural engineers. By this point, the unemployment issue provoked less concern in the industry due to rapidly growing state-sponsored labor opportunities. Not surprisingly, then, Steinlein framed his discussion of the kinds of stone and their potential use in terms of a nationalist economic interest instead. Key here is how the potential ideological significance of masonry remains outside of this promotion of particular economic policies. Steinlein begins with a discussion of how Hitler's regime had increased the reliance of German builders on stone quarried in Germany, an economic goal reversing the reliance on imported stone in the Weimar Republic but not yet achieving its potential of employing the entire stone industry within the country. In this context, he briefly mentions only two buildings specifically: Troost's House of German Art and his proposals for the Königsplatz in Munich, that is, monumental projects privileged by Hitler. Given this rhetorical frame, Steinlein then quickly moves on to a more detailed discussion of the technological aspects of stone construction, including resistance to pressure of different kinds of stone, the use of stone as facing material, and so on. Noteworthy in this discussion is the emphasis on the nationalist economic policy but also the assumption that the

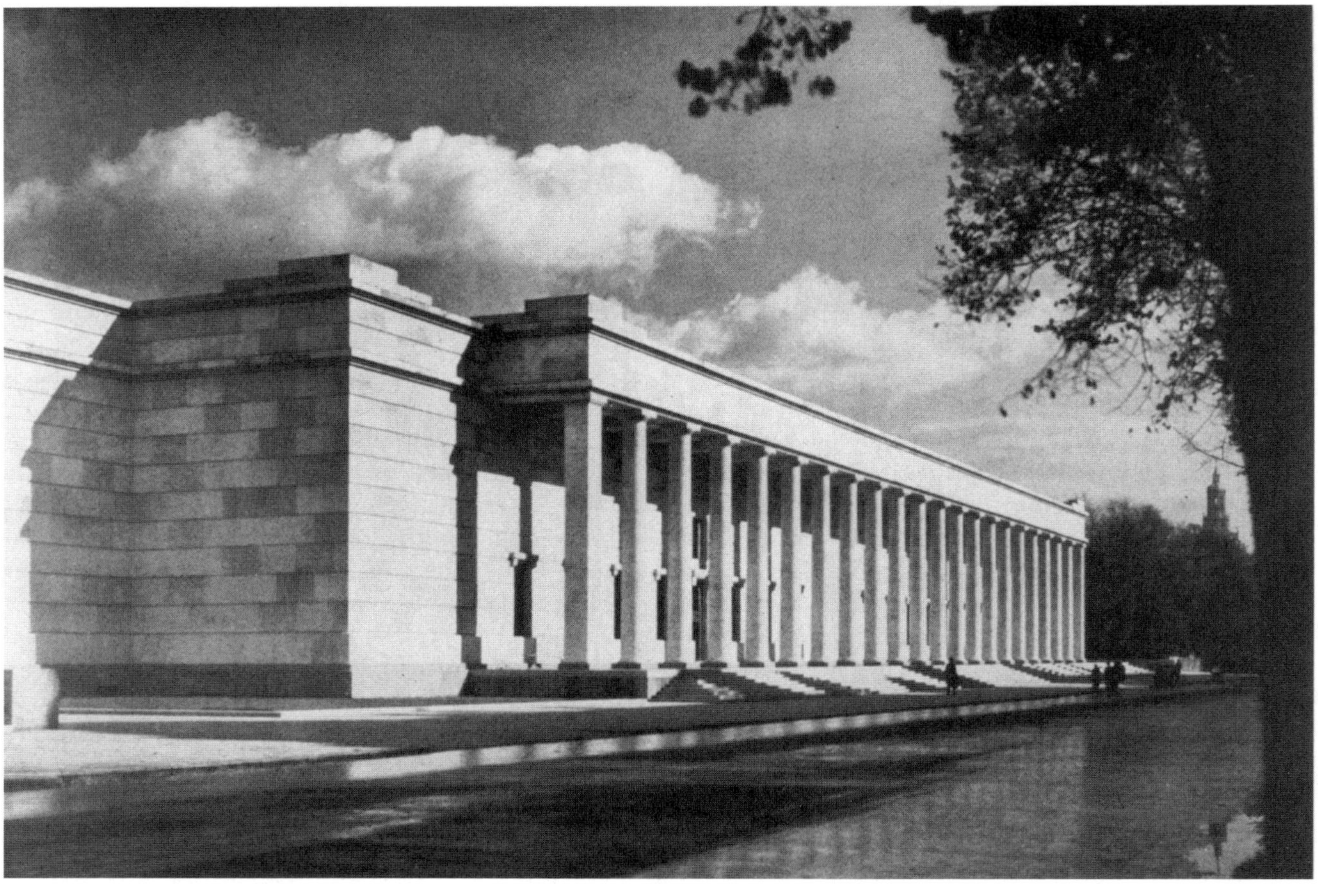

35: Paul Ludwig Troost, *Haus der deutschen Kunst*, 1933–37, Munich. Photo courtesy of Gerdy Troost, *Bauen im neuen Reich* (Bayreuth: Gauverlag Bayerische Ostmark, 1938).

main use of stone would be as a facing or decorative material, not as structural material for the building's core. Steinlein's article thus typically corresponds to this period of recovery in the building industry in which nationalist economic goals are primary and the use of stone is defined predominantly as an aesthetic element derived from Hitler's taste but not yet affected by limitations on structural steel frames.[9] The linkage between the ideologically driven cultural significance of a building and the economic or technical choices architects faced is not a part of the early promotion of masonry construction.

Yet, by the end of 1936, it was becoming more evident that the intensification of production in certain sectors of the economy was leading to shortages of key materials and a renewed need to focus on labor allocation. As preparations for war began to dominate state economic policy, attempts were made to correct these problems through the centralization of the distribution of material resources as well as the workforce. In April 1936, Hitler appointed Hermann Göring to organize the economy and put all available state and party institutions at his disposal. This resulted in Göring's Four-Year Plan (announced at the party rally in September 1936) which promoted a rapid militarization of industry including the production of structural steel. The German economy continued to operate under competitive market conditions, but the conjunction of increased political control over the economy and the interests of large private conglomerates tended toward a highly managed economic system.[10] The same process of centralization affected the building industry, most intensely by the reduction of its access to iron and cement as well as the stricter control of labor markets.

The Four-Year Plan came at a time when Hitler was formulating a much more high-profile role for monumental projects in the German building economy. While Hitler's architectural commitments were clear as early as the writing of *Mein Kampf*, it was not until the promotion of the new projects connected with the so-called "Hitler Cities" in 1937 that the influence of this aesthetic became so strongly felt in the general building economy.[11] From that point, the most important monumental projects were constructed almost in their entirety—including structural support—from granite, limestone, and marble with a brick core. But while monumental buildings were a very public focus, the promotion of stone as a structural material also came into discussions of other large-scale uses, above all the many residential estates. The preference for stone led to a strong revival of the quarrying industry up to the outbreak of war in 1939 but only for specific types of stone.[12] The building materials market, when it came to stone, depended on aesthetic decisions made by party and state leaders who, in turn, took their cues from Hitler and his architect Speer. These aesthetic decisions were concomitant with the economic limitations on the use of steel promoted by Göring's Four-Year Plan.

Hence, by 1937, the building industry was subject to political manipulation by state and party institutions greatly stressed by the huge demands of rearmament and the aesthetic debates surrounding monumental architectural policy. Gradual centralization of the industry allowed for the protection of fewer and fewer projects and for a concentration on those enterprises deemed absolutely crucial to the state. Further, the pressure on employment markets left the private economy and state projects eager for ways to maximize the output of a limited labor force. It was in the context of these conditions that architects and engineers turned to synthesizing the ideological and economic arguments for the use of masonry technology as the ideal building material (outside of industrial concerns) for the German building industry.

It is worth emphasizing the main point here: After the introduction of the material restrictions of the Four-Year Plan and the stepped-up privileging of high-profile monumental projects by Hitler and Speer, an eventual synthesis of issues and actions concerning architecture and the political economy of the state occurred. Masonry building technologies were both ideologically and economically promoted as a means of avoiding the use of steel and supporting the developing cultural goals of the state. The cultural significance of building could be used to legitimize the militarized economy. But further, the enactment of state political and economic goals concerning the building industry were in turn influenced by decisions made concerning the prioritized cultural work of monumental architecture.

This dialectic relation between political economy and architecture came about only gradually after the introduction of the Four-Year Plan and culminated in the focused promotion of architectural and militarist economic goals in 1939. In the initial stages, architects and state officials tended to weight the dual problems of access to labor and choice of materials differently. From the point of view of the economic authorities in the state, the crisis in labor markets remained the main problem to be resolved in 1936–37. Released in November 1936, the fourth order from the office of the Four-Year Plan made clear that labor allocation was the top priority that Göring expected the building industries to address to link them successfully with the requisite rearmament policy.[13]

Yet, however important labor may have been to Göring's office, material regulation— above all, the need to cut back on the use of iron and steel—occupied the concern of those in the professional architectural press. A typical example would be the anonymous article concerning "The Direction of the Building Economy" from June 1937 in *Der Deutsche Baumeister*. Here, the author's concerns centered on the need to provide different kinds of building technologies; notable, however, is not the focus on monumental building but rather on the much larger project of residential construction. For the author, steel frames must be avoided at all costs, to be replaced by such methods as reinforced concrete. But better still would be the use of wood and stone. In this early pronouncement, economic considerations related to resource distribution sound the dominant note.[14] Here, the influence of state economic policy is one way: architects and engineers are being asked to think about alternative materials for the good of rearmament. The cultural significance of specific forms and aesthetics is of course crucial for Hitler and state and party architects but not yet integrated into the discussion of economic limitations and possibilities.

Albert Speer makes this unreconciled tension between ideological projections and economic needs clear in his one major pronouncement concerning materials and the building economy in an article written in Fall 1937 for *Der Vierjahresplan,* the main organ coming out of Göring's office. The article was presciently entitled "Stone Instead of Iron" ("Stein statt Eisen").[15] Speer is certainly interested here in the ideological significance of masonry construction that follows from Hitler's own writing in *Mein Kampf*. So, for example, in the second paragraph of the article he mounts a defense of stone as *superior* to iron in relation to its ability to better represent a powerful people: "While only a few consistently used iron bridges or halls have lasted more than fifty years, the thousand year-old stone structures of Egypt and Rome still stand today as powerful reminders [*Bauzeugen*] of the past of these great peoples [*Völk*]. These structures are in many cases ruins because the human destructive mania has made them so. Nature alone could hardly have harmed them."[16] On first glance, this seems to be the same argument Hitler made in his autobiography that politically admirable societies construct the best monumental architecture. And yet, Speer is not specific here about the political efficacy of masonry but rather emphasizes its permanence. Ideological claims are broad and vague, at best, with no mention of particular buildings or even the monumental projects on which he was working such as the German Stadium at the Nuremberg Party Rally Grounds. Rather, his focus is made clear in the remainder of the article, which discusses the great flexibility of masonry construction as well as its proven worth in buildings that remain over time. Emphasizing how turning to masonry—particularly stone—allows for a conservation of steel needed for armaments work, Speer ends the article with a revival of the argument concerning autarkic policies of previous years. He reminds the reader not of stone's ideological significance but rather of the variety of clay and stone deposits available for exploitation within Nazi Germany itself. In the pages of Göring's journal, Speer is clearly indicating that the architects are falling into line with economic policy through their choice of aesthetics and building technologies.

Within the next two years, however, the pace of high-profile monumental building projects rapidly increased as more and more officials attempted to tie themselves to what by then was clearly Hitler's main peacetime interest. So, for example, designs had been completed and the cornerstones had been laid by 1938 for all of the buildings intended for the final version of the Reich Party Rally Grounds in Nuremberg, and, in January of that year, Speer publicly announced the massive plans for the rebuilding of Berlin that immediately began to be enacted. And these were merely the two most high-profile projects. In addition, as is well known, Hitler had approved and was influential in encouraging other Nazi officials to embark upon dozens of architectural projects in these prewar years that would stamp major and minor cities within Germany with the expression of the total presence of National Socialism through its locally sponsored architecture and urban planning.[17] The expansion of building projects, architects, and sites required a different definition of how such privileged architectural projects were going to have access to the key resources of labor and materials. Further, it required some flexibility of Göring and other administrators to make their economic principles fall into line with architectural policy.[18] Hence, by 1939, economic rationales alone were no longer what architects were using to define their relation to state policy. Rather, economic needs had been clearly combined with the forceful interest in and influence of the monumental building projects. It is the planned integration of the two spheres of activity that distinguishes this period leading into the war.

Myriad articles in *Der Deutsche Baumeister* attest to this new equalization of policies from the perspective of the professionals involved. A typical example would be Erich Simon, an architect in the German Labor Front (*Deutsche Arbeitsfront*), who made this position in his discussion of the building economy. Certainly, for Simon, economic efficiency and the rationalization of the building industry in line with armaments concerns were still a priority (the article appeared in March 1939, many months before the outbreak of war). "For architects the connection to the material resources [of the national economy (*Volkswirtschaft*)] plays a completely decisive role."[19] But as significant for Simon was the promotion of the ideological use of specific masonry techniques, above all stone and its association with particularly classical Roman building. He goes so far as to articulate the argument that the renunciation of steel technology is just as importantly about the rediscovery of the beauty of vaulted masonry construction.[20] Simon's article, typical for the industry at this optimistic moment, indicates how the architectural impact of a project could be seen as equally important as its political economic conditions. Within a relatively short span of time, it was not simply that issues of efficiency dictated alternative building materials; rather, it was also the case that the need for these materials was legitimized synthetically as both economically efficient and culturally significant. Such a shift is accounted for by the massive influence of the high-profile architectural concerns of the party and state on the building economy as both the economy and architecture were integrated into the militarist and expansionist goals of a Germany on the brink of war.

The coming of war in September 1939 led, however, to a very different set of conditions and policies in the building industry. The difference between pre- and postinvasion was significant; not only were certain production costs fixed but the state also implemented increasingly stringent measures in terms of the prioritization of "useful" projects. The building economy was not excepted from these measures even while Hitler pushed to have specific monumental projects continued in spite of restrictions. In the optimistic war years before 1942, articles in the architectural trade journal of *Der Deutsche Baumeister* emphasized the need of architects to become more knowledgeable about the use of diverse building technologies, the availability of building materials, and the relation between the building economy and the war effort. But as most materials were by this time already carefully regulated, the variable of greatest concern to the building economy was the labor force. Already within the first war year, the state encouraged architects and construction professionals to maximize labor output at all costs. Whereas the curtailment of peacetime building projects during the war (excepting after June 1940 Hitler's favored projects for Berlin, Nuremberg, Munich, Linz, and Hamburg) led to some relief from the worker shortage in other areas of the building economy, construction was seriously threatened by the loss of skilled and unskilled workers to military conscription. Replacements needed to be found and state officials discussed publicly the use of more foreign civilian labor from occupied territories and the use of prisoners of war. In article after article, professionals emphasized the quantity and quality of the labor force as the most pressing need in the war economy and, up to 1942, for the presumed postwar needs of the monumental building projects which seemed to be only a battle victory or two away.[21] Thus, in the early war years, the efficient use of regulated materials like steel was still a factor but the focus of debate shifted to the expansion and maximization of labor productivity. Labor became the concern that dominated the interests of the state and its architects.

The conjunction of the ideological significance of masonry technology with the needs of the militarized economy had lost much of its impact even though work on some monumental state and party projects continued at least up until the clear military setbacks on the eastern front. Even before the military defeats, Speer had signaled a clear, new direction for architectural writing during the war. For him, broad and vague associations could be drawn between the history of architecture through the centuries, the Nazi buildings then planned and under construction, and the potential for architecture's role in an expansionist Germany.[22] The balance between culture and political economy could no longer be maintained as architecture gradually became subsumed in the wartime priority of military dominance. In this sense, the narrower professional concern with justifying certain kinds of building technologies as had existed before the war became of less interest; in its stead, newer and more brutal ideological goals became the focus of government regulation and architectural practice. Here as well, the building industry worked with state policy as a key component in the military expansion and policies of oppression particularly against the European Jews. In this last chapter of the subordination of architecture to Nazi state policy, architects and planners were involved in crucial stages of concentrating, ghettoizing, and murdering millions of individuals.[23]

A reconsideration of historical political economy in relation to Hitler's state architecture indicates that aesthetic and material debates became subject to and part of the gradual radicalization of all major government policies dealing with militarization and resource management most forcefully in the years leading up to World War II. While crucial for understanding the debates around masonry in 1937–39, this is also a lesson that should make us look carefully at the political economy of other historical periods to assess more completely the relationship between art and the distribution of resources in a given society. Resources—labor, materials, and also time—are variable components that influence every art historical problem, whether it is that of the individual painter or the institutional goals of a state cultural apparatus. Seeing the functional relationship between cultural work and resources points us squarely to the intersection between art history and political economy. This intersection reveals the embeddedness of art in broader structural relations, a condition that can be used analytically to open up the possibility for art history to perform a radical critique of society. Such a critique is dependent on the question of whether art history should argue from within the box of problems raised exclusively by the artist and her or his work. Seeing this hermeneutic box as itself a construct rather than as an historical condition allows for new questions concerning the functional role of cultural work in relation to specific objects and institutions as well as to the broader social, economic, and political forces seemingly beyond the realm of art historical investigation.

NOTES

My thanks to Julie Codell for her editorial advice and for organizing the session on art and political economy for the CAA conference where these ideas were originally presented. Thanks as well to Mikkel Bolt Rasmussen and Jacob Wamberg for putting together the "Totalitarian Art and Modernity" conference at the University of Aarhus, Denmark, where a longer version of this original paper was presented and debated. Participants in these conferences and other colleagues have given me a wealth of critical feedback which has proven invaluable. In particular, I want to acknowledge Michael Thad Allen, Olaf Peters, and O. K. Werckmeister.

1. Angela Schönberger, *Die Neue Reichskanzlei von Albert Speer: Zum Zusammenhang von nationalsozialistischer Architektur und Ideologie* (Berlin: Mann Verlag, 1981); Alex Scobie, *Hitler's State Architecture* (University Park: Pennsylvania State University Press, 1990); Jochen Thies, *Architekt der Weltherrschaft: Die "Endziele" Hitlers* (Düsseldorf: Droste Verlag, 1976).

2. Charles Maier, *In Search of Stability: Explorations in Historical Political Economy* (Cambridge: Cambridge University Press, 1987), 3. See also the chapter in this volume on comparative fascist economics.

3. For the institutional and cultural development (separate from concerns of the building industry) of the professions of architect and engineer in Nazi Germany, see Eduard Führ, "Über die Kultur der Architekten und Ingenieure im 'Dritten' Deutschen Reich," in *Architektur und Ingenieurwesen zur Zeit der nationalsozialistischen Gewaltherrschaft*, ed. Ulrich Kuder (Berlin: Gebr. Mann Verlag, 1997), 53–68.

4. This brief overview of the German building economy draws on information I have presented elsewhere. See Paul B. Jaskot, *Architecture of Oppression* (London: Routledge, 2000), 15–19, 25–34.

5. See the discussion of the Bavarian situation and voter patterns before and after 1933 in Ian Kershaw, *Popular Opinion and Political Dissent in the Third Reich* (Oxford: Clarendon Press, 1983), 10–110. One report from January, 1932 produced by the building trades for the government listed the rate of unemployment in their industry at 88.6 percent, although the rate at that time could also be ascribed partially to the usual slow down in the winter months as well as the general unemployment problem. See the report on the "Beschäftigungsgrad im Baugewerbe" in Bundesarchiv (German Federal Archives, Berlin [BA]), R13/VIII, 27. Subsequent references to this archive will be BA.

6. Richard Overy, *The Nazi Economic Recovery, 1932–1938*, 2nd ed. (Cambridge: Cambridge University Press, 1996), 36–51. See also Dan Silverman, *Hitler's Economy: Nazi Work Creation Programs, 1933–1936* (Cambridge, MA: Harvard University Press, 1998). An excellent recent overview of the role of the economy in the development of National Socialist Germany is Adam Tooze, *The Wages of Destruction: The Making and Breaking of the Nazi Economy* (London: Allen Lane, 2006).

7. Franz Seidler, *Fritz Todt: Baumeister des Dritten Reiches* (Munich: F. A. Herbig Verlagsbuchhandlung, 1986), 97–159. Seidler's neoconservative approach should be viewed with caution. Nevertheless, his general observations on the building economy are backed up by contemporary pronouncements. For example, NSDAP Reichsschatzmeister Franz Xaver Schwarz pointed out the continuing problem in a memorandum of 1939: "The lack of manpower, especially in the building economy, demands a planned use of the available manpower." See the Schwarz memorandum of July 19, 1939, in BA, NS3/436, 30. See also (in this file) other orders by Schwarz sent to the SS economic administrators from 1939 to 1941 discussing similar problems.

8. Most recently, Hitler's cultural concerns and aesthetic interests are summarized in Frederic Spotts, *Hitler and the Power of Aesthetics* (Woodstock, NY: Overlook Press, 2004). See the still fundamental survey of different building types in Barbara Miller Lane, *Architecture and Politics in Germany 1918-1945* (Cambridge, MA: Harvard University Press, 1968), 185–216. For the most complete account of the ideological significance of neoclassicism and stone, see Scobie. For a comparable and compelling analysis of the political instrumentalization of masonry in the Weimar Republic that also touches on some continuities into the early Nazi period, see Christian Fuhrmeister, *Beton, Klinker, Granit: Material, Macht, Politik; eine Materialikonographie* (Berlin: Bauwesen, 2001).

9. G. Steinlein, "Vorkommen, Eigenschaften und Verwendungsarten deutscher natürlicher Gesteine," *Beilage zum "Baumeister"* no. 5 (1936): B91–93. See also Overy's discussion of the attempt to cut down on foreign financing and production in the German economy.

10. Hans-Erich Volkmann, "Die NS-Wirtschaft in Vorbereitung des Krieges," in *Ursachen und Voraussetzungen des Zweiten Weltkrieges*, ed. W. Deist et al. (Frankfurt: Fischer Taschenbuch Verlag GmbH, 1989), 329–52. For the nature of this managed economy, see Overy, 36–51, 66–67. See also the interpretation of the significance for the building economy of the first six orders from Göring's office in "Vierjahresplan und Bauwesen," *Beilage zum 'Baumeister'* 1 (1937): B14.

11. See the general overview of the five "Hitler Cities"—Berlin, Munich, Linz, Nuremberg (the Party Rally Grounds), and Hamburg—as well as reprinted documentation in Jost Dülffer, Jochen Thies, and Josef Henke, eds., *Hitlers Städte: Baupolitik im Dritten Reich* (Cologne: Böhlan Verlag, 1978). For Hitler's pronouncements on architecture, see in particular Adolf Hitler, *Mein Kampf*, trans. L. Lore (New York: Stackpole Sons, 1939), 257–63.

12. See Scobie's discussion of the relevance of stone to Hitler and the theory of "ruin value" (93–96). For specific examples of the influence of Speer and Hitler on aesthetic decisions concerning the choice of stone see the discussion of the Nuremberg Party Rally Grounds and the rebuilding of Berlin in Jaskot, *Architecture of Oppression*.

13. Anon., "Vierjahresplan und Bauwesen," *Beilage zum "Baumeister,"* no. 1 (1937): B14.

14. Anon., "Die Lenkung des Baumarktes," *Beilage zum "Baumeister,"* no. 6 (1937): B132–33.

15. Albert Speer, "Stein statt Eisen," *Der Vierjahresplan* 1, no. 3 (1937): 135–37.

16. Ibid., 136 (author's translation).

17. For an overview of Hitler's interest in a wide variety of architectural projects in these years, see Klaus Backes, *Hitler und die bildenden Künste* (Cologne: DuMont Buchverlag, 1988), 117–93. See also more recently, Spotts's summary of Hitler's aesthetic interests.

18. See, particularly, the grotesque example of the SS reorienting specific forced labor concentration camps around Speer's and Hitler's aesthetic requirements detailed in Jaskot, *Architecture of Oppression*. The interest of Nazi officials in culling favor with Hitler through adapting to his interest in cultural policy was not exclusive to architecture in this polycratic state. See, e.g., the myriad examples of art professionals' involvement with state policy and currying Hitler's attention in the two important works by Jonathan Petropoulos: *Art as Politics in the Third Reich* and *The Faustian Bargain* (Oxford: Oxford University Press, 2000).

19. Erich Simon, "Baugestaltung und Bauwirtschaft," *Der Deutsche Baumeister*, no. 3 (1939): 5 (author's translation).

20. Ibid., 5–8.

21. A review of *Der Deutsche Baumeister* reveals the prioritization of wartime and monumental building projects as well as the focus on key wartime issues like material acquisition and labor policy. See, e.g., Joachim Steffens, "Die gegenwärtigen und zukünftigen Möglichkeiten des Bauschaffens," *Der Deutsche Baumeister*, no. 1 (1942): 7–12. See, also, Christian Fuhrmeister's brief discussion of the political significance of materials for specific monuments in the Weimar and Nazi period into the war years in the useful last chapter of his book *Beton, Klinker, Granit*.

22. Albert Speer, *Neue Deutsche Baukunst* (Berlin: 1941).

23. Debra Dwork and Robert Jan van Pelt, *Auschwitz: 1270 to the Present* (New York: W. W. Norton, 1996). See, also, the overview of architecture's usefulness for anti-Semitic policy in Paul B. Jaskot, "Architecture and the Destruction of the European Jews," in *The Holocaust's Ghost: Writings on Art, Politics, Law and Education*, ed. F. C. DeCoste and Bernard Schwartz (Edmonton: University of Alberta Press, 2000), 145–64. More recently, Tim Cole has forcefully argued that we also need to consider the manipulation of space and building in the ghettoization of eastern European Jews as more central to the development of policies of oppression. See Tim Cole, *Holocaust City: The Making of a Jewish Ghetto* (New York: Routledge, 2003).

IV
A Case Study: The Political Economy of Art in America

Constructing Cultural Democracy: Ideology, Economics, and Public Art in 1930s America

Helen Langa

During the decade of the Great Depression and the New Deal, the government of the United States embarked on a unique social experiment in the political economy of art by funding an unprecedented program of state intervention into cultural production. Provoked by the financial crisis of the Great Depression to seek new means for revitalizing and enriching the nation's corporate identity, Franklin Delano Roosevelt's New Deal government supported the development and dissemination of visual art, literary works, music, and theater to a mass audience under the banner of "cultural democracy." New Deal politicians and arts administrators posed works of art as useful tools for expressing national values as well as educating, enlivening, and unifying the country's diverse communities. State-sponsored projects paid visual artists a regular salary for producing paintings, prints, and sculptures that could be displayed in public venues, underwrote mural commissions for public buildings, and supported touring exhibitions and a wide variety of educational programs. New Deal rhetoric foregrounded the importance of making America's cultural riches available to citizens frequently considered to be underprivileged in their access to the arts. It also linked individual artistic expression to ideals that joined personal liberty and national unity with a utopian valorization of culture as a unifying social good that deserved public support. Freedom of expression as a political ideal underwrote surprising tolerance for a wide variety of visual statements created under government auspices; these were mostly characterized by quiet forms of realism, but included works as diverse as Ida Abelman's abstract lithograph *Construction* (1936–39, Figure 36) and Harry Gottlieb's socially radical color silkscreen *The Strike Is Won!* (1940, Figure 37), both of which were produced for the Federal Art Project. Although not necessarily congruent, assertions of expressive artistic independence, national cohesion, and the socially beneficent functions of culture served to connect the formerly private sphere of artistic production with state-sponsored efforts to promote artistic literacy, community uplift, and the reforging of strong national identity.

In the mid-1930s, the social and political opportunities inherent in government support for the arts looked very promising to members of Roosevelt's New Deal government, although they regarded this development as a very minor aspect of their struggle with terrifying statistics of economic dissolution and human want. Proponents of "cultural democracy" emphasized that not only was spending on federal arts programs a mere fraction of the larger yearly budgets legislated to provide relief for the unemployed, but the economic costs of state support for the arts were offset by significant cultural benefits.[1] Advocates for federal intervention argued that funds appropriated for programs to support unemployed artists, musicians, writers, and performers would also facilitate new opportunities for American citizens to enjoy fine art, literature, music, dance, and theater, and these experiences would benefit all participants through their engagement with new forms of cultural expression. Discourses of cultural democracy also legitimated the inclusion of artists on federal work-relief programs by asserting that the artworks they produced had intrinsic value: as economic goods, as personal statements of individual creativity, and as cultural products that enriched the nation's corporate well-being (although this identity was defined within an unproblematic conception of shared interests that was entirely fictive).

These ideals inflected the New Deal cultural programs on several levels as state intervention in the political economy of arts production expanded during the second half of the decade.[2] However, each of the ideological constructs used to support state funding was complicated by underlying complexities and contradictions that left programs vulnerable to oppositional critique, while the pragmatic aspects of their institutional practice also produced intense public debate. Both idealism and dissent assured that the rhetoric of cultural democracy was often belied in the details of its actualization within the larger political economy of cultural development in the United States. Elitist demands for explicit standards of quality conflicted with efforts to support the economically disadvantaged. Creative individualism ran up against bureaucratic administrative policies. Left/liberal arguments for freedom of stylistic expression and political intent clashed with questions about responding

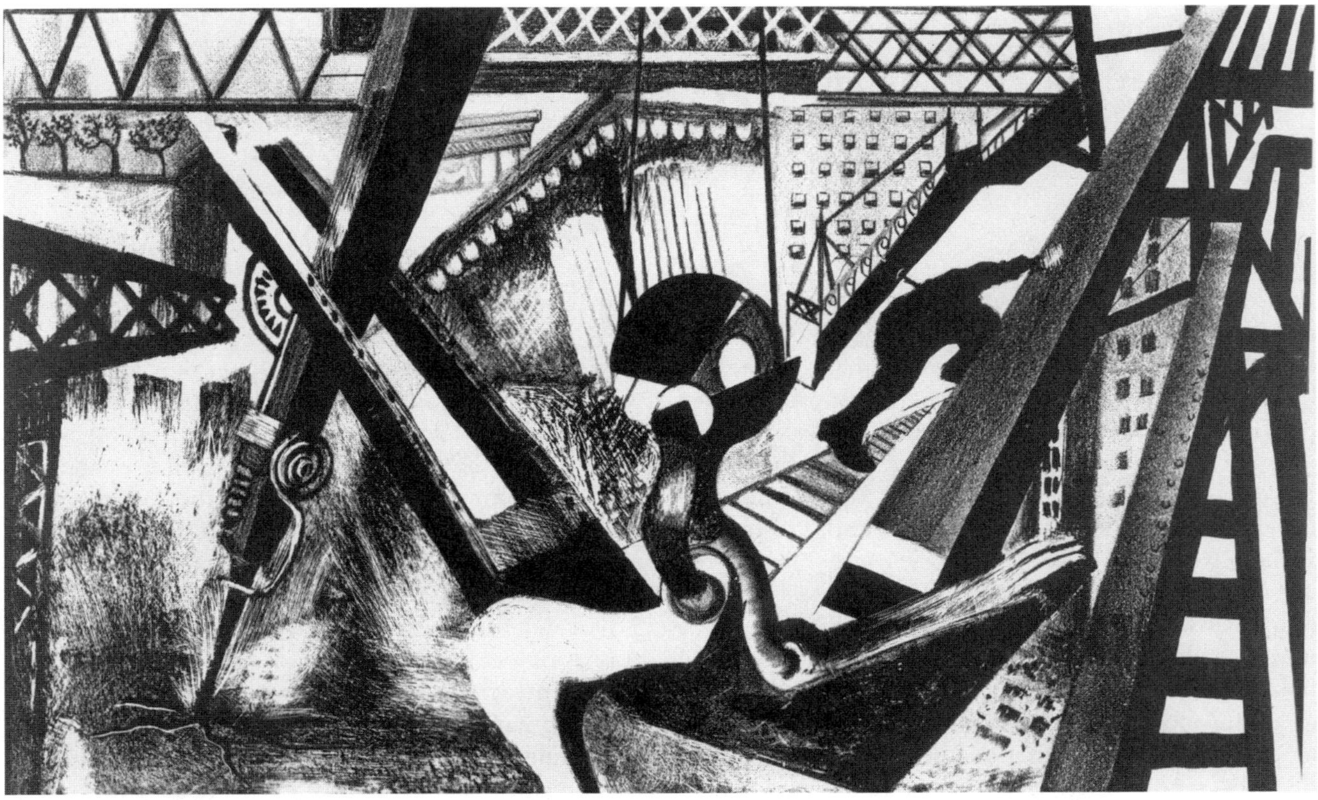

36. Ida Abelman, *Construction*, 1936–39, lithograph, WPA-FAP. Print Collection, Miriam and Ira D. Wallach Division of Art, Prints, and Photographs, The New York Public Library, Astor, Lenox, and Tilden Foundations.

to or improving public taste. Conservative rage over the representation of radical ideals combined with resentment over what was seen by some as excessive support for economically marginal products. Thus the difficulty of constructing and sustaining a state-sponsored system for funding, producing, and disseminating "democratic" art reflected significant tensions within both the political economy that shaped these art programs and the highly politicized ideology of cultural democracy itself.

A Brief Summary of the New Deal Art Programs

Since the New Deal visual art programs have been studied extensively, a brief summary of their history should suffice as introduction. Beginning in 1932, several short-term projects were established to test how federal funding for the arts might work; then in 1934–35, three long-term, nationally oriented programs were funded: the Treasury Section of Fine Arts (1934–43), the Treasury Relief Art Project (TRAP, 1935–39), and the Works Progress Administration's Federal Art Project (WPA-FAP, 1935–43). The Treasury Section commissioned 1,205 individuals and awarded 1,124 mural contracts and 289 sculpture contracts for work placed in post offices across the country and in federal buildings, mostly in Washington, DC; these were funded by one percent of the building budget, and most artists were selected in anonymous competitions.[3] TRAP commissioned art for other federal buildings, such as post offices, hospitals, and housing projects, which were already completed or whose budgets lacked money for decoration. It was run by the Treasury but funded as a relief-based program by the WPA; its products included eighty-nine murals and sixty-five sculptures; 108 painters were also commissioned to produce easel pictures.[4] The WPA-FAP was organized quite differently. It was part of a larger program, called "Federal One," that included four distinct cultural projects (Art, Music, Theater, and Writers) along with the Index of American Design, the Design Laboratory, and units that did related work: teaching, curating and producing exhibitions, and framing. Like TRAP, the WPA-FAP hired individuals who had to prove their eligibility for work-relief as well as demonstrate professional expertise in their field. Across the country, the Federal Art Project employed about

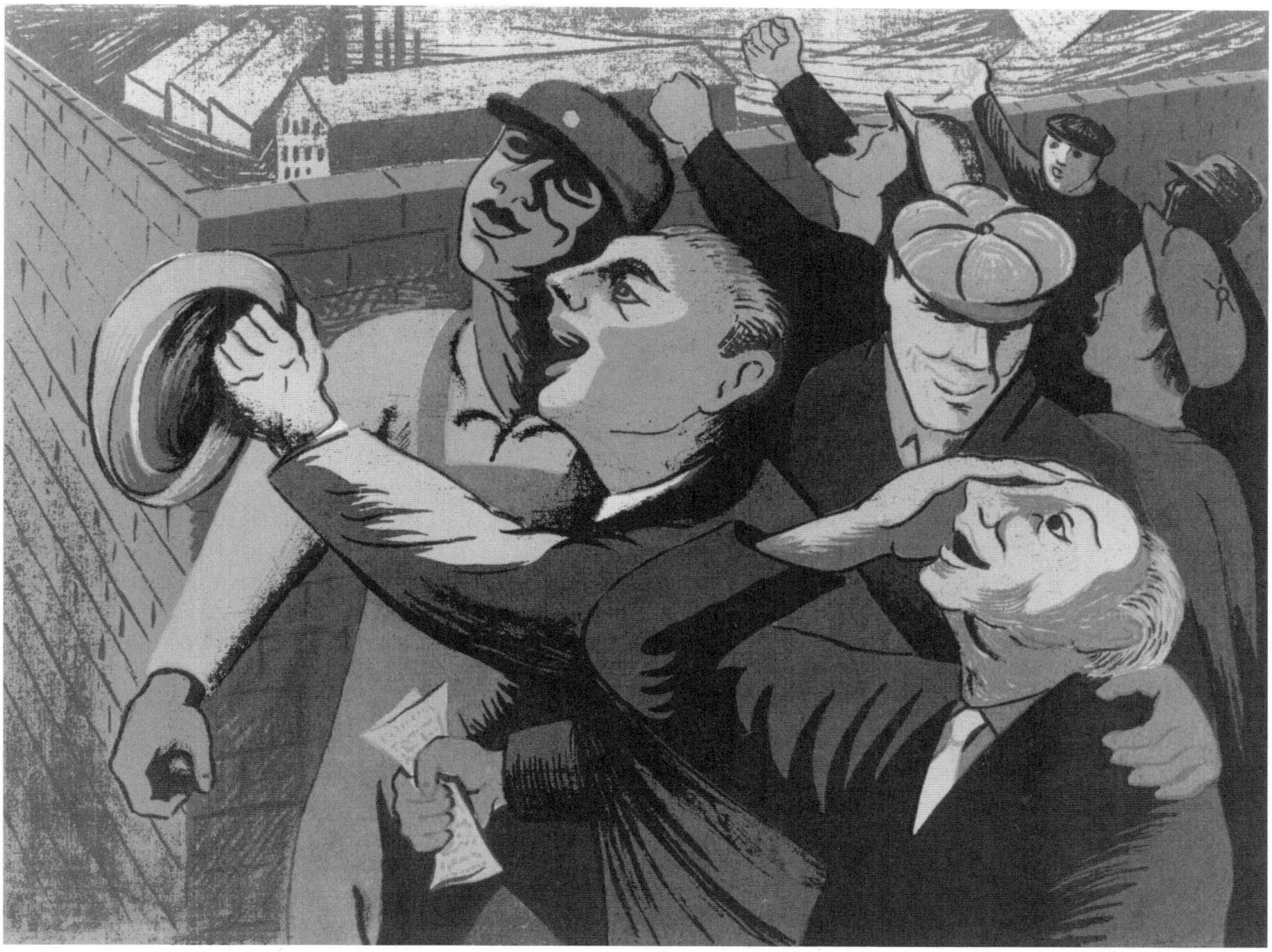

37. Harry Gottlieb, *The Strike Is Won!*, 1940, color silkscreen, WPA-FAP. Courtesy of the Ellen Sragow Gallery, New York.

5,000 visual artists who produced 2,500 murals, more than 100,000 paintings, more than 13,000 sculptures, nearly 240,000 prints, as well as theater posters and illustrations for the Index of American Design.[5] Several smaller programs ran concurrently with these, but functioned on a more limited basis. Supporters of all these nationally funded endeavors drew on the rhetoric of cultural democracy to assert their value, and they were applauded as unique experiments in state support for the arts. Yet they also faced significant challenges in meeting standards of both economic and cultural value. According to historian Richard D. McKinzie, works of art commissioned by the government had to satisfy both federal or state patrons and the public, please the artists that produced them, and meet commonly accepted standards of quality.[6] Each of these elements provoked questions related to state sponsorship of cultural goods, including widespread resistance to such seemingly frivolous expenditures during a time of economic upheaval and social anxiety. This conservative obstructionism would ultimately combine with anti-Communist red-baiting to end national support for the arts for several decades.

CONSTRUCTING CULTURAL DEMOCRACY: THREE SOURCES

Ideals of cultural democracy were the gas priming the economic motors of the New Deal art projects. The belief that democratically expanded opportunities for cultural improvement could play a significant role in the formation of national identity represented a new direction in American thought, one that was not typical of intellectual discourse before the 1930s. Its articulation reflected changing attitudes to culture and new conceptions of the political economy of art, as New Deal leaders reconsidered cultural experience as a vehicle for understanding, guiding, and reshaping the nation's social identity in a time of national crisis. As the 1930s decade opened, scholars were just beginning to rethink the meanings attributed to cultural production. Previously deployed only to describe elite accomplishments in the arts, the term "culture" was reconfigured to evoke instead the complex social environment of a whole community or country.[7] Intellectuals joined emerging interest in the individual's relationship to society, as discussed in current anthropological and sociological studies, to a revitalized focus on national history and local experience. During a time of national self-doubt, crafting a more complex understanding of the connection of America's present to its past and future seemed particularly urgent. Intellectual efforts to reassess the complexities of American identity had their creative counterpoint in new radical fiction, folk music recordings, proletarian visual art, and documentary works that joined text with photographs to portray the life patterns of varied American communities.[8]

The notion of art as the product of elite sensibility demanding both seriousness and sensitivity in its reception was not discarded, but this concept was broadened by new interest in the production of culture in more varied and class-differentiated forms, as well as the possibility of expanding access to such aesthetic experiences among a wider public audience. Moreover, the concept of cultural democracy offered new promise not only for expanded access to the arts, but for the production of works that examined, explained, or even excoriated the decade's experiences. New Deal arts administrators connected these diverse goals to the development of more cohesive national and local identities, achieved through the dissemination of democratic cultural experiences fueled by federal funding.

In arguing for this expansion of traditional views of cultural activity, advocates of cultural democracy and state support for the arts drew on three contradictory sources: continuing Progressive ideals of social improvement, Regionalist efforts to affirm local values and reject elitist urbanized forms of modernism, and leftist valorizations of art as a revolutionary weapon. They did not merge easily, since the first two drew on values tending toward the preservation of liberal capitalism and the latter on interests associated with contemporary leftist efforts to shift American culture toward socialist ideals.[9]

The legacy of Progressive-era insistence on the morally uplifting benefits of aesthetic experience played a significant role in justifying the New Deal art programs. Conviction in the value of egalitarian access to education and so-called high culture was deeply embedded in traditional American mores, and New Deal reformers argued that economic recovery and a return to national well-being were integrally connected not only to transformed fiscal and political policies but also to the continuing educational and cultural enrichment of individuals and communities.[10] Since the late nineteenth century, Progressive reformers had insisted that cultural education could improve civic life. Yet the majority of people who attended museum exhibitions and concerts or supported arts organizations were still upper-class elites who visited galleries in the company of their class peers. To reach more diverse audiences in the early twentieth century, Progressive activists in New York had established neighborhood-based exhibition and teaching venues that modeled new strategies for enhancing community participation and building democratic access to the arts, albeit through economically independent rather than state-supported institutions.[11]

Progressive goals also characterized the activities of privately funded national organizations such as the American Federation of Art (AFA), whose goals were public reeducation and intellectual improvement through cultural experience. The AFA was founded in 1909 with the goal of extending knowledge of fine art to audiences beyond the usual urban elites. The organization sent varied art exhibitions on tour around the country and published the *American Magazine of Art*. In the early 1930s, when Roosevelt's new administration was considering whether to initiate relief support for the arts, Federation leaders insisted that not only was federal intervention essential, but it could also contribute to ending the segregation of art from daily experience that kept most citizens unaware of America's culture riches.[12] The keynote speaker at the organization's twenty-fifth anniversary convention, Arnold Bennett Hall, drew on traditionally idealistic Progressive viewpoints when he argued that art experiences encouraged not only "appreciation of beauty" but also self-restraint. Hall's forceful assertion—"through the universal appeal of beauty, we find the surest pathway to the noblest impulses of the human soul"—echoed cultural ideals familiar both to Franklin Delano Roosevelt and many reformers in his administration.[13] Hall's widely shared belief in social improvement through art's supposed ability to uplift the masses assumed that working-class groups would assimilate elite Euro-American values. This ideal was easily extended to support the conviction that the arts could improve life even for those most victimized by the Depression.[14] Progressive justifications for bringing art to a wider audience joined these two concepts in uneasy relation, linking unmistakable traces of an elitist desire to improve social inferiors with egalitarian hopes for lessening the vicissitudes of economic inequity through cultural experience.

When New Deal administrators sought to justify the virtues of state-sponsored cultural democracy in speeches and essays, their rhetoric demonstrated a similar merging of elitist and egalitarian views. Holger Cahill and Edward Bruce, directors of the WPA-FAP and Treasury Section projects, shared a desire to see the state foster both artistic excellence and public accessibility, but that desire was unequally implemented. Bruce reiterated the necessity of artistic standards whereas Cahill tended to emphasize the importance of community-based involvement for both artists and the public.[15] However, Bruce did argue that the new federal art programs would benefit the country by taking the "snobbery out of art and [making] it the daily food of the average citizen."[16] When Cahill became head of the Federal Art Project in August 1935, his populist notions of cultural democracy moved its programs further in this egalitarian direction, yet still retained the goal of social improvement through enhanced aesthetic experience.[17] These concepts reshaped contemporary notions of how the political economy of art functioned within an inclusive democratic society.

Throughout his tenure as director of the WPA-FAP, Cahill insisted that aesthetic experience should not be limited to the rarified atmosphere of museums, theaters, and concert halls. Instead, he promoted understanding of the arts through community experience.[18] Believing that three-fourths of the American population were "under-privileged in the arts," he argued that state intervention through federally funded programs was one way to remedy this situation.[19] Cahill developed his goal of encouraging wider community involvement in arts institutions from two models. One was the antielitist activism of John Cotton Dana, former director of the populist Newark Museum of Art, under whom Cahill had worked as a curator. He had great admiration for Dana, who made the museum more accessible to a diverse community of urban patrons by reorganizing its downtown building and setting up branch galleries and school loan programs.[20] Cahill also drew inspiration from the egalitarian aesthetic and educational theories of John Dewey. In *Art as Experience* (1934), Dewey asserted that creative expression and community participation were as important to the flourishing of the arts as elite taste or talent. He believed that exposure to varied cultural experiences would facilitate the emergence of highly talented artists while encouraging a climate of artistic freedom and enriched social experience. Dewey stressed that art should be of its own era, because an emphasis on timeliness rather than timelessness enabled artists to participate in contemporary social discourse. Drawing on Dewey's vision, Cahill rejected the option of supporting artistic "masters" and sought instead to foster the artistic production of diverse individuals, whose works would create a "reservoir of art" in many forms.[21] Thus the primary goal of democratic support for the arts as Cahill envisioned it was not to facilitate the production of a few outstanding masterpieces but to make art "a vital, functioning part of any cultural scheme."[22]

When Cahill traveled throughout the country to drum up interest in community art centers and exhibitions, local newspaper reports suggest that this strategy inspired an enthusiastic response.[23] Speaking in Wilmington, North Carolina, he argued, "Government patronage of the arts produced the glory that remains of Greece, though it was criticized then just as President Roosevelt's WPA program for artists is criticized now. . . . The WPA project does more than provide a livelihood for artists. . . . The program tends to make art 'the property of all rather than the hobby of a few.' . . . It has helped to rediscover America's cultural past, and has brought together art interests and resources in communities."[24]

For the visual arts, this ideal was facilitated not only through support for individual artists on the WPA-FAP but also by exhibitions that brought WPA-FAP products before an expanding public audience. Between 1935 and 1939, the Federal Art Project in New York organized forty shows of work by its national participants, including muralists, painters, sculptors, and teachers. One comprehensive early exhibition was "New Horizons in American Art," shown in the autumn of 1936 to significant critical acclaim at the Museum of Modern Art in New York. Emily Genauer, writing for the art journal *Parnassus*, commented, "singular here is the paucity of studio subjects, and the concentration, instead, on the life and landscape outside the painter's door. Instead of being precious or over-refined, the works are fresh and vital."[25] A year earlier, in December 1935, the government had already opened its own Federal Art Gallery in a New York brownstone; in 1937 the gallery moved to a larger site uptown, close to leading mainstream gallery spaces on Fifty-seventh Street. Some of these exhibitions also traveled around the country to be viewed in community art centers, local museums, libraries, and other suitable venues, and others were developed by local WPA-FAP programs.[26]

Four years after the Federal Art Project was initiated, Cahill reasserted the value of cultural democracy as a motivating national ethos at the end of his introductory catalog essay for *American Art Today*, the impressive exhibition of contemporary visual art held at the 1939 New York World's Fair. He cited both public demand for arts experiences and the goal of integrating artists into the social fabric of American society as significant aspects of the nation's recovery from the Great Depression. "It would appear," he wrote, "that the desire to bring art within the reach of all as a currency for everyday living lies close to the surface in the mass of the American people. . . . Art is recovering its context in the life of contemporary society. As this tendency continues it will mean the recovery of social assurance for the artist, and for the public it will mean the possibility of participating, on a broad and democratic scale, in the experience of creative expression."[27] Cahill's expansive emphasis on diversity and vitality was reiterated in the rhetoric of cultural democracy as voiced by other New Deal arts administrators.

Growing interest in America's regional differences contributed a second perspective to efforts to expand state-sponsored cultural democracy and reshape the political economy of artistic production and consumption in the 1930s. Regionalism influenced both the Treasury Section's post office mural commissions and WPA Federal Art Project efforts to fund regional workshops, establish community art centers, and promote touring exhibitions of FAP works. The three leading regionalist artists—Thomas Hart Benton, Grant Wood, and John Stuart Curry—gained national attention when *Time* magazine featured color reproductions of their paintings in its 1934 Christmas issue. The anonymous accompanying article praised America's new regionalist painters for ending colonial deference to European culture and portraying characteristic American themes that "could be seen in their own land."[28] Wood, presented in the *Time* article as the movement's leading theorist, used his 1935 manifesto titled "Revolt Against the City" to reiterate the importance of geographical specificity and local diversity. "The American public," he argued "has readily acquired a strong interest in the distinctly indigenous art of its own land" and now demanded "an American way of looking at things."[29] Similarly, Benton commented on this new direction in American culture in 1940, at the opening of the Walker Art Center in Minneapolis, saying, "It's an exciting idea, one which seeks not to educate the people, but to bring art down off its pedestal."[30]

The belief that American artists needed to develop regionally specific and egalitarian styles that resisted the imposition of alien, "urban" values was inspired in part by the ideas of New York art critic Thomas Craven, who forcefully rejected what he viewed as the extremes of European modernist art and instead urged American artists to celebrate local and regional experience.[31] Although Craven's xenophobia and cultural chauvinism provoked significant hostility, his call for an expressly American art had substantial appeal to a nation questioning its identity in the throes of the Depression. Regionalism's emphasis on rural life, geographic specificity, and easily apprehensible style seemed to evoke goals quite similar to the rhetoric of cultural democracy.[32] Although the federal art programs never absolutely rejected modernist experimentation, it was certainly not encouraged. And many government-sponsored paintings and murals tended to represent the experience of citizens who were white, middle-class, and members of rural or small-town communities rather than exploring the full range of Americans' sociogeographic and ethnic identities.

When regionalist values were incorporated into cultural democracy's ideological mix, efforts to sustain a democratic plurality of options were at times undercut by competing priorities on the part of national administrators, artists, and the public. These divergent interests were the result of thematic, stylistic, and economic anxieties. Contestation over a narrowing of both thematic and aesthetic options is evident in many letters preserved in the records of the Treasury Section's post office mural program, although such disputes also emerged regarding mural projects funded by the WPA-FAP.[33] Concepts of what constituted good art, what subject matter was most appropriate for public consumption and local pride, and what stylistic choices and techniques an individual artist could deploy frequently set Section and FAP administrators in conflict with both artists and the very public that state-sponsored art was intended to excite and engage.[34] Mural painters faced different challenges; in some cases pressure to adapt to local tastes caused artists to repress their own values and paint work that they themselves characterized as potboilers to appease the anxieties of Section administrators, who viewed the economic continuity of their projects as dependent on public goodwill.[35] Continually faced with threatened budget cuts, federal and state administrators often found it difficult to balance personal ideals of excellence with the need to appease popular interests. Although the idea that art could function as an important arena in which to reassert a shared national identity and local allegiances held great appeal, hopes of resolving the differences between a mythic social totality constructed in patriotic rhetoric, contending local priorities, economic strictures, public taste, and artists' assertion of expressive liberty proved to be highly problematic.[36]

Leftist theories of revolutionary cultural activism also played a significant though rarely acknowledged role in shaping the meanings attributed to cultural democracy and the goals of a patriotic, nationally oriented economy of art production during the 1930s,

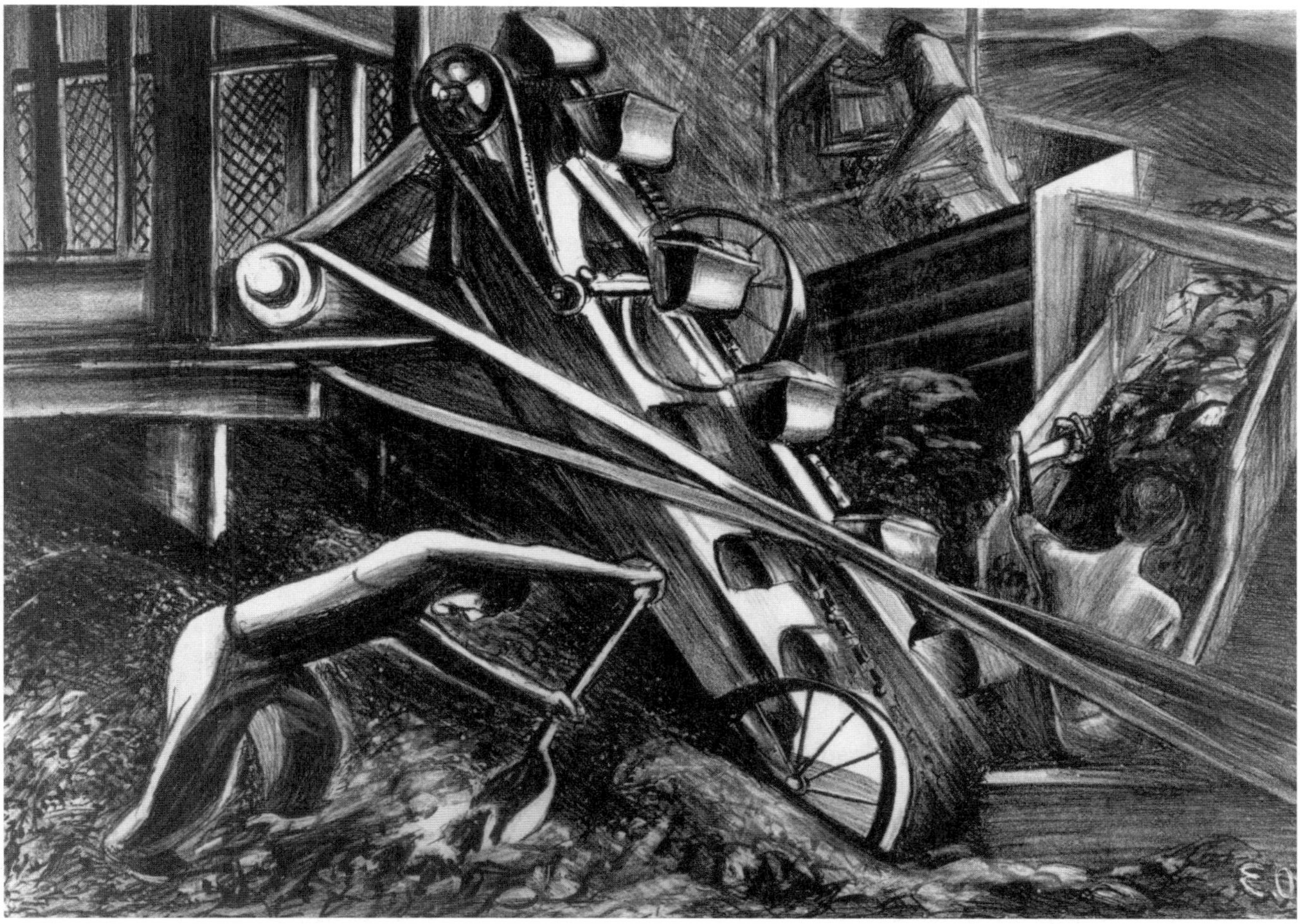

38. Elizabeth Olds, *Bootleg Coal, Pennsylvania*, 1936 lithograph, WPA-FAP. Art Collection, Harry Ransom Humanities Research Center, The University of Texas at Austin.

through the valorization of working-class identity and the notion of artists as militant cultural workers addressing themselves to a mass audience. According to traditional Marxist aesthetic theory, which the Communist Party promoted before shifting its emphasis to the more inclusive focus of the Popular Front in 1935, art should function as a "weapon of the revolution," although leftists themselves disagreed on the details of how artists could best contribute to building a socialist society.[37] Scenes of labor and industrial production, including those that seemed to critique capitalist exploitation, were produced by numerous WAP-FAP artists in both paintings and graphic art; for example, Elizabeth Olds's 1936 lithograph *Bootleg Coal, Pennsylvania* (Figure 38) depicts striking miners who turned to illegal bootleg activities to support their families. Not surprisingly, while the rhetorical concept of artists as workers was quickly adopted by proponents of the New Deal art programs, the linked call for revolutionary militancy promptly disappeared from administrative discourse. In a 1938 press release, Audrey McMahon, director of the regional Federal Art Project domain that included New York City, transformed leftist ideals into praise for a patriotic contribution to nationally oriented goals. "From the obscurity of his own individualism," she observed, "the artist has emerged to see himself as a worker and to recognize his identity in the light of a worker producing art for the American people."[38] Similarly, Lewis Mumford commented in 1936 that the artists "engaged in these WPA projects have been given something more precious than their daily bread: they have at last achieved the liberty to perform an essential function of life, in the knowledge that their work has a destination in the community."[39] Eugenie Gershoy, a printmaker, also praised the Federal Art Project for establishing contexts in which art no longer seemed an esoteric luxury but could be appreciated and used by ordinary individuals.[40] The concept of artists as workers resonated with utilitarian potency, but had to be correlated with goals that sustained the status quo rather than any radical transformation of the American political system.

Leftist views percolated into Federal Art Project rhetoric because many participating artists and supervisors were sympathetic to small-"c" communist ideals during the 1930s, although few acknowledged membership in the Communist Party.[41] Before the inauguration of the federal art programs, radical leftist artists had found encouragement for their interests through the John Reed Clubs. After its founding in 1929 by the American Communist Party, the John Reed Club had established thirty branches across the United States by 1934, and these groups became important focal points for leftist cultural organizing. Reed Club meetings provided radical artists with a forum for discussing art's role in relation to communist political doctrine and socialist ideals, but participants were not required to become party members. The New York branch was particularly active, offering discussions, classes, and exhibition opportunities.[42]

In the early 1930s, the New York John Reed Club sponsored several exhibitions with politically oriented themes, including "The Social Viewpoint in Art" (February 1933), "Hunger, Fascism, and War" (December–January 1933–34), and "Revolutionary Front—1934." These shows encouraged artists to address radical issues from proletarian perspectives and attack the inequities of American economic and social policy. Some leftist critics demanded even more explicit revolutionary content, while others rejected demands for sectarian narrowness in art.[43] After 1933 Reed Club juries tended to select more militant works, but they still endorsed a variety of stylistic and thematic choices and continued to accept submissions from amateur as well as professional artists. This stance paralleled Holger Cahill's later egalitarian concept of a pluralist cultural democracy but was obviously focused toward a different set of political priorities.

The Communist Party disbanded the John Reed Clubs in 1935, following Stalin's mandate to build a larger, more unified, liberal/leftist Popular Front against fascism in Europe. The muting of overt Marxist analysis and blurring of distinctions between leftist and liberal views encouraged formerly unaffiliated artists to ally themselves with activist groups that were no longer directly linked to socialist politics.[44] Leftist artists took leading roles in organizing the Artists' Union and the American Artists' Congress, and their ideas played a significant part in shaping policy at the WPA-FAP workshops and fomenting resistance to hostile congressional attacks. Yet despite accusations to the contrary from conservative opponents of the WPA-FAP, the party was never monolithic in its influence and few artists were doctrinaire in their use of leftist ideas. Much of the art produced by both liberals and leftists who identified with the ideal of the artist as worker did tend to be realist in style. But some leftist artists defended modernist aesthetic choices by drawing on Trotsky's arguments that art should not be under complete party control, that creative freedom was essential to artistic production, and that experimental aesthetic practices could in themselves demonstrate commitment to revolutionary social change.[45] These theoretical distinctions were hotly debated in the pages of *Art Front*, the journal of the Artists' Union, and in the *Partisan Review*. Nevertheless, after mid-decade, when the American Communist Party endorsed the idea of democratic pluralism under the aegis of the Popular Front, leftist discourse was reunited, at least in its surface manifestations, with cultural democracy's mandate to value diverse aesthetic expressions.

QUESTIONS OF RESPONSIBILITY AND POPULAR TASTE

As arts administrators sought to merge these three conceptual sources—Progressivism, regionalism, and leftism—into a coherent ideology of cultural democracy and an effective federally funded economy of art production and consumption, they found that the process of transforming the ideals of democratic accessibility and beneficent cultural experience into state-sponsored programs was fraught with complexities. One set of problems involved balancing civic and national interests (as defined by government agencies) with artists' tendencies to assert the primacy of individual self-expression. Although one goal of the New Deal art programs was to enhance a national ethos of independence and vitality, few artists except those working on mural projects understood this as essential to their purpose. Rather they turned to subjects of personal interest that reflected a vastly diverse panorama of American cultural life, from baseball to steel-making, themes that held both personal interest but also the potential of populist appeal. Indeed, many artists working for the Federal Art Project later asserted that they experienced almost complete freedom in both thematic and aesthetic choices. Those employed by the Treasury Section, by contrast, often felt more compelled to assuage both administrative and local preferences.

For artists employed on the Federal Art Project, another difficulty related to expectations regarding the governance of labor. Coming under the purview of national Works Progress Administration regulations, they had to produce evidence that they were poor enough to receive relief; many artists later recounted the humiliation they felt while undergoing the certification mandated for these positions. Once hired, they were usually required to check in daily at a central office or be counted at their studios by a peripatetic timekeeper. Numerous anecdotal narratives testify to the frustration provoked by these arrangements. Jackson Pollock supposedly once ran down the street in his pajamas to make a morning deadline, and Mabel Dwight, a successful printmaker who was then in her sixties and growing deaf, commented that she lost many nights' sleep because she feared not hearing her alarm.[46] Even if artists were counted in their own studios, the random timing of these visits kept them from going out and sketching as research for their works. Cahill requested an end to the timekeeping system as early as April 1936 and eventually it was abolished, but the bureaucratic need to account for artists' irregular schedules posed a continuing problem for FAP administrators.[47] It was resolved in part by shifting from a time-based system to one that checked artists' productivity by counting items completed. Easel painters, for example, had to turn in one work every four to six weeks, while printmakers had to submit one work a month, with leeway for supervisory approval and the actual printing process. This system was actually surprisingly lax, since artists' rate of production varied widely depending on the style, scale, and ambitiousness of a particular project, and its inaccuracy was one source of irritation for FAP opponents.

A different set of problems entailed questions of how to build interest in the visual arts among new communities of viewers while acknowledging both the realities of popular taste and the validity of diverse styles of art. Elizabeth Olds, a printmaker who worked for the WPA-FAP's Graphic Arts Division in New York, stated the obvious when she observed that "average citizens were an audience for the artist new to our time. New methods of reaching them have to be devised."[48] This necessity proved to be particularly troublesome for advocates of cultural democracy within this new federally funded economy of arts production. Access to diverse cultural opportunities did not necessarily translate into popular acceptance of unfamiliar art forms.

Both artists' and administrators' ideas about popular preferences in art were derived more from prevailing myths and ideological assumptions than from systematic sociological analysis.

Viewers' responses to public art are documented primarily in National Archive files that record controversies aroused by the Treasury Section post office murals when administrative ideals, artists' conceptions, and local community preferences did not match.[49] Although administrators wanted art destined for federally funded sites to accurately reflect local history and culture while also displaying aesthetic merit, what this meant was rarely clearly defined. Viewers often objected to the subjects that artists selected or sought to modify their interpretations. As art historian Karal Ann Marling observed, local aesthetic preferences were influenced more by movies, cartoons, and tabloid photographs than by fine art traditions. Moreover, when difficulties emerged, local people often disagreed about ameliorative remedies, further frustrating artists and supervisors.[50] Successful Section mural painters tended to emphasize easily recognizable stereotypes of site and character to avoid both local and supervisory objections. Viewers' contentious responses to federally funded murals dismayed Section administrators, who had hoped that the program would ameliorate tensions between local values and national ideals, but efforts to understand and placate viewers' expectations were not always successful.[51]

Although painters and printmakers employed by the WPA-FAP had much greater independence than muralists working for the Treasury Section, they were similarly dependent on speculation rather than specific knowledge of the public's taste. Moreover, changing social values and political discourses conditioned the definitions of audience identity developed by artists, private entrepreneurs, and federal administrators. In 1934, Reeves Lewenthal established Associated American Artists, a mail-order business that sold regionalist prints to middle-class Americans (despite its name, it was not a collective enterprise). Lewenthal viewed these works as potentially popular despite their local references because they expressed nationally valorized ideals of an American identity grounded in rural authenticity.[52] At the same time, Adolf Dehn, a leftist printmaker, observed that a new market could be developed among "every school teacher, Greenwich Village radical, every communist and New Republic culture seeker" for prints with radical, social justice subjects.[53] While regionalist and American Scene paintings and prints sold well, leftist support for radical themes emerged only late in the decade, and in limited contexts.[54]

While exactly predicting consumer desires might be difficult, it was clear that images that foregrounded positive aspects of national identity and patriotic pride were popular, as were charming or quaint genre scenes of rural and urban life, themes of modern technology such as airmail delivery, and historical subjects from the American past. Pleasant regionalist print editions produced by Associated American Artists sold out quickly, but these topics often did not match the interests of artists themselves, particularly those with bohemian or leftist values. Yet scenes of striking workers, industrial catastrophes, and suffering victims of the Depression were not equally attractive to most Americans, even those directly impacted by the Depression's economic exigencies.[55] Indeed, surveys made in the 1960s suggested that people who visited art museums rarely enjoyed art foregrounding critical social perspectives or works in radical modernist styles, both of which they found offensive and unpleasant.[56] Despite, or perhaps because of, its elitist status, casual museum-goers looked for pleasurable aesthetic stimulation and moral inspiration in viewing visual art. Works that were distressing either in subject or technique were unpopular. Most likely, similar attitudes shaped the interests of the mass public audience that proponents of cultural democracy hoped to develop thirty years earlier.[57]

Although we know that neither artists, critics, nor administrators had access to hard evidence of art consumers' preferences in the 1930s, it is useful to explore how they *imagined* public taste, and how these hypothetical conceptions influenced the implementation of state-sponsored cultural democracy. In general, neither liberals nor radicals had high expectations of the aesthetic taste of most Americans. References to the absence of even basic cultural literacy abound in the writing of administrators, artists, and critics, who agreed that most people still felt alienated by fine art, classical music, and modern dance, and arguments in favor of developing a more democratic cultural life reflected liberal efforts to remedy this perceived problem. Artists themselves viewed the public's aesthetic tastes and thematic preferences quite negatively although they tended to express this in oblique language. In an essay urging the WPA-FAP to explore mass production of fine art prints, Elizabeth Olds suggested that one of the benefits of working for the FAP was that artists could develop their ideas without having to worry about troublesome popular preferences. She added "with freedom to choose his subjects [the artist] did not need to restrict himself to gamboling kittens and succulent nymphs beside a lake (sure-fire sales)."[58] Yet despite this disparaging evaluation of the public's taste for sentimental, charming themes, Olds and her peers hoped that such values would be transformed if viewers were exposed to more interesting, modern images.

At the same time, administrators, artists, and critics also agreed that the public was unprepared to understand the aesthetic complexities of innovative modernist imagery. Elizabeth McCausland, an art critic who supported both leftist content and modernist experimentation, still saw this as a problem in 1944 when she published an essay on Picasso's art. The public tended to reject vanguard styles, she argued, because they represented an "intellectual, sophisticated idiom, removed by historical events from the understanding of the common man" and thereby "unintelligible to popular ears" (or, she might have said, eyes).[59] On this count, even those who enjoyed modernism themselves tended to agree with the nervous conservativism of Federal Art Project administrators. Public hostility to modernist styles of art posed a formidable challenge to advocates of cultural democracy and the ideal of stimulating viewers to develop new forms of educated modern taste.

Militantly leftist artists and critics, whether they upheld dominant Communist Party theories of culture or agreed with Trotskyist analyses, were no more sanguine in evaluating the preferences of contemporary audiences, and many of them worked on the federally funded New Deal art projects. Like their liberal peers, they bemoaned the fact that lack of visual literacy posed a major obstacle in the struggle to attract new viewers for contemporary art. In 1933, Meyer Schapiro, then a young art historian who had just begun teaching at Columbia University, argued that trying to reach workers by way of fine art was misguided in itself. He suggested that leftists should reject that struggle and instead use cartoons and cheap agitational prints to gain workers' attention.[60] Schapiro's ideas had changed slightly by 1936, when he published an essay titled "Public Use of Art" in *Art Front*. He reiterated that most working people did enjoy visual culture, but only in the form of comics, magazine pictures, and movies, since fine art had little appeal for them. However, he now proposed that artists could encourage workers' interest in contemporary art if they created images that directly dramatized "the life of labor and the struggle for a new society."[61] By insisting that only recognizably relevant subject matter could transform working-class viewers' evaluation of the worth of fine art, Schapiro implicitly attacked New Deal rhetoric that celebrated cultural democracy's egalitarian inclusivity and challenged the efficacy of programs intended to make high culture accessible to everyone.

Even on the broader political terrain that shaped administration of the New Deal art projects, it was precisely this question of public consumption of art, addressing both what subjects would be meaningful to viewers and how to present them aesthetically, that complicated efforts to expand public interest in art without vitiating its quality. Because they were dependent on guesses and stereotypes in trying to attract and please contemporary audiences, administrators tended to be quite cautious about the limits of public tolerance. Their anxieties were exacerbated as ideals of free democratic expression clashed with growing anger over two issues repeatedly raised by conservative opponents of public support for the arts: the supposed waste of funds appropriated for arts programs that produced inferior works and anxieties about leftist influence inflamed by anti-Communist red-baiting.

These tensions led all of the government arts programs to treat issues of public consumption gingerly by encouraging stylistic moderation and praising quietly mundane rather than politically volatile themes. This seemed a necessary step in constructing an effective political economy of art production under federal auspices. Nevertheless, a surprising number of works with overtly leftist subjects were approved by FAP supervisors.[62] Jacob Kainen, an artist employed at the WPA-FAP Graphic Arts Division workshop in New York, commented on this situation in several contexts. In a detailed essay on conditions at the workshop, he emphasized that participants were never pressured to conform to any dominant aesthetic or thematic preconceptions. The artist, he wrote "was free to select his [*sic*] own subjects and to treat them in any manner he chose. Thus a wide variety of approaches lay open to him although the prevailing mood was one of concern with his immediate milieu."[63] A similar emphasis on freedom of expression appears in recorded comments made by many other artists working for the government. However, Kainen also asserted that WPA-FAP rejection of modernist stylistic experimentation was "based upon the assumption that the people were not ready for unfamiliar expressions."[64] And on a questionnaire filled out thirty years later, he suggested that concerns about acceptable imagery and stylistic choices may indeed have contributed to the rather muted aesthetic and political character for which much FAP art was faulted by its opponents. He admitted that artists risked being fired from the projects or transferred from creative to teaching positions if supervisors thought their works were unsuited for display to mass audiences.[65] As a result of these conditions, the WPA-FAP was accused of both failing to promote high standards and suppressing innovation. Efforts by artists and administrators to avoid attack on the grounds of excessive modernity or problematic subject matter ironically became fodder for critics of cultural democracy and federal support for the arts who had little use for any form of art dependent on public funding for its sustenance.

CONSERVATIVE ATTACKS AND STRATEGIC DIFFICULTIES

By the end of the decade, the goal of modifying the capitalist economy of art production in America by adding federal support even as a temporary supplement to the weakened capitalist market had become vulnerable to critical attack on aesthetic, political, and economic grounds. The rhetoric of cultural democracy was neither able to inspire widespread public enthusiasm for state funding nor had it succeeded in convincing citizens to view this as a national priority during a time of continuing economic crisis. The unique convergence of utopian cultural and political ideals that had energized the introduction of public programs to make diverse arts experiences accessible to all Americans began to falter, and congressional hostility and red-baiting by New Deal opponents took a heavy toll on artists and administrators as they responded to threatened funding cuts and actual layoffs and closures. Ultimately, although deeper political conflicts inflamed its opponents' attacks, the difficulty of assimilating conflicting strategies for accomplishing cultural democracy's populist agenda and deep-seated doubts about the value of art to the economy as a whole posed virtually insuperable obstacles to sustaining state funding for the New Deal art programs.

The Federal Art Project in particular was targeted by conservative opponents of Roosevelt's administration almost as soon as it was established. They drew on widespread doubts about art's practical relevance to national survival and economic well-being and popular suspicion that artistic production had little relation to other forms of labor. As historian Richard McKinzie observed, "the expensive difference between putting a man to work on a sewer and putting him to work on a drawing room comedy or a mural was noted repeatedly inside and outside the government."[66] This popular hostility was vehemently contradicted by many artists, who asserted that work on the federal art programs was satisfying and useful, and that it had not only saved them from starvation but had transformed their relationship to the larger society.[67] But these idealistic claims did not impress congressional critics and other conservatives, who saw state-sponsored art programs as sites where money was wasted on works that lacked quality because subsidized art supposedly failed to offer competitive incentives for achieving excellence. The location of the WPA-FAP programs within a relief bureaucracy also led to problems such as sit-in strikes and other controversial activities by activist artists within the Artists Union and American Artists Congress, which particularly distressed many conservative congressional observers.[68]

Hostile congressmen argued that federal programs encouraged dangerous forms of social critique rather than fostering any reparational sense of national identity. Congressional opposition undercut New Deal

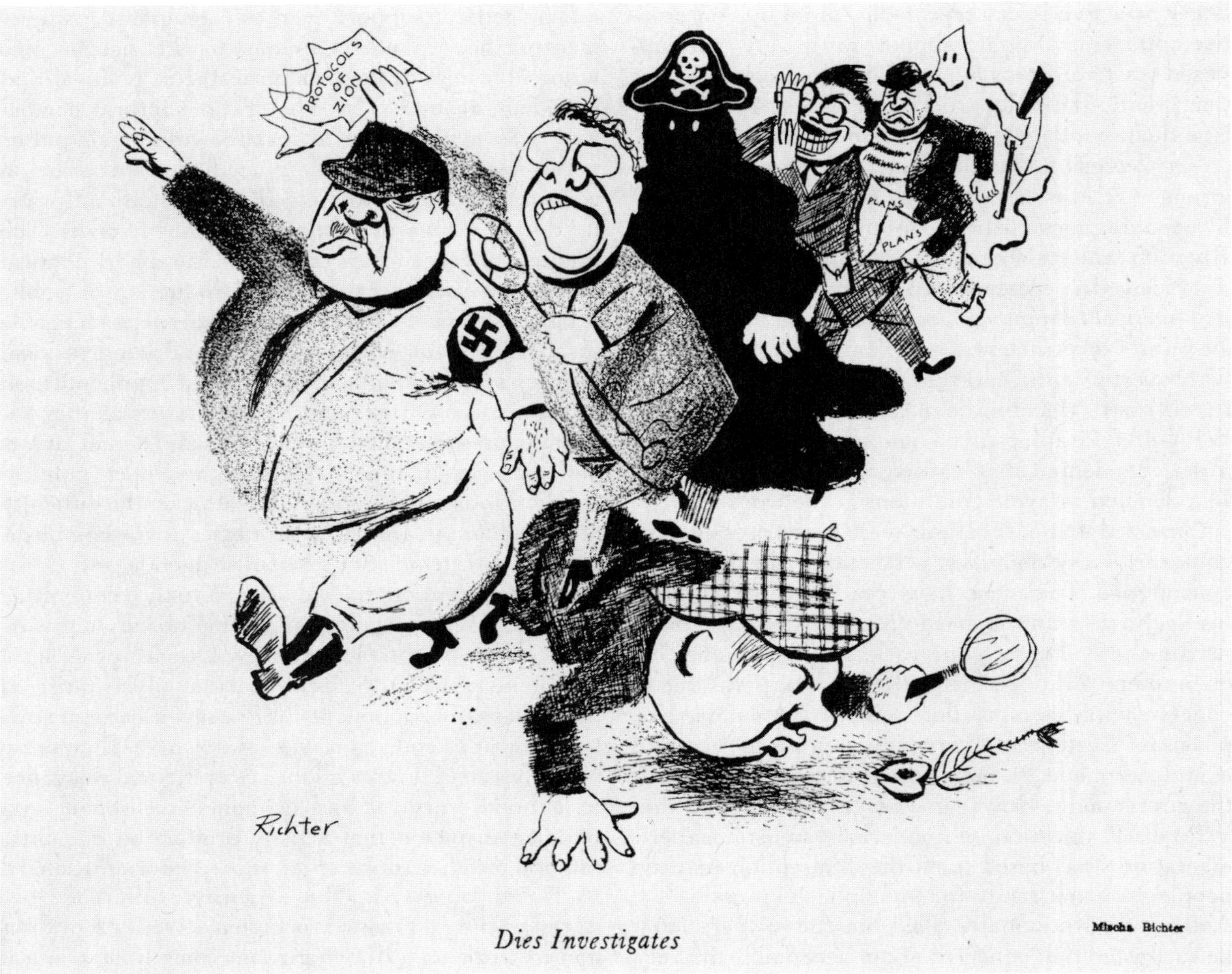

39. Mischa Richter, *Dies Investigates*, drawing reproduced in *New Masses* 30, no. 7 (February 7, 1939), 9.

efforts to promote cultural democracy from the earliest inception of these federally funded programs, as harassing legislative maneuvers restricted their reach, whittled away their funding, and undermined their validity.[69] Accusations that the projects were hotbeds of communist propaganda intensified after the Select Committee on Un-American Activities was established in the House of Representatives in 1938. Chaired by conservative representative Martin Dies, who was deeply hostile to government spending on the arts, the Committee immediately branded 640 organizations, 483 newspapers, and 280 unions as communist fronts and accused the Federal Art Project of harboring militant red agitators.[70] A satirical drawing by Mischa Richter, published in *New Masses* in 1939 (*Dies Investigates*, Figure 39), suggests that Dies's obsession with rooting out "reds" blinded the committee to more immediate threats to American democracy. Other House committees with control over WPA funding followed the Dies Committee model, and in 1940 Congress passed a bill excluding all known communists from WPA rolls.[71]

Efforts to promote the establishment of a permanent federal arts agency were equally unsuccessful.[72] The Artists' Union and the American Artists' Congress began to agitate for an independent Bureau of Fine Arts early in 1937. The concept had many supporters, because as artist Stuart Davis argued in 1938 in *American Artist* magazine, it was clear to artists that private patronage was "inadequate to establish the material basis on which a sound American artistic culture could develop."[73] In 1937 and again in 1938, sympathetic legislators introduced bills for a permanent federal art agency into Congress. However, many established artists, dealers, curators, administrators, and critics were anxious about how such a bureau would be organized. Although Holger Cahill insisted that democratic forms of cultural patronage would eventually produce outstanding artists, both liberals and conservatives accused the WPA-FAP of fostering inferior work and expressed doubts that a permanent agency would uphold higher standards of artistic taste. Forbes Watson, who was then administrator of the Treasury Section of Fine Arts, countered Cahill's optimism by protesting that good art could not be manufactured like a union product.[74] Yet as late as April 1938, Peyton Boswell, editor of the *Art Digest*, who had previously doubted the value of a federally supported, permanent fine arts agency, noted that most American artists supported the concept even if they were concerned about issues of aesthetic rigor.[75] What most artists wanted, however, did not matter. A majority of Congress adamantly opposed proposals for a permanent agency as well as continuing any federal subsidies for the arts; conservative newspaper editorials also viciously attacked the concept. In June 1938, a vote of 195 to 35 killed that year's bill proposing permanent federal support for the arts, and further consideration of the idea would not be resurrected for more than a quarter century.[76]

Conservative political maneuvering to reverse the Roosevelt administration's modestly reformist goals was largely responsible for ending federal support for the arts in the early 1940s. But it was also becoming obvious that the rhetoric of cultural democracy concealed problematic internal tensions.[77] The scant half-decade that elapsed before support ended was not sufficient time to resolve questions regarding several contentious aspects of public arts funding. For visual works, these related to defining and enforcing a universally acceptable standard of aesthetic quality, supporting varied stylistic options including modernist abstraction and surrealism, and embracing the freedom to critique contemporary social, economic, and political realities. Despite their zeal to promote new mechanisms for creating and disseminating state-funded art for a mass national audience, and the impressive numbers of works that were actually produced, administrators and artists were unable to win over the American public to support their goals.

But time was not the only problem. The valorizations of democratic freedom and unified national identity that undergirded ideals of cultural democracy could not be translated into effective public policy without confronting the diverse interests endemic to a highly stratified, capitalist society. The idea of the state as a "beneficent arbiter" of people's lives through any forms of managed production was alien to most Americans, who instead lauded an economic system that resisted government intervention in markets in the name of individual freedom.[78] Thus it was difficult to convince critics that the government could even partially reorganize the production of art as a communally beneficent system of labor. While leftist artists in particular supported this goal, curators, art dealers, and critics, each of whom had their own stake in capitalist art world structures, frequently did not. Nevertheless, whereas the rhetoric of cultural democracy asserted goals that could only be accomplished through more extended state support, the achievements of the government-sponsored art programs over a short period of time were quite impressive. The strategic mobilization of ideals of cultural democracy to legitimate state intervention in cultural production was not entirely successful, but both in its ideological premises and in the works that survive, it stands as a unique and significant experiment in reshaping the political economy of art in America to meld individual artistic expression and appreciation with federal support and national interests.

NOTES

1. The financial aspects of the various federally funded programs are discussed in numerous sources; see, e.g. William J. Barber, "'Sweet Are the Uses of Adversity': Federal Patronage of the Arts in the Great Depression," in *Economic Engagements with Art*, ed. De Marchi and Goodwin, 238 and 245. For statistics on funding and production, see Olin Dows, "The New Deal's Treasury Art Program," in O'Connor, ed., *New Deal Art Projects*, 11–49; and Bruce I. Bustard, "Artists and the Great Depression," in *A New Deal for the Arts* (Washington, DC: National Archives and Records Administration; Seattle: University of Washington Press, 1997), 1–14.

2. The basic issues for this argument were first outlined in Jane De Hart Mathews, "Arts and the People: The New Deal Quest for a Cultural Democracy," *Journal of American History* 62, no. 2 (September 1975): 316–39.

3. For Treasury Section statistics, see Dows, 20.

4. For TRAP statistics, see Dows, 27.

5. The literature on the Treasury Section and Works Progress Administration Federal Art Projects is enormous. A concise chart of the programs is provided in Marlene Park and Gerald Markowitz, *New Deal for Art* (Hamilton: Gallery Association of New York State, 1977), xii–xiii. For WPA-FAP statistics, see Dows, 43.

6. Richard D. McKinzie, *The New Deal for Artists* (Princeton, NJ: Princeton University Press, 1973), 53.

7. See Warren Susman, "The Culture of the Thirties," in *Culture as History: The Transformation of American Society in the Twentieth Century* (New York: Pantheon Books, 1973), 153.

8. From a vast number of publications, examples might include Robert and Helen Lynd's *Middletown* (1929) and *Middletown in Transition* (1937), Ruth Benedict's *Patterns of Culture* (1934), Grace Lumpkin's *To Make My Bread* (1932), and *Let Us Now Praise Famous Men* by James Agee and Walker Evans (1939).

9. For the tensions between liberal capitalism and socialist ideals in this context, see Jonathan Harris, *Federal Art and National Culture: The Politics of Identity in New Deal America* (Cambridge: Cambridge University Press, 1995); Andrew Hemingway, *Artists on the Left: American Artists and the Communist Movement, 1926–1956*

(New Haven, CT: Yale University Press, 2002), 79–85; and Helen Langa, *Radical Art: Printmaking and the Left in 1930s New York* (Berkeley and Los Angeles: University of California Press, 2004).

10. See Mathews, "Arts and the People," 316–39.

11. The institutions they established included the Educational Alliance and the People's Art Guild. See Matthew Baigell, "From Hester Street to Fifty-Seventh Street: Jewish-American Artists in New York," in *Painting a Place in America: Jewish Artists in New York 1900–1945* ed. Norman L. Kleeblatt and Susan Chevlowe (New York: The Jewish Museum, 1991), 35–36.

12. F. A. Whiting, Jr., "On Taking Part," *American Magazine of Art* 27, no. 3 (March 1934): 103.

13. Arnold Bennett Hall, "Art and Democracy," *American Magazine of Art* (May 1934), 45, annual convention issue.

14. For more on the residue of early twentieth-century culture wars over muting class, racial, and ethnic differences to established Euro-American values, see Lawrence Levine, *Highbrow/Lowbrow: The Emergence of Cultural Hierarchy in America* (Cambridge, MA: Harvard University Press, 1988), 176ff. See also Mathews, "Arts and the People," 320.

15. The differences between Bruce and Cahill were partially the result of their differing standpoints, but as Hemingway points out, they were also due to institutional constraints and distinct sources of funding: "the Treasury and its fiscally conservative secretary Morgenthau . . . and the WPA headed by the liberal Hopkins." Hemingway, *Artists on the Left*, 79.

16. Letter from Edward Bruce to Admiral Peoples (November 14, 1934) Bruce MSS, Reel D89, Archives of American Art, Smithsonian Institute. Cited in Marlene Park and Gerald R. Markowitz, *Democratic Vistas: Post Offices and Public Art in the New Deal* (Philadelphia: Temple University Press, 1984), 8, n. 16. The difficulties encountered by Bruce and the Treasury Section administrators in maintaining this emphasis on quality have been discussed in various sources. See particularly Belisario Contreras, *Tradition and Innovation in New Deal Art* (Lewisburg, PA: Bucknell University Press, 1983), 18–20; and Barbara Melosh, *Engendering Culture: Manhood and Womanhood in New Deal Public Art and Theater* (Washington, DC: Smithsonian Institution Press, 1991), 1–12.

17. For a brief summary of Cahill's role, see Audrey McMahon, "A General View of the WPA Federal Art Project in New York City and State," in O'Connor, ed., *New Deal Art Projects*, 54–56.

18. For Cahill's aesthetic sources and philosophy, see Park and Markowitz, *New Deal for Art*, 7–13; Karl E. Meyer, *The Art Museum: Power, Money, Ethics* (New York: William Morrow, 1979), 36–38; McKinzie, 80; and Francis V. O'Connor, "Introduction," in *Art for the Millions: Essays from the 1930s by Artists and Administrators of the WPA Federal Art Project* (Boston: New York Graphic Society, 1973), 16–18.

19. Holger Cahill, letter to Stuart Davis, April 13, 1937 (RG 69, Box 431), cited in Park and Markowitz, *New Deal for Art*, 10 and n. 39.

20. See Carol Duncan, "John Cotton Dana's Progressive Museum," in *Self and History: A Tribute to Linda Nochlin*, ed. Aruna D'Souza (London: Thames and Hudson, 2001), 127–36. For Cahill's reliance on Dewey's ideas, see O'Connor, "Introduction," *Art for the Millions*, 16–17.

21. Mathews, "Arts and the People," 323.

22. Holger Cahill, *New Horizons in American Art* (New York: Museum of Modern Art, 1936), 18, cited in Park and Markowitz, *New Deal for Art*, 12. For Cahill's emphasis on professionalism with respect for diversity, and reluctance to insist on any one style or thematic emphasis, see Patricia Hills, *Realism: Social Concern and Urban American Painting of the 1930s* (New York: Bread and Roses Cultural Project of the National Union of Hospital and Health Care Employees and the American Federation of Arts, 1983), 12 and McKinzie, 80.

23. Ola Mae Foushee, "North Carolina's Community Art Centers," in *Art in Action: American Art Centers and the New Deal*, ed. John Franklin White (Metuchen, NJ: Scarecrow Press, 1987), 160.

24. Holger Cahill, cited in Foushee, 160.

25. Emily Genauer, "New Horizons in American Art," *Parnassus* 8 (October 1936), 6, cited in Park and Markowitz, *New Deal for Art*, 28 and 68, n. 131.

26. See Hemingway, *Artist on the Left*, 176–79; and Langa, 33, 44–45.

27. Holger Cahill, "American Art Today," in facsimile, *American Art Today: New York World's Fair* (Poughkeepsie, NY: Apollo Press, 1987), 32.

28. "Art," *Time*, (December 21, 1934), 24–27. The essay celebrated *Time*'s first use of full-color reproductions, made possible by new printing technology.

29. Grant Wood, "Revolt Against the City," published by Frank Mott in Iowa City, 1935. Reprinted in James M. Dennis, *Grant Wood: A Study in American Art and Culture* (Columbia: University of Missouri Press, 1986), 229–35. Dennis questions whether Wood actually wrote the essay, suggesting that Mott actually penned the text. See Dennis, 41, n. 44.

30. Thomas Hart Benton, qtd. in the *Minneapolis Tribune* (January 5, 1940), cited in John Franklin White, "The Walker Art Center: A Crowning Achievement," in *Art in Action*, 21.

31. See, e.g., Thomas Craven, "Art and Propaganda," *Scribner's* 95, no. 3 (March 1934), 189–94. Reprinted in David Shapiro, *Social Realism: Art as a Weapon* (New York: Frederic Ungar, 1973), 89.

32. Many artists now associated with the regionalist or American Scene movements worked in varied parts of the country and even in urban sites, but the dominant association of Regionalism with the Midwest was common during the decade. See Nancy Heller and Julia Williams, *Painters of the American Scene* (New York: Galahad Books, 1982; orig. published as *Regionalists*, New York: Watson-Guptill, 1976), 13–33.

33. Examples of dissension over Treasury Section post office murals are discussed in detail in Melosh, *Engendering Culture*; Park and Markowitz, *Democratic Vistas*; and Karal Ann Marling, *Wall-to-Wall America: A Cultural History of Post-Office Murals in the Great Depression* (Minneapolis: University of Minnesota Press, 1982).

34. Marling, 11–14; and Melosh, 53–76.

35. Erica Beckh Rubenstein, cited in McKinzie, 55.

36. It should be acknowledged, however, that many artists did modify their original studies with only minor protest when local communities demanded changes, a fact that could signal either economic desperation or some level of compliance with the ideological goals fostered by federal patronage.

37. For an expanded discussion of the impact of the Communist Left on New Deal ideologies, see Hemingway and Langa.

38. Audrey McMahon, press release for "Art in Democracy" radio broadcast on station WEVD, 26 August 1938, WPA/FAP Department of Information (RG 69, Box 76), 7, National Archives, Washington, DC.

39. Lewis Mumford, "A Letter to the President," *New Republic* 89 (December, 30, 1936), 264.

40. Eugenie Gershoy, questionnaire, Francis V. O'Connor Papers, MF 1087, 1147, Archives of American Art, Smithsonian Institution.

41. For communist sympathies in contrast to party membership, see Michael Denning, *The Cultural Front: The Laboring of American Culture in the Twentieth Century* (London: Verso Press, 1996), 4–6; see also Hemingway and Langa.

42. See Hemingway, *Artists on the Left*, 20–24; and Langa, 19–20; also Helen A. Harrison, "John Reed Club Artists and the New Deal: Radical Responses to Roosevelt's 'Peaceful Revolution.'" *Prospects: An Annual of American Cultural Studies* 5 (1980): 240–68; and Cecile Whiting, *Antifascism in American Art* (New Haven, CT: Yale University Press, 1989), 21.

43. See John Kwait [Meyer Schapiro], "John Reed Club Art Exhibition," *New Masses* 8, no. 7 (February 1933): 23; and Louis Lozowick, "John Reed Club Show," *New Masses* 10, no. 1 (January 2, 1934): 27. For the contrasting position on the need for militancy, see Jacob Burck, "Sectarianism in Art," *New Masses* 8, no. 8 (April 1933): 26–27. After jurors tightened requirements for militancy, reviewers were more positive. See Jacob Kainen, "Revolutionary Art at the John Reed Club," *Art Front* 1, no. 2 (January 1935): 6.

44. Harrison, 249ff.

45. For Trotsky's views, see Leon Trotsky, "Art and Politics," *Partisan Review* 5, no. 3 (August–September 1938): 3–10; and Andre Breton and Diego Rivera, "Manifesto: Towards a Free Revolutionary Art," *Partisan Review* 6, no. 1 (Fall 1939): 49–53. Most recent scholarly studies dealing with the relation between cultural production and revolutionary leftist ideals tend to focus on literature rather than the visual arts. See Richard H. Pells, *Radical Visions and American Dreams: Culture and Social Thought in the Depression Years* (New York: Harper and Row, 1973), 170–92, 292–328; Laurence H. Schwartz, *Marxism and Culture: The CPUSA and Aesthetics in the 1930s* (Port Washington, NY: Kennikat Press, 1980), 83ff.; and Alan M. Wald, *The New York Intellectuals. The Rise and Decline of the Anti-Stalinist Left from the 1930s to the 1980s* (Chapel Hill: University of North Carolina Press, 1987), 91–101. Wald discusses differences between communist and Trotskyist aesthetic theories most clearly.

46. The Pollock story is apocryphal; for Dwight, see McKinzie, 85.

47. See Francis V. O'Connor, *Federal Support for the Visual Arts: The New Deal and Now* (Boston: New York Graphic Society, 1969), 100–1; for an extended discussion of FAP administrative difficulties, see McKinzie, 80–86.

48. Elizabeth Olds, "Prints for Mass Production," in O'Connor, ed., *Art for the Millions*, 142–44. Olds overlooked the sophisticated efforts of commercial artists and art directors to solicit such viewers; perhaps she believed that fine artists would be able to achieve this goal while preserving their complete creative independence. The unstable boundaries between fine art and commercial illustration, especially in relation to control over the final product, were a source of considerable tension for many artists during this period, whether they sold drawings to popular journals such as *The New Yorker*, created advertising art to earn a living, or were solicited by major design firms to create unique images for specific advertising campaigns. See Michele H. Bogart, *Artists, Advertising, and the Borders of Art* (Chicago: University of Chicago Press, 1995), 234–55.

49. Letters and memos regarding the Treasury Section mural projects are preserved at the National Archives and, as a result, the literature on New Deal murals is extensive. See esp. Virginia Mecklenberg, *The Public as Patron: A History of the Treasury Department Mural Program* (College Park: University of Maryland Art Gallery, 1979); Park and Markowitz, *Democratic Vistas*; Marling, *Wall to Wall America*; and Melosh, *Engendering Culture*.

50. See Marling, 15 and 93ff.; Park and Markowitz, *Democratic Vistas*,10–28; and Melosh, 10.

51. Mecklenburg, 10–20. For efforts to construct a positive thematic emphasis on tradition, permanence, and growth in Treasury murals, see ibid., 20.

52. See Clinton Adams, *American Lithographers 1900–1960: The Artists and Their Printers* (Albuquerque: University of New Mexico Press, 1983), 140–41; James Watrous, *A Century of American Printmaking 1880–1980* (Madison: University of Wisconsin Press, 1984), 108–9; and Fred Feretti, "The AAA and How It Grew," *ARTNews* 73, no. 2 (February 1974): 57–59.

53. Adolf Dehn, letter to George Biddle, 1934, George Biddle Papers, Archives of American Art, Smithsonian Institution. Cited in Robert C. Vitz, "Painters, Pickets, and Politics: The Artist Moves Left, 1925–1940" (PhD diss., University of North Carolina, 1971), 80–81.

54. Langa, 50–53.

55. This distaste is illustrated by the failure of earlier portfolios of prints with more radical subjects to gain success. See Langa, 16–18.

56. See Linda Nochlin, "Museums and Radicals: A History of Emergencies," *Art in America* 59, no. 4 (July–August 1971): 26–39. Nochlin cited a study by the French Centre National de la Recherche Scientifique, published in Pierre Bourdieu and Alain Darbel, *L'amour de l'art: les musées et leur public* (Paris: Editions de Minuit, 1966), as well as a study by UNESCO's International Council on Museums, published in *Museum* 22, nos. 3–4 (1969): 125–80.

57. Scholars have reached differing conclusions on whether workers were really drawn to social viewpoint art, proletarian literature, or the radical magazines of the Left. Writing in the 1970s, Richard Pells concluded that the desire to share radical ideas with working-class people represented "a device by which bourgeois intellectuals discharged their feeling of guilt and achieved a vicarious sense of militancy." Pells, 180. More recent studies have addressed complexities ignored in Pells's analysis, such as the experience of cultural producers who themselves came from working-class backgrounds, the diverse types of culture created within working-class communities in a period of changing social economies, and the shaping of those cultural forms in relation to mass media and other hegemonic cultural forces.

58. Olds, 142.

59. Elizabeth McCausland, *Picasso* (New York: ACA Gallery, 1944), 30. McCausland aired her interests in both socially concerned art and abstract modernism and innovative arts strategies in columns written for the Massachusetts newspaper, the *Springfield Republican*, but she lived in New York City after 1935.

60. See Kwait, "John Reed Art Club Exhibition," 23. For attribution of "John Kwait" as Schapiro's pseudonym, see Andrew Hemingway, "Meyer Schapiro and Marxism in the 1930s," *Oxford Art Journal* 17, no. 1 (1994), 26, n. 13; and Patricia Hills, "1936: Meyer Schapiro, *Art Front*, and the Popular Front," *Oxford Art Journal* 17, no. 1 (1994): 30.

61. Meyer Schapiro, "Public Use of Art," *Art Front* 2, no. 10 (November 1936): 4–6.

62. For more on these issues, see Langa, esp. 27–29.

63. Jacob Kainen, "The Graphic Arts Division of the WPA Federal Art Project," in O'Connor, ed., *New Deal Art Projects*, 166.

64. Kainen, "Graphic Arts Division," 173.

65. Kainen noted that he knew at least one "good" artist who was transferred because his work was deemed inappropriate; see Jacob Kainen, Questionnaire [c. 1967–68], Francis V. O'Connor Papers, MF 1088, 52. Repeated funding cuts, periodic layoffs, and the imposition of an anticommunist loyalty oath in 1938 would only have increased artists' reluctance to produce work that could place their jobs at risk.

66. McKinzie, 87.

67. Ibid., 178.

68. Barber, "Sweet Are the Uses," 252. The author further argues that dissension over centralized control within the Roosevelt administration in 1938 did not help these conflicts, as FDR sought more local diversification but administrators feared a loss of professionalization with decentralized programs (see also 247–48).

69. Congress imposed the first freeze on relief employment in March 1936, only months after the WPA-FAP was established in the fall of 1935. In June, the hiring allotment of twenty-five percent nonrelief employees was cut back to ten percent. In the spring of 1937, Congress slashed all WPA funds by twenty-five percent. In April 1938, a proposal to limit each artist to $1,000 of work-relief employment per year prompted such strong protests that it was defeated, but in July a new appropriations bill dropped the nonrelief quota to five percent. In the summer of 1939, artists were limited to eighteen consecutive months of work-relief employment, although they could resign and reapply if they requalified for relief assistance. Eighty-five percent of artists on the New York projects had worked that long and were laid off. When they reapplied, they found that because of previous cutbacks, there were only 1,000 slots for artists in 1939 instead of the 2,200 positions available in 1936, and Congress had also mandated that those who remained or were rehired must now sign a loyalty oath denying any leftist political affiliations. See McKinzie, 96 and 149, and O'Connor, *Federal Support*, 27 and 43–44.

70. Vitz, 254. See also William Leuchtenberg, *Franklin D. Roosevelt and the New Deal, 1932–1940* (New York: Harper and Row, 1963), 279.

71. McKinzie, 158–59 and 165.

72. Establishing a permanent arts agency would have stabilized many of the benefits pioneered by FAP programs, including affirmation of art's contribution to American culture, reduction of dependence on galleries, and support for art that informed public opinion instead of appeasing public taste.

73. Stuart Davis, "Toward a Democratic Culture," *American Artist* 2 (Spring 1938): 1.

74. McKinzie, 152–53.

75. See Peyton Boswell, "Comments:" *Art Digest* 12, no. 2 (October 15, 1937): 3; 12, no. 9 (February 1, 1938): 3; 12, no. 11 (March 1, 1938): 3; 12, no. 12 (March 15, 1938): 3; and 12, no. 14 (April 15, 1938): 3.

76. This was the Coffee-Pepper-Sirovich bill. See McKinzie, 154–55; and Anon. "Defeat for Fine Arts Bill," *Art Digest* 12, no. 21 (August 1, 1938): 33.

77. These years also saw conservative efforts to derail gains made by labor and consolidate the power of corporate elites who reasserted the influence of private capital. See Harris, *Federal Art*, 122.

78. Ibid., 70 and 126–27.

Cultural Democracy by Default:
The Communist Contribution to the New Deal Arts Programs

Andrew Hemingway

THE FEDERAL ARTS PROGRAMS OF THE NEW DEAL AND the Communist Party's Popular Front strategy have both been presented in retrospect as relatively short-term and expedient policies, the first out of line with the general tendency of governmental relations with art production in the United States, and the latter with the Communist Party's revolutionary aspirations. Direct state patronage of the arts as an alternative to the market did not become part of the model of a democratic polity in the U.S. in any of the normal variants, and insofar as state patronage is associated with communism, it is equated with the Stalinist model of authoritarian control of culture and has no actual democratic component. In this view, the New Deal—which certainly had no program for social revolution—inadvertently provided a space for communist propagandizing in cultural guise, while the Communist Party (CP) saw the New Deal in terms essentially defined by Moscow as a temporary ally against fascism, and infiltrated the cultural institutions it established and used them for its own political ends. But the short-term nature of the programs and the Popular Front was not immediately evident to many participants at the time, and both had to be given an ideological rationale that assumed a *permanent* shift in orientation. Moreover, as I have shown elsewhere, the specific appeal of neither was limited to the period of their operation: both had an ideological afterlife.[1] Communists and fellow travelers were able to work within the projects in part because of the genuine liberalism of administrators such as Edward Bruce, Holger Cahill, Hallie Flanagan, and Henry Alsberg on the one hand, and because the Communist Party's cultural functionaries could provide a plausible view of why the projects were truly progressive on the other. Thus the areas of overlap between the ideologies of both sides—as well as the real divergences—deserve consideration. There are things to be learned about both the political economy of the arts and the problems of cultural democracy from this exercise. In this essay I argue that the policies of both the Roosevelt administration and the Communist Party had unintended consequences in terms of popular empowerment, and that it was precisely because of this that they issued in something like cultural democracy.

The art patronage initiatives of the New Deal are associated with two planks in the administration's strategy for ameliorating the effects of the depression and hastening its end: its public works programs (Public Works of Art Project [PWAP], 1933–34; Treasury Section of Fine Arts, 1934–43) and its work relief programs (Works Progress Administration Federal Art Project [WPA-FAP], 1935–43; Treasury Relief Art Project, 1935–38).[2] Partly because the experiment of direct federal patronage lasted barely a decade, scholars have tended to assume that the administration was never deeply committed to the principle of federal involvement in the arts. Seen in this light, the arts programs are just another instance of the Roosevelt regime's commitment to "bold, persistent experimentation."[3] While it must be true that the arts were never more than a very small concern within a larger vision of greater state intervention in the economy to check irresponsible corporate power and remedy some of the grossest inequalities it caused, to the heads of the various programs they undoubtedly seemed an integral part of the New Deal's democratic agenda—however conscious they were of the fragility of their status. Edward Bruce fought tenaciously to establish the Treasury Section of Painting and Sculpture (later Treasury Section of Fine Arts) in the Treasury Procurement Division as a way of making the Public Works of Art Project experiment permanent, and—as he saw it—putting it on a sounder footing.[4] Although the WPA Federal Arts Projects had a continuing atmosphere of impermanence because of their financial dependence on the annual Emergency Relief Appropriation Acts (and the supplementary ERA Acts, as it turned out), many of those who ran them hoped to see the principle of federal support of the arts become an established feature of government, even if in a different form from the WPA, which had obvious limitations.[5]

Those who spoke for the programs may thus stand as equivalents to the Brains Truster Rexford Tugwell, as individuals whose thinking was far to the left of Roosevelt's own, and of the majority of those whom he appointed to office. Such figures were increasingly marginalized (or resigned, as in Tugwell's case), as the "social Keynesianism" of the early New Dealers gave way to the "commercial Keynesianism" of the 1940s, but they had played an important role in formulating one strand in New Deal ideology.[6] In a sense, the arts programs can be understood in the same light as the Tennessee Valley Authority (TVA), National Recovery Administration (NRA), and the Agricultural Adjustment Act (AAA), as exemplars of the radical state interventionism of the first Roosevelt administration. Although they were not declared unconstitutional by the Supreme Court like the NRA and AAA and lasted longer, like those agencies they were not part of the heritage of the New Deal, and subsequently fell victim to the conservative upsurge of the late 1930s and 1940s. But again, it is important not to see this as a fate predetermined from the outset. Just as New Deal ideologues such as Tugwell initially hoped that the NRA and AAA marked a permanent shift in relations between state and society in the U.S. toward a planned economy that would "co-ordinate and control private enterprise" because laissez-faire was incompatible with democracy in the age of monopoly capitalism, so too the administrator/ideologues of the federal art programs—Bruce, Forbes Watson, and Cahill— claimed that the era of pure market relations was over because they could not produce cultural democracy.[7] I will now lay out some of the textual evidence for this claim.

New Deal Ideology

It is no accident that some of the most radical sounding statements defining the "broad material objectives" and "philosophy of the New Deal" should be made by leading figures in the Department of Agriculture, since agriculture was the sector of the economy most at odds with the tendencies of the whole in its mode of organization, a sector particularly depressed.[8] In addition, the agricultural sector suffered from the contingencies of repeated and disastrous droughts, and, more than any other, stood for central ideological tropes in American political discourse that went back to the first days of the republic and were dramatically belied by recent experience. I exemplify such statements here through Henry Wallace's *New Frontiers* (1934) and Rexford G. Tugwell's *The Battle for Democracy* (1935), published when their authors were respectively Secretary of State and Under Secretary of State for Agriculture.[9] Much of Tugwell's book may have been formulated contemporaneously with Wallace's, since many of its chapters are addresses and articles dating from 1933–34.

The common assumption of these and other liberal texts of the period—an assumption informed both by the depth of the crisis and the example of the Bolshevik Revolution—was that the depression was a symptom of a major historical turning point. Tugwell and Wallace, together with liberals such as *New Republic* editor George Soule,[10] argued that the development of American monopoly capitalism had brought about epochal changes not only of economic organization, but also in relations between different classes and interest groups within the nation, and between them and the machinery of the state. These changes were inescapable and irreversible. (At times Tugwell sounds almost Marxist, as when he refers to "forces of change long pent" or to "the New World . . . now struggling to be born" [52, 291].)[11] In effect an "Old Order" that saw its apogee in the Republican administrations of the 1920s, and especially in that of Hoover, had reached its terminus: the Wall Street crash of 1929 was its "logical result." And its ideology—that of unqualified laissez-faire—was inconsistent with the actual practices of corporate power and effectively unworkable at both national and international levels.[12] As Tugwell put it, "There is no invisible hand. There never was" (14). The American people needed to be liberated from the "deadweight of outworn ideas and obsolete institutions" (301, cf. 318–19).

However, while a liberal writer such as Soule could look forward apparently sanguinely to a future post-capitalist society, and see the New Deal as simply the postponement of an inevitable revolutionary process, for Tugwell and Wallace, the New Deal was the revolution, a way of "making revolutionary changes without violence" (Tugwell, 52). Both of them ominously invoked the example of communism and fascism as essentially European aberrations, and argued that dictatorship and a fully planned economy ("blueprint planning" as Wallace called it) could be avoided in the United States by the renewal of democracy offered through the New Deal.[13] In effect, the administration's strategy was the extension of democracy into economic life after it had been usurped by corporate power,[14] and, the NRA and the AAA, in particular, were part of an experiment "designed to eliminate the anarchy of the competitive system" (9) and stem the drift to "economic oligarchy" (197). Although both referred to a potential threat to democracy from extremist movements, Tugwell and Wallace presented the more serious threat as coming from big business, "the wealthy troglodytes of the preceding generation," and assumed that organized labor and farmers should have more influence within the polity.[15] In an address titled "The Return to Democracy" of April 1934, Tugwell observed that democracy had been "living a precarious life amongst our business institutions" (200), but that the "beneficiaries of private industrial regimentation" (196) could not be allowed to prevail. The New Deal was the manifestation of a broad and irresistible social movement, and, correspondingly, the 1932 elections were unlike any other.[16] With them the American people had given Roosevelt a "peaceful mandate to attempt to devise a better means of distributing the national income than had previously existed" (257); with them they had "accepted the principle of a planned economic life" (167). Yet the limits of the New Deal agenda are well represented by Tugwell's claim that the task of the present was "the making over of the institutions controlled by and operated for the benefit of the few, so that regardless of their control they shall be operated for the benefit of the many" (319). While the modern corporation might have changed the meaning of the term "property," and the New Deal might aspire to place human rights above property rights, in the end, private property would remain sacrosanct.[17]

As the titles of their books indicate, Tugwell and Wallace wrapped their arguments in a mantle of Americanism and insisted on their attachment to traditional values.[18] Tugwell stressed his small town origins (140) and described himself as "thoroughly conservative"(194) in key respects. The New Deal, as both conceived it, was partly an attempt to return to a more traditional society through what was perceived as the modern method of planning. As Tugwell put it, "the land is our basic wealth"(63) and "intelligent use of the land is the first criterion of any civilization"(238). Against the "tyranny of things"(217) and the "economic regimentation"(307) of industrial labor under the "Old Order"(307), he offered a neo-Jeffersonian "vision of villages and clean small factories"(22), of "pleasant and profitable homesteads for the many rather than speculative profits for the few"(41).[19] He hoped to see a reordering of relations between city and country that would mean an end to labor in lofts and sweatshops.[20] Both invoked a full employment economy of shared abundance, and even of a society in which wages were dissociated from production.[21] The Depression was a challenge to the American people to eschew the selfish individualism of business culture and to act as a community: both stressed the importance of regionalism, and Wallace even hoped for a "modern democracy" that was "essentially a graded hierarchy of New England town meetings."[22]

The New Deal stood for "a calculated avoidance of any commitment whatever to doctrine"(92), it had no "definite objectives"(287). Rather it advanced a democratic experimentalism that was philosophically underpinned by the pragmatism of James and Dewey.[23] However, in this version it certainly stood for control of corporate power by the state in the common interest. But it stood not only for social justice, it also stood for a cultural renewal that was both national in character and regionally diverse: "If life can be made secure in each community and if the rewards of the different communities are distributed justly, there will flower in every community not only those who attain joy in daily productive work well done; but also those who paint and sing and tell stories with the peculiar flavour of their own valley, well-loved hill, or broad prairie." Science and technology made possible the "fulfilment of the individual in the unity of the whole."[24] Thus in a kind of dialectical twist, Gemeinschaft would be restored at a higher stage, and Gesellschaft would turn out to have been a passing phase.

The Ideology of the Arts Projects

Although the differences between the organization and premises of the arts projects—and particularly those between the Treasury Section of Fine Arts and the WPA Federal Art Project—were seen as important at the time, and have been treated as such by historians since, in actuality the rationales articulated by their main spokesmen were in key respects similar.[25] Nonetheless, the preference of the Left for the WPA-FAP was clear and emphatic, for reasons that will become evident.

The main spokesmen for the Treasury Section, Forbes Watson, had effectively established the basic terms of the program's rationale in defending its predecessor, the short-lived PWAP, within which he had served as technical director. As in the economy as a whole—although Watson did not make the parallel explicit—the depression in the art market was brought on by "over-production." And the fault here was partly a divergence from Americanism, since the market for modern art centered in Paris ("the highly artificialized French art market," as Watson termed it) operated with an inflated model of individualism in both practice and artist's persona, to which neither the American art buyer, nor ultimately the American artist, could relate. The heyday of this outlook was the decade beginning with the Armory Show, and a reaction against "abstract theorizing" had begun well before the Depression, issuing in a recoil toward a more realist aesthetic.[26] However, the artist's economic problems were also American, in that the art market replicated the "capitalistic system" as a whole in its intense competitiveness, and the reliance of artists on what was effectively "competitive advertising" of their own individuality to boost the value of their trademark wares. In addition, the romantic appeal of the artist's lifestyle was such that the profession was simply glutted with producers. In the face of a frenzied market that speculated in overblown reputations, the government had now stepped in to restore a healthier relationship between the artist and his public. Instead of the "mocking hollowness of an intensive competition system," the competitions for individual commissions organized by the Treasury Section offered the artist "a fair opportunity to compete with his fellow artists in a just and healthy manner."[27] By making the artist more responsible to his client—whether it be the New Deal state or the private patron—a proper relationship between artist and public would be restored. Symptomatically, however, what constituted the "public" remained undefined, languishing in the mythical realm of common sense parlance.[28] According to Watson, the PWAP had brought "the artist into far closer touch with his community and thereby into closer touch with American life," or, as his boss Bruce put it, had established "a definite democratic patronage of art."[29] They would undoubtedly have claimed the same of the Treasury Section.[30]

The tightly monitored Treasury system of patronage, which awarded commissions to individual artists for murals and sculptural decorations for federal buildings on the basis of competitions judged by "experts," presupposed an essentially formulaic notion of top-down democracy. Moreover, it looked on artists as individual providers of professional services within the market specialism of public art it created. By comparison, the WPA Federal Art Project, while its pay rates were low, was generally less prescriptive in its requirements and far more wide-ranging and diverse in its operations, involving an extensive education program as well as the employment of a much larger body of artists working in a whole range of media. It also treated all the artists it hired as wage laborers, thus opening up the possibility of unionization and collective action, and—unlike the Section—it employed artists in supervisory roles. Although the FAP was not without its proscriptions and controls, the common status of project workers as federal employees and the vitality of the Artists' Union gave the program a feeling of participatory democracy entirely absent from the Treasury's program. By contrast with Forbes Watson, the scion of a proper Boston family educated at Harvard and Columbia, its director, Holger Cahill, was the child of poor Icelandic immigrants and had no university degree. Cahill was not only closer to artistic and left-wing subcultures, he was also a more ambitious ideologue than the urbane Watson, with a more developed sociological and historical schema to explain the rationale of federal intervention in the fine arts economy.[31] Taking, as he put it, "a long view of American art," Cahill argued that its "happiest time" had been "from the middle of the seventeenth century to the second quarter of the nineteenth," when it had been "integrated fairly closely, with the basic everyday interests of American society," and there had been "a sound tradition of art patronage." However, with the coming of the industrial revolution, a "re-orientation of social and educational patterns" occurred that "brought into power new social groups with little or no tradition of art patronage," namely the "industrial millionaires." The interest of America's wealthy collectors from this class had lain almost entirely in "archaeology," an interest that issued in a museum culture essentially inimical to modern art, a culture that functioned for Cahill as the business culture of the previous generation did for Tugwell and Wallace. The Depression came as a "final blow" that practically put an end to private patronage, and, as a result, the government had stepped in with the federal art projects to prevent a process of "cultural erosion" that might otherwise have issued in a prolonged "dark age."[32]

A characteristic Cahill speech begins with the assertion: "Art is not an exotic phenomenon. It is a normal growth, deeply rooted in the life of mankind."[33] As this illustrates, Cahill's aesthetic was essentially Deweyan—a connection he made explicit in an address he gave at the philosopher's eightieth birthday celebration in New York in November 1939.[34] Like Dewey, he argued that in healthy cultures art was organically integrated with everyday life. This was not the case in the contemporary United States, due to the absence of effective patronage, as a result of which the American artist of the last hundred years had treated his work as "more and more a segregated activity, pursuing its own ends, away from the main roads of American life." Correspondingly, art had become almost exclusively a phenomenon of the large cities. The FAP, through its community art centers, set out to reverse this trend, and to take art to "under-privileged groups, which heretofore have been denied opportunities" to enjoy it. The project's larger goal was "to activize the cultural experience—to take it out of its cloistered air into a larger orbit of social usefulness," premised on the conviction that "art is [a] vital necessity of modern life," and that for the "sake of the health of our society . . . it must be built into the patterns of our culture."[35] In an untitled text of July 1937, Cahill clearly saw a continuing role for the state in securing this goal. "Because of the co-operation established in these projects between the government, the artists and the public," he wrote, "we can today envisage an art that will reach all Americans." The FAP had shown that "art for all the people is possible," and that, moreover, "that government has a responsibility in making it possible." Although the program had begun as a "compromise" between "furnishing art for America" and providing relief for artists, it had eventuated in "a cultural renaissance that brought the American audience and the American artist together in a new and sound relationship." It offered "a vision" of what "a genuine people's art functioning freely in relation to society" might be like.[36]

It will be evident from the foregoing that there are common motifs within the discourse of New Dealers such as Tugwell and Wallace and that of the arts projects administrators, which include: a sense of an historical shift brought about by the transition to monopoly capitalism, a concern with the decline of regional life and the increasingly urban character of the nation's culture, and a belief that corporate wealth played too large a role within the American polity and needed to be checked by state intervention. There was a conservative aspect to statements by both: a desire to resist the gigantism of economic institutions and bring them under democratic control and to restore a sense of community eroded by market forces. However, in the event the "more definite social machinery to bring about a council of agriculture labor, industry and consumers" that Wallace called for could not be achieved, and the "vast anonymous powers" of the modern corporations could not be checked by the mechanisms of American democracy—or at least to nothing like the extent he and Tugwell had hoped for.[37] Similarly, neither was the American ruling class nor its political representatives to be persuaded that the state should take on itself the fostering of a vital cultural democracy as an alternative to a degraded commercial mass culture and the elite culture of the museums. In the long term, the aspirations of the radical New Dealers were as chimerical as those of the Communists.

THE COMMUNIST PARTY AND THE NEW DEAL ARTS PROJECTS

The Communist Party's embrace of the New Deal was not suddenly initiated by the shift to the Popular Front strategy announced at the Seventh World Congress of the Comintern in August 1935. To begin with that ushered in the policy known as the People's Front (the term "Popular Front" being little used in the U.S.), in which the party remained highly critical of the administration as offering no secure bulwark against fascism and worked to build a Farmer-Labor Party. The swing in working-class support toward the president had caused the CP to moderate its line by the time of the 1936 elections, but it did not begin to endorse his administration in really positive terms until the shift to what it restyled as the Democratic Front in 1937.[38] Not surprisingly, the party's position on the arts programs followed a similar path. Although communist and fellow-traveling artists worked on the PWAP in 1933–34 in some numbers, the program was condemned sharply in the communist press as an attempt to buy off cultural workers with "pitifully small hand-outs from the Federal Treasury."[39] The shift in the party's stance really begins with the inauguration of the WPA arts projects, and it is linked with the more general endorsement it gave to the administration's relief programs (always qualified by the rider that they were inadequate), just as it also backed unemployment insurance and social security legislation.[40]

There was nothing intrinsically un-Leninist about the party's stance on these issues. Although Lenin had been a consistent critic of the delusions of parliamentary socialism, he argued that revolutionaries should participate in the political process to improve the lot of the proletariat where they could. This would both function as a political education for the workers at the same time as it would reveal the limitations of reformism. If the anti-Stalinist Left attacked the CP's Popular Front line, it was not because it could not be reconciled with Leninism as such, but because, initially, its Farmer-Labor strategy did not offer a sufficiently clear alternative to the New Deal, and, later, because it seemed to be abandoning its revolutionary credentials to support the administration in the interests of Soviet foreign policy.[41] For the anti-Stalinist Left, the administration remained a government of monopoly capital (incipiently fascistic, as all such regimes were), and its foreign policy stances were increasingly likely to involve the U.S. in another interimperialist war, in which hundreds of thousands of American workers would be slaughtered in the pursuit of overseas markets and control over the sources of raw materials.

Moreover, the party had compromised itself not just by its endorsement of the administration's policies, but also by its ardent espousal of Americanism. Earl Browder's notorious slogan "Communism is the Americanism of the Twentieth Century" epitomizes this.[42] In 1937, party chairman William Z. Foster claimed that the People's Front, rather than being a Comintern imposition, was built on the long-term tendency of the "American masses" to seek cross-class political alliances.[43] The following year Browder, the general secretary and de facto leader, would assert that criticism of the Moscow Trials was un-American (!) and that those who attacked the USSR were "repudiating our own American history and revolutionary heritage." In July, an editorial in the party's theoretical journal claimed that through the People's Front "we" have "become better communists and hence better Americans," and that the CP was the inheritor of the principles celebrated on the fourth.[44] Whatever the absurdity of these positions, to the party faithful they would doubtless have been reinforced by the discourse of nationalism issuing from the USSR in the 1930s, which was so difficult to reconcile with the emphatic proletarian internationalism of the previous decade. Symptomatic of this is a 1937 Soviet criticism of Sinclair Lewis's antifascist novel *It Can't Happen Here*, which observed, "One sound talk on 'Americanism' with a real Communist, who could show Sinclair Lewis what significance the country and its history have to Communists, would enlighten him, would show him that his patriotism impels the Communist to seek to free his country from the yoke of capitalism. Vulgar 'cosmopolitanism' is deeply inimical to the spirit of Marxism . . . The internationalism of communism is a negation of cosmopolitanism and a confirmation of ardent love for one's country and one's people."[45] This statement is representative of a discourse that seemed to accommodate equally the different cultures of the various peoples of the USSR under the slogan "*socialist* in content and national in form," at the same time as it served as a cloak for Greater Russian nationalism.[46] But whatever the anomalies and contradictions, it was partly because of its adoption of an Americanist discourse that the party could embrace the New Deal populism of the arts programs.

While the CP was an undemocratic party that operated in a behind-the-scenes way within the front organizations it set up, as Maurice Isserman has pointed out, the shift to the People's Front line did reconnect communism with the discourse of democratic rights, which had been so central to the socialist critique of capitalist societies in the nineteenth and early twentieth centuries. Whatever the limitations of this reconciliation, it was undoubtedly taken seriously by many of the new recruits drawn into the party during its growth phase in the later 1930s.[47] Thus, to see the People's Front only as a piece of cynical maneuvering is to view it too much through Cold War spectacles and to overlook the world of ideology within which not just ordinary party members, but even its leadership, thought and acted.[48] The question remains, however: Had the CP become a reformist party as its opponents on the Left charged? Did its leaders think there could be a gradual and peaceful transition to socialism in the United States, or could it only be brought about by armed struggle? The party leadership seems to have been divided and confused on the issue, but certainly the tendency of its chief ideologue was, time and again, to stress the current weakness of the forces working for socialism in the United States and the need to join with "non-socialist progressives" to prevent fascism so that the future destiny of the country could be decided on a democratic basis.[49] At a Lenin Memorial Meeting in January 1939, Browder observed that "nothing is farther from our minds than any abortive attempts of a small minority to impose its will upon the masses. We base ourselves completely upon the democratic masses . . . and we set no tasks that the masses are not themselves to be the moving and decisive factor in accomplishing."[50] While there were obviously other immediate factors at work, it was partly on the basis of this stance that in 1944 Browder would arrange the dissolution of the party and its supersession by the Communist Political Association. This move was based on a catastrophic misinterpretation of the nature of the wartime alliance and the future prospects of peaceful coexistence between the USSR and the capitalist powers, and it was eventually to lead to the expulsion of Browder from the reconstituted party in 1946. Nonetheless, and even allowing for the top-down character of the party's internal workings, it does seem symptomatic of the attitude of a significant proportion of its membership that he was able to push the policy through in the first place.[51]

In sum, while the Communist Party of the USA (CPUSA) remained a Stalinist organization through and through, in the period of the Democratic Front many communists and fellow travelers genuinely believed that there was a confluence between the American democratic tradition and communist politics, and that the Roosevelt administration was the necessary focus for progressive forces. This would eventually lead the party to radically shift its evaluation of the arts projects in the latter half of 1936, not only because of their relief functions, but because of the quality of the culture they promoted. In November of that year the *Daily Worker* asked rhetorically if the WPA arts projects were "just a concession on the part of capitalism, a concession to be ended slowly but surely, turning talented men and women out on the streets once again"?[52] If this were the case, the administration's bluff should be called and artists were advised to campaign for a permanent department of fine arts and for workers' control within the projects, with the artists themselves deciding who was fit to work. The following month, an editorial in the party's cultural magazine *New Masses* argued that cuts in the arts projects were not just an "assault" on the "economic security and the productivity of the artist, but upon an important phase of American culture." The cuts would not balance the budget, and they would "deprive large audiences whose growing interest in literature, painting, music, the theatre, and dance has been one of the encouraging signs of the times."[53]

These statements appeared in the phase of transition when the party was beginning to adopt a more nuanced stance on the New Deal, but still tended to take a highly critical line on the administration. By 1938 it had adopted a far more positive viewpoint and become uniformly laudatory about the projects. In March of that year, the last of a series of six articles in the *Daily Worker* hymning their achievements argued that "in our country the fight for culture has been consistently carried on by the progressives, while the reactionaries have fought bitterly to defeat all measures that would further the cultural development of the whole people," and compared the struggle for "cultural enlightenment" to that for a democratic education, "today we face the issue of extending the benefits of cultural enlightenment beyond a mere elementary education: we face the issue of making culture the common possession of the whole nation and of building a culture which shall represent and belong to all the people of the United States . . . The establishment of the Federal Arts Projects under the WPA was the first step in the direction of solving this problem."[54] A few months later, an article in the party's theoretical journal *The Communist* argued that it was crucial for the democratic front to ally itself with what it called "the cultural movement"—and by which it seems to have meant the workers within the federal arts projects, so as to end that movement's isolation from the people. The next step would be the setting up of that federal department of the fine arts that unemployed artists themselves had been calling for since 1934.[55]

Although the administration seemed to show no interest in the long-term issue of federal patronage, in 1937–38 a few liberal congressmen—namely Representatives William I. Sirovich and John M. Coffee, and Senator Claude Pepper—had adopted the idea of making the arts projects permanent as a way of achieving this end. Their efforts resulted in the so-called Coffee-Pepper Bill (aka the Federal Arts Bill), introduced in Congress in January 1938. On the basis of some support for such legislation from elements in the American Federation of Labor (AFL), Congress of Industrial Organizations (CIO), Labor's Non-Partisan League, the Farmer-Labor Party of Minnesota, and other organizations, *The Communist* claimed that the "broad masses of the people" were in favor of such legislation, and called for the Federal Arts Bill to be "made an issue in every election struggle" of that year: "This is a program to establish the rights of creative workers to live and produce their work with the assurance of reasonable remuneration based upon the social use of their work, to establish *people's sponsorship, enjoyment* and *participation in the arts as a principle of our democracy*."[56] However, in the very month that this article appeared, the Federal Arts Bill went down to a humiliating defeat in the House of Representatives by 195 votes to 35, and the 1938 elections consolidated the formation of a conservative anti–New Deal bloc in Congress for which the WPA generally and the arts projects in particular were a colossal "boondoggle."[57] As the projects came under increasing attack from the congressional Right in 1938–39, the priority became simply to defend their existing status, and the idea of making them the basis for a permanent system of federal patronage receded.[58] Moreover, in effect, the Communist Party converted to the arts projects just at the point when the strand of New Deal ideology that legitimated them was being sidelined.

FALSE PARALLELS AND UNINTENDED CONSEQUENCES

The Communist Party's backing for a federal arts bill was probably in part a response to grassroots feeling among the former members of its John Reed Clubs (superseded in 1936 by the American Artists' Congress) and the Artists' Union, and is comparable to its adaptive response to the demotic energies behind the growth of industrial unionism.[59] But tactics apart, at the ideological level it also arose from a kind of mistaken parallelism with the Soviet system. Communist critics and fellow travelers inevitably took the USSR as their model of a genuinely popular culture that was responsive to the needs of the masses. However grotesque this may seem to us now as a view of the culture of Stalinism, they believed that in the USSR artists enjoyed genuine respect as cultural workers, a generous and secure income from the state, and a healthy organic relationship with their audience. Their activities fell within the larger remit of "social and economic planning," yet, at the same time, they enjoyed a "freedom to experiment" that contrasted starkly with either the conditions of subservience to patrons demanded by market relations or with the control exercised by the federal arts programs—although the party would moderate its stance on the latter claim after 1937.[60] Thus, in the Democratic Front's imagination, Soviet artists had all the things that artists working in the free market culture of bourgeois societies lacked. Of course, communists and fellow travelers also apparently believed that the USSR enjoyed a higher form of democracy than that of the United States, an illusion reinforced by the new Soviet constitution of 1936. Thus the cultural programs of the New Deal appeared as the first steps toward the mature democratic culture that had been established under Soviet "socialism," the best that was possible within the confines of the bourgeois democratic state.

Partly because of the new acknowledgment of national cultural traditions under the Popular Front it was possible to claim that the American route to socialism would be different in some respects. In any case, the party affirmed precisely those measures through which the progressive liberals who administered the projects sought to build a more democratic culture that would reach into those areas of American society that had no contact with high culture in the past, measures such as the public art placed in high schools, hospitals, and prisons; the community art centers that took art education to slum children; and the federal theater groups that were set up in places that had never seen a theater before.[61] Liberal administrators in turn accepted working with communists partly because liberals too had misconceptions about the nature of the Soviet state—as has been amply documented—but also because they believed in a principle of democratic expression that licensed social criticism in art.[62] Their theory of art tended to be drawn from thinkers such as Veblen and Dewey and had more the flavor of prewar radicalism, in contrast to the stern instrumentalism of the Communist Party's "art is a weapon in the class struggle" line. Yet this was considerably softened under the Democratic Front, partly because the doctrines of proletarianism had been superseded by the more indeterminate creed of Socialist Realism in the USSR. But neither was sympathetic to aestheticism, and both thought art should be in some sense socially serviceable. Both were also drawn to the idea of popular traditions, even if they construed the meaning of "popular" differently. There was a significant overlap, which Holger Cahill's approving citation of the fellow-traveler Mitchell Siporin's credo for a Midwestern art in a 1939 speech illustrates: "Ours is the story of Labor and Progressivism, of Jane Addams and Mary McDowell, of Eugene Debs and Robert La Follette, Sr., of Vachel Lindsay and Theodore Dreiser, of Haymarket and Hull House."[63] Although this listing illustrated the characteristic blurring of socialism (Debs and Haymarket) and liberal progressivism (Addams and La Follette, Sr.) in Democratic Front rhetoric, from the perspective of congressional reactionaries such distinctions would have been unimportant: Siporin's Americanism would have been simply un-American. Moroever, Cahill praised the artist as "one of the most brilliant young muralists the Project has developed," despite his well-established connections with the communist movement and ostensive sympathy for labor and African Americans evident in his work.[64]

Both the party and the New Deal were responsive to larger social forces that they claimed to represent and simultaneously sought to direct. Neither fully understood those forces, which had energies that exceeded the immediate ends of both. That is to say, the artists, writers, and theater workers who came together in the projects had interests and goals that were in excess of what either the administration or the party wanted, and it was these (however inchoate) that helped to give the projects their vitality. The unionization of the arts projects workers, which was part of a larger unionization among relief employees initiated by both the socialist and communist parties via the Workers' Alliance, served to focus these energies.[65] Although the CP through the Unemployed Artists' Group of the John Reed Club was certainly the driving force behind the unionization of artists in the first instance, the party did not have the resources to entirely control the large numbers that joined any more than it could control the CIO workers that it helped to organize in the new industrial unions—and neither was it part of the logic of the Popular Front that it should do so. Thus, despite its own authoritarian structures and lack of openness about its role in the numerous fronts it initiated, the party's ostensible commitment to a radicalized vision of American democracy made it embrace the principle of the projects, and at the same time its commitment to organizing relief workers injected far more democracy into them.

Correspondingly, the administration, which had set up the projects in part as New Deal propaganda agencies, in part as make-work projects, and in part from genuine principle, had conceived them as essentially top-down structures with no inner democracy, but found itself forced to deal with project workers' unions that introduced an element of workers' power into the projects of a kind it had never envisaged. The Artists' Union, and the Workers' Alliance on the other projects, gave them a democratic content beyond that which had been intended in their conception, but which the more enlightened administrators accepted.[66] Although much of the union's work concerned pay, conditions of employment and layoffs, they also fought for freedom of expression (within certain limits) and served as a focus for the "political, social and esthetic" debates of the period through their meetings and forums, as members recalled.[67]

Testimony to this confluence between the Popular Front artists' organizations and the administration of the projects is provided by that extraordinary anthology *Art for the Millions*, which began life as a report on the Federal Art Project initiated by Cahill in 1936. Initially it was intended for publication by the Government Printing Office, but when this plan fell through it was signed up with a commercial publisher. That it was never realized has been attributed by Francis O'Connor (who edited the unwieldy corpus of manuscripts into the text we know today) to the crippling reorganization forced on the arts projects by Congress in 1939, and this is likely to have played a role.[68] *Art for the Millions* assumed, at least implicitly, that federal patronage would be permanent, and in 1939 that hope was effectively written off. But it is also likely that a volume that made so clear the connections between a New Deal agency and communist-supported organizations would have been a political liability to the administration at that juncture. In this regard it should be noted that the original editor of *Art for the Millions*, the critic Emmanuel M. Benson, was a signatory of the 1936 call for an American Artists' Congress, and was sufficiently active in that organization to be a member of the editorial committee that prepared the papers of the first congress for publication—a fact that may not be unconnected with his selection by Cahill.[69] It seems that many essays that Benson solicited would have been omitted for one reason or another, and as submitted to its publisher *Art for the Millions* would have been a third smaller than the volume O'Connor edited.[70] Thus a text by the communist Hugo Gellert titled "The Artists' Coordination Committee" and both essays on the American Artists' Congress, by Stuart Davis and Lincoln Rothschild, would have been left out, and only one of the three essays on the Artists' Union in the 1973 publication would have appeared. Even so, essays by many of the major "social artists" of the period (Julius Bloch, Philip Evergood, O. Louis Guglielmi, Jack Levine, and Mitchell Siporin among them[71]) were to be included, essays that acknowledged the political outlook of their authors in coded terms through their concern with inequality and an art of social relevance. The printmaker Mabel Dwight even spoke openly of her socialism.[72] In sum, the 1939 *Art for the Millions* would not have manifested the presence of the Left as an accepted feature of the FAP as clearly as O'Connor's anthology does, but it would still have given the House Committee on Un-American Activities—which had been investigating the projects since 1938—plenty to get its teeth into.

The CPUSA remained a Stalinist organization: it did not turn itself into a party of democratic socialism, and it is doubtful if even its most enlightened members understood the need to make such a transformation. But some of those associated with it were able to grasp a real vision of cultural democracy in the opportunities the arts programs offered. The combination of New Deal populism and the CP's Americanism (however opportunistic the impetus behind it) enabled the more farsighted to envisage a genuinely counterhegemonic culture, democratic and egalitarian, being formed under state auspices.[73] That the New Deal cultural programs contained this possibility is evident from the vehement hostility they aroused in the congressional Right. Although the projects' right-wing critics claimed there was communist propaganda in the products of the arts programs this cannot be taken seriously. Rather, what they offered was a vision of popular empowerment that to the Right was inevitably "communistic." It was this that the CP had sought to foster under the illusion that it equated with Soviet realities. That it was an illusion is beside the point.

Alan Brinkley has argued persuasively that the recession of 1937–38 forced a process of ideological adjustment within the Roosevelt administration. It effectively ended the idea, epitomized by Tugwell's *Battle for Democracy*, that the problems of modern capitalism could be resolved once and for all through state intervention and planning. In the late 1930s, New Deal liberals were divided between those who envisaged the state as having a permanent regulatory role to ensure against the instability of the market, and those who saw its role as essentially compensatory, redressing problems in the private economy without seeking to direct the mechanisms of capitalism as such. The experience of the war years weakened the appeal of a strong regulatory state among such liberals, while it restored confidence in business and resurrected the belief that a permanent growth economy was possible. These developments, together with the increasingly conservative character of Congress in the 1940s, also undercut the labor movement's ambitions to play a significant role in the counsels of government and to extend the welfare state in the postwar period. They also doomed the idea of federal art patronage in its thirties' form, as this was premised on a model of continued state action to replace, or at least supplement, market mechanisms in the cultural field. Such a program was not possible except as part of a long-term project of democratic social transformation, which the American labor movement more generally failed to realize.

In brief, the idea that there was any simple continuity between the state interventionism of the early New Deal and the postwar settlement, which resulted in a minimal welfare state provision and the hobbling of the labor movement through the Taft-Hartley Act, is unsustainable.[74] Whatever value the corporate liberal interpretation of the New Deal as a straightforward holding operation for capitalism may have, it does not match with the ideology or some of the measures of the first Roosevelt administration, including those that issued in the arts programs.[75] In relation to the long-term tendency of U.S. governments to accept corporate dominance and business principles as part and parcel of democracy and the American way, the arts projects stand out as a striking anomaly through which the subordination of artistic production to the market was for a brief period effectively challenged. Moreover, through the actions of artists mobilized by the Communist Party, something like a democratic character was achieved within the framework of state structures, even if, inevitably, in a patchy and partial way. The "triumph" of American painting in the postwar period in the form of Abstract Expressionism, came to stand as a symbol of artistic freedom in the Cold War context, but this was an essentially negative freedom asserted by artists in a situation where they had far less social power than they had briefly enjoyed as collective workers in the 1930s.[76]

NOTES

1. Andrew Hemingway, "The Debate on Art and the State in Postwar America," in *Art and Politics: Proceedings of the Third Anglo-Polish Art Historians' Conference* (Warsaw: Institut Sztuki, Polish Academy of Arts and Sciences, 1999), 151–64.

2. The Federal Art Project was one of four arts programs launched by the WPA, the others being the Federal Music, Theater, and Writers' Projects. Collectively they were known as "Federal One." See: William F. McDonald, *Federal Relief Administration and the Arts* (Columbus: Ohio State University Press, 1969); Richard D. McKinzie, *The New Deal for Artists*; Jerre Mangione, *The Dream and the Deal: The Federal Writers' Project, 1935–1943* (Boston: Little, Brown, 1972); Jane de Hart Mathews, *The Federal Theatre, 1935–1939: Plays, Relief, and Politics* (Princeton, NJ: Princeton University Press, 1967); Jane de Hart Mathews, "Arts and the People," 316–39. For the place of the arts programs in the larger scheme of things, see Anthony J. Badger, *The New Deal: The Depression Years, 1933–1940* (London: Farrar, Straus and Giroux, 1989), chapter 5.

3. The phrase is from a Roosevelt speech of 1932. See Howard Zinn, ed., *New Deal Thought* (Indianapolis, IN: Bobbs-Merrill, 1966), 83.

4. McKinzie, chapter 3. Unfortunately, there is no in-depth study of Bruce. His voluminous papers are in the Archives of American Art (AAA).

5. For funding of the arts programs, see McDonald, chapter 13. For the impermanence of the WPA and the struggles around it, see Barbara Blumberg, *The New Deal and the Unemployed: The View from New York City* (Cranbury, NJ: Associated University Presses, 1979).

6. I borrow these terms from Steve Fraser's and Gary Gerstle's introduction to their collection *The Rise and Fall of the New Deal Order, 1930–1980* (Princeton, NJ: Princeton University Press, 1989), xiv. That there was no single coherent New Deal ideology is well established—Alan Brinkley has described it as "awash in ideologies" (Fraser and Gerstle, 86). For earlier literature on this issue, see Zinn; Richard H. Pells, *Radical Visions and American Dreams*; Thomas A. Krueger and William Glidden, "The New Deal Intellectual Elite: A Collective Portrait," in *The Rich, the Well Born, and the Powerful*, ed. F. C. Jaher (Champaign-Urbana: University of Illinois Press, 1973), 338–77.

7. Rexford Tugwell, *The Battle for Democracy* (New York: Columbia University Press, 1935), 5, 197. Further page references will be cited parenthetically in text.

8. Henry A. Wallace, *New Frontiers* (New York: Reynal and Hitchcock, 1934), 281. For Wallace's summation of the New Deal, see 251–52.

9. For Tugwell, see Bernard Sternsher, *Rexford Tugwell and the New Deal* (New Brunswick, NJ: Rutgers University Press, 1964). For Wallace, see Edward L. and Frederick H. Schapsmeier, *Henry A. Wallace of Iowa: The Agrarian Years, 1910–1940* (Ames: Iowa State University Press, 1968).

10. See George Soule, *The Coming American Revolution* (New York: Macmillan, 1934). For an acute contemporary appraisal, see Felix Morrow, "Soule's Revolution," *New International* (August 1934): 61–62.

11. Tugwell had visited the USSR and was (wrongly) described as a socialist in the right-wing press.

12. See Tugwell, 289, 292, 304, 5, 170, 247; Wallace, 134, 144, 33, 41, 122. Both Tugwell and Wallace attacked the 1920s as a decade of moral confusion, see, e.g., Tugwell, 54, 61, 212.

13. Tugwell, 74–75, 203–4; Wallace, 20, 22, 245.

14. Tugwell, 290, 313; Wallace, 32, 263.

15. Wallace, 5–7; Tugwell, 313.

16. Tugwell, 290.

17. Wallace, 267–78, 251–52.

18. Tugwell, 313

19. Cf. Wallace, 274, 286.

20. Tugwell, 64.

21. Ibid., 70, 156.

22. Wallace, 283.

23. Tugwell, 200–202. On Dewey, see Tugwell, 244–45, 249. On James, see Tugwell, 75–76.

24. Wallace, 274, 277. Cf. Tugwell on the administration's "rescue of artists and the dignification of their work," 312.

25. On this area, see also Andrew Hemingway, *Artists on the Left*, 79–88, 151–53.

26. Forbes Watson, "The Public Works of Art Project: A New Deal for the Artists," *Magazine of Art* 27, no. 9 (September 1934), S29–S30.

27. Watson, "The Chance in a Thousand," *Magazine of Art* 28, no. 8 (August 1935): 470–75, 506–7.

28. Watson, "A Steady Job," *Magazine of Art* 27, no. 4 (April 1934): 168–72.

29. Watson, "The Public Works of Art Project: Federal, Republican or Democratic?," *Magazine of Art* 27, no. 1 (January 1934): 8; Edward Bruce, "Implications of the Public Works of Art Project," *Magazine of Art* 27, no. 3 (March 1934): 115.

30. Cf. Bruce's testimony before the House Committee on Patents, in Treasury Section of Painting and Sculpture Bulletin, no. 3, May/June 1935, 5–7.

31. For Cahill, see Wendy Jeffers, "Holger Cahill and American Art," *Archives of American Art Journal* 31, no. 4 (1991), 2–10; Hemingway, *Artists on the Left*, 151–53.

32. These quotes are from "Works Progress Administration, The Federal Art Project, Holger Cahill, Federal Director" (undated typescript), Holger Cahill Papers (Archives of American Art 1105: 994–1000). See also "Federal Art Project, Holger Cahill—Director," (undated typescript), National Archives, RG69, entry 1022, item 3. The main published statement of Cahill's position is his essay for the Museum of Modern Art's exhibition *New Horizons in American Art* (1936). Significantly, before the CPUSA's

shift to the People's Front, Cahill's historical view of American art had been sharply attacked in a review of the book he coedited with A. H. Barr, *Art in America in Modern Times*, in *New Masses*; see Oliver Larkin, "Art in America," *New Masses* 13, no. 12 (December 18, 1934): 23–24.

33. "Federal Art Project, Holger Cahill, Federal Director," n.p.

34. Holger Cahill, "American Resources in the Arts," in O'Connor, ed., *Art for the Millions*, 33–44. For Dewey on the ordinariness of the aesthetic, the critique of museums, and the need to recover "the continuity of esthetic experience with normal processes of living," see John Dewey, *Art as Experience* (1934) (New York: Perigree, 1980), chapter 1; on art and community, see Dewey, 80–81. Bruce also drew on Dewey to defend his program, see Hemingway, *Artists on the Left*, 81.

35. "Address of Holger Cahill . . . at the Art and Democracy Dinner, June 7, 1938, New York City" (typescript), National Archives, RG69, entry 1022, item 7. Cf. "Civic Art Centers and Galleries" (typescript), ibid.

36. "July, 1937" (untitled typescript), Cahill Papers (AAA 1105: 1218–19). In 1942, as the WPA arts programs were in their death throes, Cahill could still write: "The justification of a public art program, it seems to me, is quite simple. There are certain aspects of our civilization which cannot be carried on effectively by competitive enterprise alone." As technology leads to a civilization with increasing leisure time: "We must provide civilized leisure-time activities for the people who will have leisure on their hands, aside from the dubious juke-box esthetics which now charm so many of us." Holger Cahill to Lucy Porter, October 27, 1942 (copy) (AAA 1106: 138).

37. Wallace, 284, 268.

38. For the CPUSA and the New Deal, see Anders Stephanson, "The CPUSA Conception of the Rooseveltian State, 1933–1939," *Radical History Review* 29 (Fall 1980): 161–76; Harvey Klehr, *The Heyday of American Communism* (New York: Basic Books, 1984); Fraser M. Ottanelli, *The Communist Party of the United States: From the Depression to World War II* (New Brunswick, NJ: Rutgers University Press, 1991).

39. Editorial, *New Masses* 10, no. 1 (January 2, 1934): 4. On the communists and the PWAP, see Hemingway, *Artists on the Left*, chapter 4.

40. See Hemingway, *Artists on the Left*, 149–51.

41. V[ladimir] I[lich] Lenin, *What Is to Be Done? Burning Questions of our Movement* (1902; New York: International Publishers, 1929), esp. part 3. As Philip Rahv put it in a withering appraisal of the League of American Writers: "Within the short space of two years the 'revolutionaries' of 1935 had substituted the stars and stripes of New Deal Marxism for 'the red flag of the new materialism.'" See Philip Rahv, "Two Years of Progress—From Waldo Frank to Donald Ogden Stewart," *Partisan Review* 4, no. 3 (February 1938): 24.

42. Earl Browder, "What Is Communism?," *New Masses* 15, no. 12 (June 25, 1935): 13. Under Comintern pressure, the slogan was dropped in 1938, see Earl Browder, "Concerning American Revolutionary Traditions," *The Communist* 17, no. 12 (December 1938): 1079–85.

43. William Z. Foster, "American Origins of the People's Front," *The Communist* 16, no. 11 (December 1937): 1103–7.

44. Earl Browder, "Lessons of the Moscow Trials," *The Communist* 17, no. 4 (April 1938): 317; Editorial, "Review of the Month," 579, and Francis Franklin, "July 4th—Birthday of American Democracy," *The Communist* 17, no. 7 (July 1938): 630–41. More generally, see Earl Browder, *The People's Front* (New York: International Publishers, 1938), part 2.

45. Sergei Dinamov, "Sinclair Lewis's Communists," *International Literature*, no. 4 (April 1937): 100–1. Cf. Ivan Katayev, "The Art of the Socialist People," *International Literature* no. 6 (1936): 92–107. At the American Artists' Congress in February 1936, Margaret Bourke-White claimed: "The same spirit of hospitality [as with European artists] extends with Russia to the national minorities. In the days of the czars, their art was suppressed. Now it is encouraged to the highest degree," in "An Artist's Experience in the Soviet Union," in *Artists Against War and Fascism: Papers of the First American Artists' Congress* ed. Matthew Baigell and Julia Williams (New Brunswick, NJ: Rutgers University Press, 1986), 85. Cf. Louis Lozowick, "Aspects of Soviet Art," *New Masses* 14, no. 5 (January 29, 1935): 19, and also Lozowick's response to Lynd Ward's paper "Race, Nationality, and Art" at the 1936 Artists' Congress, Baigell and Williams, 146.

46. Joseph Stalin, *Marxism and the National-Colonial Question: A Collection of Articles and Speeches* (1934; San Francisco: Proletarian Publishers, 1975), 391.

47. Maurice Isserman, *Which Side Were You On? The American Communist Party During the Second World War* (Middletown, CT: Wesleyan University Press, 1982), 9–14. In 1939, Browder claimed that the party's Tenth National Convention of the previous year had "fixed its character as the *democratic* [my emphasis]," party of the working class, continuing the best American traditions while preparing for the socialist future." "Some Remarks on the Twentieth Anniversary of the Communist Party of the United States," *The Communist* 18, no. 9 (September 1939): 801–2.

48. As in Irving Howe and Lewis Coser, *The American Communist Party: A Critical History (1919–1957)* (Boston: Beacon Press, 1957), chapter 8.

49. "The Relation of the People's Front to the Struggle for Socialism," in Browder, *The People's Front*, 145–49. Cf. "Election Platform of the Communist Party of the USA, 1940," *The Communist* 19, no. 9 (September 1940), 796. For a critique of Browder's position on transition from a former participant in the People's Front, see Al Richmond, *A Long View from the Left: Memoirs of an American Revolutionary* (Boston: Houghton Mifflin, 1973), chapter 8.

50. Earl Browder, *Fighting for Peace* (New York: International Publishers, 1939), 225–26.

51. For this episode and the opposition to it, see Isserman, chapters 9–10. The CPA turned out to be no more democratic in its internal workings than the CPUSA, see Isserman, 191, 199, 204–5. For Browder's postwar vision, see his *Teheran: Our Path in War and Peace* (New York: International Publishers, 1944).

52. Charles E. Dexter, "The Federal Arts Projects Face an Uncertain Future," *Daily Worker*, November 18, 1936, 7.

53. "Not by Bread Alone," *New Masses* 22, no. 1 (December 29, 1936): 20.

54. John Harding, "Democracy and a National Art," *Daily Worker*, March 28, 1938, 7. The other articles had appeared on March 18 (FMP), March 22 (FTP), March 23 (FTP radio division), March 24 (FWP), March 25 (FAP). I discuss the party's shifting line on the arts projects in relation to its larger campaign for relief spending in Hemingway, *Artists on the Left*, 149–51.

55. "For a Permanent Art Project," *Art Front* 1, no. 1 (November 1934); "Artists' Union Federal Art Bill," *Art Front* 1, no. 2 (January 1935): 2 The American Artists' Congress was associated with this position from its first meeting, see Alexander R. Stavenitz, in Baigell and Williams, 180–81. In May 1938 the League of American Writers held a conference on the issue, see Alfred Davis, "Conference Today to Map Plans for Arts Bureau," *Daily Worker*, May 22, 1938. Audrey McMahon, head of the FAP in New York City and state, recalled that "Cahill and all of us were perfectly aware that the very premise of the Project was its impermanence," see O'Connor, ed., *New Deal Art Projects*, 324. Yet at the time she wrote: "It is a profoundly important factor in the understanding between the artist as an individual or as a member

of an organized group and the administrative personnel of the Federal Art Project that all have the same goal—permanency of government subvention of the artist," see "The WPA/FAP and the Organized Artist," in O'Connor, ed., *Art for the Millions*, 259.

56. C.S. Marin, "The Campaign for the Federal Arts Bill," *The Communist* 18, no. 6 (June 1938): 562–70. See also the editorial in "Culture for America," *Daily Worker*, June 13, 1938.

57. McKinzie, 150–55. For Pepper's politics, see Alex Lichtenstein, "In the Shade of the Lenin Oak: 'Colonel' Raymond Robins, Senator Claude Pepper and the Cold War," *American Communist History* 3, no. 2 (December 2004): 185–214. The Artists' Union certainly planned to campaign for another bill, see Einar Heiberg, Secretary of the Minnesota Artists' Union, in O'Connor, ed., *Art for the Millions*, 246.

58. McKinzie, chapter 9; Hemingway, *Artists on the Left*, 147–48.

59. Bert Cochran, *Labor and Communism: The Conflict that Shaped American Unions* (Princeton, NJ: Princeton University Press, 1979).

60. Bourke-White, "An Artist's Experience," and Arnold Friedman, "Government in Art," in Baigell and Williams, 156–59; Louis Lozowick, "The Artist in the USSR," *New Masses* 20, no. 5 (July 28, 1936): 18–20.

61. McKinzie, chapter 8; Mathews, *The Federal Theatre*, chapter 4; Hallie Flanagan, *Arena* (New York: Duell, Sloan and Pearce, 1940), 21–23. Among almost daily articles praising one or other aspects of the arts projects in the *Daily Worker* in 1937–38, see, e.g., Marcia Minor, "Harlem's Community Art Center," *Daily Worker*, August 1, 1938, and "A Children's Art Festival," *Daily Worker*, August 29, 1938; "30,000,000 Spectators Saw WPA Shows," *Daily Worker*, March 21, 1939; "Libraries, Hospitals and Schools Get WPA Murals," *Daily Worker*, May 12, 1939; "WPA Art Caravan Now on Grand Tour of Long Island," *Daily Worker*, August 1, 1939.

62. See Pells, 61–69 and passim; Frank A. Warren, *Liberals and Communism: The "Red Decade" Revisited* (New York: Columbia University Press, 1993).

63. Cahill, "American Resources in the Arts," 42, citing Mitchell Siporin, "Mural Art and the Midwestern Myth," in O'Connor, ed., *Art for the Millions*, 67. Cf. Holger Cahill to Mitchell Siporin, April 20, 1937, Siporin Papers (AAA 2011: 146).

64. Siporin's radicalism was more evident in his murals for the Treasury Section than in those for the WPA-FAP—Cahill regarded the artist's St. Louis post office murals (executed with Edward Millman) as "the culmination of a creative period" (meaning the New Deal cultural experiment). See Holger Cahill to Mitchell Siporin, May 11, 1942 (copy) (AAA 1107: 46). Cf. Hemingway, *Artists on the Left*, 159–69.

65. For the Workers' Alliance, see Klehr, 294–303. For the Artists' Union, see Gerald M. Monroe: "The Artists' Union of New York," DEd diss., New York University, 1971; "Artists as Militant Trade Union Workers During the Great Depression," *Archives of American Art Journal* 17, no. 1 (1974): 7-10; "Artists on the Barricades: The Militant Artists' Union Treats with the New Deal," *Archives of American Art Journal*, 18, no. 3 (1978): 20–23; O'Connor, ed., *Art for the Millions*, 237–47; Lincoln Rothshild, "Artists' Organizations of the Depression Decade," in O'Connor, ed., *New Deal Art Projects*, 198–221. The workers on neither the FTP nor the FWP managed to organize their own union as the artists did, but the Workers' Alliance was powerful in both, see Flanagan, passim; and Mangione, passim.

66. See the account of relations between the FAP administrators and the union by Audrey McMahon in O'Connor, ed., *New Deal Art Projects*, 66–67; and her "The WPA/FAP and the Organized Artist." McMahon was a warm New Dealer and member of the American Artists' Congress. The relations of some other regional FAP heads with the union were not so harmonious. For instance, Cahill was forced to replace the Illinois director Increase Robinson, see George J. Mavigliano and Richard A. Lawson, *The Federal Art Project in Illinois, 1935–1943* (Carbondale: Southern Illinois University Press, 1990), 30–45. Cahill himself had a less sanguine view of the Artists' Union in retrospect than McMahon, and seems to have been critical of both her and her running of the New York project. See Cahill, "The Reminiscences of Holger Cahill," (Columbia Oral History Collection, Columbia University, New York, 1957) 418–21, 457–63, 507–8, 537. On the other hand, it should be noted that Cahill addressed the Second American Artists' Congress in 1937, and in 1939 the organization arranged a dinner in his honor at the Brevoort Hotel in New York.

67. Robert Cronbach and Joseph Solman, in O'Connor, ed., *New Deal Art Projects*, 141, 120–21.

68. "Introduction," O'Connor, ed., *Art for the Millions*, 13–14.

69. For Benson, see ibid., 270.

70. See Appendix B, ibid., 296–303.

71. In Levine's case this was specifically encouraged by Benson, who rejected a first essay devoted to technical aspects of the artist's work, ibid., 120.

72. Mabel Dwight, "Satire in Art," in ibid., 153.

73. My argument here is not concerned with the character of the programs' products. There were inevitable constraints, such as the ban on nudes or anything directly party political within the WPA-FAP. However, I have argued elsewhere that there was a substantial measure of freedom for leftists, not just on that program, but also within the Treasury Section's. (See Hemingway, *Artists on the Left*, chapters 4 and 7.) The idea of the artist working with no constraints is facile in relation to the market, as much as in relation to art produced under state patronage for public functions. There is no such thing as absolute freedom in art production—that is simply a fantasy of bourgeois ideology.

74. Alan Brinkley, "The New Deal and the Idea of the State," and Nelson Lichtenstein, "From Corporatism to Collective Bargaining: Organized Labor and the Eclipse of Social Democracy in the Postwar Era," in Fraser and Gerstle, 85–121, 122–52.

75. For an introduction to debates around the Corporate Liberal model and its rivals, see G. William Domhoff, *The Power Elite and the State: How Policy Is Made in America* (New York: Aldine de Gruyter, 1990). Warren Carter provides an incisive analysis of the relative value of various neo-Marxist theories of the state in relation to the arts programs in his "Structure and Agency in New Deal Art: The Case of William Gropper's *Construction of a Dam*," *Object* 6 (2003–4): 5–28.

76. Cf. the contemporary critique by Walter Abell, cited in Hemingway, "The Debate on Art and the State," 158.

NASA and the Political Economy of Art, 1962–1974

Anne Collins Goodyear

As Julie Codell explains in the introduction to this volume, the political economy of art seeks to describe the value of art in a public context and to determine what benefits may accrue from its support. "Political economy of art complicates economic theories that define consumption as maximizing personal satisfaction," Codell notes, "because the political economy of art claims to express communal values or needs" (19). Taking seriously the power not only of art itself, but also its very production, to convey larger "truths," often determined by specific social or political agendas, this case study examines the rational for the creation and support of NASA's little-known "Artists Cooperation Program" during the 1960s.

The sensitivity of the space agency to the importance of the political economy is made evident in Mary A. Holman's 1974 study, *The Political Economy of the Space Program*. "NASA, perhaps more than any other science mission-oriented federal agency, has done much to try to understand the social and economic ramifications of its objectives," Holman observes.[1] Although Holman does not address NASA's art program, she clearly elaborates the organization's policy of studying and courting public support for its programs, particularly through its investment in education. In this vein, art served the interests of NASA, an organization founded to pursue the scientific and technological goal of space exploration, not so much through the creation of tangible products of exchange, but rather by shaping public perceptions of it and thus promoting the agency in the eyes of Congress and the public. By committing resources to art, which promised to outlast the ephemeral benefits of media coverage, NASA found a way to translate and communicate its objective of dominance in extraterrestrial exploration into qualities broadly compatible with human excellence. With the success of its publicly funded art program, NASA in turn offered an unlikely model for the establishment of the National Endowment for the Arts and the National Endowment for the Humanities in 1965. Perhaps most importantly, the NASA Art Program provides insight into the conjunction of two of the nation's most important and visible cultural initiatives during the course of Cold War: the production of avant-garde art and sophisticated technology.

In March 1962, several years before President Lyndon B. Johnson signed legislation establishing the National Endowment for the Arts and the National Endowment for the Humanities, James Webb, NASA's second administrator, began to put an art program into place at NASA.[2] While our understanding of many aspects of the political economy of federal arts support during the Cold War era has already benefited from scholarly attention, the NASA art program has remained absent from previous accounts of Cold War patronage. But if the NASA art program has not received the type of sustained public attention one might expect, during its first decade it nonetheless attracted some of the best-known artists and illustrators, including Robert Rauschenberg, Red Grooms, Jamie Wyeth and Norman Rockwell, and received widespread public exposure.[3]

The NASA art program provides insight into the conjunction of two of the nation's most important and visible cultural initiatives during the course of the Cold War: the production of avant-garde art and sophisticated technology, a relationship that deserves further study. As I will argue, the patronage of art promised to serve the space program by shaping public perceptions of it and thus promoting the agency in the eyes of Congress and the public. By investing in art, which promised to outlast the ephemeral benefits of media coverage, NASA hoped to reap benefits that might last for many generations.

Launching the NASA Artists' Cooperation Program

Justification for the establishment of the NASA Artists' Cooperation Program grew out of responsibilities assumed by NASA at the time of its inception. Established on October 1, 1958 by the National Aeronautics and Space Act of 1958, the civilian space agency, deliberately separated from the military, represented a direct response on the part of the United States to the Soviet victory of Sputnik, the first man-made satellite, launched almost exactly a year earlier. Charged, among other things, with "the preservation of the role of the United States as a leader in aeronautical and space activities for peaceful and scientific purposes," the act also required the agency to "provide for the widest practicable and appropriate dissemination of information concerning its activities and the results thereof."[4]

James Webb, NASA's second administrator, was well equipped to face the challenges demanded by the new era of space exploration.[5] With high-level experience both in the federal government and private industry and a strong interest in the theory of management, Webb recognized that NASA's technological goals could only be achieved in concert with an investment in cultural resources. In a letter to T. Keith Glennan, his predecessor at NASA, written the same day that the Soviet cosmonaut Yuri Gargarin became the first man in space and the first to orbit the earth, Webb confided that "[ongoing Soviet competition required the United States to] utilize every resource we have in education, communication, and transportation to build a more viable economic, political, and social structure for the free world."[6] Webb had no doubt that NASA could play a key role in the development of this infrastructure.[7]

Webb first turned his attention to art at the space agency in March 1962 when Bruce Stevenson offered NASA his portrait of Alan Shepard, the first American in space.[8] Contemplating the gift, the administrator recommended that a policy for commissioning artists be adopted "to commemorate past historic events such as Shepard's and Glenn's flight[s], as well as future historic events that we know will come to pass."[9] Even more specifically, Webb spoke to the qualities he wanted such artwork to convey, suggesting that a group portrait of the seven Mercury astronauts be commissioned that would "emphasize the team effort and the togetherness that has characterized the first group of astronauts to be trained by this nation."[10] Although the group portrait never materialized, Webb's very conception of it testifies to his recognition that artwork commissioned by NASA would serve an interpretive function, suggesting the thematic significance of particular moments in the space program.[11]

Experienced with the politics of Washington, Webb saw to it that NASA sought the input of the Commission of Fine Arts and the National Gallery in pursuing the development of an art program.[12] In consultation with the leaders of these influential art institutions, NASA invited Hereward Lester Cooke, Curator of Paintings at the National Gallery, to serve as "principal advisor" to NASA on the selection of American artists to record the U.S. space program.[13] According to a NASA memo recommending Cooke, "this level of consultancy is recommended . . . to ensure in-house cooperation at all points and, possibly, to prevent unheeded imposition of inexpert pressures on the shaping of a fine arts program."[14] Such language reflects Webb's sensitivity to the potential political pressures he faced in building a federal art program at NASA. Only a few years earlier George Dondero and a number of conservative politicians had vehemently attacked a wide range of federal art exhibitions that appeared to include "Communist" artists.[15] At NASA, Cooke joined forces with James Dean, the Director of NASA's Educational Media Division, to run the Artists' Cooperation Program.[16]

Following the recommendation of the Commission of Fine Arts, Cooke examined the Air Force's documentary art program. Assessing its strengths and weaknesses, Cooke made three recommendations that would distinguish the NASA program from this model. First, NASA would not commit itself to a commercial illustration agency, but instead would retain freedom to select any artist. This would permit NASA to solicit the work of well-established artists, thus implicitly associating the space program with the reputation of recognized talent. Accordingly, each artist would be paid an individual commission rather than be asked to "donate" his or her work in exchange for travel costs and the opportunity of witnessing a particular event. Second, unlike the Air Force, NASA would keep all preparatory sketches, which, in Cooke's view "might be used to illustrate information brochures and . . . other publications of NASA," a hope shared by NASA officials. Third, because a number of Air Force illustrators had expressed uncertainty about what to represent when arriving for an assignment, NASA would "suggest themes" to artists.[17] While the space agency would always stress the freedom granted artists involved in the art program, particularly in terms of access to its facilities, this policy of introduction made it possible, through Cooke's effusive language, to focus artists on precisely those *intangible* qualities the space agency wished to convey, as I explain below.

With regard to style, despite the recommendation of the Commission of Fine Arts that abstraction be adopted—Chairman Finley argued it "could easily be turned to something in space science and achievements"—it was the work of "realists" that was solicited in the early days of the program.[18] In 1964 Cooke actually reassured the readers of the Cape Kennedy Spaceport *News* of his intention to avoid commissioning abstract art, explaining: "We feel the material here is abstract enough."[19] Most likely eager to avoid damaging criticism from conservative congressmen, Cooke may also have felt that figurative work lent itself better to the reproduction and dissemination. As the program matured and gained support, Cooke and Dean would feel increasingly confident including a broader range of artistic styles in the program, such as those of Morris Graves and Robert Rauschenberg.

To further ensure the program's acceptance, Cooke invited the participation and the advice of three artists whom he felt would be acceptable even to a conservative audience with an anticommunist agenda: Robert McCall, a prominent aerospace illustrator active in the Air Force art program; Mitchell Jamieson, a well-known artist and illustrator who played an important role in the Navy art program during World War II; and finally, Andrew Wyeth, who had recently been hailed "America's most popular painter."[20] Writing to Wyeth in January 1963, Cooke confessed: "Frankly, I am very anxious to get this program off to a good start in the eyes of Congress here, since it may mean a lot of jobs to painters, and the prestige of your name would help."[21]

Both Jamieson and McCall joined the program, as did two young artists who had done work for the Air Force. Although Wyeth ultimately declined Cooke's invitation to work for NASA, at his suggestion Cooke commissioned Wyeth's brothers-in-law Peter Hurd and John McCoy II, both of whom had done artwork for the Air Force, and his nephew-in-law, George Weymouth. Wyeth also offered a strong recommendation of his son, Jamie, who, at age sixteen, Wyeth felt was still too young to participate in the program.[22] However, in subsequent years, Jamie Wyeth would prove a valuable contributor to the NASA art program. [23]

The painter Lamar Dodd also agreed to participate. A southern regionalist painter, Dodd had traveled extensively on behalf of the State Department, visiting Europe (including the Soviet Union), the Middle East, and Asia.[24] He had gained still further official exposure from an invitation to organize a series of radio programs on "The Visual Arts in Mid-Century America" for audiences abroad, and from his 1961 appearance on the ABC television show, *Meet the Professor*. [25] In 1962, a year before he was invited to join the NASA Artists' Cooperation Program, Dodd had also been elected the first Director of the National Council of Arts in Education.[26]

Timed to coincide with Gordon Cooper's *Mercury 9* mission, the first assignment of the NASA's Artists' Cooperation Program reflects the role it was expected to play in public "education and communication." Describing the launch as "one of the climatic activities of Project Mercury," NASA officials stressed the importance of getting "artists selected and on site at Houston and the Cape for exposure to preparatory activities."[27]

This sense of urgency reflected larger concerns. As the political scientist James Kauffman has argued, Cooper's flight occurred at a critical moment for NASA.[28] On one level, *Mercury 9* represented the end of the Mercury program and, with twenty-two earth orbits, an important step toward the American goal of reaching the moon by the end of the decade—and before the Soviets. But even more significantly, the mission offered NASA a chance to demonstrate the value of manned space flight. By late 1962 questions had resurfaced about the necessity of sending a person to the moon.[29] In the wake of John Glenn's successful orbit and the American success in the Cuban Missile Crisis, beating the Soviets in space seemed less urgent. In response to what NASA perceived as waning enthusiasm on the part of the American public for the space program, the space agency conducted an aggressive public relations campaign, fully cognizant that the flight itself was scheduled to occur just prior to congressional hearings on NASA's budget for fiscal year 1964. In an attempt to accentuate the symbolic as well as the technological importance of Cooper's flight, it was scheduled for the anniversary of Lindbergh's pioneering solo flight across the Atlantic.[30] Attempts to garner good publicity were not limited to the ground: Cooper's spacecraft was equipped with so many photographic devices the astronaut compared it to a "flying camera."[31]

Asked to assemble in Cocoa Beach, Florida, several days before the actual launch, the NASA artists enjoyed extraordinary freedom roaming about Cape Canaveral, and interested scientists and engineers invited artists to depict activity in typically restricted areas.[32] Sketches by the artists were shown to the press in June, with the promise that they would be "exhibited nationally before being placed for indefinite display in Federal buildings and museums."[33] As Cooke had proposed earlier, these drawings were also prepared for dissemination as prints and in publications.[34] Accordingly, both Peter Hurd and Paul Calle published articles describing their experience working for NASA in leading art magazines.[35]

From its earliest moments, work produced through the Artists' Cooperation Program was aimed at as large an audience as possible. This exposure was increased by the inclusion of high-profile artists such as Norman Rockwell and Robert Rauschenberg.[36] Under contract to *Look*, Norman Rockwell became involved with the NASA art program in 1964, and created a series of paintings about the Apollo project over the next five years that appeared in the pages of the magazine.[37] In 1969, Rauschenberg, who had demonstrated a long-standing interest in space exploration, accepted an invitation to respond to the launch of *Apollo 11*, and created a series of thirty-three lithographs under the title of *Stoned Moon*.[38] Shortly after witnessing the launch, Rauschenberg published a photo-essay recording his impressions of the experience.[39]

Picturing Space Exploration

While the artists involved with the NASA Artists' Cooperation Program recorded space capsules, rockets, space suits, and gantries they encountered, the message their work conveyed did not concern technology per se, but instead testified to the nontechnological associations of NASA's foray into space, such as spirituality and discovery. Whereas artists who agreed to create work for NASA were already favorably inclined toward the space program, the terms of their invitation encouraged a response that stressed awe, excitement, and even spirituality. As Lester Cooke informed them:

> The effort we are making in this country represents the frontiers not only of technical achievements, but also of the imagination. The space effort is in every way a worthy theme for the artist. Space travel started in the imagination of the artist, and it is reasonable that artists should continue to be the witnesses and recorders of our efforts in this field. . . .
>
> NASA is commissioning your imagination, and we want records of fleeting impressions and poetic by-products of thought as much as precise documents of optical experience. What is important is that the artist gives us his personal and sincere interpretation. . . .
>
> The artist, like the scientist, must reorient some of his thinking in the space environment. . . . All of our concepts of size, speed, number, mass, and even life are quaint and obsolete in this age. And have you thought of the role of man, who not only controls but is also caught in the web of the monstrous machines he has made? The metaphysical aspects of space are as fascinating as the physical and are equally within the scope of the artist.[40]

Cooke's emphasis on the "metaphysical aspects of space" reflects trends observed by Leo Marx in his celebrated 1964 study *The Machine in the Garden*, which explored the conflicted union of the machine and the pastoral ideal in American culture. Most relevant with regard to the NASA art program is Marx's analysis of the "rhetoric of the technological sublime" through which mechanical products of the industrial age, particularly the railroad, were invested with the awe-inspiring qualities traditionally associated with nature.[41] Intriguingly, the four tropes identified by Marx as part of this metaphorical transformation—"the machine and nature," "the machine and history," "the machine and the mind," and "the machine and America"—fit virtually seamlessly into an analysis of the metaphors developed by artists participating in the NASA Artists' Cooperation Program, as elaborated below.

The fascinating parity between nineteenth-century modes of response to new technologies recorded by Marx and those seized upon by artists during the 1960s suggests not only the continuity of American attitudes, but also that Marx's analysis of the historical reception of the machine reflected that of his own contemporaries. Adopting Marx's categories to interpret a wide range of artistic responses to the space program, the larger "message" conveyed by this work becomes clear: Environmentally, creatively, historically, and spiritually, NASA's programs deserved support, because they represented universal progress and the inevitable triumph of "American" values.

"The Machine and Nature"

For many artists, the relationship of space-age technology to the Florida landscape represented less a reconfiguration than a harmonious blending—the peaceful coexistence of new technology and the natural world. Deliberately or not, such images reinforced an integration of nature and technology orchestrated by NASA. In 1963, the same year that the NASA art program was first implemented, NASA established the Merritt Island National Wildlife Refuge at Kennedy Space Center to preserve the ecological balance of 140,000 acres of land it had acquired on the Florida coast.[42] This refuge, which encompasses the areas surrounding the launchpads, effectively renders these sites and their attendant technologies "machines in the garden." In *Waiting*, a watercolor sketch, Jamie Wyeth depicts the distinctive red gantries of two launchpads. Seen from a distance, the two man-made structures appear to rise naturally out of a landscape of "sandy scrub."[43] Flanking a lone palmetto tree located at the painting's center, the two gantries do not appear to be out of scale with their natural surroundings, but, instead, in harmony with them.

In William Thon's *Space Age Landscape*, the gantry actually merges with its surroundings, taking on organic qualities of its own. Even its red color has been subsumed by a dark patina. Its rusted exterior assumes the same shade as dragonflies and plant stems depicted in the foreground of the image. In a caption published alongside the painting in *Eyewitness to Space*, a lavishly illustrated account of the NASA art program, Lester

Cooke explained: "Here a gantry of the Mercury era rusts in the subtropic sea air. . . . Now it is used chiefly by sea birds who find the girders ideal nesting grounds. In the foreground, jungle growth moves in to reclaim its rights."[44] The "space age landscape" does not depict a futuristic scene, but instead suggests that even space-age technological innovations remain part of the familiar natural order. NASA's space center does not threaten the natural environment, but instead becomes part of that landscape.

The image of space-age technology being subsumed by the natural world, merging with it, and glorifying it, also characterizes Robert Rauschenberg's description of his experience watching the fueling of *Apollo 11* with liquid nitrogen: "It turned into the most beautiful icicle. . . . incredibly bright lights, the moon coming up, seeing the rocket turn into pure ice, its stripes and USA markings disappearing—and all you could hear were frogs and alligators! That combination just seemed wonderful to me. The whole project seemed one of the only things at that time not concerned with war and destruction."[45]

Several of the prints that compose *Stoned Moon*, a series of thirty-three lithographs created by Rauschenberg in response to *Apollo 11*, such as *Hybrid*, *Local Means*, and *Sky Garden* construct visual connections between the American rockets that took men to the moon and the local birds and trees that inhabited the area from which the rockets flew. As critic Lawrence Alloway suggested, Rauschenberg's juxtaposition of pictures of egrets and herons with those of *Apollo 11* includes a pun on the naturalizing nickname given to the rocket, a "bird."[46] A poster announcing publication of the series further locates the first moon shot geographically and historically. Images of each of the prints are superimposed over a print of the map of Cape Canaveral used by Rauschenberg at the launching, a reversed reproduction of a photograph of the first flight, and a picture of Buzz Aldrin walking on the moon.[47]

Artists did not restrict themselves to rendering the terrestrial landscape, but also created images speculating about sites that technology would render visible to the human eye for the first time. Several artists, such as Yeffe Kimball, Fred Messersmith, James Hendricks, Jack Perlmutter, and Lamar Dodd produced imaginary "moonscapes," claiming this new world as part of the established natural order.

"The Machine and the Mind"

Correspondence and later reflections indicate that the artists who accepted commissions from NASA were inspired by the prospect of space exploration and excited by parallels they perceived between their own activities and those of the NASA scientists. In 1964 Morris Graves conceived of a project that would coordinate the creative energies of both artists and scientists at NASA, demonstrating that artists and scientists could work together for positive scientific and aesthetic ends in the new age of space. Graves proposed integrating a jewel and a poem into the design of an Orbiting Astronomical Observatory set for launch in 1965.[48] John O'Keefe, Assistant Chief of the Theoretical Division at Goddard Space Flight Center, responded enthusiastically to the suggestion, even as he recommended modifying it slightly. He wrote to Graves: "It seemed to me that you were intending something which would be a pure statement of the meaning of art in the space context. Something which would say that this thing that we are doing is splendid in and of itself, and should shine out with what you call éclat."[49] Graves, in turn, reacted to O'Keefe's interest, with great satisfaction, explaining to Lester Cooke that O'Keefe's support, "confirms our belief that what seems to you and me purely subjective is also valid in the 'normal' imagination of [O'Keefe's] men. They seem to me to have taken to the idea as part of their creative process as searching scientists. And isn't this part of what you want as head of the NASA art program?"[50] Although Graves's project was ultimately unrealized, his approach to it indicates how the space program could be interpreted as an extension of artistic creativity.

Robert Rauschenberg's aforementioned *Stoned Moon* series also creates an analogy between the collaborative nature of the moon shot and of the creative process itself. *Sky Garden* (Figure 40), the most intricate work in the series, marked a major breakthrough in the medium of lithography. At eighty-nine inches high and forty-two inches wide, it represented the largest, hand-pulled, multicolored lithograph ever made.[51] To create this image three lithographic stones had to be laminated together, and extensive research into compatible inks and paper was required.[52] *Sky Garden* was not only an artistic triumph, but, like the moon landing, a technical one as well. Rauschenberg's perception of the relationship between NASA's triumph and his artwork is illustrated in his poetic essay "Notes on Stoned Moon," which intersperses commentary about *Apollo 11* with a description of the lithographic process. A collage of photos in the background combines images of Cape Canaveral and the moonwalk with those of the print shop.[53] In a pithy assessment of Cape Canaveral, the artist described it as "a theater where performance is all."[54]

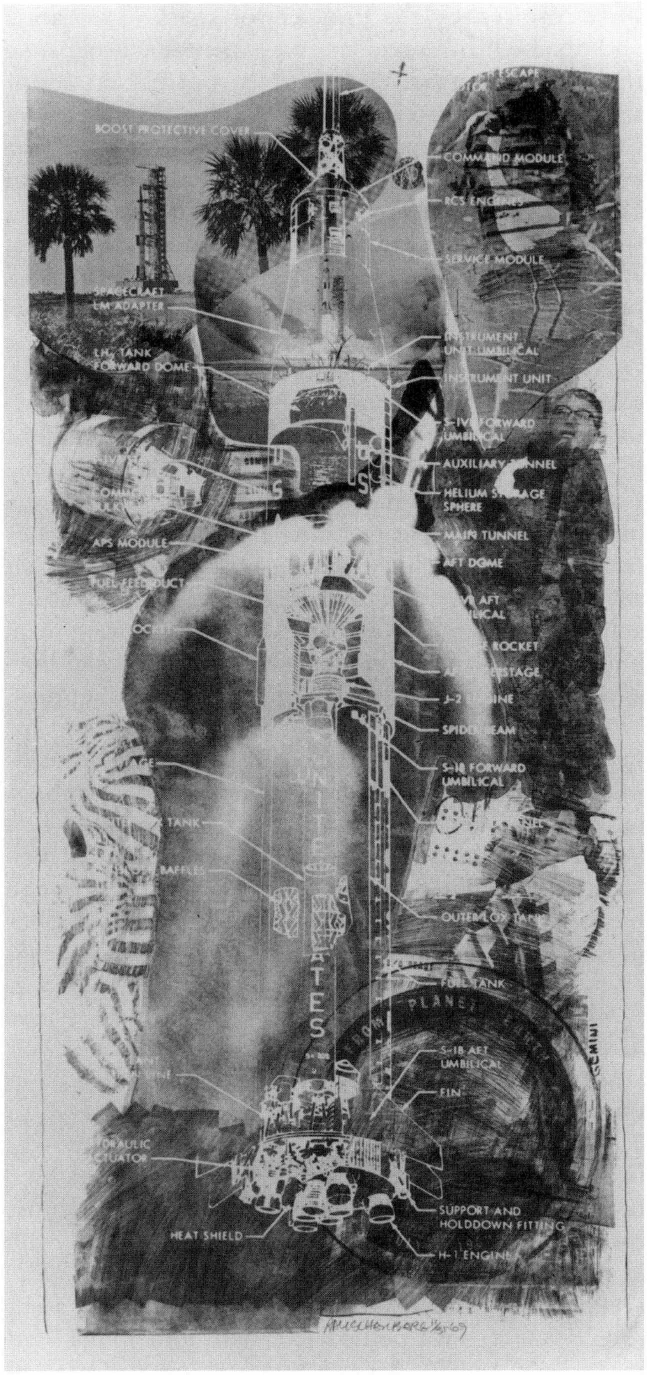

40. Robert Rauschenberg, *Sky Garden*, 1969, color lithograph and seriograph on paper, 89 × 42 in., Hirshhorn Museum and Sculpture Garden, Smithsonian Institution, Gift of the Joseph H. Hirshhorn Foundation, 1974. Photo by Lee Stalsworth. Art © Robert Rauschenberg/Licensed by VAGA, New York, NY.

"THE MACHINE AND AMERICA"

One of the best documented rhetorical tropes associated with the American space program is that of exploration.[55] The "final frontier" of space was frequently equated with the myths of the American West and Christopher Columbus's "discovery" of the continent. A 1962 NASA memo urging the rapid implementation of the art program described Webb's viewpoint in the following terms: "[The astronauts] are comparable in our time to Columbus's ships' officers in his and we feel an obligation to move swiftly to get their likenesses capably recorded for all time."[56] Lester Cooke similarly turned to the history of exploration to describe the significance of the space program, declaring: "Not since the lung-fish slithered out of the Paleozoic slime have living creatures sought to change their environment, and not since Columbus have men dared to enter more dangerous and mysterious regions."[57]

Writers seized frequently on the image of the American West. As James Kauffman has noted, a March 1962 *New York Times* editorial referred to the astronauts as "the young pioneers of the space frontier"; a year later, a *Newsweek* article attributed to the astronauts a "frontiersman's drive to stake out new territory."[58] Paul Calle's most celebrated image of the space program, *The Great Moment*, related the lunar landing to the American tradition of exploration and discovery in the West. Calle depicts the moment Neil Armstrong's foot first touched the moon's surface. The astronaut is depicted facing forward, the American flag on his left shoulder fully visible. One hand grips the ladder of the lunar module. However, the astronaut's attention is not directed at this last vestige of earth, but rather at his left boot, with which he becomes the first human being to set foot on a nonterrestrial surface. The direction of Armstrong's glance, the raking light that accentuates the texture of the moon, the bright blue color, and the relatively large shape of the boot all focus our attention on that significant step, with which Armstrong declared: "One small step for man, one giant leap for mankind." In subsequent years, Calle explained the relationship he perceived between this image and the exploration of the American West: "Although it may be difficult to compare what seems like light years apart, there are similarities. I like to use the analogy of oneness that I see between Neil Armstrong's boot sinking into the dust of the moon and the moccasined foot of a man like John Colter sinking into the snow as he entered Yellowstone River Valley for the first time."[59] The connection of the image with exploration is further accentuated by its similarity to Calle's design for the U.S. postal stamp, "First Man on the Moon," created prior to the launch of *Apollo 11*. The engraving for the stamp accompanied Armstrong and Buzz Aldrin to the moon, indexically linking the image to the activity it represents iconically.[60]

"THE MACHINE AND HISTORY"

The spiritual associations that pervade much of the work created by members of the NASA Artists' Cooperation Program mirrors the sense of religious reverence generated by humankind's first literal celestial journeys. In this way, artwork contributed to a sense of the universal historical inevitability and laudability of NASA's initiatives. Space flight thus materialized cosmic connections that had been traditionally celebrated in many cultures: American rockets quite literally joined the heavens and the earth, reconfiguring long-standing religious hierarchies. In 1962, Ray Bradbury declared: "Ancient mythologies are being reborn as mankind prepares to fuse the rockets that will celebrate his Independence of Earth and set him free upon the Moon. . . . Thus will begin a second and greater Renaissance for man so vast its repercussions cannot now be guessed. . . . Flawed man, driven from Eden, blind to God, or careless of Him, looking down the centuries for salvation, must now look only to himself for that salvation."[61]

The recasting of astronaut as new American hero forms the basis of Mitchell Jamieson's painting *First Steps*. The faceted quality of the representation of the astronaut and the background brings to mind futurist conventions for representing movement through space—in this case it seems to evoke the astronaut's emergence not just from the ocean where he had splashed down, but from a universe that has been transformed by his mere presence. The interplay of circular forms throughout the image seems to evoke the circular form of the planets and their trajectories around the sun, as well as the form of this pilot's orbit around the earth. According to Lester Cooke: "Mitchell Jamieson said that when Gordon Cooper stepped out of his scorched and fragile Mercury spacecraft, having been in space for more than twenty-two orbits, and walked onto the deck of the aircraft carrier, he suddenly seemed to be much larger than life. He seemed to represent not NASA or the United States, but all mankind, which was opening the door to a new dimension and a new future. He seemed like one of the gods of Olympus, who descends to earth

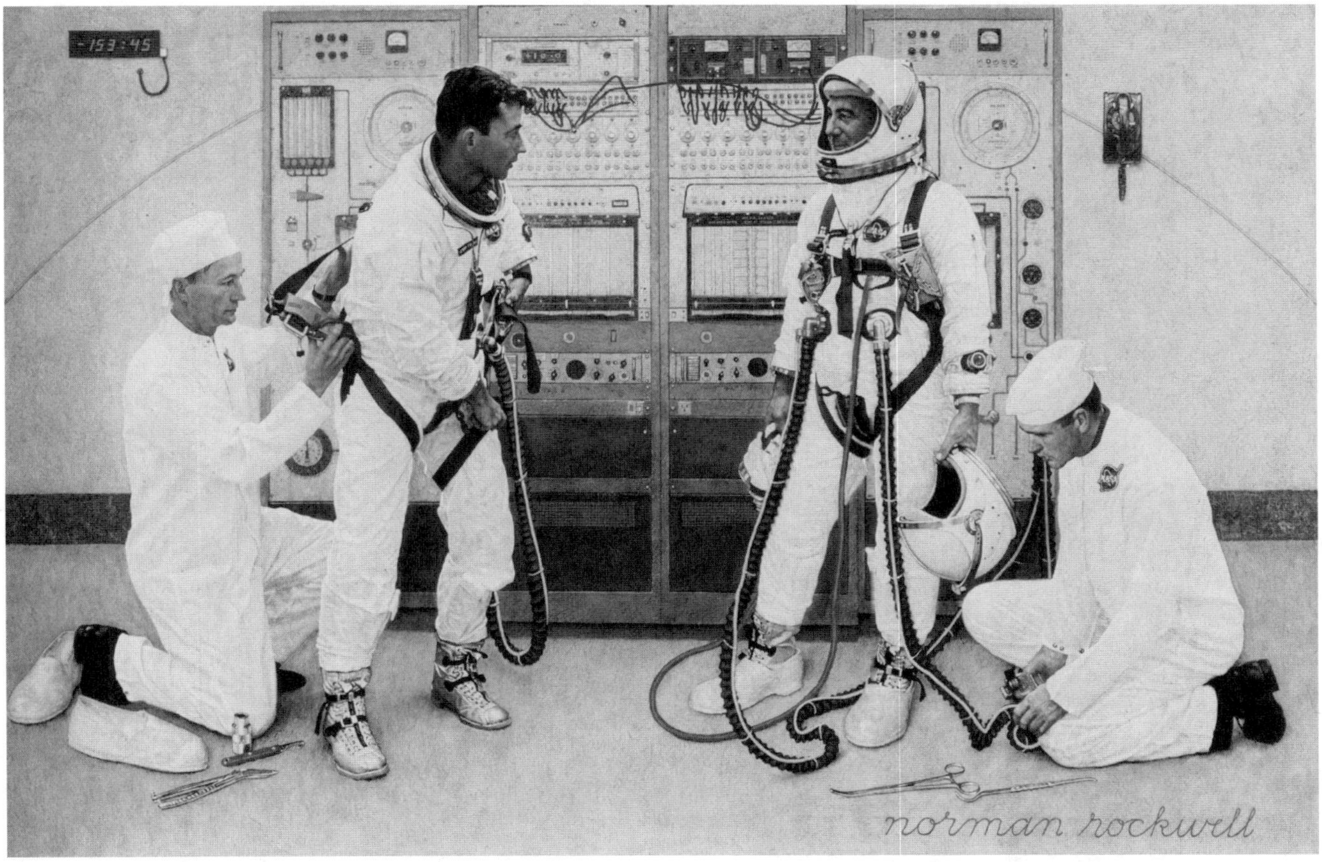

41. Norman Rockwell, *The Longest Step (Astronauts Grissom and Young Suiting Up)*, 1965, oil on canvas 33 × 52 3/8 in., National Air and Space Museum, Smithsonian Institution. Printed by permission of the Norman Rockwell Family Agency, © 1965 the Norman Rockwell Family Entities.

and mingles with mortals, but whose real home is in the skies."[62]

Norman Rockwell too created an image responding to the new spiritual order suggested by the advent of spaceflight.[63] In his painting of astronauts Gus Grissom and John Young, *The Longest Step (Astronauts Grissom and Young Suiting Up)* (Figure 41), the astronauts seem to occupy the traditional place of patron saints, honored by kneeling human patrons, in this case two suit technicians.[64] The "saints" themselves are in turn subordinated to an image of the new God, technology in the form of the computer, which here assumes the form of the crucifix.[65] The entire composition is organized in a pyramidal fashion, recalling the form of Renaissance altarpieces, such as Domenico Veneziano's *Madonna and Child with Saints*, St. Lucy Altarpiece. The blue arch in the background of *Suiting Up* evokes Raphael's *School of Athens*, apparently drawing attention to the new intellectual and spiritual order of modern America.

Like Rockwell, Lamar Dodd also infused Renaissance conventions into a number of paintings responding to the spiritual dimension of spaceflight. In *Saturn-Apollo 10-11* and *The Cosmos Awaits*, Dodd used the traditional form of the triptych, with its connotations of Christian imagery, to depict, respectively, the rocket ship supported by the gantry, and a launch. The connection of *The Cosmos Awaits* with Renaissance altarpieces is further accentuated by Dodd's incorporation of a predella and panels above the main image which seem to contrast the earthly horizon with the universe beyond into which the rocket in the center is directed. Dodd's *Apollo 9 Totality Triptych* (Figure 42) not only uses the Renaissance form of triptych

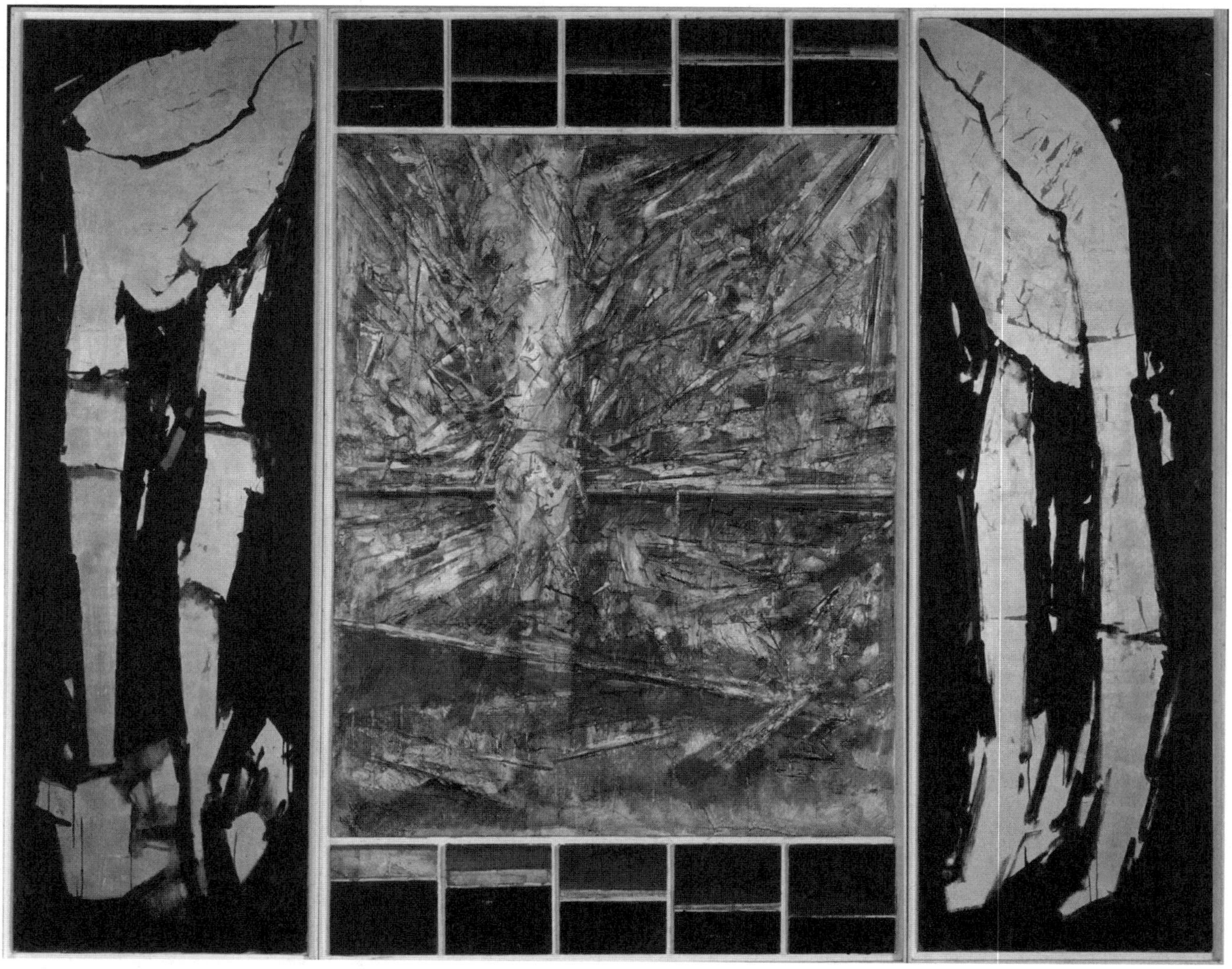

42. Lamar Dodd, *Apollo 9 Totality Triptych*, 1973–74, oil on canvas, side panels: 70 × 23½ inches; center panel: 70 × 43½ in., National Air and Space Museum, Smithsonian Institution.

and predella, but also incorporates gold paint, just as paintings of medieval icons did, enhancing the image's spiritual associations.

Peter Hurd articulated still more associations between the expression of religious sentiment in ages past and in the new age of space. Similar to Henry Adams, who was awestruck by his encounter with a dynamo at the Paris World's Fair of 1900, Hurd translated his admiration of the new machines into the terms of religious reverence, marveling at "a huge radar antennae," that "becomes a mysterious idol in contemporary metal sculpture."[66] Later, describing his reaction to the countdown, Hurd reported: "The voice of countdown is the voice of Fate itself, impersonal and inexorable."[67] The American conquest of space seemed preordained, like a mythic tale of triumph.

Concluding his essay by describing the experience of witnessing the launch of *Mercury 9*, Hurd asserted, "the thought kept occurring to me that a similar mass of effort built the great cathedrals; the same desire of man to attain his ultimate capacity. It seemed to me that the men of science today are the equivalents of those artists and artisans of the great past periods in art; that while widely different in approach, they are linked in an urge to discover the new horizons of the human spirit."[68] His watercolors of the red gantry glowing in the predawn light of launch morning, and his sketches of a radar installation and of Site 14, from which Cooper's flight would be launched, celebrate the new technological forms that human beings have wrought to reach the heavens.[69] The connection of the strange, awkward form of the gantry with revered cathedrals gives it a new significance. In *Pre-Dawn* (Figure 43) Peter Hurd celebrates the glowing form of the bright red gantry, which stretches upward into the sky. Its massive structure appears almost to touch the hazy moon, creating a vivid communion between the heavens and the earth. Hurd's poetic title refers not only to the temporal moment he represents in this image, but also to the larger significance of the historical and cultural transition into the space age. Through an artistic metaphor, the space program receives an historical—and spiritual—pedigree.

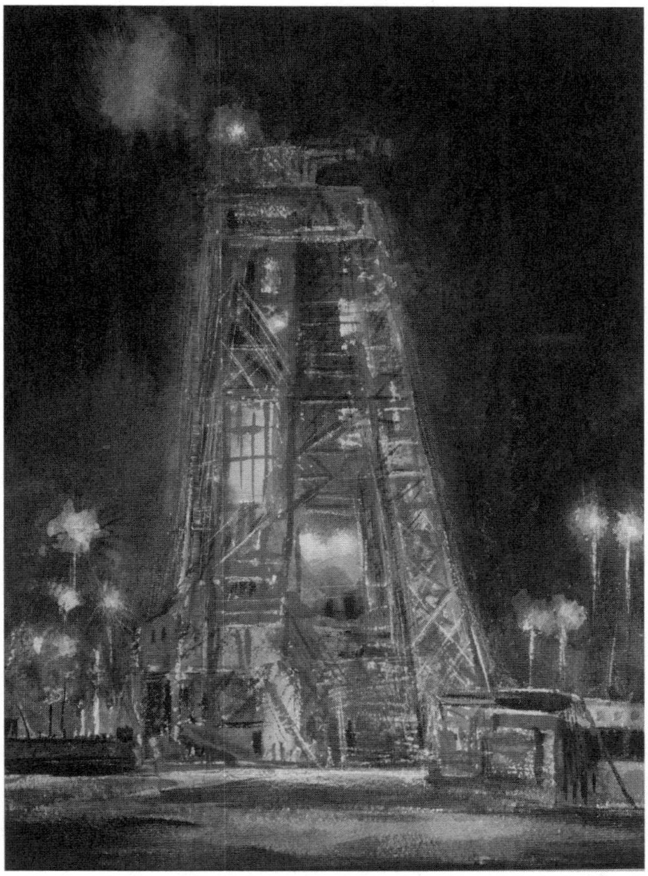

43. Peter Hurd, *Pre-Dawn*, 1963, watercolor on paper 21 × 18¼ in., National Air and Space Museum, Smithsonian Institution.

In such images, artists connected with the NASA art program gave visual form to the amazement that seems to have gripped much of the American public as spaceflight became a reality. As historian David Nye argued, the journey to see rocket launchings took on much the same character as religious pilgrimages. Travelers covered long distances to Cape Canaveral, eager to renew their faith in American technological achievement.[70] During the 1960s, as the United States sought to prove its superiority to the Soviet Union, which officially eschewed religion, millions of Americans turned out at ticker tape parades to catch glimpses of those astronauts who had actually traveled into the heavens.[71] After the *Apollo 11* astronauts, Neil Armstrong, Buzz Aldrin, and Mike Collins had returned to Earth, President Richard Nixon felt moved to describe the events of the moon landing as "the greatest week in the history of the world since Creation."[72]

Norman Mailer, commissioned by *Life* magazine to record his responses to the launch of *Apollo 11*, responded to the experience in a manner reminiscent of Henry Adams to the dynamo. Describing the sight of the Saturn V rocket waiting on the launchpad the evening before its flight, "she looked like a shrine with the lights upon her. In the distance she glowed for all the world like some white stone Madonna in the mountains, welcoming footsore travelers at dusk."[73]

THE POLITICAL AND SOCIAL SIGNIFICANCE OF THE ART PROGRAM

The image of NASA as an institution that seemed to represent the highest human ideals—spirituality, adventure, imagination, and teamwork—was conveyed not only by the works created by the art program, but by the very circumstances under which the art program was run. Perhaps most important was the very openness on which NASA prided itself, as opposed to the closed, secretive system of the Soviet Union. As James Dean has explained, artists encountered few restrictions on their movement at various NASA installations.[74] They were free to depict whatever struck them as significant in any manner.[75] Lester Cooke's letter of invitation to artists explained, "you will be completely free to draw, paint, and record whatever strikes you as significant and unique. We are commissioning not only the artist's skill, but also his perception and his imagination, and for best results neither should be dictated or forced; therefore you are free to use whatever style you wish."[76] This quality of freedom, of course, has important resonance with the democratic system itself, particularly in the context of the American struggle with the Soviet Union, and it is noteworthy that this aspect of the program was emphasized publicly.[77]

Finally, the art program also humanized the space program, by privileging the artist over the mechanical camera as a tool of public history making. The first concern was quite practical: the question of photography's ability to endure the test of time, in contrast to the more traditional media of canvas, paper, and pigment.[78] Indeed, the only stipulation NASA applied to the artists it commissioned was that they work in materials whose archival properties were proven.[79]

A more fundamental concern about technology, however, lay behind the art program. This was the belief, dating back to the nineteenth century, that artists could capture the spirit of an event in a way in which the camera, itself a product of science and technology, could not. Describing the rational for NASA's decision to commission artists in the official letter of invitation to artists, dating to 1963, Cooke explained: "When a major launch takes place at Cape Canaveral more than two hundred cameras record every split second of the blast off. Every nut, bolt and miniaturized electronic device is photographed from every angle. The artist can add very little to this in the way of factual record. But, as Daumier pointed out a century ago, the camera sees everything and understands nothing."[80] Significantly, it was precisely by testifying to the limits of technological competence that the art program succeeded in humanizing the space program, demonstrating that it was not the product of a society driven by machines, but rather of technology put in the service of the human imagination. Artistic creativity could be easily equated with scientific or technological creativity, a human rather than mechanistic characteristic. As James Dean wrote in a 1973 memo: "A technological agency able and willing to have art produced for and about itself seemed to say special things to many people. The technological space program wasn't dehumanizing. An artist could visit, work, and find beauty and understanding there."[81] James Webb himself was well aware that public enthusiasm for the space program would be linked to its human interest. In a secret report to Vice President Lyndon B. Johnson coauthored with Secretary of Defense Robert McNamara on May 8, 1961, two days after the successful space flight by Alan Shepard, the first by an American, Webb stressed: "It is man, not merely machines, in space that captures the imagination of the world."[82]

The "human values" conveyed by artist's interpretations of the space program were described to students in educational publications that incorporated reproductions of artwork commissioned by NASA. A guide to two filmstrips prepared by the National Art Education Association for NASA used art to describe the social values of the space program. The introductory remarks explain: "[These] pictures provide a *humanized account* of the people, the places, and the events where important steps in the early exploration of space took place. Through [this] art, *the air of drama and the mysticism of space pioneering are conveyed in ways that no objective recording device can match*" (my emphasis). As though responding specifically to C. P. Snow's demand for education to bridge the "gap" between the "two cultures," the guide explains that the films can be used by "art, science, and general classroom teachers."[83] An art teacher can "call special attention to the way in which an artist has worked with some particular medium," while a science teacher could "indicate certain details, ideas, or information in a given part of a frame."[84] "Reach for the Moon and Touch a Star," geared toward elementary school children, explained that this is "an adventure story" and that the artwork they will see "all add[s] together to show us how thousands of men, working together, may stretch their hands out to reach for the moon and beyond."[85] The caption accompanying a reproduction of a painting by Robert McCall in "In Sight of Giant Steps," designed for high school students, offered the following interpretation of the image: "machines do not take care of themselves, . . . without the attention of people who know what they are doing, the equipment for space is merely hardware."[86]

PUBLIC RESPONSE TO THE ARTISTS' COOPERATION PROGRAM

The American public responded enthusiastically to the NASA Artist's Cooperation Program. In 1965 Eyewitness to Space, which opened at the National Gallery of Art in Washington, DC, attracted a larger audience than any other exhibition in the museum's history, with the exception of a showing of the *Mona Lisa*.[87] Originally scheduled to run a month, Eyewitness to Space was held an extra four weeks. The exhibition then proceeded to tour the country.[88] Similar enthusiasm greeted The Artist and Space, a second exhibition of work created under the auspices of the Artists' Cooperation Program at the National Gallery of Art in late 1969, with many institutions requesting the show as organizers prepared it for travel throughout the United States.[89]

Work produced for the NASA art program also appeared in popular publications that spread word of NASA's achievements. *Eyewitness to Space*, a lavishly illustrated book describing the NASA art program, written by Lester Cooke and James Dean, proved extremely popular, quickly selling out of its first printing, and even prompting an invitation for Lester Cooke to appear on *The Mike Douglas Show*.[90] The book sought to describe the spirit of the space program through artistic interpretations of it, stressing the belief that artists could record aspects of the space program that cameras could not. A broad range of primarily positive reviews applauded this principle, concurring that the human artist produced more powerful images than mechanical devices. A representative assessment by Leonard Sanders of the *Fort Worth Star-Telegram* read: "Despite the many photographs and the cathode-tube familiarity of the U.S. space effort, the artistic interpretations by forty-seven artists who witnessed NASA efforts leave one feeling he perhaps comprehends the immensity of the space program for the first time."[91]

Eyewitness to Space figured in efforts by the U.S. government to use the art created for NASA to promote the space program abroad. As Lester Cooke noted, *Eyewitness to Space* served as "an official White House gift for foreign dignitaries," including the Vice President of China, the Prime Minister of Korea, and the Soviet Minister of Science.[92] The book also accompanied Lester Cooke on a trip sponsored by the United States Information Agency (USIA) to Eastern Europe. "Apparently East Europe is still all agog over the Apollo program," he observed.[93] Such enthusiasm abroad about the American space program was further stoked by traveling exhibitions of NASA's art collection organized by the USIA and the Art in Embassies Program.

CONCLUSION: ASSESSING THE POLITICAL BENEFITS OF NASA'S ART PROGRAM

The art program initiated by James Webb paid valuable dividends for NASA and for the nation at large via the cultural diplomacy it permitted. By aligning space exploration with the "human" qualities of spirituality, adventure, imagination, and teamwork, art created for NASA helped the agency realize what it had recognized in 1967, through a study commissioned from RAND, would be the most popular and therefore most beneficial goal for space research: to enhance national prestige by "selecting goals designed to capture the interest of the world" (Holman, 110; on RAND study, see 108–10). While Webb was not the first American official to recognize the power of art as an instrument of public policy, he may have been the first to put art in the service of science and technology. By doing so in the early 1960s, Webb stood in the vanguard of public intellectuals and politicians pushing for a closer relationship between the "two cultures," as C. P. Snow persuasively identified the divide in his 1959 book.[94] Webb's advocacy of art at NASA suggested that federal support of the arts could benefit a nation bent on impressing the world with its scientific and technological accomplishments in space, and appropriately the nation's Commission of Fine Arts congratulated the agency "for being as forward looking as they are."[95] Intriguingly, NASA's implicit identification of art as a necessary corollary to publicly supported science and technology would be adopted by advocates of the National Endowment for the Arts and Humanities. Expressing his support for the bill, Representative Frank Horton (R-NY) declared: "The Nation has reached a stage of maturity in which the arts and humanities demand equal status with science[,] and a redressing of the imbalance of the two cultures is required now."[96] A newspaper article published shortly after Johnson's public endorsement of the new arts and humanities foundation, and entered into the *Congressional Record* by Senator Claiborne Pell, a strong backer of the legislation, argued: "If we can train men's bodies to face weightlessness, they say, we should train their minds to create a culture equal to our achievements in space."[97] Leland J. Haworth, Director of the National Science Foundation, based his support for the bill on the basis of the benefits it promised scientific pursuits, perhaps most closely echoing the type of reasoning employed by Webb in his support of the NASA Artist's Cooperation program: "Federal support for the arts and humanities will . . . ultimately bring added strength and vitality to our science and technology."[98] Johnson revealed the persuasiveness of such claims when he signed the NEA and NEH into existence on September 29, 1965, placing federal funding for the arts in the context of federal funding for the sciences: "We have not always been kind, in America, to the artists and scholars who are the creators and keepers of our vision. Somehow, the scientists always seem to get the penthouse, while the arts and humanities are always down in the basement."[99]

The NASA Artists' Cooperation Program provides valuable evidence about attitudes toward the public support of the arts and the sciences during a critical moment of the Cold War, as the United States aimed to prove its superiority to the Soviet Union by beating the communists to the moon. As this study reveals, pure scientific and technological achievement alone was not sufficient for achieving national goals. In the context of the military-industrial complex, art had a critical political role to play, not only as an agent of communication, but as a signifier of the creativity and spirituality with which the United States aspired to align itself.

EPILOGUE

The best testament to the enduring political and cultural value of the NASA Art Program is its continuation to the present, despite a brief hiatus in the early 1970s. The program has not only generated a valuable collection of art by talented and well-recognized American artists, including Andy Warhol, Chakaia Booker, Annie Leibovitz, Laurie Anderson (whose recent NASA-commissioned performance work *The End of the Moon*, is represented by way of a video), William Wegman, Doug and Mike Starn, and Yvonne Jacquette, but it has also contributed a host of intangible short- and long-range assets to the space agency. In the present, the art program provides positive publicity for the space agency, allying it with prominent American artists, just as its founders had hoped. Even in the face of national tragedy, such as the loss of the Challenger and the Columbia, artists have provided lasting memorials for the fallen, helping to forestall potential bitterness by literally picturing NASA's own grief. In the long term, the art program assures NASA historical memory and cultural prestige. Through its very existence, the art program greatly increases NASA's potential appeal by providing points of access not only for those intrigued by new technologies but also for those inclined to support the arts. NASA's art program represents an investment in the space agency's future, providing a wealth of material, with an intrinsic value at once connected with, and independent from, the space agency "for future historians to dwell over," as Paul Calle predicted in 1963.[100]

NOTES

Abbreviations used in the Notes:
NASA: National Aeronautics and Space Administration
NASM: National Air and Space Museum, Smithsonian Institution, Washington, DC
NGA: National Gallery of Art, Washington, DC
SI: Smithsonian Institution, Washington, DC

This chapter was adapted from the article "Art, Technology, and the American Space Program," published in *Intertexts* 3, no. 2 by permission of Texas Tech University Press. I would like to thank the anonymous reviewers who provided helpful feedback on this essay prior to its publication here.

1. Mary A. Holman, *The Political Economy of the Space Program* (Palo Alto: Pacific Books, 1974), 169.

2. A month earlier, during February 1962, the *New York Times* had heralded John F. Kennedy's selection of August Heckscher as "Special Consultant to the President for the Arts," indicating the White House's receptivity to federal patronage of the arts. Several articles ran on Heckscher's appointment as "cultural coordinator," most prominently, a front page article by Arthur Gelb, "White House Names Heckscher to be Coordinator of Culture, *New York Times*, February 22, 1962. On this coverage, see Milton Cummings, "To Change a Nation's Cultural Policy: The Kennedy Administration and the Arts in the United States, 1961–1963," in *Public Policy and the Arts*, ed. Kevin V. Mulcahy and C. Richard Swain (Boulder, CO: Westview Press, 1982), 153.

3. For an excellent overview of this topic and the literature see Danielle Fox, "Art," in *Culture Works: The Political Economy of Culture*, ed. Richard Maxwell (Minneapolis: University of Minnesota Press, 2001), 22–59. On the topic of covert federal support of the arts, see Eva Cockcroft, "Abstract Expressionism, Weapon of the Cold War," in *Pollock and After: The Critical Debate*, ed. Francis Frascina, 2nd ed. (London: Routledge, 2000), 145–154; originally published in *Artforum* 12 (June 1974): 39–41; Serge Guilbaut, *How New York Stole the Idea of Modern Art: Abstract Expressionism, Freedom, and the Cold War*, trans. Arthur Goldhammer (Chicago: University of Chicago Press, 1983); Frances Stonor Saunders, *The Cultural Cold War: The CIA and the World of Arts and Letters* (New York: New Press, 1999). On the development of overt federal arts, see Kevin V. Mulcahy and C. Richard Swain, eds., *Public Policy and the Arts* (Boulder, CO: Westview Press, 1982); on the establishment of the National Endowment for the Arts see Livingston Biddle, *Our Government and the Arts: A Perspective from the Inside* (New York: American Council for the Arts Books, 1988). Red Grooms was an unofficial participant in the NASA art program, who received no honorarium from the space agency. However, Grooms attended the *Apollo 15* launch under the auspices of the NASA program, and in response created *Astronauts on the Moon* (1972), an enormous tableau of astronauts David Scott and James Irwin exploring the lunar surface with camera and lunar rover based on official NASA photographs. (Red Grooms, letter to Jim Dean, December 12, 1971, Art Dept. Files, Aeronautics Division, NASM, SI.) For more information on *Astronauts on the Moon*, please see Anne Collins Goodyear, "The Relationship of Art to Science and Technology in the United States, 1957–1971: Five Case Studies," PhD diss., University of Texas at Austin, 2002, 69–70; and Carter Ratcliff, *Red Grooms* (New York: Abbeville Press, 1984), 127–31. The NASA art program continues to the present, after a brief lapse from 1974–76.

4. "National Aeronautics and Space Act of 1958," excerpted in Roger D. Launius, *The History of the U.S. Civil Space Program* (Malabar, FL: Krieger, 1994), 154–58.

5. Under President Harry S. Truman, Webb headed the Bureau of the Budget and served as undersecretary of state. Both prior to and following these appointments, he held leading positions in a number of private companies, including Sperry Gyroscope Company, Republic Supply Company, and Kerr-McGee Oil Industries. Webb's background and fascination with issues of management is chronicled in his biography, W. Henry Lambright, *Powering Apollo: James E. Webb of NASA* (Baltimore: Johns Hopkins University Press, 1995).

6. James Webb, letter to T. Keith Glennan, April 12, 1961, History Office, NASA. Qtd. by Walter McDougall, *The Heavens and the Earth: A Political History of the Space Age* (1985; Baltimore: Johns Hopkins University Press, 1997), 318–19.

7. On Webb's larger social agenda, particularly regarding education, see Lambright, 99–101 and 135–41, and passim. NASA's public policy objectives, developed with regard for the economic and social implications of the space program, are discussed by Holman.

8. Bruce Stevenson, a commercial illustrator, had planned to complete a series of portraits picturing each of the original astronauts, but passed away before any others could be completed (telephone conversation with Bruce Stevenson, Jr., the artist's son, October 1999).

9. James Webb, memorandum for Hiden Cox, March 16, 1962, 1, Art Dept. Files, Aeronautics Division, NASM, SI.

10. Ibid.

11. James Dean, in a conversation with the author, confirmed that neither a group portrait nor individual portraits of the original seven *Mercury* astronauts were ever commissioned by the NASA art program (author's interview with James Dean, March 8, 1999). Webb's vision was not limited to portraiture.

12. James Webb, memorandum for Hiden Cox, March 16, 1962.

13. David E. Finley, Director of the National Gallery of Art and Chairman of the Commission of Fine Arts; Linton Wilson, Secretary of the Commission of Fine Arts; and John Walker, who succeeded Finely as Director of the National Gallery, advised NASA. On the guidance sought by NASA prior to the appointment of H. Lester Cooke, see Cooke, in his foreword to "Countdown at Canaveral," in Peter Hurd, *Art in America*, 51, no. 5 (October 1963): 60. "Countdown at Canaveral"; and NASA News Release, "First Drawings Received from NASA Artists' Cooperation Program," June 25, 1963, Art Dept. Files, Aeronautics Division, NASM, SI. Interestingly, Cooke makes mention of only Finely and Wilson, whereas the NASA news release mentions only Finely and Walker. It is possible that good politics and personal relationships played some role in the credits. For Webb's instructions and NASA's early justification of this step, see James Webb, memorandum for Hiden Cox, March 16, 1962; and Shelby Thompson, memorandum to George L. Simpson, Jr., September 20, 1962, Art Dept. Files, Aeronautics Division, NASM, SI. See Shelby Thompson memorandum to Walter L. Linglo, Jr., July 6, 1962, Art Dept. Files, Aeronautics Division, NASM, SI, on Thompson's meeting with the Fine Arts Council about how to structure the art program. In addition to being a curator, Cooke was also an artist.

14. Shelby Thompson, memorandum to George L. Simpson, Jr., September 20, 1962. Webb joined Simpson in signing off on the memo to indicate his concurrence with the suggestions put forth by Thompson.

15. It was perhaps for this reason that the same NASA memo also made note of Cooke's military service in the U.S. Air Force. Jane de Hart Mathews offers an excellent overview of the virulent resistance of George Dondero and other conservative congressmen to modern art, and particularly abstraction, which they believed was allied with communism. (Jane de Hart Mathews, "Art and Politics in Cold War America," in *Pollock and After: The Critical Debate*, ed. Francis Frascina, 2nd ed. [London: Routledge, 2000], 155–80; originally published in *The American Historical Review* 81 (Febuary–December 1976): 762–87. As James Dean, who helped to direct the art program as Director of the Educational Media Division at NASA, recalls, the climate in official Washington at the time necessitated that the expenditure of federal resources on an art program be well supported. The specter of McCarthy had not yet vanished and it was essential "to get your pedigree validated" (author's interview with James Dean, March 23, 1998). For a related comment, see also James Dean, "The Artist and Space," *Interdisciplinary Science Reviews* 3, no. 3 (1978): 245. The atmosphere of suspicion about spending of the fine arts is captured in a memo from Shelby Thompson, Director of NASA's office of Educational Programs and Services, to James Dean regarding the commissioning of artists to create a new design for the NASA Distinguished Service Award. He writes: "Since it is a United States government award, it likely would be politically wise to limit the competition to U.S. citizens. Can we also rule out Communists and Commie-front members? It would not be good for a U.S. hero award to be designed by one of the above, who would be paid U.S. tax dollars for his work, however artistically excellent it might be. *Or am I being too much like McCarthy (heaven forefend!)*?" (Shelby Thompson, memorandum to James Dean, March 4, 1963, Art Dept. Files, Aeronautics Division, NASM, SI; my emphasis).

16. Dean was promoted from Assistant to the Director of Educational Programs at NASA to Director of NASA's Educational Media Division shortly after the art program was launched. (James Dean, biographical statement, c. 1964, Art Dept. Files, Aeronautics Division, NASM, SI.) Like Cooke, Dean was also an artist himself.

17. Lester Cooke, memorandum to Shelby Thompson, undated, Art Dept. Files, Aeronautics Division, NASM, SI.

18. Cooke, memorandum to Thompson, undated. The recommendations of the Commission of Fine Arts are recorded in Shelby Thompson, memorandum for the record, July 6, 1962, Art Dept. Files, Aeronautics Division, NASM, SI. The recommendation that abstraction be adopted is particularly interesting in light of the widespread use of Abstract Expressionism to signify American "freedom" in the wake of World War II, as detailed by Guilbaut and Cockcroft.

19. Lester Cooke qtd. in "Counting Down with the Editor," *Spaceport News* 3 (January 30, 1964): 8. Cape Canaveral, which houses the Kennedy Space Center, was known as Cape Kennedy from 1963 to 1973 (Helen T. Wells, Susan H. Whiteley, and Carrie E. Karegeannes, *Origins of NASA Names*, The NASA History Series [Washington, DC: National Aeronautics and Space Administration, 1976], 149).

20. Eliot Clark, "Andrew Wyeth," *Studio* 160 (December 1960), 206. In an undated memo to Shelby Thompson explaining the backgrounds of the artists he wishes to commission, Cooke lists Wyeth's name first and refers to him as the "top ranking artist in the U.S. today." McCall is described as having "been in charge of the Air Force art program," (perhaps as a delegate within the New York Society of Illustrators), and Mitchell Jamieson is identified as having been "in charge of part of the Navy program in World War II." (Cooke, memorandum to Thompson, undated, Art Dept. Files, Aeronautics Division, NASM, SI.) Despite the historical importance of Chesley Bonestell's space paintings, he was at this time too elderly to be included in the program. However, James

Dean visited the artist at his home in Carmel, CA, and later included his work in exhibitions of the NASA Art Program at the National Gallery of Art and in the documentary book, Hereward Lester Cooke and James Dean, *Eyewitness to Space* (New York: Harry N. Abrams, 1971), discussed below. (Author's interview with James Dean, July 23, 1999.)

21. Lester Cooke, letter to Andrew Wyeth, January 24, 1963, Art Dept. Files, Aeronautics Division, NASM, SI.

22. Andrew Wyeth, letter to Lester Cooke, February 14, 1963, Art Dept. Files, Aeronautics Division, NASM, SI.

23. In 1965 Cooke and Dean would commission Jamie Wyeth to document *Gemini IV*; he would also record the *Apollo 11* launch.

24. William U. Eiland, *The Truth in Things* (Athens: University of Georgia Press, 1996), 108–18.

25. Eiland, 125–26. Among the speakers who participated in the radio series were Millard Meiss, Aline Saarinen, Lloyd Goodrich, Clement Greenberg, and Carl Zigrosser.

26. Eiland, 126.

27. Shelby Thompson, memorandum to George L. Simpson, Jr., December 21, 1962, Art Dept. Files, Aeronautics Division, NASM, SI.

28. James Kauffman, *Selling Outer Space: Kennedy, the Media, and Funding for Project Apollo, 1961–63* (Tuscaloosa: University of Alabama Press, 1994), 16, 46–47. I am much indebted to Kauffman's account of the symbolic implications of the flight for the NASA program.

29. Prior to Kennedy's challenge to place a man on the moon, scientists and politicians debated the value of manned space exploration. See McDougall, 309–16.

30. Kauffman, 46–47. Thirty-two years earlier, Amelia Earhart had similarly taken advantage of the (fifth) anniversary of Lindbergh's flight to maximize the impact of her flight from Harbor Grace, Newfoundland to Londonderry, Ireland, the first solo cross-Atlantic flight by a woman. (*Dictionary of American Biography*, s.v. "Earhart, Amelia.")

31. McDougall, 379.

32. Dean, "The Artist and Space," 250.

33. NASA News Release, June 25, 1963 and draft of the same release, prepared by Shelby Thompson, June 20, 1963, Art Dept. Files, Aeronautics Division, NASM, SI.

34. NASA News Release, June 25, 1963, Art Dept. Files, Aeronautics Division, NASM, SI.

35. The articles are as follows: Hurd, "Countdown at Canaveral," 60–72; and Paul Calle, "I Saw Atlas 9 Take Off!," *American Artist* 27, no. 8 (October 1963), 58–59, 77–79. Reproductions of artworks done in response to the launch can be found in these articles. Hurd's article was reviewed by NASA's Public Information office. In its initial draft, the article revealed its Cold War context with an aside criticizing the Russian space program. Although this was excised by NASA, Dick Mittauer enthused, "If this man [Hurd] ever decides to hang up his brushes, we'd love to have him as a feature writer in PIO" (Dick Mittauer, memorandum to James Dean, June 20, 1963, Art Dept. Files, Aeronautics Division, NASM, SI).

36. While Rockwell and Rauschenberg accepted the invitation to participate, a number of other well-known artists chose not to take part. Edward Hopper was invited to participate early in the NASA Art Program (1964), but declined due to his age (82 at the time; James Dean, "To the Moon," unpublished mss., November 7, 1998, 2–3). Thomas Hart Benton was also invited to be part of the program and to witness the *Apollo 11* launch but refused, commenting "What can I do to make a painting of a damn rocket? You'd show it better in a moving picture" (Thomas Hart Benton qtd. in William A. McWhirter, "Tom Benton at 80, Still at War with Bores and Boobs," *Life*, 67, October 3, 1969, 68–70; and author's interview with James Dean, March 23, 1998.) Other well-known artists who declined the invitation to participate in the program and witness the launch of *Apollo 11* were Willem de Kooning, who initially agreed and later balked, explaining that "he felt it would have been too much for him to have watched the launch knowing that there were three men inside," and Richard Diebenkorn, who was dealing with a divorce (author's conversation with James Dean, September 25, 1998).

37. On Rockwell's participation in the NASA Artists' Cooperation Program, see Anne Collins Goodyear, "On the Threshold of Space: Norman Rockwell's *Longest Step*," in *2001: Architecture and Design for Space, Vision and Reality*, exh. cat. (Chicago: Art Institute of Chicago; New York: Harry N. Abrams, 2001), 102–7. In addition to *The Longest Step (Astronauts Grissom and Young Suiting Up)*, 1965, Rockwell painted the following space-related paintings for *Look*: *Man on the Moon* (Portrait of an Astronaut), 1967; *Man on the Moon* (United States Space Ship on the Moon), 1967; *Apollo and Beyond* (*Apollo 11* Space Team), 1969; *The Final Impossibility: Man's Tracks on the Moon*, 1969. The paintings appeared in the following articles: Ben Kocivar, "The Longest Step, Painted for *Look* by Norman Rockwell," *Look*, April 20, 1965; John O. Osmundsen, "Man on the Moon, Painted for *Look* by Norman Rockwell," *Look*, January 10, 1967; Arthur C. Clarke, "Apollo and Beyond," *Look*, July 15, 1969; "The Final Impossibility: Man's Tracks on the Moon," *Look*, December 30, 1969. Rockwell later donated his paintings to the National Air and Space Museum, Smithsonian Institution (Norman Rockwell, letter to Mr. F. C. Durant III, October 27, 1970, Art Dept. Files, Aeronautics Division, NASM, SI).

38. On Rauschenberg's fascination with the imagery of space travel, see Anne F. Collins, "Robert Rauschenberg's Space-Age Allegory, 1959–1970," *1998 National Aerospace Conference Proceedings* (Dayton, OH: Wright State University, 1999), 82–91. Rauschenberg may also have been a good selection because of the international victory represented by his receipt of the Grand Prize at the 1964 Venice Biennale. On the cultural implications of this win see Fox, 35; and Laurie Monahan, "Cultural Cartography," *Reconstructing Modernism: Art in New York, Paris, and Montreal, 1945–1964* (Cambridge, MA: MIT Press, 1990), 369–416.

39. Robert Rauschenberg "Notes on Stoned Moon," *Studio International* 178 (December 1969): 246–7.

40. Cooke and Dean, 11–13.

41. Leo Marx, *The Machine in the Garden: Technology and the Pastoral Ideal in America* (London: Oxford University Press, 1964), 195. Marx goes so far as to observe that "the symbol of the machine incorporates a whole metaphysical system," actually inspiring the very notion of the "self-regulating" system of government established by the U.S. Constitution (165).

42. Author's conversation with Joanna Taylor, Refuge Ranger, Merritt Island National Wildlife Refuge, April 22, 1999.

43. Cooke and Dean, fig. 69.

44. Cooke and Dean, fig. 102.

45. Robert Rauschenberg, qtd. by Calvin Tomkins, *Off the Wall: Robert Rauschenberg and the Art World of Our Time* (New York: Penguin Books, 1980), 288. On Rauschenberg's fascination with the imagery of space travel, see Collins, 82–91.

46. Lawrence Alloway, "Rauschenberg's Graphic Art," in *Rauschenberg: Graphic Art*, exh. cat. (Philadelphia: Institute of Contemporary Art, 1970), 9. Reprinted in Lawrence Alloway, *Topics in American Art Since 1945* (New York: W. W. Norton, 1975).

47. James Dean pointed out to me that the map in the background is a reproduction of the one used by Rauschenberg at the launch. A close examination reveals the artist's personal notations on the map (author's conversation with James Dean, September 27, 1998).

48. An account of this project is included in Ray Kass, *Morris Graves: Vision of the Inner Eye*, exh. cat. (Washington, DC: The Phillips Collection; New York: George Braziller, 1983), 70–71. I thank Susan Lawson Bell for drawing my attention to this collaboration.

49. John O'Keefe, letter to Morris Graves, December 13, 1964, Art Dept. Files, Aeronautics Division, NASM, SI.

50. Morris Graves, letter to Lester Cooke, January 21, 1965, Art Dept. Files, Aeronautics Division, NASM, SI.

51. Riva Castleman, "Technics and Creativity," in *Technics and Creativity: Gemini G.E.L.*, exh. cat. (New York: The Museum of Modern Art, 1971), 23.

52. Ibid., 23.

53. Rauschenberg, 246–47. Rauschenberg also prepared a book of text and images based on his experience (James Dean, "The Artist and the Space Shuttle," unpublished mss. prepared for NASA, January 1990, 24). I thank James Dean for the opportunity to see this document.

54. Rauschenberg, 246.

55. For a good summary of literature dealing with the "frontier" metaphor, see Jannelle Warren-Findley, "The Collier as Commemoration: The Project Mercury Astronauts and the Collier Trophy," in *From Engineering Science to Big Science: The NACA and NASA Collier Trophy Research Project Winners*, ed. Pamela E. Mack, The NASA History Series (Washington, DC: National Aeronautics and Space Administration, 1998), 178. See also Kauffman, esp. 30–49; McCurdy, 139–61, and Stephen Pyne, "Space: The Third Great Age of Discovery," *Space: Discovery and Exploration*, ed. Martin J. Collins and Sylvia K. Kramer (Washington, DC: National Air and Space Museum, Smithsonian Institution, 1993) 17–65.

56. Thompson, memo to Simpson, December 21, 1962.

57. Cooke, letter of Invitation to artists, qtd. in Cooke and Dean, 11.

58. Kaufmann, 59.

59. Pam Hait, "The Artist's Journey," in *Paul Calle: An Artist's Journey* ed. Ginger Rener et al. (Venice, FL: Mill Pond Press, 1992), 16.

60. James Dean, "Journey into Space," in *Paul Calle*, 59.

61. Ray Bradbury, "Cry the Cosmos," *Life*, September 14, 1962, 88.

62. Cooke and Dean, figure 65.

63. See Anne Collins Goodyear, "On the Threshold of Space," 102–7.

64. I thank Susan Lawson Bell for pointing out this formal similarity (author's communication with Susan Lawson Bell, April 2, 1999).

65. Observation of Dana Bell, based on an unidentified essay (author's communication with Dana Bell, March 31, 1999).

66. Hurd, 61. Henry Adams, "The Dynamo and the Virgin," in *The Education of Henry Adams*, ed. with an intro. by Ernest Samuels (1918; Boston: Houghton Mifflin, 1973), 379–90.

67. Hurd, 64.

68. Ibid.

69. A number of the sketches and watercolors Hurd (and other NASA artists) did in response to the Cooper launch are reproduced in Hurd. Other reproductions can be found in Cooke and Dean, *Eyewitness*, and in Roger Launius and Bertram Ulrich, *NASA and the Exploration of Space* (New York: Stewart, Tabori, and Chang, 1998).

70. David E. Nye, *American Technological Sublime* (Cambridge, MA: MIT Press, 1994), 40.

71. In 1962, 50,000 people witnessed John Glenn's launch; 250,000 appeared to greet him in Washington, after he had become the first American to orbit the earth; a crowd of 4 million attended his ticker tape parade in New York (Nye, 237–38).

72. Richard Nixon, qtd. by Nye, 250.

73. Norman Mailer, *Of a Fire on the Moon* (Boston: Little, Brown, 1970), 59. Also qtd. in part by Nye, 243. I am indebted to Nye's discussion of Mailer (243–46).

74. Dean, "The Artist and Space," 250.

75. As the art program developed, Cooke and Dean no longer felt figuration was required.

76. Cooke, letter of invitation to artists, qtd. in Cooke and Dean, 13.

77. This was stressed, e.g., in Cooke and Dean, 11–26.

78. Dean, "The Artist and Space," 245.

79. Cooke, letter of invitation to artists, qtd. in Cooke and Dean, 11.

80. Cooke, letter of invitation to artists, qtd. in Dean, "The Artist and the Space Shuttle," 11–12.

81. James Dean, memorandum for the record, August 6, 1973, Art Dept. Files, Aeronautics Division, NASM, SI.

82. Lambright, 98.

83. *"Reach for the Moon and Touch a Star" and "In Sight of Giant Steps": A Guide to Accompany Two Filmstrips Prepared by a Committee of the National Art Educational Association for the National Aeronautics and Space Administration* (Washington, DC: National Art Education Association, 1967), n.p. For C. P. Snow's celebrated comments on the importance of education for bridging the divide between scientists and nonscientists see C. P. Snow, *The Two Cultures* (1959; Cambridge: Cambridge University Press, 1993), esp. 18–21, 33–40, and 50–51.

84. Filmstrip Guide, n.p.

85. Ibid.

86. Ibid.

87. A total of 67,000 people saw the show at the National Gallery of Art in Washington, DC between March 14 and May 23, 1965 (Neal Stanford, "Artists Have a Brush with Space," *Christian Science Monitor*, April 19, 1968, 1.)

88. Significantly, according to gallery records, the show was "the first such exhibition since the War [World War II] put on at the request of a government agency" (National Gallery of Art, "National Gallery of Art Exhibitions, 1941–1991," 1992, Gallery Archives, NGA).

89. Anne Cossett, memorandum to Lester Cooke, June 3, 1970, Lester Cooke Papers, Gallery Archives, NGA.

90. Lester Cooke, letter to Hans Günther Cremers, April 10, 1972, Lester Cooke Papers, Gallery Archives, NGA; and Lena Tabori, Director of Promotion, Publicity, and Advertising at Harry N. Abrams to Lester Cooke, February 29, 1972, Lester Cooke Papers, Gallery Archives, NGA. According to the letter, one invitation had already been offered (though not accepted due to short notice); a second one was being extended for March 30, 1972.

91. Leonard Sanders, "Gift Books Feature Art," *Fort Worth Star-Telegram*, December 5, 1971, Lester Cooke Papers, Gallery Archives, NGA. Reviews of the book were primarily positive. These include: Larry Rumley, "Superb Big Books of Special Interest," *Seattle Times*, November 28, 1971; Ray Bradbury, "An Art's-Eye View of Space Renaissance," *Los Angeles Times Book Review*, October 24, 1971 (also printed as "Inner Visions of Outer Space," *Chicago Sun-Times*, January 16, 1972, sec. 6, 17); Frank Getlein, "Result of NASA Art Program Revealed in a New Book," *Sunday Star*, [*Washington, DC*], October 17, 1971. Positive reviews were also carried in *American Artist*, December 1971; *Time*, December 20, 1971; *Art Direction Magazine*, November 1971. Only two reviews were critical: Clifford A. Ridley's "Capitalist Realism," *National Observer*, January 15, 1971; and Louis Vaczek's untitled review, "Technology and Culture". The reviews mentioned here are collected in Lester Cooke Papers, Gallery Archives, NGA. A letter written to James Dean by Lamar Dodd following his attendance of the College Art Association meeting in San Francisco indicates

that reception of the book was very positive among CAA members, both scholars and artists (Lamar Dodd, letter to James D. Dean, February 1, 1972, Lester Cooke Papers, Gallery Archives, NGA).

92. Lester Cooke, memorandum to J. Carter Brown and Charles P. Parkhurst, September 5, 1973, Lester Cooke Papers, Gallery Archives, NGA.

93. Lester Cooke, letter to Paul Anbinder, March 13, 1973, Lester Cooke Papers, Gallery Archives, NGA.

94. On Snow, see n. 83.

95. Shelby Thompson, memorandum for the record, July 6, 1962; the detailed account of the meeting quotes David Finley, Chairman of the Commission of Fine Arts, suggesting that "perhaps science could render service to art by giving the subject to depict."

96. *Congressional Record*, 89th Cong., 1st Sess. (1965): 36–37. Cited by Gary O. Larson, *The Reluctant Patron: The United States Government and the Arts, 1943–1965* (Philadelphia: University of Pennsylvania Press, 1983), 197.

97. Henrietta and Nelso Poynter, "Can Man Live by Technology Alone?," *St. Petersburg Times*, March 28, 1955; cited by Claiborne Pell, "National Foundation on the Arts and Humanities," *Congressional Record*, Senate (April 26, 1965): 8123–24. I thank James Dean for bringing Pell's inclusion of this material in the Congressional Record to my attention.

98. Cited in Claiborne Pell, *Establishing a National Foundation on the Arts and the Humanities*, report to accompany S. 1483, 89th Congress, S. Rept. 300, 6–7; internal quote, 1. Photocopy of report included in Progress of Legislation; Legislative Background: Arts and Humanities Foundation, Box 1, Lyndon B. Johnson (hereafter LBJ) Library.

99. "Remarks for Signing of the National Foundation for the Art and the Humanities Act of 1965," 1; Enactment and Signing; Legislative Background: Arts and Humanities Foundation, Box 1, LBJ Library. Second paragraph cited by Mary Eleanor McCombie, "Arts and Policy: The National Endowment for the Art's Art in Public Places Program, 1967–1980," PhD diss., University of Texas at Austin, 1992, 39.

100. Paul Calle, letter to Lester Cooke, June 1, 1963, Art Dept. Files, Aeronautics Division, NASM, SI.

Bibliography

Archives

Archives of American Art, Smithsonian Institution, Washington, DC: Papers of Edward Bruce (D82–92), Holger Cahill Papers (1105–1109) and Michell Siporin (2011).

Archives nationales [hereafter AN] F^{21} 845.

AN F^{21} 2381.

AN F^{21} 4403.

AN F^{21} 6160.

Biblioteca Ambrosiana, Milan, S. C. V. VIII.1: 17o.

Bodleian Library, William Holman Hunt letters, University of Oxford.

Dossier Puvis de Chavannes. Documentation Musée d'Orsay.

Geheime staatliche Archiv, Preussischer Kulturbesitz.

German Federal Archives, Berlin (BA).

Journal officiel (August 11, 1876).

Journal officiel (August 12, 1876).

Journal officiel, Chambre des Députés: Débats Parlementaires (May 24, 1885).

Journal officiel, Sénat, Débats Parlementaires (May 24, 1885).

Journal officiel, Chambre des Députés: Débats Parlementaires (May 28, 1885).

Lyndon B. Johnson Library, University of Texas at Austin, Austin, TX.

National Aeronautics and Space Administration, History Office, Washington, DC.

National Air and Space Museum, Smithsonian Institution, Washington, DC.

National Archives, Washington, DC: RG121, RG69.

National Gallery of Art, Gallery Archives, Washington, DC: Hereward Lester Cooke Papers, National Gallery of Art Exhibitions, 1941–91.

Staatliche Museen Preussischer Kulturbesitz/Zentralarchiv (SMBPK/ZA).

Books and Articles

Adams, Clinton. *American Lithographers 1900–1960: The Artists and Their Printers*. Albuquerque: University of New Mexico Press, 1983.

Adams, Henry. "The Dynamo and the Virgin." 1918. In *The Education of Henry Adams*, edited with an introduction by Ernest Samuels, 379–90. Boston: Houghton Mifflin, 1973.

Adorno, Theodor, and Max Horkheimer. *Dialectic of Enlightenment*. London: Verso, 1979.

Adorno, Theodor, and Anson G. Rabinbach. "Culture Industry Reconsidered." *New German Critique*, no. 6 (1975): 12–19.

Alberro, Alexander, and Sabeth Buchmann, eds. *Art After Conceptual Art*. Cambridge, MA: MIT Press, 2006.

Allan, D. G. C. "The Society of Arts and Government, 1754–1800: Public Encouragement of Arts, Manufactures, and Commerce in Eighteenth-Century England." *Eighteenth-Century Studies* 7, no. 4 (Summer 1974): 434–52.

———. *William Shipley: Founder of the Royal Society of Arts*. London: Scolar Press, 1968.

Allan, D. G. C., and John L. Abbott, eds. *The Virtuoso Tribe of Arts and Sciences: Studies in the Eighteenth-Century Membership of the London Society of Arts* Athens: University of Georgia Press, 1992.

Allen, Brian, ed. *Towards a Modern Art World*. London: Yale University Press, 1995.

Alloway, Lawrence. "Rauschenberg's Graphic Art." In *Rauschenberg: Graphic Art*. Exhibition catalog. Philadelphia: Institute of Contemporary Art, 1970.

Ames, Michael M. "Biculturalism in Exhibitions." *Museum Anthropology* 15, no. 2 (1991): 7–15.

Annamma, Joy, and John F. Sherry. "Disentangling the Paradoxical Alliances between Art Market and Art World." *Consumption, Markets and Culture* 6, no. 3 (September 2003): 155–81.

Anderson, Benedict. *Imagined Communities: Reflections on the Origin and Spread of Nationalism*. 2nd ed. London: Verso, 1991.

Antolini, Giovanni Antonio. *Descrizione del Foro Bonaparte*. Parma: Tipi Bodoniani, 1806.

———. *L'ordine dorico ossia il Tempio d'Ercole nella città di Cori*. Rome: Stamperia Pagliarini, 1785.

———. *Piano economico-politico del Foro Bonaparte presentato coi disegni al Comitato di Governo della Repubblica Cisalpina*. Milan: n.p., 1801.

Apple, Michael W. *Education and Power*. Boston: Routledge and Kegan Paul, 1982.

Apple, Michael W., and Lois Weis. *Ideology and Practice in Schooling*. Philadelphia: Temple University Press, 1983.

Appleton, Josie. "Who Owns Public Art?" In *Cultural Vultures: Is UK Arts Policy Damaging the Arts?*, edited by Munira Mirza, 53–70. London: Policy Exchange, 2006.

Arato, Andrew, and Jean L. Cohen. *Civil Society and Political Theory*. Cambridge, MA: MIT Press, 1992.

Art & Language. "Voices Off: Reflections on Conceptual Art." *Critical Inquiry* 33 (2006): 113– 35.

"Art into Function." *Asian Art News*, Japan Supplement, 4, no. 4 (July/August 1994): 10–13.

Arts Council of Great Britain. *Lutyens: The Work of the English Architect Sir Edwin Lutyens 1869–1944*. London: Hayward Gallery, 1981–82.

Ashton, Dore. *About Rothko*. New York: Da Capo, 1996.

Atkinson, J. B. "The Decline of Art." *Blackwood's* 138 (July 1885): 1–25.

Austin, Linda. M. *The Practical Ruskin: Economics and Audience in the Late Work*. Baltimore: Johns Hopkins University Press, 1991.

Awatere, Donna. *Maori Sovereignty*. Auckland, NZ: Broadsheet, 1984.

Baal-Teshuva, Jacob. *Christo and Jeanne-Claude*. Cologne: Tashen, 2001.

Backes, Klaus. *Hitler und die bildenden Künste*. Cologne: DuMont Buchverlag, 1988.

Backhouse, R., T. Dudley-Evans, and W. Henderson, eds. *Economics and Language*. London: Routledge, 1993.

Badger, Anthony J. *The New Deal: The Depression Years, 1933–1940*. London: Farrar, Straus and Giroux, 1989.

Baigell, Matthew. "From Hester Street to Fifty-Seventh Street: Jewish-American Artists in New York." In *Painting a Place in America: Jewish Artists in New York 1900–1945*, edited by Norman L. Kleeblatt and Susan Chevlowe, 28–71. New York: Jewish Museum, 1991.

Baigell, Matthew, and Julia Williams, eds. *Artists Against War and Fascism: Papers of the First American Artists' Congress*. New Brunswick, NJ: Rutgers University Press, 1986.

Baignères, Arthur. "Les peintures de l'Eglise Sainte-Geneviève par M. Puvis de Chavannes." *Journal officiel* (May 25, 1877), 3999.

Bailkin, Joanna. *The Culture of Property*. Chicago: University of Chicago Press, 2004.

Balisciano, Márcia L., and Steven G. Medema. "Positive Science, Normative Man: Lionel Robbins and the Political Economy of Art." In De Marchi and Goodwin, eds., *Economic Engagements with Art*, 256–84.

Barber, William J, "International Commerce in the Fine Arts and American Political Economy, 1789–1913." In De Marchi and Goodwin, eds., *Economic Engagements with Art*, 209–34.

———. "'Sweet Are the Uses of Adversity': Federal Patronage of the Arts in the Great Depression." In De Marchi and Goodwin, eds., *Economic Engagements with Art*, 235–55.

Barrell, John. *The Political Theory of Painting from Reynolds to Hazlitt: "The Body of the Public."* New Haven, CT: Yale University Press, 1986.

Barrington, Emilie (Mrs. Russell). *The Life, Letters and Works of Frederic Leighton*. 2 vols. London: George Allen, 1906.

Barry, James. *The Works of James Barry*. 2 vols. London, 1809.

Barthes, Roland. *S/Z*. New York: Hill and Wang, 1974.

Batschmann, Oskar. *The Artist in the Modern World: The Conflict between Market and Self- Expression*. New Haven, CT: Yale University Press, 1997.

Baudrillard, Jean. *For a Critique of the Political Economy of the Sign*. Translated by Charles Levin. St. Louis, MO: Telos, 1981.

———. *Simulacra and Simulation*. Ann Arbor: University of Michigan Press, 1994.

Bechtold, Brigitte H. "Introduction: Art and Political Economy." *Review of Radical Political Economics* 36, no. 4 (Fall 2004): 461–70.

Becker, Howard S. "Art as Collective Action." *American Sociological Review* 39, no. 6 (1974): 767–76.

———. *Artworlds*. Berkeley and Los Angeles: University of California Press, 1984.

———. "Art Worlds and Social Types." *American Behavioral Scientist* 19, no. 6 (1984): 703–19.

Becker, Jack. "Public Art as a Cultural Revolution." In *Public Art Forum*, 19–21. Tokyo: Public Art Research Institute, 1998.

Beddoe, Deidre. *Back to Home and Duty: Women between the Wars 1918–39*. London: Pandora, 1989.

Behne, Adolf. "Karl Scheffler und das Kronprinzenpalais." *Die Weltbühne*, June 10, 1930.

Behne, Fritz. "Kunst und Tendenz." *Völkischer Beobachter* 94 (April 24, 1929). In Koehler, 38.

Bell, Claudia. *Inventing New Zealand: Everyday Myths of Pakeha Identity*. Auckland, NZ: Penguin, 1996.

Bell, David, ed. *A Biographical Dictionary of French Political Leaders since 1870*. New York: Simon and Schuster, 1990.

Bell, Leonard. *Colonial Constructs: European Images of Maori 1840–1914*. Auckland, NZ: Auckland University Press, 1992.

Benjamin, Walter. *Illuminations*. Translated by H. Zohn. Edited by Hannah Arendt. New York: Schocken, 1969.

———. *Reflections: Essays, Aphorism, Autobiographical Writings*. Translated by Edmund Jephcott. Edited by Peter Demetz. New York: Harcourt Brace Jovanovich, 1978.

Bennett, Oliver. "Beyond Machinery: The Cultural Policies of Matthew Arnold." *History of Political Economy* 37, no. 3 (2005): 455–82.

Bennett, Tony. *The Birth of the Museum: History, Theory, Politics*. London: Routledge, 1995.

Berger, John. "The Untellable." *New Society*, May 11, 1978, 317.

Berry, Christopher J. *The Idea of Luxury: A Conceptual and Historical Investigation*. Cambridge: Cambridge University Press, 1994.

Bertoni, Franco. "L'Architettura a Faenza dalla Repubblica Cispadana alla Restaurazione: Giovanni Antonio Antolini e Pietro Tomba." In *Giuseppe Pistocchi (1744–1814) architetto giacobino*, edited by Ezzo Godoli, 63–76. Palazzo delle Esposizioni Faenza, 1974. Florence: Rotografia Fiorentina, 1974.

Besharov, Gregory. "The Outbreak of the Cost Disease: Baumol and Bowen's Founding of Cultural Economics." *History of Political Economy* 37, no. 3 (2005): 413–30.

Biddle, George. "The Artist Serves His Community." *Magazine of Art* 27, no. 9 (September 1934): S31–S32.

———. "Mural Painting in America." *Magazine of Art* 27, no. 7 (July 1934): 361–71.

Biddle, Livingston. *Our Government and the Arts: A Perspective from the Inside*. New York: American Council for the Arts Books, 1988.

Bilton, Tony, et al. *Introductory Sociology*. 3rd ed. London: Macmillan, 1996.

Black, John. *Dictionary of Economics*. Oxford: Oxford University Press, 1997.

Black, Jonathan, "'War without gloss?' Masculinity, the Feminine Ideal and the Image of the Vulnerable British Soldier in First World War Memorial Sculpture c. 1919–1925." *Objects* 2 (1999/2000): 28–46.

Blaug, Mark. Book Review of *Economic Engagements with Art*, edited by Neil De Marchi and Cranfurd D. W. Goodwin. *Journal of Cultural Economics* (May 25, 2001): 154–55.

———, ed. *The Economics of the Arts*. London: Martin Robertson, 1976.

Blumberg, Barbara. *The New Deal and the Unemployed: The View from New York City*. Cranbury, NJ: Associated University Presses, 1979.

Bode, Wilhelm von. "Eine neue deutsche Kunst in Sicht?" *Der Sammler (Unterhaltungs—und Literaturbeilage der München—Augsburger Abendzeitung)*, April 4, 1923, Adolph Donath, ed., *Der Kunstwanderer* (periodical, n.d.).

Bogart, Michele H. *Artists, Advertising, and the Borders of Art*. Chicago: University of Chicago Press, 1995.

Boime, Albert. "Caspar David Friedrich: Monk by the Sea." *Arts Magazine*, November 1986, 54–63.

Boinet, A. *Les églises parisiennes*. Vol. 3. Paris: Editions de Minuit, 1963.

Boorman, Derek. *At the Going Down of the Sun: British First World War Memorials*. York, UK: Ebor Press, 1988.

Borg, Alan. *War Memorials from Antiquity to the Present*. London: Leo Cooper, 1991.

Boswell, Peyton. "Comments." *Art Digest* 12, no. 2 (October 15, 1937): 3; 12, no. 9 (February 1, 1938): 3; 12, no. 11 (March 1, 1938): 3; 12, no. 12 (March 15, 1938): 3; and 12, no. 14 (April 15, 1938): 3.

Bourdieu, Pierre. *The Field of Cultural Production*. New York: Columbia University Press, 1993.

———. "The Field of Cultural Production, or: the Economic World Reversed." *Poetics* 12 (1983): 311–56.

Bourdieu, Pierre, and Alain Darbel. *L'Amour de l'art: Les musées et leur public*. Paris: Editions de Minuit, 1966.

Bourke, Joanna. *Dismembering the Male: Men's Bodies, Britain and the Great War*. London: Reaktion Books, 1996.

Bowlby, Rachel. "Walking, Women and Writing: Virginia Woolf as *flaneuse*." In *New Feminist Discourses: Critical Essays on Theories and Texts*, edited by Isobel Armstrong, 26–47. London: Routledge, 1992.

Bradbury, Ray. "Cry the Cosmos." *Life*, September 14, 1962, 86–94.

Bradley, James. *Religion, Revolution, and English Radicalism: Non-Conformity in Eighteenth- Century Politics and Society*. Cambridge: Cambridge University Press, 1990.

Breckman, Warren. *Marx, the Young Hegelians, and the Origins of Radical Social Theory*. Cambridge: Cambridge University Press, 1999.

Breslin, James E. B. *Mark Rothko: A Biography*. Chicago: University of Chicago Press, 1993.

Breton, André, and Diego Rivera. "Manifesto: Towards a Free Revolutionary Art." *Partisan Review* 6, no. 1 (Fall 1939): 49–53.

Brizio, Anna Maria, and Marco Rosci, eds. "Interventi urbanistici e architettonici a Milano durante il periodo napoleonico." In *Napoleone e l'Italia*, 413–27. Convegno Accademia dei Lincei Roma, 1969. Rome: L'accademia nazionale dei Lincei, 1973.

Browder, Earl. *The People's Front*. New York: International Publishers, 1938.

Brown, Maria. "Representing the Body of a Nation: The Art Exhibitions of New Zealand's National Museum." *Third Text* 16, no. 3 (2002): 285–94.

———. "Rhetorical Objects and the Stories of the Nation." In *Travelling Concepts III: Memory, Narrative, Image*, edited by Nancy Pedri, 203–15. Amsterdam: ASCA Press, 2003.

Bruce, Edward. "Implications of the Public Works of Art Project." *Magazine of Art* 27, no. 3 (March 1934): 113–15.

Brull, Steven. "Bringing Public Art to Japan." *International Herald Tribune*, March 1995, 25–26.

Buck-Morss, Susan, Julian Stallabrass, and Leonidas Donskis. *Ground Control: Technology and Utopia*. London: Black Dog Pub, 1997.

Buisson, J. "Le Salon de 1881." *Gazette des Beaux-Arts* 23, no. 6 (June 1881): 504.

Burt, Richard, ed. *The Administration of Aesthetics: Censorship, Political Criticism and the Public Sphere*. Minneapolis: University of Minnesota Press, 1994.

Bushaway, Bob. "Name Upon Name: The Great War and Remembrance." In *Myths of the English*, edited by Roy Porter, 137–67. Cambridge: Polity, 1992.

Bustard, Bruce I. *A New Deal for the Arts*. Washington, DC: National Archives and Records Administration; Seattle: University of Washington Press, 1997.

Butler, Joseph. *The Analogy of Religion, Natural and Revealed to the Constitution and Course of Nature*. London, 1788.

B. Z. am Mittag. "Bode gegen den 'Modernismus' öffentlicher Kunstpflege." April 21, 1920. Reprinted in *Germania*, Abendausgabe, April 22, 1920, as "Ein Notruf Bodes."

Cahill, Holger. "American Art Today." In *American Art Today: New York World's Fair* (facsimile), 19–32. Poughkeepsie, NY: Apollo Press, 1987.

———. "Mural America." *Architectural Record* 82, no. 3 (September 1937): 63–67.

———. *New Horizons in American Art*. New York: Museum of Modern Art, 1936.

———. "The Reminiscences of Holger Cahill." Columbia Oral History Collection, Columbia University, New York, 1957.

Cain, Peter J., and A. G. Hopkins. *British Imperialism, Innovation and Expansion, 1688–1914*. London: Longman, 1993.

Callari, Antonio, and David F. Ruccio, eds. *Postmodern Materialism and the Future of Marxist Theory: Essays in the Althusserian Tradition*. Middletown, CT: Wesleyan University Press, 1996.

Calle, Paul. "I Saw Atlas 9 Take Off!" *American Artist* 27, no. 8 (October 1963): 58–59, 77–79.

Cannadine, David. "War and Death, Grief and Mourning in Modern Britain." In *Mirrors of Mortality: Studies in the Social History of Death*, edited by Joachim Whaley, 187–252. London: Europa, 1981.

Carchetti, Guglielmo. *Frontiers in Political Economy*. London: Verso, 1991.

———. *Problems in Class Analysis*. London: Routledge, 1983.

Carrier, James G. *Gifts and Commodities*. London: Routledge, 1994.

Carter, Warren. "Structure and Agency in New Deal Art: The Case of William Gropper's *Construction of a Dam*." *Object* 6 (2003–4): 5–28.

Cassim, Julia. "Open-air, Public-art Project in Full Bloom." *Japan Times*, December, 17, 1994, 15.

Castagnary, J. "Salon de 1876." In *Salons*, vol. 2, 206–77. Paris, 1892.

Castleman, Riva. "Technics and Creativity." In *Technics and Creativity: Gemini G. E. L.* Exhibition catalog. New York: Museum of Modern Art, 1971

Cavenago, Vicenzo. *Il Lazaretto: Storia di un quartiere di Milano*. 2nd ed. Milan: NED, 1989.

Caves, Richard E. *Creative Industries: Contracts between Art and Commerce*. Cambridge, MA: Harvard University Press, 2000.

Ceadel, Martin. *Pacifism in Britain 1914–45: The Defining of a Faith*. Oxford: Clarendon Press, 1980.

Centre canadien d'architecture and Caisse nationale des monuments historiques et des sites. *Le Panthéon: Symbole des revolutions*. Paris: Picard, 1989.

Certeau, Michel de. *The Practice of Everyday Life*. Translated by Steven Rendall. Berkeley and Los Angeles: University of California Press, 1988.

Cheal, David. *The Gift Economy*. London: Routledge, 1988.

Cheere, Sir Henry. "A Plan for an Academy for Sculpture and Painting Laid before the Society of Arts." In Dr. Templeman, *Transactions*. Vol 1. London, 1754–58.

Chennevières, Philippe de. *Les décorations du Panthéon*. Paris: Aux Bureaux de *l'Artiste*, 1885.

———. *Inventaire général des richesses d'art: Volume II Monuments civils*. Paris, 1889.

Cherry, Deborah. *Painting Women: Victorian Women Artists*. London: Routledge, 1993.

Clark, Eliot. "Andrew Wyeth: America's Most Popular Painter." *Studio* 160 (December 1960): 206–9.

Clark, J. C. D. *English Society, 1660–1832*. 2nd ed. Cambridge: Cambridge University Press, 2000.

———. *The Language of Liberty, 1660–1832: Political Discourse and Social Dynamics in the Anglo-American World*. Cambridge: Cambridge University Press, 1994.

Clarke, Arthur C. "Apollo and Beyond." *Look*, July 15, 1969.

Clifford, Alan C. *Good Doctor: Philip Doddridge of Northampton*. Norwich, UK: Charenton Reformed Publisher, 2002.

Cockcroft, Eva. "Abstract Expressionism, Weapon of the Cold War." In *Pollock and After: The Critical Debate*, edited by Francis Frascina, 145–54. 2nd ed. London: Routledge, 2000.

Codell, Julie F. "'The Artist's Cause at Heart': Marion Harry Spielmann and the Late Victorian Art World." *Bulletin of the John Rylands University Library of Manchester* 71 (1989): 139–63.

———."Artists' Professional Societies: Production, Consumption and Aesthetics." In Allen, ed., *Towards a Modern Art World*, 169–87.

———. "Gentlemen Connoisseurs and Capitalists: Modern British Imperial Identity in the 1903 Delhi Durbar's Exhibition of Indian Art." In *Cultural Identities and the Aesthetics of Britishness*, edited by D. Arnold, 134–63. Manchester: Manchester University Press, 2004.

———. "Righting the Victorian Artist: The Redgraves' *A Century of Painters of the English School* and the Serialization of Art History." *Oxford Art Journal* 23, no. 2 (2000): 93–118.

———. *The Victorian Artist*. Cambridge: Cambridge University Press, 2003.

Cohen, Jean L. *Class and Civil Society: The Limits of Marxian Critical Theory*. Amherst: University of Massachusetts Press, 1982.

Cole, Tim. *Holocaust City: The Making of a Jewish Ghetto*. New York: Routledge, 2003.

A Collaboration between Architecture and Contemporary Art. Tokyo: Obayashi Corporation Public Relations Department, 1999.

Collins, Anne F. "Robert Rauschenberg's Space-Age Allegory, 1959–1970." In *1998 National Aerospace Conference Proceedings*, 82–91. Dayton, OH: Wright State University, 1999.

Commons, John. "Institutional Economics." *American Economic Review* 21 (1931): 648–57.

Compton, Ann, ed. *Charles Sargeant Jagger: War and Peace Sculpture*. London: Imperial War Museum, 1985.

Comte, Jules. "Les peintures murales du Panthéon." *L'Illustration* 1832 (April 6, 1878): 216–19.

Conklin, John. *Art Crime*. New York: Praeger, 1994.

Contreras, Belisario. *Tradition and Innovation in New Deal Art*. Lewisburg, PA: Bucknell University Press, 1983.

Cooke, Lester. Foreword to Hurd, "Countdown at Canaveral," 60.

Cooke, Lester, and James Dean. *Eyewitness to Space*. New York: Harry N. Abrams, 1971.

Cooper, C. S. *The Outdoor Monuments of London: Statues, Memorial Buildings, Tablets and War Memorials*. London: Homeland Association, 1928.

Cork, Richard. *A Bitter Truth: Avant-Garde Art and the Great War*. New Haven, CT: Yale University Press, 1994.

"Counting Down with the Editor." *Spaceport News* 3, no. 5 (January 30, 1964): 8.

Cowen, Tyler, and Alexander Tabarrok. "An Economic Theory of Avant-Garde and Popular Art, or High and Low Culture." *Southern Economic Journal* 67, no. 2 (October 2000): 232–53.

Crane, Verner W. "The Club of Honest Whigs: Friends of Science and Liberty." *William and Mary Quarterly* 23, no. 2 (April 1966): 210–33.

Crimp, Douglas. *On the Museum's Ruins*. Cambridge, MA: MIT Press, 1993.

"Culture for America." *Daily Worker*, June 13, 1938.

Cummings, Milton. "To Change a Nation's Cultural Policy: The Kennedy Administration and the Arts in the United States, 1961–1963." In *Public Policy and the Arts*, edited by Kevin V. Mulcahy and C. Richard Swain, 141–68. Boulder, CO: Westview Press, 1982.

Curl, James Steven. "The Royal Artillery Memorial at Hyde Park Corner." In Compton, ed., *Charles Sargeant Jagger*, 81–100.

Currier, Charles, trans. "Constitutional and Organic Laws of France." *Annals of the American Academy of Political and Social Sciences* 3 (March 1893): 160–69.

D., Dr. "Blick in die Kunstzeitschriften." *Der Tag*, May 20, 1930.

Dalrymple, Theodore. "An Amusement Arcade Masquerading as a Museum." *New Statesman* (February 12, 1999): 32–33.

Davies, William. "The State of English Painting." *Quarterly Review* 17 (1872): 289–336.

Davis, Stuart. "Toward a Democratic Culture." *American Artist* 2 (Spring 1938): 1.

Deacon, Malcolm. *Philip Doddridge of Northampton, 1702–51*. Northampton, UK: Northamptonshire Libraries, 1980.

Dean, James. "The Artist and Space." *Interdisciplinary Science Reviews* 3, no. 3 (1978): 244–59.

———. "The Artist and the Space Shuttle." Unpublished manuscript prepared for NASA, January 1990.

———. "Journey into Space." In Renner et al., eds., *Paul Calle*, 47–64.

Della Peruta, Franco, ed. *Storia illustrata di Milano, Vol. 5: Milano Moderna*. Milan: E. Sellino, 1993.

De Marchi, Neil, and Craufurd D. W. Goodwin, eds. *Economic Engagements with Art*. Durham, NC: Duke University Press, 1999.

De Marchi, Neil, and Jonathan A. Greene. "Adam Smith and Private Provision of the Arts." *History of Political Economy* 37, no. 3 (2005): 431–54.

Denning, Michael. *The Cultural Front: The Laboring of American Culture in the Twentieth Century*. London: Verso Press, 1996.

Dennis, James M. *Grant Wood: A Study in American Art and Culture*. Columbia: University of Missouri Press, 1986.

Dibley, Ben. "Museum, Native, Nation: Museological Narratives and Postcolonial National Identity Formation." Master's thesis, University of Auckland, 1996.

Dickey, Laurence W. "*Doux-Commerce* and the 'Mediocrity of Money' in the Context of the Wealth and Virtue Problem." In *An Inquiry into the Nature and Causes of the Wealth of Nations*, by Adam Smith, edited by Laurence W. Dickey, 243–59. Indianapolis, IN: Hackett, 1993.

———. "Economics and Ethics in Smith's Theory of Capital Accumulation." In *An Inquiry into the Nature and Causes of the Wealth of Nations*, by Adam Smith, edited by Laurence W. Dickey, 213–19. Indianapolis: Hackett, 1993.

———. "Pride, Hypocrisy and Civility in Mandeville's Social and Historical Theory." *Critical Review* (Summer 1990): 387–431.

Dickie, George. *Art and the Aesthetic: An Institutional Analysis*. Ithaca, NY: Cornell University Press, 1974.

———. *The Art Circle: A Theory of Art*. New York: Haven, 1984.

DiMaggio, Paul. *Nonprofit Enterprise in the Arts: Studies in Mission and Constraint*. Oxford: Oxford University Press, 1987.

Dines, Gail, and Jean M. Humez, eds. *Gender, Race, and Class in Media: A Text-Reader*. 2nd ed. London: Sage, 2003.

Dolfsma, Wilfred. "A Status Quo in the Economics of Art and Culture?—A View of Some Recent Developments." *De Economist* 145, no. 2 (July 1997): 243–54.

Domhoff, G. William. *The Power Elite and the State: How Policy is Made in America*. New York: Aldine de Gruyter, 1990.

Dossie, Robert. *Memoirs of Agriculture, and Other Oeconomical Arts*. 3 vols. London, 1782.

Douglas, Mary. *In the Active Voice*. London: Routledge and Kegan Paul, 1982.

———. *Risk and Blame: Essays in Cultural Theory*. London: Routledge, 1992.

Dows, Olin. "The New Deal's Treasury Art Program." In O'Connor, ed., *The New Deal Art Projects*, 11–49. Washington, DC: Smithsonian Institution Press, 1972.

Duffy, Christopher T. "The Rationale for Public Funding of a National Museum." In *Cultural Economics*, edited by Ruth Towse and Abdul Khakee, 37–48. Berlin: Springer, 1992.

Dülffer, Jost, Jochen Thies, and Josef Henke, eds. *Hitlers Städte: Baupolitik im Dritten Reich*. Cologne: Böhlan Verlag, 1978.

Dumett, Raymond E. *Gentlemanly Capitalism and British Imperialism*. London: Longman, 1999.

Duncan, Carol. *Civilizing Rituals: Inside Public Art Museums*. London: Routledge, 1995.

———. "John Cotton Dana's Progressive Museum." In *Self and History: A Tribute to Linda Nochlin*, edited by Aruna D'Souza, 127–36. New York: Thames and Hudson, 2001.

Duncan, Carol, and Alan Wallach. "The Museum of Modern Art as Late Capitalist Ritual: An Iconographic Analysis." *Marxist Perspectives* 1, no. 4 (1978): 28–51.

Dunlap, David W. "'The Gates' Promote Nothing, Except Maybe the Artists." *New York Times*, February 17, 2005, sec. B, col. 1, p. 3.

During, Simon. "Postmodernism or Postcolonialism?" *Landfall* 39 (1985): 366–80.

Dutton, Denis. "New National Museum Resembles a Junk Shop." *New Zealand Herald* (Auckland, NZ), May 21, 1998, A15.

Dwork, Deborah, and Robert Jan van Pelt. *Auschwitz: 1270 to the Present*. New York: W. W. Norton, 1996.

Eiland, William U. *The Truth in Things*. Athens: University of Georgia Press, 1996.

Elias, Julius. "Berliner Kunstglossen." *Der Tag*, June 11, 1921.

Explication des ouvrages de peinture, sculpture, architecture, gravure et lithographie des artistes vivants exposées au Palais des Champs-Elysées le 1er mai 1876. Paris: Imprimerie nationale, 1876.

L'Exposition des Beaux-Arts: Salon de 1881. Paris, 1881.

L'Exposition des oeuvres des artistes vivants: Salon de 1876: Compte rendu du Journal des Art. Paris, 1876.

Exposition universelle de 1878 à Paris: Catalogue officiel publié par le commissariat général. Volume I: Groupe I: Oeuvres d'art. Paris: Imprimerie nationale, 1878.

Fain, J. T. *Ruskin and the Economists*. Nashville, TN: Vanderbilt University Press, 1956.

Feistel-Rohmeder, Bettina. *Im Terror des Kunstbolschewismus: Urkundensammlung des "Deutschen Kunstberichtes" aus den Jahren 1927–33*. Karlsruhe: C. F. Müller, 1938.

Feretti, Fred. "The AAA and How It Grew." *ARTNews* 73, no. 2 (February 1974): 57–59.

Ferguson, Adam. *An Essay on the History of Civil Society*. Edited by Fana Oz-Salzberger. Cambridge: Cambridge University Press, 1995.

Ferriday, Peter. "The Victorian Art Market: The Profits of Painting." *Country Life*, Part 2 (June 16, 1966): 1567–78.

"The Final Impossibility: Man's Tracks on the Moon." *Look*, December 30, 1969.

Fitzgerald, Michael C. *Making Modernism: Picasso and the Creation of the Market for Twentieth Century Art*. Berkeley and Los Angeles: University of California Press, 1995.

Flanagan, Hallie. *Arena*. New York: Duell, Sloan and Pearce, 1940.

Forster-Hahn, Françoise, "The Politics of Display or the Display of Politics?" *Art Bulletin* 77 (1995): 174–79.

———. "Shrine of Art or Signature of a New Nation? The National Gallery(ies) in Berlin, 1848–1968." *Studies in the History of Art* 47 (1994): 78–99.

Forster-Hahn, Françoise, and Kurt W. Forster. *Art in Berlin 1815–1989*. Seattle: University of Washington Press, 1989.

Fouquier, Henry. *Catalogue de tableaux, aquarelles et dessins provenant de l'atelier Alexandre Cabanel*. Paris, 1889.

Foushee, Ola Mae "North Carolina's Community Art Centers." In *Art in Action: American Art Centers and The New Deal*, edited by John Franklin White, 158–66. Metuchen, NJ: Scarecrow Press, 1987.

Fox, Danielle. "Art." In *Culture Works: The Political Economy of Culture*, edited by Richard Maxwell, 22–59. Minneapolis: University of Minnesota Press, 2001.

France, Peter. "Primitivism and Enlightenment: Rousseau and the Scots." *Yearbook of English Studies* 15 (1985): 64–79.

Francis, Richard. "War Memorials." In *British Sculpture in the Twentieth Century*, edited by Sandy Nairne and Nicholas Serota, 63–65. London: Whitechapel Art Gallery, 1981.

Fraser, Steve, and Gary Gerstle, eds. *The Rise and Fall of the New Deal Order, 1930–1980*. Princeton, NJ: Princeton University Press, 1989.

Frey, B. S., and W. W. Pommerehne. *Muses and Markets: Explorations in the Economics of the Arts*. Oxford: Blackwell, 1989.

Friedrich, Paul. "Die Juryfreie Kunstschau 1923." *Berliner Börsen-Zeitung*, October 1, 1923.

Frohnmayer, John. *Leaving Town Alive: Confessions of an Arts Warrior*. New York: Houghton Mifflin, 1993.

Fruchtman, Jack, Jr. "The Apocalyptic Politics of Richard Price and Joseph Priestley: A Study in Late Eighteenth-Century English Republican Millennialism." In *Transactions of the American Philosophical Society*. Vol. 73, no. 4. Philadelphia: American Philosophical Society, 1983.

Führ, Eduard. "Über die Kultur der Architekten und Ingenieure im 'Dritten' Deutschen Reich." In *Architektur und Ingenieurwesen zur Zeit der nationalsozialistischen Gewaltherrschaft*, edited by Ulrich Kuder, 53–68. Berlin: Gebr. Mann Verlag, 1997.

Fuhrmeister, Christian. *Beton, Klinker, Granit: Materiel Macht Politik; eine Materialikonographie*. Berlin: Bauwesen, 2001.

Fullerton, Don. "Tax Policy Towards Art Museums." In *The Economics of Art Museums*, edited by Martin Feldstein, 195–235. Chicago: University of Chicago Press, 1991.

Fussell, Paul. *The Great War and Modern Memory*. Oxford: Oxford University Press, 1977.

Gagnier, Regenia. *The Insatiability of Human Wants: Economics and Aesthetics in Market Society*. Chicago: University of Chicago Press, 2000.

Gallet, Michel. *Claude-Nicolas Ledoux: 1736–1806*. Paris: Picard, 1980.

Gardiner, James. *A Class Apart: The Private Pictures of Montague Glover*. London: Serpent's Tail, 1995.

Gellner, Ernest. *Nationalism*. New York: New York University Press, 1997.

Genauer, Emily. "New Horizons in American Art." *Parnassus* 8 (October 1936): 6.

Genovese, Maria Domenica. "Milano 1796–1815: Feste pubbliche e concorsi nel primo periodo napoleonico." In *La cultura a Milano tra riformismo illuminato e rivoluzione*, edited by Raffaele De Grada et al., 99–105. Milan: Vangelista, 1989.

Giudicelli Falguières, Patrizia. "Espace privée et espace public à Milan: 1796–1814." In *Villes et Territoire pendant la Période napoléonienne: France et Italie.* Actes du colloque organisée par l'Ecole française de Rome avec la participation de la Maison des sciences de l'homme, Rome, May 3–5, 1984, 261–84. Rome: L'Ecole, 1987.

Godfrey, Tony. *Conceptual Art*. London: Phaidon, 1998.

Gollwitzer, Michael. "Francesco Milizia: Del Teatro. Ein Beitrag zur Ästhetik und Kulturgeschichte Italiens zwischen 1750 und 1790." Diss., Cologne, 1969.

Goodruff, C. H. "The Collector on the Prowl." *Blackwood's Magazine* 147 (1890): 677–87.

Goodwin, Craufurd D., ed. *Art and the Market: Roger Fry on Commerce and Art*. Ann Arbor: University of Michigan Press, 1998.

———. "The Economics of Art through Art Critics' Eyes." In De Marchi and Goodwin, eds., *Economic Engagements with Art*, 157–84.

———. "Public Support of the Arts in the History of Economics: Introduction." *History of Political Economy* 37, no. 3 (2005): 399–411.

Goodyear, Anne Collins. "Art, Technology, and the American Space Program." *Intertexts* 3, no. 2 (Fall 1999): 124–46.

———. "On the Threshold of Space: Norman Rockwell's *Longest Step*." In *2001: Architecture and Design for Space, Vision and Reality*, exhibition catalog, 102–7. Chicago: Art Institute of Chicago, 2001; New York: Harry N. Abrams, 2001.

———. "The Relationship of Art to Science and Technology in the United States, 1957–1971: Five Case Studies." PhD diss., University of Texas at Austin, 2002.

Gordon, Daniel. *Citizens without Sovereignty: Equality and Sociability in French Thought, 1670–1789*. Princeton, NJ: Princeton University Press, 1994.

Gordon, Liz, and Paul Willis. "Education, Cultural Production and Social Reproduction." *British Journal of Sociology of Education* 5, no. 2 (1984): 105–15.

Goux, Jean-Joseph. *Symbolic Economies: After Marx and Freud*. Translated by Jennifer Curtiss Gage. Ithaca, NY: Cornell University Press, 1990.

Grady, Elizabeth M. "The Politicization of Public Opinion on Modern Art at the National Gallery in Berlin, 1918–1933." PhD diss., Northwestern University, 2002.

Grandlieu, Ph. de. "N'en parlons plus!" *Le Figaro*, August 19, 1884, 1.

Grassi, Rosella. "Paolo Bargigli architetto: 1760c.–1815c." *Parma nell'arte* 1 (1982): 47–67.

Gregory, Adrian. *Silence of Memory: Armistice Day 1919–1945*. Oxford: Berg Publishers, 1994.

Gries, Christian. "Johannes Molzahn (1892–1965) und der Kampf um die Kunst im Deutschland der Weimarer Republik." PhD diss., University of Augsburg, 1996.

Griffin, Charles T., and Brenda S. Griffin. "Art Worlds and Social Types." *American Behavioral Scientist* 19, no. 6 (1984): 703–19.

Grote, Harriet. *Collected Papers*. London: John Murray, 1862.

Grunewald, Marie-Antoinette. *Paul Chenavard et la decoration du Panthéon de Paris en 1848*. Lyon: Musée des Beaux-Arts, 1977.

Guerci, Luciano. "'Democrazia rappresentativa': Definizioni e discussioni nell'Italia del triennio repubblicano 1796–1799." In *L'Europa tra illuminismo e restaurazione: Scritti in onore di Furio Diaz*, edited by Paolo Alatri, 227–75. Rome: Bulzoni, 1993.

Guilbaut, Serge. *How New York Stole the Idea of Modern Art: Abstract Expressionism, Freedom, and the Cold War*. Translated by Arthur Goldhammer. Chicago: University of Chicago Press, 1983.

Gyorgy, Peter. "Between and after Essentialism and Institutionalism." *Journal of Aesthetics and Art Criticism* 57, no. 4 (Autumn 1999): 421–37.

Haakonssen, Knud, ed. *Enlightenment and Religion: Rational Dissent in Eighteenth-Century Britain*. Cambridge: Cambridge University Press, 1996.

Habermas, Jürgen. *The Structural Transformation of the Public Sphere*. Translated by Thomas Burger. Cambridge, MA: MIT Press, 1991.

Hait, Pam. "The Artist's Journey." In Renner et al., eds., *Paul Calle*, 14–45.

Hall, Arnold Bennett. "Art and Democracy." *American Magazine of Art*, May 1934, 44–45, annual convention issue.

Hallé, Charles E. *Notes from a Painter's Life*. London: J. Murray, 1909.

Harper, Jenny. "For the Sake of Your Art." *Dominion* (Wellington, NZ), June 2, 1999, 10.

Harries, Meirion, and Susie Harries. *The War Artists: British Official War Art of the Twentieth Century*. London: Michael Joseph and Imperial War Museum, 1983.

Harris, Jonathan, ed. *Art, Money, Parties: New Institutions in the Political Economy of Contemporary Art*. Tate Liverpool Critical Forum. Vol. 7. Liverpool: Liverpool University Press, 2004.

———. *Federal Art and National Culture: The Politics of Identity in New Deal America*. Cambridge: Cambridge University Press, 1995.

Harris, Wendell V. "A Handlist of Nineteenth-Century London Art Societies and Their Predecessors." *Nineteenth-Century Studies* 18 (2004): 139–62.

Harrison, Helen A. "John Reed Club Artists and the New Deal: Radical Responses to Roosevelt's 'Peaceful Revolution.'" *Prospects: An Annual of American Cultural Studies* 5 (1980): 240–68.

Hart, Solomon A. *The Reminiscences of Solomon Alex Hart, R. A.* Edited by Alexander Brodie. London: Wyman and Sons, 1882.

Harvey, Charles, and Jon Press. *William Morris: Design and Enterprise in Victorian Britain*. Manchester, UK: Manchester University Press, 1991.

Harvey, David. *The Condition of Postmodernity: An Enquiry into the Origins of Cultural Change*. London: Blackwell, 1989.

———. "From Space to Place and Back Again: Reflections on the Condition of Postmodernity." In John Bird et al., eds., *Mapping the Future*, 3–29.

———. *Limits to Capital*. London: Verso, 1999.

Haskell, Francis. "An Italian Patron of French Neo-Classic Art." In *Past and Present in Art and Taste: Selected Essays*. New Haven, CT: Yale University Press, 1987.

———. "More about Sommariva." *Burlington Magazine*, October 1972, 691–95.

Hay, Ian. *Their Name Liveth: The Book of the Scottish National War Memorial*. London: John Lane, 1931.

Hayden, Dolores. *The Power of Place in Urban Landscape as Public History*. Cambridge, MA: MIT Press, 1995.

Hearder, Harry. *Italy in the Age of the Risorgimento: 1790–1870*. Longman History of Italy 6. London: Longman 1980.

Heilbrun, James, and Charles M. Gray. *The Economics of Art and Culture*. 2nd ed. Cambridge: Cambridge University Press, 2001.

Heller, Nancy, and Julia Williams. *Painters of the American Scene*. New York: Galahad Books, 1982.

Hemingway, Andrew. *Artists on the Left: American Artists and the Communist Movement, 1926–1956*. New Haven, CT: Yale University Press, 2002.

———. "The Debate on Art and the State in Postwar America." In *Art and Politics: Proceedings of the Third Anglo-Polish Art Historians' Conference*, 151–64. Warsaw: Institut Sztuki, Polish Academy of Arts and Sciences, 1999.

———. "Meyer Schapiro and Marxism in the 1930s." *Oxford Art Journal* 17, no. 1 (1994): 13–29.

Henderson, Willie. *Economics as Literature*. New York: Routledge, 1995.

———. *John Ruskin's Political Economy*. New York: Routledge, 2000.

Henderson, W., T. Dudley-Evans, and R. Backhouse, eds. *Economics and Language*. London: Routledge, 1993.

Herman, Edward S., and Noam Chomsky. *Manufacturing Consent: The Political Economy of the Mass Media*. New York: Pantheon Books, 1988.

Heuss, Theodor. "Kunst, Revolution, Staatsform: Randbemerkungen." *Deutsche Allgemeine Zeitung*, April 2, 1919.

Hills, Patricia. "1936: Meyer Schapiro, *Art Front*, and the Popular Front." *Oxford Art Journal* 17, no. 1 (1994): 30–41.

———. *Social Concern and Urban Realism: American Painting of the 1930s*. New York: Bread and Roses Cultural Project of the National Union of Hospital and Health Care Employees and the American Federation of Arts, 1983.

Hirsch, Fred. *The Social Limits to Growth*. Cambridge, MA: Harvard University Press, 1976.

Hirschman, Albert O. *The Passions and the Interests: Political Arguments for Capitalism before Its Triumph*. Princeton, NJ: Princeton University Press, 1977.

———. "Rival Views of Market Society." In *Rival Views of Market Society and Other Recent Essays*, 109–17. Cambridge, MA: Harvard University Press, 1992.

Hitler, Adolf. *Mein Kampf*. Translated by L. Lore. New York: Stackpole Sons, 1939.

———. *Mein Kampf*. Introduction by D. C. Watt. Translated by Ralph Manheim. London: Hutchinson, 1969. Originally published as Hitler, *Mein Kampf: Eine Abrechnung*. Munich: Zentralverlag der NSDAP, F. Eher Nachf, 1925–27.

Hodgson, G. M. *Economics and Institutions: A Manifesto for a Modern Institutional Economics*. Cambridge: Polity Press, 1988.

Hodgson, G. M., W. J. Samuels, and M. R. Tool, eds. *The Elgar Companion to Institutional and Evolutionary Economics*. Aldershot, UK: Edward Elgar, 1994.

Holman, Mary A. *The Political Economy of the Space Program*. Palo Alto, CA: Pacific Books, 1974.

Homberger, E. "The Story of the Cenotaph." *Times Literary Supplement*, November 12, 1976, 1429–30.

Horgan, Joanne C. *Museum of New Zealand: Report of the Interviews*. Boston: E. Verner John and Associates, 1988.

Hoving, Thomas. *False Impressions: The Hunt for Big-Time Art Fakes*. New York: Simon and Schuster, 1996.

Howson, Susan. "Lionel Robbins's 'Art and the State.'" *History of Political Economy* 37, no. 3 (2005): 617–46.

Hughes, Gordon. "Measuring the Economic Value of the Arts." *Policy Studies* 9 (Spring 1989): 33–45.

Huish, Marcus B. "Ten Years of British Art." *Nineteenth Century* 27 (1890): 102–18.

———. "Whence This Great Multitude of Painters?" *Nineteenth Century* 32 (1892): 720–32.

Hume, David. *Essays: Moral, Political, and Literary*. Indianapolis, IN: Liberty Classics, 1987.

Hurd, Peter. "Countdown at Canaveral." *Art in America* 51, no. 5 (October 1963): 60–72.

Hynes, Samuel. *A War Imagined: The First World War and English Culture*. London: Bodley Head, 1991.

Ishii, Toru. "Greeting." In *Sculpture and Foliage*. Tokyo: Spatial Design Consultants, 1991.

Isserman, Maurice. *Which Side Were You On? The American Communist Party During the Second World War*. Middletown, CT: Wesleyan University Press, 1982.

Itoi, Kay. "A Forest of Public Art." *Sculpture* 15 (April 1996): 26–30.

"James Clarke Hook." *Art Journal* 7 (1856): 41–44.

Jameson, Fredric *Postmodernism or, the Cultural Logic of Late Capitalism*. Raleigh, NC: Duke University Press, 1991.

Jaskot, Paul B. "Architecture and the Destruction of the European Jews." In *The Holocaust's Ghost: Writings on Art, Politics, Law and Education*, edited by F. C. DeCoste and Bernard Schwartz, 145–64. Edmonton: University of Alberta Press, 2000.

———. *Architecture of Oppression*. London: Routledge, 2000.

Jeffers, Wendy. "Holger Cahill and American Art." *Archives of American Art Journal* 31, no. 4 (1991): 2–5.

Jones, Kimberly. "Resurrecting History: Jean-Paul Laurens and the Politics of History Painting During the French Third Republic, 1871–1914." PhD diss., University of Maryland, 1996.

Jones, Mark, ed. *Fake? The Art of Deception*. Berkeley and Los Angeles: University of California Press, 1990.

Jopling, Louise. "On the Education of the Artistic Faculty." In *Education and Professions*, vol. 1, The Women's Library, edited by Ethel M. M. McKenna, 103–72. London: Chapman and Hall, 1903.

Joy, Annamma, and John F. Sherry. "Disentangling the Paradoxical Alliances between Art Market and Art World." *Consumption, Markets and Culture* 6, no. 3 (September 2003): 155–81.

Junge, Henrike, ed. *Avantgarde und Pulikum: Zur Rezeption avantgardistischer Kunst in Deutschland 1905–1933*. Cologne: Böhlau Verlag, 1992.

Justi, Ludwig. "Kunst und Politik." *Kunstchronik und Kunstmarkt*, n.s., 57, no. 35 (May 26, 1922): 569–74.

———. *Neue Kunst: Ein Führer zu den Gemälden der sogenannten Expressionisten in der National-Galerie*. Berlin: Amtliche Veröffentlichungen der National-Galerie im Verlag von Julius Bard, 1921.

Kainen, Jacob. "The Graphic Arts Division of the WPA Federal Art Project." In *The New Deal Art Projects: An Anthology of Memoirs*, edited by Francis V. O'Connor. Washington, DC: Smithsonian Institution Press, 1972.

———. "Revolutionary Art at the John Reed Club." *Art Front* 1, no. 2 (January 1935): 6.

Kannès, Gianluca. "Un acquarello per il Foro Bonaparte in Milano ed altri inediti di G.A. Antolini." *Storia della Città* 7, no. 22 (April–June 1982): 85.

———. "Il Foro Bonaparte tra l'Antolini e il Canonica: Un progetto di concorso ma non di esecuzione." In *Milano Parco Sempione: Spazio, pubblico, progetto, architettura 1796/1980*, Triennale de Milano, 106–13. Milan: n.p., 1980.

Karp, Ivan. Introduction to *Museums and Communities: The Politics of Public Culture*, edited by Ivan Karp, Christine Mullen Kreamer, and Steven D. Lavine, 1–17. Washington, DC: Smithsonian Institution Press, 1992.

Kass, Ray. *Morris Graves: Vision of the Inner Eye*. Exhibition catalog. Washington, DC, The Phillips Collection, April 9–May 29, 1983. New York: George Braziller, 1983.

Kastner, Jeffrey, and Brian Wallis, eds. *Land and Environmental Art*. London: Phaidon, 1998.

Kauffman, James. *Selling Outer Space: Kennedy, the Media, and Funding for Project Apollo, 1961–63*. Tuscaloosa: University of Alabama Press, 1994.

Keane, John. *Democracy and Civil Society*. London: Verso, 1988.

Kernot, Bernie. "Te Maori Te Hokinga Mai: Some Reflections." *Art Galleries and Museums Association of New Zealand Journal* 18, no. 2 (1987): 3–7.

Kershaw, Ian. *Popular Opinion and Political Dissent in the Third Reich*. Oxford: Clarendon Press, 1983.

Kim, Joohoan. "From Commodity Production to Sign Production: A Triple Triangle Model for Marx's Semiotics and Peirce's Economics." *Semiotica* 132, no. 1 (2000): 75–101.

Kimura, Mitsuhiro, and Fram Kitagawa, supervisors. *A "New Century" for City and Public Art: Faret Tachikawa Art Project*. Tokyo: Gendaikikakushitsu Publishers, 1995.

King, Alexander M. *Memorials of the Great War in Britain: The Symbolism and Politics of Remembrance*. Oxford: Berg, 1998.

———. "The Politics of Meaning in the Commemoration of the First World War in Britain, 1914–39." PhD thesis, University College, University of London, 1993.

———. "Remembering and Forgetting in Public Memorial of the Great War." In *The Art of Forgetting*, edited by Adrian Forty and Susanne Kuchler, 147–69. Oxford: Berg, 1999.

Klamer, Arjo ed. *The Value of Culture: On the Relationship between Economics and Arts*. Amsterdam: Amsterdam University Press, 1996.

Klehr, Harvey. *The Heyday of American Communism*. New York: Basic Books, 1984.

Klein, Iris. *Vom kosmogonischen zum völkischen Eros: Eine sozialgeschichtliche Analyse bürgerlich-liberaler Kunstkritik in der Zeit von 1917 bis 1936*. Munich: Tuduv, 1991.

Kocivar, Ben. "The Longest Step, Painted for *Look* by Norman Rockwell." *Look*, April 20, 1965.

Koehler, Gerhard. *Kunstanschauung und Kunstkritik in der nationalsozialistischen Presse: Die Kritik im Feuilleton des "Völkischen Beobachters" 1920–1932*. Munich: Zentralverlag der NSDAP, Franz Eher Nachf, 1937.

Krauss, Rosalind. *The Originality of the Avant-Garde and Other Myths*. Cambridge, MA: MIT Press, 1985.

Krueger, Thomas A., and William Glidden. "The New Deal Intellectual Elite: A Collective Portrait." In *The Rich, the Well Born, and the Powerful*, edited by F. C. Jaher, 338–77. Champaign-Urbana: University of Illinois Press, 1973.

Kubsch, Hugo. "Vom Corinth bis Klee." *Deutsche Tageszeitung*, August 8, 1931.

"Kunst unterm Knüppel: Preußens Verdienste um die bildenden Künste." *Berlin am Morgen*, April 22, 1932.

"Die Künstler an den Reichskanzler: Van Gogh und der Ruf nach einer Notverordnung." *Berliner Tageblatt*, April 28, 1932.

Kwait, John [Meyer Schapiro]. "John Reed Club Art Exhibition." *New Masses* 8, no. 7 (February 1933): 23.

Lacy, Suzanne, ed. *Mapping the Terrain: New Genre Public Art*. Seattle, WA: Bay Press, 1995.

Lafenestre, Georges. "Alexandre Cabanel." *Gazette des Beaux-Arts* 1 (April 1889): 265–80.

Laidley, William J. *The Origin and First Two Years of the New English Art Club*. London: Bodley Head, 1907.

Lambright, W. Henry. *Powering Apollo: James E. Webb of NASA*. Baltimore: Johns Hopkins University Press, 1995.

Langa, Helen. *Radical Art: Printmaking and the Left in 1930s New York*. Berkeley and Los Angeles: University of California Press, 2004.

Laqueur, Thomas. "Memory and Naming in the Great War." In *Commemorations: The Politics of National Identity*, edited by John R. Gillis, 150–67. Princeton, NJ: Princeton University Press, 1994.

Larkin, Oliver. "Art in America." *New Masses* 13, no. 12 (December 18, 1934): 23–24.

Larson, Gary O. *The Reluctant Patron: The United States Government and the Arts, 1943–1965*. Philadelphia: University of Pennsylvania Press, 1983.

Larson, Magali S. *The Rise of Professionalism: A Sociological Analysis*. Berkeley and Los Angeles: University of California Press, 1977.

Launius, Roger D. *The History of the U.S. Civil Space Program*. Malabar, FL: Krieger, 1994.

Launius, Roger D., and Bertram Ulrich. *NASA and the Exploration of Space*. New York: Stewart, Tabori, and Chang, 1998.

Leadbeater, Charles. *Living on Thin Air: The New Economy*. London: Penguin Books, 2000.

Lee, A. "Ruskin and Political Economy: *Unto This Last*." In *New Approaches to Ruskin: Thirteen Essays*, edited by Robert Hewison. London: Routledge and Kegan Paul, 1981.

Leith, James A. *Space and Revolution: Projects for Monuments, Squares, and Public Buildings in France 1789–1799*. Montreal: McGill-Queen's University Press, 1991.

Lenin, V[ladimir] I[lich]. *What Is to Be Done? Burning Questions of Our Movement*. 1902. New York: International Publishers, 1929.

"Die Lenkung des Baumarktes." *Beilage zum "Baumeister,"* no. 6 (1937): B132–33.

Leslie, G. D. "The Artist in Relation to His Work." *Art Journal*, n.s., 21 (1882): 69–72.

"A Letter to the Members of the Society for the Encouragement of Arts, Manufactures, and Commerce." London, 1761.

Leuchtenberg, William. *Franklin D. Roosevelt and the New Deal, 1932–1940*. New York: Harper and Row, 1963.

Levine, Lawrence. *Highbrow/Lowbrow: The Emergence of Cultural Hierarchy in America*. Cambridge, MA: Harvard University Press, 1988.

Lichtenstein, Peter M. *An Introduction to Post-Keynesian and Marxian Theories of Value and Price*. Armonk, NY: M. E. Sharpe, 1983.

Lilienthal, David E. *TVA: Democracy on the March*. Harmondsworth: Penguin, 1944.

Lippard, Lucy. *Six Years: The Dematerialization of the Art Object from 1966 to 1972: A Cross-Reference Book of Information on Some Esthetic Boundaries*. Berkeley and Los Angeles: University of California Press, 1977.

Lloyd, David W. *Battlefield Tourism. Pilgrimage and the Commemoration of the Great War in Britain, Australia and Canada 1919–39*. Oxford: Berg 1998.

Locke, Robert R. *French Legitimists and the Politics of Moral Order in the Early Third Republic*. Princeton, NJ: Princeton University Press, 1986.

Longworth, Philip. *The Unending Vigil: A History of the Commonwealth War Graves Commission 1917–67*. London: Constable, 1967.

Lough, John. *An Introduction to Nineteenth-Century France*. London: Longman Group, 1978.

Lovejoy, Arthur O., and George Boas. *Primitivism and Related Ideas in Antiquity*. Baltimore: Johns Hopkins University Press, 1935.

Lozowick, Louis. "John Reed Club Show." *New Masses* 10, no. 1 (January 2, 1934): 27.

Luhman. Niklas. *Art as a Social System*. Stanford, CA: Stanford University Press, 2000.

Luke, Timothy W. "From Commodity Aesthetics to Ecology Aesthetics: Arts and the Environmental Crisis." *Art Journal* 51, no. 2 (Summer 1992): 72–76.

Lutyens, Mary. "Selling the Missionary." *Apollo* 86 (November 1967): 380–87.

Maas, Harro. "Pacifying the Workman: Ruskin and Jevons on Labor and Popular Culture." In De Marchi and Goodwin, eds., *Economic Engagements with Art*, 85–120.

Macleod, Dianne Sachko. *Art and the Victorian Middle Class: Money and the Making of Cultural Identity*. Cambridge: Cambridge University Press, 1996.

Macpherson, James. *The Poems of Ossian and Related Works*. Edited by Howard Gaskill with introduction by Fiona Stafford. Edinburgh: Edinburgh University Press, 1996.

Maier, Charles. *In Search of Stability: Explorations in Historical Political Economy*. Cambridge: Cambridge University Press, 1987.

Mailer, Norman. *Of a Fire on the Moon*. Boston: Little, Brown, 1970.

Malvern, Sue. "'For King and Country': Frampton's *Edith Cavell* 1915–1920, and the Writing of Gender in Memorials to the Great War." In *Sculpture and the Pursuit of the Modern Ideal in Britain, c. 1880–1930*, edited by David J. Getsy, 219–44. Aldershot, UK: Ashgate Press, 2004.

———. "War, Memory and Museums: Art and Artefacts in the Imperial War Museum." *History Workshop Journal* 49 (2000): 177–203.

———. *Witnessing, Testimony and Remembrance: Modern Art, Britain and the Great War*. London: Yale University Press, 2004.

Mangione, Jerre. *The Dream and the Deal: The Federal Writers' Project, 1935–1943*. Boston: Little, Brown, 1972.

Mannheim, Karl. *Ideology & Utopia: An Introduction to the Sociology of Knowledge*. New York: Harcourt, 1936.

Marin, C. S. "The Campaign for the Federal Arts Bill." *The Communist* 18, no. 6 (June 1938): 562–70.

Marling, Karal Ann. *Wall-to-Wall America: A Cultural History of Post-Office Murals in the Great Depression*. Minneapolis: University of Minnesota Press, 1982.

Marsh, Jan, and Pamela Gerrish Nunn. *Pre-Raphaelite Women Artists*. Manchester: Manchester City Art Galleries, 1997.

———. *Women Artists and the Pre-Raphaelite Movement*. London: Virago, 1989.

Marx, Leo. *The Machine in the Garden: Technology and the Pastoral Ideal in America*. London: Oxford University Press, 1964.

Mathews, Jane de Hart. "Art and Politics in Cold War America." In *Pollock and After: The Critical Debate*, edited by Francis Frascina, 2nd ed., 155–80. London: Routledge, 2000.

———. "Arts and the People: The New Deal Quest for Cultural Democracy." *Journal of American History* 62, no. 2 (September 1975): 316–39.

———. *The Federal Theatre, 1935–1939: Plays, Relief, and Politics*. Princeton, NJ: Princeton University Press, 1967.

Mathieu, Thomas. *Kunstauffassungen und Kulturpolitik im Nationalsozialismus, Studien zu Adolf Hitler, Joseph Goebbels, Alfred Rosenberg, Baldur von Schirach, Heinrich Himmler, Albert Speer, Wilhelm Frick*. Saarbrücken: Pfau Verlag, 1997.

Mavigliano, George J., and Richard A. Lawson. *The Federal Art Project in Illinois, 1935–1943*. Carbondale: Southern Illinois University Press, 1990.

Maxwell, Richard, ed. *Culture Works: The Political Economy of Culture*. Minneapolis: University of Minnesota Press, 2001.

Mazzocca, Fernando. "G. B. Sommariva o il Borghese Mecenate." *Itinerari* 2 (1981): 145–277.

McCausland, Elizabeth. *Picasso*. New York: ACA Gallery, 1944.

McCombie, Mary Eleanor. "Arts and Policy: The National Endowment for the Art's Art in Public Places Program, 1967–1980," PhD diss., University of Texas at Austin, 1992.

McCurdy, Howard. *Space and the American Imagination*. Washington, DC: Smithsonian Institution Press, 1997.

McDermott Miller Ltd. *Non-users of Museums in New Zealand: A Survey and Guide for Museums*. Wellington, NZ: Museum Directors Federation of Aotearoa New Zealand, 1996.

McDonald, William F. *Federal Relief Administration and the Arts*. Columbus: Ohio State University Press, 1969.

McDougall, Walter. *The Heavens and the Earth: A Political History of the Space Age*. 1985. Baltimore: Johns Hopkins University Press, 1997.

McKinzie, Richard D. *The New Deal for Artists*. Princeton, NJ: Princeton University Press, 1973.

McMahon, Audrey. "A General View of the WPA Federal Art Project in New York City and State." In O'Connor, ed., *The New Deal Art Projects*.

McWhirter, William A. "Tom Benton at 80, Still at War with Bores and Boobs." *Life*, October 3, 1969, 64–70.

Mead, Sidney (Hirini) Moko. *Magnificent Te Maori. Te Maori Whakahirahira*. Auckland, NZ: Heinemann, 1986.

———, ed. *Te Maori: Maori Art from New Zealand Collections*. Auckland, NZ: Heinemann; New York: American Federation of Arts, 1984.

Mecklenburg, Virginia. *The Public as Patron: A History of the Treasury Department Mural Program*. College Park: University of Maryland Art Gallery, 1979.

Melosh, Barbara. *Engendering Culture: Manhood and Womanhood in New Deal Public Art and Theater*. Washington, DC: Smithsonian Institution Press, 1991.

Memmo, Andrea. *Elementi di Architettura Lodoliana o sia l'arte del fabbricare con solidità scientifica e con eleganza non capricciosa*. Rome: Pagliarini, 1786.

Merker, Reinhard, *Die bildenden Künste im Nationalsozialismus: Kulturideologie, Kulturpolitik, Kulturproduktion*. Cologne: DuMont Buchverlag, 1983.

Meyer, Karl E. *The Art Museum: Power, Money, Ethics*. New York: William Morrow, 1979.

Mezzanotte, Paolo. "L'architettura dal 1796 alla caduta del Regno Italico." In *Storia di Milano*, vol. 13, 478–522. Turin: Fond. Treccani degli Alfieri per la Storia di Milano, 1959.

Michalski, Sergiusz. *Public Monuments: Art in Political Bondage, 1870–1997*. London: Reaktion Books, 1998.

Miles, Malcolm. *Art, Space and the City: Public Art and Urban Futures*. London: Routledge, 1997.

———, ed. *Art for Public Places*. Winchester, UK: Winchester School of Art Press, 1989.

Milizia, Francesco. *Del Teatro*. Rome, 1771; Veniza: Giambattista Pasquali, 1773.

———. *Principi di architettura civile*. 3 vols. Finale: Stamperia di Jacopo de' Rossi, 1781. Reprint, "Collana anastatica 3." 5 vols. Milan: Sapere, 2000.

———. *Principi di architettura civile*. Edited by Giovanni A. Antolini. Milan, 1817. Reprint, Milan: Mazzotta, 1972.

———. *Trattato completo, formale e materiale del teatro*. 2nd ed. Venice: n.p., 1794. Reprint, Bologna: Forni, 1969.

Miller Lane, Barbara. *Architecture and Politics in Germany 1918–1945*. Cambridge, MA: Harvard University Press, 1968.

Mills, Ernestine. *The Life and Letters of Frederic Shields, 1833–1911*. London: Longmans, Green, 1912.

Moggridge, D. E. "Keynes, the Arts, and the State." *History of Political Economy* 37, no. 3 (2005): 535–55.

Monahan, Laurie. "Cultural Cartography." In *Reconstructing Modernism: Art in New York, Paris, and Montreal, 1945–1964*, edited by Serge Gibaut, 369–416. Cambridge, MA: MIT Press, 1990.

Monroe, Ann. "CVJ Corporation." *Wall Street Journal*, July 12, 1984, sec. 1, col. 1, p. 1.

Monroe, Gerald M. "Artists as Militant Trade Union Workers During the Great Depression." *Archives of American Art Journal* 17, no. 1 (1974): 7–10.

———. "Artists on the Barricades: The Militant Artists' Union Treats with the New Deal." *Archives of American Art Journal* 18, no. 3 (1978): 20–23.

———."The Artists' Union of New York." D.Ed diss., New York University, 1971.

Moore, Gregory C. G. "Evangelical Aesthete: Ruskin and the Public Provision of Art." *History of Political Economy* 37, no. 3 (2005): 483–508.

Moriarty, Christine. "Christian Iconography and First World War Memorials." *Imperial War Museum Review* 6 (1991): 63–75.

Morrow, Felix. "Soule's Revolution." *New International*, August 1934, 61–62.

Mort, Frank. "Mapping Sexual London: The Wolfenden Committee on Homosexual Offences and Prostitution 1954–57." *New Formations: A Journal of Culture/Theory/Politics* 37 (1999): 92–113.

Mossetto, Gianfranco. *Aesthetics and Economics*. Dordrecht, Netherlands: Kluwer Academic Publishers, 1993.

Mulcahy, Kevin V., and C. Richard Swain, eds. *Public Policy and the Arts*. Boulder, CO: Westview Press, 1982.

Musée Fabre. *Dessins d'Alexandre Cabanel 1823–1889*. Montpellier, France: Musée Fabre, 1989.

Museum of Modern Art, New York. *New Horizons in American Art*. New York, 1936.

Museum of New Zealand. Project Development Board. *A Concept for the Museum of New Zealand Te Papa Tongarewa*. Wellington, NZ: Museum of New Zealand, 1989.

Museum of New Zealand Te Papa Tongarewa. *Admission Charges: The Issues: Audience New Zealand, Identity New Zealand*. Compiled by Mark Lindsay. Wellington, NZ: Museum of New Zealand Te Papa Tongarewa, 1994.

———. The Exchange-Concept Design. Archives of the Museum of New Zealand Te Papa Tongarewa, 1995.

———. *Museum of New Zealand Te Papa Tongarewa Annual Report 1996–1997*. Wellington, NZ: Museum of New Zealand Te Papa Tongarewa, 1997.

———. *Museum of New Zealand Te Papa Tongarewa Annual Report 1998*. Wellington, NZ: Museum of New Zealand Te Papa Tongarewa, 1998.

———. *Museum of New Zealand Te Papa Tongarewa Annual Report 1998–1999*. Wellington, NZ: Museum of New Zealand Te Papa Tongarewa, 1999.

———. *Museum of New Zealand Te Papa Tongarewa Annual Report 1999–2000*. Wellington, NZ: Museum of New Zealand Te Papa Tongarewa, 2000.

———. *Parade—90% Developed Design Part One A*. Archives of the Museum of New Zealand Te Papa Tongarewa, 1996.

———. "Press Kit: Parade." *Te Papa Our Place*. Museum of New Zealand Te Papa Tongarewa. http://tepapa.govt.nz/communications/press_releases/pr_parade.html

Myerscough, John. *The Economic Importance of the Arts in Britain*. London: Policy Studies Institute, 1988.

Napoléon I. *Correspondance de Napoléon Ier publié par ordre de l'Empereur Napoléon III*. Edited by A. Du Casse. 32 vols. Paris: Impremerie Imperial, 1858–69.

Naumann, Ruth, Lyn Harrison, and Te Kaponga Winiata. *Te Mana o Te Tiriti: The Living Treaty*. 1990. Auckland, NZ: New House Publishers, 1997.

Newall, Christopher. *Victorian Watercolors*. Oxford: Phaidon, 1987.

Newton, Douglas. "Old Wines in New Bottles, and the Reverse." In *Museums and the Making of "Ourselves": The Roles of Objects in National Identity*, edited by F. E. S. Kaplan, 269–90. London: Leicester University Press, 1994.

New Zealand Ministry for Culture and Heritage. *Report of Specific Issues Relating to the Museum of New Zealand Te Papa Tongarewa*. By Des Griffin, Chris Saines, and T. L. Rodney Wilson. June 16, 2000.

Nochlin, Linda. "Museums and Radicals: A History of Emergencies." *Art in America* 59, no. 4 (July–August 1971): 26–39.

Noth, Winfred. *Handbook of Semiotics*. Bloomington: Indiana University Press, 1995.

Nye, David E. *American Technological Sublime*. Cambridge, MA: MIT Press, 1994.

Obayashi Head Office Art Project Catalogue. *A Collaboration between Architecture and Contemporary Art*, 1999.

O'Connor, Francis V., ed. *Art for the Millions: Essays from the 1930s by Artists and Administrators of the WPA Federal Art Project*. Boston: New York Graphic Society, 1973.

———. *Federal Support for the Visual Arts: The New Deal and Now*. Boston: New York Graphic Society, 1969.

———, ed. *The New Deal Art Projects: An Anthology of Memoirs*. Washington, DC: Smithsonian Institution, 1972.

O'Doherty, Brian. *Inside the White Cube: The Ideology of the Gallery Space*. Santa Monica, CA: Lapis, 1986.

"L'oeuvre de M. Puvis de Chavannes au Panthéon." *La France*, December 11, 1877, 3.

O'Hara, Phillip Anthony. "The Revival of Political Economy and its Main Protagonists: 1960s to the Present." *History of Economics Review* 37 (Winter 2003): 140–51.

Olds, Elizabeth. "Prints for Mass Production." In O'Connor, ed., *Art for the Millions*.

Oliphant, Margaret. "An Artist's Autobiography." *Blackwood's Magazine* 136 (November 1884): 614–31.

Osborne, Catherine. "The Public Eye." *Asahi Evening News*, Weekend, September 8, 1994.

Osmundsen, John O. "Man on the Moon, Painted for *Look* by Norman Rockwell." *Look*, January 10, 1967.

Ottanelli, Fraser M. *The Communist Party of the United States: From the Depression to World War II*. New Brunswick, NJ: Rutgers University Press, 1991.

Overy, Richard. *The Nazi Economic Recovery, 1932–1938*. Rev. 2nd ed. Cambridge: Cambridge University Press, 1996.

Ozouf, Mona. "La fête révolutionnaire et l'espace urbain." In *Stadt und Fest: Zu Geschichte und Gegenwart europäischer Festkultur*, edited by Paul Hugger, 89–108. Unterägeri, Switzerland: W and H; Stuttgart: J. B. Metzler, 1987.

Park, Marlene, and Gerald Markowitz. *Democratic Vistas: Post Offices and Public Art in the New Deal*. Philadelphia: Temple University Press, 1984.

———. *New Deal for Art*. Hamilton: Gallery Association of New York State, 1977.

Parker, Irene. *Dissenting Academies in England: Their Rise and Progress and Their Place among the Educational Systems of the Country*. Cambridge: Cambridge University Press, 1914. Reprint, New York: Octagon Books, 1969.

Patetta, Luciano, ed. *Idea della magnificenza civile: Architettura a Milano 1770–1848*. Rotonda di Via Bersana Milano, October–November 1978. Milan: Electa, 1978.

Patris d'Uckermann, René. *Ernest Hébert*. Paris: Réunion des musées nationaux, 1982.

Peacock, A., and S. Cameron, eds. *National Arts and Media Strategy Unit*. London: Arts Council of England, 1991.

Pearson, David. *A Dream Deferred: The Origins of Ethnic Conflict in New Zealand*. Wellington, NZ: Allen and Unwin, 1990.

Pells, Richard H. *Radical Visions and American Dreams: Culture and Social Thought in the Depression Years*. New York: Harper and Row, 1973.

Penn, William. *The Political Writings of William Penn*. Indianapolis, IN: Liberty Fund, 2002.

Petrie, Brian. *Puvis de Chavannes*. Brookfield, VT: Ashgate, 1997.

Petropoulos, Jonathan. *Art as Politics in the Third Reich*. Chapel Hill: University of North Carolina Press, 1996.

———. *The Faustian Bargain*. Oxford: Oxford University Press, 2000.

Pfeifer, Eva. *Das Hitlerbild im Spiegel einiger konservatier Zeitungen in den Jahren 1929–1933*. Heidelberg: Ruprecht-Karl Universität, 1966.

Pick, Daniel. *The Rationalisation of Slaughter in the Modern Age*. New Haven, CT: Yale University Press, 1993.

Pile, Steve. *The Body and the City: Psychoanalysis, Space and Subjectivity*. London: Routledge, 1996.

Pingeot, Anne. "Le decor sculpte du Panthéon sous le Second Empire et le IIIe République." In *Panthéon: Symbole des revolutions*, 259–69. Paris: Picard, 1989.

Pistocchi, Giuseppe. "Riflessioni architettoniche sopra il premiato disegno della trionfale colonna de erigersi in Milano." Milan, 1800. In *Giuseppe Pistocchi (1744–1814) architetto giacobino*, edited by Ezzo Godoli, 89–92. Faenza: Palazzo delle Esposizioni 1974; Florence: Rotografia Fiorentina, 1977.

Pocock, J. G. A. "Cambridge Paradigms and Scotch Philosophers: A Study of the Relations between the Civic Humanist and the Civil Jurisprudential Interpretation of Eighteenth-Century Social Thought." In *Wealth & Virtue: The Shaping of Political Economy in the Scottish Enlightenment*, edited by I. Hont and M. Ignatieff, 235–52. Cambridge: Cambridge University Press, 1981.

———. *Virtue, Commerce, and History*. Cambridge: Cambridge University Press, 1985.

Port, M. H. *Imperial London: Civil Government Building in London 1851–1915*. New Haven, CT: Yale University Press, 1995.

Postlethwait, Malachy. *Universal Dictionary of Trade and Commerce*. 3 vols. London, 1730– 55.

Potts, Alex. "Male Phantasy and Modern Sculpture." *Oxford Art Journal* 15, no. 2 (1992): 38–47.

Powell, Walter W., and Paul J. Dimaggio, eds. *The New Institutionalism in Organizational Analysis*. Chicago: University of Chicago Press, 1991.

Pressly, William L. "A Chapel of Natural and Revealed Religion: James Barry's Series for the Society's Great Room Reinterpreted." *Journal of the Royal Society for the Encouragement of Arts, Manufactures, and Commerce* 132 (1984): 543–47, 634–37.

———. *James Barry: The Artist as Hero*. London: Tate Gallery, 1983.

———. *The Life and Art of James Barry*. New Haven, CT: Yale University Press, 1981.

Price, Aimée Brown. *Pierre Puvis de Chavannes*. New York: Rizzoli, 1994.

Price, Richard. *The Evidence for a Future Period of Improvement in the State of Mankind, with the means and Duty of Improving It, in a Discourse Delivered on Wednesday, the 25th of April, 1787 at the Meeting-House in the Old Jewry, London, to the Supporters of a New Academical Institution Among Protestant Dissenters*. London, 1787. In *Political Writings*, edited by D. O. Thomas, 152–75. Cambridge: Cambridge University Press, 1991.

———. *Observations on the Importance of the American Revolution and The Means of making it a Benefit to the World*. London, 1785. In *Political Writings*, edited by D. O. Thomas, 20–75. Cambridge: Cambridge University Press, 1991.

Priestley, Joseph. *An Essay on the First Principles of Government, and on the Nature of Political, Civil, and Religious Liberty*, 2nd ed. London, 1771. In *Political Writings*, edited by Peter Miller. Cambridge: Cambridge University Press, 1993.

———. *Institutes of Natural and Revealed Religion*. 2 vols. London, 1772–73.

Project Development Team for the National Museum of New Zealand/Te Marae Taonga o Aotearoa. *Nga Taonga o te Motu: Te Marae Taonga o Aotearoa. Treasures of the Nation: National Museum of New Zealand: A Plan for Development*. Wellington, NZ: Department of Internal Affairs, 1985.

Prouvaire, Jean. "Peintures sacrées." In *La République des lettres: Le Salon de 1876*, 180–81. Paris, 1876.

Pullan, Ann. "Public Goods or Private Interests? The British Institution in the Early Nineteenth Century." In *Art in Bourgeois Society, 1790–1850*, ed. A. Hemingway and W. Vaughan, 27–44. Cambridge: Cambridge University Press, 1998.

Puppi, Lionello, ed. *Prato della Valle: Due millenni di storia di un'avventura urbana*. Padua: Signum, 1986.

Pyne, Stephen. "Space: The Third Great Age of Discovery." In *Space: Discovery and Exploration*, edited by Martin J. Collins and Sylvia K. Kramer, 17–65. Washington, DC: National Air and Space Museum, Smithsonian Institution, 1993.

Quatremère de Quincy, Antoine Chrysostome. "Architecture." In *Encyclopédie Méthodique*. Vol. 1. Paris, 1801.

Quilter, Harry. "The Relation of Criticism to Production in Art." *National Review* 2, no. 25 (June 1895): 466–81.

Radicchio, Vincenzo. *Descrizione della general idea . . . dall'eccellentissimo signore Andrea Memmo . . . sul materiale del Prato, che denominavasi della Valle*. Rome: Antonio Fulgoni, 1786.

Ranger, Terence, and Eric J. Hobsbawm, eds. *The Invention of Tradition*. Cambridge: Cambridge University Press, 1992.

Raspi Serra, Joselita, ed. *Paestum and the Doric Revival 1750–1813: Essential Outline of an Approach*. 2 vols. Rome: Centro Di, 1986.

Ratcliff, Carter. *Red Grooms*. New York: Abbeville Press, 1984.

Rauschenberg, Robert. "Notes on Stoned Moon." *Studio International* 178 (December 1969): 246–47.

"Reach for the Moon and Touch a Star" and "In Sight of Giant Steps": A Guide to Accompany Two Filmstrips Prepared by a Committee of the National Art Educational Association for the National Aeronautics and Space Administration. Washington, DC: National Art Education Association, 1967.

Redgrave, F. M. *Richard Redgrave, C. B. R. A.* London: Cassell, 1891.

Redgrave, Richard, and Samuel Redgrave. *A Century of Painters of the English School*. 2 vols. London: Smith, Elder, 1866.

Rees, Helen. "Art Exports and the Construction of National Heritage in Late-Victorian and Edwardian Great Britain." In De Marchi and Goodwin, eds., *Economic Engagements with Art*, 187–208.

Reitlinger, Gerald. *The Economics of Taste. Vol. 1: The Rise and Fall of Picture Prices, 1760–1960*. London: Barrie and Rockliff, 1961.

Renner, Ginger, et al., eds. *Paul Calle: An Artist's Journey*. Venice, FL: Mill Pond Press, 1992.

Review of Radical Political Economics 36, no. 4 (2004), special art and political economy issue.

Reynolds, Ada M. *The Life and Work of Frank Holl*. London: Methuen, 1912.

Richer, Jean. "Une collaboration inconnue: La description du Panthéon de Paul Chenavard par Gautier et Nerval." *Archives des lettres modernes* 3, no. 48 (1963).

Rider, C. "Art, Ethics and Economics." *Review of Social Economy* 57 (1999): 263–82.

Roberts, Marion, with Chris Marsh and Miffa Salter. *Public Art in Private Places: Commercial Benefits and Public Policy*. London: University of Westminster Press, 1993.

Rohault de Fleury, H. *Historique de la Basilique du Sacré Coeur: Pièces et documents*. Vol. 1. Paris: F. Levé, 1903.

Roos, Jane Mayo. "Aristocracy in the Arts: Philippe de Chennevières and the Salons of the Mid 1870s." *Art Journal* 48, no. 1 (Spring 1989): 53–62.

———. "Rodin, Hugo and the Panthéon: Art and Politics in the Third Republic." PhD diss., Columbia University, 1981.

———. "Rodin's Monument to Victor Hugo: Art and Politics in the Third Republic." *Art Bulletin* 68, no. 4 (December 1986): 632–56.

Rose, Jonathan. "Was Capitalism Good for Victorian Literature?" *Victorian Studies* 46, no. 3 (Spring 2004): 489–501.

Rose, Margaret A. *Marx's Lost Aesthetic: Karl Marx and the Visual Arts*. Cambridge: Cambridge University Press, 1984.

Ross, Robert. *Present and Future Prospects of English Art*. Lecture delivered before the Sandon Studios Society, Liverpool, October 10, 1910. London: Sandon Studios Society, 1911.

Rossi, Aldo. *Scritti scelti sull'architettura e la città: 1956–1972*. Edited by Rosaldo Bonicalzi. Milan: Cooperativa libreraria universitaria del politecnico, 1975.

Rossi-Pinelli, Orietta. "Il Foro Bonaparte: Progetto e fallimento di una città degli uguali." *Ricerche di storia dell'arte* 3 (1976): 43–65.

Rota, Ettore. "L'età napoleonica: 1796–1814." In *Storia di Milano*. 18 vols. Turin: Fond. Treccani degli Alfieri per la Storia di Milano, 1953–96.

Rothfield, Lawrence, ed. *Unsettling "Sensation": Arts-Policy Lessons from the Brooklyn Museum of Art Controversy*. New Brunswick, NJ: Rutgers University Press, 2001.

Rousseau, Jean-Jacques. *Lettre à d'Alembert sur les spectacles*. Paris: Garnier freres, 1926.

Ruskin, John. *Works of John Ruskin*. Edited by E. T. Cook and Alexander Wedderburn. 39 vols. London: G. Allen, 1903–12.

Rutherford, David. *Dictionary of Economics*. London: Routledge, 1995. "Le Salon de 1876." *Zigzags*, May 7, 1876, 4.

Samuel, Raphael, ed. *Patriotisms. Britain 1900–1939: The Making and Unmaking of British National Identity. Volume 1: History and Politics*. London: Routledge, 1989.

Saunders, Frances Stonor. *The Cultural Cold War: The CIA and the World of Arts and Letters*. New York: New Press, 1999.

Sawyer, Paul. *Ruskin's Poetic Argument: The Design of the Major Works*. Ithaca, NY: Cornell University Press, 1985.

Schabas, Margaret. "Victorian Economics and the Science of the Mind." In *Victorian Science in Context*, edited by B. Lightman, 72–93. Chicago: University of Chicago Press, 1997.

Schapiro, Meyer. "Public Use of Art." *Art Front* 2, no. 10 (November 1936): 4–6.

Schapsmeier, Edward L., and Frederick H. Schapsmeier. *Henry A. Wallace of Iowa: The Agrarian Years, 1910–1940*. Ames: Iowa State University Press, 1968.

Scheffler, Karl. *Berliner Museumskrieg*. Berlin: Bruno Cassirer, 1921.

Schönberger, Angela. *Die Neue Reichskanzlei von Albert Speer: Zum Zusammenhang von nationalsozialistischer Architektur und Ideologie*. Berlin: Mann Verlag, 1981.

Schotter, Andrew. *The Economic Theory of Social Institutions*. Cambridge: Cambridge University Press, 1981.

Schuster, J. Mark Davidson. "The Public Interest in the Art Museum's Public." In *Art in Museums*, edited by Susan Pearce, 109–42. London: Athlone, 1995.

Schwartz, Lawrence H. *Marxism and Culture. The CPUSA and Aesthetics in the 1930s*. Port Washington, NY: Kennikat Press, 1980.

Scobie, Alex. *Hitler's State Architecture*. University Park: Pennsylvania State University Press, 1990.

Scotti, Aurora. *Il Foro Bonaparte: Un' utopia giacobina a Milano*. Translated by R. E. Wolf. Milan: F. M. Ricci, 1989.

Segawa, Ritsuko, Sachiko Kodama, and Yasuko Maekawa, eds. *Public Art Proposals I, II, III*. Tokyo: International Contemporary Art Fair, Japan, 1992, 1993, 1994.

Seidler, Franz. *Fritz Todt: Baumeister des Dritten Reiches*. Munich: F. A. Herbig Verlagsbuchhandlung, 1986.

Selwood, Sara. *The Benefits of Public Art*. London: Policy Studies Institute, 1995.

———. "Unreliable evidence: The Rhetorics of Data Collectoon in the Cultural Sector." In *Cultural Vultures: Is UK Arts Policy Damaging the Arts?*, edited by Munira Mirzas, 38–52. London: Policy Exchange, 2006.

Shapiro, David. *Social Realism: Art as a Weapon*. New York: Frederic Ungar, 1973.

Sherburne, J. C. *John Ruskin, or The Ambiguities of Abundance: A Study in Social and Economic Criticism*. Cambridge, MA: Harvard University Press, 1972.

Sherman, Daniel J. *The Construction of Memory in Interwar France*. Chicago: University of Chicago Press, 1999.

Shinjuku i-LAND Public Art Project CD. Tokyo: Housing and Urban Development Corp., 1996.

Silverman, Dan. *Hitler's Economy: Nazi Work Creation Programs, 1933–1936*. Cambridge, MA: Harvard University Press, 1998.

Simmons, P. L. "Art-Aids to Commerce." *Art Journal*, n.s., 11 (1872): 295–96.

Simon, Erich. "Baugestaltung und Bauwirtschaft." *Der Deutsche Baumeister*, no. 3 (1939): 5–8.

Simoncini, Giorgio. "Aspetti della politica napoleonica dei lavori pubblici in Italia." In *Villes et Territoire pendant la Période napolèonienne: France et Italie*. Actes du colloque organisée par l'Ecole française de Rome avec la participation de la Maison des sciences de l'homme, Rome, May 3–5, 1984, 1–21. Rome: L'Ecole, 1987.

———. *La città nell'età dell'illuminismo: Le capitali italiane*. Florence: L. S. Olschki, 1996.

Sloane, Joseph C. "Paul-Marc-Joseph Chenavard, artiste de 1848." PhD diss., University of North Carolina, 1962.

Smallfield, Frederic. "A Private View of Private Views." *Temple Bar* 74 (June 1885): 252–57.

Smith, Adam. *An Inquiry into the Nature and Causes of the Wealth of Nations*. Edited by Laurence W. Dickey. Indianapolis, IN: Hackett, 1993.

Snow, C. P. *The Two Cultures*. 1959. Cambridge: Cambridge University Press, 1993.

Soland, Brigitte. *Becoming Modern: Young Women and the Reconstruction of Womanhood in the 1920s*. Princeton, NJ: Princeton University Press, 2000.

Soldini, Jean. "Il Foro Bonaparte di Luigi Canonica." *Storia della Città* 7, no. 22 (1982): 89–94.

Solkin, David H. *Painting for Money: The Visual Arts and the Public Sphere in Eighteenth- Century England*. New Haven, CT: Yale University Press, 1992.

Soule, George. *The Coming American Revolution*. New York: Macmillan, 1934.

Spadafora, David. *The Idea of Progress in Eighteenth-Century Britain*. New Haven, CT: Yale University Press, 1990.

Sparrow, William Shaw. *Advertising and British Art*. London: John Lane, 1924.

Speer, Albert. *Neue Deutsche Baukunst*. Berlin: Volk und Reich Verlag, 1941.

———. "Stein statt Eisen." *Der Vierjahresplan* 1, no. 3 (1937): 135–37.

Spoonley, Paul. "Constructing Ourselves: The Post-colonial Politics of Pakeha." In *Justice and Identity: Antipodean Practices*, edited by Margaret Wilson and Anna Yeatman, 96–115. Wellington, NZ: Bridget Williams Books, 1995.

Spotts, Frederic. *Hitler and the Power of Aesthetics*. Woodstock, NY: Overlook Press, 2004.

Sraffa, Piero. *The Production of Commodities by Means of Commodities*. Cambridge: Cambridge University Press, 1960.

Stafford, Fiona. *The Sublime Savage: A Study of James Macpherson and the Poems of Ossian*. Edinburgh: Edinburgh University Press, 1988.

Stalin, Joseph. *Marxism and the National-Colonial Question: A Collection of Articles and Speeches*. 1934. San Francisco: Proletarian Publishers, 1975.

Stallybrass, Peter, and Allon White. *The Politics and Poetics of Transgression*. Ithaca, NY: Cornell University Press, 1986.

Statistics New Zealand. *New Zealand Official Yearbook 1997*. Wellington, NZ: Government Printer, 1997.

Steffens, Joachim "Die gegenwärtigen und zukünftigen Möglichkeiten des Bauschaffens." *Der Deutsche Baumeister*, no. 1 (1942): 7–12.

Steinlein, G., "Vorkommen, Eigenschaften und Verwendungsarten deutscher natürlicher Gesteine." *Beilage zum "Baumeister,"* no. 5 (1936): B91–93.

Stendhal [Beyle, Henri]. *Œuvres intimes*. Paris: Gallimard, 1955.

Stephanson, Anders. "The CPUSA Conception of the Rooseveltian State, 1933–1939." *Radical History Review* 29 (Fall 1980): 161–76.

Sternsher, Bernard. *Rexford Tugwell and the New Deal*. New Brunswick, NJ: Rutgers University Press, 1964.

Stimson, Blake, and Alexander Alberro, eds. *Conceptual Art: A Critical Anthology*. Cambridge, MA: MIT Press, 1999.

Suderburg, Erika, ed. *Space, Site, Intervention: Situating Installation Art*. Minneapolis: University of Minnesota Press, 2000.

Sugimura, Sokichi. "Art at City Corners." *The Aurora, Kansai Forum* 21 (1997): 1–8.

———. "The Art: From Appreciation to City Making and Revelation." *Public Art* 2 (1994).

Susman, Warren. *Culture as History: The Transformation of American Society in the Twentieth Century*. New York: Pantheon Books, 1973.

Sveiby, Karl Erick. *The New Organizational Wealth*. San Francisco: Berrett-Koehler, 1997.

Swarte, Victor de. *Lettres sur le Salon de 1876*. Saint-Omer, France: n.p., n.d.

Tagg, John. *Grounds of Dispute: Art History, Cultural Politics, and the Discursive Field*. Minneapolis: University of Minnesota Press, 1992.

Takeda, Naoki. *Public Art in Japan*. Translated by Taiko Chandler. Tokyo: Seibundo Shinkousha, 1995.

Tapsell, Paul. "Taonga: A Tribal Response to Museums." PhD diss., University of Oxford, 1998.

Tate, Trudi. *Modernism, History and the First World War*. Manchester: Manchester University Press, 1998.

Thackara, Davina, ed. *The Benefits of Public Art*. Public Art Forum Symposium transcript, 27.

Thies, Jochen. *Architekt der Weltherrschaft: Die "Endziele" Hitlers*. Düsseldorf: Droste Verlag, 1976.

Thomas, Nicholas. *Colonialism's Culture: Anthropology, Travel and Government*. Cambridge: Polity Press, 1994.

———. *Possessions: Indigenous Art/Colonial Culture*. London: Thames and Hudson, 1999.

Throsby, David. *Economics and Culture*. Cambridge: Cambridge University Press, 2001.

———. "The Production and Consumption of the Arts: A View of Cultural Economics." *Journal of Economic Literature* 1 (1994): 1–29.

Todd, Margo. *Christian Humanism and the Puritan Social Order*. Cambridge: Cambridge University Press, 1987.

———. "Seneca and the Protestant Mind: The Influence of Stoicism on Puritan Ethics." *Archive für Reformationsgeschichte 74* (1983): 182–99.

Tomkins, Calvin. *Off the Wall: Robert Rauschenberg and the Art World of Our Time*. New York: Penguin Books, 1980.

Tramposch, William. "Exact Imagining: The Museum as a Journey." *Museum News* 77, no. 2 (1998): 44–49.

———. "Te Papa: Reinventing the Museum." *Museum Management and Curatorship* 17 (1998): 339–50.

Trotsky, Leon. "Art and Politics." *Partisan Review* 5, no. 3 (August/September 1938): 3–10.

Tugwell, Rexford G. *The Battle for Democracy*. New York: Columbia University Press, 1935.

Upchurch, Anna. "William Morris and the Case of Public Support of the Arts." *History of Political Economy* 37, no. 3 (2005): 509–34.

Vachon, Maurice. "Les peintures de M. Puvis de Chavannes au Panthéon." *La France*, May 28, 1877, 2.

Vaisse, Pierre. "La peinture monumentale au Panthéon sous la IIIe république." In *Le Panthéon: symbole des revolutions*, 252–58. Paris: Picard, 1989.

———. "Styles et sujets dans la peinture officielle de la IIIe République: Ferdinand Humbert au Panthéon." *Bulletin de la Société de l'Histoire de l'art français* (1977): 297–311.

———. *La troisième république et les peintres*. Paris: Flammarion, 1995.

Veblen, Thorsten. *The Theory of the Leisure Class: An Economic Study in the Evolution of Institutions*. New York: Macmillan, 1899.

Vergnette, François. "Anticléricalisme et naturalisme au Panthéon: Le décor de Jean-Paul Laurens." *Histoire de l'art* 28 (December 1994): 51–56.

Veron, Th. *Mémorial de l'art et des artistes de mon temps: Le Salon de 1876*. Paris, 1876. "Vierjahresplan und Bauwesen." *Beilage zum "Baumeister,"* no. 1 (1937): B14.

Viner, Jacob. *The Role of Providence in the Social Order: An Essay in Intellectual History*. Princeton, NJ: Princeton University Press, 1972.

Vitruvius. *Ten Books on Architecture*. Translated by Ingrid D. Rowland. Commentary and illustrations by Thomas Noble Howe. New York: Cambridge University Press, 1999.

Vitz, Robert C. "Painters, Pickets, and Politics: The Artist Moves Left, 1925–1940." PhD diss., University of North Carolina at Chapel Hill, 1971.

Vogel, Harold L. *Entertainment Industry Economics*. 4th ed. Cambridge: Cambridge University Press, 1998.

Völkischer Beobachter. "Kampf gegen den Kunstbolschewismus." Vol. 64. June 14–15, 1925. In *Kunstanschauung und Kunstkritik in der nationalsozialistischen Presse: Die Kritik im Feuilleton des "Voelkischen Beobachters" 1920–1932*, by Gerhard Koehler. Munich: Zentralverlag der NSDAP, Franz Eher Nachf, 1937.

Volkmann, Hans-Erich. "Die NS-Wirtschaft in Vorbereitung des Krieges." In *Ursachen und Voraussetzungen des Zweiten Weltkrieges*, edited by Wilhelm Deist et al. Frankfurt: Fischer Taschenbuch Verlag GmbH, 1989, 329–52.

Wald, Alan M. *The New York Intellectuals: The Rise and Decline of the Anti-Stalinist Left from the 1930s to the 1980s*. Chapel Hill: University of North Carolina Press, 1987.

Walker, John A. *Art and Outrage: Provocation, Controversy and the Visual Arts*. London: Pluto, 1999.

Walker, Ranginui. *Ka Whawhai Tonu Matou: Struggle Without End*. Auckland, NZ: Penguin, 1990.

Wall, Mattie. "Te Hokinga Mai." *Art Galleries and Museums Association of New Zealand Journal* 17, no. 3 (1986): 18.

Wallace, Henry. *New Frontiers*. New York: Reynal and Hitchcock, 1934.

Wallis, Brian. "Selling Nations: International Exhibitions and Cultural Diplomacy." In *Museum Culture: Histories, Discourses, Spectacles*, edited by Daniel J. Sherman and Irit Rogoff, 256–81. London: Routledge, 1994.

Ward, Henrietta Mary Ada. *Memories of Ninety Years*. Edited by Isabel G. McAllister. London: Hutchinson, 1924.

Warren, Frank A. *Liberals and Communism: The "Red Decade" Revisited*. New York: Columbia University Press, 1993.

Warren-Findley, Jannelle. "The Collier as Commemoration: The Project Mercury Astronauts and the Collier Trophy." In *From Engineering Science to Big Science: The NACA and NASA Collier Trophy Research Project Winners*, edited by Pamela E. Mack. The NASA History Series. Washington, DC: National Aeronautics and Space Administration, 1998.

Watrous, James. *A Century of American Printmaking 1880–1980*. Madison: University of Wisconsin Press, 1984.

Watson, Forbes. "The Chance in a Thousand." *Magazine of Art* 28, no. 8 (August 1935): 470–75, 506–7.

———. "The Federal Works of Art Project: Federal Republican or Democratic?" *Magazine of Art* 27, no. 1 (January 1934): 6–9.

———. "The Innocent Bystander." *Magazine of Art* 27, no. 11 (November 1934): 601–6.

———. "A Steady Job." *Magazine of Art* 27, no. 4 (April 1934): 168–72.

———. "The Public Works of Art Project: A New Deal for the Artists." *Magazine of Art* 27, no. 9 (September 1934, Supplement): 29–30.

———. "The Public Works of Art Project: Federal, Republican or Democratic?" *Magazine of Art* 27, no. 1 (January 1934): 8.

———. "The USA Challenges Artists." *Parnassus* 6, no. 1 (June 1933): 275.

Watts, Michael R. *The Dissenters: From the Reformation to the French Revolution*. Oxford: Clarendon Press, 1978.

Waugh, Evelyn. *The Diaries of Evelyn Waugh*. Edited by Michael Davie. Harmondsworth, UK: Penguin Books, 1982.

Weber, Max. *The Protestant Ethic and the Spirit of Capitalism*. London: Routledge, 1930.

Wells, Helen T., Susan H. Whiteley, and Carrie E. Karegeannes. *Origins of NASA Names*. The NASA History Series. Washington, DC: National Aeronautics and Space Administration, 1976.

Westfall, Carroll W. "Antolini's Foro Bonaparte in Milan." *Journal of the Warburg and Courtauld Institutes* 32 (1969): 366–85.

Weyergraf-Serra, Clara, and Martha Buskirk, eds. *The Destruction of Tilted Arc: Documents*. Cambridge, MA: MIT Press, 1991.

White, John Franklin, ed. *Art in Action: American Art Centers and the New Deal*. Metuchen, NJ: Scarecrow Press, 1987.

White, Michael V. "Obscure Objects of Desire? Nineteenth-Century British Economists and the Price(s) of 'Rare Art.'" In De Marchi and Goodwin, eds., *Economic Engagements with Art*, 57–84.

Whiting, Cecil. *Antifascism in American Art*. New Haven, CT: Yale University Press, 1989.

Whiting, F. A., Jr. "On Taking Part." *American Magazine of Art* 27, no. 3 (March 1934): 103.

Williams, Paul. "Parade: Reformulating Art and Identity at Te Papa, Museum of New Zealand." *Open Museum Journal* 3 (May 2001): 1–28.

Williams, Raymond. *The Country and the City*. Oxford: Oxford University Press, 1973.

Wilson, Margaret and Anna Yeatman. Introduction to *Justice and Identity: Antipodean Practices*, edited by Margaret Wilson and Anna Yeatman, i–xvi. Wellington, NZ: Bridget Williams Books.

Winter, Jay. *Sites of Memory, Sites of Mourning: The Great War in European Cultural History*. Cambridge: Cambridge University Press, 1996.

Witkin, Robert. *Art and Social Structure*. Cambridge: Polity Press, 1995.

Wolff, Janet. *Aesthetics and the Sociology of Art*. 2nd ed. Ann Arbor: University of Michigan Press, 1993.

———. *The Social Production of Art*. New York: New York University Press, 1993.

Wood, Grant. "Revolt Against the City." In Dennis, *Grant Wood*, 229–35.

Woodmansee, Martha, and Mark Osteen, eds. *The New Economic Criticism: Studies at the Intersection of Literature and Economics*. London: Routledge, 1999.

Woolf, Virginia. *Street Haunting: A London Adventure*. San Francisco: Westgate Press, 1930.

Wright, Philip. "The Quality of Visitors' Experience in Art Museums." In *The New Museology*, edited by Peter Vergo, 119–48. London: Reaktion, 1989.

Wykes, David L. "The Contribution of the Dissenting Academy to the Emergence of Rational Dissent." In *Enlightenment and Religion: Rational Dissent in Eighteenth-Century Britain*, edited by Knud Haakonssen, 99–139. Cambridge: Cambridge University Press, 1996.

Xenophon. *A Dialogue on Devotion after the Manner of Xenophon; in which The Reasonableness, Pleasure and Advantages of it are considered. To which is prefixed, A Conversation of Socrates, Wherein he proves A God and a Providence*. Translated by Thomas Amory. London, 1746.

———. *The Science of Good Husbandry: Or, the Oeconomics of Xenophon*. Translated by R. Bradley. London, 1727.

Yanal, Robert, ed. *Institutions of Art: Reconsiderations of George Dickie's Philosophy*. University Park: Pennsylvania State University Press, 1994.

Yoshimoto, Mitsuhiro, and Mami Kataoka. "Incorporating the Arts into Urban Development." *NLI Research*, no. 73 (December 1994): 9.

Zaghi, Carlo. *Il Direttorio Francese e la Repubblica Cisalpina*. 2 vols. Rome: Istituto storico italiana per l'età moderna e contemporanea, 1992.

———. *L'Italia di Napoleone dalla Cisalpina al Regno*. 1969. Turin: UTET, 1986.

Zelizer, Viviana A. "Beyond the Polemics on the Market: Establishing a Theoretical and Empirical Agenda." *Sociological Forum* 3 (Fall 1988): 614–34.

———. *The Social Meaning of Money*. New York: Basic Books, 1994.

Zinn, Howard, ed. *New Deal Thought*. Indianapolis, IN: Bobbs-Merrill, 1966.

Zola, Emile. *Salons*. Geneva: Librarie E. Droz, 1959.

Zukin, Sharon. *Loft Living: Culture and Capital in Urban Change*. New Brunswick, NJ: Rutgers University Press 1989.

Zukin, Sharon, and Paul DiMaggio, eds. *Structures of Capital: The Social Organization of the Economy*. Cambridge: Cambridge University Press, 1990.

Contributors

MARIA E. BROWN is an independent scholar living in Australia. Her research interests focus on cultural representations in art museums, a subject on which she has written several articles published in *Third Text*, *The Chicago Art Journal*, and the *Journal of the Museums Association of New Zealand*. Her chapter, "Art in New Zealand's New National Museum," appears in *Travelling Concepts III: Memory, Image and Narrative*, edited by Nancy Pedri (2003), 203–15.

JULIE F. CODELL is Professor of Art History at Arizona State University. She has published widely on Victorian culture and India under the Raj in professional journals, scholarly anthologies, and encyclopedias. She wrote *The Victorian Artist* (2003); edited *The Political Economy of Art* (FDUP, 2008), *Imperial Co-Histories: National Identities in the British and Colonial Press* (FDUP, 2002), *Photography and the Imperial Durbars of British India* (2008), and *Genre, Gender, Race, and World Cinema* (2007); and coedited *Encountering the Victorian Press* (with L. Brake, 2004) and *Orientalism Transposed: The Impact of the Colonies on British Culture* (with D. Macleod, 1998; currently being translated into Japanese (2008). She is completing a manuscript on the Delhi coronation durbars, 1877–1911, for which she has received fellowships from the NEH, American Institute for Indian Studies, Getty Foundation, and the Huntington Library.

ANNE COLLINS GOODYEAR is Assistant Curator of Prints and Drawings at the National Portrait Gallery, Smithsonian Institution. She has published articles related to her dissertation in *Science in Context* and *Intertexts*, and forthcoming essays will appear in *Leonardo* (2007), and in *Cold War Modern: Art and Design in a Divided World*, edited by David Crowley and Jane Pavitt (2008). Goodyear is the author of essays in *Reconsidering a Century of Flight*, edited by Roger Launius and Janet R. Daly Bednarek (2003) and exhibition catalogs for the North Carolina Museum of Art's *Defying Gravity: Contemporary Art and Flight* (2003) and the Art Institute of Chicago's *2001: Architecture and Design for Space, Vision and Reality* (2001). She coedited *Flight: A Celebration of 100 Years in Art and Literature* (2003). Her essay "The Portrait, the Photograph, and the Index," recently appeared in *Photography Theory*, edited by James Elkins (2006). She is cocurator of the upcoming National Portrait Gallery exhibition "Inventing Marcel Duchamp: The Dynamics of Portraiture" and will serve as coeditor and essayist for the exhibition catalog (2008).

ELIZABETH M. GRADY is Adjunct Professor of Art History at the Fashion Institute of Technology (SUNY), Special Assistant to the Estate of Diane Arbus, Curatorial Assistant at the Whitney Museum of American Art, and works as an independent curator. She has organized several exhibitions in the last several years at nonprofit organizations in New York and Philadelphia, including the summer show at the Morgan Lehman Gallery, New York, on the formation of American national identity, and a show of sculpture and installation work at the Soap Factory in Minneapolis, which opened in September 2007. Recent publications include critical essays in catalogs of the work of emerging and mid-career artists (2006), and an essay on the representation of competing economic and political systems and worldviews in contemporary painting in the catalog for the Whitney's Remote Viewing exhibition in summer 2005.

DANIEL R. GUERNSEY is Associate Professor of Art History in the School of Art and Art History at Florida International–Miami. He is the author of *The Artist and the State, 1777–1855: The Politics of Universal History in British and French Painting* (2007) as well as articles on James Barry and Gustave Courbet. His other scholarly interests include the history of liberal political economy and early socialism. His current research examines the aesthetic theory of Pierre-Joseph Proudhon.

ANDREW HEMINGWAY is a Professor in the History of Art at University College–London. He has published widely in many professional journals and scholarly anthologies. He is the author of *The Norwich School of Painters, 1803–33* (1979); *Landscape Imagery and Urban Culture in Early Nineteenth-Century Britain* (1992); and *Artists on the Left: American Artists and the Communist Movement, 1926–56* (2002). He is the editor of *Marxism and the History of Art: From William Morris to the New Left* (2006), and coeditor, with William Vaughan, of *Art in Bourgeois Society, 1790–1850* (1998).

JOACHIM HOMANN is Curator at the Picker Art Gallery at Colgate University. He earned his PhD in 2004 from the State Academy of Design in Karlsruhe, Germany, with a dissertation on the constitution of public space in Milan during the Habsburgian and Napoleonic eras. He received graduate fellowships at the University of Hamburg, Germany, and at the Busch-Reisinger Museum, Harvard University. Most recently, he taught at the University of Texas at El Paso. Homann organized exhibitions on artists Natalia Goncharova, Roberto Matta, and Francisco Toledo, among others. He cofounded and served as editor of H-Arthist, an e-mail list for art historians within the University of Michigan's humanities network.

PAUL B. JASKOT is Associate Professor of Art History in the Department of Art and Art History at DePaul University. He is the author of *The Architecture of Oppression: The SS, Forced Labor and the Nazi Monumental Building Economy* (2000) as well as many articles on architecture and politics during the Third Reich. Other scholarly interests include the history of modern German art and architecture and Marxist art history. His current research focuses on the political reception of the Nazi past and postwar German art. In conjunction with this project, he coedited (with Gavriel Rosenfeld) an anthology entitled *Beyond Berlin: 12 Postwar German Cities Confront the Nazi Past* (2007).

HELEN LANGA is Associate Professor of Art History at American University in Washington, D.C. She has published numerous articles on the cultural and political meanings of 1930s prints and the work of women artists within sociocultural contexts. Her book *Radical Art: Printmaking and the Left in 1930s New York* (2004) discussed the constructed nature of images of labor, antiracist, and antifascist images and addressed issues of cultural democracy and federal rhetoric about prints for a new mass audience. Other scholarly interests focused on the 1930s include gendered ideologies, leftist interventions, and the relation of religion and social justice interests in American visual culture.

ANN Z. LI is the US-based Director of the Pont Aven School of Contemporary Art in France and teaches social informatics at Baruch College of the City University of New York. She has coauthored a studio foundations textbook and her research has ranged from the architectural history of the Colonial British port city in Asia to the role of geospatial information in assessing environmental media policy.

ELIZABETH NORMAN, retired Senior Lecturer in art history at Sheffield Hallam University, has a PhD from the University of Leeds on the culture and management of public art in Japan, the result of more than twelve years of research and eight study visits to Japan. She has published in Japanese as well as in British and American journals and delivered papers on public art in Japan at international annual conferences of the Association of Asian Studies and at the Public Art Research Institute, Tokyo. Currently she is the coauthor of a volume for a national survey of publicly sited sculpture headed by the Public Monuments and Sculpture Association, London (forthcoming).

CHERYL K. SNAY is Assistant Curator of Prints and Drawings at the Jack S. Blanton Museum of Art, University of Texas at Austin, where she is currently organizing the exhibition, *A Century of Grace: 19th-Century European Masterworks from the Dahesh Museum of Art*. Prior to this, she was a research associate for a nineteenth-century French drawings project organized by The Baltimore Museum of Art and the Walters Art Museum, which included a circulating exhibition with a catalog, *The Essence of Line: French Drawings from Ingres to Degas* (2005) and online searchable database. She published her findings on previously unidentified drawings related to Bourbon Restoration monuments in *The Burlington Magazine*, and her studies on American collectors of French drawings in *Master Drawings*. She was a consultant to the National Gallery of Art, Washington, DC, on their film *Henri de Toulouse-Lautrec and Montmartre* (2005).

ANDREW P. STEPHENSON teaches visual theories at the University of East London. He has published articles on British art and design of the late nineteenth and twentieth centuries, most recently "Posing and Performance: The Problematics of Homosocial Visibility and Its Articulations in the Late Nineteenth-Century London Artworld," in *Visual Culture in Britain* (2007); "Palimpsestic Promenades: Memorial Sculpture and the Urban Consumption of Space in Post–1918 London," in *The Journal of the Australian and New Zealand Art Association* (2005); and "A Keen Sight for the Signs of the Races: John Singer Sargent, 'Whiteness' and the Fashioning of Anglo-Performativity," in *Visual Culture in Britain* (2005). He is coeditor with Amelia Jones of *Performing the Body/Performing the Text* (1999) and is currently working on a study of British modernism from 1920 to 1940 and *Patrilenes: Masculine Self-Fashioning and Artistic Performance in Britain 1850–1910*.

Index